Excel
for Windows® 95

MAY 7 1999

UNLEASHED

Paul McFedries

SAMS
PUBLISHING

201 West 103rd Street
Indianapolis, IN 46290

To Karen (skish!)

Copyright © 1995 by Sams Publishing

FIRST EDITION

International Standard Book Number: 0-672-30739-1

Library of Congress Catalog Card Number: 95-70098

98 97 96 95   4 3 2 1

Interpretation of the printing code: the rightmost double-digit number is the year of the book's printing; the rightmost single-digit, the number of the book's printing. For example, a printing code of 95-1 shows that the first printing of the book occurred in 1995.

Composed in AGaramond, Futura, Helvetica, and MCPdigital by Macmillan Computer Publishing

Printed in the United States of America

Publisher and President	Richard K. Swadley
Acquisitions Manager	Greg Wiegand
Development Manager	Dean Miller
Managing Editor	Cindy Morrow
Marketing Manager	Gregg Bushyeager

Acquisitions Editor
Rosemarie Graham

Development Editor
Sharon Cox

Software Development Specialist
Steve Straiger

Production Editor
Gayle L. Johnson

Copy Editors
Cheri Clark, James Grass, Bart Reed, Joe Williams

Technical Reviewer
Thomas Hayes

Editorial Coordinator
Bill Whitmer

Technical Edit Coordinator
Lynette Quinn

Formatter
Frank Sinclair

Editorial Assistant
Sharon Cox

Cover Designer
Jason Grisham

Book Designer
Alyssa Yesh

Production Team Supervisor
Brad Chinn

Production
Mary Ann Abramson, Angela D. Bannan, Carol Bowers, Michael Brummit, Heather Butler, Charlotte Clapp, Jeanne Clark, Terrie Deemer, Mike Dietsch, Terri Edwards, Judy Everly, George Hanlin, Louisa Klucznik, Ayanna Lacey, Kevin Laseau, Erika Millen, Casey Price, Bobbi Satterfield, Susan Van Ness, Mark Walchle, Paul Wilson

Indexers
Jeanne Clark, Cheryl Dietsch, Bront Davis

Overview

Part V Unleashing Spreadsheet Applications with VBA

Part VI Appendixes

Contents

Part V Unleashing Spreadsheet Applications with VBA

Part VI Appendixes

Acknowledgments

Robert Pirsig, in *Zen and the Art of Motorcycle Maintenance,* wrote that "a person who sees Quality and feels it as he works is a person who cares." If this book is a quality product, it's because the people at Sams cared enough to make it so.

I'd like to thank Acquisitions Editor Rosemarie Graham for, well, acquiring me and for pulling the project together. Special thanks goes to Development Editor Sharon Cox for doing a great job despite having to wear so many hats. Many thanks, also, to Production Editor Gayle Johnson for her insightful comments and unfailing good humor; to Copy Editors Cheri Clark, Joe Williams, Jim Grass, and Bart Reed for their uncanny ability to find my dumb mistakes; and to Technical Editor Thomas Hayes for making sure my instructions cut the technical mustard.

About the Author

Paul McFedries runs his own computer consulting firm, specializing in spreadsheet and database applications. He also is a freelance writer who has authored or coauthored more than 20 books, including *DOS for the Guru Wanna-Be, Excel 5 Super Book,* and *Navigating the Internet, Third Edition.* He can be reached via e-mail at paulmcf@hookup.net.

Introduction

Before Windows 3.0 was introduced in 1990, Windows languished in the PC never-never land of good ideas whose time had not come. Its clunky interface and not-ready-for-prime-time features ensured that it would remain a mere curiosity in a world in love with the DOS command line.

Sharing this software oblivion was Excel, one of the first major packages that took full advantage of the Windows environment. Originally ported from a highly successful Macintosh version, the first couple of releases of Excel waited patiently in the wings while its DOS peers (especially Lotus 1-2-3) took their bows on center stage.

When Microsoft introduced Windows 3.0 in the spring of 1990, the reaction from computer users everywhere was nothing short of overwhelming. Millions of people seeking increased productivity and an easy-to-use interface (not to mention a great game of Solitaire) followed Microsoft's vision of the PC environment of the future.

Excel, too, soon released its own version 3.0, and it rode Windows' coattails to the top of the Windows spreadsheet charts. People from all walks of life suddenly discovered that spreadsheets didn't have to be ugly and unintuitive. Why, Excel almost made number-crunching a pleasure (almost). Then, when versions 4.0 and 5.0 shipped over the next few years, it was a case of the best getting better. Everyone wondered what Excel could possibly do for an encore.

Excel

Welcome to Version 7.0

With the release of Excel 7.0, Microsoft's software designers have proven that they still have plenty of tricks up their sleeves. Although Excel 7.0 isn't a radical redesign (if it ain't broke...), a fistful of new and improved features will please everyone from spreadsheet novices to power users. Here's a summary of just a few of these new toys:

Support for Windows 95: The true *raison d'être* for Excel 7.0, of course, is Windows 95. The new version is a 32-bit program that takes full advantage of some of Windows 95's most advanced features. On a more mundane level, Excel supports Windows 95 innovations such as long filenames, Microsoft Exchange, and the new and improved Open and Save As dialog boxes (from which you can create folders, rename files, and perform other basic file maintenance).

Easier file management: Actually, Excel's Open dialog box, shown in Figure I.1, is an enhanced version of the standard Windows 95 Open dialog box. You can use it to preview worksheets before opening them, set up a list of "favorite" folders, and perform sophisticated file searches.

FIGURE I.1.

Excel's Open dialog box is a souped-up version of the standard Windows 95 Open dialog box.

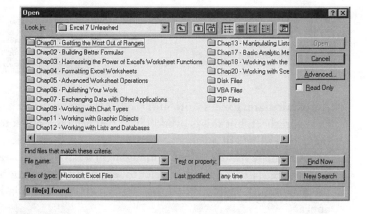

Speed, speed, and more speed: Thanks to 32-bit code and lots of performance tweaking, Excel 7.0 is much faster than any of its predecessors (up to 40 percent faster for certain types of operations).

AutoCorrect: First introduced in Word for Windows 6, AutoCorrect is now available in Excel. This handy feature corrects your spelling on-the-fly as you type text into a cell, text box, chart title, or just about anywhere else. AutoCorrect comes with over 400 predefined corrections (such as changing *teh* to *the* or *wtih* to *with*), but you also can define custom corrections for your own frequent faux pas. (Select the **T**ools | **A**utoCorrect command to display the AutoCorrect dialog box, shown in Figure I.2.)

FIGURE I.2.

Use the AutoCorrect dialog box to customize AutoCorrect.

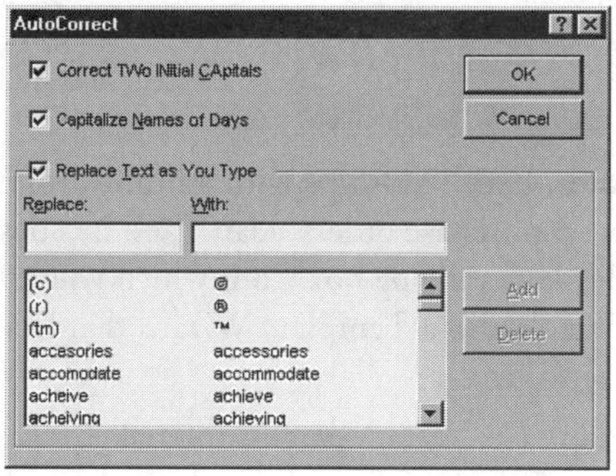

AutoComplete: This feature promises to take at least some of the drudgery out of data entry. As you're typing text into a cell, Excel examines the entries in the column above the cell. If the first few letters match an existing entry, AutoComplete kicks in and uses the existing entry to complete the cell for you (see Figure I.3). If you right-click on a cell and choose Pick from the list, AutoComplete will display a list of the unique entries in the column above the cell.

FIGURE I.3.

AutoComplete fills in a cell entry automatically based on the entries in the column above.

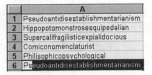

AutoCalculate: Excel's AutoSum toolbar button makes it easy to add a SUM() formula to a worksheet, but this is overkill if all you need is a quick total for a few cells. To make these kinds of quick-and-dirty calculations even easier, Excel 7.0 presents the AutoCalculate feature. When you highlight a range of cells, the sum appears automatically in the status bar. If you prefer to see another calculation (such as the average or the maximum), right-click on the sum and choose a calculation from the menu that appears.

AutoFilter's Top Ten lists: The AutoFilter feature introduced in Excel 5.0 made it easy to filter a list without having to set up a separate criteria range. Excel 7.0 adds an extra level of convenience to AutoFilter by letting you filter the list to show only the top or bottom values. Even though it's called the Top 10 filter, you can use it to display any number of top or bottom values, based on either the values themselves or a percentage (for example, the top five percent of test scores). Selecting Top 10 from an AutoFilter drop-down list displays the Top 10 AutoFilter dialog box, shown in Figure I.4.

FIGURE I.4.

Use the Top 10 AutoFilter dialog box to customize the Top 10 AutoFilter.

Templates: Excel 7.0 ships with a number of customizable templates for things such as invoices, purchase orders, loans, and business plans. Selecting the **F**ile | **N**ew command displays a dialog box from which you can preview and choose the template you need. There's also a Template Wizard that lets you easily link fields in a template with worksheet cells.

Data Map: The Data Map feature makes it easy to chart geographical data, as shown in Figure I.5. Excel 7.0 comes with predefined maps that include cities, states, countries, and even large airports.

Improved drag-and-drop: Excel 7.0 now lets you drag a range and drop it on either another worksheet in the same workbook (hold down Alt and drop the range on the worksheet tab) or on a different workbook (drop the range on the workbook's window).

CellTips: If you have a note attached to a cell, you can now view the first few lines of the note by placing the mouse pointer over the cell. After a second or two, a box appears (called a *CellTip*) that shows you the note.

FIGURE I.5.

An example of a data map.

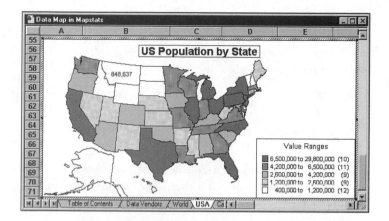

ScrollTips: To make it easier to navigate a large worksheet using the scroll bars, Excel 7.0 includes a new feature called *ScrollTips*. A ScrollTip is a small box that appears whenever you drag either the vertical or horizontal scroll box. The ScrollTip tells you which row will appear at the top of the window (in the case of the vertical scroll bar) or which column will appear on the left side of the window (in the case of the horizontal scroll bar) when you release the mouse button (see Figure I.6).

FIGURE I.6.

ScrollTips appear when you drag either the horizontal or vertical scroll box.

Improved numeric formatting: Excel 7.0's numeric formats are easier to understand and work with. The codes (such as #) have been moved behind the scenes, replaced with dialog box options and sample formats. There are also extra predefined formats for common items such as ZIP codes, phone numbers, and social security numbers.

Shared lists: Shared lists are Excel databases that you can store (or share) on a network. You can make them accessible to other people on the network, and multiple people can edit and update the information in the list.

What You Should Know Before Reading This Book

My goal in writing *Excel for Windows 95 Unleashed* was to give you complete coverage of Excel's intermediate-to-advanced features. This means that I bypass basic topics such as entering and editing data (which I assume you already know how to do) in favor of more complex operations such as worksheet auditing, outlines, lists, data analysis, and Visual Basic for Applications.

I've tried to keep the chapters focused on the topic at hand and unburdened with long-winded theoretical discussions. For the most part, each chapter gets right down to brass tacks without much fuss and bother. To keep the chapters uncluttered, I've made a few assumptions about what you know and don't know:

- I assume you have knowledge of rudimentary computer concepts such as files and folders.

- I assume you're familiar with Windows and that you know how to launch applications and use accessories such as Control Panel.

- I assume you're comfortable with the basic Windows 95 interface. This book doesn't tell you how to work with things such as pulldown menus, dialog boxes, and the Excel Help system.

- I assume you can operate peripherals attached to your computer, such as the keyboard, mouse, printer, and modem.

- I assume you've installed Excel and are ready to dive in at a moment's notice.

- I assume you've used Excel for a while and are comfortable with basic data entry, editing, and formulas.

- I assume you have a brain and are willing to use it.

How This Book Is Organized

To help you find the information you need, *Excel for Windows 95 Unleashed* is divided into five parts that group related tasks. The next few sections offer a summary of each part.

Part I: Unleashing Excel's Day-to-Day Operations

The eight chapters in Part I take Excel's day-to-day drudgeries (such as working with ranges and formulas) and extend them so that you can exploit their full power. You'll learn advanced techniques for ranges, formulas, and functions, as well as how to protect your data. Other chapters discuss such power tools as templates, outlines, and linking, as well as using dialog box controls on worksheets. The last two chapters show you how to exchange data with other applications (including Lotus 1-2-3) and how to customize Excel to suit the way you work.

Part II: Unleashing Excel's Charting and Graphics Capabilities

Part II gives you an in-depth tour of Excel's charting and graphics features. Chapter 9 shows you how to create and format charts—including 3-D charts and the new Data Map feature—as well as how to take advantage of chart overlays. Chapter 10 discusses numerous techniques for enhancing your charts, and Chapter 11 covers topics such as drawing lines and shapes and formatting graphic objects.

Part III: Unleashing Excel's Databases and Lists

Part III introduces you to Excel lists and external databases. In Chapter 12 you'll learn basic skills such as creating and sorting a list, using a data form, and filtering list records, as well as more advanced skills including subtotals and list functions. Chapters 13 and 14 give you complete coverage of pivot tables, from creating them to customizing them. Chapters 15 and 16 explore Microsoft Query and show you how to use it to access external databases and create sophisticated queries.

Part IV: Unleashing Excel's Data Analysis Wizardry

Part IV shows you how to get the most out of Excel's impressive array of analytic features. Chapter 17 covers basic analysis techniques such as what-if, Goal Seek, iteration, and trend analysis (including a complete Sales Forecasting model). The rest of the chapters cover Excel's powerful analytical tools: Analysis Toolpak, Solver, and Scenario Manager.

Part V: Unleashing Spreadsheet Applications with VBA

Part V introduces you to Visual Basic for Applications, Excel's macro programming language. First you learn how to record simple VBA macros, and then I show you how to add your own code to make your programs more powerful and flexible. You'll also learn how to build custom dialog boxes, menus, and toolbars; how to program lists and external databases; how to make VBA respond to events; how to work with other applications; how to debug your macros; and more.

Part VI: Appendixes

I've also tacked on a few extra goodies at the end of this book. The appendixes include coverage of the Excel 4 macro language (Appendix A), a complete listing of Visual Basic for Applications' statements and functions (Appendixes B and C), and the Windows ANSI character set (Appendix D).

About the CD

This book comes with a CD-ROM that includes the following:

- All the VBA code from the listings in Part V.
- Miscellaneous files from examples used in this book.
- Version 5.5 of the Baarns Utilities, an impressive collection of Excel utilities designed to make Excel more powerful and easier to use. Version 5.5 loads faster, uses fewer resources, and has more tools than previous versions.

This Book's Special Features and Conventions

Excel for Windows 95 Unleashed is designed to give you the information you need without making you wade through ponderous explanations and interminable technical background. To make your life easier, this book includes various features and conventions that help you get the most out of the book and Excel itself.

Steps: Throughout the book, each Excel task is summarized in a step-by-step procedure.

Commands: I use the following style for Excel menu commands: **File | O**pen. This means that you pull down the **F**ile menu and select the **O**pen command. Accelerator keys for menus and commands appear in bold.

Dialog box controls: Dialog box controls have bold accelerator keys—for example, **C**lose.

Things you type: Whenever I suggest that you type something, what you type appears in a monospace font.

Visual Basic keywords: Keywords reserved in the Visual Basic language appear in monospace—for example, `Function`.

Functions: Excel worksheet and macro functions appear in capital letters and are followed by parentheses: `SUM()`. When I list the arguments you can use with a function, *required* arguments appear in ***bold italic monospace***, and *optional* arguments appear in *italic monospace:* `CELL(`***info_type***`,`*reference*`)`.

The code continuation character (➥): When a line of code is too long to fit on one line of this book, it is broken at a convenient place, and the code continuation character appears at the beginning of the next line.

An underscore at the end of a code line: This is VBA's *line continuation character*, and it's used to spread a single VBA statement over multiple lines. This is handy if you have a lengthy statement that would otherwise extend past the right side of the window. When you use the line-continuation character, make sure you insert a space before the underscore.

Three vertical dots: When you see three vertical dots separating lines of code, this indicates that some of the code has been omitted for the sake of brevity.

The Excel 7 icon: This icon highlights features new to Excel 7.

Excel **7**

The CD icon: This icon tells you that the file being discussed is available on the CD that comes with this book.

This book also uses the following boxes to draw your attention to important (or merely interesting) information.

> **NOTE**
>
> The Note box presents asides that give you more information about the topic under discussion. These tidbits provide extra insights that give you a better understanding of the task at hand. In many cases, they refer you to other sections of the book for more information.

> **TIP**
>
> The Tip box tells you about Excel methods that are easier, faster, or more efficient than the standard methods.

> **CAUTION**
>
> The all-important Caution box tells you about potential accidents waiting to happen. There are always ways to mess things up when you're working with computers. These boxes help you avoid at least some of the pitfalls.

PART

I

Unleashing Excel's Day-to-Day Operations

Getting the Most Out of Ranges

1

Other than performing data-entry chores, you probably spend most of your Excel life working with ranges in some way. Whether you're copying, moving, formatting, naming, or filling them, ranges are a big part of Excel's day-to-day operations. And why not? After all, working with a range of cells is a lot easier than working with each cell individually. For example, suppose that you want to know the average of a column of numbers running from B1 to B30. You *could* enter all 30 cells as arguments in the AVERAGE function, but I'm assuming that you have a life to lead away from your computer screen. Typing =AVERAGE(B1:B30) is decidedly quicker (and almost certainly more accurate).

In other words, ranges save time and they save wear and tear on your typing fingers. But there's more to ranges than that. Ranges are powerful tools that can unlock the hidden power of Excel. So the more you know about ranges, the more you'll get out of your Excel investment. This chapter reviews some range basics and then takes you beyond the range routine and shows you some techniques for taking full advantage of Excel's range capabilities.

A Review of Excel's Range Selection Techniques

As you work with Excel, you'll come across three situations in which you'll select a cell range:

- When a dialog box field requires a range input
- While entering a function argument
- Before selecting a command that uses a range input

In a dialog box field or function argument, the most straightforward way to select a range is to enter the range coordinates by hand. Just type the address of the upper-left cell (called the *anchor cell*), followed by a colon, and then the address of the lower-right cell. To use this method, you either must be able to see the range you want to select, or you must know in advance the range coordinates you want. Because often this is not the case, most people don't type the range coordinates directly; instead, they select ranges using either the mouse or the keyboard.

Selecting a Range with the Mouse

Although you can use either the mouse or the keyboard to select a range, you'll find that the mouse makes the job much easier. The following sections take you through several methods you can use to select a range with the mouse.

Selecting a Contiguous Range with the Mouse

A rectangular, contiguous grouping of cells is the most common type of range. To use the mouse to select such a range, follow these steps:

1. Point the mouse at the upper-left cell of the range (this cell is called the *anchor*); then press and hold down the left mouse button.

2. With the left mouse button still pressed, drag the mouse pointer to the lower-right cell of the range. The cell selector remains around the anchor cell, and Excel highlights the other cells in the range in reverse video. The formula bar's Name box shows the number of rows and columns you've selected, as shown in Figure 1.1.

FIGURE 1.1.

As you select a range, the Name box shows the number of rows and columns you've selected.

The Name box shows the number of rows and columns selected

Five rows are selected

Four columns are selected

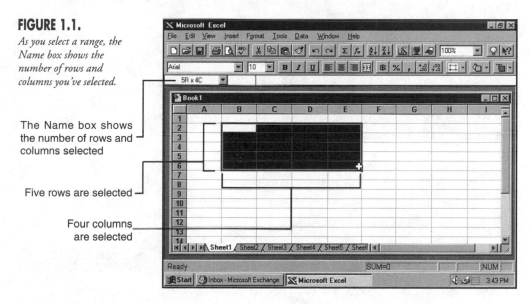

3. Release the mouse button. The cells remain selected to show the range you've defined, and the Name box shows the address of the anchor cell.

TIP

Do you have to start over if you select the wrong lower-right corner and your range ends up either too big or too small? Not at all. Just hold down the Shift key and click on the correct lower-right cell. The range adjusts automatically.

Selecting a Row or Column with the Mouse

Using the worksheet row and column headings, you can quickly select a range that consists of an entire row or column. For a row, click on the row's heading; for a column, click on the column's heading. If you need to select adjacent rows or columns, just drag the mouse pointer across the appropriate headings.

What if you want to select every row and every column (or, in other words, the entire worksheet)? Easy: just click the Select All button near the upper-left corner of the sheet (see Figure 1.2).

FIGURE 1.2.

Click the Select All button to select the entire worksheet.

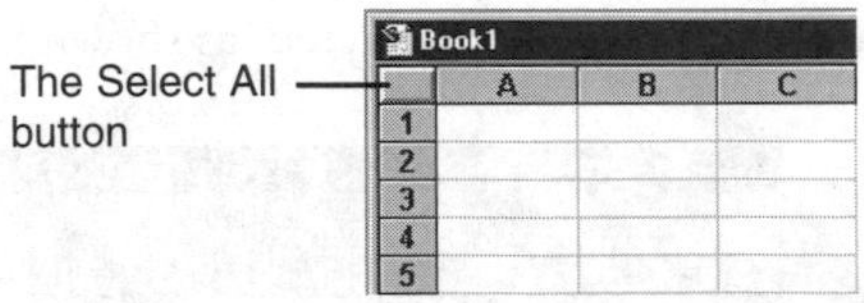

The Select All button

Selecting a Range in Extend Mode with the Mouse

An alternative method uses the mouse with the F8 key to select a rectangular, contiguous range. You can do this by following these steps:

1. Click on the upper-left cell of the range.
2. Press F8. Excel enters Extend mode (you'll see EXT in the status bar).
3. Click on the lower-right cell of the range. Excel selects the entire range.
4. Press F8 again to turn off Extend mode.

> **TIP**
>
> After selecting a large range, you'll often no longer see the active cell because you've scrolled it off the screen. If you need to see the active cell before continuing, you can either use the scroll bars to bring it into view or press Ctrl-Backspace.

Selecting a Noncontiguous Range with the Mouse

If the cells you want to work with are scattered willy-nilly throughout the sheet, you'll need to combine them into a noncontiguous range. The secret to defining a noncontiguous range is to hold down the Ctrl key while selecting the cells. The following steps gives you the details.

> **CAUTION**
>
> Be careful when selecting cells with this method. After you've selected a cell, the only way to deselect it is by starting over.

1. Select the first cell or the first rectangular range you want to include in the non-contiguous range. If you're selecting a rectangular range, you can use any of the methods described earlier.

2. Press and hold down the Ctrl key.

3. Select the other cells or rectangular ranges you want to include in the noncontiguous range. Note, however, that for subsequent rectangular ranges, you can't use the Extend mode procedure.

4. When you've finished selecting cells, release the Ctrl key.

CAUTION

Always press and hold down the Ctrl key *after* you've selected your first cell or range. Otherwise, Excel includes the currently selected cell or range as part of the noncontiguous range. This action could create a circular reference in a function if you were defining the range as one of the function's arguments. (Not sure what a "circular reference" is? Don't sweat it: I'll explain it all in Chapter 2, "Building Better Formulas.")

Selecting Cell Ranges with the Keyboard

If your mouse is buried under paperwork, or if you just prefer to use your keyboard, you still have lots of range selection methods at your disposal. In fact, you have no fewer than three methods to choose from, as described in the next few sections.

Selecting a Contiguous Range with the Keyboard

If the cells you want to work with form a rectangular, contiguous block, here's how to select them from the keyboard:

1. Use the arrow keys to select the upper-left cell of the range (this is the anchor cell).

2. Press and hold down the Shift key.

3. Use the arrow keys (or Page Up and Page Down if the range is a large one) to highlight the rest of the cells.

4. Release the Shift key.

TIP

If you want to select a contiguous range that contains data, there's an easier way to select the entire range. First, move to the upper-left cell and hold down the Shift key.

> Press Ctrl-down arrow to select the contiguous cells below the upper-left cell, and then press Ctrl-right arrow to select the contiguous cells to the right of the selected cells.

TIP

If you select a range large enough that all the cells don't fit on the screen, you can scroll through the selected cells by activating the Scroll Lock key. When Scroll Lock is on, pressing the arrow keys (or Page Up and Page Down) scrolls you through the cells while keeping the selection intact.

Selecting a Row or a Column with the Keyboard

Selecting an entire row or column from the keyboard is a snap. Just select a cell in the row or column you want, and then press either Ctrl-Spacebar to select the current column or Shift-Spacebar to select the current row.

If you want to select the entire worksheet, press Ctrl-A.

Selecting a Noncontiguous Range with the Keyboard

If you need to select a noncontiguous range with the keyboard, follow these steps:

1. Select the first cell or range you want to include in the noncontiguous range.
2. Press Shift-F8 to enter Add mode. (ADD appears in the status line.)
3. Select the next cell or range you want to include in the noncontiguous range.
4. Repeat steps 2 and 3 until you've selected the entire range.

Working with 3-D Ranges

A *3-D range* is a range selected on multiple sheets. This is a powerful concept because it means that you can select a range on two or more sheets and then enter data, apply formatting, or give a command, and the operation will affect all the ranges at once.

To create a 3-D range, you first need to group the worksheets you want to work with. To select multiple sheets, you can use any of the following techniques:

- ■ To select adjacent sheets, click on the tab of the first sheet, hold down the Shift key, and click on the tab of the last sheet.
- ■ To select noncontiguous sheets, hold down the Ctrl key and click on the tab of each sheet you want to include in the group.

■ To select all the sheets in a workbook, right-click on any sheet tab and click on the Select All Sheets command.

When you've selected your sheets, each tab is highlighted and [Group] appears in the workbook title bar. To ungroup the sheets, click on a tab that isn't in the group. Alternatively, you can right-click on one of the group's tabs and select the Ungroup Sheets command from the shortcut menu.

With the sheets now grouped, you create your 3-D range simply by activating any of the grouped sheets and then selecting a range using any of the techniques we just ran through. Excel selects the same cells in all the other sheets in the group. (If you're from Missouri, the "Show Me" state, you can prove it for yourself by activating the other sheets in the group.)

You can also type in a 3-D range by hand when, say, entering a formula. Here's the general format for a 3-D reference:

```
FirstSheet:LastSheet!ULCorner:LRCorner
```

Here, FirstSheet is the name of the first sheet in the 3-D range, LastSheet is the name of the last sheet, and ULCorner and LRCorner define the cell range you want to work with on each sheet. For example, to specify the range A1:E10 on worksheets Sheet1, Sheet2, and Sheet3, use the following reference:

```
Sheet1:Sheet3!A1:E10
```

You'll normally use 3-D references in worksheet functions that accept them. These functions include AVERAGE(), COUNT(), COUNTA(), MAX(), MIN(), PRODUCT(), STDEV(), STDEVP(), SUM(), VAR(), and VARP().

Advanced Range Selection Techniques

So much for the basic, garden-variety range selection techniques. Now I'll show you a few advanced techniques that can make your selection chores faster and easier.

Using Go To to Select a Range

For very large ranges, Excel's **Edit | G**o To command comes in handy. You normally use **Go To** to jump quickly to a specific cell address or range name. The following steps show you how to exploit the power of Go To to select a range:

1. Select the upper-left cell of the range.
2. Select the **Edit | G**o To command or press Ctrl-G. The Go To dialog box appears, as shown in Figure 1.3.

FIGURE 1.3.

You can use the Go To dialog box to easily select a large range.

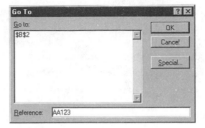

3. Use the **R**eference text box to enter the cell address of the lower-right corner of the range.

> **TIP**
>
> You also can select a range using **G**o To by entering the range coordinates in the **R**eference text box.

4. Hold down the Shift key and select OK. Excel selects the range.

> **TIP**
>
> Another way to select very large ranges is to select the **V**iew | **Z**oom command and select a reduced magnification in the Zoom dialog box (say, **50%** or **25%**). You can then use this "big picture" view to select your range.

Using the Go To Special Dialog Box

You normally select cells according to their position within a worksheet, but Excel includes a powerful feature that enables you to select cells according to their contents or other special properties. If you select the **E**dit | **G**o To command and then click the **S**pecial button in the Go To dialog box, the Go To Special dialog box appears, as shown in Figure 1.4.

FIGURE 1.4.

Use the Go To Special dialog box to select cells according to their contents, formula relationships, and more.

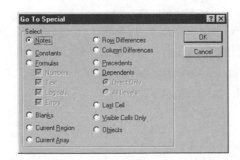

Selecting Cells by Type

The Go To Special dialog box contains four options to select cells according to the type of contents they contain. Table 1.1 summarizes these options.

Table 1.1. Options for selecting a cell by type.

Option	*Description*
Notes	Selects all cells that contain a note.
Constants	Selects all cells that contain constants of the types specified in one or more of the check boxes listed under the **Formulas** option.
Formulas	Selects all cells containing formulas that produce results of the types specified in one or more of the following four check boxes:
	Numbers Selects all cells that contain numbers.
	Text Selects all cells that contain text.
	Lo**g**icals Selects all cells that contain logical values.
	Errors Selects all cells that contain errors.
Blan**k**s	Selects all cells that are blank.

> **TIP**
>
> You can also press Ctrl-? to select all cells containing notes.

Selecting Adjacent Cells

If you need to select cells adjacent to the active cell, the Select Special dialog box gives you two options. Choose the Current **R**egion option to select a rectangular range that includes all the nonblank cells that touch the active cell.

If the active cell is part of an array, choose the Current **A**rray option to select all the cells in the array. (For an in-depth discussion of Excel arrays, head for Chapter 2 and read the "Working with Arrays" section.)

> **TIP**
>
> The shortcut key for selecting the current region is Ctrl-*. For the current array, you can press Ctrl-/.

Selecting Cells by Differences

Excel also enables you to select cells by comparing rows or columns of data and selecting only those cells that are different. The following steps show you how it's done:

1. Select the rows or columns you want to compare. (Make sure that the active cell is in the row or column with the comparison values you want to use.)

2. Display the Go To Special dialog box, and select one of the following options:

    Row Differences — This option uses the data in the active cell's column as the comparison values. Excel selects the cells in the corresponding rows that are different.

    Column Differences — This option uses the data in the active cell's row as the comparison values. Excel selects the cells in the corresponding columns that are different.

3. Select OK.

> **TIP**
>
> Excel provides a couple of handy shortcut keys for these options. Ctrl-\ selects row differences and Ctrl-| selects column differences.

For example, Figure 1.5 shows a selected range of numbers. Suppose that you wanted to compare the numbers in columns B and C with those in column A and select the ones in B and C that are different. Because you're comparing rows of data, you would select the Row Differences option from the Select Special dialog box. Figure 1.6 shows the results.

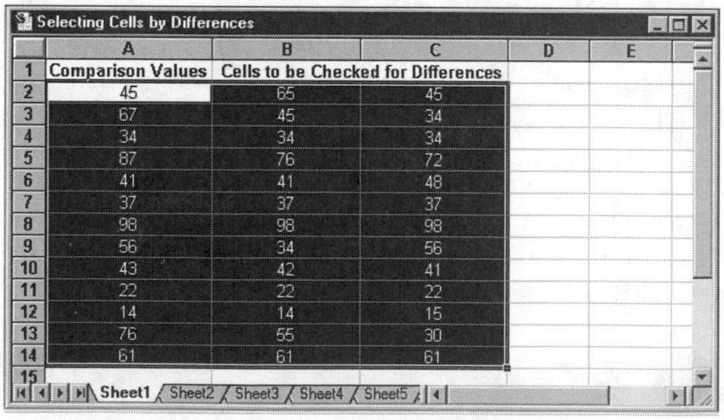

FIGURE 1.5.

The Go To Special feature can compare rows (or columns) of data and select only the different cells.

	A	B	C	D	E
1	Comparison Values	Cells to be Checked for Differences			
2	45	65	45		
3	67	45	34		
4	34	34	34		
5	87	76	72		
6	41	41	48		
7	37	37	37		
8	98	98	98		
9	56	34	56		
10	43	42	41		
11	22	22	22		
12	14	14	15		
13	76	55	30		
14	61	61	61		
15					

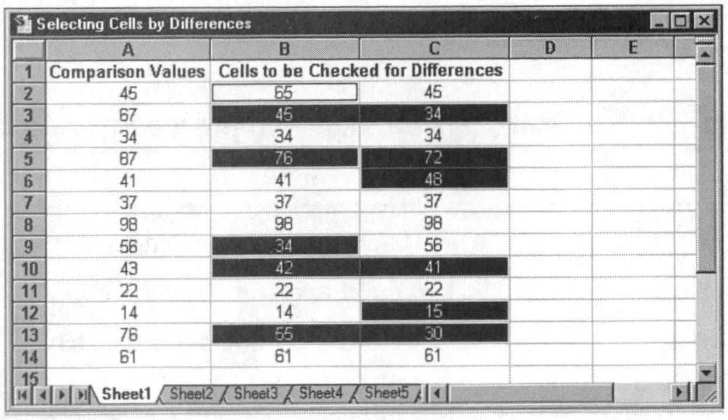

FIGURE 1.6.

The results of the Go To Special operation.

	A	B	C	D	E
1	Comparison Values	Cells to be Checked for Differences			
2	45	65	45		
3	67	45	34		
4	34	34	34		
5	87	76	72		
6	41	41	48		
7	37	37	37		
8	98	98	98		
9	56	34	56		
10	43	42	41		
11	22	22	22		
12	14	14	15		
13	76	55	30		
14	61	61	61		
15					

Sheet1 / Sheet2 / Sheet3 / Sheet4 / Sheet5

Selecting Cells by Reference

If a cell contains a formula, Excel defines the cell's *precedents* as those cells that the formula refers to. For example, if cell A4 contains the formula =SUM(A1:A3), then cells A1, A2, and A3 are the precedents of A4. A *direct* precedent is a cell referred to explicitly in the formula. In the preceding example, A1, A2, and A3 are direct precedents of A4. An *indirect* precedent is a cell referred to by a precedent. For example, if cell A1 contains the formula =B3*2, cell B3 is an indirect precedent of cell A4.

Excel also defines a cell's *dependents* as those cells with a formula that refers to the cell. In the preceding example, cell A4 would be a dependent of cell A1. (Think of it this way: the value that appears in cell A4 *depends on* the value that's entered into cell A1.) Like precedents, dependents can be direct or indirect.

The Go To Special dialog box enables you to select precedents and dependents as described in these steps:

1. Select the range you want to work with.
2. Display the Go To Special dialog box.
3. Select either the **P**recedents or the **D**ependents option.
4. Select the D**i**rect Only option to select only direct precedents or dependents. If you need to select both the direct and the indirect precedents or dependents, select the All Levels option.
5. Select OK.

Table 1.2 lists the shortcut keys you can use to select precedents and dependents.

Table 1.2. Shortcut keys for selecting precedents and dependents.

Shortcut Key	Description
Ctrl-[	Selects direct precedents.
Ctrl-]	Selects direct dependents.
Ctrl-{	Selects all levels of precedents.
Ctrl-}	Selects all levels of dependents.

Other Go To Special Options

The Go To Special dialog box also includes a few more options for your range selection pleasure:

Option	Description
Last Cell	Selects the last cell in the worksheet (that is, the lower-right corner) that contains data or formatting.
Visible Cells Only	Selects only cells that are unhidden.
Objects	Selects all the worksheet's graphic objects.

TIP

To select the last cell quickly, press Ctrl-End. For the visible cells, press Alt-;.

Using Range Names

Although ranges enable you to work efficiently with large groups of cells, there are some disadvantages to using ranges:

■ You can't work with more than one range at a time. Each time you want to use a range, you have to redefine its coordinates.

■ Range notation is unintuitive. To know what a formula such as =SUM(E6:E10) is adding, you have to look at the range itself.

■ A slight mistake in defining a range can lead to disastrous results, especially when you're erasing a range.

You can overcome these problems by using range names. You can assign names of up to 255 characters to any single cell or range on your spreadsheet. To include the range in a formula or range command, you use the name instead of selecting the range or typing in its coordinates. You can create as many range names as you like, and you can even assign multiple names to the same range.

Range names also make your formulas intuitive and easy to read. For example, by assigning the name AugustSales to a range such as E6:E10, the purpose of a formula such as =SUM(AugustSales) becomes immediately clear. Range names also increase the accuracy of your range operations because you don't have to specify range coordinates.

Besides overcoming the problems mentioned earlier, range names also bring several advantages to the table:

- Names are easier to remember than range coordinates.
- Names don't change when you move a range to another part of the worksheet.
- Named ranges adjust automatically whenever you insert or delete rows or columns within the range.
- Names make it easier to navigate a worksheet. You can use the Go To command to jump to a named range quickly.
- You can use worksheet labels to create range names quickly.

Defining a Range Name

Besides having a maximum length of 255 characters, range names must also follow these guidelines:

- The name must begin with either a letter or the underscore character (_). For the rest of the name, you can use any combination of characters, numbers, or symbols, except spaces. For multiple-word names, separate the words by using the underscore character or by mixing case (for example, CostOfGoods). Excel doesn't distinguish between uppercase and lowercase letters in range names.
- Don't use cell addresses or any of the operator symbols (such as +, –, *, /, <, >, and &), because these could cause confusion if you use the name in a formula.
- To make typing easier, try to keep your names as short as possible while still retaining their meaning. TotalProfit93 is faster to type than Total_Profit_For_Fiscal_Year_93, and it's certainly clearer than the more cryptic TotPft93.

With these guidelines in mind, follow these steps to define a range name:

1. Select the range you want to name.
2. Select the **Insert | Name | Define** command. The Define Name dialog box appears, as shown in Figure 1.7.

FIGURE 1.7.

Use the Define Name dialog box to define a name for the selected range.

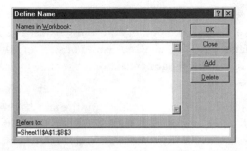

If you're in a hurry, you can press Ctrl-F3 to open the Define Name dialog box quickly.

3. Enter the range name in the Names in **W**orkbook text box.

When defining a range name, always enter at least the first letter of the name in uppercase. Why? Well, it will prove invaluable later when you need to troubleshoot your formulas. The idea is that you type the range name entirely in lowercase letters when you insert it into a formula. When you accept the formula, Excel then converts the name to the case you used when you first defined it. If the name remains in lowercase letters, Excel doesn't recognize the name, so it's likely you misspelled the name when typing it.

4. If, for some reason, the range displayed in the **R**efers to box is incorrect, you can use one of two methods to change it:

   ■ Type the correct range address (be sure to begin the address with an equals sign).

   ■ Move the cursor into the **R**efers to box, delete the existing address, and then use the mouse or keyboard to select a new range on the worksheet.

If you need to move around inside the **R**efers to box with the arrow keys (say, to edit the existing range address), first press F2 to put Excel into Edit mode. If you don't, Excel remains in Point mode, and the program assumes that you're trying to select a cell on the worksheet.

5. Click the **A**dd button. Excel adds the name to the Names in **W**orkbook list.

6. Repeat steps 3 through 5 for any other ranges you want to name.

7. When you're done, click the Close button to return to the worksheet.

NOTE

Range nameså are available to all the sheets in a workbook. This means, for example, that a formula in Sheet1 can refer to a named range in Sheet16 simply by using the name directly. If you need to use the same name in different sheets, you can create *sheet-level* names. These kinds of names are preceded by the name of the worksheet and an exclamation mark. For example, Sheet1!Sales refers to a range named Sales in Sheet1, and Sheet2!Sales refers to a range named Sales in Sheet2.

If the named range exists in a different workbook, you must precede the name with the name of the file in single quotation marks. For example, if the Mortgage Amortization workbook contains a range named Rate, you use the following entry to refer to this range in a different workbook:

```
'Mortgage Amortization'!Rate
```

Working with the Name Box

The Name box in Excel's formula bar (see Figure 1.1) gives you some extra features that help make it easier to work with range names:

- After you've defined a name, it appears in the Name box whenever you select the range.

- The Name box doubles as a drop-down list. To select a named range quickly, drop the list down and select the name you want. Excel moves to the range and selects the cells.

- You also can use the Name box as an easy way to define a range name. Just select the range and click inside the Name box to display the insertion point. Enter the name you want to use, and then press Enter. Excel defines the new name automatically.

Using Worksheet Text to Define Names

When you select the **I**nsert | **N**ame | **D**efine command, Excel sometimes suggests a name for the selected range. For example, Figure 1.8 shows that Excel has suggested the name Advertising for the range C6:E6. As you can see, Advertising is the row heading of the selected range, so Excel has used an adjacent text entry to make an educated guess about what you'll want to use as a name.

FIGURE 1.8.

Excel uses adjacent text to guess at the range name you want to use.

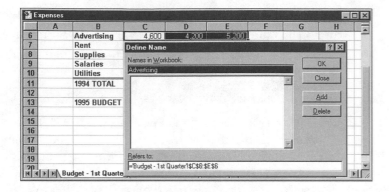

Instead of waiting for Excel to guess, you can tell the program explicitly to use adjacent text as a range name. The following procedure shows you the appropriate steps:

1. Select the range of cells you want to name, including the appropriate text cells that you want to use as the range names (see Figure 1.9).

FIGURE 1.9.

Include the text you want to use as names when you select the range.

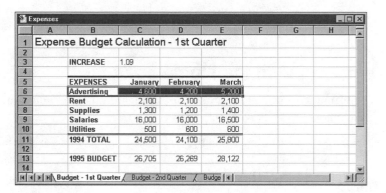

2. Select the **I**nsert | **N**ame | **C**reate command. Excel displays the Create Names dialog box, shown in Figure 1.10.

FIGURE 1.10.

Use the Create Names dialog box to specify the location of the text to use as a range name.

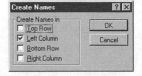

TIP

The shortcut key for the Create Names dialog box is Ctrl-Shift-F3.

3. Excel guesses where the text for the range name is located and activates the appropriate check box (**Left Column** in the preceding example). If this isn't the check box you want, deactivate it and then activate the appropriate one.

4. Select OK.

NOTE

If the text you want to use as a range name contains any illegal characters (such as a space), Excel replaces those characters with an underscore (_).

When naming ranges from text, you're not restricted to working with just columns or rows. You can select ranges that include both row and column headings, and Excel will happily assign names to each row and column. For example, in Figure 1.11, the Create Names dialog box appears with both the **Top Row** and **Left Column** check boxes activated.

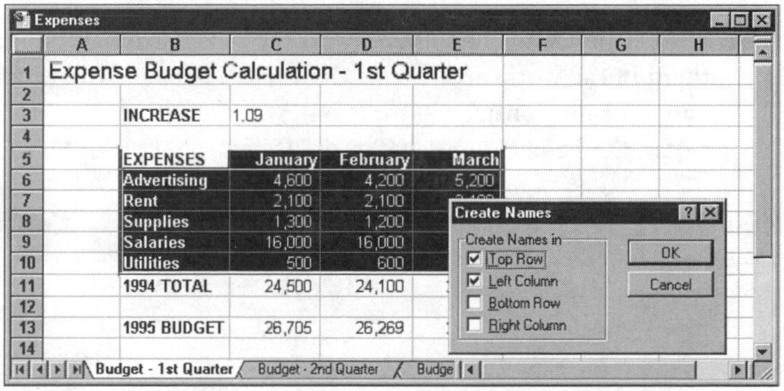

FIGURE 1.11.

Excel can create names for rows and columns at the same time.

NOTE

When you define names for the rows and columns in a range, you can refer to each cell as the intersection of two ranges. For example, in Figure 1.11, cell C7 would be January Rent. See "Using Excel's Reference Operators," later in this chapter, for more information about the intersection operator.

Naming Constants

One of the best ways to make your worksheets comprehensible is to define names for every constant value. For example, if your worksheet uses an interest rate variable in several formulas, you can define a constant named Rate and use the name in your formulas to make them more readable. There are two ways to do this:

■ Set aside an area of your worksheet for constants, and name the individual cells. For example, Figure 1.12 shows a worksheet with three named constants: Rate (cell B5), Term (Cell B6), and Amount (cell B7). Notice how the formula in cell E5 refers to each constant by name.

FIGURE 1.12.

Grouping formula constants and naming them makes worksheets easy to read.

	A	B	C	D	E	F	G	H
1								
2	**Loan Amortization**							
3								
4	Constants:			Period	Payment	Interest	Principal	
5	Rate	8%		1	(313.36)	(66.67)	(246.70)	
6	Term	3		2	(313.36)	(65.02)	(248.34)	
7	Amount	10,000		3	(313.36)	(63.37)	(250.00)	
8				4	(313.36)	(61.70)	(251.66)	
9				5	(313.36)	(60.02)	(253.34)	
10				6	(313.36)	(58.33)	(255.03)	
11				7	(313.36)	(56.63)	(256.73)	
12				8	(313.36)	(54.92)	(258.44)	
13				9	(313.36)	(53.20)	(260.17)	
14				10	(313.36)	(51.46)	(261.90)	

Amortization Schedule — Amortization / Sheet2 / Sheet3 / Sheet4 / S

■ If you don't want to clutter a worksheet, you can name constants without entering them in the worksheet. Select the **I**nsert | **N**ame | **D**efine command. Then enter a name for the constant in the Names in **W**orkbook text box, and enter an equals sign (=) and the constant's value in the **R**efers to text box. Figure 1.13 shows an example.

FIGURE 1.13.

You can create and name constants in the Define Name dialog box.

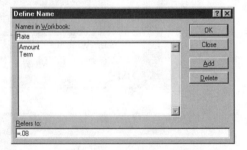

Pasting a List of Range Names in a Worksheet

If you need to document a worksheet for others to read (or figure out the worksheet yourself a few months from now), you can paste a list of the worksheet's range names. This list includes the name and the range it represents (or the value it represents, if the name refers to a constant). Follow these steps to paste a list of range names:

1. Move the cell pointer to an empty area of the worksheet that's large enough to accept the list without overwriting any other data.

2. Select the **I**nsert | **N**ame | **P**aste command. Excel displays the Paste Name dialog box.

TIP

You also can press F3 to display the Paste Name dialog box.

3. Select the Paste **L**ist button. Excel pastes the worksheet's names and ranges.

Changing a Range Name

If you need to change the name of one or more ranges, you can use one of two methods:

- If you've changed some row or column labels, just redefine the range names based on the new text, and delete the old names (as described in the next section).

- Select the Insert | **N**ame | **D**efine command. Highlight the name you want to change in the Names in **W**orkbook list, make your changes in the text box, and click the **A**dd button.

CAUTION

Note that these methods don't actually change the name of the range. Instead, they just define a new name for the range while leaving the old name intact. This also means that any formulas that refer to the original range name won't get changed.

Deleting a Range Name

If you no longer need a range name, you should delete the name from the worksheet to avoid cluttering the name list. The following procedure outlines the necessary steps:

1. Select the Insert | **N**ame | **D**efine command to display the Define Name dialog box.
2. In the Names in **W**orkbook list, select the name you want to delete.
3. Select **D**elete. Excel deletes the name from the list.
4. Repeat steps 2 and 3 for any other names you want to delete.
5. When you're done, select OK.

Data Entry in a Range

If you know in advance the range you'll use for data entry, you can save yourself some time and keystrokes by selecting the range before you begin. As you enter your data in each cell, use the keys listed in Table 1.3 to navigate the range.

Table 1.3. Navigation keys for a selected range.

Key	Result
Enter	Moves down one row.
Shift-Enter	Moves up one row.
Tab	Moves right one column.
Shift-Tab	Moves left one column.
Ctrl-. (period)	Moves from corner to corner in the range.
Ctrl-Alt-right arrow	Moves to the next range in a noncontiguous selection.
Ctrl-Alt-left arrow	Moves to the preceding range in a noncontiguous selection.

The advantage of this technique is that the active cell never leaves the range. For example, if you press Enter after adding data to a cell in the last row of the range, the active cell moves back to the top row and over one column.

Filling a Range

If you need to fill a range with a particular value or formula, Excel gives you two methods:

- Select the range you want to fill, type the value or formula, and press Ctrl-Enter. Excel fills the entire range with whatever you entered in the formula bar.

- Enter the initial value or formula, select the range you want to fill (including the initial cell), and select the **Edit | Fill** command. Then select the appropriate command from the cascade that appears. For example, if you're filling a range down from the initial cell, select the **Down** command. If multiple sheets are selected, use the **Edit | Fill | Across Worksheets** command to fill the range in each worksheet.

> **TIP**
>
> Press Ctrl-R to select the **Edit | Fill | Right** command or Ctrl-D to select the **Edit | Fill | Down** command.

Using the Fill Handle

The *fill handle* is the small black square in the bottom-right corner of the active cell or range. This handy little tool can do many useful things, including creating a series of text or numeric values and filling, clearing, inserting, and deleting ranges. The next few sections show you how to use the fill handle to perform each of these operations.

Using AutoFill to Create Text and Numeric Series

Worksheets often use text series (such as January, February, March; or Sunday, Monday, Tuesday) and numeric series (such as 1, 3, 5; or 1993, 1994, 1995). Instead of entering these series by hand, you can use the fill handle to create them automatically. This handy feature is called *AutoFill.* The following steps show you how it works:

1. For a text series, select the first cell of the range you want to use, and enter the initial value. For a numeric series, enter the first two values and then select both cells.

2. Position the mouse pointer over the fill handle. The pointer changes to a plus sign (+).

3. Drag the mouse pointer until the gray border encompasses the range you want to fill. If you're not sure where to stop, look at the formula bar's Name box, which shows you the series value of the last selected cell.

4. Release the mouse button. Excel fills in the range with the series.

Figure 1.14 shows several series created with the fill handle (the shaded cells are the initial fill values). Notice, in particular, that Excel increments any text value that includes a numeric component (such as Quarter 1 and Customer 1001).

FIGURE 1.14.

Some sample series created with the fill handle. Shaded entries are the initial fill values.

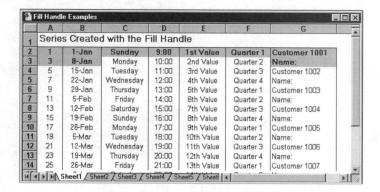

Here are a few guidelines to keep in mind when using the fill handle to create a series:

- Dragging the handle down or to the right increments the values. Dragging it up or to the left decrements the values.

- The fill handle recognizes standard abbreviations such as Jan and Sun.

- To vary the series interval for a text series, enter the first two values of the series, and then select both of them before dragging. For example, entering 1st and 3rd produces the series 1st, 3rd, 5th, and so on.

- If you use three or more numbers as the initial values for the fill handle series, Excel creates a "best fit" or "trend" line. To learn more about using Excel for trend analysis, see Chapter 17, "Basic Analytic Methods."

Creating a Custom AutoFill List

As you've seen, Excel recognizes certain values (for example, January, Sunday, 1st Quarter) as part of a larger list. When you drag the fill handle from a cell containing one of these values, Excel fills the cells with the appropriate series. However, you're not stuck with just the few lists that Excel recognized out of the box. You're free to define your own AutoFill lists, as described in the following steps:

1. Select the **Tools | O**ptions command to display the Options dialog box.

2. Select the Custom Lists tab.

3. In the Custom **L**ists box, select NEW LIST. An insertion point appears in the List **E**ntries box.

4. Type an item from your list into the List **E**ntries box and press Enter. Repeat this step for each item. (Make sure that you add the items in the order in which you want them to appear in the series.) Figure 1.15 shows an example.

FIGURE 1.15.

Use the Custom Lists tab to create your own custom lists.

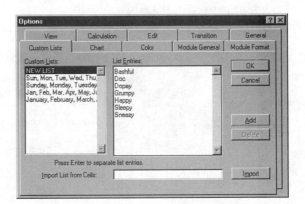

5. Select **A**dd to add the list to the Custom **L**ists box.

6. Select OK to return to the worksheet.

TIP

If you already have the list in a worksheet range, don't bother entering each item by hand. Instead, activate the **I**mport List from Cells edit box, and enter a reference to the range (you can either type the reference or select the cells directly on the worksheet). Click the Im**p**ort button to add the list to the Custom **L**ists box.

> **NOTE**
>
> If you need to delete a custom list, highlight it in the Custom **L**ists box, and then select the **D**elete button.

Filling a Range

You can use the fill handle to fill a range with a value or formula. Just enter your initial values or formulas, select them, and then drag the fill handle over the destination range. (I'm assuming here that the data you're copying won't create a series.) When you release the mouse button, Excel fills the range.

Note that if the initial cell contains a formula with relative references (which I'll talk about in Chapter 2), Excel adjusts the references accordingly. For example, suppose that the initial cell contains the formula =A1. If you fill down, the next cell will contain the formula =A2, the next will contain =A3, and so on.

Creating a Series

Instead of using the fill handle to create a series, you can use Excel's Series command to gain a little more control over the whole process. Follow these steps:

1. Select the first cell you want to use for the series, and enter the starting value. If you want to create a series out of a particular pattern (such as 2, 4, 6,...), fill in enough cells to define the pattern.

2. Select the entire range you want to fill.

3. Select the **E**dit | **F**ill | **S**eries command. Excel displays the Series dialog box, shown in Figure 1.16.

FIGURE 1.16.

Use the Series dialog box to define the series you want to create.

4. In the Series in group, select **R**ows to create the series in rows starting from the active cell, or **C**olumns to create the series in columns.

5. Use the Type group to enter the type of series you want. You have the following options:

Linear   This option finds the next series value by adding the step value (see step 7) to the preceding value in the series.

Growth   This option finds the next series value by multiplying the preceding value by the step value.

Date   This option creates a series of dates based on the option you select in the Date Unit group (Day, Weekday, Month, or Year).

AutoFill   This option works much like the fill handle does. You can use it to extend a numeric pattern or a text series (for example, Qtr1, Qtr2, Qtr3).

6. If you want to extend a series trend, activate the Trend check box. (See Chapter 17 for a discussion of trend analysis.) This option is available only if you selected a Linear or Growth series type.

7. If you selected a Linear, Growth, or Date series type, enter a number in the Step Value box. This number is what Excel uses to increment each value in the series.

8. To place a limit on the series, enter the appropriate number in the Stop Value box.

9. Select OK. Excel fills in the series and returns you to the worksheet.

Figure 1.17 shows some sample column series. The Growth series stops at cell C14 (value 128) because the next term in the series (256) is greater than the stop value of 250. The Day series fills the range with every second date (because the step value is 2). The Weekday series is slightly different; the dates are sequential, but weekends are skipped.

FIGURE 1.17.

Some sample column series generated with the Series command.

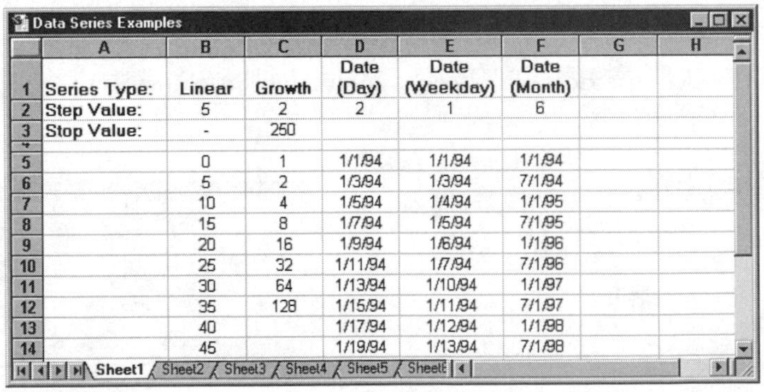

	A	B	C	D Date (Day)	E Date (Weekday)	F Date (Month)	G	H
1	Series Type:	Linear	Growth					
2	Step Value:	5	2	2	1	6		
3	Stop Value:	-	250					
5		0	1	1/1/94	1/1/94	1/1/94		
6		5	2	1/3/94	1/3/94	7/1/94		
7		10	4	1/5/94	1/4/94	1/1/95		
8		15	8	1/7/94	1/5/94	7/1/95		
9		20	16	1/9/94	1/6/94	1/1/96		
10		25	32	1/11/94	1/7/94	7/1/96		
11		30	64	1/13/94	1/10/94	1/1/97		
12		35	128	1/15/94	1/11/94	7/1/97		
13		40		1/17/94	1/12/94	1/1/98		
14		45		1/19/94	1/13/94	7/1/98		

Data Series Examples   Sheet1 / Sheet2 / Sheet3 / Sheet4 / Sheet5 / Sheet6

Copying a Range

The quickest way to become productive with Excel is to avoid reinventing your worksheet wheels. If you have a formula that works, or a piece of formatting that you've put a lot of effort into, don't start from scratch to create something similar. Instead, make a copy and then adjust the copy as necessary.

Fortunately, Excel offers all kinds of ways to make copies of your worksheet ranges. Most of these methods involve the Copy command, but I'll begin by showing you the very handy drag-and-drop method.

Using Drag-and-Drop to Copy a Range

If you have a mouse, you can use it to copy a range by selecting the range and then dragging it to the appropriate destination. There are no menus to maneuver and no risks of accidentally overwriting data because you can see exactly where the copied range will go. The following steps show you how to copy a range:

1. Select the range you want to copy.
2. Hold down the Ctrl key.
3. Move the mouse pointer over any edge of the selection (except the fill handle!). You'll know you've positioned the mouse pointer correctly when it changes to an arrow with a plus sign (+).
4. With Ctrl still held down, begin dragging the mouse pointer to the destination range. Excel displays a gray outline that shows you the border of the copy.
5. When you've positioned the range border properly in the destination area, release the mouse button and then the Ctrl key (in that order). Excel pastes a copy of the original range.

NOTE

If you can't get drag-and-drop to work, you need to turn it on. Select the **T**ools | **O**ptions command, select the Edit tab, and activate the Allow Cell **D**rag and Drop check box.

Copying a Range with the Copy Command

If you don't have a mouse kicking around, or if you prefer the pull-down menu approach, you can copy a range using the Copy command.

CAUTION

Before copying a range, look at the destination area and make sure that you won't be overwriting any nonblank cells. Remember that you can use the Undo command if you accidentally destroy some data. If you want to insert the range among some existing cells, see the section later in this chapter titled "Inserting a Copy of a Range."

Follow these steps to copy a range using the Copy command:

1. Select the range you want to copy.

2. Select the **E**dit | **C**opy command. Excel copies the contents of the range to the Clipboard and displays a moving border around the range.

3. Select the upper-left cell of the destination range.

4. Select the **E**dit | **P**aste command. Excel pastes the range from the Clipboard to your destination.

Copying Shortcuts

Because copying a range is one of the most common worksheet tasks, Excel gives you a fistful of shortcut methods to help you get the job done quickly. Here's a summary:

■ The toolbar method:

 Click on this tool on the Standard toolbar to copy the contents of the selected range to the Clipboard.

 Click on this tool on the Standard toolbar to paste the contents of the Clipboard into the destination range.

■ The shortcut keys method:

Press Ctrl-C to copy the selected range, and press Ctrl-V to paste it. If you're going to paste the copied range only once, you can just press Enter instead of selecting **E**dit | **P**aste or pressing Ctrl-V.

■ The shortcut menu method:

Right-click inside a selected range or cell to display the Range shortcut menu. Then select **C**opy or **P**aste as needed.

Making Multiple Copies of a Range

If you need to make multiple copies of a range, you *could* execute a separate Paste command for each destination, but Excel offers an easier way. The following procedure gives the steps:

1. Select the range you want to copy.

2. Copy the range to the Clipboard using any of the methods described earlier.

3. Select the upper-left cell for each destination range (see Figure 1.18). The cells you select can be contiguous or noncontiguous.

4. Select the **E**dit | **P**aste command. Excel pastes the range from the Clipboard to each destination, as shown in Figure 1.19.

FIGURE 1.18.

To paste multiple copies, select the upper-left cell for each destination range.

Copied range

Destination cells

FIGURE 1.19.

When you execute the Paste command, Excel copies the range to each destination.

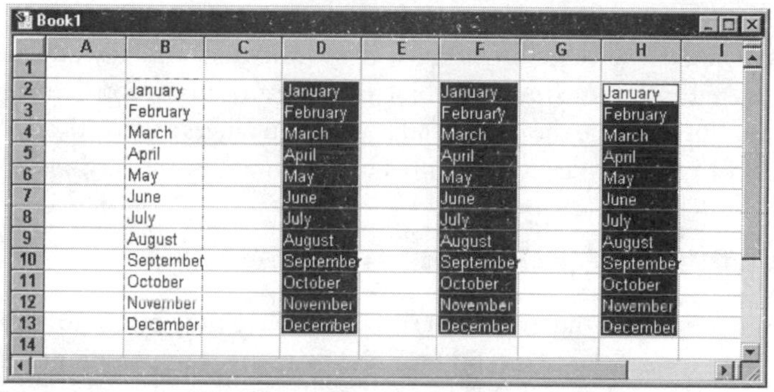

Inserting a Copy of a Range

If you don't want a pasted range to overwrite existing cells, you can tell Excel to *insert* the range. In this case, Excel moves the existing cells out of harm's way before pasting the range from the Clipboard. (As you'll see, you have control over where Excel moves the existing cells.) Follow these steps to insert a copy of a range:

1. Select the range you want to copy.
2. Use any of the methods described earlier in this chapter to copy the range to the Clipboard.
3. Select the upper-left cell of the destination range.
4. Select the **Insert | Copied Cells** command. Excel displays the Insert Paste dialog box to enable you to choose where to move the existing cells that would otherwise be overwritten (see Figure 1.20).

FIGURE 1.20.

Use the Insert Paste dialog box to tell Excel which direction to move the existing cells.

You also can insert a copied range by right-clicking on the destination cell and selecting the Insert Copied Cells command from the shortcut menu.

5. Select Shift Cells **R**ight to move the cells to the right or Shift Cells **D**own to move them down.

6. Select OK. Excel shifts the existing cells and then pastes the range from the Clipboard.

Advanced Range Copying

The copying techniques we've looked at so far normally copy the entire contents of each cell in the range: the value or formula, the formatting, and any attached cell notes. If you like, you can tell Excel to copy only some of these attributes, you can transpose rows and columns, or you can combine the source and destination ranges arithmetically. All this is possible with Excel's **E**dit | Paste **S**pecial command. These techniques are outlined in the next three sections.

Copying Selected Cell Attributes

When rearranging a worksheet, you can save time by combining cell attributes. For example, if you need to copy several formulas to a range but you don't want to disturb the existing formatting, you can tell Excel to copy only the formulas.

If you want to copy only selected cell attributes, follow these steps:

1. Select the range you want to work with, and then copy it to the Clipboard.

2. Select the destination range.

3. Select the **E**dit | Paste **S**pecial command. Excel displays the Paste Special dialog box, shown in Figure 1.21.

FIGURE 1.21.

Use the Paste Special dialog box to select the cell attributes you want to copy.

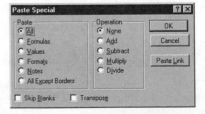

You also can display the Paste Special dialog box by right-clicking on the destination range and selecting the Paste Special command from the shortcut menu.

4. In the Paste group, select the attribute you want to paste into the destination range:

All	Pastes all the cell attributes
Formulas	Pastes only the cell formulas
Values	Converts the cell formulas to values and pastes only the values
Forma**t**s	Pastes only the cell formatting
Notes	Pastes only the cell notes
All Ex**c**ept Borders	Pastes all the cell attributes except the cell's border formatting

5. If you don't want Excel to paste any blank cells included in the selection, activate the Skip **B**lanks check box.

6. Select OK to paste the range.

Combining the Source and Destination Arithmetically

Excel enables you to combine two ranges arithmetically. For example, suppose that you have a range of constants that you want to double. Instead of creating formulas that multiply each cell by two (or, even worse, doubling each cell by hand), you can create a range of the same size that consists of nothing but twos. You then combine this new range with the old one and tell Excel to multiply them. The following steps show you what to do:

1. Select the destination range. (Make sure that it's the same shape as the source range.)

2. Type the constant you want to use, and then press Ctrl-Enter. Excel fills the destination range with the number you entered.

3. Copy the source range to the Clipboard.

4. Select the destination range again.

5. Select the **E**dit | Paste **S**pecial command to display the Paste Special dialog box.

6. Use the following options in the Operation group to select the arithmetic operator you want to use:

None	Performs no operation
Add	Adds the destination cells to the source cells
Subtract	Subtracts the source cells from the destination cells
Multiply	Multiplies the source cells by the destination cells
Divide	Divides the destination cells by the source cells

7. If you don't want Excel to include any blank cells in the operation, activate the Skip **B**lanks check box.

8. Select OK. Excel pastes the results of the operation into the destination range.

Transposing Rows and Columns

If you have row data that you would prefer to see in columns (or vice versa), you can use the Edit | Paste Special command to transpose the data, no problem. Follow these steps:

1. Copy the source cells to the Clipboard.
2. Select the upper-left corner of the destination range.
3. Select the Edit | Paste Special command to display the Paste Special dialog box.
4. Activate the Transpose check box.
5. Select OK. Excel transposes the source range, as shown in Figure 1.22.

FIGURE 1.22.

You can use the Edit | Paste Special command to transpose rows and columns.

Copied range

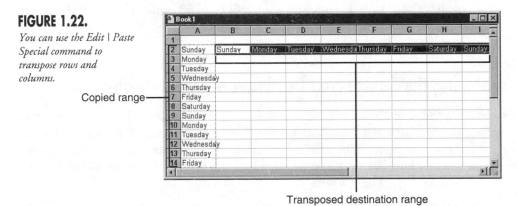

Transposed destination range

Moving a Range

Moving a range is very similar to copying a range, except that the source range gets deleted when all is said and done. You also have the choice of using drag-and-drop or the menu commands.

Using Drag-and-Drop to Move a Range

The drag-and-drop method for moving a range is identical to the one you learned for copying a range, except that you don't have to hold down the Ctrl key. Follow these steps:

1. Select the range you want to move.
2. Move the mouse pointer over any edge of the selection until you see the pointer change to an arrow.
3. Drag the mouse pointer to the destination range. Excel displays a gray outline that shows the border of the copy.
4. When you've positioned the range border properly in the destination area, release the mouse button.

5. If your moved range will paste over any nonblank cells, Excel asks whether you want to replace the contents of the destination cells (see Figure 1.23). If everything looks reasonable, select OK to continue. Excel deletes the original range and pastes it in the destination.

FIGURE 1.23.

Excel warns you if the dropped range will obliterate any existing nonblank cells.

Using the Menu Commands to Move a Range

To move a range with the menu commands, you need to cut the range to the Clipboard and then paste it. The following procedure details the steps involved.

> **CAUTION**
>
> As with copying, you need to be careful when moving ranges so that you don't write over any existing data. If necessary, you can always insert the range using the Insert | Cut Cells command. If you do make a mistake, be sure to select the Edit | Undo command right away.

1. Select the range you want to move.
2. Select the **Edit | Cut** command. Excel cuts the contents of the range to the Clipboard and displays a moving border around the range.
3. Select the upper-left cell of the destination range.
4. Select the **Edit | Paste** command. Excel pastes the range from the Clipboard to your destination.

> **TIP**
>
> For faster range moving, press Ctrl-X instead of selecting the **Edit | Cut** command, or right-click on the source range and select the **Cut** command from the Range shortcut menu. You can also click the Cut button on the Standard toolbar.

Inserting and Deleting a Range

When you begin a worksheet, you generally use rows and columns sequentially as you add data, labels, and formulas. More often than not, however, you'll need to go back and add some values or text that you forgot or that you need for another part of the worksheet. When this happens, you need to insert ranges into your spreadsheet to make room for your new information. Conversely, you often have to remove old or unnecessary data from a spreadsheet, which requires you to delete ranges. The next few sections describe various and sundry methods for inserting and deleting ranges in Excel.

Inserting an Entire Row or Column

The easiest way to insert a range into a worksheet is to insert an entire row or column. The following steps show you how it's done:

1. Select the row or column before which you want to insert the new row or column. If you want to insert multiple rows or columns, select the appropriate number of rows or columns, as shown in Figure 1.24.

FIGURE 1.24.

Two rows have been selected at the point where two new rows are to be inserted.

Summary of Quarterly Sales and Expenses

	A	B	C	D	E	F	G	H	I	J
1										
2		Quarterly Expenses					Quarterly Sales			
3										
4		January	February	March			January	February	March	
5	Advertising	13,800	12,600	15,600		East	48,550	44,600	50,200	
6	Freight	8,700	8,250	9,100		West	42,100	40,900	43,750	
7	Rent	6,300	6,300	6,300		Midwest	38,500	37,800	40,050	
8	Supplies	3,900	3,600	4,200		South	43,750	41,400	45,650	
9	Salaries	48,000	48,000	49,500		TOTAL	172,900	164,700	179,650	
10	Travel	8,400	7,200	9,000						
11	Vehicles	1,500	1,800	1,800						
12	TOTAL	90,600	87,750	95,500						
13										
14										

1st Quarter / 2nd Quarter / 3rd Quarter / 4th Quarter

> **TIP**
>
> Press Ctrl-Spacebar to select an entire column, or Shift-Spacebar to select an entire row.

2. If you're inserting rows, select the **Insert | Rows** command. Excel shifts the selected rows down, as shown in Figure 1.25. If you're inserting columns, select the **Insert | Columns** command instead. In this case, Excel shifts the selected columns to the right.

FIGURE 1.25.

When you insert rows, Excel shifts the existing cells down.

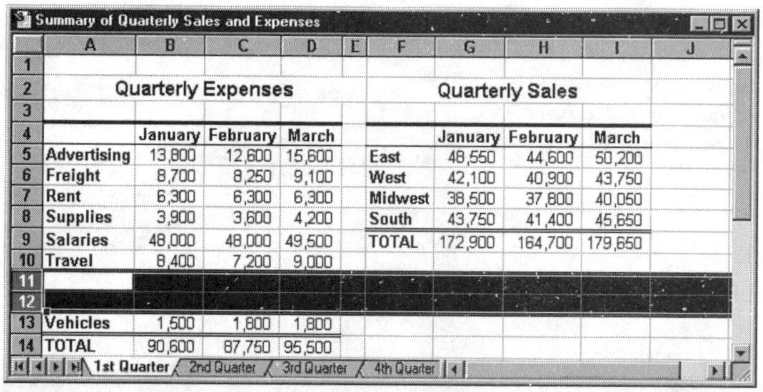

> **TIP**
>
> As soon as you've selected a row or column, press Ctrl-+ (plus sign) to insert a row or column quickly. You also can right-click on the range and then select Insert from the shortcut menu.

Inserting a Row or Column with the Fill Handle

You can use the fill handle we looked at earlier to insert entire rows and columns effortlessly. Begin by selecting the row or column where you want to perform the insertion. You'll see that the first cell in the row or column contains the fill handle. Next, hold down the Shift key and drag the fill handle in the direction in which you want to insert the rows or columns. The number of rows or columns you drag across determines the number of rows or columns that get inserted. When you release both the mouse button and the Shift key, Excel performs the insertion, no questions asked.

Inserting a Cell or Range

In some worksheets, you might need to insert only a single cell or a range of cells so as not to disturb the arrangement of surrounding data. For example, suppose that you want to add a Repair line between Rent and Supplies in the Quarterly Expenses table in Figure 1.26. You don't want to add an entire row because it would create a gap in the Quarterly Sales table. Instead, you can insert a range that covers just the area you need. Follow these steps to see how this works:

1. Select the range where you want the new range to appear. In the Quarterly Expenses example, you would select the range A8:D8 (see Figure 1.26).

2. Select the **Insert | Cells** command. Excel displays the Insert dialog box, shown in Figure 1.27.

FIGURE 1.26.

When you insert cells in the Quarterly Expenses table, you don't want to disturb the Quarterly Sales table.

	A	B	C	D	E	F	G	H	I	J
2		Quarterly Expenses					Quarterly Sales			
3										
4		January	February	March			January	February	March	
5	Advertising	13,800	12,600	15,600		East	48,550	44,600	50,200	
6	Freight	8,700	8,250	9,100		West	42,100	40,900	43,750	
7	Rent	6,300	6,300	6,300		Midwest	38,500	37,800	40,050	
8	Supplies	3,900	3,600	4,200		South	43,750	41,400	45,650	
9	Salaries	48,000	48,000	49,500		TOTAL	172,900	164,700	179,650	
10	Travel	8,400	7,200	9,000						
11	Vehicles	1,500	1,800	1,800						
12	TOTAL	90,600	87,750	95,500						
13										
14										

Summary of Quarterly Sales and Expenses

1st Quarter / 2nd Quarter / 3rd Quarter / 4th Quarter

FIGURE 1.27.

Use the Insert dialog box to tell Excel which to shift the existing cells.

Insert

Insert
- ○ Shift Cells Right
- ● Shift Cells Down
- ○ Entire Row
- ○ Entire Column

OK
Cancel

3. Select either Shift Cells **R**ight or Shift Cells **D**own, as appropriate.

4. Select OK. Excel inserts the range (see Figure 1.28).

FIGURE 1.28.

Excel has shifted the existing cells down to create room for the new range.

	A	B	C	D	E	F	G	H	I	J
1										
2		Quarterly Expenses					Quarterly Sales			
3										
4		January	February	March			January	February	March	
5	Advertising	13,800	12,600	15,600		East	48,550	44,600	50,200	
6	Freight	8,700	8,250	9,100		West	42,100	40,900	43,750	
7	Rent	6,300	6,300	6,300		Midwest	38,500	37,800	40,050	
8						South	43,750	41,400	45,650	
9	Supplies	3,900	3,600	4,200		TOTAL	172,900	164,700	179,650	
10	Salaries	48,000	48,000	49,500						
11	Travel	8,400	7,200	9,000						
12	Vehicles	1,500	1,800	1,800						
13	TOTAL	90,600	87,750	95,500						
14										

Summary of Quarterly Sales and Expenses

1st Quarter / 2nd Quarter / 3rd Quarter / 4th Quarter

Inserting a Range with the Fill Handle

The fill handle also comes in handy when you are inserting a range. Select the range in which you want the insertion to occur, hold down the Shift key, and drag the fill handle over the area where you want the new range inserted. When you release the mouse button and the Shift key, Excel inserts the range.

Deleting an Entire Row or Column

Deleting a row or column is similar to inserting. In this case, however, you need to exercise a little more caution because a hasty deletion can have disastrous effects on your worksheet. (However, keep in mind that you can always select the **Edit | Undo** command if you make any mistakes.)

The following procedure shows you how to delete a row or column:

1. Select the row or column you want to delete.
2. Select the **Edit | Delete** command. Excel deletes the row or column and shifts the remaining data appropriately.

> **TIP**
>
> To delete a selected row or column quickly, press Ctrl-– (minus sign). You also can right-click on the range and select Delete from the shortcut menu.

Deleting a Cell or Range

If you need to delete only one cell or a range to avoid trashing any surrounding data, follow these steps:

1. Select the cell or range you want to delete.
2. Select the **Edit | Delete** command. Excel displays the Delete dialog box, shown in Figure 1.29.

FIGURE 1.29.

Use the Delete dialog box to let Excel know which way to adjust the remaining cells after it has performed the deletion.

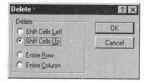

3. Select either Shift Cells **L**eft or Shift Cells **U**p, as appropriate.
4. Select OK. Excel deletes the range.

Clearing a Range

As you've seen, deleting a range actually removes the cells from the worksheet. What if you want the cells to remain, but you want their contents or formats cleared? For that, you can use Excel's Clear command, as described in the following steps:

1. Select the range you want to clear.
2. Select the **Edit | Clear** command. Excel displays a submenu of Clear commands.
3. Select either **All**, **Formats**, **Contents**, or **Notes**, as appropriate.

> **TIP**
>
> To delete the contents of the selected range quickly, press Delete. You also can right-click on the range and select Clear Contents from the Range shortcut menu.

Clearing a Range with the Fill Handle

To clear the values and formulas in a range with the fill handle, you can use either of the following two techniques:

- If you want to clear only the values and formulas in a range, select the range and then drag the fill handle into the range and over the cells you want to clear. Excel grays out the cells as you select them. When you release the mouse button, Excel clears the cells' values and formulas.

- If you want to scrub everything from the range (values, formulas, formats, and notes), select the range and then hold down the Ctrl key. Next, drag the fill handle into the range and over each cell you want to clear. Excel clears the cells when you release the mouse button.

Using Excel's Reference Operators

As you probably know, Excel has various operators that you use for building formulas (such as +, *, and &). We'll talk more about them in the next chapter, but I'd like to close our look at ranges by talking about Excel's three *reference operators*. You use these operators when working with cell references, as discussed in the next three sections.

Using the Range Operator

The *range* operator is just the familiar colon (:) that you've been using all along. All you do is insert a colon between two references, and Excel creates a range (for example, A1:C5). Nothing too surprising there.

Until now, though, you've probably been creating your ranges by using the reference on the left side of the colon to define the upper-left corner of the range and the reference on the right side of the colon to define the lower-right corner. There are other ways to create ranges with the range operator, however. Table 1.4 points out a few of them.

Table 1.4. Sample ranges created with the range operator.

Range	What It Refers To
A:A	Column A (that is, the entire column)
A:C	Columns A through C
1:1	Row 1
1:5	Rows 1 through 5

You also can use a range name on either side of the colon. In this case, the named range becomes a *corner* for the larger range. For example, Figure 1.30 shows a worksheet with the named range Rent that refers to B7:D7. Table 1.5 shows some sample ranges you can create with Rent as one corner.

FIGURE 1.30.

The named range Rent used in Table 1.5.

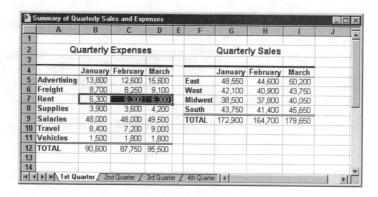

Table 1.5. Sample ranges created with a range name.

Range	What It Refers To
Rent:A1	A1:D7
Rent:G2	B2:G7
Rent:E10	B7:E10
Rent:A13	A7:D13

Using the Intersection Operator

If you have ranges that overlap, you can use the *intersection* operator (a space) to refer to the overlapping cells. For example, Figure 1.31 shows two ranges: C4:E9 and D8:G11. To refer to the overlapping cells (D8:E9), you would use the following notation: C4:E9 D8:G11.

FIGURE 1.31.

The intersection operator returns the intersecting cells of two ranges.

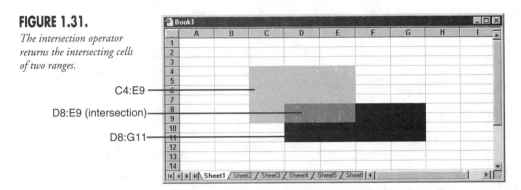

If you've named the ranges on your worksheet, the intersection operator can make things much easier to read because you can refer to individual cells by using the names of the cell's row and column. For example, in Figure 1.32, the range B5:B12 is named January and the range B7:D7 is named Rent. This means that you can refer to cell B7 as January Rent (see cell H11).

FIGURE 1.32.

After you name ranges, you can combine row and column headings to create intersecting names for individual cells.

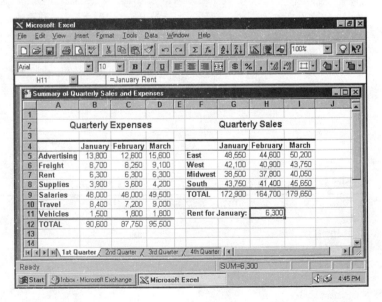

> **CAUTION**
>
> If you try to define an intersection name and Excel displays #NULL! in the cell, it means the two ranges don't have any overlapping cells.

Using the Union Operator

To create a reference that combines two or more ranges, use the *union* operator (,). For example, Figure 1.33 shows the range C4:E9,D8:G11, which is the union of C4:E9 and D8:G11.

FIGURE 1.33.

Use the union operator to create a single reference that combines two or more ranges.

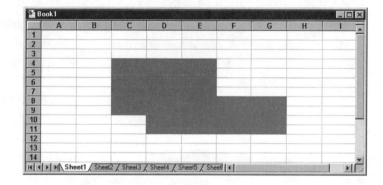

Summary

This chapter showed you how to get the most out of your worksheet ranges. I showed you a number of ways to select a range with both the mouse and the keyboard. I also told you about range names, the fill handle, creating a series, copying and moving a range, and how to use Excel's reference operators. For related range information, see the following chapters:

- In Chapter 2, "Building Better Formulas," I'll show you how to work with a special type of range called an *array*.

- Functions often use range arguments, and you'll be learning about functions in Chapter 3, "Harnessing the Power of Excel's Worksheet Functions."

- To make your ranges look their best, you need to know how to format them. You'll find all kinds of formatting techniques in Chapter 4, "Formatting Excel Worksheets."

Building Better Formulas

2

A worksheet is merely a lifeless collection of numbers and text until you define some kind of relationship among the various entries. You do this by creating *formulas* that perform calculations and produce results. This chapter takes you through some formula basics, shows you a number of techniques for building powerful formulas, and talks about troubleshooting and auditing formulas.

Understanding Formula Basics

Most worksheets are created to provide answers to specific questions: What is the company's profit? Are expenses over or under budget, and by how much? What is the future value of an investment? How big will my bonus be this year? You can answer these questions, and an infinite variety of others, by using Excel formulas.

All Excel formulas have the same general structure: an equals sign (=), followed by one or more *operands*—which can be a value, a cell reference, a range, a range name, or a function name—separated by one or more *operators*—the symbols that combine the operators, such as the plus sign (+) and the greater-than sign (>).

Excel divides formulas into four groups: arithmetic, comparison, text, and reference. Each group has its own set of operators, and you use each group in different ways. In the next few sections, I'll show you how to use each type of formula.

Using Arithmetic Formulas

Arithmetic formulas are by far the most common type of formula. They combine numbers, cell addresses, and function results with mathematical operators to perform calculations. I've summarized the mathematical operators used in arithmetic formulas in Table 2.1.

Table 2.1. The arithmetic operators.

Operator	Name	Example	Result
+	Addition	=10+5	15
−	Subtraction	=10-5	5
−	Negation	=-10	−10
*	Multiplication	=10*5	50
/	Division	=10/5	2
%	Percentage	=10%	0.1
^	Exponentiation	=10^5	100000

Most of these operators are straightforward, but the exponentiation operator might require further explanation. The formula =x^y means that the value x is raised to the power y. For example, the formula =3^2 produces the result 9 (that is, 3*3=9). Similarly, the formula =2^4 produces 16 (that is, 2*2*2*2=16).

Using Comparison Formulas

A *comparison formula* is a statement that compares two or more numbers, text strings, cell contents, or function results. If the statement is true, the result of the formula is given the logical value TRUE (which is equivalent to any nonzero value). If the statement is false, the formula returns the logical value FALSE (which is equivalent to 0). Table 2.2 summarizes the operators you can use in logical formulas.

Table 2.2. Comparison formula operators.

Operator	Name	Example	Result
=	Equal to	=10=5	FALSE
>	Greater than	=10>5	TRUE
<	Less than	=10<5	FALSE
>=	Greater than or equal to	="a">="b"	FALSE
<=	Less than or equal to	="a"<="b"	TRUE
<>	Not equal to	="a"<>"b"	TRUE

There are many uses for comparison formulas. For example, you can determine whether to pay a salesperson a bonus by using a comparison formula to compare his actual sales with a predetermined quota. If the sales are greater than the quota, the rep is awarded the bonus. You also can monitor credit collection. For example, if the amount a customer owes is more than 150 days past due, you might send the invoice to a collection agency.

Using Text Formulas

So far, I've discussed formulas that calculate or make comparisons and return values. A *text formula* is a formula that returns text. Text formulas use the ampersand (&) operator to work with text cells, text strings enclosed in quotation marks, and text function results.

One way to use text formulas is to concatenate text strings. For example, if you enter the formula ="soft"&"ware" into a cell, Excel displays software. Note that the quotation marks and ampersand are not shown in the result. You also can use & to combine cells that contain text. For example, if A1 contains the text Ben and A2 contains Jerry, then entering the formula =A1&" and " &A2 returns Ben and Jerry. I show you other uses for text formulas in Chapter 3, "Harnessing the Power of Excel's Worksheet Functions."

Using Reference Formulas

The reference operators combine two cell references or ranges to create a single joint reference. I discussed reference formulas in detail in Chapter 1, "Getting the Most Out of Ranges," but Table 2.3 gives you a quick summary.

Table 2.3. Reference formula operators.

Operator	Name	Description
: (colon)	Range	Produces a range from two cell references (for example, A1:C5).
(space)	Intersection	Produces a range that is the intersection of two ranges (for example, A1:C5 B2:E8).
, (comma)	Union	Produces a range that is the union of two ranges (for example, A1:C5,B2:E8).

Understanding Operator Precedence

You'll often use simple formulas that contain just two values and a single operator. In practice, however, most formulas you use will have a number of values and operators. In these more complex expressions, the order in which the calculations are performed becomes crucial. For example, consider the formula =3+5^2. If you calculate from left to right, the answer you get is 64 (3+5 equals 8 and 8^2 equals 64). However, if you perform the exponentiation first and then the addition, the result is 28 (5^2 equals 25 and 3+25 equals 28). As this example shows, a single formula can produce multiple answers depending on the order in which you perform the calculations.

To control this problem, Excel evaluates a formula according to a predefined *order of precedence*. This order of precedence enables Excel to calculate a formula unambiguously by determining which part of the formula it calculates first, which part second, and so on.

The Order of Precedence

Excel's order of precedence is determined by the various formula operators I outlined earlier. Table 2.4 summarizes the complete order of precedence used by Excel.

Table 2.4. Excel's order of precedence.

Operator	Operation	Order of Precedence
:	Range	First
(space)	Intersection	Second

Operator	*Operation*	*Order of Precedence*
,	Union	Third
–	Negation	Fourth
%	Percentage	Fifth
^	Exponentiation	Sixth
* and /	Multiplication and division	Seventh
+ and –	Addition and subtraction	Eighth
&	Concatenation	Ninth
= < > <= >= <>	Comparison	Tenth

From this table, you can see that Excel performs exponentiation before addition. Therefore, the correct answer for the formula =3+5^2, given earlier, is 28. Notice, as well, that some operators in Table 2.4 have the same order of precedence (for example, multiplication and division). This means that it doesn't matter in which order these operators are evaluated. For example, consider the formula =5*10/2. If you perform the multiplication first, the answer you get is 25 (5*10 equals 50, and 50/2 equals 25). If you perform the division first, you also get an answer of 25 (10/2 equals 5, and 5*5 equals 25). By convention, Excel evaluates operators with the same order of precedence from left to right.

Controlling the Order of Precedence

There are times when you want to override the order of precedence. For example, suppose that you want to create a formula that calculates the pretax cost of an item. If you bought something for $10.65, including 7 percent sales tax, and you want to find the cost of the item less the tax, you use the formula =10.65/1.07, which gives you the correct answer of $9.95. In general, this is the formula:

$$\text{Pre-tax cost} = \frac{\text{Total Cost}}{1 + \text{Tax Rate}}$$

Figure 2.1 shows how you might implement such a formula. Cell B5 displays the Total Cost variable, and cell B6 displays the Tax Rate variable. Given these parameters, your first instinct might be to use the formula =B5/1+B6 to calculate the original cost. This formula is shown in cell E9, and the result is given in cell D9. As you can see, this answer is incorrect. What happened? Well, according to the rules of precedence, Excel performs division before addition, so the value in B5 first is divided by 1 and then is added to the value in B6. To get the correct answer, you must override the order of precedence so that the addition 1+B6 is performed first. You do this by surrounding that part of the formula with parentheses, as shown in cell E10. When this is done, you get the correct answer (cell D10).

FIGURE 2.1.

Use parentheses to control the order of precedence in your formulas.

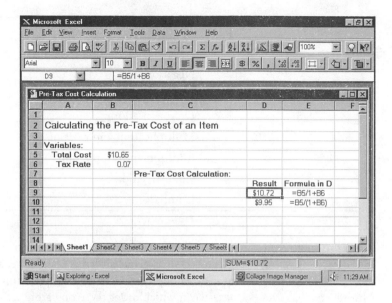

In general, you can use parentheses to control the order that Excel uses to calculate formulas. Terms inside parentheses are always calculated first; terms outside parentheses are calculated sequentially (according to the order of precedence). To gain even more control over your formulas, you can place parentheses inside one another; this is called *nesting* parentheses. Excel always evaluates the innermost set of parentheses first. Here are a few sample formulas:

Formula	First Step	Second Step	Third Step	Result
3^(15/5)*2-5	3^3*2–5	27*2–5	54–5	49
3^((15/5)*2-5)	3^(3*2–5)	3^(6–5)	3^1	3
3^(15/(5*2-5))	3^(15/(10–5))	3^(15/5)	3^3	27

Notice that the order of precedence rules also hold within parentheses. For example, in the expression (5*2–5), the term 5*2 is calculated before 5 is subtracted.

Using parentheses to determine the order of calculations enables you to gain full control over Excel formulas. This way, you can make sure that the answer given by a formula is the one you want.

CAUTION

One of the most common mistakes when using parentheses in formulas is to forget to close a parenthetic term with a right parenthesis. If you do this, Excel generates a `Parentheses do not match` message. To make sure that you've closed each parenthetic term, count all the left and right parentheses. If these totals don't match, you know you've left out a parenthesis.

Controlling Worksheet Calculation

Excel always calculates a formula when you confirm its entry, and the program normally recalculates existing formulas automatically whenever their data changes. This behavior is fine for small worksheets, but it can slow you down if you have a complex model that takes several seconds or even several minutes to recalculate. To turn off this automatic recalculation, follow these steps:

1. Select the **T**ools | **O**ptions command. The Options dialog box appears.

2. Select the Calculation tab to display the Calculation options, as shown in Figure 2.2.

FIGURE 2.2.

Select the Calculation tab in the Options dialog box to control worksheet calculations.

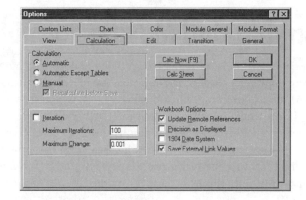

3. To disable automatic recalculation, select the **M**anual option. If you would prefer to leave automatic calculation on except for data tables, select the Automatic Except **T**ables option instead.

4. If you chose **M**anual, you also can decide not to recalculate before saving the worksheet. Just turn off the Recalculate before Save check box.

5. Select OK.

With manual calculation turned on, you'll see a `Calculate` message appear in the status bar whenever your worksheet data changes and your formula results need to be updated. When you want to recalculate, select **T**ools | **O**ptions and choose one of the following options from the Calculation tab:

- Click the Calc **N**ow button to recalculate every open worksheet.
- Click the Calc **S**heet button to recalculate only the active worksheet.

TIP

To recalculate the open worksheets without bothering with the Options dialog box, press F9. If you want to calculate only the active worksheet, press Shift-F9.

If you want to recalculate only part of your worksheet while manual calculation is turned on, you have two options:

■ To recalculate a single formula, select the cell containing the formula, activate the formula bar, and then confirm the cell (by pressing Enter or clicking the Enter button).

■ To recalculate a range, select the range, select the **E**dit | **R**eplace command, and enter an equals sign (=) in both the Fi**n**d What and **R**eplace With boxes. (Make sure that the Find Entire Cells **O**nly check box is deactivated.) When you select Replace **A**ll, Excel "replaces" the equals sign in each formula with another equals sign. This doesn't change anything, but it forces Excel to recalculate each formula.

Copying and Moving Formulas

I showed you various techniques for copying and moving ranges. The procedures for copying and moving ranges that contain formulas are identical, but the results are not always straightforward. For an example, check out Figure 2.3, which shows a list of expense data for a company. The formula in cell C11 totals the January expenses. The idea behind this worksheet is to calculate a new expense budget number for 1995 as a percentage increase of the actual 1994 total. Cell C3 displays the INCREASE variable (in this case, the increase being used is 9 percent). The formula that calculates the 1995 BUDGET number (cell C13 for the month of January) multiplies the 1994 TOTAL by the INCREASE (that is, =C11*C3).

FIGURE 2.3.

A budget expenses worksheet.

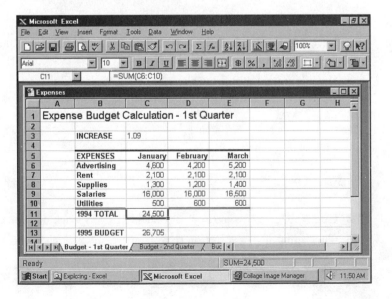

The next step is to calculate the 1994 TOTAL expenses and the 1995 BUDGET figure for February. You could just type each new formula, but you learned in the preceding chapter that you can copy a cell much more quickly. Figure 2.4 shows the results when you copy the contents of cell C11 into cell D11. As you can see, Excel adjusts the range in the formula's SUM() function so that only the February expenses are totaled. How did Excel know to do this? To answer this question, you need to know about Excel's relative reference format.

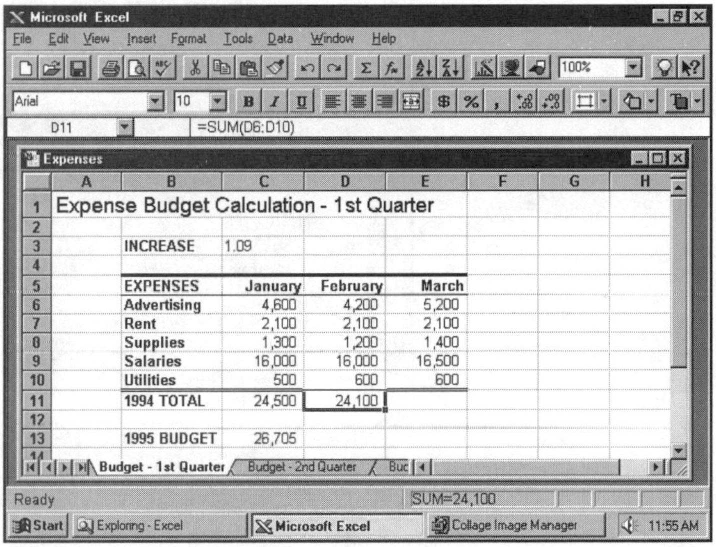

FIGURE 2.4.

When you copy the January 1994 TOTAL formula to February, Excel automatically adjusts the range reference.

Understanding Relative Reference Format

When you use a cell reference in a formula, Excel looks at the cell address relative to the location of the formula. For example, suppose that you have the formula =A1*2 in cell A2. To Excel, this formula says, "Multiply the contents of the cell one row above this one by 2." This is called the *relative reference format*, and it's the default format for Excel. This means that if you copy this formula to cell A5, the relative reference is still "Multiply the contents of the cell one row above this one by 2," but the formula changes to =A4*2, because A4 is one row above A5.

Figure 2.4 shows why this format is useful. You had to copy only the formula in cell C11 to cell D11 and, thanks to relative referencing, everything comes out perfectly. To get the expense total for March, you would just have to paste the same formula into cell E11. You'll find that this way of handling copy operations will save you incredible amounts of time when you're building your worksheet models.

However, you need to exercise some care when copying or moving formulas. Let's see what happens if we return to the budget expense worksheet and try copying the 1995 BUDGET formula in cell C13 to cell D13. Figure 2.5 shows that the result is 0! What happened? The formula bar shows the problem: the new formula is =D11*D3. Cell D11 is the February 1994

TOTAL, and that's fine, but instead of the INCREASE cell (C3), the formula refers to a blank cell (D3). Excel treats blank cells as 0, so the answer is 0. The problem is the relative reference format. When the formula was copied, Excel assumed that the new formula should refer to cell D3. To see how you can correct this problem, you need to learn about another format: the *absolute reference format*.

FIGURE 2.5.

Copying the January 1994 BUDGET formula to February creates a problem.

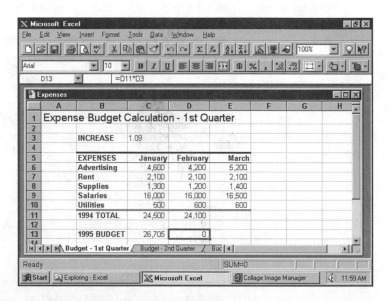

NOTE

The relative reference format problem doesn't occur when you move a formula. When you move a formula, Excel assumes that you want to keep the same cell references.

Understanding Absolute Reference Format

When you refer to a cell in a formula using the absolute reference format, Excel uses the physical address of the cell. You tell the program that you want to use an absolute reference by placing dollar signs ($) before the row and column of the cell address. To return to the example in the preceding section, Excel interprets the formula =$A$1*2 as "Multiply the contents of cell A1 by 2." No matter where you copy or move this formula, the cell reference doesn't change. The cell address is said to be *anchored*.

To fix the budget expense worksheet, we need to anchor the INCREASE variable. To do this, change the January 1995 BUDGET formula in cell C13 to read =C11*$C$3. After you've made this change, try copying the formula again to the February 1995 BUDGET column. You should get the proper value this time.

> **CAUTION**
>
> Most range names refer to absolute cell references. This means that when you copy a formula that uses a range name, the copied formula will use the same range name as the original, which might produce errors in your worksheet.

You also should know that you can enter a cell reference using a mixed reference format. In this format, you anchor either the cell's row (by placing the dollar sign in front of the row address only—for example, B$6) or its column (by placing the dollar sign in front of the column address only—for example, $B6).

> **TIP**
>
> You can quickly change the reference format of a cell address by using the F4 key. When editing a formula, place the cursor to the left of the cell address, and keep pressing F4. Excel cycles through the various formats.

Copying a Formula Without Adjusting Relative References

If you need to copy a formula but don't want the formula's relative references to change, you can use three methods:

- If you want to copy a formula from the cell above, select the lower cell and press Ctrl-' (apostrophe).

- Activate the formula bar and use the mouse or keyboard to highlight the entire formula. Next, copy the formula to the Clipboard (by selecting **E**dit | **C**opy or by pressing Ctrl-C); then press the Esc key to deactivate the formula bar. Finally, select the cell in which you want the copy to appear, and paste the formula there.

- Activate the formula bar and type an apostrophe (') at the beginning of the formula (to the left of the equals sign) to convert it to text. Press Enter to confirm the edit, copy the cell, and then paste it in the desired location. Now, delete the apostrophe from both the source and the destination cells to convert the text back to a formula.

Displaying Worksheet Formulas

By default, Excel displays the results of a formula, rather than the formula itself, in cells. If you need to see a formula, you can simply choose the appropriate cell and look at the formula bar. However, there will be times when you'll want to see all the formulas in a worksheet (such as when you're troubleshooting your work). To display your worksheet's formula, follow these steps:

1. Select the **T**ools | **O**ptions command. The Options dialog box appears.
2. Select the View tab.
3. Activate the Formulas check box.
4. Select OK. Excel displays the worksheet formulas.

TIP

You can also press Ctrl-' (backquote) to toggle a worksheet between values and formulas.

NOTE

For more information about troubleshooting formulas, see "Troubleshooting Formulas," later in this chapter.

Converting a Formula to a Value

If a cell contains a formula whose value will never change, you can convert the formula to that value. This frees up memory for your worksheet because values use much less memory than formulas do. For example, you might have formulas in part of your worksheet that use values from a previous fiscal year. Because these numbers aren't likely to change, you can safely convert the formulas to their values. To do this, follow these steps:

1. Select the cell containing the formula you want to convert.
2. Double-click on the cell or press F2 to activate in-cell editing.
3. Press F9. The formula changes to its value.
4. Press Enter or click on the Enter box. Excel changes the cell to the value.

You'll often need to use the result of a formula in several places. If a formula is in cell C5, for example, you can display its result in other cells by entering =C5 in each of the cells. This is the best method if you think the formula result might change, because if it does, Excel updates the other cells automatically. However, if you're sure the result won't change, you can copy only the value of the formula into the other cells. Use the following procedure to do this:

> **CAUTION**
>
> If your worksheet is set to manual calculation, make sure that you update your formulas (by pressing F9) before copying the values of your formulas.

1. Select the cell that contains the formula.
2. Copy the cell.
3. Select the cell or cells to which you want to copy the value.
4. Select the **E**dit | Paste **S**pecial command. The Paste Special dialog box appears.
5. Activate the **V**alues option button in the Paste group.
6. Select OK. Excel pastes the cell's value to each cell you selected.

Working with Arrays

An *array* is a group of cells or values that Excel treats as a unit. You create arrays either by using a function that returns an array result (such as DOCUMENTS(); see the section in this chapter titled "Functions That Use or Return Arrays"), or by entering an *array formula,* which is a single formula that either uses an array as an argument or enters its results in multiple cells.

Using Array Formulas

Here's a simple example that illustrates how array formulas work. In the Expenses workbook shown in Figure 2.6, the 1995 BUDGET totals are calculated using a separate formula for each month as shown here:

January 1995 BUDGET	=C11*$C$3
February 1995 BUDGET	=D11*$C$3
March 1995 BUDGET	=E11*$C$3

You can replace all three formulas with a single array formula by following these steps:

1. Select the range that you want to use for the array formula. In the 1995 BUDGET example, you select C13:E13.
2. Type the formula, and in the places where you would normally enter a cell reference, type a range reference that includes the cells you want to use. *Don't,* I repeat, *don't* press Enter when you're done. In the example, you enter =C11:E11*$C$3.
3. To enter the formula as an array, press Ctrl-Shift-Enter.

FIGURE 2.6.

This worksheet uses three separate formulas to calculate the 1995 BUDGET figures.

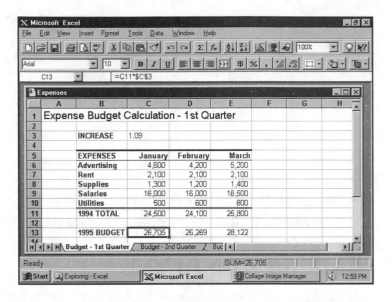

The 1995 BUDGET cells (C13, D13, and E13) now all contain the same formula:

`{=C11:E11*$C$3}`

Notice that the formula is surrounded by braces ({ }). This identifies the formula as an array formula. (When you enter array formulas, you never need to enter these braces yourself; Excel adds them automatically.)

NOTE

Because Excel treats arrays as a unit, you can't move or delete part of an array. If you need to work with an array, you must select the whole thing. If you want to reduce the size of an array, select it, activate the formula bar, and then press Ctrl-Enter to change the entry to a normal formula. You can then select the smaller range and reenter the array formula.

TIP

To select an array quickly, activate one of its cells and press Ctrl-/.

Understanding Array Formulas

To understand how Excel processes an array, you need to keep in mind that Excel always sets up a correspondence between the array cells and the cells of whatever range you entered into the array formula. In the 1994 BUDGET example, the array consists of cells C13, D13, and E13, and the range used in the formula consists of cells C11, D11, and E11. Excel sets up a correspondence between array cell C13 and input cell C11, D13 and D11, and E13 and E11. To calculate the value of cell C13 (the January 1994 BUDGET), for example, Excel just grabs the input value from cell C11 and substitutes that in the formula. Figure 2.7 shows a diagram of this process.

FIGURE 2.7.

When processing an array formula, Excel sets up a correspondence between the array cells and the range used in the formula.

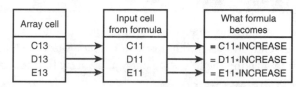

Array formulas can be confusing, but if you keep these correspondences in mind, you should have no trouble figuring out what's going on.

Array Formulas That Operate on Multiple Ranges

In the preceding example, the array formula operated on a single range, but array formulas also can operate on multiple ranges. For example, consider the Invoice Template worksheet shown in Figure 2.8. The totals in the Extension column (cells F12 through F16) are generated by a series of formulas that multiply the item's price by the quantity ordered. For example, the formula in cell F12 is this:

=B12*E12

FIGURE 2.8.

This worksheet uses several formulas to calculate the extended totals for each line.

You can replace all these formulas by making the following entry as an array formula into the range F12:F16:

=B12:B16*E12:E16

Again, you've created the array formula by replacing each cell reference with the corresponding ranges (and by pressing Ctrl-Shift-Enter).

> **NOTE**
>
> You don't have to enter array formulas in multiple cells. For example, if you don't need the Extended totals in the Invoice Template worksheet, you can still calculate the Subtotal by making the following entry as an array formula in cell F17:
>
> =SUM(B12:B16*E12:E16)

Using Array Constants

In the array formulas you've seen so far, the array arguments have been cell ranges. You also can use constant values as array arguments. This procedure enables you to input values into a formula without having them clutter your worksheet.

To enter an array constant in a formula, enter the values right in the formula, and observe the following guidelines:

- Enclose the values in braces ({}).
- If you want Excel to treat the values as a row, separate each value with a semicolon.
- If you want Excel to treat the values as a column, separate each value with a comma.

For example, the following array constant is the equivalent of entering the individual values in a column on your worksheet:

{1;2;3;4}

Similarly, the following array constant is equivalent to entering the values in a worksheet range of three columns and two rows:

{1,2,3;4,5,6}

As a practical example, Figure 2.9 shows two different array formulas. The one on the left (used in the range E4:E7) calculates various loan payments given the different interest rates in the range C5:C8. The array formula on the right (used in the range F4:F7) does the same thing, but the interest rate values are entered as an array constant directly in the formula.

FIGURE 2.9.

*Using array constants in
your array formulas means
you don't have to clutter
your worksheet with the
input values.*

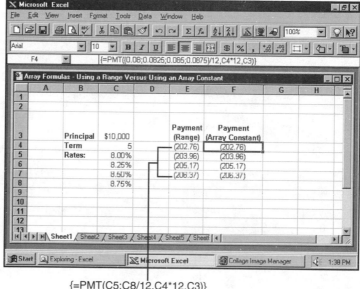

{=PMT(C5:C8/12,C4*12,C3)}

Functions That Use or Return Arrays

Many of Excel's worksheet functions either require an array argument or return an array result
(or both). Table 2.5 lists several of these functions and explains how each one uses arrays.

Table 2.5. Some Excel functions that use arrays.

What the Function Uses	*Array Argument?*	*Returns Array Result?*
COLUMN()	No	Yes, if the argument is a range
COLUMNS()	Yes	No
CONSOLIDATE()	Yes	No
DOCUMENTS()	No	Yes, if multiple documents are open
FILES()	No	Yes
GROWTH()	Yes	Yes
HLOOKUP()	Yes	No
INDEX()	Yes	Yes
LINEST()	No	Yes
LOGEST()	No	Yes
LOOKUP()	Yes	No

continues

Table 2.5. continued

What the Function Uses	Array Argument?	Returns Array Result?
MATCH()	Yes	No
MDETERM()	Yes	No
MINVERSE()	No	Yes
MMULT()	No	Yes
NAMES()	No	Yes
ROW()	No	Yes, if the argument is a range
ROWS()	Yes	No
SUMPRODUCT()	Yes	No
TRANSPOSE()	Yes	Yes
TREND()	Yes	Yes
VLOOKUP()	Yes	No
WINDOWS()	No	Yes
WORKGROUP()	Yes	No

When you use functions that return arrays, be sure to select a range large enough to hold the resulting array, and then enter the function as an array formula.

Working with Range Names in Formulas

You probably use range names often in your formulas. After all, a cell that contains the formula =Sales-Expenses is much more comprehensible than one that contains the more cryptic formula =F12-F2. The next few sections show you a few techniques that will make it easier for you to use range names in formulas.

Pasting a Name into a Formula

One way to enter a range name in a formula is to type the name in the formula bar. But what if you can't remember the name? Or what if the name is long and you've got a deadline looming? For these kinds of situations, Excel has a feature that enables you to select the name you want from a list and paste it right into the formula. The following procedure gives you the details:

1. In the formula bar, place the insertion point where you want the name to appear.
2. Select the **Insert | Name | Paste** command. Excel displays the Paste Name dialog box, shown in Figure 2.10.

FIGURE 2.10.
Use the Paste Name dialog box to paste a range name into a formula.

> **TIP**
>
> A quick way to display the Paste Name dialog box is to press F3.

3. Use the Paste **N**ame list to highlight the range name you want to use.
4. Select OK. Excel pastes the name in the formula bar.

> **TIP**
>
> You can bypass the Paste Name dialog box by using the Name box in the formula bar. When you're ready to paste a name, drop down the Name list and select the name you want.

Applying Names to Formulas

If you've been using ranges in your formulas, and you name those ranges later, Excel doesn't automatically apply the new names to the formulas. Instead of substituting the appropriate names by hand, you can get Excel to do the dirty work for you. Follow these steps to apply the new range names to your existing formulas:

1. Select the range in which you want to apply the names, or select a single cell if you want to apply the names to the entire worksheet.
2. Select the **I**nsert | **N**ame | **A**pply command. Excel displays the Apply Names dialog box, shown in Figure 2.11.

FIGURE 2.11.
Use the Apply Names dialog box to select the names you want to apply to your formula ranges.

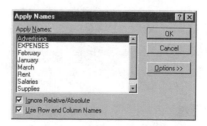

3. Select the names you want applied from the Apply Names list.

4. Activate the **I**gnore Relative/Absolute check box to ignore relative and absolute references when applying names. (See the next section for more information on this option.)

5. The **U**se Row and Column Names check box tells Excel whether to use the worksheet's row and column names when applying names. If you activate this check box, you also can click the Options button to see more choices. (See the section in this chapter titled "Using Row and Column Names When Applying Names" for details.)

6. Select OK to apply the names.

Ignoring Relative and Absolute References When Applying Names

If you deactivate the **I**gnore Relative/Absolute option in the Apply Names dialog box, Excel only replaces relative range references with names that refer to relative references, and it only replaces absolute range references with names that refer to absolute references. If you leave this option activated, Excel ignores relative and absolute reference formats when applying names to a formula.

For example, suppose that you have a formula such as =SUM(A1:A10) and a range named Sales that refers to $A$1:$A$10. With the Ignore Relative/Absolute option turned off, Excel will not apply the name Sales to the range in the formula; Sales refers to an absolute range, and the formula contains a relative range. Unless you think you'll be moving your formulas around, you should leave the **I**gnore Relative/Absolute option activated.

Using Row and Column Names When Applying Names

For extra clarity in your formulas, leave the **U**se Row and Column Names check box activated in the Apply Names dialog box. This option tells Excel to rename all cell references that can be described as the intersection of a named row and a named column. In Figure 2.12, for example, the range C6:C13 is named January, and the range C7:E7 is named Rent. This means that cell C7—the intersection of these two ranges—can be referenced as January Rent.

> **NOTE**
>
> The space character is Excel's intersection operator. For more information, see Chapter 1.

FIGURE 2.12.

The intersection of the January and Rent ranges (cell C7) can be referenced as January Rent.

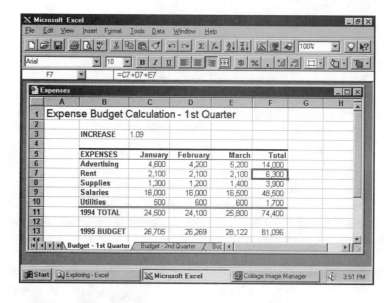

The Total for the Rent row (cell F7) currently contains the formula =C7+D7+E7. If you applied range names to this worksheet and selected the Use Row and Column Names option, you would think this formula would be changed to this:

```
=January Rent + February Rent + March Rent
```

If you try this, however, you'll get a slightly different formula, as shown in Figure 2.13.

FIGURE 2.13.

The Total Rent (cell F7) formula after applying names.

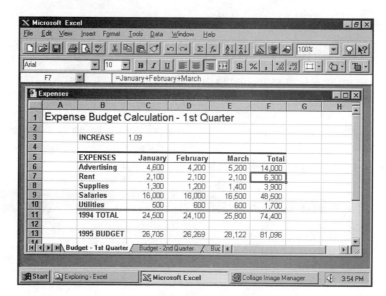

The reason for this is that when Excel is applying names, it omits the row name if the formula is in the same row. (It also omits the column name if the formula is in the same column.) In cell F7, for example, Excel omits Rent in each term because F7 is in the Rent row.

Omitting row headings isn't a problem in a small model, but it can be confusing in a large worksheet, where you might not be able to see the names of the rows. Therefore, if you're applying names to a large worksheet, you'll probably prefer to include the row headings when applying names.

If you click the **O**ptions button in the Apply Names dialog box, the expanded dialog box (shown in Figure 2.14) includes extra options that enable you to include column (and row) headings. To include column names, deactivate the Omit **C**olumn Name if Same Column check box. You can include rows by deactivating the Omit **R**ow Name if Same Row check box. The expanded dialog box also enables you to choose the order of names in the reference (Ro**w** Column or Co**l**umn Row).

FIGURE 2.14.

The expanded Apply Names dialog box.

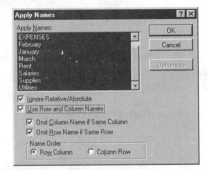

Avoiding #NAME Errors When Deleting Range Names

If you've used a range name in a formula and then you delete that name, Excel generates a #NAME error. Wouldn't it be better if Excel just converted the name to its appropriate cell reference in each formula, the way Lotus 1-2-3 does? Possibly, but there is an advantage to Excel's seemingly inconvenient approach. By generating an error, Excel enables you to catch range names that you delete by accident. Because Excel leaves the names in the formula, you can recover by simply redefining the original range name.

> **NOTE**
>
> Redefining the original range name becomes problematic if you can't remember the appropriate range coordinates. This is why it's always a good idea to paste a list of range names and their references into each of your worksheets. (I showed you how to do this back in Chapter 1; see the section titled "Pasting a List of Range Names in a Worksheet.")

If you don't need this safety net, there *is* a way to make Excel convert deleted range names into their cell references. Just select the **T**ools | **O**ptions command, and select the Transition tab in the Options dialog box that appears. Activate the Transition Formula Entry check box, and then select OK. This action tells Excel to treat your formula entries the same way Lotus 1-2-3 does. Specifically, in formulas that use a deleted range name, the name automatically gets converted to its appropriate range reference. As an added bonus, Excel also performs the following automatic conversions:

- If you enter a range reference in a formula, the reference gets converted to a range name (provided, of course, that a name exists).

- If you define a name for a range, Excel converts any existing range references into the new name. This enables you to avoid the Apply Names feature, discussed earlier.

Naming Formulas

In Chapter 1, I showed you how to set up names for often-used constants. You can apply a similar naming concept for frequently used formulas, and as with the constants, the formula doesn't physically have to appear in a cell. This not only saves memory, but it often makes your worksheets easier to read as well. Follow these steps to name a formula:

1. Select the **I**nsert | **N**ame | **D**efine command. Excel displays the Define Name dialog box.

2. Enter the name you want to use for the formula in the Names in **W**orkbook edit box.

3. In the **R**efers to box, enter the formula exactly as you would in the formula bar.

> **TIP**
>
> Press F2 to put Excel into Edit mode before you move around inside the **R**efers to box with the arrow keys. If you don't press F2 first, Excel assumes that you're trying to select a cell on the worksheet.

4. Select OK.

Now you can enter the formula name in your worksheet cells (rather than the formula itself). For example, following is the formula for the volume of a sphere (r is the radius of the sphere):

$4\pi r^3/3$

So assuming that you have a cell named Radius somewhere in the workbook, you could create a formula named, say, SphereVolume and make the following entry in the **R**efers to box of the Define Name dialog box:

```
=(4*PI()*Radius^3)/3
```

NOTE

To see some good examples of named formulas, refer to the later section of this chapter titled "An Example: The Game of Life, Excel Style."

Working with Links in Formulas

If you have data in one workbook that you want to use in another, you can set up a link between them. This action enables your formulas to use references to cells or ranges in the other workbook. When the other data changes, Excel automatically updates the link.

For example, Figure 2.15 shows two linked workbooks. The Budget Summary sheet in the 1995 Budget - Summary workbook includes data from the Details worksheet in the 1995 Budget workbook. Specifically, the formula shown for cell B2 in 1995 Budget - Summary contains an external reference to cell R7 in the Details worksheet of 1995 Budget. If the value in R7 changes, Excel immediately updates the 1995 Budget - Summary workbook.

FIGURE 2.15.

Two linked workbooks.

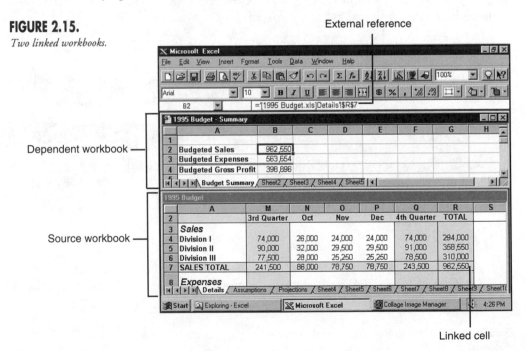

> **NOTE**
>
> The workbook that contains the external reference is called the *dependent* workbook (or the *client* workbook). The workbook that contains the original data is called the *source* workbook (or the *server* workbook).

Understanding External References

There's no big mystery behind Excel links. You set up links by including an external reference to a cell or range in another workbook (or in another worksheet from the same workbook). In my case, all I did was enter an equals sign in cell B2 of the Budget Summary worksheet, and then I clicked on cell R7 in the Details worksheet.

The only thing you need to be comfortable with is the structure of an external reference. Here's the syntax:

```
'path[workbookname]sheetname'!reference
```

`path`	The drive and directory in which the workbook is located. You need to include the path only when the workbook is closed.
`workbookname`	The name of the workbook, including an extension. Always enclose the workbook name in square brackets ([ ]). You can omit `workbookname` if you're referencing a cell or range in another sheet of the same workbook.
`sheetname`	The name of the worksheet's tab. You can omit `sheetname` if `reference` is a defined name in the same workbook.
`reference`	A cell or range reference, or a defined name.

For example, if you close the 1995 Budget workbook, Excel automatically changes the external reference shown in Figure 2.15 to this:

```
='C:\My Documents\Worksheets\[1995 Budget.xls]Details'!$R$7
```

> **NOTE**
>
> You need the single quotation marks around the path, workbook name, and sheet name only if the workbook is closed or if the path, workbook, or sheet name contains spaces. If in doubt, include the single quotation marks anyway; Excel happily ignores them if they're not required.

Updating Links

The purpose of a link is to avoid duplicating formulas and data in multiple worksheets. If one workbook contains the information you need, you can use a link to reference the data without re-creating it in another workbook.

To be useful, however, the data in the dependent workbook should always reflect what actually is in the source workbook. You can make sure of this by updating the link as explained here:

- If both the source and the dependent workbooks are open, Excel automatically updates the link whenever the data in the source file changes.

- If the source workbook is open when you open the dependent workbook, Excel automatically updates the links again.

- If the source workbook is closed when you open the dependent workbook, Excel displays a dialog box asking whether you want to update the links. Select Yes to update or No to cancel.

- If you didn't update a link when you opened the dependent document, you can update it any time by selecting the **Edit | Links** command. In the Links dialog box that appears (see Figure 2.16), highlight the link and then select the **Update Now** button.

FIGURE 2.16.

Use the Links dialog box to update the linked data in the source workbook.

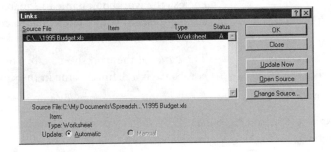

Editing Links

If the name of the source document changes, you'll need to edit the link to keep the data up-to-date. You can edit the external reference directly, or you can change the source by following these steps:

1. With the dependent workbook active, select the **Edit | Links** command to display the Links dialog box.

2. Highlight the link you want to change.

3. Select the **Change** Source button. Excel displays the Change Links dialog box.

4. Select the new source document, and then select OK to return to the Links dialog box.

5. Select Close to return to the workbook.

Troubleshooting Formulas

Despite your best efforts, the odd error might appear in your formulas from time to time. These errors can be mathematical (for example, dividing by zero), or Excel might simply be incapable of interpreting the formula. In the latter case, problems can be caught while you're entering the formula. For example, if you try to enter a formula that has unbalanced parentheses, Excel won't accept the entry; it displays an error message instead.

> **TIP**
>
> If you try to enter an incorrect formula, Excel won't enable you to do anything else until you either fix the problem or cancel the operation (which means you lose your work). If the formula is complex, you might not be able to see the problem right away. Rather than deleting all your work, place an apostrophe (') at the beginning of the formula to convert it to text. This way, you can save your work while you try to figure out the problem.

Excel's Error Values

For other kinds of errors, Excel displays one of the following error values in the cell:

#DIV/0!   This error almost always means that the cell's formula is trying to divide by 0. The cause is usually a reference to a cell that either is blank or contains the value 0. Check the cell's precedents to look for possible culprits. You'll also see #DIV/0! if you enter an inappropriate argument in some functions. MOD(), for example, returns #DIV/0! if the second argument is 0.

> **NOTE**
>
> To check items such as cell precedents and dependents, see the section later in this chapter titled "Auditing a Worksheet."

#N/A   This value is short for "not available," and it means that the formula couldn't return a legitimate result. You usually see #N/A when you use an inappropriate argument (or if you omit an argument) in a function.

HLOOKUP() and VLOOKUP(), for example, return #N/A if the lookup value is smaller than the first value in the lookup range.

#NAME?   You see the #NAME? error when Excel doesn't recognize a name you used in a formula. Make sure that you've defined the name and that you've spelled it correctly. You also see #NAME? if you enter a string without surrounding it with quotation marks, or if you enter a range and accidentally omit the colon.

#NULL!   Excel displays this error when you use the intersection operator (see Chapter 1) on two ranges that have no cells in common.

#NUM!   This error means there's a problem with a number in your formula. For example, you see #NUM! if you enter a negative number as the argument for the SQRT() or LOG() functions.

#REF!   The #REF! error means that your formula contains an invalid reference. You usually see this error when you delete a cell to which the formula refers. You need to add the cell back in or adjust the formula reference.

#VALUE!   When Excel generates a #VALUE! error, you've used an inappropriate argument in a function. For example, you might have entered a string rather than a number or reference.

Troubleshooting Techniques

Tracking down formula errors is one of the necessary evils you'll face when building your worksheets. To make this chore a little easier, this section presents the following simple techniques you can use to sniff out problems:

- To help you avoid mismatched parentheses, Excel provides two visual clues in the formula bar. The first clue occurs when you type a right parenthesis. Excel highlights both the right parenthesis and its corresponding left parenthesis. If you type what you think is the last right parenthesis and Excel doesn't highlight the first left parenthesis, your parentheses are unbalanced. The second clue occurs when you use the left and right arrow keys to navigate a formula. When you cross over a parenthesis, Excel highlights the other parenthesis in the pair.

- When entering function names and defined names, use all lowercase letters. If Excel recognizes a name, it converts the function to all uppercase and the defined name to its original case. If no conversion occurs, you misspelled the name, you haven't defined it yet, or you're using a function from an add-in macro that isn't loaded.

> **TIP**
>
> You also can use the **I**nsert | **F**unction (shortcut key Shift-F3) or **I**nsert | **N**ame | **P**aste (shortcut key F3) commands to enter functions and names safely.

■ You can calculate complex formulas one term at a time. In the formula bar, highlight the term you want to calculate, and then press F9. Excel converts the highlighted section into its value. Make sure that you press the Esc key when you're done to avoid entering the formula with just the calculated values.

Auditing a Worksheet

Some formula errors are the result of referencing other cells that contain errors or inappropriate values. To find out, you can use Excel auditing features to trace cell precedents, dependents, and errors.

How Auditing Works

If a formula refers to a number of cells, and some of those cells also refer to other cells, tracking down the source of a problem can become a nightmare. To help out, Excel's auditing features can create *tracers*—arrows that literally point out the cells involved in a formula. You can use tracers to find three kinds of cells:

Precedents   Cells that are directly or indirectly referenced in a formula. For example, suppose that cell B4 contains the formula =B2; then B2 is a direct precedent of B4. Now suppose that cell B2 contains the formula =A2/2; this makes A2 a direct precedent of B2, but it's also an *indirect* precedent of cell B4.

Dependents   Cells that are directly or indirectly referenced by a formula. In the preceding example, cell B2 is a direct dependent of A2, and B4 is an indirect dependent of A2.

Errors   Cells that contain an error value and are directly or indirectly referenced in a formula (and therefore cause the same error to appear in the formula).

Figure 2.17 shows a worksheet with three examples of tracer arrows:

■ Cell B4 contains the formula =B2, and B2 contains =A2/2. The arrows (they're blue on-screen) point out the precedents (direct and indirect) of B4.

■ Cell D4 contains the formula =D2, and D2 contains =D1/0. The latter produces the #DIV/0! error. Therefore, the same error appears in cell D4. The arrow (it's red on-screen) is pointing out the source of the error.

■ Cell G4 contains the formula =Sheet2!A1. Excel displays the dashed arrow with the worksheet icon whenever the precedent or dependent exists on a different worksheet.

FIGURE 2.17.

The three types of tracer arrows.

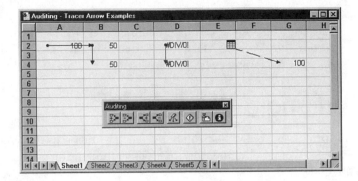

Tracing Cell Precedents

To trace cell precedents, follow these steps:

1. Select the cell containing the formula whose precedents you want to trace.
2. Select the **Tools | Auditing | T**race Precedents command. Excel adds a tracer arrow to each direct precedent.

    You also can click on this tool on the Auditing toolbar to trace precedents.

3. Keep repeating step 2 to see more levels of precedents.

TIP

You also can trace precedents by double-clicking on the cell, provided you turn off in-cell editing. You do this by selecting the **T**ools | **O**ptions command and then deactivating the Edit Directly in Cell check box in the Edit tab. Now when you double-click on a cell, Excel selects the cell's precedents.

Tracing Cell Dependents

Here are the steps to follow to trace cell dependents:

1. Select the cell whose dependents you want to trace.
2. Select the **T**ools | **A**uditing | Trace **D**ependents command. Excel adds a tracer arrow to each direct dependent.

    You also can trace dependents by clicking on this tool on the Auditing toolbar.

3. Keep repeating step 2 to see more levels of dependents.

Tracing Cell Errors

To trace cell errors, follow these steps:

1. Select the cell containing the error you want to trace.

2. Select the **T**ools | **A**uditing | Trace **E**rror command. Excel adds a tracer arrow to each cell that produced the error.

 You also can click on this tool on the Auditing toolbar to trace errors.

Removing Tracer Arrows

To remove the tracer arrows, you have three choices:

■ Select the **T**ools | **A**uditing | Remove **A**ll Arrows command to remove all the tracer arrows.

■ Click on the Remove All Arrows tool on the Auditing toolbar to remove all tracer arrows.

 The Auditing toolbar's Remove All Arrows tool.

■ Use the following buttons on the Auditing toolbar to remove precedent and dependent arrows one level at a time.

 Click on the Remove Precedent Arrows tool on the Auditing toolbar to remove precedent arrows one level at a time.

 Click on the Remove Dependent Arrows tool on the Auditing toolbar to remove dependent arrows one level at a time.

An Example: The Game of Life, Excel Style

To illustrate some of the concepts discussed in this chapter, let's look at a spreadsheet model that's both fun and highly addictive. (Don't try this one if you have deadlines to meet!) It's an Excel version of the popular game called Life. This is a game in which living cells survive, die, or are reborn based on simple rules that take into account overcrowding and isolation. A habitat is set up where you can watch the population through successive generations. After a while, the birth and death of individual cells become secondary to the spellbinding patterns that always seem to emerge. You can use any of the 10 initial populations supplied with the game, or you can create your own populations.

Don't worry; this project isn't totally frivolous because there are also plenty of more serious things to learn. For example, you'll explore concepts such as named formulas and relative range names. You can even perform your own life experiments using Life.xls, which is on the CD.

NOTE

Life.xls has several macros that together constitute the underlying engine of the Life application. To learn how these macros operate, see Appendix A, "An Excel 4.0 Macro Language Primer."

What Is the Game of Life?

The Game of Life was invented by the Cambridge mathematician John Horton Conway in the 1960s. It involves a two-dimensional, gridlike world populated with *cells*. The fate of each cell depends entirely on how many *neighbors* it has; a neighbor is any other immediately adjacent living cell.

As you might expect, you use individual worksheet cells to represent the Life cells. A living cell is represented by a *nonzero* worksheet cell; a dead cell, by a worksheet cell containing *zero*.

Three simple rules determine the destiny of each cell:

- A living cell survives into the next generation if it has either two or three neighbors.
- A living cell dies if it has four or more neighbors (overpopulation), or if it has either one or zero neighbors (isolation).
- A dead cell is reborn if it has exactly three neighbors (you can, if you want, think of them as the mother, father, and doctor).

In Life, you apply each of these rules to every cell in the population *simultaneously*. In other words, you don't start with one cell, determine whether it lives or dies, and then move on to the next. Instead, you take a snapshot of the population at a given moment and apply the rules to all the cells at once. This is called a *generation*. When the calculations are done, you remove the dead cells, add the reborn ones, and start again. Because each generation takes only a second or two (depending on the speed of your computer), it's easy to watch dozens of generations to see what fate befalls your population.

Playing the Game of Life

When you open the Life.xls file, the worksheet and dialog box shown in Figure 2.18 appear. The bordered worksheet area is called the *Habitat*. It's the Life world where the cells live and die. You can use the Life dialog box to select an initial population, clear the Habitat, or create your own world.

FIGURE 2.18.

The Life worksheet and dialog box.

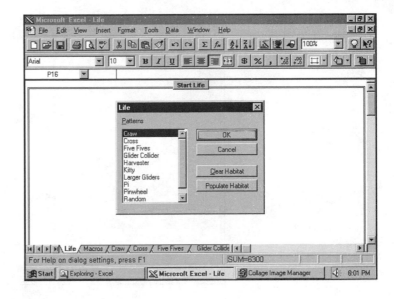

Before looking under the hood of the Life application, let's see how the game is played. The next two sections give you the basics.

Playing with the Predefined Population Patterns

Life comes with 10 predefined population patterns. These are initial populations that demonstrate how Life works. Here's how to run Life using one of these patterns:

1. Open the Life.xls file. If it's already open but the Life dialog box isn't on your screen, click the Start Life button.

2. Select an initial population pattern from the Patterns list. Figure 2.19 shows the initial population for the Five Fives pattern.

TIP

To start with something different every time, try the Random pattern.

---

3. Select OK. The initial population is seeded, and the generations begin. The status bar tells you how many generations have passed and what the current population is. Figure 2.20 shows the Five Fives pattern after 60 generations.

FIGURE 2.19.

The initial population for the Five Fives pattern.

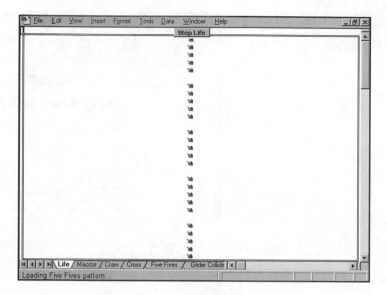

FIGURE 2.20.

The Five Fives pattern after 60 generations.

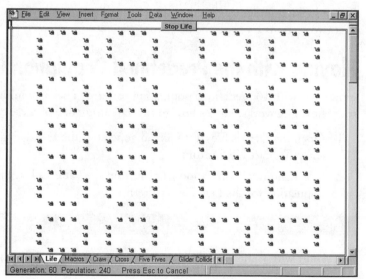

4. Press Esc to stop the game and return to the Life dialog box.

Creating Your Own Population

If you want to enter your own population, follow these steps:

1. Open the Life.xls file (or click on Start Life to display the Life dialog box).
2. To start with a fresh habitat, click the Clear Habitat button.

3. Click the **P**opulate Habitat button. Life removes the dialog box and activates the Habitat.

4. To create a living cell, select a worksheet cell inside the Habitat and either press the Insert key or double-click on the cell. You can remove the cell by pressing Insert or double-clicking again.

5. After you enter all the living cells you want for your initial population, press Enter to start the game. (If you prefer to return to the Life dialog box, select Start Life or press the Esc key.)

6. Click on Stop Life or press the Esc key to stop the game and return to the Life dialog box.

The Facts of Life

Breaking down the Life application into the following four areas makes it easier to understand: the Habitat, the Neighbor Table, the New Generation Table, and the Macros sheet.

The Habitat

As was mentioned earlier, the *Habitat* is the Life world where the cells live, die, and are reborn. There's nothing terribly complicated about this area. To designate a living cell, the program enters a 9 in one of the worksheet cells. Why a 9? The Habitat is formatted with the Wingdings font, and a 9 prints a small mouse, which was the most lifelike symbol I could find. For dead cells, the program enters a 0 (which displays as a blank because I turned off the zeros for this worksheet).

The Neighbor Table

To find out what happens to each cell, you have to look at its neighbors. In this case, you have to examine the worksheet cells surrounding each cell in the Habitat. For example, consider cell C3. To find out whether it lives, dies, or is reborn in the next generation, you have to count the number of neighbors that exist in its eight surrounding cells: B2, C2, D2, B3, D3, B4, C4, and D4. This is the job of the *Neighbor Table*.

The Neighbor Table consists of the range B43:AD71, and each cell in this table corresponds to a cell in the Habitat. After each generation, the Neighbor Table tells you how many neighbors each cell in the Habitat has. You can then use this data to create the next generation.

Every cell in the Neighbor Table has what appears to be the same formula:

```
=Neighbors
```

Neighbors is the defined name for the formula that calculates how many neighbors each cell has. Figure 2.21 illustrates how this works. The selected cell is C44, which corresponds to C3 in the Habitat. As you can see in the Define Name dialog box, the Neighbors formula is as follows:

```
=SUM(Life!B2:D2,Life!B3,Life!D3,Life!B4:D4)
```

FIGURE 2.21.

The Neighbor Table and the Neighbors formula.

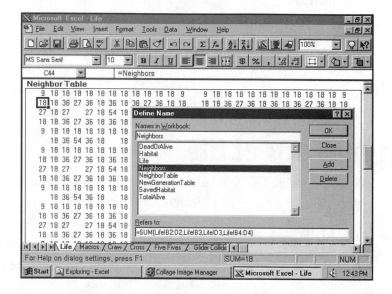

This formula adds the values of the cells surrounding C3. Because dead cells have the value 0 and live cells have the value 9, we can tell how many living neighbors C3 has. (Technically, the formula gives the number of neighbors multiplied by 9; this is why the values you see in the Neighbor Table in Figure 2.21 are all multiples of 9.)

Note that Neighbors is a relative range name. The references in the formula are relative, so they change for each cell in the Neighbor Table. For example, the Neighbors formula for cell D44 (which counts the neighbors for cell D3 in the Habitat), is this:

```
=SUM(Life!C2:E2,Life!C3,Life!E3,Life!C4:E4)
```

The other thing to note about the Neighbor Table is that the formulas overlap. This overlap creates circular references, so you have to control the calculations manually (as you'll see later).

The New Generation Table

After you know how many neighbors each cell has, you need to apply the Life rules to determine the fate of the cell. This is accomplished by the *New Generation Table*. This table has the coordinates B74:AD102, and each cell corresponds to a cell in the Neighbor Table (and so, indirectly, to a cell in the Habitat).

Like the Neighbor Table, the New Generation Table also appears to have the same formula in every cell:

```
=DeadOrAlive
```

This is another named formula, but this one applies the Life rules to determine whether the corresponding Habitat cell is dead or alive in the next generation. In Figure 2.22, cell C75 is selected, which corresponds to C44 in the Neighbor Table and C3 in the Habitat.

FIGURE 2.22.

The New Generation Table and the DeadOrAlive formula.

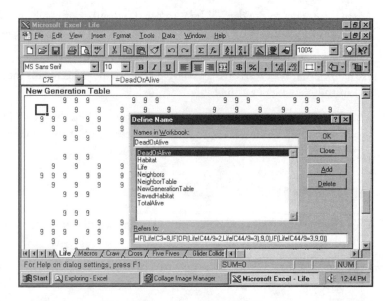

As you can see, this formula is a real mouthful. Here's a revised version in which I've taken out all the references to the Life worksheet:

```
=IF(C3=9,IF(OR(C44/9=2,C44/9=3),9,0),IF(C44/9=3,9,0))
```

NOTE

Unfamiliar with the IF() and OR() functions? No problem. I'll explain them in detail in the next chapter.

The main IF() function tests whether the cell is currently alive (C3=9). If it is, the following IF() function is executed:

```
IF(OR(C44/9=2,C44/9=3),9,0)
```

C44 is the corresponding Neighbor Table cell that tells you how many neighbors the Habitat cell has. Recall that these are in multiples of 9, so you have to divide C44 by 9 to get the true number. This IF() function says if the cell now has either two or three neighbors (that is, if it will survive into the next generation), enter a 9 in the New Generation Table cell; otherwise, enter a 0 (that is, it dies).

If the Habitat cell is currently dead, the second part of the main IF() function executes instead:

```
IF(C44/9=3,9,0)
```

Again, you have to divide C44 by 9 to get the number of neighbors. If the result is 3 (that is, the dead cell has enough neighbors to be reborn), enter a 9 in the New Generation Table cell; otherwise, enter a 0 (the cell remains dead).

Note, too, that DeadOrAlive is a relative range name. This means the formula changes for each cell in the New Generation Table.

The final step is to create the new generation by copying the New Generation Table and pasting it onto the Habitat. Because the New Generation Table consists of 0s and 9s, these will appear as dead or alive cells, respectively, in the Habitat.

Summary

This chapter showed you how to build better formulas in Excel. For related information on formulas, see the following chapters:

- You'll find you use ranges extensively in your formulas. To make sure that your range skills are at their peak, see Chapter 1, "Getting the Most Out of Ranges."

- Your formula arsenal won't be complete until you know how to wield Excel's impressive function library. You'll find basic function know-how and lots of examples of formulas that use functions in Chapter 3, "Harnessing the Power of Excel's Worksheet Functions."

- To make your formula results look their best, you need to know how to format your worksheets. You'll find all kinds of formatting techniques in Chapter 4, "Formatting Excel Worksheets."

- See Appendix A, "An Excel 4.0 Macro Language Primer," to learn about the macros that make the Life application tick.

Harnessing the Power of Excel's Worksheet Functions

3

This chapter introduces you to Excel's built-in worksheet functions. You'll learn what the functions are, what they can do, and how to use them. We'll also take a quick tour through each of Excel's nine function categories, and I'll show you lots of practical examples of functions in action.

About Excel's Functions

Functions are formulas that have been predefined by Excel. They're designed to take you beyond the basic arithmetic and text formulas you've seen so far. They do this in three ways:

- Functions make simple but cumbersome formulas easier to use. For example, suppose that you want to add a list of 100 numbers in a column starting at cell A1 and finishing at cell A100. Even if you wanted to, you wouldn't be able to enter 100 separate additions in a cell because you would run out of room (recall that cells are limited to 255 characters). Luckily, there's an alternative: the SUM() function. With this function, you would simply enter =SUM(A1:A100).

- Functions enable you to include complex mathematical expressions in your worksheets that otherwise would be impossible to construct using simple arithmetic operators. For example, determining a mortgage payment given the principal, interest, and term is a complicated matter at best, but Excel's PMT() function does it without breaking a sweat.

- Functions enable you to include data in your applications that you couldn't access otherwise. For example, the INFO() function can tell you how much memory is available on your system, what operating system you're using, what version number it is, and more.

As you can see, functions are a powerful addition to your worksheet-building arsenal. With the proper use of these tools, there is no practical limit to the kinds of models you can create.

The Structure of a Function

Every function has the same basic form:

FUNCTION(argument1, argument2, ...)

The function begins with the function name (SUM or PMT, for example), which is followed by a list of *arguments* separated by commas and enclosed in parentheses. The arguments are the function's inputs—the data it uses to perform its calculations.

For example, the FV() function determines the future value of a regular investment based on three required arguments and two optional ones:

FV(***rate,nper,pmt***, *pv, type*)

rate	The fixed rate of interest over the term of the investment.
nper	The number of deposits over the term of the investment.
pmt	The amount you'll deposit each time.
pv	The present value of the investment.
type	When the deposits are due (0 for the beginning of the period; 1 for the end of the period).

> **NOTE**
>
> Throughout this book, when I introduce a new function, I show the argument syntax and then describe each argument (as I just did with the FV() function). In the syntax line, I show the function's required arguments in **bold italic monospace** type and the optional arguments in *regular italic monospace* type.

After processing these inputs, FV() returns the total value of the investment at the end of the term. Figure 3.1 shows a simple future-value calculator that uses this function. (In case you're wondering, I entered the Payment value in cell B4 as negative because Excel always treats any money you have to pay as a negative number.)

FIGURE 3.1.

The FV() function in action.

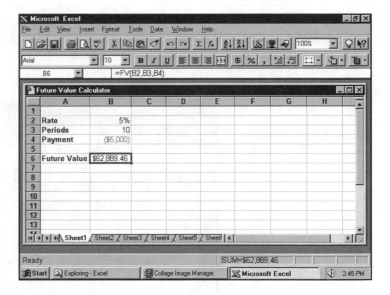

Entering Functions

You enter functions as you do any other data, but you must follow these rules:

- You can enter the function name in either uppercase or lowercase letters. Excel always converts function names to uppercase.

- Always enclose function arguments in parentheses.

- Always separate multiple arguments with commas. (You might want to add a space after each comma to make the functions more readable.)

- You can use a function as an argument for another function. This is called *nesting* functions. For example, the function AVERAGE(SUM(A1:A10), SUM(B1:B15)) sums two columns of numbers and returns the average of the two sums.

Using the Function Wizard

Although normally you'll type your functions by hand, there might be times when you can't remember the spelling of a function or the arguments it takes. To help out, Excel provides a tool called the Function Wizard. It enables you to select the function you want from a list and prompts you to enter the appropriate arguments. The following procedure shows you how the Function Wizard works:

1. To start a formula with a function, select the Function Wizard tool in the Standard toolbar. Excel activates the formula bar, enters an equals sign and the most recently used function in the cell, and displays the Function Wizard - Step 1 of 2 dialog box, shown in Figure 3.2.

FIGURE 3.2.

Use the first Function Wizard dialog box to select a function.

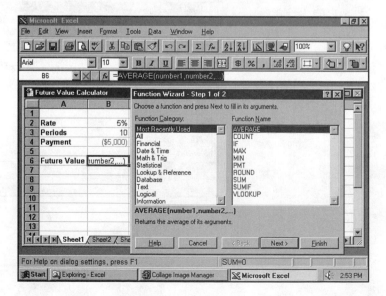

If the Standard toolbar isn't displayed, you can activate the Function Wizard by clicking on the Function Wizard box on the formula bar.

 The Function Wizard icon.

TIP

To skip Step 1 of the Function Wizard, enter the name of the function in the cell, and then either select the Function Wizard button or press Ctrl-A.

---

2. In the Function **C**ategory list, select the type of function you need. If you're not sure, select All.

3. Select the function you want to use from the Function **N**ame list.

4. If you don't want to paste the function's arguments, select the **F**inish button to return to the worksheet. Otherwise, select the Next > button. Excel displays the Function Wizard - Step 2 of 2 dialog box.

5. For each required argument and each optional argument you want to use, enter a value or cell reference in the appropriate text box. Excel shows the current argument values and the current function value (see Figure 3.3).

6. When you're done, select **F**inish. Excel pastes the function and its arguments into the cell.

FIGURE 3.3.

Use the second Function Wizard dialog box to enter values for the function's arguments.

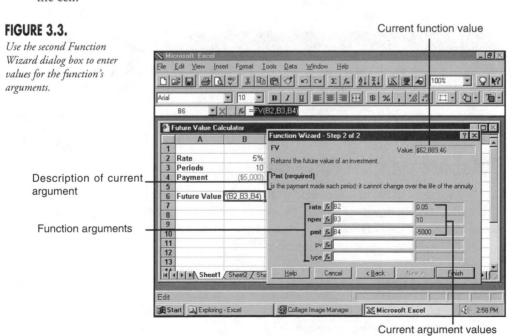

Using Excel's Functions

Excel has various function categories, including these:

- Database and list
- Date and time
- Financial
- Information
- Logical
- Lookup and reference
- Math and trigonometry
- Statistical
- Text

> **NOTE**
>
> Many Excel functions are available only by loading the Analysis Toolpak add-in macro. See Chapter 18, "Working with the Analysis Toolpak," for more information.

The following sections give you a brief overview of each function category, along with some examples.

> **NOTE**
>
> If you can't find what you need among Excel's built-in functions, you can create your own. See Chapter 21, "Getting Started with VBA," to learn how to create functions with Visual Basic for Applications.

Database and List Functions

Excel's database and list functions help you analyze database information. They return values such as the maximum and minimum quantities in a field, and the average of a field. I won't discuss these functions in detail here, because I talk about them in Chapter 12, "Working with Lists and Databases."

Date and Time Functions

The date and time functions enable you to convert dates and times to serial numbers and perform operations on those numbers. This capability is useful for such things as accounts receivable aging, project scheduling, and time management applications. Table 3.1 lists a few of the most commonly used date and time functions. (For the **serial_number** arguments, you can use any valid Excel date.)

Table 3.1. Common date and time functions.

Function	Description
DATE(**year**,**month**,**day**)	Returns the serial number of a date, in which **year** is a number from 1900 to 2078, **month** is a number representing the month of the year, and **day** is a number representing the day of the month.
DATEVALUE(**date_text**)	Converts a date from text to a serial number.
DAY(**serial_number**)	Extracts the day component from the date given by **serial_number**.
EDATE(**start_date**, **months**)*	Returns the serial number of a date that is the specified number of **months** before or after **start_date**.
EOMONTH(**start_date**, **months**)*	Returns the serial number of the last day of the month that is the specified number of **months** before or after **start_date**.
HOUR(**serial_number**)	Extracts the hour component from the time given by **serial_number**.
MINUTE(**serial_number**)	Extracts the minute component from the time given by **serial_number**.
MONTH(**serial_number**)	Extracts the month component from the date given by **serial_number** (January = 1).
NETWORKDAYS(**start_date**, **end_date**, holidays)*	Returns the number of working days between **start_date** and **end_date**. Doesn't include weekends and any dates specified by holidays.
NOW()	Returns the serial number of the current date and time.
SECOND(**serial_number**)	Extracts the seconds component from the time given by **serial_number**.
TIME(**hour**,**minute**,**second**)	Returns the serial number of a time, in which **hour** is a number between 0 and 23, and **minute** and **second** are numbers between 0 and 59.
TIMEVALUE(**time_text**)	Converts a time from text to a serial number.

continues

Table 3.1. continued

Function	Description
TODAY()	Returns the serial number of the current date.
WEEKDAY(*serial_number*)	Converts a serial number to a day of the week (Sunday = 1).
WEEKNUM(*serial_number*, *return_type*)*	Returns a number that corresponds to where the week that includes *serial_number* falls numerically during the year. Use 1 for *return_type* if your weeks begin on Sunday. Use 2 if your weeks begin on Monday.
WORKDAY(*start_date*, *days*, *holidays*)*	Returns the serial number of the day that is *days* working days from *start_date*. Weekends and *holidays* are excluded.
YEAR(*serial_number*)	Extracts the year component from the date given by *serial_number*.

*Function is part of the Analysis Toolpak

Determining the Number of Days an Invoice Is Past Due

If you use Excel to store accounts receivable data, you'll need to calculate the number of days that overdue invoices are past due. Figure 3.4 shows a simple implementation of an accounts receivable database. For each invoice, the due date is calculated by adding 30 to the invoice date. Column E uses the TODAY() function to calculate the number of days each invoice is past due. Later in this chapter, when we discuss the IF() and AND() functions, I'll show you more sophisticated formulas for calculating the invoice date, due date, and invoice aging.

Determining a Person's Birthday Given His Birth Date

If you know a person's birth date, determining his birthday is easy: just keep the month and day the same and substitute the current year for the year of his birth. To accomplish this in a formula, you could use the following:

```
=DATE(YEAR(NOW()),MONTH(Birthdate),DAY(Birthdate))
```

Here, I'm assuming that the person's date of birth is in a cell named BirthDate. The YEAR(NOW()) component extracts the current year, and MONTH(Birthdate) and DAY(Birthdate) extract the month and day, respectively, from the person's date of birth. Combine these into the DATE() function, and you have his birthday.

FIGURE 3.4.

This worksheet uses the TODAY( ) function to calculate the number of days an invoice is past due.

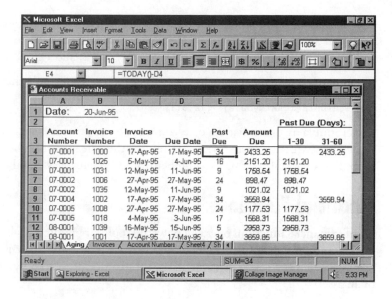

Calculating a Person's Age

If you have a person's birth date entered into a cell named Birthdate, and you need to calculate how old she is, you might think the following formula would do the job:

```
=YEAR(NOW())-YEAR(Birthdate)
```

This works, but only if the person's birthday has already passed this year. If she hasn't had her birthday yet, this formula reports her age as being one year greater than it really is.

To solve this problem, we need to take into account whether the person's birthday has passed. To see how we do this, check out the following logical expression:

```
=DATE(YEAR(NOW()),MONTH(Birthdate),DAY(Birthdate))>NOW()
```

This expression asks whether the person's birthday for this year (which we derive using the formula from the preceding section) is greater than today's date. If it is, the expression returns logical TRUE, which is equivalent to 1; if it isn't, the expression returns logical FALSE, which is equivalent to 0. In other words, we can get the person's true age just by subtracting the result of the logical expression from our original formula, like so:

```
=YEAR(NOW())-YEAR(Birthdate)-(DATE(YEAR(NOW()),MONTH(Birthdate),
➥DAY(Birthdate))>NOW())
```

Calculating Julian Dates

Excel has built-in functions that convert a given date into a numerical day of the week (the WEEKDAY( ) function) and that return the numerical ranking of the week in which a given date falls (the WEEKNUM() function). However, Excel doesn't have a function that calculates the Julian date for a given date—the numerical ranking of the date for the year in which it falls. For example, the Julian date of January 1 is 1, January 2 is 2, and February 1 is 32.

If you need to use Julian dates in your business, here's a formula that will do the job:

```
=MyDate-DATE(YEAR(MyDate)-1,12,31)
```

This formula assumes that the date you want to work with is in a cell named MyDate. The expression DATE(YEAR(MyDate),12,31) returns the date serial number for December 31 of the preceding year. Subtracting this number from MyDate gives you the Julian number.

Financial Functions

Excel's financial functions offer you powerful tools for building applications that manage both business and personal finances. You can use these functions to calculate such things as the internal rate of return of an investment, the future value of an annuity, or the yearly depreciation of an asset.

Although Excel has dozens of financial functions that use many different arguments, the following list covers the arguments you'll use most frequently:

rate	The fixed rate of interest over the term of the loan or investment.
nper	The number of payments or deposit periods over the term of the loan or investment.
pmt	The periodic payment or deposit.
pv	The present value of the loan (the principal) or the initial deposit in an investment.
fv	The future value of the loan or investment.
type	The type of payment or deposit. Use 0 (the default) for end-of-period payments or deposits, and use 1 for beginning-of-period payments or deposits.

For most financial functions, the following rules apply:

- The underlying unit of both the interest rate and the period must be the same. For example, if the *rate* is the annual interest rate, you must express *nper* in years. Similarly, if you have a monthly interest rate, you must express *nper* in months.

- You enter money you receive as a positive quantity, and you enter money you pay as a negative quantity. For example, you always enter the loan principal as a positive number because it's money you receive from the bank.

- The *nper* argument should always be a positive integer quantity.

Table 3.2 lists a few common financial functions.

Table 3.2. Common financial functions.

Function	Description
CUMIPMT(*rate*,*nper*,*pv*,*start*,*end*,*type*)*	Returns the cumulative interest paid on a loan between **start** and **end**.
CUMPRINC(*rate*,*nper*,*pv*,*start*,*end*,*type*)*	Returns the cumulative principal paid on a loan between **start** and **end**.
DB(*cost*,*salvage*,*life*,*period*,*month*)	Returns the depreciation of an asset over a specified period using the fixed-declining balance method.
DDB(*cost*,*salvage*,*life*,*period*,*factor*)	Returns the depreciation of an asset over a specified period using the double-declining balance method.
EFFECT(*nominal_rate*,*npery*)*	Returns the effective annual interest rate given the nominal annual interest rate and the number of yearly compounding periods.
FV(*rate*,*nper*,*pmt*,*pv*,*type*)	Returns the future value of an investment or loan.
IPMT(*rate*,*per*,*nper*,*pv*,*fv*,*type*)	Returns the interest payment for a specified period of a loan.
IRR(*values*,*guess*)	Returns the internal rate of return for a series of cash flows.
MIRR(*values*,*finance_rate*,*reinvest_rate*)	Returns the modified internal rate of return for a series of periodic cash flows.
NOMINAL(*effect_rate*,*npery*)*	Returns the nominal annual interest rate given the effective annual interest rate and the number of yearly compounding periods.
NPER(*rate*,*pmt*,*pv*,*fv*,*type*)	Returns the number of periods for an investment or loan.
NPV(*rate*,*value1*,*value2*...)	Returns the net present value of an investment based on a series of cash flows and a discount rate.
PMT(*rate*,*nper*,*pv*,*fv*,*type*)	Returns the periodic payment for a loan or investment.
PPMT(*rate*,*per*,*nper*,*pv*,*fv*,*type*)	Returns the principal payment for a specified period of a loan.

continues

Table 3.2. continued

Function	Description
PV(*rate*,*nper*,*pmt*,fv,type)	Returns the present value of an investment.
RATE(*nper*,*pmt*,*pv*,fv,type,guess)	Returns the periodic interest rate for a loan or investment
SLN(*cost*,*salvage*,*life*)	Returns the straight-line depreciation of an asset over one period.
SYD(*cost*,*salvage*,*life*,*period*)	Returns sum-of-years digits depreciation of an asset over a specified period.

*Function is part of the Analysis Toolpak

Building an Amortization Schedule

Figure 3.5 shows a loan amortization schedule. The Amount, Rate, and Term variables represent the *pv*, *rate*, and *nper* arguments, respectively. Column E shows the monthly payment, column F the monthly interest, and column G the monthly principal. (Column D, the Period, is used by the PPMT() and IPMT() functions for the *per* argument.) In each function, notice how I divided the annual interest rate by 12 ($B$4/12) to get the monthly rate, and how I multiplied the term by 12 ($B$5*12) to get the number of months in the loan. This enables me to determine the monthly payment.

FIGURE 3.5.

A loan amortization schedule built with the functions PMT(), PPMT(), and IPMT().

=PPMT($B$3/12,D4,$B$4*12,$B$5)

=IPMT($B$3/12,D4,$B$4*12,$B$5)

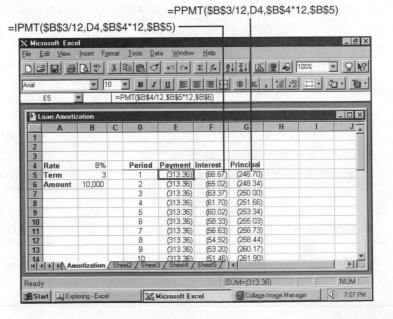

Allowing for Extra Monthly Mortgage Payments

Many mortgages today allow you to pay an extra amount each month that gets applied directly to the principal. Before you decide to take on the financial burden of these extra payments, though, you probably want two questions answered:

■ How much quicker will I pay off the mortgage?

■ How much money will I save over the amortization period?

Both questions are easily answered using Excel's financial functions. Consider the mortgage analysis model I've set up in Figure 3.6. The Data side shows all the numbers needed for our calculations: the principal (cell C6), the rate (C8), the number of years in the term (C9), and the extra monthly principal payment (C10; notice that you enter this as a negative number).

FIGURE 3.6.

A mortgage analysis worksheet that calculates the effect of making extra monthly payments toward the principal.

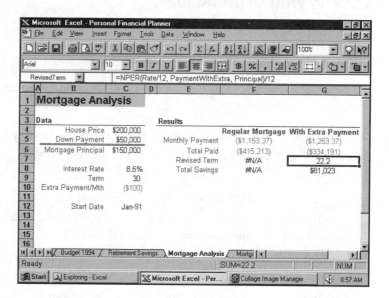

The Results side shows the results of various calculations. For the Monthly Payment, I calculated two values:

■ Cell F5 uses the PMT() function to calculate the monthly outlay without the extra principal payment.

■ Cell G5 (named PaymentWithExtra) shows the total monthly payment including the extra principal payment (=F5+C10).

To figure out the revised term, we use the following NPER() function in cell G7:

```
=NPER(Rate/12, PaymentWithExtra, Principal)/12
```

The *rate* argument is Rate (cell C8) divided by 12 (which gives the monthly interest rate), the *pmt* argument is the PaymentWithExtra cell (G5), and the *pv* argument is the Principal cell (C6). In this case, NPER() returns the number of months in the revised term, so we divide the whole thing by 12 to get the number of years. As you can see, even paying as little as $100 extra each month saves nearly eight years on the amortization.

Calculating the total savings is now straightforward. The total paid for the regular mortgage is just the monthly payment multiplied by the number of months in the term. In Figure 3.6, the total is $415,213 (cell F6). The total paid with the extra payment is the revised monthly payment (G5) multiplied by the number of months in the revised term. As you can see in Figure 3.6, the total paid is $334,191, for a total savings of $81,023.

Dealing with Depreciation

If you need to factor in the declining value of capital equipment into your budget or planning worksheets, you'll be pleased to know that Excel has no fewer than five different functions that calculate depreciation. This section examines the functions and explains their differences.

Here's a list of the various arguments used in the depreciation functions:

cost	The initial cost of the asset.
salvage	The asset's value at the end of the depreciation period.
life	The number of periods over which the asset is to be depreciated.
period	The period for which you want to calculate the depreciation.
fv	The future value of the loan or investment.
factor	The rate at which the balance declines. The default value is two (the double-declining balance method).
month	The number of months in the first year of the depreciation.

The SLN() function uses the straight-line depreciation method, which assumes that the asset declines in value by the same amount each year throughout its useful life.

The SYD() function implements the little-used sum-of-the-year's-digits method, in which earlier years of the asset's useful life carry a greater depreciation expense than later years.

The DB() function uses the fixed-declining balance method, which depreciates the asset at a fixed rate over the asset's useful life. DB() uses the optional *month* argument so that you can specify the number of months the asset was used in the first year. The default value is 12, but if you use any number less than 12, you have to extend the depreciation schedule by one period past the asset's useful life. (This procedure enables you to take into account the portion of the useful life you omitted from the first year.)

The DDB() function uses the double-declining balance method, which, like SYD(), also calculates an accelerated depreciation schedule. The extra argument *factor* determines the rate at which the balance declines. The default value is 2, which gives you the double-declining balance method. To use a different declining balance method, change the *factor* argument.

The final depreciation function is `VDB()`, which uses the variable-declining balance method:

`VDB(`***`cost`***`, `***`salvage`***`, `***`life`***`, `***`start_period`***`, `***`end_period`***`, `*`factor`*`, `*`no_switch`*`)`

`VDB()` is similar to `DDB()`, except that the ***period*** argument is replaced by a ***start_period*** and an ***end_period***. The advantage of this is that you can easily allow for assets acquired during the fiscal year. For example, if you purchase a machine at the end of the first quarter, your first year depreciation should cover only the three quarters the machine was in use. This would mean entering 0 for the ***start_period*** and 0.75 for the ***end_period***. The next period would run from 0.75 to 1.75, and so on.

As an example, Figure 3.7 shows several depreciation schedules for an asset with an initial cost of $8,000, a salvage cost of $2,000, and a useful life of three years. Each schedule was derived using a different depreciation function. The Depreciation Functions:1 window shows the results, and the Depreciation Functions:2 window shows the formulas used for the `DB()`, `DDB()`, and `VDB()` functions. Note that the `VDB()` schedule uses a declining balance rate of 1.5.

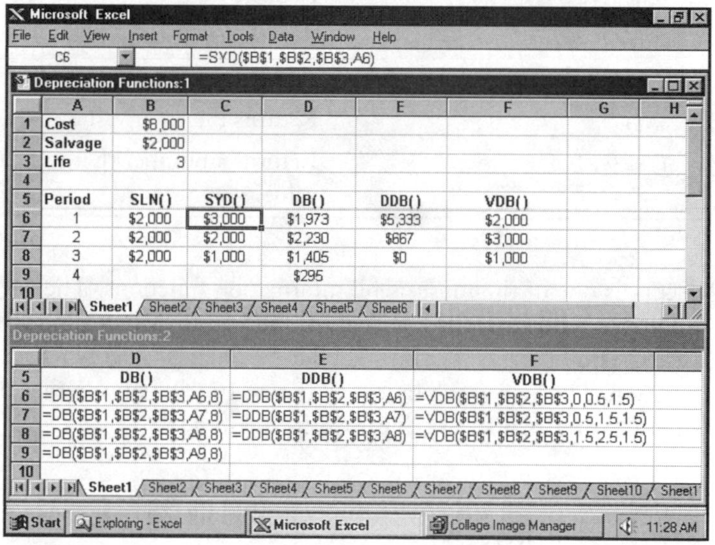

	A	B	C	D	E	F
1	Cost	$8,000				
2	Salvage	$2,000				
3	Life	3				
4						
5	Period	SLN()	SYD()	DB()	DDB()	VDB()
6	1	$2,000	$3,000	$1,973	$5,333	$2,000
7	2	$2,000	$2,000	$2,230	$667	$3,000
8	3	$2,000	$1,000	$1,405	$0	$1,000
9	4			$295		

	D	E	F
5	DB()	DDB()	VDB()
6	=DB($B$1,$B$2,$B$3,A6,8)	=DDB($B$1,$B$2,$B$3,A6)	=VDB($B$1,$B$2,$B$3,0,0.5,1.5)
7	=DB($B$1,$B$2,$B$3,A7,8)	=DDB($B$1,$B$2,$B$3,A7)	=VDB($B$1,$B$2,$B$3,0.5,1.5,1.5)
8	=DB($B$1,$B$2,$B$3,A8,8)	=DDB($B$1,$B$2,$B$3,A8)	=VDB($B$1,$B$2,$B$3,1.5,2.5,1.5)
9	=DB($B$1,$B$2,$B$3,A9,8)		

FIGURE 3.7.
Schedules for Excel's various depreciation functions.

Information Functions

Excel's information functions return data concerning cells, worksheets, and formula results. They're mostly used in macros to test for particular conditions, such as which version of Excel the user has. Table 3.3 lists all the information functions.

Table 3.3. Excel's information functions.

Function	Description
CELL(*info_type*,*reference*)	Returns information about various cell attributes, including formatting, contents, and location.
ERROR.TYPE(*error_val*)	Returns a number corresponding to an error type.
INFO(*type_text*)	Returns information about the operating system and environment.
ISBLANK(*value*)	Returns TRUE if the value is blank.
ISERR(*value*)	Returns TRUE if the value is any error value except #NA.
ISERROR(*value*)	Returns TRUE if the value is any error value.
ISLOGICAL(*value*)	Returns TRUE if the value is a logical value.
ISNA(*value*)	Returns TRUE if the value is the #NA error value.
ISNONTEXT(*value*)	Returns TRUE if the value is not text.
ISNUMBER(*value*)	Returns TRUE if the value is a number.
ISREF(*value*)	Returns TRUE if the value is a reference.
ISTEXT(*value*)	Returns TRUE if the value is text.
N(*value*)	Returns the value converted to a number.
NA()	Returns the error value #NA.
TYPE(*value*)	Returns a number that indicates the data type of the value.

CELL() is one of the most useful information functions. The *info_type* argument is a string value that represents the information you want to know about a particular cell. Some sample attributes are "address," "row," "col," and "contents." Figure 3.8 illustrates how to use the CELL() function. The "type" attribute used in row 10 tells you whether the cell contains a value (v), a label (l), or a blank (b). The "width" attribute in row 11 tells you the width of the cell's column.

Logical Functions

You can use the logical functions to create decision-making formulas. You can test whether a certain condition exists within your spreadsheet and have the program take specific actions based on the result. For example, you can test cell contents to see whether they're numbers or labels, or you can test formula results for errors. Table 3.4 summarizes Excel's logical functions.

FIGURE 3.8.

Some examples of the CELL() function.

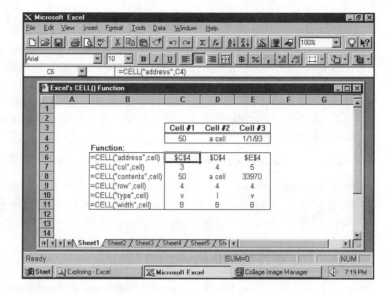

Table 3.4. Excel's logical functions.

Function	Description
AND(*logical1*,*logical2*,...)	Returns TRUE if all the arguments are true.
FALSE()	Returns FALSE.
IF(*logical_test*,*true_expr*,*false_expr*)	Performs a logical test and returns a value based on the result.
NOT(*logical*)	Reverses the logical value of the argument.
OR(*logical1*,*logical2*,...)	Returns TRUE if any argument is true.
TRUE()	Returns TRUE.

Let's examine one of the most powerful logical functions: IF(). As you can see from Table 3.4, this function takes the form IF(***logical_test***,***true_expr***,*false_expr*), in which ***logical_test*** is the logical expression to be tested. The argument ***true_expr*** is the value returned if ***logical_test*** is true, and *false_expr* is the value returned if ***logical_test*** is false.

For example, consider the following formula:

```
=IF(A1>=1000, "It's big!", "It's not!")
```

The logical expression A1>=1000 is used as the test. If this proves to be true (that is, if the value in cell A1 is greater than or equal to 1,000), the function returns the string It's big!; if the condition is false, the function returns It's not!.

Avoiding Division by Zero

As you saw in Chapter 2, "Building Better Formulas," Excel displays the #DIV/0! error if a formula tries to divide a quantity by zero. To avoid this error, you can use IF() to test the divisor and ensure that it's nonzero before performing your division. For example, the basic equation for calculating gross margin is (Sales – Expenses)/Sales. To make sure that Sales isn't zero, use the following formula (I'm assuming here that you have cells named Sales and Expenses that contain the appropriate values):

```
=IF(Sales<>0, (Sales - Expenses)/Sales, "Sales are zero!")
```

If the logical expression Sales<>0 is true, that means Sales is nonzero, so the gross margin calculation can proceed. If Sales<>0 is false, the Sales value is zero, so the message Sales are zero! is displayed instead.

Testing for a Flawed Pentium Chip

In the fall of 1994, all heck broke loose in the computing world when it was revealed that Intel had been shipping Pentium chips that contained an error in their floating-point division routines. Debates raged for months as to the seriousness of the problem and the frequency with which it would appear in the real world.

If you're wondering whether you (or the people you share your worksheets with) have one of the flawed Pentium chips, here's a simple IF() function that will let you know:

```
=IF(4195835-(4195835/3145727)*3145727<>0, "Flawed Pentium alert!", "You're cool!")
```

Using Logical Functions to Improve the Aging Worksheet

Let's see how we can use logical functions to develop a "smarter" accounts receivable aging worksheet.

For starters, our due date calculation just adds 30 to the invoice date. However, we would prefer to avoid setting a due date that falls on a weekend. So we need to test whether the invoice date plus 30 falls on a Saturday or Sunday. The WEEKDAY() function will help because it returns 7 if the date is a Saturday, and 1 if the date is a Sunday.

So to check for a Saturday, we could use the following formula:

```
=IF(WEEKDAY(C4+30)=7, C4+32, C4+30)
```

Here, I'm assuming that the invoice date resides in cell C4. If WEEKDAY(C4+30) returns 7, the date is a Saturday, so we add 32 to C4 instead (this makes the due date the following Monday). Otherwise, we just add 30 days as usual.

Checking for a Sunday is similar:

```
=IF(WEEKDAY(C4+30)=1, C4+31, C4+30)
```

The problem, though, is that we need to combine these two tests into a single formula. To do that, we can *nest* one IF() function inside another. Here's how it works:

```
=IF(WEEKDAY(C4+30)=7, C4+32, IF(WEEKDAY(C4+30)=1, C4+31, C4+30))
```

The main IF() checks to see whether the date is a Saturday. If it is, we add 32 days to C4; otherwise, we run the second IF(), which checks for Sunday.

For cash-flow purposes, we also need to correlate the invoice amounts with the number of days past due. Ideally, we would like to see a list of invoice amounts that are fewer than 30 days past due, between 31 and 60 days past due, and so on. Figure 3.9 shows one way to set up accounts receivable aging.

FIGURE 3.9.

Using IF() and AND() to arrange past-due invoices.

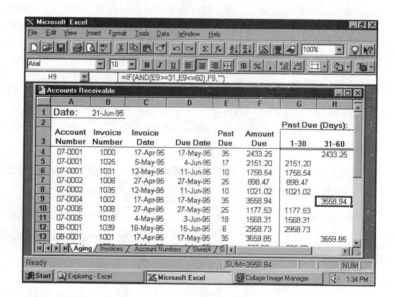

For the invoice amounts shown in column G (1–30 days), we use the following formula (this is the formula that appears in G4):

```
=IF(E4<=30, F4, "")
```

If the number of days the invoice is past due (cell E4) is less than or equal to 30, display the amount (cell F4). Otherwise, just display a blank.

The amounts in column H (31–60 days) are a little trickier. Here, we need to check whether the number of days past due is greater than or equal to 31 days *and* less than or equal to 60 days. To accomplish this, we can press the AND() function into service:

```
=IF(AND(E4>=31, E4<=60), F4, "")
```

The AND() function checks two logical expressions: E4>=31 and E4<=60. If both are true, AND() returns TRUE, and the IF() function displays the invoice amount. If one of the logical expressions isn't true (or if they're both not true), AND() returns FALSE, and the IF() function displays a blank.

Determining Whether a Value Appears in a List

Many spreadsheet applications require you to look up a value in a list. For example, you might have a table of customer discounts in which the percentage discount is based on the number of units ordered. For each customer order, you need to look up the appropriate discount, based on the total units in the order. Similarly, a teacher might convert a raw test score into a letter grade by referring to a table of conversions.

The array formulas you learned about in the preceding chapter offer some tricks for looking up values. For example, suppose that you want to know whether a certain value exists in an array. You can use the following general formula, entered into a single cell as an array:

`=OR(value=range)`

Here, *value* is the value you want to search for, and *range* is the range of cells in which to search. For example, Figure 3.10 shows a list of customers with overdue accounts. You enter the account number of the customer in cell B1, and cell B2 tells you whether the number appears in the list.

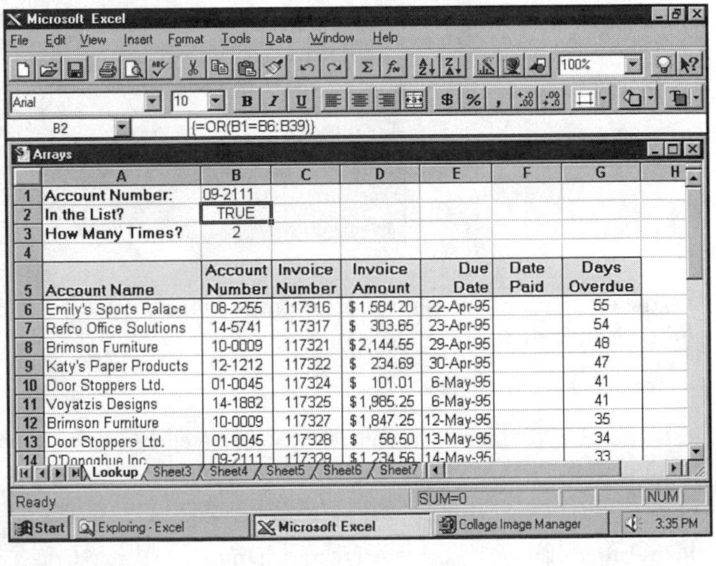

FIGURE 3.10.

An array formula that tells you whether a value appears in a list.

Here's the array formula in cell B2:

`{=OR(B1=B6:B39)}`

The OR() function returns TRUE if any one of its arguments is true. The array formula checks each value in the range B6:B39 to see whether it equals the value in B1. If any one of those comparisons is true, OR() returns TRUE. Therefore, you'll know that the value is in the list.

NOTE

Recall from Chapter 2 that you don't include the braces ({ }) when you enter an array formula. Just type the formula without the braces, and then press Ctrl-Shift-Enter.

TIP

As a similar example, following is an array formula that returns TRUE if a particular account number is *not* in the list:

`{=AND(B1<>B6:B39)}`

I'll leave figuring out how this formula works as an exercise for you.

Now you know how to find out whether a value appears in a list, but what if you need to know how many times the value appears? The following formula does the job:

`=SUM(IF(value=range,1,0))`

Again, `value` is the value you want to look up, and `range` is the range for searching. In this formula, the `IF()` function compares `value` with every cell in `range`. The values that match return 1, and the `SUM()` function adds up all the 1s. The final total is the number of occurrences of `value`. Figure 3.11 shows this formula in action (cell B3) using the list of overdue invoices.

FIGURE 3.11.

An array formula that counts the number of times a value appears in a list.

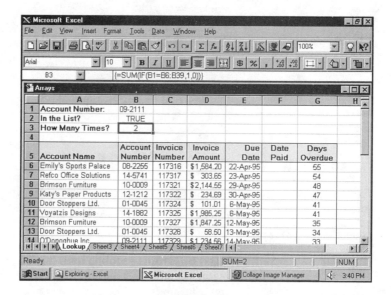

Lookup and Reference Functions

The lookup functions (such as LOOKUP(), MATCH(), and INDEX()) are powerful tools that enable you to retrieve values from lists and tables. The reference functions are useful for determining cell contents and obtaining information about ranges. Table 3.5 lists some commonly used lookup and reference functions.

Table 3.5. Some of Excel's lookup and reference functions.

Function	*Description*
AREAS(***reference***)	Returns the number of areas in a reference.
CHOOSE(***num***,***value1***,value2,...)	Uses ***num*** to select one of the list of arguments given by ***value1***, value2, and so on.
COLUMN(*reference*)	Returns the column number of a reference.
COLUMNS(***array***)	Returns the number of columns in an array.
HLOOKUP(***value***,***table***,***row_num***)	Searches for ***lookup_value*** in ***table*** and returns the value in the ***row_num*** row.
INDEX(***table***,***row_num***,***col_num***,***area_num***)	Looks in ***table*** and returns the value of the cell at the intersection of row ***row_num*** and column ***col_num***.
MATCH(***value***,***range***,***match_type***)	Searches ***range*** for ***value*** and, if found, returns the relative position of ***value*** in ***range***.
ROW(*reference*)	Returns the row number of a reference.
ROWS(***array***)	Returns the number of rows in an array.
VLOOKUP(***value***,***table***,***col_num***)	Searches for ***lookup_value*** in ***table*** and returns the value in the ***col_num*** row.

More About the Handy *CHOOSE()* Function

Excel's CHOOSE() function enables you to select a value from a list. Here is this function's syntax:

CHOOSE(***num***, *value1*, value2,...)

    num   Determines which of the values in the list is returned. If ***num*** is 1, ***value1*** is returned. If ***num*** is 2, ***value2*** is returned (and so on). ***num*** must be a number (or a formula or function that returns a number) between 1 and 29.

> **value1**,value2... Signifies the list of up to 29 values from which CHOOSE() selects the return value. The values can be numbers, text strings, references, names, formulas, or functions.

For example, the following formula returns the text string "Place":

```
=CHOOSE(2,"Win, "Place", "Show")
```

Calculating Weighted Questionnaire Results

One common use for CHOOSE() is to calculate weighted questionnaire responses. For example, suppose that you just completed a survey in which the respondents had to enter a value between 1 and 5 for each question. Some questions and answers are more important than others, so each question is assigned a set of weights. You use these weighted responses for your data. How do you assign the weights? The easiest way is to set up a CHOOSE() function for each question. For instance, suppose that question 1 uses the following weights for answers 1 through 5: 1.5, 2.3, 1.0, 1.8, and 0.5. If so, the following formula can be used to derive the weighted response:

```
=CHOOSE(Question1, 1.5, 2.3, 1.0, 1.8, 0.5)
```

(Assume that the answer for question 1 is in a cell named Question1.)

Calculating the Day of the Week

As you saw earlier, Excel's WEEKDAY() function returns a number that corresponds to the day of the week, in which Sunday is 1, Monday is 2, and so on.

What if you want to know the actual day (not the number) of the week? If you need to display only the day of the week, you can format the cell as dddd. If you need to use the day of the week in a formula, you need a way to convert the WEEKDAY() result into the appropriate string. Fortunately, the CHOOSE() function makes this process easy. For example, suppose that cell B5 contains a date. You can find the day of the week it represents with the following formula:

```
=CHOOSE(WEEKDAY(B5),"Sun","Mon","Tue","Wed","Thu","Fri","Sat")
```

I've used abbreviations for each day to save space, but you can use whatever you like.

Looking Up Values in Tables

In many worksheet formulas, the value of one argument often depends on the value of another. For example, in a formula that calculates an invoice total, the customer's discount might depend on the number of units purchased. The usual way to handle this kind of problem is to look up the appropriate value in a table. Excel has two functions that do just that: VLOOKUP() and HLOOKUP().

The VLOOKUP() function works by looking in the first column of a table for the value you specify. (The V in VLOOKUP() stands for "vertical.") More specifically, the VLOOKUP() function looks for the largest value that is less than or equal to the one you specify. It then looks across the appropriate number of columns (which you specify) and returns whatever value it finds there.

Here's the full syntax for VLOOKUP():

VLOOKUP(*value*, *table*, *col_num*)

value	The value you want to find in the first column of *table*. You can enter a number, a string, or a reference. Excel looks for the largest value that's less than or equal to *value*.
table	The table to use for the lookup. You can use a range reference or a name.
col_num	If VLOOKUP() finds a match, *col_num* is the column number in the table that contains the data you want returned (in which the first column is column 1).

> **CAUTION**
>
> To get reliable results from VLOOKUP(), the values in the first column of the table must be in alphabetical or numerical order.

Figure 3.12 shows a worksheet that uses VLOOKUP() to determine the discount a customer gets on an order, based on the number of units purchased. For example, cell D4 uses the following formula:

=VLOOKUP(A4, $H$5:$I$11,2)

FIGURE 3.12.

A worksheet that uses VLOOKUP() to look up a customer's discount in a discount schedule.

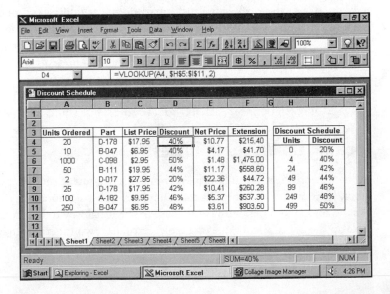

Cell A4 contains the number of units purchased (20), and the range $H$5:$I$11 is the discount schedule table. VLOOKUP() searches down the first column (H5:H11) for the largest value that is less than or equal to 20. The first such cell is H6 (because the value in H7—24—is larger than 20). VLOOKUP() therefore moves to the second column (because we specified *col_num* to be 2) of the table (cell I6) and grabs the value there (40%).

The HLOOKUP() function is similar, except that it works by looking in the first row of a table for the largest value that is less than or equal to the one you specify. (The H in HLOOKUP() stands for "horizontal.") If successful, this function then looks down the specified number of rows and returns the value it finds there. Here's the syntax for HLOOKUP():

HLOOKUP(*value, table, row_num*)

value	The value to find in the first row of *table*. You can enter a number, a string, or a reference. Excel looks for the largest value that's less than or equal to *value*.
table	The table you want to use for the lookup. You can use a range reference or a name.
row_num	If HLOOKUP() finds a match, this is the row number in the table that contains the data you want returned (in which the first row is row 1).

CAUTION

As with VLOOKUP(), HLOOKUP() works reliably only when the values in the first row of the table are in alphabetical or numerical order.

Finding Exact Matches

VLOOKUP() and HLOOKUP() have two major drawbacks as lookup tools:

- They look only for the largest entries that are less than or equal to the value you enter as an argument. In most lookups, you'll probably want to find an exact match.
- The column or row that these functions use for searching must be in alphabetical or numerical order. You can sort the table, but that isn't always convenient.

To get around these limitations, you need to use two more functions: MATCH() and INDEX().

The MATCH() function looks through a row or column of cells for a value. If MATCH() finds an exact match, it returns the relative position of the match in the row or column. Here's the syntax:

MATCH(*value, range, type*)

value	The value you want to find. You can use a number, string, reference, or logical value.
range	The row or column of cells you want to use for the lookup.
type	Specifies how you want Excel to match *value* with the entries in *range*. You have three choices:

0	Finds the first value that exactly matches *value*. *range* can be in any order.
1	Finds the largest value that's less than or equal to *value*. *range* must be in ascending order. This is the default value.
−1	Finds the smallest value that is greater than or equal to *value*. *range* must be in descending order.

TIP

Another advantage you get with MATCH() is that you can use the usual wildcard characters within the *value* argument (provided that *type* is 0 and *value* is text). You can use the question mark (?) for single characters and the asterisk (*) for multiple characters.

Normally you don't use the MATCH() function by itself; rather, you combine it with the INDEX() function. INDEX() returns the value of a cell at the intersection of a row and column inside a reference. Here's the syntax for INDEX():

```
INDEX(reference, row_num, col_num, area_num)
```

reference	A reference to one or more cell ranges.
row_num	The number of the row in *reference* from which to return a value. You can omit *row_num* if *reference* is a single row.
col_num	The number of the column in *reference* from which to return a value. You can omit *col_num* if *reference* is a single column.
area_num	If you entered more than one range for *reference*, *area_num* is the range you want to use. The first range you entered is 1, the second is 2, and so on.

The idea is that you use MATCH() to get *row_num* or *col_num* (depending on how your table is laid out) and then use INDEX() to return the value you need. For example, Figure 3.13 shows a simple data-entry screen that automatically adds a customer name after the user enters the account number. The function that accomplishes this is in cell B4:

```
=INDEX(D3:E18,MATCH(B2,D3:D18,0),2)
```

FIGURE 3.13.

A simple data-entry worksheet that uses INDEX() and MATCH() to look up a customer's name based on the entered account number.

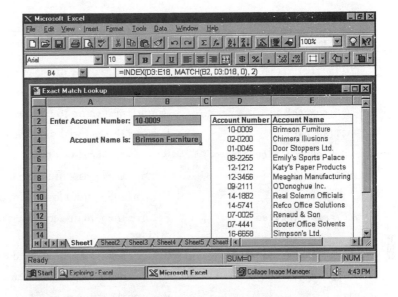

Math and Trigonometric Functions

Excel boasts dozens of math functions that perform tasks such as calculating square roots and logarithms and generating random numbers. The trigonometric functions take an angle argument and calculate values such as its sine, cosine, and arctangent. Table 3.6 lists a few of the most common math and trig functions.

Table 3.6. Common math and trig functions.

Function	Description
ABS(***number***)	Returns the absolute value of ***number***.
CEILING(***number***,***significance***)	Rounds ***number*** up to the nearest integer.
COMBIN(***number***,***number_chosen***)*	Returns the number of possible ways that ***number*** objects can be combined in groups of ***number_chosen***.

continues

Table 3.6. continued

Function	Description
COS(*angle*)	Returns the cosine of *angle* (expressed in radians).
EXP(*number*)	Returns *e* raised to the power of *number*.
EVEN(*number*)	Rounds *number* up to the nearest even integer.
FACT(*number*)	Returns the factorial of *number*.
FLOOR(*number*,*significance*)	Rounds *number* down to the nearest integer.
INT(*number*)	Rounds *number* down to the nearest integer.
LN(*number*)	Returns the natural logarithm of *number*.
MOD(*number*,*divisor*)	Returns the remainder of *number* after dividing by *divisor*.
MROUND(*number*,*multiple*)*	Rounds *number* to the desired *multiple*.
ODD(*number*)	Rounds *number* up to the nearest odd integer.
PI()	Returns the value pi.
RAND()	Returns a random number between 0 and 1.
RANDBETWEEN(*bottom*,*top*)*	Returns a random number between *bottom* and *top*.
ROUND(*number*,*num_digits*)	Rounds *number* to a specified number of digits.
SIN(*angle*)	Returns the sine of *angle* (expressed in radians).
SQRT(*number*)	Returns the positive square root of *number*.
SUM(*number1*,*number2*,...)	Returns the sum of the arguments.
TAN(*angle*)	Returns the tangent of *angle* (expressed in radians).
TRUNC(*number*,*num_digits*)	Truncates *number* to an integer.

*Function is part of the Analysis Toolpak

A Closer Look at the Rounding Functions

Let's look at the differences between seven of Excel's rounding functions: ROUND(), CEILING(), FLOOR(), EVEN(), ODD(), INT(), and TRUNC().

The most common rounding function is ROUND(), which takes two arguments, *number* and *num_digits*. *num_digits* specifies the number of digits you want *number* rounded to, as explained here:

- If *num_digits* is greater than 0, Excel rounds *number* to *num_digits* decimal places.
- If *num_digits* is 0, Excel rounds *number* to the nearest integer.
- If *num_digits* is less than 0, Excel rounds *number* to *num_digits* to the left of the decimal point.

Table 3.7 demonstrates the effect of the *num_digits* argument on the results of the ROUND() function. Here, *number* is 1234.5678.

Table 3.7. The ROUND() function.

num_digits	Result
3	1234.568
2	1234.57
1	1234.6
0	1235
−1	1230
−2	1200
−3	1000

The CEILING() and FLOOR() functions take two arguments, *number* and *significance*. These functions round the value given by *number* to a multiple of the value given by *significance*. The difference is that CEILING() rounds *away* from zero, and FLOOR() rounds *toward* zero. For example, CEILING(1.56, 0.1) returns 1.6, and CEILING(-2.33, -0.5) returns −2.5. Similarly, FLOOR(1.56, 0.1) returns 1.5, and FLOOR(-2.33, -0.5) returns −2.0.

> **CAUTION**
>
> For the CEILING() and FLOOR() functions, both arguments must have the same sign or they'll return the error value #NUM!. Also, if you enter a 0 for the second argument of the FLOOR() function, you'll get the error #DIV/0!.

The EVEN() and ODD() functions round a single numeric argument away from zero. EVEN() rounds the number to the next even number, and ODD() rounds it to the next odd number. For example, EVEN(14.2) returns 16 and EVEN(-23) returns −24. Similarly, ODD(58.1) returns 59 and ODD(-6) returns −7.

The INT() and TRUNC() functions are similar in that you can use both to convert a value to its integer portion. For example, INT(6.75) returns 6 and TRUNC(3.6) returns 3. However, these functions have two major differences that you should keep in mind:

- For negative values, INT() returns the next number *away* from zero. For example, INT(-3.42) returns −4. If you just want to lop off the decimal part, you need to use TRUNC() instead.

■ TRUNC() can take a second argument—*num_digits*—that you can use to specify the number of decimal places to leave on. For example, TRUNC(123.456, 2) returns 123.45.

> **NOTE**
>
> As if these rounding functions weren't enough, the Analysis Toolpak add-in macro supplies another rounding function: MROUND(**number,multiple**). This handy function rounds **number** to the nearest multiple of the value given by **multiple**. See Chapter 18 for details.

Using Rounding to Prevent Calculation Errors

Most of us are comfortable dealing with numbers in decimal—or base 10—format (the odd hexadecimal-loving computer pro notwithstanding). Computers, however, prefer to work in the simpler confines of the binary—or base 2— system. So when you plug a value into a cell or formula, Excel converts it from decimal to its binary equivalent, makes its calculations, and then converts the binary result back into decimal format.

This procedure is fine for integers because all decimal integer values have an exact binary equivalent. However, there are many non-integer values that don't have an exact equivalent in the binary world. Excel can only approximate these numbers, and this approximation can lead to errors in your formulas. For example, try entering the following formula into any worksheet cell:

```
=0.01=(2.02-2.01)
```

This formula compares the value 0.01 with the expression 2.02-2.01. These should be equal, of course, but when you enter the formula, Excel returns a FALSE result! What gives?

The problem is that, in converting the expression 2.02-2.01 into binary and back again, Excel picks up a stray digit in its travels. To see it, enter the formula =2.02-2.01 in a cell and then format it to show 16 decimal places. (I'll talk about numeric formats in the next chapter.) You should see the following, surprising, result:

```
0.0100000000000002
```

That wanton 2 in the 16th decimal place is what threw off our original calculation. To fix the problem, use the TRUNC() function (or possibly the ROUND() function, depending on the situation) to lop off the extra digits to the right of the decimal point. For example, the following formula produces a TRUE result:

```
=0.01=TRUNC(2.02-2.01, 2)
```

Calculating Cumulative Totals

Many worksheets need to calculate cumulative totals. Most budget worksheets, for example, show cumulative totals for sales and expenses over the course of the fiscal year. Similarly, loan amortizations often show the cumulative interest and principal paid over the life of the loan.

Calculating these straightforward cumulative totals is easy. See the worksheet shown in Figure 3.14. Column F tracks the cumulative interest on the loan, and cell F6 contains the following SUM() formula:

```
=SUM($D$7:D7)
```

This formula just sums cell D7, which is no great feat. However, when you fill the range F7:F54 with this formula, the left part of the SUM() range ($D$7) remains anchored; the right side (D7) is relative and therefore changes. So, for example, the corresponding formula in cell F10 would be this:

```
=SUM($D$7:D10)
```

FIGURE 3.14.

A worksheet that calculates cumulative totals.

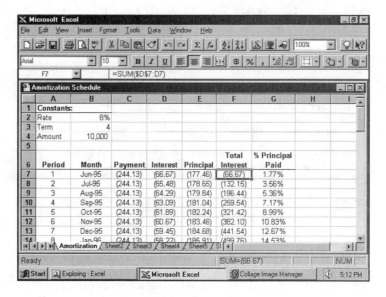

In case you're wondering, column G tracks the percentage of the total principal that's been paid off so far. Here's the formula used in cell G7:

```
=SUM($E$7:E7)/$B$4*-1
```

The SUM($E$7:E7) part calculates the cumulative principal paid. To get the percentage, we just divide by the total principal (cell B4). The whole thing is multiplied by −1 to return a positive percentage.

Summing Only the Positive or Negative Values in a Range

If you have a range of numbers that contains both positive and negative values, what do you do if you need a total of only the negative values? Or only the positive ones? You could enter the individual cells into a SUM() function, but there's an easier way that uses a simple array formula.

To sum the negative values in a range, you would use the following formula:

```
{=SUM((range<0)*range)}
```

Here, *range* is a range reference or named range. The *range<0* test returns 1 for those range values that are less than 0; otherwise, it returns 0. Therefore, only negative values get included in the SUM().

Similarly, you would use the following array formula to sum only the positive values in *range*:

```
{=SUM((range>0)*range)}
```

Determining Whether a Year Is a Leap Year

If you need to determine whether a given year is a leap year, the MOD() function makes it easy. MOD() calculates the remainder (or modulus) after dividing one number into another. Here's the syntax for this more-useful-than-you-think function:

```
MOD(number, divisor)
```

> *number*   The dividend (that is, the number to be divided).
>
> *divisor*   The number by which you want to divide *number*.

For example, MOD(24,10) equals 4 (that is, 24 divided by 10 is 2 with remainder 4).

Leap years (with some exceptions) are years divisible by 4. So a year is a leap year if the following formula returns 0:

```
=MOD(year, 4)
```

In this case, *year* is a four-digit year number (or a cell that contains a year). This formula works for the years 1901 to 2099, which should take care of most people's needs. The formula doesn't work for 1900 and 2100, because those years, despite being divisible by four, aren't leap years. The general rule is that a year is a leap year if it's divisible by 4 and it's not divisible by 100, *unless* it's also divisible by 400. Therefore, because 1900 and 2100 are divisible by 100 and not by 400, they aren't leap years. The year 2000, however, is a leap year. If you want a formula that takes the full rule into account, use the following formula:

```
=(MOD(year, 4)=0)-(MOD(year, 100)=0)+(MOD(year, 400)=0)
```

The three parts of the formula that compare a MOD() function to 0 return 1 or 0. Therefore, the result of this formula will always be 0 for leap years and nonzero for all other years.

Statistical Functions

The statistical functions calculate all the standard statistical measures such as average, maximum, minimum, and standard deviation. For most of the statistical functions, you supply a list of values (called a *sample* or *population*). You can enter individual values or cells, or you can specify a range. Table 3.8 lists a few of the statistical functions.

Table 3.8. Common statistical functions.

Function	Description
AVERAGE(**number1**,number2,...)	Returns the average.
CORREL(**array1**,**array2**)	Returns the correlation coefficient.
COUNT(**value1**,value2,...)	Counts the numbers in the argument list.
COUNTA(**value1**,value2,...)	Counts the values in the argument list.
FORECAST(**x**,**known_y's**,**known_x's**)	Returns a forecast value for **x** based a linear regression of the arrays **known_y's** and **known_x's**.
FREQUENCY(**data_array**,**bins_array**)	Returns a frequency distribution.
LARGE(**array**,**k**)	Returns the **k**th largest value in **array**.
LINEST(**known_y's**,known_x's,const,stats)	Uses the least squares method to calculate a straight-line fit through your data.
MAX(**number1**,number2,...)	Returns the maximum value.
MEDIAN(**number1**,number2,...)	Returns the median value.
MIN(**number1**,number2,...)	Returns the minimum value.
MODE(**number1**,number2,...)	Returns the most common value.
PERCENTILE(**array**,**k**)	Returns the **k**th percentile of the values in **array**.
RANK(**number**,**ref**,order)	Returns the rank of a number in a list.
SMALL(**array**,**k**)	Returns the **k**th smallest value in **array**.
STDEV(**number1**,number2,...)	Returns the standard deviation based on a sample.
STDEVP(**number1**,number2,...)	Returns the standard deviation based on an entire population.

continues

114

Table 3.8. continued

Function	Description
TREND(**known_y's**,*known_x's*,*new_x's*,*const*)	Returns values along a linear trend.
VAR(**number1**,*number2*,...)	Returns the variance based on a sample.
VARP(**number1**,*number2*,...)	Returns the variance based on an entire population.

Figure 3.15 illustrates the use of several statistical functions.

FIGURE 3.15.

Examples of statistical functions.

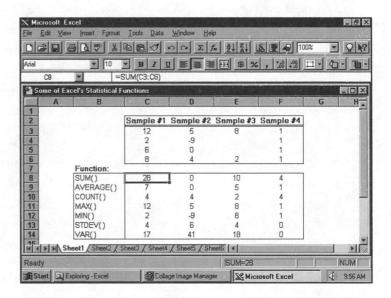

Text Functions

Excel's text functions enable you to manipulate text strings and labels. With these functions, you can convert numbers to strings, change lowercase letters to uppercase (and vice versa), compare two strings, and more. Table 3.9 summarizes several of the most useful text functions.

Table 3.9. Some text functions.

Function	Description
CHAR(**number**)	Returns the character that corresponds to the ANSI code given by **number**.
CLEAN(**text**)	Removes all nonprintable characters from **text**.

Function	Description
CODE(*text*)	Returns the ANSI code for the first character in *text*.
EXACT(*text1*,*text2*)	Compares two strings to see whether they are identical.
FIND(*find*,*within*,*start_num*)	Returns the character position of the text *find* within the text *within*. FIND() is case-sensitive.
LEFT(*text*,*num*)	Returns the leftmost *num* characters from *text*.
LEN(*text*)	Returns the length of *text*.
LOWER(*text*)	Converts *text* to lowercase.
MID(*text*,*start_num*,*num*)	Returns a *num* characters from *text* starting at *start_num*.
PROPER(*text*)	Converts *text* to proper case (first letter of each word capitalized).
RIGHT(*text*,*num*)	Returns the rightmost *num.* characters from *text*.
SEARCH(*find*,*within*,*start_num*)	Returns the character position of the text *find* within the text *within*. SEARCH() is not case-sensitive.
T(*value*)	Converts *value* to text.
TEXT(*value*,*format*)	Formats *value* and converts it to text.
TRIM(*text*)	Removes excess spaces from *text*.
UPPER(*text*)	Converts *text* to uppercase.
VALUE(*text*)	Converts *text* to a number.

Figure 3.16 demonstrates several of the text functions.

Generating a Series of Letters

Excel's Fill handle and **D**ata | **S**eries command are great for generating a series of numbers or dates, but they don't do the job when you need a series of letters (such as a, b, c, and so on). However, you can use the CHAR() function in an array formula for generating a series.

The CHAR(*number*) function's purpose is to convert a character's ANSI code *number* into the character itself. For example, CHAR(162) returns the cents symbol (¢), and CHAR(188) returns the one-quarter symbol (¼).

FIGURE 3.16.

Examples of Excel's text functions.

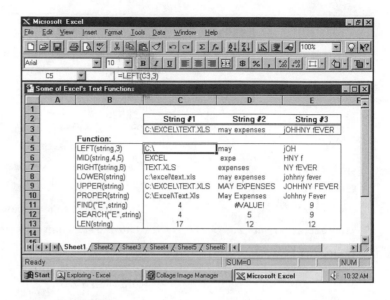

We're concerned with the characters a through z (which correspond to ANSI codes 97 to 122) and A through Z (65 to 90). To generate a series of these letters, follow these steps:

1. Select the range you want to use for the series.

2. Activate in-cell editing by pressing F2.

3. Type the following formula:

   ```
   =CHAR(97+ROW(range)-ROW(first_cell))
   ```

   In this formula, *range* is the range you selected in step 1, and *first_cell* is a reference to the first cell in *range*. For example, if the selected range is B10:B20, you would type this:

   ```
   =CHAR(97+ROW(B10:B20)-ROW(B10))
   ```

> **NOTE**
>
> I'm assuming that you've selected a column for your series. If you've selected a row, replace the ROW() functions in the formula with COLUMN().

4. Press Ctrl-Shift-Enter to enter the formula as an array.

Because you entered this as an array formula, the ROW(*range*)-ROW(*first_cell*) calculation generates a series of numbers (0, 1, 2, and so on) that represent the offset of each cell in the range from the first cell. These offsets are added to 97 to produce the appropriate ANSI codes for the lowercase letters. If you want uppercase letters, replace the 97 with 65.

> **TIP**
>
> If you want to generate your letters starting in row 1, you can use the following version of the formula:
>
> `{=CHAR(96+ROW(range))}`

Extracting a Substring

Excel's text functions make it easy to extract substrings from larger strings. For example, you can use the LEFT() and RIGHT() functions to grab a specified number of characters at the beginning or end of the string. But what if you're not sure how many characters you need to extract? Suppose that you have a column of cells that contain people's names, like this:

```
Lorraine O'Donoghue
Karen Hammond
Vince Durbin
Katy Renaud
Paul Richardson
```

If you want to sort these cells by last name, you need to extract the last names into a new column and sort using that column as the primary key. (For more sorting information, turn to Chapter 12.) The RIGHT() function won't cut it because the surnames all have various lengths.

The solution is to use the FIND() function to find the space that separates the first and last names, and then use the MID() function to extract everything to the right of the space. First off, here's the FIND() function that locates the space (assuming that the name is in cell A1):

```
FIND(" ",A1)
```

For "Lorraine O'Donoghue," this function returns 9.

The MID() function takes three arguments:

text	The string to use for the extraction (A1 in our example).
start_num	The character position to start extracting. We want to start immediately after the space, so we'll use the expression `FIND(" ",A1)+1`.
num	The number of characters to extract. In our case, the number of characters to extract is the total length of the string—LEN(A1)—minus the position of the space—FIND(" ",A1).

So here's our formula, in all its glory:

```
=MID(A1, FIND(" ", A11)+1, LEN(A1)-FIND(" ", A1))
```

A Date Conversion Formula

If you import mainframe or server data into your worksheets, or if you import online service data such as stock market quotes, you'll often end up with date formats that Excel can't handle. One common example is the YYMMDD format (for example, 950930).

To convert this value into a date that Excel can work with, you can use the LEFT(), MID(), and RIGHT() functions. If the unrecognized date is in cell A1, LEFT(A1,2) will extract the year, MID(A1,3,2) will extract the month, and RIGHT(A1,2) will extract the day. Plugging these functions into a DATE() function gives Excel a date it can handle:

```
=DATE(LEFT(A1,2), MID(A1,3,2), RIGHT(A1,2))
```

Formatting Dates Used in Strings

Many people like to annotate their workbooks by setting Excel in manual calculation mode and entering a NOW() function into a cell. The NOW() function won't update unless you save or recalculate the sheet, so you always know when the sheet was last updated.

Instead of just entering NOW() by itself, you might find it better to preface the date with an explanatory string, such as This workbook last updated:. To do this, you can enter the following formula:

```
="This workbook last updated: " & NOW()
```

Unfortunately, your output will look something like this:

```
This workbook last updated: 34872.51001
```

The number 34872.51001 is Excel's internal representation of a date and time. (The number to the left of the decimal is the date, and the number to the right of the decimal is the time.) To get a properly formatted date and time, use the TEXT(*value*,*format*) function, in which *value* is the data you want to format, and *format* is a string representing the type of formatting to use. For example, to format the results of the NOW() function in the MM/DD/YY HH:MM format, use the following formula:

```
="This workbook last updated: " & TEXT(NOW(), "mm/dd/yy hh:mm")
```

Here's the output:

```
This workbook last updated: 09/30/95 12:14
```

Summary

This chapter took you on a tour of Excel's extensive function library. For related information on functions, see the following chapters:

- Many Excel functions take range arguments. To learn more about ranges and range names, see Chapter 1, "Getting the Most Out of Ranges."

- Most functions appear as part of larger formulas. To get more information on using formulas in Excel—especially the arrays that are used by lots of functions—see Chapter 2, "Building Better Formulas."

- I'll talk about Excel's database functions in Chapter 12, "Working with Lists and Databases."

- I'll discuss some of Excel's statistical functions in more depth in Chapter 17, "Basic Analytic Methods." Also, I'll look at some of the Analysis Toolpak's functions in Chapter 18, "Working with the Analysis Toolpak."

- If you would like to try your hand at creating your own user-defined functions, you can learn all you need to know in Chapter 21, "Getting Started with VBA."

Formatting Excel Worksheets

Most worksheets are drab, lifeless conglomerations of numbers, formulas, and text. Real ho-hum stuff. If you'll be sharing your sheets with others, either via e-mail, fax, floppy disk, or presentation, your numbers will have much more impact if they're nicely formatted and presented in an eye-catching layout. This chapter shows you how merely adding a few fonts, a few colors, and a few styles can turn even the most prosaic worksheet into a thing of beauty.

Not planning on showing off your work to anyone? That's no reason to ignore formatting. As you'll see in this chapter, Excel has features such as multiple views, window panes, numeric formats, and cell notes that can help you work with any sheet, even those that are "for your eyes only."

Formatting Numbers, Dates, and Times

One of the best ways to improve the readability of your worksheets is to display your data in a format that is logical, consistent, and straightforward. Formatting currency amounts with leading dollar signs, percentages with trailing percent signs, and large numbers with commas are a few of the ways you can improve your spreadsheet style.

This section shows you how to format numbers, dates, and times using Excel's built-in formatting options. You'll also learn how to create your own formats to gain maximum control over the appearance of your data.

Numeric Display Formats

When you enter numbers in a worksheet, Excel removes any leading or trailing zeros. For example, if you enter 0123.4500, Excel displays 123.45. The exception to this rule occurs when you enter a number that is wider than the cell. In this case, Excel tailors the number to fit in the cell either by rounding off some decimal places or by using scientific notation. A number such as 123.45678 is displayed as 123.4568, and 123456789 is displayed as 1.23+08. In both cases, the number is changed for display purposes only; Excel still retains the original number internally.

When you create a worksheet, each cell uses this format, known as the *general* number format, by default. If you want your numbers to appear differently, you can choose from among Excel's seven categories of numeric formats: Number, Currency, Accounting, Percentage, Fraction, Scientific, and Special.

> **Number formats:** The number formats have three components: the number of decimal places (0 to 30), whether or not the thousands separator (,) is used, and how negative numbers are displayed. For negative numbers, you can display the number with a leading minus sign, in red, surrounded by parentheses, or in red surrounded by parentheses.

Currency formats: The currency formats are similar to the number formats, except that the thousands separator is always used, and you have the option of displaying the numbers with a leading dollar sign ($).

Accounting formats: With the accounting formats, you can select the number of decimal places and whether to display a leading dollar sign. If you do use a dollar sign, Excel displays it flush-left in the cell. All negative entries are displayed surrounded by parentheses.

Percentage formats: The percentage formats display the number multiplied by 100 with a percent sign (%) to the right of the number. For example, .506 is displayed as 50.6%. You can display 0 to 30 decimal places.

Fraction formats: The fraction formats enable you to express decimal quantities as fractions. There are nine fraction formats in all, including displaying the number as halves, quarters, eighths, sixteenths, tenths, and hundredths.

Scientific formats: The scientific formats display the most significant number to the left of the decimal, 2 to 30 decimal places to the right of the decimal, and then the exponent. So 123000 is displayed as 1.23E+05.

Special formats: The special formats are a collection designed to take care of special cases. Here's a list of the special formats with some examples:

Format	Enter This	What It Displays As
ZIP Code	1234	01234
ZIP Code + 4	123456789	12345–6789
Phone Number	1234567890	(123) 456–7890
Social Security Number	123456789	123–45–6789

Changing Numeric Formats

The quickest way to format numbers is to specify the format as you enter your data. For example, if you begin a dollar amount with a dollar sign ($), Excel automatically formats the number as currency. Similarly, if you type a percent sign (%) after a number, Excel automatically formats the number as a percentage. Here are a few more examples of this technique. Note that you can enter a negative value using either the negative sign (–) or parentheses.

Number Entered	Number Displayed	Format Used
$1234.567	$1,234.57	Currency
($1234.5)	($1,234.50)	Currency
10%	10%	Percentage
123E+02	1.23E+04	Scientific
5 3/4	5 3/4	Fraction
0 3/4	3/4	Fraction
3/4	4–Mar	Date

NOTE

Excel interprets a simple fraction such as 3/4 as a date (March 4, in this case). Always include a leading zero, followed by a space, if you want to enter a simple fraction from the formula bar.

Specifying the numeric format as you enter a number is fast and efficient because Excel guesses the format you want to use. Unfortunately, Excel sometimes guesses wrong (for example, interpreting a simple fraction as a date). In any case, you don't have access to all the available formats (for example, displaying negative dollar amounts in red). To overcome these limitations, you can select your numeric formats from the Number tab in the Format Cells dialog box, as shown in the following steps:

To open the Format Cells dialog box and select a format, follow the steps in this procedure:

1. Select the cell or range of cells you want the new format to apply to.

2. Select Format | Cells. The Format Cells dialog box appears.

TIP

To open the Format Cells dialog box quickly, either right-click on the cell or range and then select the Format Cells command from the shortcut menu, or press Ctrl-1.

3. If necessary, select the Number tab, shown in Figure 4.1.

FIGURE 4.1.

Use the Number tab in the Format Cells dialog box to select a numeric format.

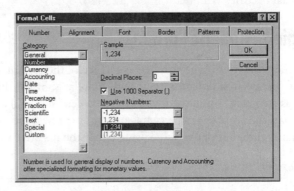

4. Select a format category from the Category list box. Excel displays the various options available for the category you choose.

5. Select the formatting options you want to use. The Sample information box shows a sample of the format applied to the current cell's contents.

6. Select OK. Excel returns you to the worksheet with the new formatting applied.

As an alternative to the Format Cells dialog box, Excel offers several keyboard shortcuts for setting the numeric format. Select the cell or range you want to format, and use one of the key combinations listed in Table 4.1.

Table 4.1. Shortcut keys for selecting numeric formats.

Shortcut Key	Format
Ctrl-~	General
Ctrl-!	Number (two decimal places; using thousands separator)
Ctrl-$	Currency (two decimal places; using dollar sign; negative numbers surrounded by parentheses)
Ctrl-%	Percentage (no decimal places)
Ctrl-^	Scientific (two decimal places)

If your mouse is nearby, you can use the tools in the Formatting toolbar as another method of selecting numeric formats. Here are the four available tools:

Button	Name	Format
$	Currency Style	Accounting (two decimal places; using dollar sign)
%	Percent Style	Percentage (no decimal places)
,	Comma Style	Number (two decimal places; using thousands separator)
+.0 .00	Increase Decimal	Increases the number of decimal places in the current format
.00 +.0	Decrease Decimal	Decreases the number of decimal places in the current format

Customizing Numeric Formats

Excel numeric formats give you lots of control over how your numbers are displayed, but they have their limitations. For example, no built-in format enables you to display a different currency symbol (the British pound sign, £, for example) or display temperatures using, say, the degree symbol.

To overcome these limitations, you need to create your own custom numeric formats. You can do this either by editing an existing format or by entering your own from scratch. The formatting syntax and symbols are explained in detail later in this section.

Every Excel numeric format, whether built-in or customized, has the following syntax:

`positive format;negative format;zero format;text format`

The four parts, separated by semicolons, determine how various numbers are presented. The first part defines how a positive number is displayed, the second part defines how a negative number is displayed, the third part defines how zero is displayed, and the fourth part defines how text is displayed. If you leave out one or more of these parts, numbers are controlled as shown here:

Number of Parts Used	Format Syntax
Three	`positive format;negative format;zero format`
Two	`positive and zero format; negative format`
One	`positive, negative, and zero format`

Table 4.2 lists the special symbols you use to define each of these parts.

Table 4.2. Numeric formatting symbols.

Symbol	Description
General	Displays the number with the General format.
#	Holds a place for a digit and displays the digit exactly as typed. Displays nothing if no number is entered.
0	Holds a place for a digit and displays the digit exactly as typed. Displays zero if no number is entered.
?	Holds a place for a digit and displays the digit exactly as typed. Displays a space if no number is entered.
. (period)	Sets the location of the decimal point.
, (comma)	Sets the location of the thousands separator. Marks only the location of the first thousand.
%	Multiplies the number by 100 (for display only) and adds the percent (%) character.
E+ e+ E– e–	Displays the number in scientific format. E– and e– place a minus sign in the exponent; E+ and e+ place a plus sign in the exponent.
/ (slash)	Sets the location of the fraction separator.

Symbol	Description
$ ( ) : – + (space)	Displays the character.
*	Repeats whatever character immediately follows the asterisk until the cell is full. Doesn't replace other symbols or numbers.
_ (underscore)	Inserts a blank space the width of whatever character follows the underscore.
\ (backslash)	Inserts the character that follows the backslash.
"*text*"	Inserts the *text* that appears within the quotation marks.
@	Holds a place for text.
[*COLOR*]	Displays the cell contents in the specified color. See "Using Color in Worksheets," later in this chapter.
[*condition value*]	Uses conditional statements to specify when the format is to be used.

Before looking at some examples, let's run through the basic procedure. To customize a numeric format, select the cell or range you want to format, and then follow these steps:

1. Display the Number tab in the Format Cells dialog box using one of the methods outlined in the preceding section.
2. In the **C**ategory list, select Custom.
3. If you're editing an existing format, highlight it in the **T**ype list box.
4. Edit or enter your format code.
5. Select OK. Excel returns you to the worksheet with the custom format applied.

Excel stores each new format definition in the Custom category. If you edited an existing format, the original format is left intact, and the new format is added to the list. You can select the custom formats the same way you select the built-in formats. To use your custom format in other workbooks, you copy a cell containing the format to that workbook. See "Working with Cell Formats," later in this chapter, to learn about copying and moving cell formats. Figure 4.2 shows a dozen examples of custom formats.

The formats in Example 1 show how you can reduce a large number to a smaller, more readable one by using the thousands separator. A format such as 0,000.0 would display, say, 12300 as 12,300.0. If you remove the three zeros between the comma and the decimal (to get the format 0,.0), Excel displays the number as 12.3 (although it still uses the original number in calculations). In essence, you've told Excel to express the number in thousands. To express a larger number in millions, you just add a second thousands separator.

FIGURE 4.2.

Sample custom numeric formats.

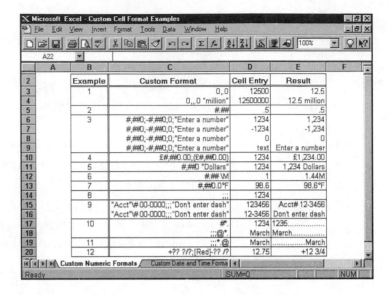

Use the format in Example 2 when you don't want to display any leading or trailing zeros.

Example 3 shows a four-part format. The first three parts define how Excel should display positive numbers, negative numbers, and zero. The fourth part displays the message Enter a number if the user enters text in the cell.

In Example 4, the British pound sign (£) is used in place of the dollar sign. To enter the pound sign, press Alt-0163 on the keyboard's numeric keypad. (This won't work if you use the numbers along the top of the keyboard.) Table 4.3 shows some common ANSI characters you can use. (See Appendix D, "The Windows ANSI Character Set," for the complete ANSI character set.)

Table 4.3. ANSI character key combinations.

Key Combination	ANSI Character
Alt-0163	£
Alt-0162	¢
Alt-0165	¥
Alt-0169	©
Alt-0174	®
Alt-0176	°

Example 5 adds the text string "Dollars" to the format.

In Example 6, an M is appended to any number, which is useful if your spreadsheet units are in megabytes.

Example 7 uses the degree symbol (°) to display temperatures.

The three semicolons used in Example 8 result in no number being displayed.

Example 9 shows that you can get a number sign (#) to display in your formats by preceding # with a backslash (\).

In Example 10, you see a trick for creating dot trailers. Recall that the asterisk (*) symbol fills the cell with whatever character follows it. So creating a dot trailer is a simple matter of adding "*." to the end of the format.

Example 11 shows a similar technique that creates a dot leader. Here the first three semicolons display nothing; then comes "*.", which runs dots from the beginning of the cell up to the text (represented by the @ sign).

Finally, Example 12 shows a format that's useful for entering stock quotations.

Hiding Zeros

Worksheets look less cluttered and are easier to read if you hide unnecessary zeros. Excel enables you to hide zeros either throughout the entire worksheet or only in selected cells.

To hide all zeros, select **Tools** | **Options**, click on the View tab in the Options dialog box, and deactivate the **Z**ero Values check box.

To hide zeros in selected cells, create a custom format that uses the following format syntax:

`positive format;negative format;`

The extra semicolon at the end acts as a placeholder for the zero format. Because there's no definition for a zero value, nothing is displayed. For example, the format $#,##0.00_); ($#,##0.00); displays standard dollar values, but it leaves the cell blank if it contains zero.

> **TIP**
>
> If your worksheet contains only integers (no fractions or decimal places), you can use the format #,### to hide zeros.

Using Condition Values

The action of the formats you've seen so far have depended on whether the cell contents were positive, negative, zero, or text. Although this is fine for most applications, there are times when you need to format a cell based on different conditions. For example, you might want only specific numbers, or numbers within a certain range, to take on a particular format. You can achieve this effect by using the [*condition value*] format symbol. With this symbol, you set up conditional statements using the logical operators =, <, >, <=, >=, and <>, and the appropriate numbers. You then assign these conditions to each part of your format definition.

For example, suppose that you have a worksheet for which the data must be within the range –1,000 to 1,000. To flag numbers outside this range, you set up the following format:

```
[>=1000]"Error: Value >= 1,000";[<=-1000]"Error: Value <= -1,000";0.00
```

The first part defines the format for numbers greater than or equal to 1,000 (an error message). The second part defines the format for numbers less than or equal to –1,000 (also an error message). The third part defines the format for all other numbers (0.00).

Date and Time Display Formats

If you include dates or times in your worksheets, you need to make sure that they're presented in a readable, unambiguous format. For example, most people would interpret the date 8/5/94 as August 5, 1994. However, in some countries this date would mean May 8, 1994. Similarly, if you use the time 2:45, do you mean AM or PM? To avoid these kinds of problems, you can use Excel's built-in date and time formats, listed in Table 4.4.

Table 4.4. Excel's date and time formats.

Format	Display
m/d	8/3
m/d/yy	8/3/95
mm/dd/yy	08/03/95
d-mmm	3-Aug
d-mmm-yy	3-Aug-95
dd-mmm-yy	03-Aug-95
mmm-yy	Aug-95
mmmm-yy	August-95
mmmm d, yyyy	August 3, 1995
h:mm AM/PM	3:10 PM
h:mm:ss AM/PM	3:10:45 PM
h:mm	15:10
h:mm:ss	15:10:45
mm:ss.0	10:45.7

Format	Display
[h]:[mm]:[ss]	25:61:61
m/d/yy h:mm AM/PM	8/23/94 3:10 PM
m/d/yy h:mm	8/23/94 15:10

The [h]:[mm]:[ss] format might require a bit more explanation. You use this format when you want to display hours greater than 24 or minutes and seconds greater than 60. For example, suppose you have an application in which you need to sum several time values (such as the time you've spent working on a project). If you add, say, 10:00 and 15:00, Excel normally shows the total as 1:00 (since, by default, Excel restarts times at 0 when they hit 24:00). To display the result properly (that is, as 25:00), use the format [h]:00.

You use the same methods you used for numeric formats to select date and time formats. In particular, you can specify the date and time format as you input your data. For example, entering Jan-94 automatically formats the cell with the mmm-yy format. Also, you can use the following shortcut keys:

Shortcut Key	Format
Ctrl-#	d–mmm–yy
Ctrl-@	h:mm AM/PM
Ctrl-;	Current date (m/d/yy)
Ctrl-:	Current time (h:mm AM/PM)

> **TIP**
>
> Excel for the Macintosh uses a different date system than Excel for Windows uses. If you share files between these environments, you need to use Macintosh dates in your Excel for Windows worksheets to maintain the correct dates when you move from one system to another. Select **T**ools | **O**ptions, click on the Calculation tab, and check the 1904 **D**ate System check box.

Customizing Date and Time Formats

Although the built-in date and time formats are fine for most applications, you might need to create your own custom formats. For example, you might want to display the day of the week (for example, "Friday"). Custom date and time formats generally are simpler to create than custom numeric formats. There are fewer formatting symbols, and you usually don't need to specify different formats for different conditions. Table 4.5 lists the date and time formatting symbols.

Table 4.5. The date and time formatting symbols.

Symbol	Description
	Date Formats
d	Day number without a leading zero (1 to 31)
dd	Day number with a leading zero (01 to 31)
ddd	Three-letter day abbreviation (Mon, for example)
dddd	Full day name (Monday, for example)
m	Month number without a leading zero (1 to 12)
mm	Month number with a leading zero (01 to 12)
mmm	Three-letter month abbreviation (Aug, for example)
mmmm	Full month name (August, for example)
yy	Two-digit year (00 to 99)
yyyy	Full year (1900 to 2078)
	Time Formats
h	Hour without a leading zero (0 to 24)
hh	Hour with a leading zero (00 to 24)
m	Minute without a leading zero (0 to 59)
mm	Minute with a leading zero (00 to 59)
s	Second without a leading zero (0 to 59)
ss	Second with a leading zero (00 to 59)
AM/PM, am/pm, A/P	Displays the time using a 12-hour clock
/ : . –	Symbols used to separate parts of dates or times
[*COLOR*]	Displays the date or time in the color specified
[*condition value*]	Uses conditional statements to specify when the format is to be used

Figure 4.3 shows some examples of custom date and time formats.

Deleting Custom Formats

The best way to become familiar with custom formats is to try your own experiments. Just remember, however, that Excel stores each format you try. If you find that your list of custom formats is getting a bit unwieldy or that it's cluttered with unused formats, you can delete formats by following the steps outlined here:

FIGURE 4.3.

*Sample custom date and
time formats.*

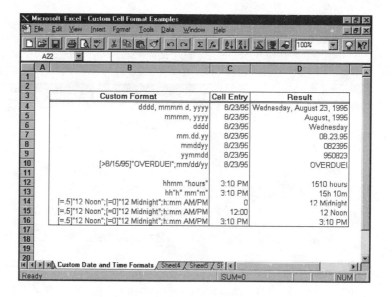

1. Choose Format | Cells, and then select the Number tab in the Options dialog box.

2. Select the Custom category.

3. Highlight the format in the **T**ype list box. (Note that you can delete only the formats you've created yourself.)

4. Select the **D**elete button. Excel removes the format from the list.

5. To delete other formats, repeat steps 2 through 4.

6. Select OK. Excel returns you to the spreadsheet.

Working with Fonts

Assigning appropriate formats to your worksheet numbers can greatly enhance the readability of your data. But no matter how skillfully you've applied your formatting, a worksheet full of numbers still causes the eyes of your audience to glaze over very quickly. The next step in creating a presentation-quality report is to surround your numbers with attractive labels and headings.

This section shows you how to work with Excel's extensive font capabilities. You'll learn about the various font attributes and how to apply them to your worksheets. Throughout this section, the emphasis is on selecting fonts that improve the impact and effectiveness of your worksheets.

Learning About Fonts

The characters you enter into your Excel worksheets have several attributes: the *typeface*, the *type size*, and the *type style*. Taken all together, these attributes define the character's *font*.

The first of these attributes, the typeface, refers to a distinctive graphical design of letters and numbers. Typefaces differ according to the shape and thickness of characters, as well as a number of other stylistic features. As Figure 4.4 shows, typefaces can be very different.

FIGURE 4.4.

Some sample typefaces.

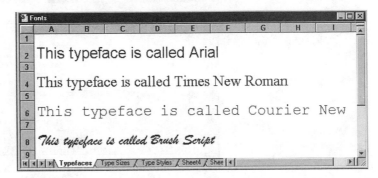

All typefaces are classified as either *serif, sans serif,* or *decorative.* A serif typeface contains fine cross strokes, or "feet," at the end of each main character stroke. For example, look at the capital T in the Times New Roman typeface in Figure 4.4. A sans serif typeface, such as the Arial example in Figure 4.4, doesn't contain these cross strokes. Decorative typefaces, such as Brush Script in Figure 4.4, have unique designs that are used for special effects. Here are some general rules for selecting worksheet typefaces:

- Use sans serif typefaces for numbers, headings, and titles. Sans serif characters tend to be wider and cleaner looking than their serif counterparts, which is helpful when you're displaying numbers or brief but large text entries. (A sans serif typeface—Arial—is the default typeface used by Excel.)

- Use serif typefaces for lengthy sections of text. The elegant serif design makes smaller characters easy to read.

- When choosing a typeface for a report, take your audience into consideration. If you're presenting the report to a business group, you should use more conservative typefaces, such as Bookman, Century Schoolbook, or Times New Roman. In more relaxed settings, you can try Avant Garde or even (in small doses) a calligraphic font such as Lucida Calligraphy.

- Try to limit yourself to two typefaces (at most) in a single worksheet. Using more makes your reports look jumbled and confusing. It's much more effective to vary type size and style within a single typeface than to use many different typefaces.

NOTE

The number of typefaces you have available depends, in some cases, on the printer you use and whether you have a printer font cartridge or a font management program installed on your computer. The TrueType software built into Windows 95 is an example of a font management program. It gives you five font families: Arial, Courier New, Symbol, Times New Roman, and Wingdings.

The next font attribute is the size of the typeface. Type size, the measure of the height of a font, is measured in points. There are 72 points in an inch, so selecting a type size of 72 gives you letters approximately one inch high. (Technically, type size is measured from the highest point of a tall letter, such as *h*, to the lowest point of a descending letter, such as *y*.) Figure 4.5 shows a few sample type sizes.

FIGURE 4.5.

Some sample type sizes.

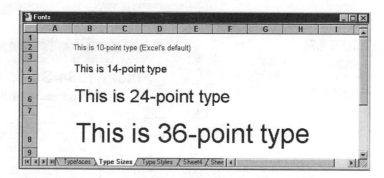

Use different type sizes in your worksheets to differentiate titles and headings from data:

- Use 24- or even 36-point type for worksheet titles, but remember that your title must fit on a single page. If your report has a subtitle, use a type size that's slightly smaller than the one used in the main title. For example, if your title is in 24-point type, make the subtitle 18-point type.

- Column and row labels look good in 12- or 14-point type, but, again, watch the size. If your labels are too large, you'll have to widen your columns accordingly.

- For most reports, the standard 10-point type is fine for your data, although you'll probably have to switch to a larger type (such as 12-point) if you plan to present your work on a slide or overhead.

The type style of a font refers to attributes such as regular, bold, and italic. Figure 4.6 shows examples of each of these attributes.

Use any of these type styles to make sections of your worksheet stand out. Bold often is used for worksheet titles, and headings often are displayed as both bold and italic. In general, however, you should use these styles sparingly, because overuse diminishes their impact. Other type styles (often called type *effects*) include underlining, strikethrough, superscript, and subscript.

Figure 4.7 shows an Excel spreadsheet that implements many of the features described in this chapter. As you can see, fonts are a powerful way to improve your worksheet design. The next section shows you how to implement fonts in Excel.

FIGURE 4.6.
Some type style attributes.

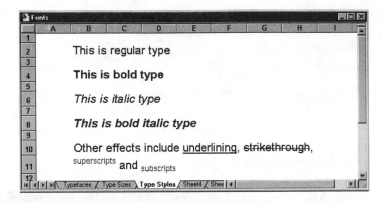

FIGURE 4.7.
Using fonts effectively can greatly improve the look of your worksheets.

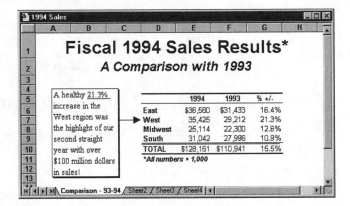

Using Fonts

With Excel, you can use up to 256 different fonts on a single worksheet, although, in practice, a presentation-quality report should use only a few fonts. (Remember that a font is a specific combination of typeface, size, and style. This means that 10-point Arial is a different font from 24-point Arial Bold.)

To select a font, follow these steps:

1. Select a cell, a range, or a group of characters inside a cell.

> **NOTE**
>
> To select characters inside a cell, press F2 or double-click on the cell to activate in-cell editing. Then use the mouse or the keyboard to highlight the characters you want to format. Note that you can format individual cell characters only if the cell contains text. The characters in formulas and numbers all use the same formatting.

2. Select the Format | Cells command, and then select the Font tab in the Format Cells dialog box, shown in Figure 4.8.

FIGURE 4.8.

Use the Font tab to set your font options.

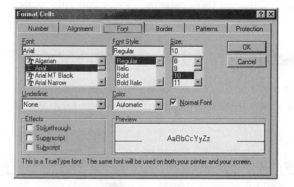

3. Select a typeface from the **F**ont list box (the terms *font* and *typeface* often are used interchangeably). Excel shows printer fonts with a printer graphic beside them, and TrueType fonts have the double-T TrueType logo beside them.

4. Select a font style from the **Fo**nt Style list box.

5. Select a type size from the **S**ize list box.

6. Select any other font options you want to use.

> **TIP**
>
> Activate the **N**ormal Font check box to select Excel's default font. See the section "Working with Cell Formats," later in this chapter, to learn how to change the default font.

7. Select OK. Excel returns you to the worksheet and formats the cells with the font you chose.

Selecting Fonts with the Formatting Toolbar

Besides using the Font tab, you can set many of the font attributes using the Formatting toolbar, which contains the following font tools:

Arial ▼   Use the Font drop-down list box to select a typeface.

10 ▼   Use the Font Size drop-down list box to select a font size.

B   Click on the Bold tool to apply the bold font style.

Click on the Italic tool to apply the italic font style.

 Click on the Underline tool to apply the underline font style.

Selecting Font Attributes with Shortcut Keys

If you don't have a mouse or if you prefer to use the keyboard, you can use the various keyboard shortcuts that Excel provides to select font attributes. Table 4.6 lists these shortcut key combinations.

Table 4.6. Shortcut keys for selecting font attributes.

Shortcut Keys	Result
Ctrl-2 or Ctrl-B	Toggles the bold style on or off
Ctrl-3 or Ctrl-I	Toggles the italic style on or off
Ctrl-4 or Ctrl-U	Toggles the underline effect on or off
Ctrl-5	Toggles the strikethrough effect on or off

Aligning Cell Contents

When you place data in an unformatted cell, Excel aligns text entries with the left edge of the cell, numbers and dates with the right edge of the cell, and error and logical values in the center of the cell. This is the default General alignment scheme. Although this format is useful for distinguishing text entries from numerical ones, it tends to make a worksheet look messy and poorly organized. To remedy this problem, Excel gives you various alignment options.

You set alignment attributes by selecting the Format | Cells command and then displaying the Alignment tab in the Format Cells dialog box, shown in Figure 4.9.

FIGURE 4.9.

Use the Alignment tab to align the contents of your cells.

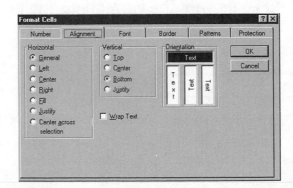

This tab is divided into four areas: Horizontal, Vertical, Orientation, and **W**rap Text. The Horizontal section contains the following options (see Figure 4.10 for an example of each option):

General	Uses the default alignment settings.
Left	Left-aligns the cell contents.
Center	Centers the cell contents.
Right	Right-aligns the cell contents.
Fill	Repeats the contents of the cell until the cell is filled.
Justify	Aligns the cell contents with the left and right edges of the cell. For text entries longer than the cell width, the cell height is increased to accommodate the text.
Center **a**cross selection	Centers the cell contents across the selected range.

FIGURE 4.10.

The horizontal alignment options.

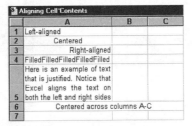

Excel's Formatting toolbar also boasts several buttons that can make your alignment chores a bit easier:

 Click on this tool to left-align cell contents.

 Click on this tool to center cell contents.

 Click on this tool to right-align cell contents.

 Click on this tool to center a cell across the selection.

If you increase the height of a row (as explained later in the section titled "Working with Columns and Rows"), the Vertical section of the Alignment tab enables you to position cell entries vertically using the following options (see Figure 4.11 for an example of each option):

Top	Aligns the cell contents with the top of the cell.
Center	Aligns the cell contents with the center of the cell.

Bottom	Aligns the cell contents with the bottom of the cell.
Justify	Justifies the cell contents vertically.

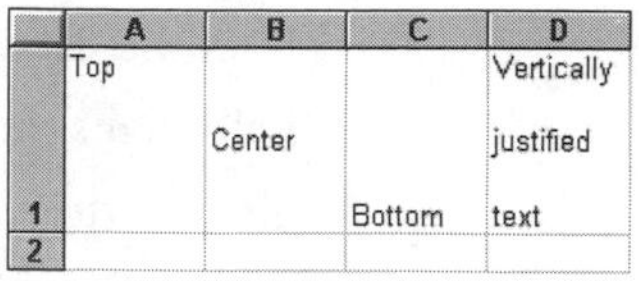

FIGURE 4.11.

The vertical alignment options.

	A	B	C	D
	Top			Vertically
		Center		justified
1			Bottom	text
2				

The Orientation section of the Alignment tab enables you to orient your cell entries in four ways: left-to-right (normal), vertically, sideways with characters running from bottom to top, and sideways with characters running from top to bottom (although this doesn't necessarily mean the top and bottom of the cell boundaries). Figure 4.12 shows an example of each option.

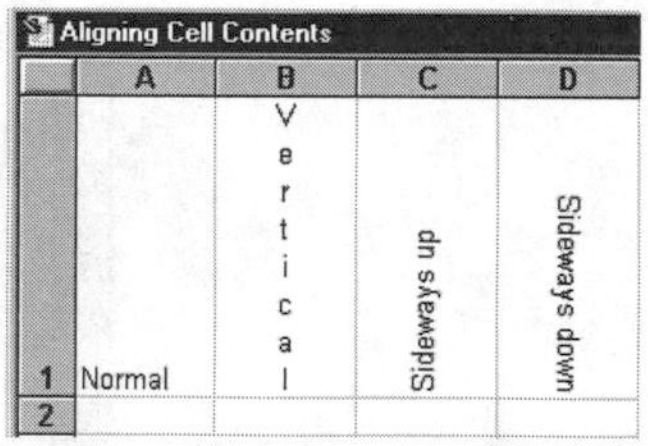

FIGURE 4.12.

The orientation alignment options.

NOTE

If you choose either the vertical or the sideways orientation with a long text entry, you have to adjust the height of the cell to see all the text. See "Working with Columns and Rows," later in this chapter, for instructions on adjusting row height.

The final option in the Alignment tab is the **W**rap Text check box, which enables you to wrap long cell entries so that they're displayed on multiple lines in a single cell (see Figure 4.13). You can left-align, center, right-align, or justify wrapped entries.

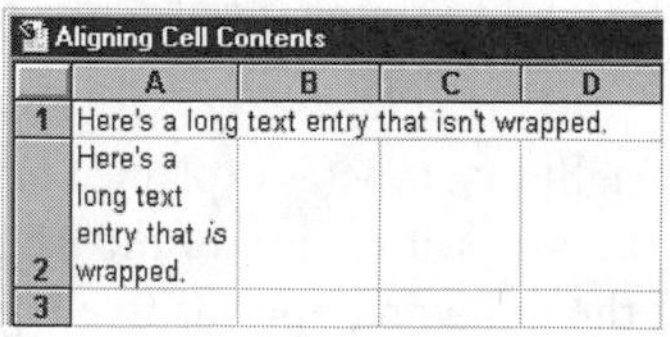

FIGURE 4.13.

The Word Wrap alignment option.

	A	B	C	D
1	Here's a long text entry that isn't wrapped.			
2	Here's a long text entry that *is* wrapped.			
3				

Working with Cell Borders

Excel enables you to place borders of various weights and patterns around your worksheet cells. This is useful for enclosing different parts of the worksheet, defining data entry areas, and marking totals.

You apply cell borders by selecting Format | Cells and then displaying the Border tab in the Format Cells dialog box, shown in Figure 4.14. This tab is divided into three sections: Border, Style, and Color (I'll discuss colors in the section "Using Color in Worksheets").

FIGURE 4.14.

The Border tab in the Format Cells dialog box.

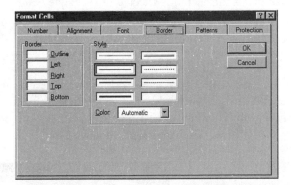

The Style section contains the eight border styles you can use. The Border section applies the chosen style using the following five options:

Outline	Applies the currently selected border style to the outer edges of the selected range.
Left	Applies the currently selected border style to the left edge of each cell in the selected range.
Right	Applies the currently selected border style to the right edge of each cell in the selected range.

Top   Applies the currently selected border style to the top edge of each cell in the selected range.

Bottom   Applies the currently selected border style to the bottom edge of each cell in the selected range.

> **TIP**
>
> Press Ctrl-& (ampersand) to put an outline border around the selected cells. Press Ctrl-_ (underscore) to remove all borders from the selected cells.

Follow these steps to apply a border to a cell or range:

1. Select the cell or range to be bordered.
2. Select Format | Cells, then select the Border tab in the Format Cells dialog box.
3. Select the border location from the Border section of the dialog box. Excel displays a sample of the currently selected border style beside the Border option.
4. Select a different border style if necessary. When you select a style, a sample appears in the box to the left of the selected Border option.
5. Select OK. Excel returns you to the worksheet with the borders applied.

Figure 4.15 shows how you can use cell borders to create an invoice form. In a business document such as this, your borders should be strictly functional. You should avoid the merely decorative, and, as in Figure 4.15, you should make your borders serve a purpose, whether it's marking a data area or separating parts of the form.

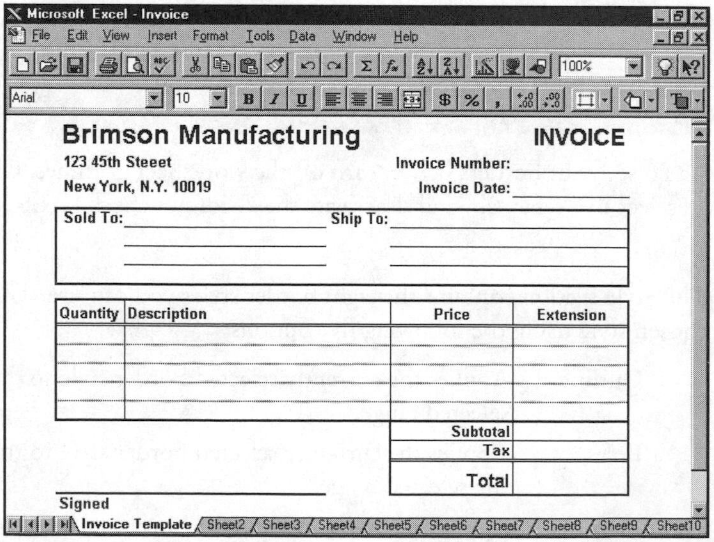

FIGURE 4.15.

Using cell borders to create an invoice form.

Using the Borders Tear-Off Tool

Excel's toolbars include a few tear-off tools that can make your formatting chores easier. The Borders tool on the Formatting toolbar is an example:

 The Borders tool from the Formatting toolbar.

You can use a tear-off tool in one of two ways:

■ As a drop-down list. Click on the arrow to display a box of formatting options. In the Borders tool, for example, the box displays a dozen common border combinations.

■ As a floating toolbar. If you position the mouse pointer anywhere inside the dropped-down box, hold down the left mouse button, and then drag the pointer outside the box. The box "tears off" from the toolbar. When you release the mouse button, Excel displays the box as a floating toolbar. This makes it easy to make selections when you're doing a lot of formatting.

Working with Cell Patterns

One of the most effective ways to make an area of your worksheet stand out is to apply a pattern or shading to the cells. By shading titles, headings, and important results, you give your reports a polished, professional appearance.

Excel offers 18 different patterns, which you apply by using the Patterns tab in the Format Cells dialog box, shown in Figure 4.16. This dialog box is divided into three areas:

Color   This area sets the background color.

Pattern   This drop-down list box contains the 18 cell patterns and several boxes for selecting the foreground color—that is, the color of the pattern itself. See "Using Color in Worksheets," later in this chapter, for details.

Sample   This area shows how the currently selected pattern options will appear on the worksheet.

FIGURE 4.16.

The Patterns tab in the Format Cells dialog box.

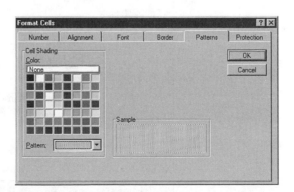

To apply a pattern to a cell or a range of cells, select Format | Cells, display the Patterns tab in the Format Cells dialog box, and then select your pattern from the **P**attern list. When you select OK, Excel returns you to the worksheet with the patterns applied.

Figure 4.17 shows the Brimson Manufacturing invoice with some shading effects. Figure 4.18 shows another application of cell patterns. In this example, patterns are used to create a timeline (also known as a Gantt chart) for a project management application. Each project task is listed on the left, and the bars show where each task starts and ends. You can use different cell patterns to represent tasks not yet started, tasks partially completed, tasks fully completed, and tasks delayed.

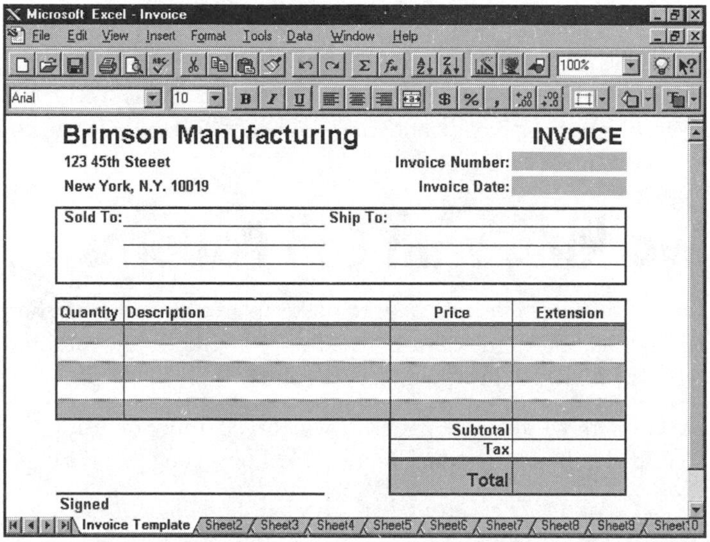

FIGURE 4.17.

The Brimson Manufacturing invoice with shading effects.

FIGURE 4.18.

Using cell patterns to create a Gantt chart.

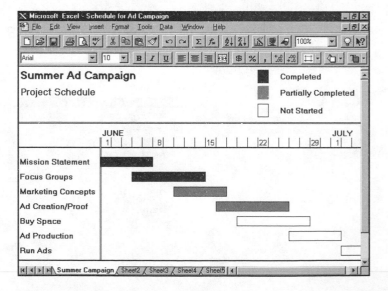

Working with Columns and Rows

An easy way to improve the appearance of your worksheet is to manipulate its rows and columns. This section teaches you how to adjust column widths and row heights. It also explains how to hide and unhide entire rows and columns, gridlines, and headings.

Adjusting Column Widths

You can use column width adjustments to improve the appearance of your worksheet in various ways:

- When you're faced with a truncated text entry or a number that Excel shows as ######, you can enlarge the column so that the entry will be displayed in full.

- If your worksheet contains many numbers, you can widen the columns to spread out the numbers and make the worksheet less cluttered.

- You can make your columns smaller so that the entire worksheet fits on-screen or on a single printed page.

- You can adjust the column width so that the entire worksheet creates a grid for a timeline chart (again, see Figure 4.18).

TIP

If you have a column of numbers in which one number (such as a date) is wider than the column and appears as ######, you don't need to widen the column to accommodate the number. Instead, use the TEXT() function to display the number as text. This allows the number to flow into the next column (provided, of course, that the next column is empty). I discussed the TEXT() function in Chapter 3, "Harnessing the Power of Excel's Worksheet Functions," in the section called "Text Functions."

Excel measures column width in characters. When you create a new worksheet, each column uses a standard width of 8.43 characters. The actual column width you see on-screen depends on the width of the default font. For example, the standard column width with 10-point Arial (7 pixels per character unit) is only half the size of the standard width with 20-point Arial (14 pixels per character unit). (For instructions on how to change the default font, see "Working with Cell Formats," later in this chapter.) You can use any of the following four methods to adjust your column widths:

- Enter a specific column width.
- Use the mouse to set the column width.
- Set the standard width for all columns.
- Have Excel set the width automatically with the AutoFit feature.

Method One: Entering a Specific Column Width

Excel enables you to set column widths as short as 0 characters or as long as 255 characters. To enter a column width, follow these steps:

1. Select at least one cell in each column that you want to adjust.
2. Select Format | Column | Width. Excel displays the Column Width dialog box, shown in Figure 4.19. The Column Width edit box shows the width of the selected columns. (This box is blank if you've chosen columns with varying widths.)

FIGURE 4.19.

Use the Column Width dialog box to set the width for the selected columns.

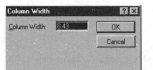

TIP

To quickly open the Column Width dialog box, right-click on the column header, and then choose Column Width from the shortcut menu.

3. Enter the desired width in the Column Width edit box.
4. Select OK. Excel sets the column width and returns you to the worksheet.

When entering column widths, you can use an integer or a decimal number. If, however, you enter a width such as 10.1 and call up the Column Width dialog box for the same column, you'll notice that the Column Width edit box actually says 10.14. What happened is that Excel adjusted the column width to the nearest pixel. For 10-point Arial (Excel's default font), a character unit has 7 pixels, or roughly 0.143 characters per pixel. This means that Excel will round a column width of 10.1 to 10.14. Similarly, a width of 9.35 is rounded down to 9.29.

Method Two: Using the Mouse to Set the Column Width

You can bypass the Column Width dialog box by using the mouse to drag a column to the width you want. The following procedure lists the steps that are involved:

1. Move the mouse pointer to the column header area, and position the pointer at the right edge of the column you want to adjust. The mouse pointer changes to the shape shown in Figure 4.20.
2. Press and hold down the left mouse button. The formula bar's Name box displays the current column width, and the column's right gridline turns into a dashed line, as shown in Figure 4.20.

FIGURE 4.20.

You can use the mouse to adjust the column width.

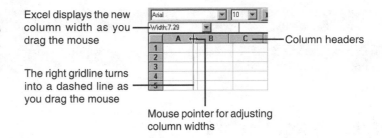

Excel displays the new column width as you drag the mouse

Column headers

The right gridline turns into a dashed line as you drag the mouse

Mouse pointer for adjusting column widths

3. Drag the pointer left or right to the desired width. As you move the pointer, the formula bar displays the new width.

4. Release the mouse button. Excel adjusts the column width accordingly.

You can use this technique to set the width of several columns at once. For every column you want to adjust, select the entire column and then perform the preceding steps on any one column. Excel applies the new width to each selected column.

Method Three: Setting the Standard Width for All the Columns

Using Excel's standard font, the standard column width is 8.43. You can change this width by following these steps:

1. Select the Format | Column | Standard Width command. Excel displays the Standard Width dialog box, shown in Figure 4.21.

FIGURE 4.21.

Use the Standard Width dialog box to set the width for all the worksheet's columns.

2. Enter the desired width in the Standard Column Width edit box.

3. Select OK. Excel applies the new column width to all the columns in the worksheet (except those not using the standard width).

Method Four: Using Excel's AutoFit Feature

If you have a long column of entries of varying widths, it might take you a few tries to get the optimum column width. To avoid guesswork, you can have Excel set the width automatically using the AutoFit feature. When you use this feature, Excel examines the column's contents and sets the width slightly larger than the longest entry.

To use AutoFit, select each column you want to adjust, and then select the Format | Column | AutoFit Selection command. Excel adjusts the columns to their optimal width and returns you to the worksheet.

> **TIP**
>
> To quickly set the AutoFit width, position the mouse pointer at the right edge of the column header and double-click.

Adjusting Row Height

You can set the height of your worksheet rows by using techniques similar to those used for adjusting column widths. Excel normally adjusts row heights automatically to accommodate the tallest font in a row. However, you can make your own height adjustments to give your worksheet more breathing room or to reduce the amount of space taken up by unused rows.

> **CAUTION**
>
> When reducing a row height, always keep the height larger than the tallest font to avoid cutting off the tops of any characters.

Excel measures row height in points—the same units used for type size. When you create a new worksheet, Excel assigns a standard row height of 12.75 points, which is high enough to accommodate the default 10-point Arial font. If you were to change the default font to 20-point Arial, each row height would increase accordingly.

You can use any of these three methods to adjust row heights:

- Enter a specific row height.
- Use the mouse to set the row height.
- Have Excel set the height automatically using the AutoFit feature.

Method One: Entering a Specific Row Height

Excel enables you to set row heights as small as 0 points or as large as 409 points. To enter a row height, follow these steps:

1. Select at least one cell in each row you want to adjust.
2. Select the Format | Row | Height command. Excel displays the Row Height dialog box, shown in Figure 4.22. The Row Height edit box shows the height of the selected rows. (This box is blank if you've chosen rows with varying heights.)

FIGURE 4.22.

Use the Row Height dialog box to set the height for the selected rows.

TIP

To quickly open the Row Height dialog box, right-click on the row header, and then choose Row Height from the shortcut menu.

---

3. Enter the height you want in the **R**ow Height edit box.

4. Select OK. Excel sets the row height and returns you to the worksheet.

Method Two: Using the Mouse to Set the Row Height

You can avoid the **R**ow Height dialog box by using the mouse to drag a row to the height you want. Here's how it's done:

1. Move the mouse pointer to the row header area, and position the pointer at the bottom edge of the row you want to adjust. The mouse pointer changes to the shape shown in Figure 4.23.

FIGURE 4.23.

You can use the mouse to adjust the row height.

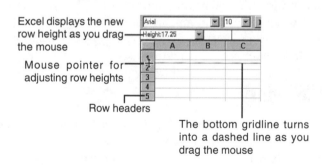

Excel displays the new row height as you drag the mouse

Mouse pointer for adjusting row heights

Row headers

The bottom gridline turns into a dashed line as you drag the mouse

2. Press and hold down the left mouse button. The formula bar displays the current row height, and the row's bottom gridline turns into a dashed line, as shown in Figure 4.23.

3. Drag the pointer up or down to reach the desired height. As you move the pointer, the formula bar displays the new height.

4. Release the mouse button. Excel adjusts the row height accordingly.

You can use this technique to set the height of several rows at once. For every row you want to adjust, select the entire row and then perform the preceding steps on any one row. Excel applies the new height to each row.

Method Three: Using Excel's AutoFit Feature

If you've made several font changes and height adjustments to a long row of entries, you might need to try several times to set an optimum row height. To save time, you can use Excel's AutoFit feature to set the height automatically to the best fit.

To try it out, select each row you want to adjust, and then select Format | **R**ow | **A**utoFit. Excel adjusts the rows to their optimal height and returns you to the worksheet.

> **TIP**
>
> To quickly set the AutoFit height, position the mouse pointer at the bottom edge of the row header and double-click.

Hiding Columns and Rows

Your worksheets might contain confidential information (such as payroll figures) or unimportant information (such as the period numbers used when calculating interest payments). In either case, you can hide the appropriate columns or rows when showing your worksheet to others. The data remains intact but isn't displayed on-screen. The next two sections show you how to hide and unhide columns and rows.

Hiding Columns

Hiding a column is equivalent to setting the column width to 0. Instead of adjusting the column width directly, however, you can hide the current column (or multiple columns if you first select a cell in each column) by using any of the following techniques:

- Select the Format | **C**olumn | **H**ide command.
- Press Ctrl-0 (zero).
- Right-click on the column header, and then choose **H**ide from the shortcut menu.
- Position the mouse pointer on the right edge of the column header, and drag the pointer to the left, past the left edge of the column header.

When you hide a column, the column letter no longer appears in the headers. For example, Figure 4.24 shows a worksheet with confidential payroll information in columns C, D, and E. Figure 4.25 shows the same worksheet with these columns hidden and their letters missing from the column headers. However, you still can refer to cells in the hidden columns in formulas and searches.

FIGURE 4.24.
Columns C, D, and E contain confidential information.

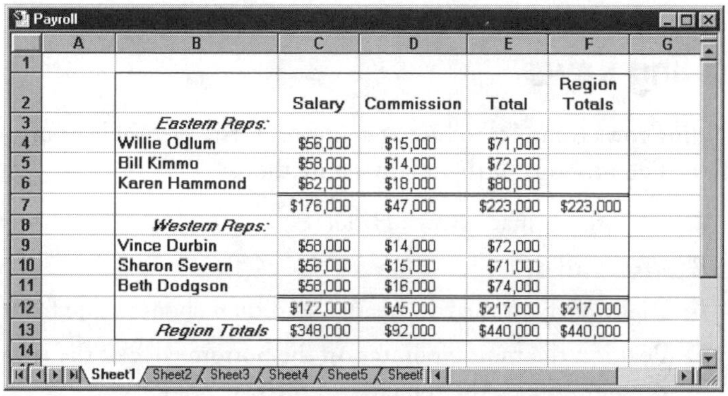

Payroll

	A	B	C	D	E	F	G
1							
2			Salary	Commission	Total	Region Totals	
3		*Eastern Reps:*					
4		Willie Odlum	$56,000	$15,000	$71,000		
5		Bill Kimmo	$58,000	$14,000	$72,000		
6		Karen Hammond	$62,000	$18,000	$80,000		
7			$176,000	$47,000	$223,000	$223,000	
8		*Western Reps:*					
9		Vince Durbin	$58,000	$14,000	$72,000		
10		Sharon Severn	$56,000	$15,000	$71,000		
11		Beth Dodgson	$58,000	$16,000	$74,000		
12			$172,000	$45,000	$217,000	$217,000	
13		*Region Totals*	$348,000	$92,000	$440,000	$440,000	
14							

Sheet1 / Sheet2 / Sheet3 / Sheet4 / Sheet5 / Sheet6

FIGURE 4.25.
The same worksheet with columns C, D, and E hidden.

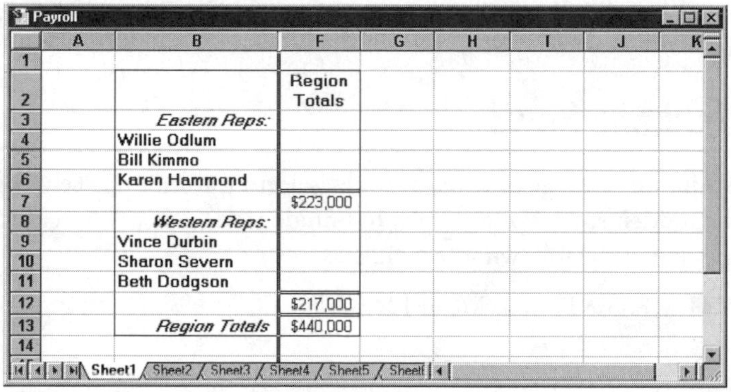

Payroll

	A	B	F	G	H	I	J	K
1								
2			Region Totals					
3		*Eastern Reps:*						
4		Willie Odlum						
5		Bill Kimmo						
6		Karen Hammond						
7			$223,000					
8		*Western Reps:*						
9		Vince Durbin						
10		Sharon Severn						
11		Beth Dodgson						
12			$217,000					
13		*Region Totals*	$440,000					
14								

Sheet1 / Sheet2 / Sheet3 / Sheet4 / Sheet5 / Sheet6

Unhiding Columns

To unhide a range of columns, first select at least one cell from each column on either side of the hidden columns. For example, to unhide columns C, D, and E, select a cell in columns B and F. Then use any of the following techniques:

- Choose F**o**rmat | **C**olumn | **U**nhide.
- Press Ctrl-).
- Right-click on the selection, and choose Unhide from the shortcut menu.

What do you do, though, if you want to unhide just a single column out of a group of hidden columns (for example, column C out of columns C, D, and E)? Here are the steps to follow:

1. Choose the **E**dit | **G**o To command, or press F5. Excel displays the Go To dialog box.
2. Enter a cell address in the column you want to unhide. For example, to unhide column C, enter `C1`.

3. Select OK. Excel moves to the cell address.

4. Choose F**o**rmat | **C**olumn | **U**nhide or Ctrl-). Excel unhides the column and returns you to the worksheet.

Hiding Rows

Hiding rows is similar to hiding columns. First, select at least one cell in every row you want to hide. Then try one of the following methods:

■ Choose F**o**rmat | **R**ow | **H**ide.

■ Press Ctrl-9.

■ Right-click on the row header, and then choose **H**ide from the shortcut menu.

■ Position the mouse pointer on the bottom edge of the row header, and drag the pointer up past the top edge of the row header.

As with columns, when you hide a row, the row letter no longer appears in the headers. However, you still can refer to cells in the hidden rows in formulas and searches.

Unhiding Rows

To unhide a range of rows, begin by selecting at least one cell from each row on either side of the hidden rows. For example, to unhide rows 3, 4, and 5, select a cell in rows 2 and 6. Then use one of the following techniques:

■ Choose F**o**rmat | **R**ow | **U**nhide.

■ Press Ctrl-(.

■ Right-click on the selected rows, and choose Unhide from the shortcut menu.

If you want to unhide a single row out of a group of hidden rows (for example, row 3 out of rows 3, 4, and 5), use the following procedure:

1. Choose the **E**dit | **G**o To command, or press F5 to display the Go To dialog box.

2. Enter a cell address in the row you want to unhide. For example, to unhide row 3, enter A3.

3. Select OK. Excel moves to the cell address.

4. Choose F**o**rmat | **R**ow | **U**nhide, or press Ctrl-(. Excel unhides the rows and returns you to the worksheet.

Hiding Gridlines and Headers

Excel enables you to hide both your worksheet gridlines and the row and column headers. This feature is useful for displaying your worksheet to others on-screen or on an overhead, or for a data-entry application. Removing gridlines also helps your cell border and shading effects show up better.

The following steps show you how to remove your worksheet gridlines and headers:

1. Select the **T**ools | **O**ptions command, and in the Options dialog box that appears, select the View tab.
2. To remove gridlines, deactivate the **G**ridlines check box.
3. To remove the headers, deactivate the Row and Column H**e**aders check box.
4. Select OK. Excel returns you to the worksheet with your chosen display options in effect.

To restore gridlines or row and column headers, repeat the preceding steps and activate the appropriate check boxes.

Using Color in Worksheets

The previous sections in this chapter have shown you how to turn a plain, unformatted worksheet into an attractive, professional-quality report. The final touch involves adding just the right amount of color to your presentation. With colors, you can emphasize important results, shape the layout of your page, and add subtle psychological effects.

If you don't have access to a color printer, you can use color in your worksheets for on-screen presentations or to convert worksheets and charts to overheads or slides using an off-site graphics service.

Excel's Color Palette

When applying colors to your worksheet elements, Excel enables you to choose from a palette of 56 colors. Figure 4.26 shows the default palette. Later in this chapter, you'll learn how to customize this palette with your own colors.

FIGURE 4.26.

Excel's 56-color palette.

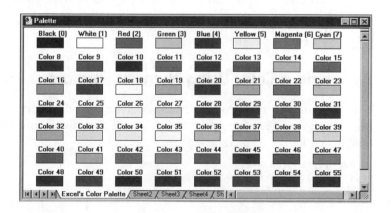

NOTE

The palette colors on your system appear differently, depending on whether you're using a 16- or 256-color video driver. The 256-color driver shows the palette as solid colors (as shown in Figure 4.25), and the 16-color driver shows colors 16 through 55 as patterns.

Because this book's black-and-white reproduction doesn't show the actual palette colors, I've included the file Palette.xls on the CD.

Assigning Colors to Cell Contents

You can use any of the palette colors to format individual cell entries. Colors make worksheet titles and headings stand out and also emphasize interesting results. You can use two methods to change the color of cell contents:

■ Assign font colors.

■ Use color symbols in custom numeric and date formats.

Assigning a Font Color

To apply a font color to a cell's contents, follow these steps:

1. Select the group of characters inside a cell, the entire cell, or the range that you want to format.

2. Choose the Format | Cells command, and select the Font tab in the Format Cells dialog box.

3. Select a color from the Color drop-down list. The font in the Preview box changes color to match your selection.

4. Select OK. Excel returns you to the worksheet with the color applied.

You also can use the Font Color tear-off tool in the Formatting toolbar to assign a color to a cell's contents.

Assigning a Color Using Numeric Formats

You can gain even more control over the coloring of cell entries by using numeric formats. Recall the following currency formats from the "Formatting Numbers, Dates, and Times" section, earlier in this chapter:

```
$#,##0_);[RED]($#,##0)
$#,##0.00_);[RED]($#,##0.00)
```

In each example, the second part of the format applies the color red to any negative amount. By creating your own custom formats, you can apply a color to any number or range of numbers. Table 4.7 lists the nine color symbols you can use in your custom numeric color formats.

Table 4.7. The color symbols to use in numeric formats.

Symbol	Color
[BLACK]	Black
[WHITE]	White
[RED]	Red
[GREEN]	Green
[BLUE]	Blue
[YELLOW]	Yellow
[MAGENTA]	Magenta
[CYAN]	Cyan
[COLOR *n*]	A color from the color palette, in which *n* is a number between 0 and 55 (see Figure 4.26)

The following format displays positive numbers in blue, negative numbers in red, zero values in green, and text in magenta:

```
[BLUE]0.00;[RED]-0.00;[GREEN]0;[MAGENTA]
```

You can add condition values to your formats to handle just about any situation. For example, if you have an accounts receivable worksheet that contains a column showing the number of days that invoices are past due, use the following format to display numbers over 90 in magenta:

```
[>90] [MAGENTA]###;###
```

Assigning Colors to Borders and Patterns

Earlier in this chapter, you learned that using cell borders and patterns can make your worksheets appear more organized and dynamic. You can extend these advantages by applying colors to your borders and cell patterns.

To try this out, first select the cell or range of cells you want to format. Then select the Format | Cells command to display the Format Cells dialog box. Then use either of the following techniques:

■ To apply a border color, select the Border tab and choose the color you want from the **C**olor drop-down list.

- To apply a pattern color, first select the Patterns tab. To apply a background color, choose one of the boxes in the **C**olor section. To apply a foreground color, choose a color from the **P**attern drop-down list.

When you're done, select OK to return to the worksheet with the color applied.

 You also can use the Color tear-off tool in the Formatting toolbar to assign a background color to a cell pattern.

By mixing the pattern and its foreground and background colors, you can create different shades of any palette color. Figure 4.27 shows an example. In each of the Result columns, the foreground color used is Dark Cyan. The cells in the Result row (B6:L6) are a combination of the patterns and colors shown in the Pattern row (B2:L2), the Foreground Color row (B3:L3), and the Background Color row (B4:L4). The foreground color used throughout is Dark Cyan. This is the color from which we'll derive the different shades.

FIGURE 4.27.

Use the dot patterns with dark or light background colors to produce shades of the foreground color.

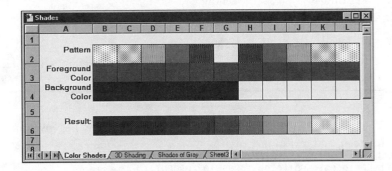

In the first five columns (B6:F6), the background color is black, and the pattern varies from the widely spaced dots of the pattern in cell B2 to the tightly spaced dots of the pattern in cell F2. As you can see, the colors in the Result row become progressively lighter. Why does this happen? Well, recall that the dots in any pattern use the current foreground color. Since the pattern in G2 has relatively few dots, the result is dominated by the background color (black, in this case). As we move from left to right, the dots in the patterns become more numerous. The upshot is that we see more of the foreground color and less of the background color, which makes the result appear lighter.

This sequence culminates in column G, where the pattern (G2) is solid. This means, by definition, that there is no background color, so the result (cell G6) is a pure palette color (Dark Cyan).

In the last five columns (H6:L6), the background color is switched to white and we run through the patterns in reverse order. Again, as you move from left to right, the resulting color becomes lighter because the background color (white) increasingly dominates the result. With this simple trick, you get an additional 10 "colors" for every palette color.

Creating 3-D Effects

You can use contrasting border and pattern colors to achieve impressive 3-D effects in your worksheets. Begin by coloring each cell in the worksheet with a neutral color (not too dark, not too light), such as gray. (Depending on which color you use, you might have to make most of your cell contents bold to make them show up properly.) With 3-D effects, you can format an area to look as though it's raised up from the worksheet or sunken into the worksheet.

To create a raised effect, follow these steps:

1. Select the top row of cells in the range. In the Border tab of the Format Cells dialog box, add a border to the **T**op, and select white from the **C**olor list.

2. Select the left column of cells in the range. In the Border tab, add a border to the **L**eft, and select white from the **C**olor list.

> **NOTE**
>
> When you perform this procedure, you'll notice that some of the Border boxes are grayed. This is normal. It means that only some of the selected cells have the border applied.

3. Select the bottom row of cells in the range. In the Border tab, add a border to the **B**ottom, and select black from the **C**olor list.

4. Select the right column of cells in the range. In the Border tab, add a border to the **R**ight, and select black from the **C**olor list.

Here are the steps to follow to create a sunken effect:

1. Select the top row of cells in the range. In the Border tab of the Format Cells dialog box, add a border to the **T**op, and select black from the **C**olor list.

2. Select the left column of cells in the range. In the Border tab, add a border to the **L**eft, and select black from the **C**olor list.

3. Select the bottom row of cells in the range. In the Border tab, add a border to the **B**ottom, and select white from the **C**olor list.

4. Select the right column of cells in the range. In the Border tab, add a border to the **R**ight, and select white from the **C**olor list.

Figure 4.28 shows a worksheet formatted with 3-D effects.

FIGURE 4.28.

You can use borders and shading to create 3-D effects.

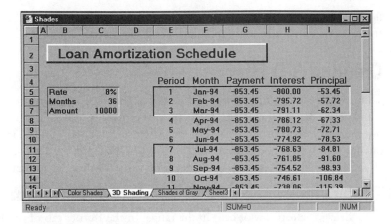

Assigning Colors to Gridlines

For something a little different, you can change the color of your worksheet gridlines. The following procedure lists the appropriate steps:

1. Select **Tools** | **Options** and then select the View tab from the Options dialog box.
2. Select a color from the **Color** drop-down list under the **G**ridlines check box.
3. Select OK. Excel returns you to the worksheet with the new color applied.

Customizing the Color Palette

As you've seen in this section, you use the Excel color palette in lots of Excel nooks and crannies. The 56 default colors are usually fine for most applications, and you might never need another color. However, if a particular shade would be just right for your presentation, Excel enables you to customize the color palette.

> **TIP**
>
> If you use your corporate colors in presentations, you can create a custom palette containing several hues and shades of your company's colors.

You customize your own colors using the Color Picker dialog box, shown in Figure 4.29. You can use one of two methods to select a color. The first method utilizes the fact that you can create any color in the spectrum by mixing the colors red, green, and blue. The Color Picker dialog box enables you to enter specific numbers between 0 and 255 for each of these colors. A lower number means the color is less intense, and a higher number means the color is more intense.

FIGURE 4.29.

The Color Picker dialog box.

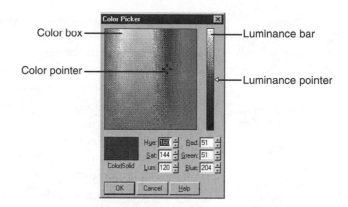

To give you some idea of how this works, Table 4.8 lists the first eight colors of the default palette and their respective red, green, and blue numbers.

Table 4.8. The red, green, and blue numbers for eight default palette colors.

Color	Red	Green	Blue
Black	0	0	0
White	255	255	255
Red	255	0	0
Green	0	255	0
Blue	0	0	255
Yellow	255	255	0
Magenta	255	0	255
Cyan	0	255	255

NOTE

Whenever the **Red**, **Green**, and **Blue** values are equal, you get a gray-scale color. Lower numbers produce darker grays, and higher numbers produce lighter grays.

The second method for selecting colors involves setting three different attributes: hue, saturation, and luminance.

Hue	This number (which is more or less equivalent to the term *color*) measures the position on the color spectrum. Lower numbers indicate a position near the red end, and higher numbers move through the yellow, green, blue, and violet parts of the spectrum. As you increase the hue, the color pointer moves from left to right.
Saturation	This number is a measure of the purity of a given hue. A saturation setting of 240 means that the hue is a pure color. Lower numbers indicate that more gray is mixed with the hue until, at 0, the color becomes part of the gray scale. As you increase the saturation, the color pointer moves toward the top of the color box.
Luminance	This number is a measure of the brightness of a color. Lower numbers are darker, and higher numbers are brighter. The luminance bar to the right of the color box shows the luminance scale for the selected color. As you increase the luminance, the slider moves toward the top of the bar.

Following is the procedure to create a custom palette:

1. Choose **Tools | O**ptions and then select the Color tab from the Options dialog box. The Color tab displays all 56 colors in the Excel palette.

2. Select the color you want to change.

> **TIP**
>
> If you need to reset the palette to the default colors, select the **R**eset button.

3. Select **M**odify. The Color Picker dialog box appears with the selected color's numbers displayed.

4. To select a new color, enter the appropriate values in the text boxes. You also can use the mouse to move the color pointer in the color box and move the slider up or down the luminance bar.

5. (Optional) The Color|Solid box shows the selected color on the left and the nearest solid color on the right (if you're using a 16-color video driver). If you want to use the solid color, double-click on it.

6. Select OK. Excel returns you to the Color tab.

7. Repeat steps 2 through 6 to customize other colors in the palette.

8. When you finish, select OK. Excel returns you to the worksheet with the new palette in effect.

> **NOTE**
>
> To use your new colors in custom numeric formats, refer to the palette number. For example, if you replace black in the default palette, refer to the new color as [COLOR 1] in your format definitions.

Copying Custom Color Palettes

You can copy custom color palettes created in other workbooks by following these steps:

1. Open the workbook that contains the custom color palette.
2. Open the workbook into which you want to copy the custom palette.
3. Choose the **T**ools | **O**ptions command, and select the Color tab in the Options dialog box.
4. In the **C**opy Colors from drop-down list, select the workbook that contains the custom colors you want to copy. The Color tab displays the color palette from the selected workbook.
5. Select OK. Excel copies the color palette into the current workbook.

> **NOTE**
>
> Save color schemes you use frequently (such as your company's colors or the colors of major clients) in their own workbooks. You then can copy the colors into your current worksheet whenever you need them.

Using Color Effectively

Now you know how to apply colors to your Excel worksheets, but that's only half the battle. Colors that are poorly matched or improperly applied can make a presentation look worse, not better. This section examines a few basics for effectively using colors in your worksheets.

With so many colors available, the temptation is to go overboard and use a dozen different hues on each page. However, using too many colors can confuse your audience and even cause eye fatigue. Try to stick to three or four colors at most. If you must use more, try to use different shades of three or four hues.

Before finalizing your color scheme, you need to ensure that the colors you've selected work well together. For example, blue and black are often difficult to distinguish, and green/red combinations clash. Other color combinations to avoid are red/blue, green/blue, and brown/black. On the other hand, color combinations such as red/yellow, gray/red, and blue/yellow go well together, as do contrasting shades of the same color, such as black and gray.

> **NOTE**
>
> Another good reason to avoid using too much green and red in your worksheets is that approximately eight percent of the male population suffers from red-green color blindness.

When selecting colors, think about the psychological impact that your scheme will have on your audience. Studies have shown that "cool" colors such as blue and gray evoke a sense of dependability and trust. Use these colors for business meetings. For presentations that require a little more excitement, "warm" colors such as red, yellow, and orange can evoke a festive, fun atmosphere. For a safe, comfortable ambiance, try using brown and yellow. For an environmental touch, use green and brown.

After you've settled on a color scheme, use it consistently throughout your presentation. Charts, clip art, and slides should all use the same colors.

Working with Cell Formats

As you've seen, Excel contains powerful formatting features that can make your worksheets look their best. The problem is that you can end up spending more time working on the appearance of a spreadsheet than on the actual data. To remedy this problem, Excel offers a number of features that make your cell formatting faster and more efficient.

This section shows you how to display cell format information, copy and move existing formats, define format styles, and use Excel's handy AutoFormat and Format Painter features.

Displaying Cell Format Information

With so many formatting options available, it's easy to lose track of which cells are formatted with which options. To help, Excel provides an Info window that can show you the attributes of any cell. To use the Info window to learn about a cell's formatting, follow these steps:

1. Move to the cell you want to use.
2. Select the **T**ools | **O**ptions command, and then select the View tab in the Options dialog box.
3. Activate the Info **W**indow check box.
4. Select OK. Excel displays the Info window and the Info window menu bar.
5. Select the **I**nfo | Forma**t** command. Excel displays the cell format information in the Info window.

Figure 4.30 shows an Info window displaying the format options of cell I5 from the 3D Shading worksheet.

FIGURE 4.30.

The Info window displaying cell formats.

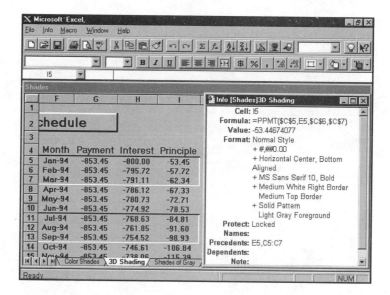

Copying Cell Formats

After you've formatted a cell the way you want it, you can use the same format in other parts of your worksheet by copying the entire cell. When you copy a cell, Excel pastes both the cell contents and the cell format to the new location.

If, however, you want to copy only the formatting and not the contents, Excel gives you two methods:

- Use Paste Special to paste formats.
- Use the Format Painter to apply existing formats to a selected range.

Copying Formats with Paste Special

To copy only formats to a destination, use the Paste Special command, as described in the following steps:

1. Select the cell or range you want to copy.
2. Choose the **E**dit | **C**opy command.

3. Select the destination range.

4. Choose the **E**dit | Paste **S**pecial command. Excel displays the Paste Special dialog box.

5. In the Paste section, select Format**s**.

6. Select OK. Excel copies only the formats from the original cells.

Copying Cell Formats with the Format Painter

Excel's Format Painter tool enables you to easily apply an existing format to a selected range. The following procedure shows you how it's done:

1. Select the cell or range that contains the format you want to copy (see Figure 4.31).

FIGURE 4.31.

Select the range containing the format you want to copy.

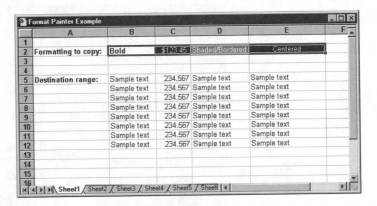

2. Click on the Format Painter tool in the Standard toolbar. A small paintbrush appears beside the mouse pointer.

 The Format Painter tool.

3. Drag the mouse pointer over the range to which you want to copy the format (see Figure 4.32).

FIGURE 4.32.

Select the Format Painter tool, and then drag the mouse pointer over the range to which you want to copy the format.

4. Release the mouse button. Excel copies the format from the original range into the destination range, as shown in Figure 4.33.

FIGURE 4.33.

When you release the button, Excel pastes the original format into the destination range.

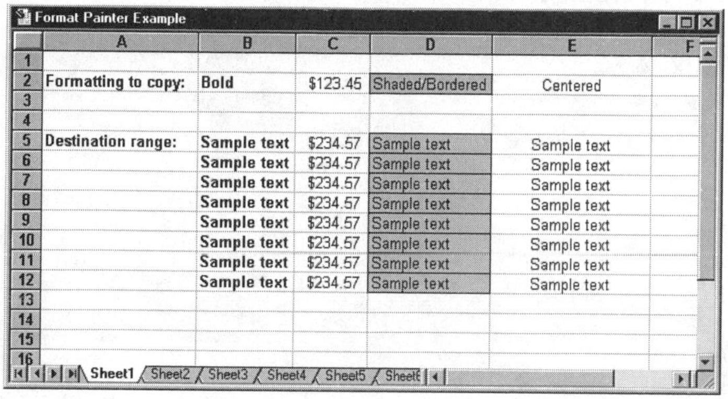

	A	B	C	D	E
1					
2	Formatting to copy:	Bold	$123.45	Shaded/Bordered	Centered
3					
4					
5	Destination range:	Sample text	$234.57	Sample text	Sample text
6		Sample text	$234.57	Sample text	Sample text
7		Sample text	$234.57	Sample text	Sample text
8		Sample text	$234.57	Sample text	Sample text
9		Sample text	$234.57	Sample text	Sample text
10		Sample text	$234.57	Sample text	Sample text
11		Sample text	$234.57	Sample text	Sample text
12		Sample text	$234.57	Sample text	Sample text

Clearing Cell Formats

Clearing only the format in a cell (and leaving the contents intact) is easy. Just select the cell or range that contains the formats you want to clear, and then choose the **E**dit | Cle**a**r | **F**ormats command.

Working with Styles

Depending on the options you choose, formatting a single cell or range can take dozens of mouse clicks or keystrokes. If you plan to use a specific formatting combination repeatedly, don't re-invent the wheel each time. Using Excel's Style feature, you can summarize any combination of formatting options under a single style name and then apply the whole combination in a single operation.

Styles also save time if you need to reformat your document. Normally, you would have to select every cell containing the format you want to change (including blank cells) and then make the adjustments. With styles, you just redefine the style, and Excel updates all the associated cells automatically.

A style can contain most of the formatting features you've learned about in this chapter, including fonts, alignment, borders, and patterns, as well as number, date, and time formats. Excel also comes with several built-in styles: Comma, Comma [0], Currency, Currency [0], Percent, and Normal. Normal is the default style for the entire workbook.

Applying a Style

Here are the steps to follow to apply a style:

1. Select the cell or range you want to format.
2. Select the Format | Style command. Excel displays the Style dialog box, shown in Figure 4.34.

FIGURE 4.34.

Use the Style dialog box to apply a style.

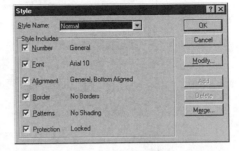

3. Select the style you want from the Style Name drop-down list. A description of the formatting options included in the selected style appears in the Style Includes group.
4. If you don't want to use some part of the style, deactivate the appropriate check box in the Style Includes group.
5. Select OK. Excel applies the style to the selected cells.

When you apply a style to a cell, Excel overwrites the cell's existing format. Similarly, if you apply a style first and then format the cell, the new formatting overwrites the style. In both cases, however, only defined attributes change. For example, if you apply the Percent style to a cell already formatted as left-aligned, the alignment doesn't change.

Creating a Style

Besides using the built-in styles supplied by Excel, you can define your own styles to suit your needs. Any style you create appears in the Style Name list for that workbook. Excel provides three ways to define styles:

- By example
- By definition
- By merging styles from another document

NOTE

It's a good idea to create a style for frequently used sections of your worksheet. For example, a Heading style would contain attributes of your worksheet headings, and a Title style would contain your worksheet title format.

Creating a Style by Example

If you have a cell that contains a format combination you want to use as a style, you can tell Excel to define a new style based on the cell format. This is called the *style by example* method, and you follow these steps to use it:

1. Select the cell that contains the format combination you want to turn into a style.
2. Select the Format | Style command to display the Style dialog box.
3. Type the new style name in the **S**tyle Name edit box.
4. Select OK. Excel creates the new style.

You can select multiple cells to use as an example. In this case, Excel assigns only formats that the cells have in common. For example, suppose that you have one cell that's left-aligned with a border and another that's left-aligned without a border. If you select both cells to use as your example, Excel defines the new style as left-aligned only.

Creating a Style by Definition

The second method for creating a style involves setting the specific format options using the Style dialog box. This is called the *style by definition* method. Follow these steps to create a style by definition:

1. Select the Format | Style command to display the Style dialog box.
2. Enter the new style name in the **S**tyle Name edit box.
3. Select the **M**odify button. Excel displays the Format Cells dialog box.
4. Use the tabs in the Format Cells dialog box to select your style options. When you're done, Select OK to return to the Style dialog box.
5. To accept the new style, click the **A**dd button.
6. To create more styles, repeat steps 2 through 5. Otherwise, you can either apply the new style to the selected cells by selecting OK, or exit the dialog without applying the style by selecting Close.

Merging Styles from Another Document

The third method for creating styles involves copying the existing styles from another document into the current workbook. This is called *merging* styles. This method is useful if you have other workbooks in which you've already defined several styles. Instead of defining them again in the current workbook, you simply merge them. Before continuing, you need to open the workbook containing the styles, and the workbook receiving the styles must be the active window. The following procedure shows you how to merge styles:

1. Select the **Format | S**tyle command to display the Style dialog box.
2. Select the **Merge** button. The Merge Styles dialog box appears with a list of the currently open workbooks.
3. Select the workbook with the styles you want to copy.
4. Select OK. Excel copies the styles from the file and returns you to the Style dialog box.
5. To apply a new style, select it from the **St**yle Name list box, and then select OK. Otherwise, select Close.

CAUTION

If the receiving workbook contains a style with the same name as a style that's being merged, Excel displays a warning box. Select **Y**es to overwrite the existing styles or **No** to merge all styles except those with the same name.

NOTE

If you have a number of styles you use frequently, create a workbook to store the styles. To use these styles in the current workbook, just merge them from the styles workbook.

Redefining a Style

As you've seen, styles can save time when you have to apply many formats to a worksheet. Styles also can save time by making it easier to reformat your documents. If you've used styles to format a worksheet, just redefine the style, and Excel automatically updates every cell containing the style to match the new style definition. You also can redefine any of Excel's built-in styles, including the Normal style, which is the default used for all cells in any new worksheet. You can redefine styles in two ways:

- By example
- By definition

Redefining a Style by Example

You can use the *style by example* method to redefine an existing style. Follow these steps:

1. Select a cell that contains the format you want to use to redefine the style.

2. Choose the Format | Style command to display the Style dialog box.

3. In the Style Name edit box, type the name of the style you want to redefine. (You must type the name, not merely select it from the list.)

4. Select OK. Excel redefines the style and updates all the workbook cells that use the style.

Redefining a Style by Definition

Here are the steps to follow to use the *style by definition* method to redefine an existing style:

1. Choose the Format | Style command to display the Style dialog box.

2. Select the style that you want to redefine from the Style Name list.

3. Select the Modify button to display the Format Cells dialog box.

4. Make your changes to the style attributes, and then select OK to return to the Style dialog box.

5. Select OK. Excel redefines the style.

Deleting a Style

To keep your style lists to a minimum, you should delete any styles you no longer use. When you delete a style, any associated cells revert to the Normal style. (Any other formatting options you added on top of the style remain in effect, however.) Follow these steps to delete a style from a worksheet:

1. Select the Format | Style command to display the Style dialog box.

2. Pick out the style you want to delete from the Style Name list box.

3. Select the Delete button. Excel deletes the style and converts every cell in the workbook that uses the style to Normal.

4. Repeat steps 2 and 3 to delete other styles.

5. Select OK.

NOTE

You can't delete the Normal style.

Using the AutoFormat Feature

Excel offers a feature that enables you to format any worksheet range easily. This feature, called *AutoFormat*, can automatically apply certain predefined format combinations to create attractive, professional-quality tables and lists.

There are 16 predefined AutoFormat combinations. Each combination uses selected format options to display numbers, fonts, borders, and patterns and to set cell alignment, column width, and row height. AutoFormat doesn't just apply a single format combination to each cell. Instead, it applies separate formatting for row and column headings, data, and summary lines (for example, subtotals and totals). If you have formatting that you want left intact, you can tell Excel to leave out the appropriate format options from the automatic format. For example, if you've already set up your font options, you can exclude the font formats from the AutoFormat table.

> **CAUTION**
>
> You can't apply an AutoFormat to a single cell or to a noncontiguous range. If you try, Excel displays an error message. You can, however, select a single cell if it's within a table. Excel detects the surrounding table automatically.

Here are the basic steps to follow to use the AutoFormat feature:

1. Select the range you want to format.
2. Select the **Fo**rmat | **A**utoFormat command. Excel displays the AutoFormat dialog box, shown in Figure 4.35.

FIGURE 4.35.

The AutoFormat dialog box.

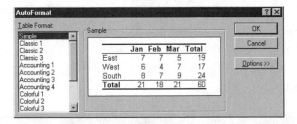

3. Select a format combination from the **T**able Format list box. An example of each format appears in the Sample box.
4. To exclude formatting, click the **O**ptions button, and in the Formats to Apply section that appears, uncheck the format types you want to exclude. The displayed example adjusts accordingly.
5. Select OK. Excel applies the formatting to the range you selected.

When using the AutoFormat feature, keep the following points in mind:

- AutoFormat usually assumes that the top row and the left column in your range contain the range headings. To avoid improper formatting, be sure to include your headings when you select the range.

- Each table format uses the typeface defined in the Normal font. To use a different typeface in all your AutoFormat tables, change the Normal font to the typeface you want.

- The Classic table formats are designed to be used in any worksheet to make your data more readable. Headings and totals are set off with borders or shading.

- The Financial table formats can be used in any worksheet that contains currency values. Initial data values and totals are formatted as currency.

- The Colorful table formats are suitable for on-screen or slide presentations or for reports produced on a color printer.

- The List table formats can be used with lists and databases. Shading and borders are used to make the data more readable.

- The 3D Effects table formats give your worksheets a professional-quality appearance suitable for any presentation.

Adding Comments with Text Boxes and Notes

This chapter has shown you many techniques for making your worksheets clearer and more readable. However, a well-organized worksheet can be difficult to read if you use formulas and calculations that are obscure to other users. Because you can't always be there to explain your work, Excel enables you to add comments to your documents in the form of *text boxes*, *text notes*, and *sound notes*. You use text boxes to add explanatory remarks that sit "on top" of the worksheet. You use text notes to attach comments to individual cells. If your computer has a sound card, you can record sound notes and attach them to a cell. This section shows you how to work with all three kinds of objects.

Working with Text Boxes

Many people like to add handwritten comments directly to their printed worksheets or on sticky notes. For a more professional look, or for times when you're presenting your work on-screen or as a slide presentation, add an Excel text box to your worksheet. A text box is a block of text that sits on the worksheet. The text box is a graphic "object," so you can position, size, edit, and format it independently of the worksheet cells. (For more information on Excel's graphic objects, especially on object properties and formatting, see Chapter 11, "Working with Graphic Objects.")

Adding a Text Box

To create a text box, follow these steps:

1. Click on the Text Box tool in the Drawing toolbar. (If you don't see the Drawing toolbar on-screen, right-click on any toolbar and then select Drawing from the shortcut menu.) If you want to create more than one text box, double-click on the tool. The regular mouse pointer changes to a crosshair pointer.

 The Text Box tool from the Drawing toolbar.

2. Position the pointer where you want the top-left corner of the text box to be.

3. Drag the mouse pointer to where you want the bottom-right corner of the text box to be. As you drag the pointer, Excel draws an outline of the box.

> **TIP**
>
> To make the text box a square, hold down Shift while dragging the pointer. To align the text box with the worksheet gridlines, hold down the Alt key while dragging the pointer.

4. Release the mouse button. If you're drawing only one box, Excel places a blinking insertion-point cursor in the upper-left corner of the box. If you double-clicked on the Text Box tool but you want to draw only a single box, skip to step 6.

5. If you're creating more boxes, repeat steps 2 through 4. When you've finished, click on the first box in which you want to enter text.

6. Type your text in the box. The text automatically wraps and scrolls within the box.

7. To add text to another box, click on the box and enter the text you want.

8. When you're finished, click on an empty area of the worksheet or press the Esc key.

> **NOTE**
>
> Use text boxes for short explanations or to point out key worksheet results. For longer, more technical comments, attach a text note or a sound note to a cell. (See the sections "Working with Text Notes" and "Working with Sound Notes," later in this chapter.)

Editing and Formatting Text Box Text

After you've added a text box to a worksheet, you're free to edit and format the text contained in the box. To edit the contents of a text box, follow these steps:

1. Click on the text box you want to edit.

2. Click inside the text box to position the cursor for inserting text, or highlight the text you want to change.

3. Edit or format the text using the same techniques you use for editing and formatting cell contents.

CAUTION

If you click only once on the text box and then begin typing, Excel replaces the entire contents of the box with your typing. If this happens, immediately select the **Edit** | **U**ndo Typing command or press Ctrl-Z.

4. When you're finished, click outside the box or press the Esc key.

TIP

When editing a text box, press Enter to start a new line. To enter a tab, press Ctrl-Tab.

NOTE

An ideal use for text boxes is to show others your worksheet formulas. To enter a formula in a text box, select the cell, highlight the formula in the cell, and select **Edit** | **C**opy. Position the cursor inside the text box, and select **Edit** | **P**aste to enter the formula into the box.

Deleting a Text Box

If your worksheet contains a text box or arrow that you no longer need, you can delete the object by clicking on it and then selecting the **Edit** | **C**ut command (or you can press Delete).

TIP

In some cases, you might prefer hiding text boxes instead of deleting them. To do this, select the **Tools** | **O**ptions command, and then select the View tab in the Options dialog box. In the Objects group, select Hi**d**e All.

Working with Text Notes

If you don't want to display comments on your worksheet, you can attach text notes to specific cells. These notes remain hidden and can be viewed only by displaying the Cell Note dialog box or by hovering the mouse pointer over the cell. A note indicator marks each cell that contains a note.

A text note is similar to a footnote in a book or report. A text note can be as long as you like, so you can use it for a lengthy explanation of your worksheet assumptions—without interfering with the appearance of the document. You also can use text notes for technical explanations, analyses of worksheet results, or just your name.

> **NOTE**
>
> For audited worksheets, enter the name of the person who created the worksheet, the auditor, and the date of the last revision in a text note. Use a consistent cell for the note, such as A1. Be sure to protect each worksheet so that no unauthorized revisions can be made. For more information on protecting worksheets, see Chapter 5, "Advanced Worksheet Topics."

Adding a Text Note

Here are the steps to follow to add text notes to your worksheet cells:

1. Select the cell to which you want to add the note.
2. Select the **I**nsert | **N**ote command. Excel displays the Cell Note dialog box, shown in Figure 4.36.

FIGURE 4.36.

The Cell Note dialog box.

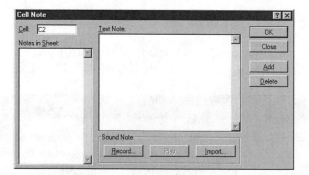

3. Enter the note in the **T**ext Note box.
4. Select the **A**dd button. Excel displays the cell address and the first few characters of the note in the Notes in **S**heet list box.

5. To add a note to another cell, enter the cell address in the **C**ell box (or use the arrow keys to select a cell), and repeat steps 3 and 4.

6. Select OK. Excel returns you to the worksheet.

When you add a text note to a cell, a small red square (called a *note indicator*) appears in the upper-right corner of the cell.

TIP

You can turn off the note indicators if you're presenting your worksheet on-screen. Select the **T**ools | **O**ptions command. Then select the View tab and deactivate the **N**ote Indicator check box.

Viewing a Text Note

To view a text note, Excel gives you two choices:

■ Select the cell containing the note, and then choose the **I**nsert | **N**ote command (or press Shift-F2) to display the Cell Note dialog box. The note attached to the selected cell appears in the **T**ext Note box, as shown in Figure 4.37.

FIGURE 4.37.

Select the text note you want to view from the Cell Note dialog box.

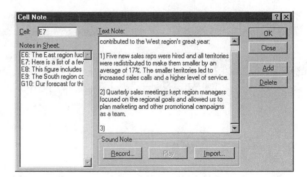

■ Position your mouse pointer over the cell containing the note. After a second or two, a box appears that shows the note text (the first 12 lines only; see Figure 4.38).

Excel

TIP

If you're not sure which cell contains the note you want, use the **E**dit | **F**ind command to search for a word or phrase from the note. In the Find dialog box, enter the word or phrase in the **Fi**nd What box, and select Notes from the **L**ook in drop-down list.

FIGURE 4.38.

If you let the mouse pointer linger over a cell containing a note, the note appears on-screen.

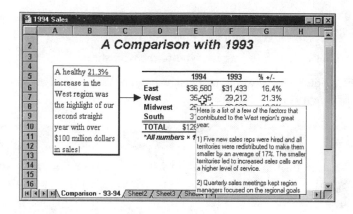

Copying a Text Note

If you need to copy a text note to another cell, follow these steps:

1. Select the **Insert | Note** command to display the Cell Note dialog box.

2. Select the note you want to copy from the Notes in **S**heet list box.

3. In the **C**ell box, enter the address of the cell to which you want to copy the note.

4. Select OK. Excel copies the note to the new cell.

TIP

You also can copy a text note using the cut-and-paste method. Select the cell containing the note, and choose **E**dit | **C**opy. Select the destination cell, and choose **E**dit | Paste **S**pecial. In the Paste Special dialog box, activate **N**otes and then select OK.

Deleting a Text Note

If your worksheet contains notes that you no longer need, you can delete them by using any of the following methods:

- Select the cell containing the note, and then select the **E**dit | Clear | **N**otes command.

- In the Cell Note dialog box, select the note you want to delete from the Notes in **S**heet list box, and then select the **D**elete button. In this case, Excel displays a message warning you that the note will be permanently deleted. Select OK.

- To delete all the notes in a worksheet, choose the **E**dit | **G**o To command, select the **S**pecial button to display the Go To Special dialog box, activate the Notes option, and then select OK. This sequence tells Excel to select all cells in the worksheet that contain notes. Then select the **E**dit | Clear | **N**otes command.

You also can select all the cells with text notes by pressing Ctrl-? (question mark).

Working with Sound Notes

Text notes can convey information, but they lack the nuances and subtleties of the human voice. To really get your point across, you can record messages and insert them as a note in a cell. This section shows you how to work with sound notes in your worksheets.

To make voice recordings, you need a sound card with a microphone jack.

Recording a Sound Note

To record a sound note, follow these steps:

1. Select the cell in which you want to add the sound note.

2. Select the **I**nsert | **N**ote command to display the Cell Note dialog box.

3. In the Sound Note group, select the **R**ecord button. Excel displays the Record dialog box, shown in Figure 4.39.

FIGURE 4.39.

*Use the Record dialog box
to record sound notes.*

4. Select the **R**ecord button and speak your message into the microphone. Your notes can be up to 1 minute and 11 seconds long. If you need to stop the recording temporarily, click the **P**ause button.

5. When you've finished, select the **S**top button.

6. To play back the message, select the **P**lay button.

7. When you're satisfied with your recording, select OK to return to the Cell Note dialog box.

8. Select OK to return to the worksheet. Excel places a cell note indicator in the top-right corner of the cell.

Playing a Sound Note

To play a sound note (again, you must have the appropriate hardware and software to play a sound note), follow these steps:

1. Select the **I**nsert | **Not**e command to display the Cell Note dialog box.
2. In the Notes in **S**heet list, highlight the cell containing the sound note you want to hear. (A sound note appears as an asterisk beside the cell address.)
3. Select the **P**lay button.

Erasing a Sound Note

If you want to rerecord a sound note, you need to erase the old one by following these steps:

1. Select the **I**nsert | **Not**e command to display the Cell Note dialog box.
2. In the Notes in **S**heet list, highlight the cell containing the sound note you want to erase.
3. Select the **E**rase button. Excel erases the recording.

Summary

This chapter showed you how to make your worksheets look their best by taking advantage of Excel's impressive array of formatting options. For more formatting-related information, check out these chapters:

■ Worksheet templates and start-up sheets give you easy access to your formats. See Chapter 5, "Advanced Worksheet Topics," for information about working with Excel templates.

■ After you've gotten your worksheet looking good, you might want to present it to others. Chapter 6, "Printing Your Work," tells you how to print worksheets, create reports, and put together an Excel slide show.

■ Sometimes the best way to convey your worksheet data is through a chart. Chapter 9, "Working with Chart Types," and Chapter 10, "Enhancing Charts," tell you all you need to know.

■ For more information on Excel's graphic objects, especially on object properties and formatting, see Chapter 11, "Working with Graphic Objects."

Advanced
Worksheet Topics

5

IN THIS CHAPTER

Although many of Excel's advanced features are designed with specific groups of users in mind (scientists, engineers, and so on), others are intended to make everyone's life easier. These tools reward a bit of effort in the short term with improved productivity in the long term. Such is the case with the features that are the subjects of this chapter: worksheet views, data protection, templates, outlines, dialog controls on worksheets, and Excel's multiuser workbook options. All of these features have two things in common: they can make your day-to-day work more efficient, and they can help you get more out of your Excel investment.

Changing the Worksheet View

When you work with large and complex worksheets, only a small part of the total document fits into a single window. The result is that you spend a lot of time scrolling through your worksheet and jumping back and forth between data areas. What you need is a way to simultaneously view separate parts of a worksheet.

The next few sections show you how to do just that. With Excel, you can view a single workbook in multiple windows, split a single window into multiple panes, and even view the same worksheet with different formatting and display options.

Displaying Multiple Workbook Windows

As a user of the Windows environment, you know what an advantage it is to have multiple applications running in their own windows. Most Windows applications take this concept a step further by enabling you to open multiple documents in their own windows. However, Excel goes one better by enabling you to open multiple windows for the *same* document.

When you open a second window on a workbook, you're not opening a new file; you're viewing the same file twice. You can navigate independently in each window, so you can display different parts of a workbook at the same time. Excel even enables you to change the workbook display for every window.

> **NOTE**
>
> You can change a value in one part of the workbook and watch its effect in another part. This capability is invaluable for what-if analysis. See Chapter 17, "Basic Analytic Methods," for more information on what-if analysis.

Opening a New Workbook Window

To open another window for the current workbook, select the **Window | New** Window command. When Excel opens a new window, it changes the names appearing in the workbook title bar. Excel appends :1 to the title of the original window, and it appends :2 to the title of the second window. Figure 5.1 shows an example using the 1994 Sales workbook. Notice that the original window now has the title 1994 Sales:1, and the new window has the title 1994 Sales:2.

FIGURE 5.1.

Two windows containing the same workbook.

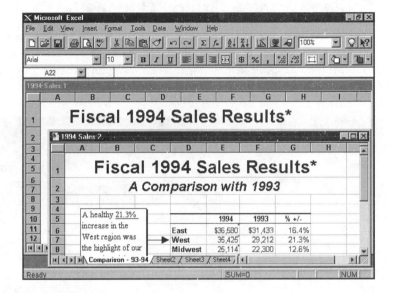

The number of windows you can open for a workbook is limited by your computer's memory. (With Windows 95's improved memory handling, however, you shouldn't have any trouble opening up as many windows as you need.) Any window you open can be moved and sized to suit your taste. Because each window is a view of the same workbook, any editing or formatting changes you make in one window are automatically reflected in all the other windows.

NOTE

You can use multiple windows to make data entry easier. Open one window for the data-entry area, and then use other windows to display, say, a list of data codes (for example, part numbers or general ledger accounts).

Navigating Workbook Windows

After you've opened two or more windows, you'll need to switch between them. Use any of the following techniques to navigate among workbook windows:

- Click on any visible part of a window to activate it.
- Pull down the **W**indow menu and select one of the windows listed at the bottom of the menu. Excel displays a check mark beside the currently active window.

■ Press Ctrl-Tab to move to the next window. Press Ctrl-Shift-Tab to move to the preceding window.

Setting Window Display Options

One of the most useful aspects of multiple workbook windows is that you can set different display options (such as showing gridlines or row and column headers) in each window. For example, you can troubleshoot formula errors by displaying formulas in one window and results in another. Figure 5.2 shows an example.

FIGURE 5.2.

You can set different display options in each workbook window, such as displaying formulas in one window and results in another.

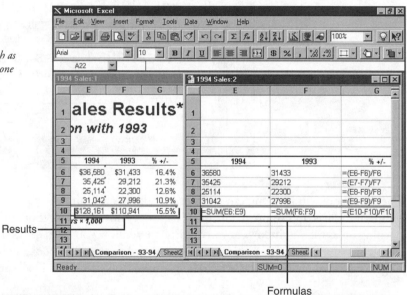

> **TIP**
>
> To quickly toggle the display between formulas and results, press Ctrl-' (backquote).

Follow these steps to set display options for a window:

1. Activate the window in which you want to change the display.

2. Select the **T**ools | **O**ptions command, and then select the View tab in the Options dialog box.

3. Use the controls in the Window Options group to set up the window the way you want. For example, activate the Formulas check box to display worksheet formulas.

4. Select OK. Excel returns you to the window with the new options in effect.

Arranging Workbook Windows

One of the problems with having several windows open at once is that they tend to get in each other's way. In most cases, it's preferable to give each window its own portion of the work area. Even though you can move and size windows yourself, you might prefer to have Excel handle this task for you. You can do this by selecting the **W**indow | **A**rrange command to display the Arrange Windows dialog box, shown in Figure 5.3. The Arrange section contains the following options:

Tiled	Divides the work area into rectangles of approximately equal size (called tiles) and assigns each open window to a tile.
Horizontal	Divides the work area into horizontal strips of equal size and assigns each open window to a strip.
Vertical	Divides the work area into vertical strips of equal size and assigns each open window to a strip.
Cascade	Arranges the windows so that they overlap each other and so that you can see each window's title bar.

FIGURE 5.3.

Use the Arrange Windows dialog box to arrange your open windows.

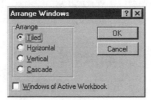

If you have other workbooks open at the same time and you want to arrange only the current workbook windows, activate the **W**indows of Active Workbook check box in the Arrange Windows dialog box. This tells Excel to apply the selected Arrange option to the current workbook windows only. When you're done, select OK to arrange the windows.

If you don't want to include a window in an arrangement, activate the window and select the **W**indow | **H**ide command. Excel removes the window from the screen, but the window remains open in memory. To view the window again, select **W**indow | **U**nhide and select the window from the Unhide dialog box that appears.

Closing a Workbook Window

If you find your work area getting cluttered with open windows, you can close a window by using any of the following techniques:

- Click the window's Close button (the × in the upper-right corner).
- Double-click the window's Control-menu button (that's the icon in the upper-left corner of the window.

■ Press Alt — (hyphen) to open the window's Control menu, and then select Close.

■ Press Ctrl-F4.

Displaying Multiple Worksheet Panes

Another way to simultaneously view different parts of a large worksheet is to use Excel's Split feature. You can use Split to divide a worksheet into two or four *panes* in which each pane displays a different area of the sheet. The panes simultaneously scroll horizontally and vertically. You also can freeze the panes to keep a worksheet area in view at all times.

Splitting a Worksheet into Panes

Depending on the type of split you want, you can use one of the following two methods to split your worksheets:

■ Use the **W**indow | **S**plit command to split the worksheet into four panes at the selected cell. (Later, you can adjust the split to two panes if you like.)

■ Use the horizontal or vertical split boxes to split the worksheet into two panes at a position you specify (horizontally or vertically).

Using the Split Command

When you use the Split command, Excel splits the worksheet into four panes at the currently selected cell. How do you know which cell to select? Look at Figure 5.4, which shows the Amortization worksheet with cell C6 selected.

FIGURE 5.4.

The Amortization worksheet before splitting.

	A	B	C	D	E	F	G	H
1				**Loan Amortization Schedule**				
2	Rate	8%						
3	Months	48						
4	Amount	$10,000						
5	Period	Month	Payment	Interest	Principal	Total Interest	Prinicipal % Paid	
6	1	Jun-93	($244.13)	($66.67)	($177.46)	$66.67	1.77%	
7	2	Jul-93	($244.13)	($65.48)	($178.65)	$132.15	3.56%	
8	3	Aug-93	($244.13)	($64.29)	($179.84)	$196.44	5.36%	
9	4	Sep-93	($244.13)	($63.09)	($181.04)	$259.54	7.17%	
10	5	Oct-93	($244.13)	($61.89)	($182.24)	$321.42	8.99%	
11	6	Nov-93	($244.13)	($60.67)	($183.46)	$382.10	10.83%	
12	7	Dec-93	($244.13)	($59.45)	($184.68)	$441.54	12.67%	
13	8	Jan-94	($244.13)	($58.22)	($185.91)	$499.76	14.53%	
14	9	Feb-94	($244.13)	($56.98)	($187.15)	$556.74	16.40%	

When the worksheet is split—by selecting the **W**indow | **S**plit command—the results are as shown in Figure 5.5. Notice that Excel places the *horizontal split bar* on the top edge of the selected cell's row and the *vertical split bar* on the left edge of the selected cell's column. This feature is convenient because now the loan variables are in the upper-left pane, the periods and months are in the lower-left pane, the title and column headings are in the upper-right pane, and the loan data is in the lower-right pane. The panes are synchronized so that as you move down through the loan data, the period and month values also move down.

FIGURE 5.5.

The Amortization worksheet after splitting.

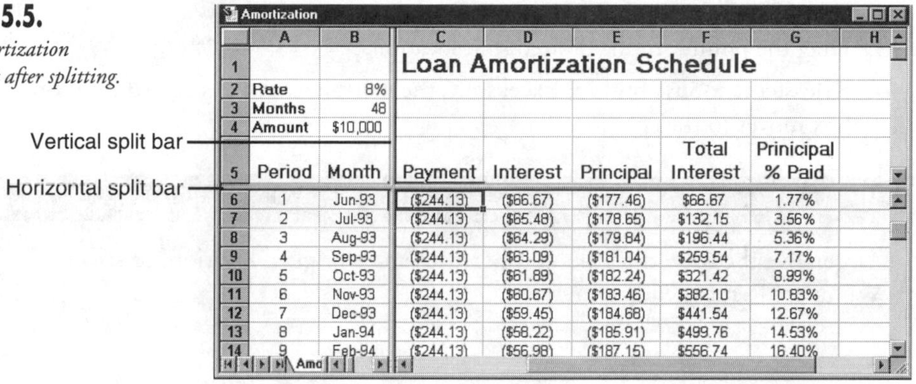

Vertical split bar

Horizontal split bar

If the split isn't where you want it, you can always use your mouse to drag the vertical or horizontal split bar. To move both bars at the same time, drag the intersection point.

Using the Window Split Boxes

Using the mouse, you can use the horizontal and vertical split boxes to create a two-pane split. The horizontal split box is the small button located between the vertical scroll bar's up arrow and the window's Close button (see Figure 5.6). The vertical split box is the small button to the right of the horizontal scroll bar's right arrow (again, see Figure 5.6).

FIGURE 5.6.

You can use the split boxes to split a worksheet.

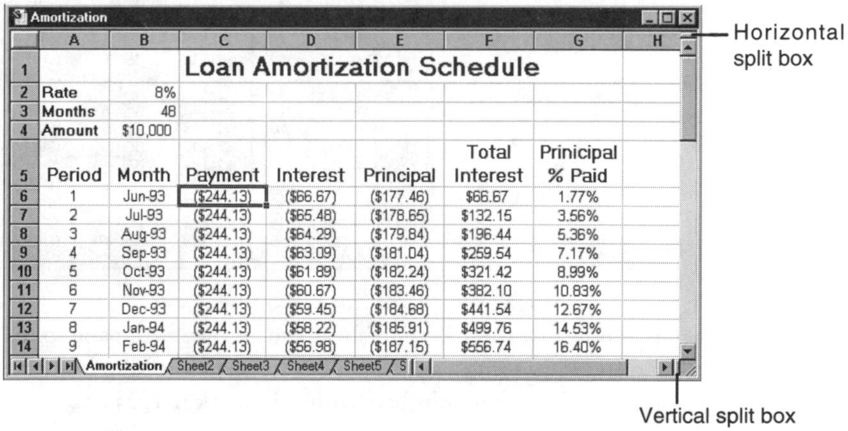

Horizontal split box

Vertical split box

Follow these steps to split a worksheet using the split boxes:

1. Position the mouse pointer on the split box you want. The pointer changes to a two-sided arrow.

2. Press and hold the left mouse button. Excel displays a light gray bar to indicate the current split position.

3. Drag the pointer to the desired split location.

4. Release the mouse button. Excel splits the worksheet at the selected location. The split box moves to the split location.

> **TIP**
>
> To remove the split, drag the split box back to its original location, or select the **W**indow | Remove **S**plit command.

Freezing Worksheet Titles

One of the problems with viewing multiple panes is that the work area can get confusing when some of the panes contain the same cells. For example, Figure 5.7 shows the Amortization worksheet split into four panes, each of which contains cell C8 in its upper-left corner. Clearly, such a display is meaningless. To prevent this situation from happening, you can *freeze* your panes so that areas displaying worksheet titles or column headings remain in place.

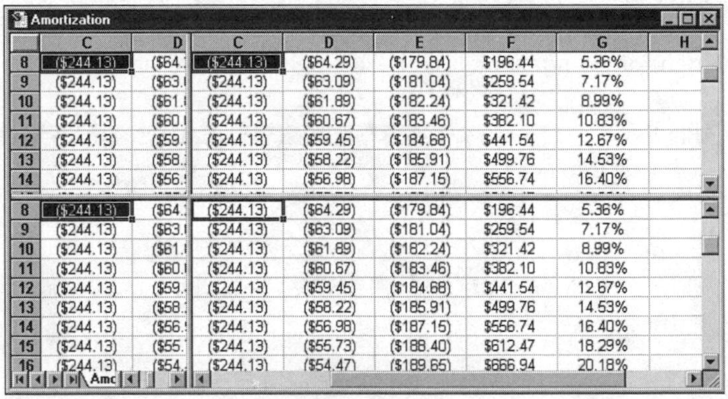

FIGURE 5.7.

Split worksheets often can become confusing.

To try it out, first split the worksheet and arrange each pane so that it shows the desired information (titles, headings, and so on). Now select the **W**indow | **F**reeze Panes command. Excel replaces the thick gray split bars with thin black freeze bars.

Figure 5.8 shows the Amortization worksheet with frozen panes. In this case, the panes were frozen from the split position shown in Figure 5.5. For this example, the frozen panes provide the following advantages:

- No matter where you move up or down in the worksheet, the column headings and loan variables remain visible.

- As you move up or down in the worksheet, the values in the bottom panes remain synchronized.

- No matter where you move left or right in the worksheet, the period and month values remain visible.

- As you move left or right in the worksheet, the values in the two right panes remain synchronized.

FIGURE 5.8.

The Amortization worksheet with frozen panes.

	A	B	C	D	E	F	G	H
1			**Loan Amortization Schedule**					
2	Rate	8%						
3	Months	48						
4	Amount	$10,000						
5	Period	Month	Payment	Interest	Principal	Total Interest	Prinicipal % Paid	
6	1	Jun-93	($244.13)	($66.67)	($177.46)	$66.67	1.77%	
7	2	Jul-93	($244.13)	($65.48)	($170.00)	$132.15	3.58%	
8	3	Aug-93	($244.13)	($64.29)	($179.84)	$196.44	5.36%	
9	4	Sep-93	($244.13)	($63.09)	($181.04)	$259.54	7.17%	
10	5	Oct-93	($244.13)	($61.89)	($182.24)	$321.42	8.99%	
11	6	Nov-93	($244.13)	($60.67)	($183.46)	$382.10	10.83%	
12	7	Dec-93	($244.13)	($59.45)	($184.68)	$441.54	12.67%	
13	8	Jan-94	($244.13)	($58.22)	($185.91)	$499.76	14.53%	
14	9	Feb-94	($244.13)	($56.98)	($187.15)	$556.74	16.40%	

TIP

To unfreeze panes without removing the splits, select the **Window | Unfreeze Panes** command. To unfreeze panes *and* remove the splits, select the **Window | Remove Split** command.

Zooming In and Out

So far, you've seen various methods for viewing your workbooks. Most of these techniques help you work easily with large spreadsheets by enabling you to simultaneously view different parts of the document. Even though this is very valuable, what you often need is the capability to see the big picture, because even the largest window can display only a few dozen cells at most. Excel offers a Zoom feature that enables you to see your workbooks with various degrees of *magnification*.

With Zoom, a magnification value of 100 percent represents the normal workbook view. If you select a lower magnification, Zoom scales each cell smaller by the amount you specify and therefore displays more cells in the window. For example, if you choose the 50 percent magnification, the workbook cells become smaller by half. If you choose a higher magnification, Zoom scales each cell larger. All your data and formatting options remain intact, and you can make changes to the workbook at any magnification.

Follow these steps to use the Zoom feature:

1. Select the **View | Z**oom command. Excel displays the Zoom dialog box, shown in Figure 5.9.

FIGURE 5.9.

Use the Zoom dialog box to zoom in or out of your workbook.

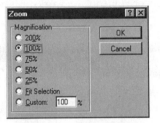

2. Select the option you want from the Magnification group. The **F**it Selection option scales the workbook so that the selected range fits inside the window. The **C**ustom option enables you to enter your own magnification (a number between 10 and 400).

3. Select OK. Excel adjusts the Zoom magnification and redisplays the workbook.

 You also can use the Zoom tool on the Standard toolbar to select a magnification.

Displaying Multiple Workbook Views

Displaying the same file in multiple windows or panes is a great way to manage large workbooks. Unfortunately, managing the windows can be time-consuming. You have to open each window, scroll to the worksheet area you want, set your display options, size the window, and position it where you can see it. Of course, you can save your window configurations with the workbook, and Excel will reinstate them every time you open the file. However, you might not want all those windows active all the time. The solution is to create different views of your workbooks.

A *view* is a specific workbook configuration that can include the window size and position, panes and frozen titles, zoom magnification, selected cells, display options, row heights and column widths (including hidden rows and columns), and print settings. After you've saved a view, you can conveniently recall it any time from a list of views.

> **TIP**
>
> The first view you create should be of your worksheet in its basic configuration (give it the name "Normal"). This way, you can always revert to this configuration from your other views.

Creating a View

You use Excel's View Manager to create workbook views. The following procedure shows you the steps to follow:

1. Set up your workbook (or one of your workbook windows) with the view configuration you want.
2. Choose the **View | View** Manager command. Excel displays the View Manager dialog box.
3. Select the **Add** button. Excel displays the Add View dialog box, shown in Figure 5.10.

FIGURE 5.10.

Use the Add View dialog box to name the new view.

4. Enter a name for the view in the **Name** text box. The name must begin with a letter.
5. In the View Includes section, select the extra settings you want to include in the view.
6. Select OK. Excel saves the view and returns you to the workbook.

Displaying a View

One of the main advantages to views is that you can display them only when you need them. Excel makes displaying views easy, as the following steps show:

1. Select the **View** | **V**iew Manager command to display the View Manager dialog box.
2. Use the **V**iews list to highlight the view you want to use.
3. Select the **S**how button. Excel displays the view.

Deleting a View

To delete a workbook view, follow these steps:

1. Select the **View** | **V**iew Manager command to display the View Manager dialog box.
2. Use the **V**iews list to highlight the view you want to delete.
3. Select the **D**elete button. Excel asks you to confirm that you want to delete the view.
4. Select OK to delete the view.
5. Repeat steps 2 through 4 to delete other views.
6. Select Close to return to the workbook.

Using Workspace Files

Although Excel's worksheet tabs mean that you'll probably have fewer files open at once, there will still be plenty of times when you need multiple workbooks open. If you regularly use the same workbooks, you can create a *workspace file* that contains not only the workbooks, but also their current position. When you open the workspace file, Excel opens the specified workbooks and positions them accordingly. Follow these steps to save a workspace file:

1. Open the workbooks you want to use, and position them where you want them to appear.
2. Select the **F**ile | Save **W**orkspace command. Excel displays the Save Workspace dialog box.
3. Use the Save **i**n list to select a location for the file.

TIP

If you want the file opened automatically when you start Excel, save it in the \Excel\XLStart directory.

---

4. Enter a name for the file in the File **n**ame box.
5. Select **S**ave.

After you save a workspace file, you can open it at any time just like a regular Excel file.

CAUTION

If you make changes to the workspace (such as closing a file or changing the position of a window), you need to follow the preceding steps again to save the new settings.

Using Outlines

Outlines? In a spreadsheet? Yes, those same creatures that caused you so much grief in high school English class also are available in Excel. In a worksheet outline, though, you can *collapse* sections of the sheet to display only summary cells (such as quarterly or regional totals, for example), or you can *expand* hidden sections to show the underlying detail.

The worksheet in Figure 5.11 displays monthly budget figures for various sales and expense items. The columns include quarterly subtotals and, although you can't see it in Figure 5.11, a grand total. The rows include subtotals for sales, expenses, and gross profit.

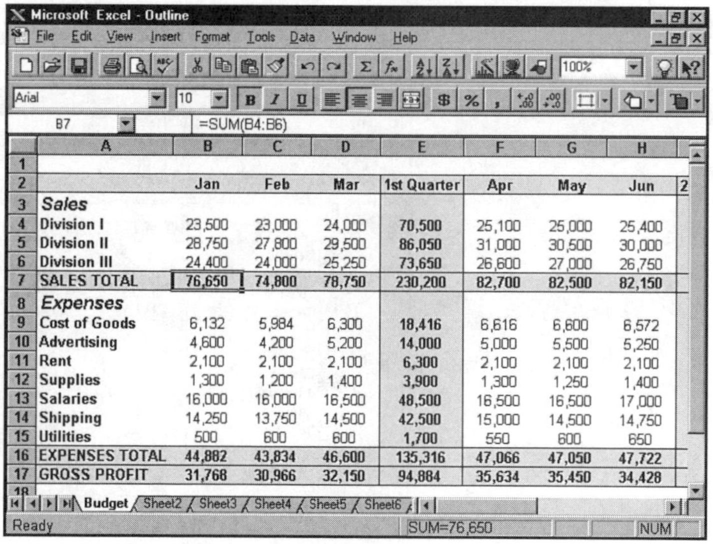

	A	B	C	D	E	F	G	H
1								
2		Jan	Feb	Mar	1st Quarter	Apr	May	Jun
3	*Sales*							
4	Division I	23,500	23,000	24,000	70,500	25,100	25,000	25,400
5	Division II	28,750	27,800	29,500	86,050	31,000	30,500	30,000
6	Division III	24,400	24,000	25,250	73,650	26,600	27,000	26,750
7	SALES TOTAL	76,650	74,800	78,750	230,200	82,700	82,500	82,150
8	*Expenses*							
9	Cost of Goods	6,132	5,984	6,300	18,416	6,616	6,600	6,572
10	Advertising	4,600	4,200	5,200	14,000	5,000	5,500	5,250
11	Rent	2,100	2,100	2,100	6,300	2,100	2,100	2,100
12	Supplies	1,300	1,200	1,400	3,900	1,300	1,250	1,400
13	Salaries	16,000	16,000	16,500	48,500	16,500	16,500	17,000
14	Shipping	14,250	13,750	14,500	42,500	15,000	14,500	14,750
15	Utilities	500	600	600	1,700	550	600	650
16	EXPENSES TOTAL	44,882	43,834	46,600	135,316	47,066	47,050	47,722
17	GROSS PROFIT	31,768	30,966	32,150	94,884	35,634	35,450	34,428

FIGURE 5.11.
A budget worksheet showing detail and summary data.

Suppose that you don't want to see so much detail. For example, you might need to see only the quarterly totals for each row, or you might want to hide the salary figures for a presentation you're making. An outline is the easiest way to do this. Figure 5.12 shows the same worksheet with an outline added (I'll explain shortly what the various symbols mean). Using this outline, you can hide whatever details you don't need to see. Figure 5.13 shows the worksheet with data hidden for the individual months and salaries. You can go even further. The view in Figure 5.14 shows only the sales and expenses totals and the grand totals.

FIGURE 5.12.

The budget worksheet with outlining added.

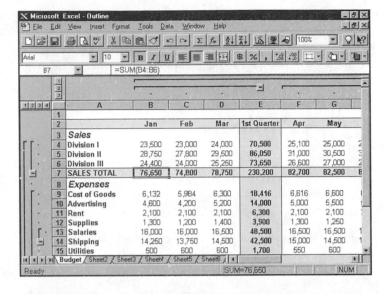

FIGURE 5.13.

Outlining enables you to hide detail data you don't need to see.

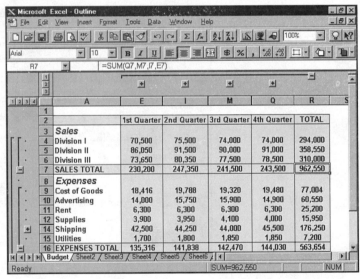

FIGURE 5.14.

Outlines usually have several levels that enable you to hide even subtotals.

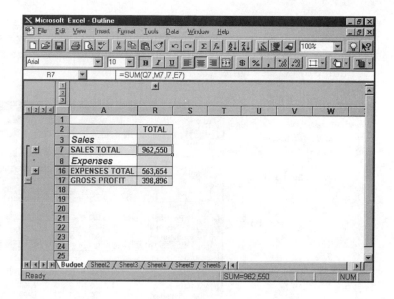

One of the big advantages of outlines is that as soon as you've hidden some data, you can work with the visible cells as though they were a single range. This means that you can format those cells quickly, print them, create charts, and so on.

Creating an Outline Automatically

The easiest way to create an outline is to have Excel do it for you. (You can create an outline manually too, as you'll see later.) Before you create an outline, you need to make sure that your worksheet is a candidate for outlining. There are two main criteria:

- The worksheet must contain formulas that reference cells or ranges directly adjacent to the formula cell. Worksheets with SUM() functions that subtotal cells above or to the left (such as the budget worksheet presented earlier) are particularly good candidates for outlining.

- There must be a consistent pattern to the direction of the formula references. For example, you can outline a worksheet containing formulas that always reference cells above or to the left. However, you can't outline a worksheet with, for example, SUM() functions that reference ranges above and below a formula cell.

After you determine that your worksheet is outline material, select the range of cells you want to outline. If you want to outline the entire worksheet, select only a single cell. Then choose the **D**ata | **G**roup and Outline | **A**uto Outline command. Excel creates the outline and displays the outline tools (see Figure 5.15).

FIGURE 5.15.

When you create an outline, Excel adds outline tools to the worksheet.

Level symbols —

Level bars —

Collapse symbols —

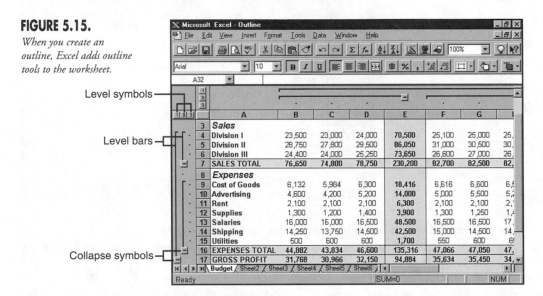

Understanding the Outline Tools

When Excel creates an outline, it divides your worksheet into a hierarchy of *levels*. These levels range from the worksheet detail (the lowest level) to the grand totals (the highest level). Excel outlines can handle up to eight levels of data.

In the Budget worksheet, for example, Excel created three levels for both the column and the row data:

- In the columns, the monthly figures are the details, so they're the lowest level (level 3). The quarterly totals are the first summary data, so they're the next level (level 2). Finally, the grand totals are the highest level (level 1).

- In the rows, the individual sales and expense items are the details (level 3). The sales and expenses subtotals are the next level (level 2). The Gross Profit row is the highest level (level 1).

> **NOTE**
>
> Somewhat confusingly, Excel has set things up so that lower outline levels have higher level numbers. The way I remember it is that the higher the number, the more detail the level contains.

To help you work with your outlines, Excel adds the following tools to your worksheet:

Level bars: These bars indicate the data included in the current level. Click on a bar to hide the rows or columns marked by a bar.

Collapse symbol: Click on this symbol to hide (or *collapse*) the rows or columns marked by the attached level bar.

Expand symbol: When you collapse a level, the collapse symbol changes to an expand symbol (+). Click on this symbol to display (or *expand*) the hidden rows or columns.

Level symbols: These symbols tell you which level each level bar is on. Click on a level symbol to display all the detail data for that level.

TIP

To toggle the outline symbols on and off, press Ctrl-8.

Creating an Outline Manually

If you examine Figure 5.12 closely, you'll see that the Budget worksheet's rows have *four* outline levels, whereas the rows in Figure 5.15 have only three. Where did the extra level come from? I added it manually because I needed some way of collapsing the Salaries row. Because this row isn't a subtotal or some other formula, Excel ignores it (rightfully so) when creating an automatic outline.

If you would like more control over the outlining process, you easily can do it yourself. The idea is that you selectively *group* or *ungroup* rows or columns. When you group a range, you assign it to a lower outline level (that is, you give it a higher level number). When you ungroup a range, you assign it to a higher outline level.

Grouping Rows and Columns

The following procedure shows you how to group rows and columns:

1. If your detail data is in rows, select the rows you want to group. You can select at least one cell in each row, or you can select entire rows, thus saving a step later (see Figure 5.16). If your detail data is in columns, select the columns you want to group.

TIP

To select an entire row, click on the row heading or press Shift-Spacebar. To select an entire column, click on the column heading or press Ctrl-Spacebar.

FIGURE 5.16.

*The Sales detail rows
selected for grouping.*

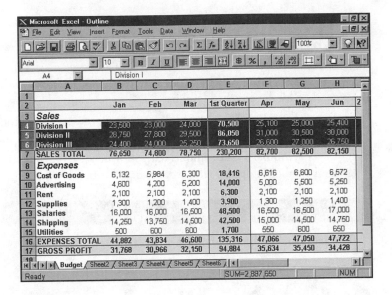

2. To group the selection, use any of the following techniques:

   ■ Select the **D**ata | **G**roup and Outline | **G**roup command.

   ■ Press Alt-Shift-right arrow.

   ■ Click the Group button on the Query and Pivot toolbar.

    The Group button.

   If you selected something other than entire rows or columns, Excel displays the Group
   dialog box, shown in Figure 5.17. Proceed to step 3 to deal with this dialog box.

FIGURE 5.17.

*If you didn't select entire
rows or columns, Excel
displays the dialog box.*

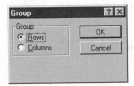

   If you selected entire rows or columns, Excel groups the selection and adds the outline
   symbols to the sheet, as shown in Figure 5.18. In this case, you can skip to step 4.

3. In the Group dialog box, select either **R**ows or **C**olumns, and then select OK to create
   the group.

4. Repeat steps 1 through 3 either to group other rows or columns or to move existing
   groups to a lower outline level.

FIGURE 5.18.

When you group a selection, Excel adds the appropriate outline symbols to the worksheet.

	A	B	C	D	E	F	G	H
1								
2		Jan	Feb	Mar	1st Quarter	Apr	May	Jun
3	*Sales*							
4	Division I	23,500	23,000	24,000	**70,500**	25,100	25,000	25,40
5	Division II	28,750	27,800	29,500	**86,050**	31,000	30,500	30,00
6	Division III	24,400	24,000	25,250	**73,650**	26,600	27,000	26,75
7	SALES TOTAL	76,650	74,800	78,750	**230,200**	82,700	82,500	82,15
8	*Expenses*							
9	Cost of Goods	6,132	5,984	6,300	**18,416**	6,616	6,600	6,57
10	Advertising	4,800	4,200	5,200	**14,000**	5,000	5,500	5,25
11	Rent	2,100	2,100	2,100	**6,300**	2,100	2,100	2,10
12	Supplies	1,300	1,200	1,400	**3,900**	1,300	1,250	1,40
13	Salaries	16,000	16,000	16,500	**48,500**	16,500	16,500	17,00
14	Shipping	14,250	13,750	14,500	**42,500**	15,000	14,500	14,75
15	Utilities	500	600	600	**1,700**	550	600	650
16	EXPENSES TOTAL	44,882	43,834	46,600	**135,316**	47,066	47,050	47,72
17	GROSS PROFIT	31,768	30,966	32,150	**94,884**	35,634	35,450	34,42

Ready SUM=2,887,650 NUM

Ungrouping Rows and Columns

If you make a mistake when grouping a selection, or you need to make adjustments to your outline levels, here's how to ungroup rows and columns:

1. If you're working with rows, select the rows you want to ungroup. Again, you can save a step if you select the entire row. If you're working with columns, select the columns you want to ungroup.

2. To ungroup the selection, use any one of the following techniques:

   ■ Select the **D**ata | **G**roup and Outline | **U**ngroup command.

   ■ Press Alt-Shift-left arrow.

   ■ Click the Ungroup button on the Query and Pivot toolbar.

    The Ungroup button.

   If you selected entire rows or columns, Excel ungroups the selection and removes the outline symbols. In this case, you can skip to step 4.

   If you selected something other than entire rows or columns, Excel displays the Ungroup dialog box. Proceed to step 3 to deal with this dialog box.

3. In the Ungroup dialog box, select either **R**ows or **C**olumns, and then select OK to ungroup the selection.

4. Repeat steps 1 through 3 either to ungroup other rows or columns or to move existing groups to a higher outline level.

Hiding and Showing Detail Data

The whole purpose of an outline is to enable you to move easily between views of greater or lesser detail. The next two sections tell you how to hide and show detail data in an outline.

Hiding Detail Data

To hide details in an outline, you have three methods to choose from:

■ Click on the collapse symbol at the bottom (for rows) or right (for columns) of the level bar that encompasses the detail data.

■ Select a cell in a row or column marked with a collapse symbol, and then select the **D**ata | **G**roup and Outline | **H**ide Detail command.

■ Select a cell in a row or column marked with a collapse symbol, and click on the Hide Detail tool on the Query and Pivot toolbar.

 The Hide Detail button.

Showing Detail Data

To show collapsed detail, you have no fewer than four methods to choose from:

■ Click on the appropriate expand symbol.

■ To see the detail for an entire level, click on the level marker.

■ Select a cell in a row or column marked with an expand symbol, and then select the **D**ata | **G**roup and Outline | **S**how Detail command.

■ Select a cell in a row or column marked with an expand symbol, and then click on the Show Detail tool on the Query and Pivot toolbar.

 The Show Detail button.

Selecting Outline Data

When you collapse an outline level, the data is only temporarily hidden from view. If you select the outline, your selection includes the collapsed cells. If you want to copy, print, or chart only the visible cells, you need to follow these steps:

1. Hide the outline data you don't need.

2. Select the outline cells you want to work with.

3. Select the **E**dit | **G**o To command to display the Go To dialog box.

4. Select the **S**pecial button. Excel displays the Go To Special dialog box.

5. Activate the **V**isible Cells Only option button.

6. Select OK. Excel modifies your selection to include only those cells in the selection that are part of the expanded outline.

> **TIP**
>
> You also can select visible cells by pressing Alt-; (semicolon).

Removing an Outline

You can remove selected rows or columns from an outline, or you can remove the entire outline. Follow these steps:

1. If you want to remove only part of an outline, select the appropriate rows or columns. If you want to remove the entire outline, select a single cell.

2. Select the **D**ata | **G**roup and Outline | **C**lear Outline command. Excel adjusts or removes the outline.

Consolidating Multisheet Data

Many businesses create worksheets for a specific task and then distribute them to various departments. The most common example is budgeting. Accounting will create a generic "budget" template that each department or division in the company must fill out and return. Similarly, you often see worksheets distributed for inventory requirements, sales forecasting, survey data, experimental results, and more.

Creating these worksheets, distributing them, and filling them in are all straightforward operations. The tricky part, however, comes when the sheets are returned to the originating department, and all the new data must be combined into a summary report showing company-wide totals. This task is called *consolidating* the data, and it's often no picnic, especially for large worksheets. However, as you'll soon see, Excel has some powerful features that can take the drudgery out of consolidation.

Excel can consolidate your data using one of the following two methods:

Consolidating by position: With this method, Excel consolidates the data from several worksheets using the same range coordinates on each sheet. You would use this method if the worksheets you're consolidating have an identical layout.

Consolidating by category: This method tells Excel to consolidate the data by looking for identical row and column labels in each sheet. So, for example, if one worksheet lists monthly Gizmo sales in row 1 and another lists monthly Gizmo sales in row 5, you can still consolidate as long as both sheets have a "Gizmo" label at the beginning of these rows.

In both cases, you specify one or more *source ranges* (the ranges that contain the data you want to consolidate) and a *destination range* (the range where the consolidated data will appear). The next couple of sections take you through the detail for both consolidation methods.

Consolidating by Position

If the sheets you're working with have the same layout, consolidating by position is the easiest way to go. For example, check out the three workbooks—Division I Budget, Division II Budget, and Division III Budget—shown in Figure 5.19. As you can see, each sheet uses the same row and column labels, so they're perfect candidates for consolidation by position.

FIGURE 5.19.

When your worksheets are laid out identically, use consolidation by position.

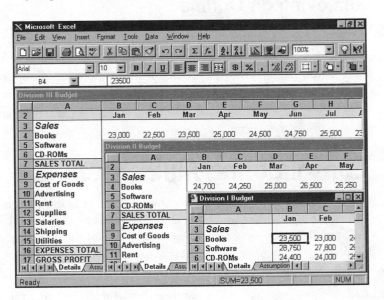

Begin by creating a new worksheet that has the same layout as the sheets you're consolidating. Figure 5.20 shows a new Consolidation workbook that I'll use to consolidate the three budget sheets.

As an example, let's see how you would go about consolidating the sales data in the three budget worksheets shown in Figure 5.19. We're dealing with three source ranges:

> '[Division I Budget]Details'!B4:M6
>
> '[Division II Budget]Details'!B4:M6
>
> '[Division III Budget]Details'!B4:M6

With the consolidation sheet active, follow these steps to consolidate by position:

1. Select the upper-left corner of the destination range. In the Consolidate By Position worksheet, select cell B4.

FIGURE 5.20.

When consolidating by position, create a separate consolidation worksheet that uses the same layout as the sheets you're consolidating.

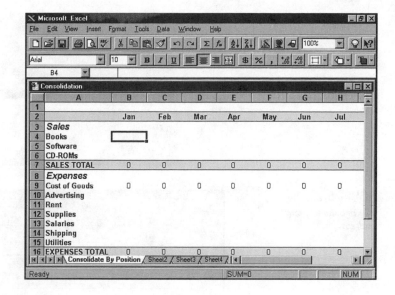

2. Choose the **D**ata | Co**n**solidate command. Excel displays the Consolidate dialog box.

3. Use the **F**unction drop-down list to select the operation to use during the consolidation. You'll use Sum most of the time, but Excel has 10 other operations to choose from, including Count, Average, Max, and Min.

4. In the **R**eference text box, enter a reference for one of the source ranges. Use one of the following methods:

   ■ Type the range coordinates by hand. If the source range is in another workbook, be sure to include the workbook name enclosed in square brackets, as shown earlier. If the workbook is in a different drive or folder, include the full path to the workbook as well.

   ■ If the sheet is open, activate it (either by clicking on it or by selecting it from the **W**indow menu), and then use your mouse to highlight the range.

   ■ If the workbook isn't open, select the **B**rowse button, highlight the file in the Browse dialog box, and then select OK. Excel adds the workbook path to the **R**eference box. Fill in the sheet name and the range coordinates.

5. Select the **A**dd button to add the range to the All References box, as shown in Figure 5.21.

6. Repeat steps 4 and 5 to add all the source ranges.

7. If you want the consolidated data to change whenever you make changes to the source data, activate the Create Links to **S**ource Data check box.

8. Select OK. Excel gathers the data, consolidates it, and then adds it to the destination range (see Figure 5.22).

FIGURE 5.21.

The Consolidate dialog box with several source ranges added.

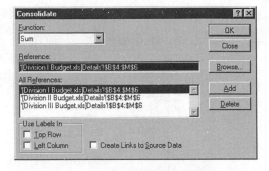

FIGURE 5.22.

The consolidated sales budgets.

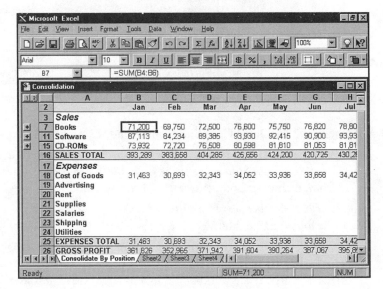

If you chose not to create links to the source data in step 7, Excel just fills the destination range with the consolidation totals. If you did create links, however, Excel does three things:

- Adds link formulas to the destination range for each cell in the source ranges you selected. (See the section titled "Working with Links in Formulas" in Chapter 2, "Building Better Formulas," for details on link formulas.)

- Consolidates the data by adding SUM() functions (or whatever operation you selected in the Function list) that total the results of the link formulas.

- Outlines the consolidation worksheet and hides the link formulas, as you can see in Figure 5.22.

If you display the Level 1 data, you'll see the linked formulas. For example, Figure 5.23 shows the detail for the consolidated sales number for Books in January (cell B7). The detail in cells B4, B5, and B6 contain formulas that link to the corresponding cells in the three budget worksheets (for example, '[Division I Budget.xls]Details'!$B$4).

FIGURE 5.23.

The detail (linked formulas) for the consolidated data.

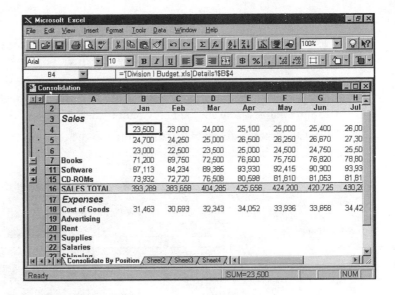

Consolidating by Category

If your worksheets don't use the same layout, you need to tell Excel to consolidate the data *by category*. In this case, Excel examines each of your source ranges and consolidates data that uses the same row or column labels. For example, take a look at the Sales rows in the three worksheets shown in Figure 5.24. As you can see, Division C sells Books, Software, Videos, and CD-ROMs; Division B sells Books and CD-ROMs; and Division A sells Software, Books, and Videos. Here's how you go about consolidating these numbers (note that I'm skipping over some of the details given in the preceding section):

1. Create or select a new worksheet for the consolidation, and select the upper-left corner of the destination range. It isn't necessary to enter labels for the consolidated data because Excel does it for you automatically. If, however, you want to see the labels in a particular order, it's OK to enter them yourself. (Just make sure, however, that you spell the labels exactly as they're spelled in the source worksheets.)

2. Select the **D**ata | Co**n**solidate command to display the Consolidate dialog box.

3. Use the **F**unction drop-down list to select the operation to use during the consolidation.

4. In the **R**eference text box, enter a reference for one of the source ranges. In this case, make sure that you include in each range the row and column labels for the data.

5. Select the **A**dd button to add the range to the All References box.

6. Repeat steps 4 and 5 to add all the source ranges.

7. If you want the consolidated data to change whenever you make changes to the source data, activate the Create Links to **S**ource Data check box.

8. If you want Excel to use the data labels in the top row of the selected ranges, activate the **T**op Row check box. If you want Excel to use the data labels in the left column of the source ranges, activate the **L**eft Column check box.

9. Select OK. Excel gathers the data according to the row and column labels, consolidates it, and then adds it to the destination range (see Figure 5.25).

FIGURE 5.24.

Each division sells a different mix of products, so we need to consolidate by category.

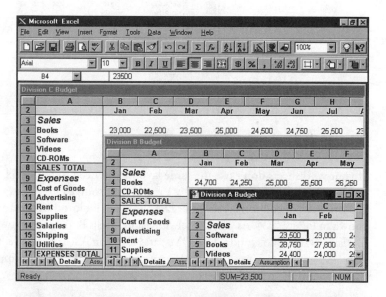

FIGURE 5.25.

The sales numbers consolidated by category.

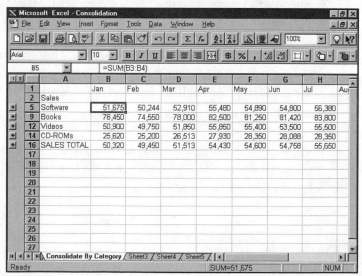

> **NOTE**
>
> Pivot tables are often better for consolidating data by category. See Chapter 13, "Creating Pivot Tables," to find out how they work.

Protecting Worksheet Data

When you've labored long and hard to get your worksheet formulas or formatting just right, the last thing you need is to have a cell or range accidentally deleted or copied over. You can prevent this difficulty by using Excel's worksheet protection features, which enable you to prevent changes to anything from a single cell to an entire workbook.

Protecting Individual Cells, Objects, and Scenarios

Protecting cells, objects, and scenarios in Excel is a two-step process:

1. Set up the item's protection formatting. You have three options:

   ■ Cells, objects, and scenarios can be either *locked* or *unlocked*. As soon as protection is turned on (see step 2), a locked item can't be changed, deleted, moved, or copied over.

   ■ Cell formulas and scenarios can be either *hidden* or *visible*. With protection on, a hidden formula doesn't appear in the formula bar when the cell is selected; a hidden scenario doesn't appear in the Scenario Manager dialog box.

> **NOTE**
>
> Unfamiliar with scenarios? You'll learn all about them in Chapter 20, "Working with Scenarios."

   ■ Text boxes, macro buttons, and some worksheet dialog box controls (see the section later in this chapter titled "Using Dialog Box Controls on a Worksheet") also can have *locked text*, which prevents the text they contain from being altered.

2. Turn on the worksheet protection.

These steps are covered in more detail in the following sections.

Setting Up Protection Formatting for Cells

By default, all worksheet cells are formatted as locked and visible. This means that you have three options when setting up your protection formatting:

■ If you want to protect every cell, leave the formatting as it is, and turn on the worksheet protection.

■ If you want certain cells unlocked (for data entry, for example), select the appropriate cells and unlock them before turning on worksheet protection. Similarly, if you want certain cells hidden, select the cells and hide them.

■ If you want only selected cells locked, select all the cells and unlock them. Then select the cells you want protected and lock them. To keep only selected formulas visible, hide every formula and then make the appropriate range visible.

Here are the steps to follow to set up protection formatting for worksheet cells:

1. Select the cells for which you want to adjust the protection formatting.

2. Select the Format | Cells command, and in the Format Cells dialog box, activate the Protection tab. Excel displays protection options for the range (see Figure 5.26).

FIGURE 5.26.

Use the Protection tab in the Format Cells dialog box to set up the protection formatting for individual worksheet cells.

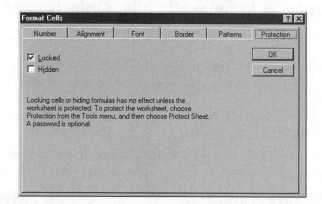

3. To lock the cells' contents, activate the **L**ocked check box. To unlock cells, deactivate this check box.

4. To hide the cells' formulas, activate the **H**idden check box. To make the cells' formulas visible, deactivate the check box.

TIP

Hiding a formula prevents only the formula from being displayed in the formula bar; the results appear inside the cell itself. If you also want to hide the cell's contents, create an empty custom numeric format (;;;), and assign this format to the cell. For details on creating a custom numeric format, see Chapter 4, "Formatting Excel Worksheets."

---

5. Select OK.

Setting Up Protection Formatting for Objects

Excel locks all worksheet objects by default (and it locks the text in text boxes, macro buttons, and some worksheet dialog box controls; see the section in this chapter titled "Using Dialog Box Controls on a Worksheet"). As with cells, you have three options for protecting objects:

- If you want to protect every object, leave the formatting as it is, and turn on the worksheet protection.
- If you want certain objects unlocked, select the appropriate objects and unlock them before turning on worksheet protection.
- If you want only selected objects locked, select all the objects and unlock them. Then select the objects you want protected and lock them.

TIP

To select all the objects in a sheet, choose the **Edit | Go** To command, click the **S**pecial button in the Go To dialog box, and then activate the O**bj**ects option.

Follow these steps to set up protection formatting for worksheet objects:

1. Select the objects for which you want to adjust the protection formatting.
2. Select the Fo**r**mat | Obj**e**ct command, and in the Format Object dialog box, activate the Protection tab. Excel displays protection options for objects.
3. To lock the objects, activate the **L**ocked check box. To unlock them, deactivate this check box.
4. For text boxes or macro buttons, activate the Lock **T**ext check box to protect the text. Deactivate this check box to unlock the text.
5. Select OK.

Setting Up Protection Formatting for Scenarios

Similar to cells, scenarios are normally locked and visible. You can't work with scenarios in groups, however, so you must set up their protection formatting individually. The following procedure shows you the steps:

1. Select the **T**ools | S**c**enarios command. The Scenario Manager dialog box appears.
2. Highlight the scenario in the S**c**enarios list, and then click the **E**dit button. Excel displays the Edit Scenario dialog box, shown in Figure 5.27.

FIGURE 5.27.

Use the Edit Scenario dialog box to set up protection formatting for a scenario.

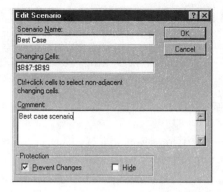

3. To lock the scenario, activate the **P**revent Changes check box. To unlock it, deactivate this check box.

4. To hide the scenario, activate the **Hid**e check box; deactivate it to unhide the scenario.

5. Select OK. Excel displays the Scenario Values dialog box.

6. Enter new values, if necessary, and then select OK.

7. Repeat steps 2 through 6 to set the protection formatting for other scenarios.

8. When you're done, select Close to return to the worksheet.

Protecting a Worksheet

At this point, you've formatted the cells, objects, or scenarios for protection. To activate the protection, follow these steps:

1. Select the **T**ools | **P**rotection | **P**rotect Sheet command. Excel displays the Protect Sheet dialog box, shown in Figure 5.28.

FIGURE 5.28.

Use the Protect Sheet dialog box to activate your protection formatting.

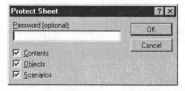

2. For added security, you can enter a password in the **P**assword text box. This means that no one can turn off the worksheet's protection without first entering the password. If you decide to enter a password, keep the following guidelines in mind:

   ■ When you enter a password, Excel masks it with asterisks. If you're not sure whether you entered the word correctly, don't worry. Excel asks you to confirm it.

- Passwords can be up to 255 characters long, and you can use any combination of letters, numbers, spaces, and other symbols.

- Use a password that's meaningful to you so that it's easier to remember. Don't, however, use a password that's easy for someone else to guess (such as your name or your spouse's name).

CAUTION

If you forget your password, there's no way to retrieve it, and you'll never be able to access your worksheet. As a precaution, you might want to write down your password and store it in a safe place.

- Excel differentiates between uppercase and lowercase letters, so remember the capitalization you use.

3. Select what you want to protect: **C**ontents, **O**bjects, or **S**cenarios.

4. Select OK.

5. If you entered a password, Excel asks you to confirm it. Reenter the password and then select OK.

TIP

To navigate only the unlocked cells in a protected document, use the Tab key (or Shift-Tab to move backward). The tab avoids the locked cells altogether (which you can still move to by using the arrow keys or the mouse) and always jumps to the next unlocked cell. If you happen to be on the last unlocked cell, the tab wraps around to the first unlocked cell.

To turn off the protection, select the **T**ools | **P**rotection | Un**p**rotect Sheet command. If you entered a password, Excel displays the Unprotect Sheet dialog box. Type the password in the **P**assword text box, and then select OK.

Protecting Windows and Workbook Structures

You also can protect your windows and workbook structures. When you protect a window, Excel takes the following actions:

- Hides the window's maximize and minimize buttons, Control-menu box, and borders. This means the window can't be moved, sized, or closed.

- Disables the **W**indow menu's **N**ew Window, **S**plit, and **F**reeze Panes commands when the window is active. The **A**rrange command remains active, but it has no effect on the protected window. The **H**ide and **U**nhide commands remain active.

When you protect a workbook's structure, Excel takes the following actions:

- Disables the **E**dit menu's De**l**ete Sheet and **M**ove or Copy Sheet commands.
- Prevents the **I**nsert menu's **W**orksheet, **Ch**art, and **M**acro commands from having any effect on the workbook.
- Keeps the Scenario Manager from creating a summary report.

Follow these steps to protect windows and workbook structures:

1. Activate the window or workbook you want to protect.
2. Select the **T**ools | **P**rotection | Protect **W**orkbook command. Excel displays the Protect Workbook dialog box, shown in Figure 5.29.

FIGURE 5.29.

Use the Protect Workbook dialog box to protect your workbook structure and windows.

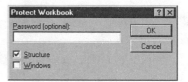

3. Enter a password in the **P**assword text box, if required. Follow the same guidelines outlined in the preceding section.
4. Select what you want to protect: **S**tructure or **W**indows.
5. Select OK.
6. If you entered a password, Excel asks you to confirm it. Reenter the password and select OK.

Protecting a File

For workbooks with confidential data, merely protecting cells or sheets might not be enough. For a higher level of security, Excel gives you three options (listed in order of increasing security):

- You can have Excel recommend that a workbook be opened as read-only. A read-only document can be changed, but you can't save your changes. Or, more accurately, you can save changes, but only to a file with a different name. The original file always remains intact. Note that Excel only recommends that the file be opened as read-only. You also can open the file with full read/write privileges.
- You can assign a password for saving changes. Users who know this password (the write reservation password) are assigned write privileges and can save changes to the workbook. All others can open the file only as read-only.
- You can assign a password for opening a document. A password is useful for workbooks with confidential information, such as payroll data. Only users who know the password can open the file.

To set these security options, follow these steps:

1. Activate the workbook and select the **F**ile | Save **A**s command (or press F12).
2. In the Save As dialog box, click the **O**ptions button. Excel displays the Save Options dialog box, shown in Figure 5.30.

FIGURE 5.30.

Use the Save Options dialog box to set up various levels of security for a worksheet file.

3. If you want Excel to recommend that the file be opened as read-only, activate the **R**ead-Only Recommended check box.
4. To restrict the write privileges when the worksheet is opened, enter a password in the **W**rite Reservation Password edit box.
5. To prevent unauthorized users from opening the file, enter a password in the **P**rotection Password edit box.

> **NOTE**
>
> When entering passwords, follow the same guidelines outlined earlier for worksheet protection.

6. Select OK.
7. If you entered passwords, Excel asks you to confirm them. Reenter the passwords and select OK. Excel returns you to the Save As dialog box.
8. Select OK. Excel asks whether you want to replace the existing file.
9. Select OK.

Working with Templates

A *template* is a document that contains a basic layout (sheets, labels, formulas, formatting, styles, names, and so on) that you can use as a skeleton for similar documents. A template ensures that worksheets, charts, or macro sheets that you use frequently all have a consistent look and feel. For example, if you need to consolidate budget numbers from various departments (as described earlier in this chapter), your task will be much easier if all the worksheets have the same layout. To that end, you can issue each department a budget template containing the worksheet layout you want everyone to use.

Creating a Template

Creating a template is similar to creating any other workbook. The following procedure outlines the required steps:

1. Set up the workbook with the settings you want to preserve in the template. You can either use an existing document or create a new one from scratch.

2. Select the **File** | Save **As** command to display the Save As dialog box.

3. Enter a name for the template in the File **n**ame text box (you don't need to add an extension; see step 5).

4. In the Save File as Type drop-down list, select the Template option. Excel displays the Templates folder.

5. Use the Save **in** list to select the folder for the template. The templates that ship with Excel are stored in the Spreadsheet Solutions folder.

TIP

If you save the template in your Excel startup folder (usually the \Excel\XLStart subfolder), you can open it quickly by selecting the **File** | **N**ew command (see the next section).

6. Select **S**ave.

Creating a New Document Based on a Template

After you've created a template, you can use either of the following methods to create a new document based on the template:

■ If you saved the template in your Excel startup directory, select the **File** | **N**ew command to display the New dialog box, shown in Figure 5.31. In the General tab, highlight the template and select OK. (The Workbook template, by the way, creates a default Excel workbook.)

■ To use one of Excel's built-in templates, select **File** | **N**ew, select the Spreadsheet Solutions tab in the New dialog box, highlight the template, and then select OK.

In both cases, Excel opens a copy of the file, gives the window the same name as the template, and adds a number. The number indicates how many times you've used this template to create a new document in the current Excel session. For example, if the template is called Budget, the first new document you create is called Budget1, the second is Budget2, and so on.

FIGURE 5.31.

When you save a template in the startup directory, its name appears in the New dialog box.

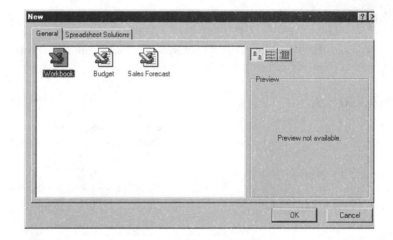

Customizing the Startup Workbook

By default, Excel opens a workbook called Book1 when you start the program. This default workbook is referred to as the *startup workbook*. If you find yourself constantly changing the default formatting, display options, or other settings, you can create a customized version of the startup workbook by following these steps:

1. Open a new workbook (or an existing one), and specify the settings you want to use for your startup document.
2. Follow the steps outlined earlier to save the sheet as a template with the name Book. You must save the template to your startup directory (usually \Excel\XLStart).
3. Select OK.

Now, whenever you start Excel, the program automatically opens a copy of the Book template with your customized settings.

Making Changes to a Template

When you want to make changes to a template, use the **F**ile | **O**pen command, highlight the template, and select **O**pen. After the template is open, you can make changes as you would to any other workbook. When you finish, save the file. (You don't need to specify the Template type this time, because Excel automatically saves the file as a template.)

Using Dialog Box Controls on a Worksheet

One of Excel's slickest features is that it enables you to place dialog box controls such as spinners, check boxes, and list boxes directly on a worksheet. You can then link the values returned by these controls to a cell to create an elegant method for entering data.

Using the Forms Toolbar

You add the dialog box controls by selecting tools from the Forms toolbar, shown in Figure 5.32. Following is a summary of the tools you can use to place controls on a worksheet.

FIGURE 5.32.

Use the Forms toolbar to draw dialog box controls on a worksheet.

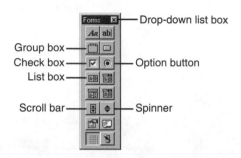

NOTE

The following descriptions are purposely brief. For a more complete discussion of each control, see Chapter 25, "Creating a Custom User Interface."

Group box	Creates a box to hold option buttons.
Check box	Creates a check box. If activated, a check box returns the value TRUE in its linked cell. If it's deactivated, it returns FALSE.
Option button	Creates an option button. In each group of option buttons, the user can select only one option. The returned value is a number indicating which option button was activated. The value 1 represents the first button added to the group, 2 signifies the second button, and so on.
List box	Creates a list box from which the user can select an item. The items in the list are defined by the values in a specified worksheet range, and the value returned to the linked cell is the number of the item chosen.
Drop-down list box	Creates a drop-down list box. This box is similar to a list box; however, the control shows only one item at a time until it's dropped down.
Scroll bar	Creates a scroll bar control. Unlike window scroll bars, a scroll bar control can be used to select a number from a range of values. Clicking on the arrows or dragging the scroll box changes the value of the control. This value is what gets returned to the linked cell.

| Spinner | Creates a spinner. Similar to a scroll bar, you can use a spinner to select a number between a maximum and minimum value by clicking on the arrows. The number is returned to the linked cell. |

NOTE

You can add a command button to a worksheet, but you have to assign a macro to it. See Chapter 21, "Getting Started with VBA," to learn how to create macro buttons.

Adding a Control to a Worksheet

You add controls to a worksheet using the same steps you use to create any graphic object. I'll be taking you through the specific steps for Excel's other graphic objects in Chapter 11, "Working with Graphic Objects," but here's a quick preview for dialog box controls:

1. In the Forms toolbar, click on the control you want to create. The mouse pointer changes to a crosshair.

2. Move the pointer onto the worksheet, and drag the mouse pointer to create the object.

3. Excel assigns a default caption to group boxes, check boxes, and option buttons. To edit this caption, click on the control and edit the text accordingly. When you're done, click outside the control.

After you've added a control, you can move it and size it as needed, as described in Chapter 11.

CAUTION

The controls you add are "live" in the sense that when you click on them, you're working the control (activating it and changing its value). To select a control for sizing or moving, you need to hold down the Ctrl key before clicking on the control.

Linking a Control to a Cell Value

To use the dialog box controls for inputting data, you need to associate each control with a worksheet cell. The following procedure shows you how it's done:

1. Select the control you want to work with. (Again, remember to hold down the Ctrl key before you click on the control.)

2. Select the Format | Object command to display the Format Object dialog box.

You also can click on the Properties tool in the Forms toolbar to display the Format Object dialog box.

3. Activate the Control tab and then use the Cell **L**ink box to enter the cell's reference. You can either type the reference or select it directly on the worksheet.

4. Select OK to return to the worksheet.

Figure 5.33 shows a worksheet with several controls and their corresponding linked cells. (To make things a little clearer, I added the numbers you see beside the scroll bar and spinner; they don't come with the control.)

Working with List Boxes

List boxes and drop-down lists are different from other controls because you also have to specify a range that contains the items to appear in the list. The following steps show you how it's done:

1. Enter the list items in a range.

2. Add the list control to the sheet (if you haven't done so already), and then select it.

3. Select the F**o**rmat | Obj**e**ct command to display the Format Object dialog box.

4. Activate the Control tab, and then use the **I**nput Range box to enter a reference to the range of items. You can either type in the reference or select it directly on the worksheet.

5. Select OK to return to the worksheet.

FIGURE 5.33.

A worksheet with several controls and their corresponding linked cells.

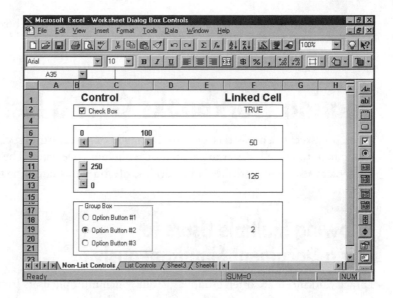

Figure 5.34 shows a worksheet with a list box and a drop-down list. The list used by both controls is the range A2:A8. Notice that the linked cells display the number of the list selection, not the selection itself. To get the selected list item, you can use the INDEX() function with the following syntax:

INDEX(*list_range*, *list_selection*)

list_range	The range used in the list box or drop-down list.
list_selection	The number of the item selected in the list.

FIGURE 5.34.

A worksheet with a list box and drop-down list control.

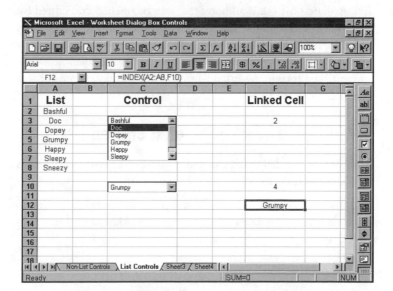

For example, to find out the item selected from the drop-down list box in Figure 5.34, you use the following formula:

```
=INDEX(A2:A8,F10)
```

Sharing Workbooks Over a Network

If you use Excel in a networked environment, you can use features such as shared lists and electronic mail to make it easier to collaborate with your colleagues. The next few sections finish our look at advanced worksheet and workbook features by examining these workgroup-related options.

Allowing Multiple Users to Edit a Document Simultaneously

Larger worksheets are often group efforts in which multiple users from multiple departments have a hand in the finished product. One way to do this is to send the document to a user (say, via e-mail, as we'll discuss later), have her update it, and then send it to the next person. This is an inefficient way to work for two reasons:

- Only one person ever works on the document at a time.
- If someone who has already worked on the spreadsheet needs to make a change, she has to find the person who has it now, get it from him, and then send it to the next person.

Fortunately, Excel 7 for Windows 95 implements a simple solution to this inefficiency: *shared lists.* A shared list is a workbook that can be opened and edited by multiple users at the same time. It's called a shared "list" because it's designed for collaborations that involve Excel lists and databases. Specifically, when you're working in a shared list, you can only enter data, insert and delete ranges, and sort the data. All other operations—including formatting ranges and entering formulas—are off-limits. (Technically, you *can* enter formulas, but Excel won't save them.)

Setting Up a Workbook as a Shared List

After you've decided that a particular workbook needs to be used as a shared list, you must run through two tasks to get things set up properly.

The first task is to decide on a location for all your shared lists. This should be a shared network resource, such as a server or a shared workgroup folder.

The second task is to designate the workbook as a shared list. Here's how it's done:

1. Set up the workbook the way you want it, including data labels and formatting.

2. Select the **File | Sh**ared Lists command. Excel displays the Shared Lists dialog box, shown in Figure 5.35.

FIGURE 5.35.

Use the Shared Lists dialog box to set up your workbook as a shared list.

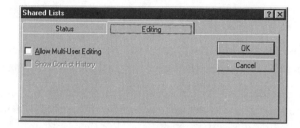

3. In the Editing tab, activate the **A**llow Multi-User Editing check box, and then select OK. Excel warns you that the operation will result in a save.

4. Select OK. If this is the first time you've set up a shared list, the User Identification dialog box appears and asks you to enter a user name.

5. Change the default user name, if needed, and then select OK. Excel returns you to the workbook and displays [Shared] in the workbook's title bar.

> **NOTE**
>
> The default user name displayed by Excel is your Excel user name. To change your Excel user name, choose the **Tools | O**ptions command, select the General tab, and then edit the User **N**ame text box.

Working with a Shared List

After your workbook is set up as a shared list, others from your network or workgroup are free to open the workbook in their own versions of Excel 7 for Windows 95. (If you try to open a shared list from a previous version of Excel, you'll be able to open the file only as read-only.) As mentioned earlier, shared list operations are limited to data entry, range insertions and deletions, and sorting.

To see the other users currently working with the shared list, select the **File | Sh**ared List command, and then select the Status tab in the Shared Lists dialog box. The list box displays the names of all users who have the workbook open (see Figure 5.36). When you're done, select OK to return to the workbook.

FIGURE 5.36.

The Status tab tells you the user names of the people who currently have the shared list open.

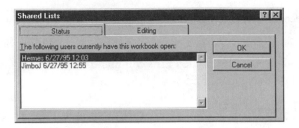

To update a shared list with each user's changes, select the File | Save command. If the save includes changes made by another user, a dialog box message appears to let you know.

If two or more users have made conflicting changes, the Conflict Resolution dialog box appears to ask you which change to accept (see Figure 5.37). Select the Use **m**y changes button to save the workbook with your edits, or select the Use **t**hese changes button to accept the changes made by the other user. You can also view a worksheet that lists conflicts you've had with this shared list (and which conflicting values were accepted) by selecting File | S**h**ared List, activating the Show **C**onflict History check box in the Editing tab, and then selecting OK. Excel adds a sheet named Conflict History to the end of the workbook.

FIGURE 5.37.

The Conflict Resolution dialog box appears if two or more users have made changes to the same cell.

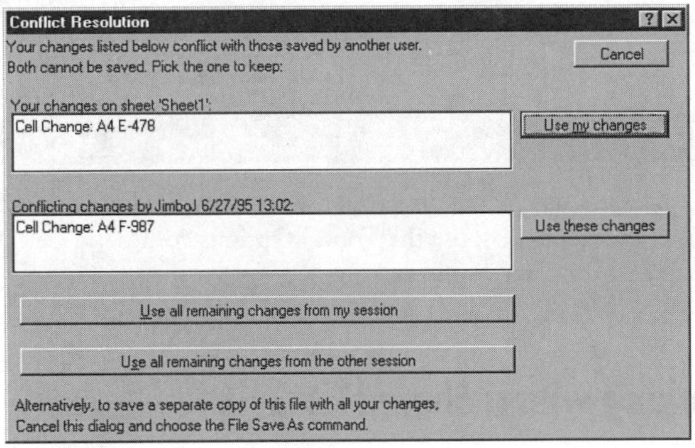

Exchanging Workbooks Via E-Mail

Shared lists are handy for maintaining databases and for efficient multiuser data entry, but they won't meet all your workbook-sharing needs. For example, you might want a colleague to make more substantial changes to a workbook (such as formatting or formula building). Or you might just want a few people in your workgroup to examine a spreadsheet, make comments or sign off on it, and then send it back to you. For these types of operations, you need to use e-mail. The good news, though, is that you can do all your e-mailing right from the comfort of your Excel window. The next few sections fill you in on the details.

Attaching a Workbook to an E-Mail Message

If you want a colleague to have a copy of a workbook, you can attach the workbook file to an e-mail message addressed to that person. The recipient can be a person on your network, the Microsoft Network, or even the Internet (depending on how Microsoft Exchange is set up and whether your network has a gateway to e-mail systems outside your own). Here's how it's done from Excel:

1. Open the workbook you want to send.
2. Select the **File | Send** command.
3. Excel might ask you which Exchange profile you want to use. If so, choose the profile and then select OK.
4. In the Microsoft Exchange window that appears, you'll see that your workbook is shown as an attachment, as shown in Figure 5.38. Fill in the other fields (To, Cc, Subject, message) as necessary.

FIGURE 5.38.

When you send a workbook, it appears as an attachment in an Exchange message.

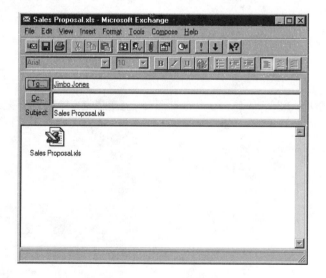

5. When you're ready, select **File | Send** or press Ctrl-Enter to send the message.

NOTE

If you want to send only, say, a range of cells, copy the range to the Clipboard and then load Microsoft Exchange. Start a new message, select the message area, and then paste the range from the Clipboard.

Routing a Workbook

If you need input from several colleagues, you *could* send separate e-mail messages to each person with the workbook attached, but Excel gives you an easier method: *routing*. When you route a workbook, you specify a series of recipients on a *routing slip*. Excel sends the document to the first person on the routing slip. When that person is done with the workbook, he sends it, and the routing slip automatically addresses it to the next routing slip recipient. The workbook eventually finds its way back after each person has added his two cents' worth.

Here's how to add a routing slip to a workbook:

1. Open the workbook you want to route.

2. Select the **File | Add R**outing Slip command.

3. Excel might ask you which Exchange profile you want to use. If so, choose the profile and then select OK.

4. Select the **Ad**dress button to display the Address Book.

5. In the order in which you want the workbook routed, select a recipient and then select **To**–>. When you're done, select OK.

6. Adjust the **S**ubject text, if necessary, and enter an explanatory message in the **M**essage Text area, as shown in Figure 5.39.

FIGURE 5.39.

Use the Routing Slip dialog box to select your recipients and set a few other routing options.

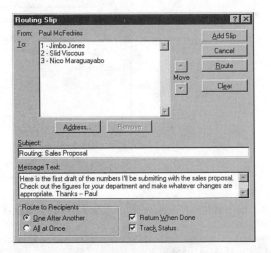

7. If you want the workbook returned to you after the last recipient has worked with it, keep the Return **W**hen Done check box active. If you would like to receive a message each time a recipient routes the workbook to the next person, leave the Trac**k** Status check box active.

8. When you're ready, select the **R**oute button.

When the first recipient receives the message, she opens the file, makes her changes (or whatever), and then selects File | Send. Exchange routes the workbook to the next recipient automatically.

Summary

This chapter showed you some advanced techniques for dealing with Excel worksheets and workbooks. We talked about changing the worksheet view, using outlines, consolidating data, protecting worksheets and workbooks, working with templates, using worksheet dialog box controls, and employing Excel's workgroup features. If you're still hungry for more information, here are a few other places to check:

- Multiple worksheet views are handy for simple what-if analyses. See Chapter 17, "Basic Analytic Methods," for more information on what-if analysis.

- Data consolidation can add link formulas to the destination range for each cell in the source ranges you selected. See the section titled "Working with Links in Formulas" in Chapter 2, "Building Better Formulas," for details about link formulas.

- Pivot tables are often better for consolidating data by category. See Chapter 13, "Creating Pivot Tables," and Chapter 14, "Customizing Pivot Tables," to find out how they work.

- I showed you how to protect your scenarios. If you have scenarios to protect, you can find out how to do it in Chapter 20, "Working with Scenarios."

- For a more in-depth discussion of worksheet dialog box controls, see Chapter 25, "Creating a Custom User Interface."

- You can add a command button to a worksheet, but you have to assign a macro to it. See Chapter 21, "Getting Started with VBA," to learn how to create macro buttons.

- To learn how to move, size, and delete graphic objects such as worksheet dialog box controls, head for Chapter 11, "Working with Graphic Objects."

Printing Your Work

6

IN THIS CHAPTER

After you've entered your data, built your formulas, formatted your ranges, and set up your worksheet just so, you'll often want to print a hard copy for distribution or for filing. This chapter guides you through both the basics and the advanced options of Excel's printing features. You'll learn how to select page setup options, define a print area, preview the print job, set up reports, and, of course, send your creation to a printer or file.

Selecting Page Setup Options

Before printing, you need to decide how you want your worksheet pages to appear. This includes deciding the paper orientation (landscape or portrait) and the size of your margins. To set these options, select the File | Page Setup command to display the Page Setup dialog box. The next few sections explain most of the options in this dialog box. When you're finished choosing your options, select OK to return to the document or Print to send it to the printer.

Changing the Page Options

The Page Setup dialog box has a Page tab (see Figure 6.1) that gives you options for altering the look and dimensions of your printed pages. Let's take a look at each option in detail.

FIGURE 6.1.

Use the Page Setup dialog box to control the look of your printed worksheet pages.

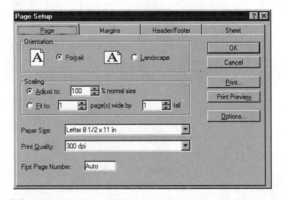

I'll save the options in the Scaling group until later in this chapter. See the section titled "Fitting More Data on a Page."

Setting the Page Orientation

The *page orientation* determines how Excel lays out the worksheet data on the page. The Page tab gives you two options:

Portrait	If you activate this option, Excel prints the worksheet along the short side of the page (this is the normal page orientation). Assuming Excel's default margin sizes of 0.75 inches on the left and right and 1 inch on the top and bottom, and the default 8.5-inch by 11-inch letter-size paper setting, this orientation gives you a print area that's 7 inches wide and 9 inches high on each page.
Landscape	Select this option to make Excel print along the long side of the page. With the default margins on letter-size paper, this orientation gives you a print area 9 1/2 inches wide and 6 1/2 inches high.

Selecting a Different Paper Size

Use the Page tab's Paper Size drop-down list to select a different paper size for your printout. The options in this list include standard letter size (8 1/2 × 11) and legal size (8 1/2 × 14). Depending on the currently selected printer, you might see other sizes too. Make sure that the size you select matches the paper loaded in the printer.

Adjusting the Print Quality

Use the Print Quality drop-down list to set the quality of the worksheet printout. If you're printing a final draft, select the highest available setting (which might be 300 dpi or 600 dpi, depending on your printer) for the best-looking output. If you're just printing a copy to see how things look, you can save some ink (or toner, if you have a laser printer) by selecting a lower number (say, 150 dpi or even 75 dpi).

Setting the Starting Page Number

If the document you're printing is part of a larger report, you might want to start your page numbers at a number other than 1. For example, if you've already printed the first 10 pages of a report, you'll probably want the next page to start at page number 11.

To adjust the first page number, enter the appropriate number in the Page tab's First Page Number text box.

Setting Page Margins

The *page margins* are the blank areas that surround the printed text on a page. By default, Excel makes the left and right margins 0.75 inches and the top and bottom margins 1 inch, but you can override that if you like. Why would you want to do such a thing? Here are a few good reasons:

■ If someone else will be making notes on the page, it helps to include bigger margins (to give that person more room to write).

■ Smaller margins all around mean that you get more text on a page. On a long worksheet, this could save you a few pages when you print.

■ If you have a worksheet that won't quite fit on a page, you could decrease the appropriate margins enough to fit the extra lines onto a single page. (You should read the section titled "Fitting More Data on a Page," later in this chapter, to learn some other ways to squeeze more data on a page.)

To adjust the margins, first select the Margins tab in the Page Setup dialog box, shown in Figure 6.2. You can then select the following options:

Margins	The **T**op, **B**ottom, **L**eft, and **R**ight spinners enable you to enter your new margin values.
From Edge	These options control how far the headers and footers appear from the edge of the page. Use He**a**der to set the distance from the top of the page to the top of the header. Use **F**ooter to set the distance from the bottom of the page to the bottom of the footer.
Center on Page	These options tell Excel to center the printout between the margins. Activate the Hori**z**ontally check box to center between the left and right margins; activate the **V**ertically check box to center between the top and bottom margins.

FIGURE 6.2.

Use the Margins tab to change the size of your page margins.

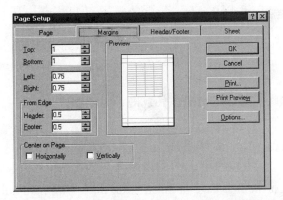

Adding a Header or Footer

You can add headers or footers that display information at the top (for a header) or bottom (for a footer) of every printed page. This feature is useful for keeping track of such items as page numbers and the current date and time. The next two sections show you how to work with Excel's predefined and custom headers and footers.

Adding a Predefined Header or Footer

Excel has various predefined headers and footers that can display page numbers, workbook and worksheet names, file revision dates, authors, and more. Follow these steps to add one of these headers or footers:

1. Select the Header/Footer tab in the Page Setup dialog box, shown in Figure 6.3.

FIGURE 6.3.

Use the Header/Footer tab to define a header and footer for your printout.

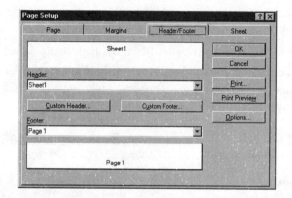

2. Use the Header drop-down list to select a predefined header. Your selection appears in the header box above the list. Here's a summary of Excel's predefined headers (Left, Center, and Right tell you how the data is aligned in the header):

General Form	Left	Center	Right
Page *x*		Page 1	
Page *x* of *y*		Page 1 of 5	
Sheet title		Sheet1	
Confidential, *Date*, Page *x*	Confidential	8/23/95	Page 1
Sheet *title*, Page *x*		Sheet1	Page 1
Sheet title, Confidential, Page *x*	Sheet1	Confidential	Page 1
Page *x*, *Sheet title*		Page 1	Sheet1
User name, Sheet title, Date	Jimbo	Sheet1	8/23/95
Prepared by *user name Date*, Page *x*	Prepared by Jimbo	8/23/95	Page 1

3. Use the **F**ooter drop-down list to select a predefined footer. Your choice appears in the footer box below the list. (You have the same predefined options as you do with the header.)

Creating a Custom Header or Footer

If none of the predefined headers or footers fits the bill, you can create your own custom version. You can enter seven different items in a customized header or footer: text (such as a workbook title or other explanatory comments), the current page number and total page count, the date and time, and the workbook and worksheet tab names. You can specify a font for any of these items, and you can place the items on the left or right side of the page, or in the center. The following procedure shows you the necessary steps:

1. Select the Header/Footer tab in the Page Setup dialog box.
2. To create a custom header, select the **C**ustom Header button to display the Header dialog box, shown in Figure 6.4. To create a custom footer, select the **C**ustom Footer button to display the Footer dialog box.

FIGURE 6.4.

Use the Header dialog box to create a custom header. The Footer dialog box works like the Header dialog box.

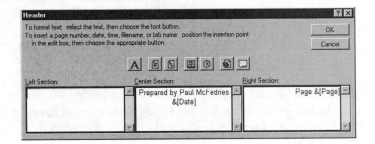

3. Select either the **L**eft Section, **C**enter Section, or **R**ight Section text box.
4. Enter text or select one of the following buttons to insert a code:

Button	Code	Description
	&[Page]	Page number
	&[Pages]	Page count
	&[Date]	Current date
	&[Time]	Current time
	&[File]	Workbook filename

&[Tab]   Worksheet tab name

5. (Optional) Select any text you want to format, and then click the Font button. In the font dialog box that appears, enter the font options you want to use, and then select OK to return to the Header or Footer dialog box.

    The Font button.

6. Repeat steps 3 through 5 to enter any other text or codes.

7. Select OK. Excel returns you to the Page Setup dialog box and displays the header or footer in the appropriate box.

NOTE

If you want to see your header or footer before printing the workbook, select the Print Preview button. I'll discuss the Print Preview feature in depth later in this chapter.

Adjusting the Appearance of Each Page

The Sheet tab in the Page Setup dialog box gives you several options that affect the look of your printed pages (see Figure 6.5). The next few sections take you through each option.

FIGURE 6.5.

The Sheet tab's options control the look of your printout.

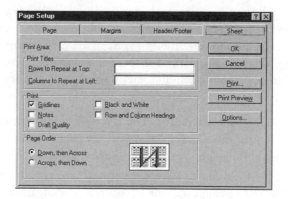

Defining a Print Area

After you have your pages laid out the way you want, you need to decide how much of the workbook you want to print. By default, Excel prints the selected worksheets, but you can also choose to print the entire workbook.

If, however, you prefer to print only a part of a sheet, you need to define a *print area*. A print area is a special range that defines the cells you want to print. To set it up, first select the Print Area text box in the Sheet tab. Then type the range you want to print, or use your mouse or keyboard to select the range on the worksheet. You can enter as many ranges as you need.

There's another way to set the print area that doesn't involve the Page Setup dialog box. In the worksheet, select the range you want to print, and then select the **F**ile | Pri**n**t Area | **S**et Print Area command.

When you return to the worksheet, you'll see that Excel displays a dotted line around the range to mark the print area and names the range Print_Area.

Removing a Print Area

If you no longer need a print area, you can remove it with any of the following methods:

- Define a different print area.
- Select the **F**ile | Pri**n**t Area | **C**lear Print Area command.
- Select the **I**nsert | **N**ame | **D**efine command, and delete the Print_Area name.
- Select the **F**ile | Page Set**u**p command, activate the Sheet tab, and delete the reference from the Print **A**rea text box.

Defining Titles to Print on Every Page

If your printout covers more than a single page, your row and column titles normally print only on the first page. This setup can make the subsequent pages confusing and difficult to read. To get around this problem, you can tell Excel to print the appropriate row and column headings on every page. If you select one or more rows, they'll print at the top of each page; if you select one or more columns, they'll print on the left of each page. Use either or both of the following methods to define the titles you want to print on every page:

- In the **R**ows to Repeat at Top text box, type the range for the column headings that you want to appear at the top of each page. You also can select the range on the worksheet using the mouse or the keyboard.
- In the **C**olumns to Repeat at Left text box, type the range for the row headings that you want to appear at the left of each page. Again, you also can use the mouse or the keyboard to select the range directly on the worksheet.

Excel defines the name Print_Titles for the ranges you entered.

Removing Print Titles

To turn off print titles, take either of the following actions:

- Select the **I**nsert | **N**ame | **D**efine command, and delete the Print_Titles name.

■ Select the File | Page Setup command, and then delete the references from the **R**ows to Repeat at Top and **C**olumns to Repeat at Left text boxes.

Controlling the Look of the Printed Pages

The Print group contains several check boxes that determine how your printed pages appear. Here's a rundown:

Gridlines	Excel normally prints the worksheet gridlines (unless you've turned off the gridlines). If you prefer not to see the gridlines on your printout, deactivate the **G**ridlines check box.

NOTE

To turn off worksheet gridlines, select the **T**ools | **O**ptions command, activate the View tab, and then deactivate the **G**ridlines check box.

Notes	If your workbook contains cell notes, activate this check box to print the notes with the workbook.
Draft **Q**uality	For faster (but lower-quality) printing, activate this check box. Excel speeds up printing by suppressing gridlines and some graphics in the printout.
Black and White	If you've added any color formatting to your cells or charts, most printers print these colors as patterns. If this isn't the look you want, activate this check box to tell Excel to print these colors as shades of gray or, in the case of text, as black and white.
Row and Column Headings	If you're printing the worksheet as documentation, you probably want to print the row and columns headings too. (This is especially true if you display the document's formulas before printing.) You can do this by activating this check box.

Changing the Print Order

The options in the Page Order group control how Excel prints ranges that are larger than a single page. If the **D**own, then Across option is selected, Excel works its way down through the range when printing the pages. It then jumps back to the top of the range, moves over to the next group of columns, and works down again.

If you prefer to print across the range first, and then down through the rows, activate the Across option, and then the Down option.

Previewing the Printout

You can't see page elements such as margins, headers, and footers in Excel's normal screen display. Because these features play such a large part in determining the look of your printouts, Excel offers a Print Preview feature. This feature shows you a scaled-down, full-page version of your worksheet pages. Print Preview enables you to get the "big picture" so that you can see the effect of each of the page layout and print options you've selected. You also have easy access to the Page Setup dialog box, where you can make changes and immediately see the effect on the printout. Print Preview also enables you to adjust your margins visually using the mouse, and, finally, you also can print from the preview screen.

To see the preview screen, select the **F**ile | Print Pre**v**iew command. You'll see a screen similar to the one shown in Figure 6.6.

 Mouse users can display the Print Preview screen by clicking the Print Preview button on the Standard toolbar.

FIGURE 6.6.

Excel's Print Preview screen.

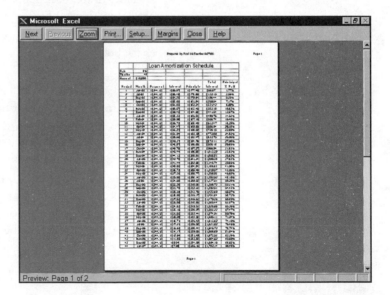

Changing the Print Preview Magnification

When you start Print Preview, Excel displays the first page of the printout full size. To toggle between full size and actual size (that is, the actual size of the printed page), you can take the following actions:

- Select the **Z**oom button. To return to the full-page view, select **Z**oom again.
- Move the mouse pointer onto the page so that the pointer changes to a magnifying glass. Position the pointer over the area you want to zoom in on, and then click. To return to the full-page view, click on the sheet again.

Navigating the Print Preview Pages

When you're working with the Print Preview pages full size, you can display other pages in your printout by selecting the **N**ext and **P**revious buttons. You also can use the keys listed in Table 6.1.

Table 6.1. Navigating Print Preview in full-size mode.

Key	Result
Down arrow	Moves to the next page.
Up arrow	Moves to the previous page.
End	Moves to the last page.
Home	Moves to the first page.

When you're viewing a page actual size, use the scroll bars to move around the page using the mouse. With the keyboard, use the keys listed in Table 6.2.

Table 6.2. Navigating Print Preview in actual-size mode.

Key	Result
Arrow key	Moves left, right, down, or up.
Ctrl-right arrow, or End	Moves to the right side of the page.
Ctrl-left arrow, or Home	Moves to the left side of the page.
Ctrl-down arrow	Moves to the bottom of the page.
Ctrl-up arrow	Moves to the top of the page.
Ctrl-End	Moves to the bottom-right corner of the page.
Ctrl-Home	Moves to the top-left corner of the page.

Adjusting Page Margins and Column Widths in Print Preview

One of the big advantages of Print Preview is that it enables you to change your page margins and column widths easily. If you select the **M**argins button, Excel displays margin and column *handles* at the top of the screen and indicates the margins with dotted lines (see Figure 6.7). By dragging the handles, you can change the margins and columns visually.

FIGURE 6.7.

In Print Preview, select the Margins button to change the page margins and column widths by dragging the handles that appear at the top of the screen.

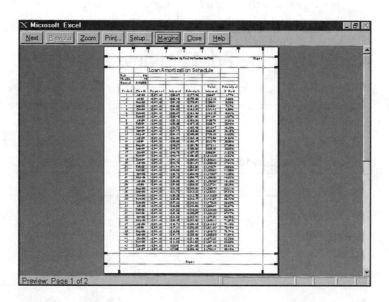

Follow these steps to adjust your page margins or column widths:

1. In the Print Preview screen, select the **M**argins button.
2. Position the mouse pointer over the handle of the margin or column you want to adjust. The pointer changes to a two-sided arrow with a line through it. Note that, if you press and hold down the left mouse button, Excel displays the current margin size or column width in the status bar.
3. Drag the handle to the new location.
4. Repeat steps 2 and 3 for the other margins or columns you want to adjust.

Other Print Preview Buttons

The Print Preview screen also includes these three buttons:

Prin**t**   This button displays the Print dialog box. I'll explain the various options in this dialog box in the next section.

| Setup | This button displays the Page Setup dialog box (discussed earlier in this chapter). If you change any Page Setup options, Excel shows you the effect of the new settings when you return to Print Preview. |
| Close | This button exits Print Preview and returns you to the worksheet. |

Printing a Worksheet

After setting up your pages, defining your print area and print titles, and previewing the output, you're ready to start printing. Before you do, though, make sure that your printer is turned on and ready to receive output (it should be online, have enough paper, and so on). Then select the **File | Print** command to display the Print dialog box, shown in Figure 6.8.

FIGURE 6.8.

Use the Print dialog box to specify your print options.

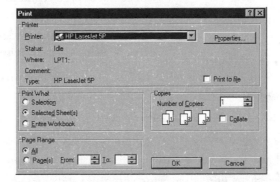

TIP

You can bypass the menus and display the Print dialog box directly by pressing Ctrl-P.

Here's a summary of the various options available in the Print dialog box:

| **P**rinter | Use this drop-down list to choose a different printer. |

CAUTION

If you choose the **P**roperties button for the printer you select, any adjustments you make to the printer options will affect *all* documents in *all* your Windows applications. To change settings for individual worksheets only, use the **F**ile | Page Setup command.

| Print to file | Activate this check box when you're printing to a file rather than the printer. See "Printing to a Text File," later in this chapter, for details. |

Print What	Use these option buttons to determine how much of the workbook you want to print. Selection prints the selected range, Selected Sheet(s) prints the current sheet group, and Entire Workbook prints everything.
Number of Copies	Use this spinner to enter the number of copies you want Excel to print.
Collate	Use this option to control how Excel prints multiple copies of a multipage document. For example, suppose that you want two copies of a three-page document. If Collate is activated, each copy of the entire document is printed at one time. If Collate is deactivated, you'll get two copies of page 1, then two copies of page 2, and then two copies of page 3.
Page Range	Use this option to select the number of pages to print. Select All to print everything, and select Page(s) to print a range of pages (which you specify with the From and To spinners).

The following procedure gives you the complete rundown of the steps involved in printing an Excel workbook:

1. Make sure that your printer is turned on and is online.
2. Open or activate the workbook you want to print.
3. If necessary, select the range or worksheets you want to print.
4. Select the File | Page Setup command and enter your page layout options.
5. If you don't want to print the entire document, use the Sheet tab's Print Area box to select the range you want to print.
6. If you want row or column titles to appear on every page, use the Sheet tab's Rows to Repeat at Top and Columns to Repeat at Left text boxes to select them.
7. Select OK to return to the worksheet.
8. Select the File | Print command to display the Print dialog box.
9. Enter your print options.
10. Select OK to print the document.

 Click the Print button on the Standard toolbar to print the workbook without displaying the Print dialog box.

Adjusting Page Breaks

Excel breaks up large worksheets into pages in which the size of each page is a function of the paper size, the default font, and the margin settings in the Page Setup dialog box. Using these parameters, Excel sets automatic page breaks to delineate the print area for each page. Although you can't adjust automatic page breaks, you can override them using manual page breaks. This enables you to control which data is printed on each page.

> **TIP**
>
> To see Excel's automatic page breaks before printing, select the **Tools | O**ptions command, select the View tab, and then activate the A**u**tomatic Page Breaks option.

Before setting a manual page break, you need to position the cell pointer correctly. Figure 6.9 uses the Page Breaks workbook to illustrate the correct cell positions:

- In the Both Breaks worksheet, the cell pointer is on cell C10. Inserting a manual page break here creates a horizontal break above the cell and a vertical break to the left of the cell.

- In the Horizontal Break worksheet, the break is inserted with the cell pointer in the first column (cell A5). Here, Excel inserts only a horizontal page break above the cell.

- In the Vertical Break worksheet, the break is inserted with the cell pointer in the first row (cell C1). In this case, Excel inserts only a vertical page break to the left of the cell.

FIGURE 6.9.

The correct cell positions for inserting manual page breaks.

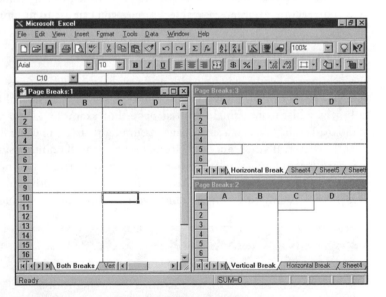

> **TIP**
>
> You can make it a bit easier to see the page breaks if you turn off the worksheet gridlines. Select the **Tools | O**ptions command, select the View tab, and then deactivate the **G**ridlines check box.

To insert a manual page break, position the cell pointer appropriately for the break you want, and then select the Insert | Page **B**reak command. Excel inserts the page break at the cell you selected.

To remove manual page breaks, first move to any cell immediately below a horizontal page break or immediately to the right of a vertical page break. Then select the Insert | Remove Page **B**reak command.

> **NOTE**
>
> Automatic and manual page breaks appear as dashed lines on your worksheet. You can tell the two kinds of page breaks apart by noting that automatic page breaks use smaller dashes with more space between each dash.

Fitting More Data on a Page

When you print a worksheet, you often end up with a couple of rows or columns that can't fit on a page. These are printed on a separate page, which usually is inconvenient and unattractive. This section examines several techniques you can use to fit more information on a page.

Adjusting the Normal Font

A worksheet's default column width and row height are functions of the *font* defined in the Normal style. In general, the smaller the type size of the Normal font, the more rows and columns will fit on a single printed page. For example, 10-point Arial prints about 49 standard-height rows on a single page (assuming that you're using 8 1/2-inch by 11-inch paper). However, if you reduce the Normal type size to 8 points, a single page prints about 56 standard-height rows. Similarly, using a narrower font increases the number of columns printed per page. For example, 10-point Arial prints 9 standard-width columns per page, but this increases to 11 standard-width columns if you use 10-point Times New Roman.

> **NOTE**
>
> For instructions on adjusting the Normal style, head for Chapter 4, "Formatting Excel Worksheets," and read the section titled "Working with Styles."

Setting Smaller Margins

Because margins determine the amount of space surrounding your printed data, reducing margin size (as described earlier in this chapter) means more room on each page for printing. For example, reducing all four margins (right, left, top, and bottom) to 0.25 inches increases the number of columns printed from 9 to 11 and the number of rows from 49 to 57 (assuming that 10-point Arial is the Normal font).

Changing the Paper Size and Orientation

If you're having trouble fitting all your rows on a page, try printing on longer paper. Changing the paper size from 8 1/2 by 11 inches to 8 1/2 by 14 inches increases the number of rows per page from 49 to 65 (based on 10-point Arial). Use the Page Setup dialog box to select a paper size.

If you're having trouble getting all your columns to fit on a page, change the *paper orientation* from portrait to landscape in the Page Setup dialog box. When you switch to landscape orientation, Excel prints the worksheet sideways and increases the number of columns per page from 9 to 13. Just remember that this orientation reduces the number of rows printed per page.

Adjusting Rows and Columns

Make sure that your rows are no taller (and your columns no wider) than they need to be. Select the entire print area, and select both the Format | Row | AutoFit and the Format | Column | AutoFit Selection commands. Also, hiding any unnecessary rows and columns enables you to fit more important information on each page.

> **NOTE**
>
> You also can use row adjustments to reduce the number of lines printed per page. For example, if you want to produce a double-spaced report, select every row in the print area, and select the Format | Row | Height command to double the height of each row.

Scaling Your Worksheet

If you have a PostScript printer or any other printer that accepts scaleable fonts, you can scale your worksheets to fit on one page. When you specify a percentage reduction, Excel shrinks the printed worksheet proportionally and maintains all your layout and formatting options. (You also can enlarge your worksheets.) The following procedure outlines the steps to follow:

1. Select the File | Page Setup command, and then select the Page tab in the Page Setup dialog box.

2. In the Scaling section, select the Adjust to option, and then use the spinner beside it to enter a percentage. To reduce the printout, enter a value between 10 and 100. To enlarge the printout, enter a value between 100 and 400.

3. Select OK.

If you have to use a lot of trial and error to get the proper reduction setting, you can save some time by having Excel do the work for you. You just specify the number of pages you want for the document, and Excel handles the reduction automatically. If necessary, you can enter both a length and a width for the printout. Here's how you do it:

1. Select **F**ile | Page Se**t**up, and then select the Page tab in the Page Setup dialog box.

2. In the Scaling section, select the **F**it to option, and use its spinners to enter the number of pages wide and tall you want the printout to be.

3. Select OK.

> **TIP**
>
> Even if your printer doesn't support scaleable fonts, you can still scale your worksheets to fit a page. Select the entire print area, hold down the Shift key while you select **E**dit | **C**opy Picture, and select the options you want from the Copy Picture dialog box. Select OK to return to the worksheet. Finally, paste the picture and scale it to the size you want. See Chapter 11, "Working with Graphic Objects," for more information about working with pictures.

Printing Text Colors

Excel normally prints all text in black, no matter what color the text is on-screen. If you have a PostScript printer, however, you can get text colors to print in shades of gray by installing one of Window 95's color printer drivers. Here are the steps you need to follow:

1. Select Windows 95's Start button, open the **S**ettings folder, and then select Printers. The Printers folder appears.

2. Select the Add Printer icon. Windows 95 starts up the Add Printer Wizard.

3. Select Next > to move on to the next Wizard dialog box.

4. If the Wizard asks whether you want to set up a **L**ocal printer or a **N**etwork printer, activate the appropriate option and then select Next >.

5. Use the **M**anufacturers list to choose a printer manufacturer, use the **P**rinters list to choose a color PostScript printer (see Figure 6.10), and then select Next >. Here are some examples:

Manufacturer	Printer
Digital	Digital Colormate PS
HP	HP PaintJet XL300 PostScript
IBM	IBM 4079 Color Jetprinter PS
Kodak	KODAK ColorEase PS Printer
NEC	Colormate PS
QMS	ColorScript 100 Model 10

FIGURE 6.10.

Use this Add Printer Wizard dialog box to select a driver for a color PostScript printer.

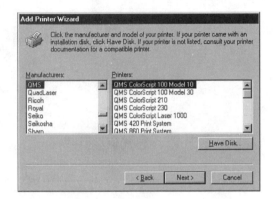

6. In the next Add Printer Wizard dialog box, highlight the port to which your printer is attached, and then select Next >.

7. Use the **P**rinter name text box to enter a name for the printer (this is the name that will appear in the **P**rinter drop-down list in Excel's Print dialog box), and then select Next >.

8. When the Wizard asks whether you want to print a text page, activate **N**o and then select Finish.

9. If the Wizard asks you for one of your Windows 95 disks, insert the disk and select OK. Windows installs the driver for the printer and returns you to the Printers folder.

10. Select **F**ile | **C**lose to close the Printers folder.

When you're back in Excel, you can print colored text by choosing the **F**ile | **P**rint command and then using the **P**rinter drop-down list to select the color PostScript printer. Figure 6.11 shows a sample printout using this technique.

FIGURE 6.11.
Text colors printed as shades of gray.

This is blue text

This is red text

This is magenta text

This is green text

This is yellow text

Printing to a Text File

You can print your worksheets to a text file by using Excel's Print to File feature. This feature is handy if you want to print a worksheet on an off-site printer, such as a color printer, a PostScript printer, or a Linotronic printer. You just select the appropriate printer driver (as outlined in the preceding section) and print the worksheet to a file (I'll show you how to do this in a second). When you get to the printer site, use DOS to copy the file to the printer. The output will be exactly the same as if it were printed directly from Excel.

> **NOTE**
>
> Use this technique to copy worksheets to a file for printing later on a typesetting machine. Find out whether your typesetter uses a Linotronic or Compugraphic model. Select the appropriate printer driver, and then print the worksheet to a disk.

Here are the steps to follow to print a workbook to a file:

1. Select the **F**ile | **P**rint command to display the Print dialog box.
2. Use the **P**rinter drop-down list to select the printer driver you want to use.
3. Activate the Print to **f**ile check box.
4. Select OK. Excel displays the Print to File dialog box, shown in Figure 6.12.
5. Use the File **n**ame text box to enter a name for the file, and use the **F**olders list to select a location.
6. Select OK. Excel copies the worksheet to the file.

FIGURE 6.12.

Use the Print to File dialog box to enter a filename for the printout.

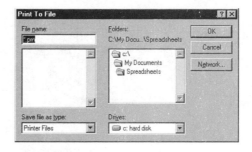

Working with Reports

In Chapter 5, "Advanced Worksheet Topics," in the section titled "Changing the Worksheet View," you learned how to create different *views* of your worksheets. A view, you'll recall, contains specific settings for the display options, window position and size, row height and column width, and so on. These different views are real time-savers when you're manipulating a worksheet on-screen. Excel also includes a feature called the *Report Manager* that enables you to put together a sequence of views and print them in a *report*. For maximum flexibility, you can specify different print settings with each view and use these settings when printing your reports.

This section introduces you to Excel reports and shows you how to create, edit, and print your own reports.

Creating Reports

If you're using views to create your report, you first need to define the print settings for each view. You can define page setup options, headers, footers, and even different printers (on different printer ports). Here are some guidelines to follow when defining your view print settings:

- Use the header or footer to display a title for each view.
- If a view is designed to show only a section of a worksheet (such as a list of account codes), be sure to set up a Print_Area range to restrict the printout to the view's data.
- Set up your Print_Title range and page breaks as needed with each view.

When you create a report, you enter a report name and then define the various *sections* of the report. (A section is a specific worksheet view, a scenario, or a combination of the two.) The following procedure outlines the steps you need to run through:

1. Select the **V**iew | **R**eport Manager command. Excel displays the Report Manager dialog box.
2. Select the **A**dd button. Excel displays the Add Report dialog box, shown in Figure 6.13.

FIGURE 6.13.

Use the Add Report dialog box to define your report sections.

3. Enter a name for the report in the **R**eport Name text box.

4. Use the **S**heet drop-down list to select a worksheet to include in the report.

5. If you have a view to include in the report, select it from the **V**iew drop-down list.

6. If you have a scenario to include, select it from the Sce**n**ario drop-down list box.

7. Select the **A**dd button. Excel displays the selected worksheet, view, and scenario in the Sections in this Report list.

8. Repeat steps 4 through 7 to include other sections in the report.

9. Activate the Use **C**ontinuous Page Numbers check box to print the report with consecutive page numbers.

10. Select OK. Excel returns you to the Print Report dialog box and adds the report to the **R**eports list.

11. Select **C**lose to return to the workbook.

TIP

You can document your complex workbooks by printing hard copies of the results, formulas, variables used, and range names. Set up a view for each component, and then create a report called "Documentation."

Editing Reports

Your reports print in the order in which you selected the sections. If you want to change that order—or make any other modifications—you can edit your reports by following these steps:

1. Select the **V**iew | **R**eport Manager command to display the Print Report dialog box.

2. In the **R**eports list box, highlight the report you want to edit.

3. Select the **Edit** button. Excel displays the Edit Report dialog box (which is identical to the Add Report dialog box).

4. To add a section (or to use a different combination of worksheets, views, and scenarios), choose the worksheet, view, and scenario from the Section to Add group, and then select the **Add** button.

5. To change the section order, highlight the appropriate section in the Sections in this Report list, and use the Move **Up** and Move **Down** buttons to place the section where you want it.

6. To delete a section, highlight the section in the Sections in this Report list, and select the De**l**ete button.

7. Select OK. Excel returns you to the Print Report dialog box.

8. Select the **Close** button to return to the workbook.

Printing Reports

When you've defined the report to your satisfaction, you can print it by following these steps:

1. Select the **View** | **R**eport Manager command to display the Print Report dialog box.

2. In the **R**eports list box, highlight the report you want to print.

3. Select the **P**rint button. Excel displays the Print dialog box.

4. Use the **C**opies text box to enter the number of copies you want.

5. Select OK. Excel prints the report.

Deleting Reports

The following procedure shows you how to delete a report you no longer need:

1. Select the **View** | **R**eport Manager command to display the Print Report dialog box.

2. In the **R**eports list box, highlight the report you want to delete.

3. Select the De**l**ete button. Excel asks you to confirm the deletion (see Figure 6.14).

FIGURE 6.14.

Excel asks you to confirm a report deletion.

4. Select OK to proceed with the deletion. Excel removes the report from the **R**eports list.

5. Repeat steps 2 through 4 for other reports you want to delete.

6. Select **C**lose. Excel returns you to the workbook.

Summary

This chapter showed you the ins and outs of printing Excel worksheets and reports. You went on a thorough tour of the Page Setup dialog box. I also showed you how to use Print Preview, adjust page breaks, print text colors, and print to a text file. Here is a list of chapters that have related information on printing:

- For instructions on adjusting the Normal style, head for Chapter 4, "Formatting Excel Worksheets."

- To get lots of information on worksheet views, turn to Chapter 5, "Advanced Worksheet Topics."

- To learn how to print worksheets programmatically, see Chapter 24, "Manipulating Excel with VBA." You can even use VBA to display the Print dialog box. You'll find out how in Chapter 23, "Controlling VBA Code and Interacting with the User."

Exchanging Data with Other Applications

7

Excel doesn't exist in a vacuum. You often have to import data to Excel from other applications (such as a database file or a text file from a mainframe). And just as often you have to export Excel data to other programs (such as a word processor or a presentation graphics package). Although these tasks usually are straightforward, you still can run into some problems. Excel therefore provides some features that can help you avoid these problems. This chapter looks at the various ways you can exchange data between Excel and other applications.

Exchanging Data with Windows Applications

To use text and graphics from another Windows application in Excel (or to use Excel data in another Windows application), you can use any of the following methods:

Cut and paste using the Clipboard: With this method, you cut or copy data from one Windows application and paste it into another.

Linking: With this method, you use a special paste command that sets up a link between the original data and the new copy. When you change the original data, the linked copy is updated automatically.

Embedding: With this method, you create a copy of a file or object from another application and paste the copy into Excel as an embedded object. This embedded copy contains not only the data but also all the underlying information associated with the originating application (file structure, formatting codes, and so on).

These methods are described in the next three sections.

> **NOTE**
>
> Linking and embedding are possible only with applications that support the object linking and embedding (OLE) standard.

Using the Clipboard

The *Clipboard* is a temporary storage location in memory for cut or copied data. It can store text, numbers, graphics, or anything you can cut or copy in a Windows application. You then can switch to a different program and paste the Clipboard data. If you don't want to embed or link the data, follow these steps to exchange data using the Clipboard:

1. Activate the application containing the original data.

2. Select the data, and then select either the **E**dit | **C**ut or the **E**dit | **C**opy command. The data is transferred to the Clipboard. Figure 7.1 shows a table in Word for Windows that has been selected and copied.

FIGURE 7.1.

A Word for Windows table that has been selected and copied to the Clipboard.

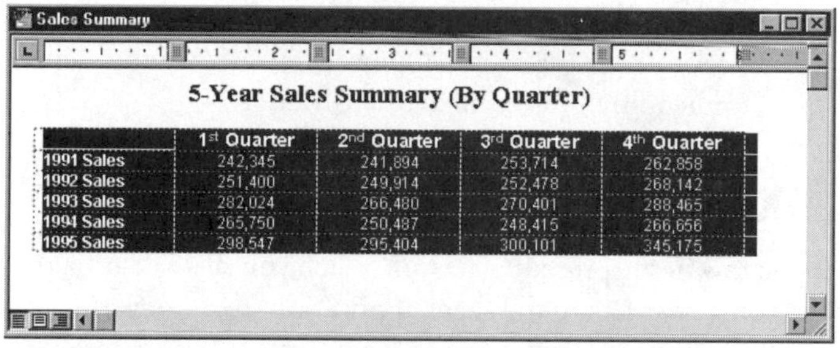

TIP

If you want to copy an Excel range to another application as a picture, select the range, hold down the Shift key, and select the **Edit | Copy** Picture command. For more details on this procedure, head for Chapter 11, "Working with Graphic Objects," and read the section titled "Working with Cell Pictures."

---

3. Switch to the application that you want to receive the data.

4. Move to where you want the data to appear, and select the **Edit | Paste** command. The data is pasted from the Clipboard. Figure 7.2 shows the Word for Windows table pasted into an Excel worksheet.

FIGURE 7.2.

The Word for Windows table pasted into an Excel worksheet.

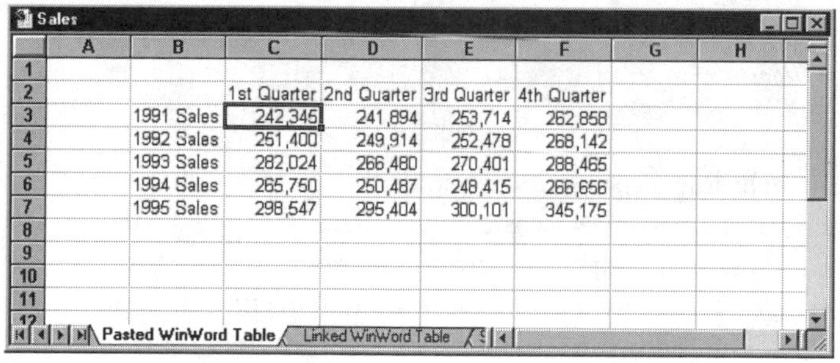

If you're pasting text into Excel, follow these guidelines when you select a location for the text:

- If you want to place the text in a text box, double-click on the text box to get the insertion point, and then position the insertion point where you want the text to appear.

- If you want to position the text within a single cell (provided that there are fewer than 255 characters in the selection), activate either in-cell editing or the formula bar, and then position the insertion point.

■ If you've selected any object before pasting (such as a graphics image or text box), Excel embeds the text as a Picture object. (See the section in this chapter titled "Embedding Objects in a Worksheet.")

Linking Data

As you saw in the preceding section, when you share data via the Clipboard method, Windows sends only raw data to the client application. In other words, if you use the normal Paste command to paste data from a server file into a client application, you must manually change the copied data in the client file whenever the data in the server file is changed.

> **NOTE**
>
> Let's take a second to make sure that you're comfortable with the terminology used with object linking and embedding.
>
> For starters, an *object* is anything you can cut or copy in an application. It can be a section of text, a worksheet range, a bitmap, a sound file, or just about any data you create in an application.
>
> The program you use to create the object is called the *server application* (or sometimes the *source application* or the *object application*).
>
> The program that receives the linked or embedded object is called the *client application* (or sometimes the *destination application* or the *container application*).
>
> A document that contains objects from different applications is called a *compound document.*

By including a special *link* reference when you perform the paste, however, you can eliminate this extra work, because the link updates the copied data automatically. This link tells the client application where the document came from so that the link can check the server file for changes. If the server file has been altered, the link automatically updates the client application's copy. The following procedure shows you how to copy and link data in Excel:

1. Activate the application containing the original data (the *server*).
2. Select the data, and then select **E**dit | **C**opy to copy the data to the Clipboard.
3. Switch to Excel (the *client*), and activate the cell or object that you want to receive the data.
4. Select the **E**dit | Paste **S**pecial command. Excel displays the Paste Special dialog box, shown in Figure 7.3.
5. In the **A**s list, select the format you want to use for the copied data. The options you see depend on the type of data. If you're pasting text, be sure to select Text.
6. Activate the Paste **L**ink option.

FIGURE 7.3.

Use the Paste Special dialog box to select the type of object to paste and to set up the link.

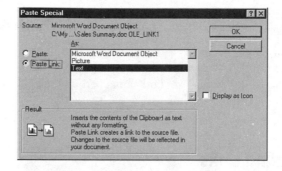

7. Select OK. Excel pastes the data and sets up the link.

CAUTION

If Excel displays the #REF! error when you link the server data, automatic updating of remote references probably has been turned off. To turn it on, select the **T**ools | **O**ptions command, select the Calculation tab in the Options dialog box, and activate the Update **R**emote References check box.

Figure 7.4 shows the same Word for Windows table, but this time it was pasted with a link. The array formula displayed in the formula bar is called a *remote reference formula*. It tells Excel where the server document is located so that it can update the link when necessary. (See the section "The Relationship Between Linking and Word Bookmarks," later in this chapter, for more details about these remote reference formulas.)

FIGURE 7.4.

The Word for Windows table pasted with a link.

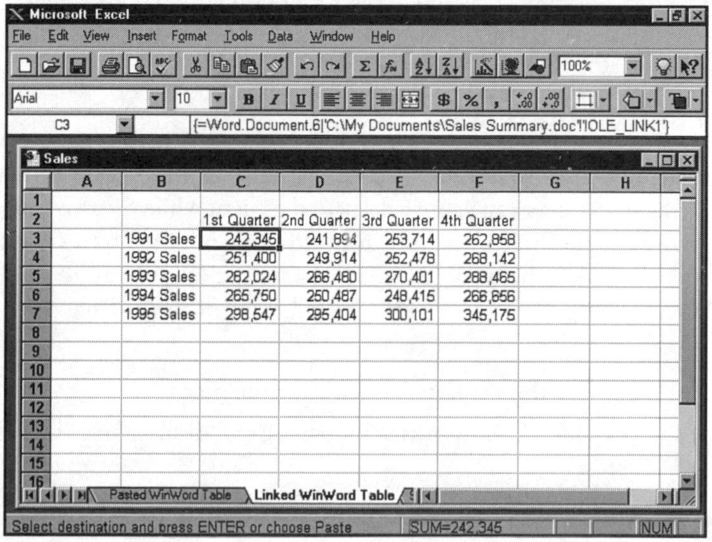

> **NOTE**
>
> You can, of course, use Excel as the server application and link Excel data to a client program. The steps you follow are similar to those in the preceding section. Some applications have a Paste Link command on their Edit menu that enables you to paste and link at the same time.

Updating Links

After you've pasted and linked some data, Excel maintains the links as detailed here:

■ If both the server application and the Excel client workbook are open, Excel updates the link automatically whenever the data in the server file changes.

■ When you open a client workbook that contains automatic links (see the next section), Excel displays a dialog box asking whether you want to update the links. Select **Y**es to update or **N**o to cancel.

> **NOTE**
>
> If you don't want Excel to ask whether to update links, select the **T**ools | **O**ptions command, and select the Edit tab in the Options dialog box. Deactivate the Ask to Update Automatic Links check box, and then select OK.

■ If you didn't update a link when you opened the client workbook, you can update it at any time by selecting the **E**dit | **L**inks command. Then, in the Links dialog box that appears, highlight the link and select the **U**pdate Now button.

Controlling a Link

The problem with linked objects is that they tend to slow you down. Even the smallest change in the server data can cause a delay in the client while the two programs exchange pleasantries. Many people therefore prefer to control the link themselves by switching from an *automatic* link (in which the data gets updated automatically) to a *manual* link (in which the data gets updated only when you say so). The following procedure shows you how to convert to a manual link:

1. Activate the workbook containing the link.
2. Select the **E**dit | **L**inks command. Excel displays the Links dialog box, shown in Figure 7.5.
3. Highlight the link you want to change.

FIGURE 7.5.

Use the Links dialog box to change a link from automatic to manual.

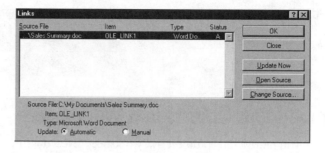

4. Activate the **M**anual option.

5. Select OK.

With a manual link established, you can update the link by displaying the Links dialog box, highlighting the link, and selecting the **U**pdate Now button.

TIP

If a workbook contains many links, you might not want to convert them all to manual. Instead, select the **T**ools | **O**ptions command, and in the Calculation tab, deactivate the **U**pdate Remote References check box. This setting prevents Excel from updating any link, even if you select the **U**pdate Now button in the Links dialog box.

Editing a Link

If the name of the server document changes, you need to edit the link to keep the data up-to-date. One way to edit the link is to edit the external reference directly. Remember, though, that you're dealing with an array formula. You therefore must select the entire array (a quick way to do this is to activate one of the array cells and press Ctrl-/), edit the formula, and then press Ctrl-Shift-Enter.

Alternatively, you can change the source by following these steps:

1. With the client workbook active, select the **E**dit | **Link**s command to display the Links dialog box.

2. Highlight the link you want to change.

3. Select the **C**hange Source button. Excel displays the Change Links dialog box, shown in Figure 7.6.

4. Enter a reference for the new server document, and then select OK to return to the Links dialog box.

5. Select Close to return to the workbook.

FIGURE 7.6.

*Use the Change Links
dialog box to edit the
reference to the server
document.*

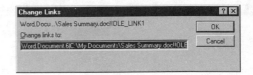

Embedding Objects in a Worksheet

When you paste a linked object in a worksheet, Excel doesn't paste the data. Instead, it sets up a remote reference formula that *points to* the data. If Excel can't find the server file—for example, if the file has been moved, renamed, or deleted—the link breaks and Excel displays a #NAME? error in any cell that used the remote reference.

Embedding differs from linking in that embedded data becomes part of the worksheet. There is no link to the original server document, so it doesn't matter what happens to the original document. In fact, there is no need for a server file at all because the embedded object maintains its native format. Also, you can easily start the server application by double-clicking on one of its objects in the client worksheet. The downside to this convenience is that storing all the information about an embedded object increases the size of the workbook accordingly.

> **NOTE**
>
> In applications that support the OLE standard, an *object* is, in simplest terms, any data you can place on the Clipboard. It could be a section of text, a graphics image, a chart, or anything else you can select and copy.

There are three ways to embed an object in a worksheet:

- Copy the object from the server application, and paste it in the worksheet as an embedded object.
- Insert a new embedded object from within Excel.
- Insert an existing file as an embedded object from within Excel.

Embedding an Object by Pasting

If the object you want to embed already exists, you can place it on the Clipboard and then embed it in the worksheet using the Paste Special command. The following procedure shows you the steps to work through:

1. Activate the server application, and open or create the document that contains the object.

2. Select the object you want to embed.

3. Select the **Edit | Copy** command to place the data on the Clipboard.

4. Activate Excel and open or create the worksheet that you want to receive the data.

5. Select the cell where you want to paste the data.

6. Select the **Edit | Paste Special** command to display the Paste Special dialog box.

7. In the **As** list, select the option that pastes the data as an embedded object. You generally look for one of two clues, depending on the server application:

   ■ The data type contains the word *Object.*

   ■ The data type contains the name of the server application.

8. If you want to see the data in the worksheet, skip to step 10. Otherwise, you can display the object as an icon by activating the **D**isplay as Icon check box. The default icon and the Change **I**con button appear (see Figure 7.7).

FIGURE 7.7.

*You can display an
embedded object as an icon.*

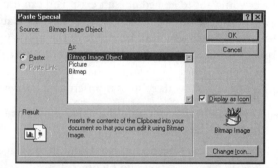

Why would you want to display the object as an icon? The most common reason is that you don't need to see the data all the time. For example, the object might contain explanatory text for a worksheet model. If users of the model need to read the text, they can double-click on the icon.

9. To choose a different icon, select Change **I**con, and then select the image from the Change Icon dialog box. To use a different icon file, select the **B**rowse button, and then select the file from the Browse dialog box. Select OK until you return to the Paste Special dialog box.

10. Select OK. Excel embeds the object in the worksheet.

Figure 7.8 shows a worksheet with a Paint object embedded normally and as an icon.

FIGURE 7.8.

A Paintbrush object embedded normally and as an icon.

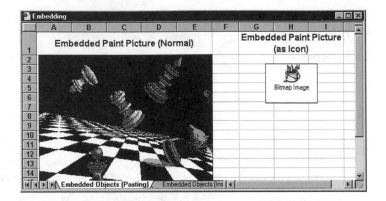

Embedding a New Object by Inserting

If the object you want to embed doesn't exist, you can use Excel to create a new object in the server application and embed it without creating a separate server document. This is, in fact, the only way to embed an object from one of the mini-applications that ship with Excel and other products. Programs such as Microsoft WordArt are not standalone applications, so you can't create separate files. You can use these programs' objects only by inserting them in the client application. Follow these steps to insert a new server object in an Excel worksheet:

1. Select the cell where you want the object embedded. (This cell represents the upper-left corner of the object.)

2. Select the **Insert | O**bject command, and in the Object dialog box that appears, select the Create New tab, shown in Figure 7.9.

FIGURE 7.9.

Use the Create New tab to create a new object for embedding.

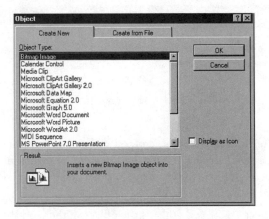

3. In the **O**bject Type list, select the type of object you want to create.

NOTE

You can display the new object as an icon by activating the Display as Icon check box.

4. Select OK. Excel starts the server application.

5. Create the object you want to embed.

6. Exit the server application. Depending on the program you're using, you usually can exit by using one of the following techniques:

   ■ Click outside the object's frame.

   ■ Select the **File | Exit & Return to** *Worksheet* command, in which *Worksheet* is the name of the active Excel worksheet. In this case, the server application asks whether you want to update the embedded object. Select **Yes**.

TIP

In some server applications, you can embed the object without leaving the application by selecting the **File | Update** command.

Figure 7.10 shows a Microsoft WordArt object embedded in a worksheet.

FIGURE 7.10.

A new WordArt object embedded in a worksheet.

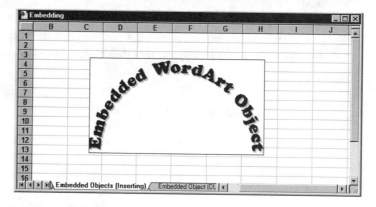

Embedding a File by Inserting

You can insert an entire existing file (as opposed to an object within a file) as an embedded object. This feature is useful if you want to make changes to the file from within Excel without disturbing the original. Follow these steps:

1. Select the cell where you want to embed the object. (This cell represents the upper-left corner of the object.)

2. Select the **I**nsert | **O**bject command, and in the Object dialog box that appears, select the Create from File tab.

3. Use the File **N**ame text box to enter the path for the file you want to insert. If you're not sure, select the **B**rowse button, highlight the file in the Browse dialog box, and then select In**s**ert.

4. If you want the file to appear as an icon, activate the Display as Icon check box.

5. Select OK. Excel embeds the file.

Editing an Embedded Object

If you need to make changes to an embedded object, you can start the server application and automatically load the object by using either of the following methods:

- Double-click on the object.
- Select the object, and then select the **E**dit | *ObjectType* **O**bject | **E**dit command, in which *ObjectType* is the type of object you selected (for example, WordArt or Document).
- Right-click on the object, and then select *ObjectType* **O**bject | **E**dit command, in which *ObjectType* is the type of object you selected.

> **NOTE**
>
> If you double-click on some embedded objects (such as a sound file or a video file), Windows plays the object instead of editing it. In this case, you can edit the object only by choosing the **E**dit | *ObjectType* **O**bject | **E**dit command.

Should You Link or Embed?

Perhaps the most confusing aspect of OLE is determining under what circumstances you should link your objects or embed them. The answer lies in how OLE treats the source data. As I mentioned earlier, when you link an object, OLE doesn't bother sending the data to the client program. Instead, it only sends a reference that tells the client application which file contains the source data. This is enough to maintain the link between the two applications. When you embed an object, however, Windows crams the actual data (and a few other goodies) into the client document.

So you should link your objects if any of the following conditions apply:

- You want to keep your client documents small. The client just gets the link information, and not the data itself, so there's much less overhead associated with linking.

■ The object still needs some work. If you haven't yet completed the object, you should link it so that any further modifications are updated in the client document.

■ You're sure the server file won't be moved or deleted. To maintain the link, OLE requires that the server document remain in the same place. If it gets moved or deleted, the link is broken.

■ You need to keep the server file as a separate document in case you want to make changes to it later, or in case you need it for more OLE operations. You're free to link an object to as many client files as you like. If you think you'll be using the server data in different places, you should link it to maintain a separate file.

■ You won't be sending the client file via e-mail or floppy disk. Again, OLE expects the linked server data to appear in a specific place. If you send the client document to someone else, that person might not have the proper server file to maintain the link.

Similarly, you should embed your objects if any of the following conditions applies:

■ You don't care how big your client files get. Embedding works best in situations in which you have lots of hard disk space and lots of memory.

■ You don't need to keep the server file as a separate document. If you need to use the server data only once, embedding it means you can get rid of the server file and reduce the clutter on your hard disk.

■ You'll be sending the client document and you want to ensure that the object arrives intact. If you send a file containing an embedded object, the other person will see the data complete and unaltered.

Working with OLE 2 Applications

The latest version of object linking and embedding—version 2—includes many new features that make embedded objects even easier to create and maintain. Here's a summary of just a few of these features:

Drag and drop objects between applications: You can move information between two open OLE 2 applications simply by dragging selected data from one application and dropping it in the other. If you want to copy the data, you need to hold down the Ctrl key while dragging.

In-place inserting: If you select an OLE 2 object from the Create New tab in the Object dialog box, Excel activates *in-place* inserting. This means that instead of displaying the server application in a separate window, certain features of the Excel window are temporarily hidden so that the server's features can be displayed:

■ Excel's title bar changes to the name of the server application.

■ The Excel menu bar (with the exception of the **F**ile and **W**indow menus) is replaced by the server's menu bar.

■ The Excel toolbars are replaced by the server's toolbars.

■ Any other features you need for creating the server object (such as the Ruler in Word for Windows) are also added to the window.

To exit in-place editing and embed the object, click outside the object frame. Figure 7.11 shows what happens to the Excel window when you insert a Word for Windows (version 6 or later) document object.

FIGURE 7.11.

The Excel window displays many features of the Word for Windows window when you insert a Word document object.

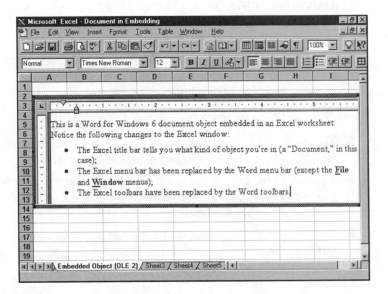

In-place editing: When you edit an OLE 2 object, the object remains where it is, and the Excel window changes as it does with in-place inserting. Make your changes and then click outside the object to complete the edit.

Exchanging Data with the Other Microsoft Office Programs

As you might expect, Excel data sharing works best with the other programs that come with the Microsoft Office suite: Word, PowerPoint, and Access. In the Office 95 package, the links between these programs are even tighter and more integrated than before. Microsoft's goal with this new Office suite (and, indeed, with all of Windows 95) is to turn the user's attention away from working with applications and more toward working with documents. This is a laudable goal, because for too long now, we users have been shaping our documents to fit the application we were using, rather than the other way around. We need to start thinking of applications as mere tools that help us achieve a particular result.

To that end, the Office applications boast three features that can help us focus on our documents:

- The applications themselves share a common user interface. For example, the menu structures and toolbar buttons in all the office programs are nearly identical. Also, many of the Office programs share common modules, such as the spell checker.

- Support for OLE 2 in all the Office applications makes it easier to create and maintain compound documents.

- The addition of the Binder application (which we'll talk about a little later) makes it easy to combine related documents from multiple applications into a single file for distribution.

Although most of your Office data-sharing will follow the basic OLE steps we looked at in the preceding few sections, a few shortcuts and techniques are specific to the Office applications. The next few sections fill you in on the details.

Working with Word

As the word processor in the Office group, Microsoft Word is a popular choice as a client application because worksheets, ranges, and charts are often used to back up statements in a proposal or memo. However, exchanging data between Word and Excel isn't always straightforward because, depending on how you paste the information, it's often hard to predict the result. To help out, the next couple of sections tell you exactly what to expect when sharing data between Word and Excel.

Exporting an Excel Range to Word

When you copy a range in Excel and then select Word's Edit | Paste Special command, the Paste Special dialog box gives you five data types to use for the paste. To help you decide which option is best for you, Table 7.1 summarizes each data type.

Table 7.1. Data types available for pasting an Excel range.

Data Type	Description
Microsoft Excel Worksheet Object	Embeds the range as a Worksheet object.
Formatted Text (RTF)	Pastes the range as a Word table and preserves existing formatting.
Unformatted Text	Pastes the range as plain text with tabs separating each column and linefeeds separating each row.

continues

Table 7.1. continued

Data Type	Description
Picture	Inserts the range as a picture. Use this data type rather than Bitmap to preserve memory and keep screen redraws fast.
Bitmap	Inserts the range as a bitmap image. The only advantage over the Picture data type is that the bitmap image shows you exactly what the Excel range looks like.

TIP

When an Excel range is on the Clipboard, selecting Word's **E**dit | **P**aste command is the same as selecting Edit | Paste **S**pecial and choosing the Formatted Text (RTF) option.

NOTE

If you copy an Excel chart to the Clipboard, Word's Paste Special dialog box offers you three data types: Microsoft Excel Chart Object, Picture, and Bitmap.

Creating a New Excel Worksheet in Word

Earlier I showed you how to embed a new object in a client document by using the client application's **I**nsert | **O**bject command. If you want to embed a new Excel worksheet object in a Word document, you can select Word's **I**nsert | **O**bject command and choose Microsoft Excel Worksheet as the object type. If you have a mouse handy, however, Word gives you an even easier way to embed a new worksheet object, as shown in these steps:

1. In Word, position the insertion-point cursor at the spot where you want the worksheet object to appear.
2. Move the mouse pointer over the Insert Microsoft Excel Worksheet button in Word's Standard toolbar, and then press and hold down the left mouse button. A grid appears below the toolbar.

3. Each grid cell represents a cell in the range. To define the size of the range you want, drag the mouse pointer into the grid and highlight the appropriate number of rows and columns you want (see Figure 7.12).

FIGURE 7.12.

Drag the mouse pointer into the grid to define the number of rows and columns in your embedded range.

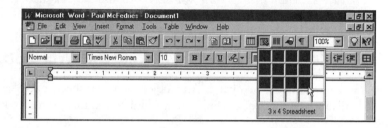

4. Release the mouse button. Word embeds the range and activates in-place inserting.

5. Enter your data, formulas, and formatting using the Excel menus, toolbars, and formula bar.

6. When you're done, click outside the object.

Importing Text from Word

Copying Word text to the Clipboard and then pasting it into Excel is straightforward. The Paste Special dialog box gives you a choice of three data types, as described in Table 7.2.

Table 7.2. Data types available for pasting Word text.

Data Type	Description
Microsoft Word Document Object	Embeds the text as a Document object.
Picture	Inserts the text as a picture.
Text	Pastes the text as unformatted text. Places text separated by tabs into separate columns; places paragraphs into separate rows.

TIP

When Word text is on the Clipboard, selecting Excel's **Edit** | **P**aste command is the same as selecting **Edit** | Paste **S**pecial and choosing the Text data type.

> **NOTE**
>
> If you copy a Word table to the Clipboard and you would prefer to insert the content of each table cell into its own worksheet cell, use the Text data type when pasting.

The Relationship Between Linking and Word Bookmarks

As you saw earlier, when you link an object in a worksheet, Excel sets up a remote reference formula to keep track of the link. For a Word object, this formula takes the following general form:

```
=Word.Document.6¦DocumentName!''!BookmarkName'
```

Here, *DocumentName* is the full pathname of the Word document containing the original text, and *BookmarkName* is the name of a special bookmark that Excel creates in the Word document. For example, if this is the first time you've linked text from a particular document, Excel creates a bookmark named OLE_LINK1. (To prove this for yourself, display the Word document, select the **E**dit | **B**ookmark command, highlight the OLE_LINK1 bookmark in the Bookmark dialog box, and then select the **G**o To button. Word takes you right to the linked text.)

If you already have bookmarks set up in a Word document, you can create your own remote reference formulas from scratch. Here's how it's done:

1. In Excel, select a range with enough rows to hold all the paragraphs in your bookmarked text. (If the text contains tabs, you'll need to select enough columns as well.)

2. In the formula bar, enter the remote reference formula. Make sure that you enter the full pathname for the document (the drive, folder, and filename), as well as the bookmark name.

3. Press Ctrl-Shift-Enter. Excel pastes the text into the selected range.

Working with PowerPoint

Exchanging data between Excel and PowerPoint uses methods similar to those for Word. Here are a few things to bear in mind:

■ When you're pasting a range, PowerPoint's Paste Special dialog box gives you the same data type choices as does Word.

■ PowerPoint tends to insert worksheets and charts as rather small objects. To see the range properly, you need to increase the size of the object.

- If you want to insert a new worksheet object into a slide, you can use PowerPoint's Insert Microsoft Excel Worksheet button on its Standard toolbar. This button works just like the one on Word's Standard toolbar.

Working with Access

If your database needs to extend only to simple, flat-file tables, Excel's built-in database capabilities probably will do the job for you. (See Chapter 12, "Working with Lists and Databases," to learn Excel's database ropes.) For larger table and relational features, however, you'll want to use a more sophisticated application such as Access. The next couple of sections show you how to share data between Excel and Access.

Exporting Excel Data to Access

To get Excel data into Access, you can use either the Clipboard or the Import Spreadsheet Wizard feature in Access.

To use the Clipboard method, you need to set up an Access table with the same number of fields as there are columns in the range you want to copy. When that's done, follow these steps to paste the data into the table:

1. In Excel, copy the data to the Clipboard.

2. In Access, open the table (Datasheet view), move to the new record at the bottom of the table, and select the first field.

3. Select the **Edit | Paste Append** command. Access pastes the data into the table and displays a dialog box letting you know how many records are about to be added.

4. Select **Yes** to return to the table.

> **CAUTION**
>
> If the Excel range you're copying has more columns than there are fields in the Access table, Access ignores the extra columns.

To use the Import Spreadsheet Wizard method, follow these steps:

1. In Excel, close the workbook you'll be importing, if it's currently open.

2. In Access, select the **File | Get External Data | Import** command. Access displays the Import dialog box.

3. Highlight Microsoft Excel in the Files of **type** list.

4. Highlight the workbook you want to import, and then select Import. Access starts the Import Spreadsheet Wizard, shown in Figure 7.13.

FIGURE 7.13.

Use the first Import Spreadsheet Wizard dialog box to tell Access the name of the worksheet or range you want to import.

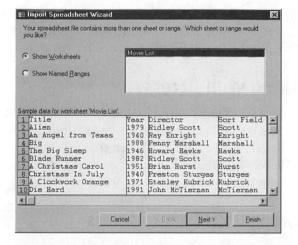

TIP

You can bypass steps 1 through 4 if you've loaded Excel's AccessLinks add-in file. With this add-in loaded, select a cell inside the table you want to export and then choose the **Data | Convert** to Access command to start the Import Spreadsheet Wizard.

---

5. Either activate the Show **W**orksheets option and highlight the worksheet you want to import, or activate the Show Named **R**anges option and highlight the named range you want to import. When you're done, select **N**ext > to display the next Import Spreadsheet Wizard dialog box.

6. If the first row of the worksheet or range contains the field names you want to use, activate the **i**nclude Field Names on First Row check box.

7. Use the Start Importing Data at **R**ow text box to specify the first row to import, and then select **N**ext > to display the next Import Spreadsheet Wizard dialog box, shown in Figure 7.14.

8. For each field (column), enter a Field **N**ame and specify whether the field should be **I**ndexed. If you want the Wizard to bypass a field, activate the Do not import field (**S**kip) check box. To select a different field, click on the field's header. When you're done, select **N**ext > to move to the next dialog box.

9. The next Wizard dialog box lets you specify a primary key for the new table. You have three choices (select **N**ext > after you've made your choice):

   ■ Let **A**ccess add Primary Key: Choose this option to tell Access to create a new field (called ID) to use as the primary key.

■ **C**hoose my own Primary Key: Choose this option to select a primary key from one of the existing fields (which you select from the associated drop-down list).

■ **N**o Primary Key: Choose this option if you don't want to specify a primary key for the new table.

FIGURE 7.14.

Use this Import Spreadsheet Wizard dialog box to specify information about each field you're importing.

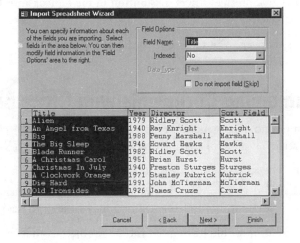

10. In the final Import Spreadsheet Wizard dialog box, enter a name for the new table in the Import to Table text box. If you would like the Wizard to analyze the structure of the table (to look for data redundancies and other relational issues), activate the check box. When you're ready, select **F**inish. Access creates the new table and displays a dialog box to let you know.

11. Select OK to return to the database.

Importing Data from Access

Getting table records from Access to Excel can also be done in one of two ways: with the Clipboard or with the Analyze It With MS Excel feature. Here's a rundown of the Clipboard method:

1. In Access, open the table (Datasheet view), and select the records you want to import.

2. Select **E**dit | **C**opy to place the records on the Clipboard.

3. In Excel, select the destination for the records.

4. Select **E**dit | **P**aste. Excel pastes the field names in the current row and the records in separate rows below.

The Analyze It With MS Excel feature can convert an Access database object into an Excel worksheet and open the new sheet in Excel all in one step. To try it out, open the datasheet, form, or report that you want to convert, and then do one of the following:

- Select the **T**ools | Office**L**inks | **A**nalyze It With MS Excel command.
- Click on the OfficeLinks button in the toolbar and then select Analyze It With MS Excel.

Access converts the table into an Excel worksheet, activates Excel, and then loads the new worksheet.

Combining Documents with Office Binder

Compound documents are easiest to work with if the objects linked or embedded inside them are relatively small. Inserting a large worksheet into, say, Word has two disadvantages:

- The large sheet clutters the document and makes it hard to scroll.
- Word scales down wide ranges so that they'll fit inside the page margins. If the object is scaled too much, the text becomes difficult to read.

One solution would be to insert the range object as an icon. This method works, but it's not as convenient as seeing the full range.

A better solution is the Binder program that ships with Microsoft Office 95. A binder document is a special container file designed to hold entire files from other applications. For example, suppose that you are putting together a sales proposal. It might include several memos written in Word, some worksheets and charts built in Excel, and a slide show created in PowerPoint. Rather than embedding all of these files into a single Word or Excel compound document, you can insert everything into a binder file. The binder displays an icon for each file, and when you click on an icon, Binder displays the contents of the file in its native format.

Starting Binder

To get Binder started, select the Start button, open the Start menu's **P**rograms folder, open the Microsoft Office folder, and then select Microsoft Binder. The Binder window appears, as shown in Figure 7.15.

Each file you add to the binder is called a *section*. The icons for each section appear in the column that runs down the left side of the window. The contents of each section are shown in the large gray area to the right.

FIGURE 7.15.
The Binder window.

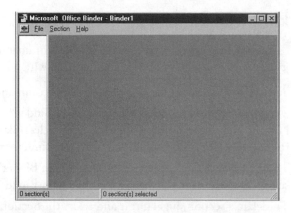

Adding a Section to the Binder

To add a section to the binder, you have two choices:

■ Add an existing file as a section. You do this by selecting the **S**ection | Add from **F**ile command, highlighting the file in the Add from File dialog box, and then selecting A**d**d.

■ Add a new, blank section. In this case, select the **S**ection | **A**dd command, highlight the type of file in the Add Section dialog box, and then select OK.

Figure 7.16 shows a binder with several sections added. To display the contents of a section, just click on its icon. Binder is an OLE 2 application, so it activates in-place editing: it opens the section's application, displays the application's menus and toolbars, and then displays the file in its native format. You're free to work with the file as you normally would in the application.

FIGURE 7.16.
Click on a section to display the contents of the file in its native format.

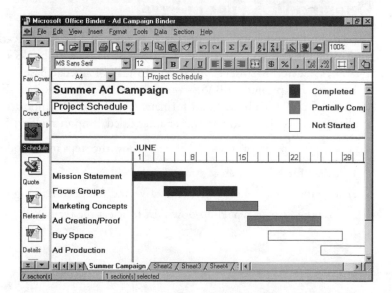

Working with Binder

Binder's File and Section menus contain all kinds of commands for working with sections. Here's a quick summary of the sorts of things you can do with a Binder file:

- To save the file, select the **F**ile | **S**ave Binder command (or press Ctrl-S).
- To start a new binder, select the **F**ile | **N**ew Binder command (or press Ctrl-N). In the New Binder dialog box that appears, either select Blank Binder in the General tab or select one of the binder templates from the Binders tab.
- To open an existing binder, select **F**ile | **O**pen Binder (or press Ctrl-O), and then select the binder file you want from the Open Binder dialog box.
- To delete a section, highlight it and select the **S**ection | **D**elete command. (Note that doing so deletes only the section from the binder. It doesn't delete the underlying file.)
- To rearrange the order of a section, either drag its icon to the new location, or select the **S**ection | **R**earrange command and then use the Rearrange Sections dialog box to move the sections.
- To hide a section, click on it and then select **S**ection | **H**ide.

Exchanging Data with DOS Applications

Many Excel users have a foot in both the Windows and the DOS camps. They use some Windows applications (such as Excel), but they also use some DOS programs (such as dBASE or WordPerfect). If you're one of those people, this section shows you how to exchange data between Excel and a DOS application.

Opening DOS Files in Excel

Excel can open and work with files from the following DOS applications: Lotus 1-2-3 (as described in the section of this chapter titled "Moving Workbooks Between Excel and Lotus 1-2-3"), Quattro Pro, Microsoft Works, dBASE (or any database management program, such as FoxPro, that produces dBASE-compatible files), and files in DIF (Data Interchange Format) and SYLK (Symbolic Link) formats. (Excel also can import text files created by DOS applications. See the section in this chapter titled "Importing Text Files.")

To open a file for one of these programs, follow the steps in the following procedure.

1. Select the **F**ile | **O**pen command.
2. Use the Look **i**n list to select the drive and folder containing the file you want to open.
3. Use the Files of **t**ype drop-down list to select the type of file you want to open.

4. Highlight the filename.

5. Select **O**pen.

> **NOTE**
>
> If Excel doesn't recognize the structure of the file you're opening, the Text Import Wizard dialog box might appear. See the section in this chapter titled "Importing Text Files" to learn how to use the Text Import Wizard.

Copying Text from a DOS Application

The best way to copy text from a DOS application is to place the program in a window and highlight the text you want. The following procedure takes you through the required steps:

1. Switch to the DOS application and place it in a window (if it's not already in a window) by pressing Alt-Enter.

> **NOTE**
>
> If the DOS application is running in graphics mode, when you copy a section of the screen, you're copying a graphic image of the text, not the text itself. If you want text only, make sure that the program is running in character mode before continuing.

2. When the text you want to copy is on-screen, pull down the window's Control menu (by clicking on the Control-menu box or by pressing Alt-Spacebar), and select the **E**dit | Ma**r**k command. A blinking cursor appears just below the Control menu box.

3. Highlight the information you want to copy.

4. Press Enter to copy the selection.

5. Switch to Excel and select the cell or object that you want to receive the text.

6. Select the **E**dit | **P**aste command. Excel pastes the text.

> **NOTE**
>
> If you want to copy a graphic image from a DOS application, activate the program and press the Print Screen key. Because this method copies the *entire* window (scroll bars, title bar, and all), you might first want to edit the image in a dedicated graphics program such as Paint.

Pasting Excel Data to a DOS Application

Follow these steps to paste Excel data to a DOS application:

1. Select the data you want to copy, and then choose the **Edit | Copy** command. This action places the data into the Clipboard.

2. Switch to the DOS application and place it in a window.

3. Position the cursor where you want the data to appear.

4. Pull down the window's Control menu, and select the **Edit | Paste** command. The Clipboard copies the data to the application and places a Tab between each cell's data.

Importing Text Files

When you import text data, Excel usually breaks up the file according to the position of the carriage-return and line-feed characters. This means that each line in the text file gets inserted into a cell. In most cases, this is not the behavior you want. For example, if you've downloaded some stock data, you need the date, volume, and pricing values in separate columns.

Instead of making you divide each line by hand, Excel includes a TextWizard tool that can parse text files in the usual step-by-step fashion of the Wizards. How you use the TextWizard depends on the format of the text. There are two possibilities:

Delimited text: Each field is separated by characters such as commas, spaces, or tabs.

Fixed width text: The fields are aligned in columns.

If you're not sure which type of file you're dealing with, just start the TextWizard as described in either of the following two procedures. In most cases, the TextWizard can determine the data type for you.

To import a text file (or to convert worksheet text into columns), follow these steps:

1. To open the text file, select the **File | Open** command, and then select the file from the Open dialog box. (To help out, select the Text Files option from the List Files of **T**ype list.) Excel displays the Text Import Wizard - Step 1 of 3 dialog box, shown in Figure 7.17.

   Or, if you want to convert worksheet text, select the text and select the **D**ata | T**e**xt to Columns command. Excel displays the Convert Text to Columns Wizard - Step 1 of 3 dialog box.

2. In the Original Data Type group, activate either **D**elimited or Fixed **W**idth.

3. If you're importing a text file, enter a number in the Start Import at **R**ow spinner, and then select the file's native environment from the File **O**rigin drop-down list.

4. Select the Next > button to move to the Wizard's Step 2 dialog box, shown in Figure 7.18.

FIGURE 7.17.

Use the Text Import Wizard - Step 1 of 3 dialog box to select the type of text file you're importing.

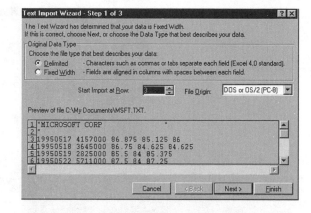

FIGURE 7.18.

The Text Import Wizard - Step 2 of 3 dialog box for delimited data.

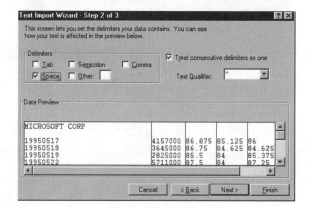

5. If you're using a delimited file, select the appropriate delimiting character from the Delimiters check boxes. If the data includes text in quotation marks, select the appropriate quotation mark character from the Text **Q**ualifier list.

   If you're using a fixed-width file, you can set up the column breaks by using the following techniques:

   ■ To create a column break, click inside the Data Preview area at the spot where you want the break to occur.

   ■ To move a column break, drag it to the new location.

   ■ To delete a column break, double-click on it.

6. Select the Next > button to move to the Wizard's Step 3 dialog box, shown in Figure 7.19.

7. Select each column and then choose one of the options from the Column Data Format group. (You select a column by clicking on the column header.) If you don't want a column imported, activate the Do Not **I**mport Column (Skip) option.

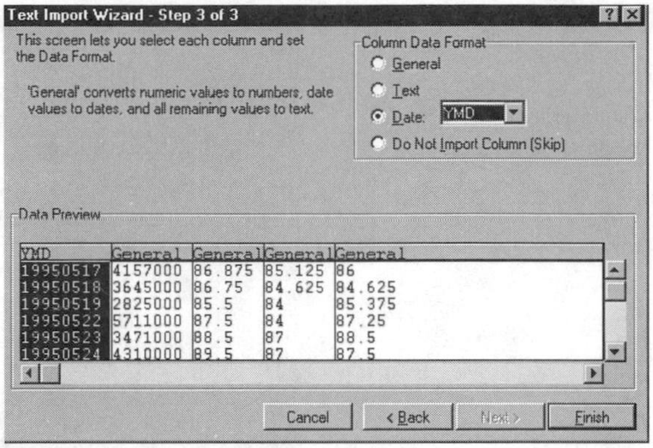

FIGURE 7.19.

Use the Step 3 of 3 dialog box to select and format the columns.

8. Select **Finish**. Excel imports the text file, as shown in Figure 7.20.

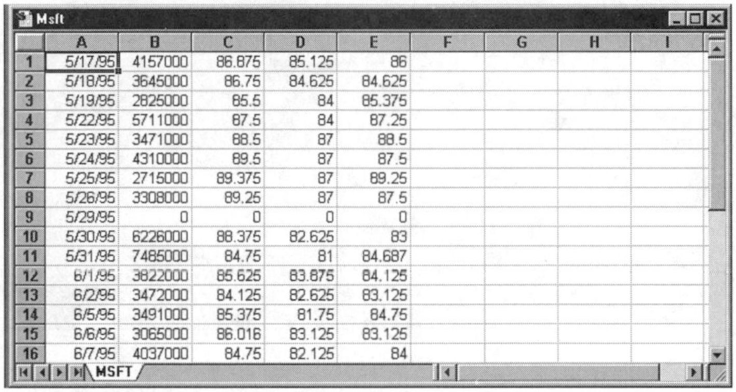

FIGURE 7.20.

The text file imported into Excel.

Notes for Lotus 1-2-3 Users Switching to Excel

Microsoft recognized early on that many people using Excel would not be first-time spreadsheet users, but instead would be users of other spreadsheet programs who decided to switch to Excel. Because Lotus 1-2-3 is the dominant spreadsheet in the DOS market, it was reasonable to assume that most people making the switch would be former 1-2-3 users.

With this fact in mind, Microsoft has included a fistful of features to make the transition from 1-2-3 to Excel as smooth and untroubled as possible. Here are a few of these features:

- Excel's Help system includes not only a tutorial designed specifically for former 1-2-3 users, but also a feature that enables you to enter 1-2-3 keystrokes and commands and then see how to do the same thing in Excel.

- You can set up Excel to accept 1-2-3-style formulas and navigation keys.
- Excel reads 1-2-3's .FMT files so that your careful formatting is preserved when you load a file into Excel.
- Excel has a macro translator that enables you to run most of your 1-2-3 macros in Excel without modification.

This section covers just the features you need to know to get started using Excel. To learn more about working with 1-2-3 files, see the section "Moving Workbooks Between Excel and Lotus 1-2-3," later in this chapter.

The Basic Differences Between Excel and 1-2-3

If you're switching to Excel from one of the DOS versions of 1-2-3, the most obvious differences you'll see are those related to the Windows environment: being able to open multiple worksheets and display each in its own movable and sizable window; navigating a sheet using scroll bars; and using pull-down menus to select commands.

Probably the biggest difference between Excel and 1-2-3 for DOS is the basic procedure you use to implement most commands. In 1-2-3, first you select a command, and then you select the cell or range to use with the command. In Excel, this procedure is reversed: first you select the range, and then you select the command. This procedure might seem strange at first, but it has one big advantage: when the command finishes, the range is still selected. You therefore can immediately apply another command to the same group of cells.

You'll find that Excel uses slightly different terminology for many commands and features. Table 7.3 lists a few common Lotus terms and their Excel equivalents.

Table 7.3. Excel equivalents for common 1-2-3 terminology.

1-2-3 Term	Excel Equivalent
@function	Function
Address	Reference
Border	Row and column headings
Cell pointer	Active cell
Control panel	Menu bar, formula bar
Cursor	Insertion point
Data range	Data series
Data table 1	One-input table
Data table 2	Two-input table

continues

Table 7.3. continued

1-2-3 Term	Excel Equivalent
Database	List
Formula criteria	Computed criteria
Global	Workspace
Graph	Chart
Highlight	Select
Input range	List range
Label	Text
Label prefix	Alignment
Logical 0	FALSE
Logical 1	TRUE
Output range	Extract range
Print range	Print area
Prompt	Dialog box
Range highlight	Selected range
Target cell	Dependent cell

Navigating Excel

As you'll see later, you can use the Help system to learn Excel while still using 1-2-3 commands and keyboard techniques. If you need to get up to speed quickly, however, you can set up Excel to use a different set of navigation keys that more closely resemble those you're used to working with.

Before doing that, however, you should learn the keys that are the same in Lotus and Excel. Table 7.4 lists them.

Table 7.4. Compatible 1-2-3 and Excel keys.

Key	Function
Right arrow	Moves right one column
Left arrow	Moves left one column
Up arrow	Moves up one row
Down arrow	Moves down one row

Key	Function
Page Up	Moves up one page
Page Down	Moves down one page
F1	Displays Help
F2	Edits the current cell
F4	Toggles the reference format
F5	Activates Go To
F6	Moves to the next pane (or window, in Excel)
F9	Calculates the worksheet

To try out the alternative keys, select the **T**ools | **O**ptions command, and in the Transition tab, activate the Transition Navigation **K**eys check box. Select OK to put this new option into effect. Table 7.5 presents a list of the keys that change when you activate this option.

Table 7.5. Keys that change when you select the Transition Navigation Keys option.

Key	Normal Excel Function	Alternative Function
Home	Moves to the first cell	Moves to cell A1 in the row
Tab	Moves right one column	Moves right one page
Shift-Tab	Moves left one column	Moves left one page
Ctrl-right arrow	Moves right to next block	Moves right one screen of data
Ctrl-left arrow	Moves left to next block	Moves left one screen of data
"	N/A	Right-aligns the cell text
^	N/A	Centers the cell text
\	N/A	Fills the cell with the characters that follow

NOTE

You can use 1-2-3's left-align prefix (') regardless of whether the Transition Navigation Keys option is selected.

Entering Formulas

An Excel formula is fundamentally the same as a 1-2-3 formula: it's a series of values or functions separated by operators that calculates a final result. Without modifying Excel, you can enter most formulas exactly as in 1-2-3. However, Excel converts the formula to its native format. Here are the differences to expect:

- Excel formulas begin with an equals sign (=) rather than a plus sign (+). You can start an Excel formula with a plus sign, but Excel adds an equals sign to the beginning of the formula.

- Excel functions don't use the @ prefix. You can still use it if you like, but Excel strips it when you confirm the formula.

- Excel range references use a colon (:) between two cell addresses rather than the double dots (..) you used in 1-2-3. Again, you can use the dot notation, but Excel converts it to a colon.

To make formula entry even more similar to that in 1-2-3, Excel has a Transition Formula Entry feature that changes how Excel uses range names in formulas. Excel automatically selects this option when you open a 1-2-3 spreadsheet, but you can use it with Excel worksheets by selecting the **T**ools | **O**ptions command and then activating the Transition Formula Entry check box in the Transition tab. See "Excel Changes Its Settings When You Import a 1-2-3 File," later in this chapter, for an explanation of the changes this option provides.

Another feature you can use to make Excel more like 1-2-3 is the Transition Formula Evaluation setting. You activate this option by selecting the **T**ools | **O**ptions command. Then, in the Transition tab, you activate the Transition Formula Evaluation check box. This setting controls aspects of how Excel treats certain worksheet values and functions. Again, see the "Excel Changes Its Settings When You Import a 1-2-3 File" section for a summary.

> **CAUTION**
>
> If you plan to use Transition Formula Entry and Transition Formula Evaluation in a worksheet, set these options before you enter any data, and leave them on. Switching them on and off can throw off the worksheet calculations.

Using the Help System to Learn Excel

One of the biggest hurdles you face when you move to a new application is overcoming your ingrained keyboard habits. What felt natural and smooth in your old program will feel strange and uncomfortable in the new one. Of course, because humans are such adaptable creatures, you'll get used to things fairly quickly and soon will find yourself wondering how you ever could have used that clunky old application.

To ease the transition, Excel's Help system provides a feature that shows you how to perform Lotus 1-2-3 tasks in Excel. You can either see a demonstration of the task in Excel or read a text box created by the Help system that contains instructions.

Demonstrating Excel Commands

To see a demonstration of the Excel equivalent of a 1-2-3 command, follow these steps:

1. Select the **H**elp | Lotus 1-2-3 Help command. Excel displays the Help for Lotus 1-2-3 Users dialog box, shown in Figure 7.21.

FIGURE 7.21.

Use the Help for Lotus 1-2-3 Users dialog box to see a demonstration of the Excel equivalent of a 1-2-3 command.

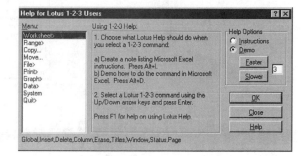

2. Make sure that the **D**emo option is selected in the Help Options group.
3. In the **M**enu list, select the 1-2-3 command you want demonstrated.
4. Select OK.
5. Excel might ask you for more information. Enter the required data and select OK. Excel then performs the demonstration.

TIP

You can adjust the speed of the demonstration. Display the Help for Lotus 1-2-3 Users dialog box, and then, before starting the demonstration, select either the **F**aster or the **S**lower button.

Displaying Instructions for Excel Commands

To create a text box containing the instructions for an Excel equivalent of a 1-2-3 command, follow these steps:

1. Select the **H**elp | Lotus 1-2-3 Help command to display the Help for Lotus 1-2-3 Users dialog box.

2. Activate the **I**nstructions option in the Help Options group.

3. In the **M**enu list, select the 1-2-3 command you want demonstrated.

4. Select OK. Excel creates the text box, as shown in Figure 7.22.

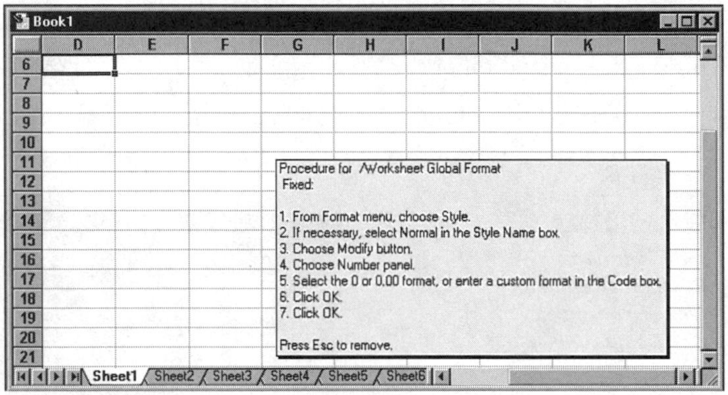

FIGURE 7.22.

The Help system can create a text box containing the instructions for an Excel equivalent of a 1-2-3 command.

Moving Workbooks Between Excel and Lotus 1-2-3

If it's not overly dramatic to discuss software in terms of geopolitical forces, I can summarize the current struggle for domination in the spreadsheet market as the struggle between two countries: Excel (in Windows) and Lotus 1-2-3 (in DOS). Both countries seek to expand their borders and increase their populations by offering new perks and features and by encouraging immigration with attractive incentives and entitlement programs.

Even though their governments might have declared a spreadsheet war, the citizens of both countries still need to work together and cross each other's borders with a minimum of culture shock. In this section, I show you how to make Excel and 1-2-3 work together. I also show you how to transfer files back and forth so that you preserve not only worksheet accuracy but also your careful formatting.

Many offices today use a mixture of Excel and 1-2-3. For example, the Accounting department might use 1-2-3 exclusively, whereas the Sales and Marketing departments might have switched to Excel when they converted their machines to Windows. Both types of users often need to exchange information, so it's important that the transition be as smooth as possible. Excel recognized this fact long ago and thus made it easy to import 1-2-3 files into Excel and to export Excel files to 1-2-3 format. You have to watch out for some pitfalls, however. I'll discuss these later.

Importing a 1-2-3 File into Excel

Excel can import 1-2-3 files that are in the following formats:

Lotus Release	Format
1A	WKS
2. x	WK1
2.3, 2.4 (formatting)	FMT
3.x	WK3
3.1, 3.1+ (formatting)	FM3
4.x	WK4
1-2-3/W	WK3, FM3

To import a 1-2-3 file, follow these steps:

1. Select the **File** | **O**pen command.
2. Use the Look **in** list to select the drive and folder containing the 1-2-3 file you want to import.
3. To see only 1-2-3 files in the list, select Lotus 1-2-3 Files from the Files of **t**ype drop-down list.
4. Highlight the file you want to import.
5. Select OK.

How Excel Imports 1-2-3 Files

Excel usually imports 1-2-3 files without fuss, but you should be aware of the following characteristics of the importing process:

- 3-D worksheets (WK3 format) are imported as multiple-tab workbooks. The 3-D formulas are preserved, and each 3-D level is given its own workbook tab.
- If Excel can't interpret a formula, it uses the calculated value of the formula.
- If the worksheet's FMT or FM3 formatting file has the same name as the worksheet and is in the same directory, Excel reads the formatting and tries to duplicate it.
- If the worksheet has no formatting file, Excel uses Courier 10 as the Normal style font.
- Unprotected cells appear in a blue font.
- Formula comments (that is, any text that follows a semicolon in a formula) get imported into a cell note.

Figure 7.23 shows a typical 1-2-3 worksheet (without an associated FMT file) imported into Excel.

FIGURE 7.23.

A 1-2-3 worksheet imported into Excel.

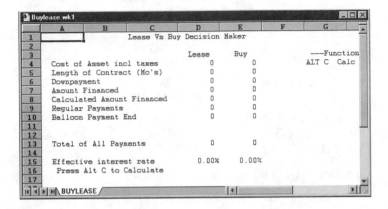

Excel Changes Its Settings When You Import a 1-2-3 File

When you import a 1-2-3 file, Excel changes some option settings to make using a 1-2-3 worksheet easier for you. The settings it changes are in the Transition tab of the Options dialog box, shown in Figure 7.24. You can display this dialog box by selecting the **T**ools | **O**ptions command.

FIGURE 7.24.

The Transition tab in the Options dialog box controls settings that make Excel operate more like 1-2-3.

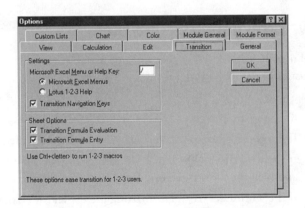

Here's a rundown of some of the options in the Transition tab:

Transition Navigation **K**eys: This option changes the functions of some Excel keystrokes. See Table 7.5 for a list of the changes.

Transition **F**ormula Evaluation: Excel also activates this check box. This option causes Excel to handle formula evaluation in the following ways:

- If the lookup value in the HLOOKUP() and VLOOKUP() functions is text, Excel does three things differently: (1) it looks for exact matches rather than the largest value that is less than or equal to the lookup value; (2) the row or column you're using for the search can be in any order; and (3) if the third argument (the one that tells Excel how many rows or columns into the table to look for the desired value) is 1, Excel returns the offset of the matched lookup value, not the value itself. For example, if you're using VLOOKUP() and the lookup value is in the fourth row of the lookup column, Excel returns 4 if VLOOKUP()'s third argument is 1.

- Conditional tests return 1 rather than TRUE and 0 rather than FALSE.

- When one of the MOD() function's arguments is negative, MOD() returns different values depending on the setting of this check box. For example, the formula =MOD(-24,10) returns 6 when Transition Formula Evaluation is off and – 4 when it's on.

- Text strings are assigned the value 0.

- You can't concatenate numeric values. If you try to, Excel returns a #VALUE! error.

- You can't use string functions on numeric values. If you try to, Excel returns a #VALUE! error.

Transition Formula Entry: Excel activates this check box if there are any macro names on the worksheet. This option causes Excel to handle formula entry in the following ways:

- If you enter a reference that corresponds to a named range you've defined, Excel automatically converts the reference to the appropriate name after you confirm the entry. Note that this feature works only for contiguous ranges. Because Excel enables you to define noncontiguous ranges, this feature might not always work.

- If a formula contains a range name, activating the formula bar changes the name to its underlying reference.

- If you delete a range name, formulas containing the name automatically convert to their underlying reference.

- If you add a dollar sign ($) before a range name, Excel makes the name absolute.

CAUTION

After you've opened a 1-2-3 worksheet, don't change the settings of these three check boxes. Changing them while you are working on the sheet can throw off the worksheet calculations.

> **NOTE**
>
> You should be aware that Excel also turns off its automatic number formatting feature when you're working with a 1-2-3 worksheet. In an Excel worksheet, if you enter 3-mar-94, Excel knows you've entered a date and formats the cell automatically with the dd-mmm-yy format. In a Lotus 1-2-3 worksheet, however, entering 3-mar-94 produces a #NAME? error.

Saving a 1-2-3 Worksheet as an Excel File

If you apply Excel-specific formatting or features to a 1-2-3 worksheet, you lose these changes when you save the sheet in a 1-2-3 format. If you want to keep these nontranslatable changes, you need to save the file in Excel's format. (You can't just rename the file with an .XLS extension.) The following procedure takes you through the steps:

1. Select the File | Save As command. Excel displays the Save As dialog box.
2. In the Save as type drop-down list, select Microsoft Excel Workbook.
3. If necessary, use the Save in list to select a location for the file.
4. Use the File name box to enter a name for the worksheet (Excel adds its default .XLS extension automatically).
5. Select OK. Excel converts the file into an Excel worksheet.

Exporting an Excel File in 1-2-3 Format

If you need to export an Excel file in 1-2-3 format, work through the steps in the following procedure:

1. Select the File | Save As command to display the Save As dialog box.
2. In the Save as type drop-down list, select one of the Lotus 1-2-3 file formats. If you want to create a Lotus formatting file as well, make sure that you select either the WK3,FM3 (1-2-3) or the WK1,FMT (1-2-3) option.
3. If necessary, use the Save in list to select a location for the file.
4. Use the File name box to enter a name for the worksheet (Excel automatically adds the required extension).
5. Select OK. Excel converts the file into a Lotus worksheet.

Some Notes About Exporting Excel Files to 1-2-3

Exporting Excel files, like importing 1-2-3 files, is generally straightforward. You should, however, keep the following points in mind when exporting your Excel workbooks:

■ If you select a 1-2-3 format other than WK3, Excel exports only the active sheet.

■ If Excel can't convert a formula into something 1-2-3 understands, it exports the value of the formula instead.

■ References to noncontiguous ranges are not exported (because they're not supported by 1-2-3). Intersection and union operators also are not exported.

■ The WKS format can handle only 2,048 rows, and the WK1 and WK3 formats can handle only 8,192 rows. References above these limits are wrapped around to the top of the worksheet. For example, converting a sheet with a reference to A8193 into the WK1 format changes the reference to A1. Because this effect probably is undesirable, you should adjust the layout of the worksheet before exporting it.

■ All Excel error values are exported as 1-2-3's @ERR function, except #N/A, which is exported as the @NA function.

■ Named constants and formulas are not exported. Excel converts the name to the constant or formula instead.

■ Arrays are not exported. Excel uses the values in the array instead.

Summary

This chapter showed you various methods for sharing data between Excel and your other applications. I showed you the basic cut-and-paste Clipboard technique, various object linking and embedding methods, and a few techniques for exchanging data with DOS applications. We also looked at the Office Binder, importation of text files, and some special Lotus 1-2-3 considerations.

Here are some other chapters to check out for related information:

■ For a complete rundown of the various controls found in the Options dialog box, see Chapter 8, "Customizing Excel."

■ If the data you want exists in an external database file, you'll need to learn the querying techniques found in Chapter 15, "Using Microsoft Query," and Chapter 16, "Creating Advanced Queries."

■ To learn how to create pictures (both linked and unlinked) of worksheet cells, see Chapter 11, "Working with Graphic Objects."

■ If you would like to try your hand at controlling data sharing via VBA (including OLE automation), Chapter 28, "Working with Other Applications: OLE, DDE, and More," is the place to look.

Customizing Excel

8

The Microsoft programmers designed Excel so that the commands and features most commonly used by most people are within easy reach. This means that the setup of the menu system and toolbars reflects what the ordinary user might want. However, no one qualifies as an ordinary user—we all work with Excel in our own way. What one person uses every day, another needs only once a year; one user's obscure technical feature is another's bread and butter.

To address these differences, Excel provides what might be the most customizable interface on the market today. Excel has dozens of settings you can use to control everything from automatic recalculation to display of zero values. The Menu Editor enables you to create custom menus either by deleting some of Excel's built-in commands or by adding new commands and attaching macros to them. You can also easily configure the toolbars simply by dragging buttons on or off a toolbar. You can even create your own button faces with the Button Editor. This chapter explores all of these customization features.

Customizing Excel's Options

In some of the earlier chapters, I introduced you to the Options dialog box and showed you how to modify some of Excel's default settings. To get our customization tour off to a good start, this section takes a comprehensive look at every option available in this dialog box.

Displaying the Options Dialog Box

To get started, you need to display the Options dialog box by selecting the **T**ools | **O**ptions command. In this dialog box, shown in Figure 8.1, you use the 10 tabs to modify Excel's settings and default values.

FIGURE 8.1.

You can use the Options dialog box to change dozens of Excel's default settings.

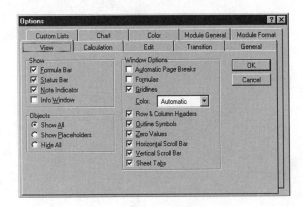

In case you need a briefing at this point, here's a summary of the navigation techniques for a multilevel tabbed dialog box:

- Using the mouse, click on a tab to select it.
- Using the keyboard, press Ctrl-Tab to move right and Ctrl-Shift-Tab to move left.
- If the tab name is selected, you can press the right-arrow key to move right, the left-arrow key to move left, the up-arrow key to move up, and the down-arrow key to move down.

When you finish choosing your options, select OK to return to the worksheet.

Changing the View

The View tab options control several display settings for the Excel screen, workbooks, objects, and windows.

The Show group has four check boxes:

Formula Bar: Deactivate this check box to hide the formula bar. If you use in-cell editing, turning off the formula bar gives you more room on-screen. The downside is that you lose access to the Name box and the Function Wizard button. You also can hide the formula bar by deactivating the **View | Formula Bar** command.

Status Bar: Deactivate this check box to hide the status bar and give yourself some extra screen real estate. You also can hide the status bar by deactivating the **View | Status Bar** command.

TIP

If you want to maximize the work area, the easiest way to do it is to select the **View | Full Screen** command. This command removes everything from the screen except the menu bar, row and column headers, scroll bars, and sheet tabs (as you'll soon see, you can use the View tab to turn off these items as well). To return to the normal view, either click the Full Screen toolbar button or select **View | Full Screen** again.

Note Indicator: Deactivate this check box to remove the small red squares that Excel places in the upper-right corner of cells that have notes attached to them.

Info Window: Activate this check box to display the Info window, which gives you information about various cell properties. Figure 8.2 shows the Info window containing data for cell R7 in the 1995 Budget worksheet. Use the **Info** menu (which appears when you activate the Info window) to select which properties you want displayed.

FIGURE 8.2.

*The Info window can show
you many properties of the
active cell.*

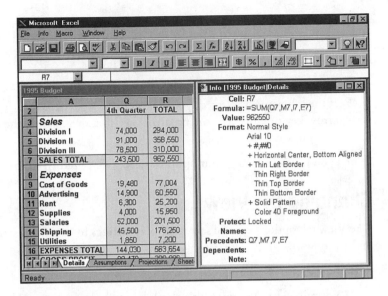

The Objects group in the View tab sets the display options for worksheet objects. If you have a worksheet with a lot of graphics, these options can make it easier to scroll through the sheet. Select Show **P**laceholders to show a gray box where the graphics would normally be. Select Hi**d**e All to hide the graphics entirely. When you want to display the graphic objects normally, select the Show **A**ll option.

TIP

You also can cycle through these options without displaying the Options dialog box. Just press Ctrl-6 repeatedly.

The nine check boxes in the Window Options group control the display of each Excel window:

Automatic Page Breaks: Activate this check box to display the dashed lines that mark the borders of each printed page.

Formulas: Activate this check box to display cell formulas rather than values.

TIP

You also can toggle between formulas and values by pressing Ctrl-` (backquote).

Gridlines: Use this check box to toggle gridlines on and off. When gridlines are on, you can use the **C**olor drop-down list to select a color for the gridlines.

Click this button on the Forms toolbar to toggle gridlines on and off.

Row and Column Headers: Use this check box to toggle the row and column headers on and off.

Outline Symbols: If the current worksheet is outlined, use this check box to toggle the outline symbols on and off.

> **TIP**
>
> You also can press Ctrl-8 to toggle outline symbols on and off.

Zero Values: Deactivate this check box to hide cells containing zero.

Horizontal Scroll Bar: Use this check box to toggle the horizontal scroll bar on and off.

Vertical Scroll Bar: Use this check box to toggle the vertical scroll bar on and off.

Sheet Tabs: Use this check box to toggle the sheet tabs on and off.

Changing the Calculation Options

The Calculation tab options contain several settings used to control worksheet calculations, as shown in Figure 8.3.

FIGURE 8.3.

Use the Calculation tab to work with Excel's calculation settings.

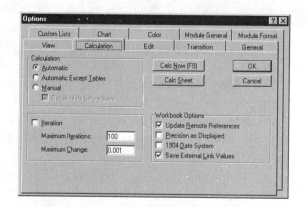

You use the Calculation group options to set the calculation mode, which determines when Excel recalculates a worksheet. See Chapter 2, "Building Better Formulas," to learn about the various Excel calculation modes.

Activating the Iteration check box sets up the worksheet for iterative calculations. For an example, see the material on circular reference formulas in Chapter 17, "Basic Analytic Methods." You also can use the Maximum Iterations and Maximum Change text boxes with Goal Seek (which I also cover in Chapter 17).

The Workbook Options group contains the following options:

Update Remote References: This check box controls whether Excel recalculates formulas that contain references to other applications. If you find that remote references are increasing the time Excel takes to recalculate formulas, deactivate this option. On the other hand, if your links display the #REF! error, you need to activate this check box.

Precision as Displayed: When this check box is deactivated (the default), Excel stores values with full (15-digit) precision. When you activate this check box, Excel uses the displayed value in each cell to determine the precision it uses. For example, if a cell contains 1234.567, Excel uses three-digit precision for the cell.

1904 Date System: Activate this check box to calculate dates using January 2, 1904, as the starting point (rather than January 1, 1900). Because Excel for the Macintosh uses the 1904 date system, this option enables you to work with the same worksheet in both the PC and the Mac environments.

Save External Link Values: If this check box is activated (the default) and a workbook contains links to another workbook, Excel saves copies of the linked values from the server workbook in the client workbook. If a large amount of data is involved, the dependent workbook might get bloated beyond a reasonable size. If this happens, deactivate this check box to prevent Excel from storing the source values.

Changing the Editing Options

The options in the Edit tab, shown in Figure 8.4, control various cell and range editing settings:

Edit Directly in Cell: This check box toggles in-cell editing on and off. If you turn in-cell editing off, Excel's double-click behavior changes: if the cell contains a note, the Cell Note dialog box appears; if the cell contains a formula, the formula's precedents are selected.

Allow Cell Drag and Drop: This check box toggles Excel's drag-and-drop feature. When this check box is activated, you can move or copy a range by dragging it with the mouse pointer.

Alert before Overwriting Cells: When you use drag-and-drop to move or copy a range, Excel warns you if nonblank cells in the destination range will be overwritten. Deactivate this check box to disable this warning.

Move Selection after Enter: If you activate this check box, Excel moves down one row when you press Enter to confirm a cell entry (or it moves up one row when you press Shift-Enter). If you deactivate this check box, Excel stays on the same cell when you press Enter (or Shift-Enter).

FIGURE 8.4.

The Edit tab options control Excel's editing settings.

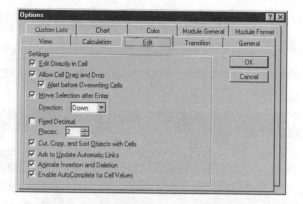

Fixed Decimal: Activate this check box to cause Excel to automatically insert a decimal place into numbers you enter. Use the **P**laces spinner to specify the location of the decimal. For example, if **P**laces is 2, Excel converts a number entered as 12345 to 123.45.

Cut, Copy, and Sort **O**bjects with Cells: Activate this check box to keep graphic objects together with their underlying cells when you cut or copy the cells or when you sort or filter a list.

Ask to **U**pdate Automatic Links: When you open a workbook that contains automatic links to a server document in another application (see Chapter 7, "Exchanging Data with Other Applications"), Excel displays a dialog box asking whether you want to update the links. Deactivate this check box to prevent this dialog box from appearing.

A**n**imate Insertion and Deletion: When this check box is activated (the default), Excel animates range inserting and deleting. In a deletion, for example, Excel removes the range and then shows the adjacent cells moving to their new position. To turn off this behavior, deactivate this check box.

Enable Auto**C**omplete for Cell Values: With this check box activated (the default), Excel attempts to complete your cell entries automatically by examining existing cells in the same column. For example, suppose that you enter ACME Coyote Supplies in cell A1. If you then move down to cell A2 and enter A, Excel fills in the rest of the cell with ACME Coyote Supplies.

Changing the Lotus 1-2-3 Transition Options

The options in the Transition tab control settings that make it easier to switch from Lotus 1-2-3 to Excel. See Chapter 7 (especially the section called "Notes for Lotus 1-2-3 Users Switching to Excel") for details.

Changing the General Workspace Options

The controls on the General tab, shown in Figure 8.5, affect miscellaneous workspace options:

Reference Style: Select A**1** to use A1-style references or R1**C**1 to use R1C1-style references.

NOTE

The normal A1 style that you're accustomed to numbers a worksheet's rows from 1 to 16384 and assigns the letters A through IV to the worksheet's 256 columns. In R1C1 style, though, Excel numbers both the rows and the columns. In general, the notation R*x*C*y* refers to the cell at row *x* and column *y*. Here are some examples:

A1 Style	R1C1 Style
$A$1	R1C1
$D$8	R8C4
$B$4:$E$10	R4C2:R10C5
$B:$B	C2 (that is, column B)
$3:$3	R3 (that is, row 3)

As you can see, these are all absolute references. To use relative references in R1C1 notation, enclose the numbers in square brackets. For example, R[2]C[2] refers to the cell two rows down and two columns to the right of the active cell. Similarly, R[–1]C[–3] refers to the cell one row above the active cell and three columns to the left. Here are a few more examples of relative references:

Relative Reference	Description
R[1]C[–1]	One row down and one column left
R[–5]C[3]	Five rows up and three columns right
R[2]C	Two rows down, same column
RC[–1]	Same row, one column left
R	The current row
C	The current column

Menus: Activate the **R**ecently Used File List check box to display at the bottom of the **F**ile menu a list of the last four files you used. If you prefer the Excel 4.0 menu structure, activate the Microsoft **E**xcel 4.0 Menus check box.

Ignore Other Applications: Activate this check box to cause Excel to ignore Dynamic Data Exchange (DDE) requests from other applications.

Reset Tip**W**izard: The TipWizard is a toolbar that displays tips related to actions you've recently performed in Excel. Activate this check box to clear the list of tips.

Click on this tool on the Standard toolbar to display the TipWizard.

FIGURE 8.5.

*The General tab controls
various workspace options.*

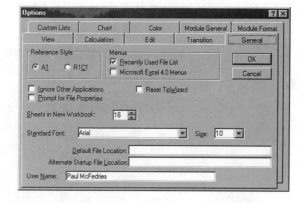

Prompt for File Properties: Activate this check box to have Excel display the Properties dialog box whenever you save a new workbook.

Sheets in New Workbook: This option specifies the default number of sheets in new workbooks. You can enter a number between 1 and 255.

Standard Font: This drop-down list contains the typefaces available on your system. The typeface you select becomes the one Excel uses for all new worksheets and workbooks. You also can set the default type size by selecting a number in the Size list.

Default File Location: This option determines the initial folder that appears when you first display the Open or Save As dialog boxes. To make it easy to find your Excel documents, save them all in a single folder and enter the full path in this text box.

Alternate Startup File Location: Excel uses the \Excel\XLStart folder as its default startup location. Any files placed in this directory are opened automatically when you start Excel, and any templates in this directory appear in the New dialog box. Use this text box to specify a startup directory in addition to \Excel\XLStart.

User **N**ame: In this text box, enter the user name you want displayed in the Properties dialog box, scenarios, views, and file sharing.

The Custom Lists Tab

You can use the Custom Lists tab to create your own lists for AutoFill series. I showed you how to create custom lists with this tab in Chapter 1, "Getting the Most Out of Ranges," in the section "Creating a Custom AutoFill List."

Changing the Chart Options

The Chart tab, shown in Figure 8.6, controls several default chart settings. (Note that the Chart tab's options are available only if you've activated a chart, as described in Chapter 9, "Working with Chart Types.")

FIGURE 8.6.

The Chart tab controls various default chart settings.

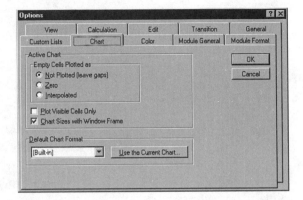

Empty Cells Plotted as: This group specifies how Excel should handle blank cells in a data series. Select **N**ot Plotted to ignore blanks, **Z**ero to plot blanks as zeros, and **I**nterpolated to have Excel draw a straight line between the points on either side of the blank cell.

Plot Visible Cells Only: Excel normally includes in a chart cells that you've hidden yourself or that have been hidden by an outline or filter. Deactivate this check box to exclude hidden cells from the chart data series.

Chart Sizes with Window Frame: If your chart is displayed in a separate chart sheet, activate this check box to cause Excel to change the size of the chart whenever you change the size of the window. You also can size a chart with its window frame by selecting the **V**iew | Sized with **W**indow command. (This command is available only when you activate a chart sheet.)

Default Chart Format: This group determines the chart type for new charts that are created using the Default Chart button. See Chapter 9 for instructions.

Working with Custom Color Palettes

You can use the Color tab to customize Excel's default 56-color palette. For the full details, see the section "Using Color in Worksheets" in Chapter 4, "Formatting Excel Worksheets."

Changing the General Module Options

If you use Visual Basic for Applications, the options in the Module General tab, shown in Figure 8.7, control several module sheet settings:

Auto Indent: If this check box is activated, Visual Basic indents the next line to the same point as the line you just entered. If it's deactivated, Visual Basic moves the insertion point to the beginning of each new line.

FIGURE 8.7.

The Module General tab controls the default settings for Visual Basic modules.

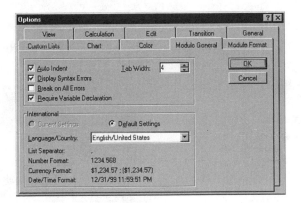

Tab Width: Use this option to set the number of spaces Visual Basic moves whenever you press the Tab key in a module.

Display Syntax Errors: Activate this check box to force Visual Basic to check the syntax of each line when you enter it. If a mistake is detected, a dialog box pops up to warn you.

Break on All Errors: Activate this check box to force Excel to halt execution if any procedure in the current module contains an error.

Require Variable Declaration: When this check box is activated, it adds the following statement to the top of each new module:

```
Option Explicit
```

This statement tells Visual Basic to generate an error if you try to use an undeclared variable.

International: This group controls the international settings used in the module. Select **C**urrent Settings to use the settings defined in the Windows Control Panel. Select **D**efault Settings and choose an item from the **L**anguage/Country list to specify settings for Visual Basic modules only.

Changing the Module Format Options

Visual Basic displays text such as keywords, comments, and syntax errors in a different color. The Module Format tab, shown in Figure 8.8, enables you to customize these colors as well as the font used in a module. The following procedure shows you how to use this tab to format the appearance of module code:

1. Use the **F**ont list to select a typeface for the code.

2. Use the **S**ize list to select a type size.

3. Use the **C**ode Colors list to select the type of code you want to work with.

4. Use the **F**oreground and **B**ackground lists to select the colors to use for the code type you selected in step 3.

5. Repeat steps 3 and 4 to set the colors for other code types.

FIGURE 8.8.

Use the Module Format options to format the text in your Visual Basic modules.

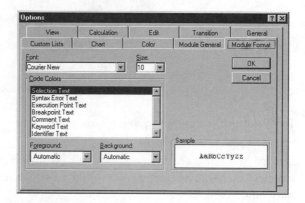

Customizing Excel's Menus

Excel comes with a powerful tool called the Menu Editor. This feature enables you to modify Excel's menus or create your own from scratch. Here's a list of some of the things you can do with the Menu Editor:

- Add commands to or delete commands from an existing menu or shortcut menu.

- Create your own custom menus and attach them to any menu bar.

- Delete menus from any menu bar.

- Create your own menu bars.

The next few sections show you how to do all this and more.

Starting the Menu Editor

To start the Menu Editor, follow these steps:

1. Either activate an existing Visual Basic module or create a new one by selecting the **I**nsert | **M**acro | **M**odule command.

2. Select the **T**ools | Menu E**d**itor command. Excel displays the Menu Editor dialog box, shown in Figure 8.9.

 You also can click on this tool on the Visual Basic toolbar to start the Menu Editor.

FIGURE 8.9.

Use the Menu Editor to customize Excel's menus.

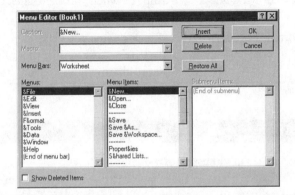

The Menu Editor dialog box contains the following features:

Caption	A text box containing the name of the item currently highlighted in the Menu Items list.
Macro	A text box in which you enter the name of the macro you want to attach to a custom menu item.
Menu **B**ars	A list containing the name of the current menu bar.
M**e**nus	A list of the menus in the current menu bar.
Menu I**t**ems	A list of the menu items in the highlighted menu.
S**u**bmenu Items	A list of items on the submenu attached to the highlighted menu item.

When working with menu bars, you can use either a custom menu bar you created or one of the built-in menu bars listed in Table 8.1.

Table 8.1. Excel's built-in menu bars.

Menu Bar	Description
Worksheet	Appears when a worksheet is active.
Chart	Appears when a chart is active.
No Documents Open	Appears when there are no open workbooks.
Visual Basic Module	Appears when a Visual Basic module is active.
Shortcut Menus 1	Appears when you right-click a toolbar, tool, cell, row or column header, workbook tab, window title bar, or desktop.
Shortcut Menus 2	Appears when you right-click a drawn object, macro button, or text box.
Shortcut Menus 3	Appears when you right-click the following chart elements: data series, text, arrow, plot area, gridline, floor, legend, or the entire chart.

NOTE

Excel stores your customized menus in the current workbook. If you close the workbook, Excel reverts to the default menus. If you want your custom menus to appear all the time, you can use either the Personal Macro Workbook (unhide the file Personal.xls) or a template that you store in the startup directory (see the section titled "Working with Templates" in Chapter 5, "Advanced Worksheet Topics").

Customizing an Existing Menu

You can customize an existing Excel menu either by adding new commands to run your macros or by deleting some of Excel's built-in commands.

Adding a Command to a Menu

To add a command to an existing menu, follow these steps:

1. Start the Menu Editor as described earlier.
2. Use the Menu **B**ars list to select the menu bar or shortcut menu group you want to work with.
3. Use the M**e**nus list to select the menu you want to add the command to.

4. Use the Menu Items list to select where on the menu you want the command added:

   ■ To add the command to the end of the menu, select the [End of menu] item.

   ■ Otherwise, select the command above which you want the new command to appear.

5. Select the **I**nsert button. Excel adds a blank command and activates the **C**aption text box.

6. Use the **C**aption box to enter a name for the command. Type an ampersand (&) before the letter you want to use as an accelerator key for the command. To add a separator bar, type a hyphen (–).

7. To attach a macro to the command, move to the **M**acro drop-down list and either type the name or select it from the list. If the macro resides in another workbook, be sure to include the name of the workbook (for example, Personal.xls!ToggleGridlines).

8. Select OK. Excel adds the command.

NOTE

If you add the command to any menu bar other than the Visual Basic Module menu bar, you must activate the appropriate sheet to see your changes. For example, if you add a command to the Worksheet menu bar, activate a worksheet.

Adding Submenu Commands

After you've added a command, you can attach a submenu by following these steps:

1. Start the Menu Editor as described earlier.

2. Use the Menu **B**ars list to select the menu bar or shortcut menu group you want to work with.

3. Use the M**e**nus list to select the menu that contains the submenu command.

4. Use the Menu **It**ems list to select the submenu command.

5. Use the S**u**bmenu Items list to select where on the submenu you want the command added:

   ■ To add the command to the end of the submenu, select the [End of submenu] item.

   ■ Otherwise, select the command above which you want the new command to appear.

6. Select the **I**nsert button. Excel adds a blank command and activates the **C**aption text box.

7. Use the **C**aption box to enter a name for the command. Type an ampersand (&) before the letter you want to use as an accelerator key for the command. To add a separator bar, type a hyphen (–).

8. To attach a macro to the command, move to the **M**acro drop-down list and either type the name or select it from the list. If the macro resides in another workbook, be sure to include the name of the workbook (for example, Personal.xls!ToggleGridlines).

9. Repeat steps 5 through 8 to add other commands to the submenu.

10. Select OK. Excel creates the submenu.

Deleting a Command from a Menu

The following procedure shows you the steps to follow to delete a command from an existing menu:

1. Start the Menu Editor.

2. Select the menu bar or shortcut menu group you want to work with from the Menu **B**ars list.

3. Select the menu that contains the command you want to delete.

4. Highlight the command in the Menu **I**tems list.

5. Select the **D**elete button. Excel deletes the command.

6. Select OK to return to the module.

CAUTION

Excel doesn't ask for confirmation before deleting a command. If you accidentally delete a custom command, select the Cancel button. If you accidentally delete a built-in command, see the section later in this chapter titled "Undeleting a Built-In Menu or Command."

Customizing an Existing Menu Bar

The Menu Editor enables you to customize any of Excel's menu bars the same way you customize an individual menu. You can add new menus and delete existing menus.

Adding a Menu to a Menu Bar

If you want to add some macros to Excel's menu structure, you might not want to clutter the existing menus with all kinds of new commands. The alternative is to create an entirely new menu and add it to a menu bar. Here are the steps to follow:

1. Start the Menu Editor.

2. Select the menu bar or shortcut menu group you want to work with from the Menu **B**ars list.

3. Use the M**e**nus list to select where on the menu bar you want the menu added:

   ■ To add the menu to the end of the menu bar, select the [End of menu bar] item.

   ■ Otherwise, select the menu to the left of which you want the new command to appear.

4. Select the **I**nsert button. Excel adds a blank menu and activates the **C**aption text box.

5. Use the **C**aption box to enter a name for the menu. As with commands, type an ampersand (&) before the letter you want to use as an accelerator key for the menu.

6. Follow the procedures outlined earlier, in the section called "Customizing an Existing Menu," to add commands to the new menu.

7. Select OK. Excel adds the menu.

Deleting a Menu from a Menu Bar

The following procedure shows you the steps to work through to delete a menu from an existing menu bar:

1. Start the Menu Editor.

2. Use the Menu **B**ars list to select the menu bar or shortcut menu group you want to work with.

3. Use the M**e**nus list to select the menu you want to delete.

4. Select the **D**elete button. Excel deletes the command.

5. Select OK to return to the module.

> **CAUTION**
>
> As with menu commands, Excel doesn't ask for confirmation before deleting a menu. If you accidentally delete a custom menu, select Cancel. If you accidentally delete a built-in menu, see the section later in this chapter titled "Undeleting a Built-In Menu or Command."

Working with Custom Menu Bars

The Menu Editor also enables you to create your own custom menu bars from scratch and to delete any custom menu bars you no longer need (although you can't delete any of the built-in menu bars).

Creating a Custom Menu Bar

If you're building a custom application in Excel, you'll often need to satisfy two goals:

- Give your users easy access to commands that directly affect the application.
- Hide any other Excel commands that are not related to the application.

One of the best ways to accomplish this goal is to create a custom menu bar that includes only the commands you want the user to see. Follow these steps to create a custom menu bar:

1. Start the Menu Editor.
2. In the Menu **B**ars list, select one of the menu bars or shortcut menu groups (it doesn't matter which one) to clear any selections you might have in the other lists.
3. Select the **I**nsert button. Excel creates a blank menu bar and activates the **C**aption text box.
4. Enter a name for the new menu bar.
5. Follow the steps outlined earlier to add new menus and commands to the menu bar.
6. Select OK.

Deleting a Custom Menu Bar

If you no longer need a custom menu bar, follow these steps to delete it:

1. Start the Menu Editor.
2. In the Menu **B**ars list, select the custom menu bar you want to delete.
3. Select the **D**elete button. Excel deletes the menu bar.
4. Select OK.

Undeleting a Built-In Menu or Command

If you delete any of Excel's built-in menus or commands, you can restore them by following these steps:

1. Start the Menu Editor.
2. Activate the **S**how Deleted Items check box. The deleted menus or commands appear in grayed text.

3. Highlight the menu or command you want to restore.

4. Select the Un**d**elete button. Excel restores the command.

5. Select OK to return to the module.

Customizing Excel's Toolbars

Excel's tabbed dialog boxes and revamped menu structure make it much easier to find the commands and features you want. But you still can't beat the toolbars for making short work of common tasks. The problem is that Excel has 13 displayable toolbars, and there's a finite amount of screen real estate to work with (especially if you use Excel in VGA mode). The solution is to customize the toolbars so that they display buttons for only the features you use the most.

Setting Toolbar Options

Before you learn how to customize toolbars, you should know about a few toolbar options. Select the **V**iew | **T**oolbars command to have Excel display the Toolbars dialog box, shown in Figure 8.10.

FIGURE 8.10.

Use the Toolbars dialog box to set toolbar options.

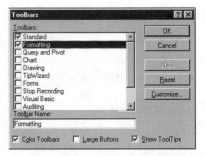

TIP

You also can display the Toolbars dialog box by right-clicking on a toolbar and selecting the Toolbars command from the shortcut menu.

Along the bottom of the Toolbars dialog box, you see the following check boxes:

Color Toolbars: Excel usually displays color in some of the toolbar buttons. If you don't have a color screen, you might be able to see these buttons better if you deactivate the C**o**lor Toolbars check box.

Large Buttons: The toolbar buttons can be quite small in higher video resolutions. You can increase the size of the buttons by activating the **L**arge Buttons check box.

Show ToolTips: The ToolTips that appear when the mouse pointer lingers for a second or two over a button are convenient when you're first learning the lay of the toolbar land. After a while, however, you might find them distracting. You can turn them off by deactivating the **S**how ToolTips check box.

Select OK to put any options you change into effect.

Customizing an Existing Toolbar

With the Toolbars dialog box displayed, use the following techniques to modify any displayed toolbar:

- To move a button to a different location, drag it within the toolbar. If you drag the button only slightly, you create a space between buttons.
- To change the size of a toolbar drop-down list, click on it and drag either the left or the right edge.
- To delete a button, drag it off the toolbar.

Adding a Button to a Toolbar

Excel actually has more toolbar buttons than the ones you see on its default toolbars. In fact, most Excel features have their own buttons, and it's possible to add any of these buttons to a toolbar. For example, if you regularly use Excel's worksheet protection, you can add the Lock Cell button that toggles protection on and off. This method is more convenient than constantly selecting the **T**ools | **P**rotection | **P**rotect Sheet command.

You add buttons to a toolbar by using the Customize dialog box, shown in Figure 8.11. This dialog box is divided into three sections:

Categories	Excel divides all its toolbar buttons into the 14 categories contained in this list. The Custom category contains buttons you can use for your macros.
Buttons	The available buttons in the selected category.
Description	If you select a button, Excel displays a description of the button's function at the bottom of the dialog box.

To add buttons to a toolbar, follow these steps:

1. Display the toolbar you want to add buttons to.
2. Select the **V**iew | **T**oolbars command to display the Toolbars dialog box.
3. Select the **C**ustomize button to display the Customize dialog box.

FIGURE 8.11.

Use the Customize dialog box to add buttons to a toolbar.

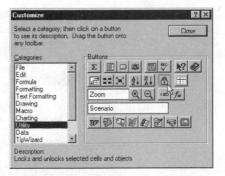

A quick way to display the Customize dialog box is to right-click on a toolbar and select the Customize command from the shortcut menu.

4. Use the **C**ategories list to select a button category.

5. Drag the button you want to add from the Buttons section to the toolbar location. Excel inserts the button between the existing buttons.

6. Repeat steps 4 and 5 to add other buttons.

7. When you're done, select the Close button.

Assigning a Macro to a Button

If you want to assign a macro to a button, you can assign it either to one of Excel's built-in buttons or to one of the custom buttons.

If you have a macro that mimics or improves on an existing Excel feature, you can assign the macro to the feature's toolbar button by following these steps:

1. Display the toolbar that contains the button you want to work with.

2. Select the **View** | **T**oolbars command to display the Toolbars dialog box.

3. Select the button.

4. Select the **Tools** | **Assign** Macro command. Excel displays the Assign Macro dialog box, shown in Figure 8.12.

You can display the Assign Macro dialog box also by right-clicking on the button and selecting the Assign Macro command from the shortcut menu.

FIGURE 8.12.

Use the Assign Macro dialog box to assign a macro to a toolbar button.

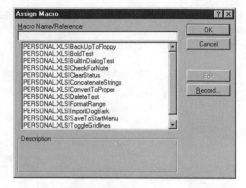

5. Select the macro from the **M**acro Name/Reference list.

   Alternatively, to record the macro, click the **R**ecord button and record the macro as you normally would. When you finish recording the macro, Excel assigns the macro to the button you selected and then returns you to the worksheet.

6. If you selected a macro from the list, select OK to return to the Customize dialog box, and then select Close to return to the workbook.

Instead of altering the behavior of Excel's built-in buttons, you can add a new button by using one of those available in the Custom category. The following procedure shows you how to assign a macro to one of these buttons:

1. Display the toolbar you want to use for the custom button.

2. Select the **V**iew | **T**oolbars command to display the Toolbars dialog box.

3. Select the **C**ustomize button, and then select Custom from the **C**ategories list.

4. Drag the custom button you want to use to the toolbar. When you release the button, Excel displays the Assign Macro dialog box.

5. Select the macro from the **M**acro Name/Reference list.

   Alternatively, to record the macro, click the **R**ecord button and record the macro as you normally would. When you finish recording the macro, Excel assigns the macro to the button you selected and then returns you to the worksheet.

6. If you selected a macro from the list, select OK to return to the Customize dialog box, and then select Close to return to the workbook.

Resetting a Toolbar

If you've customized one of Excel's built-in toolbars, you reset it to its default configuration by following these steps:

1. Select the **V**iew | **T**oolbars command to display the Toolbars dialog box.

2. In the **T**oolbars list, highlight the toolbar you want to reset.

3. Select the **R**eset button.

4. Select OK.

Creating a New Toolbar

Rather than messing around with Excel's own toolbars, you might prefer to create a toolbar from scratch and add built-in and custom buttons to it. Here are the steps to follow:

1. Select the **V**iew | **T**oolbars command to display the Toolbars dialog box.

2. In the Tool**b**ar Name text box, enter the name you want to use for the toolbar.

3. Select the **N**ew button. Excel displays a new, empty toolbar and displays the Customize dialog box, shown in Figure 8.13.

FIGURE 8.13.

When you create a new toolbar, Excel displays it and opens the Customize dialog box.

New toolbar

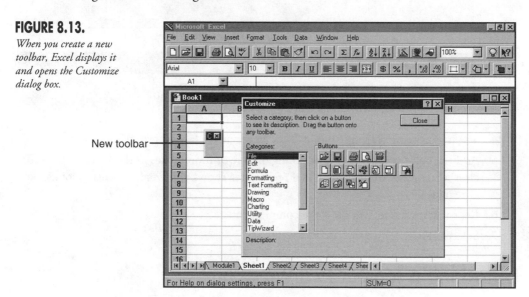

4. Add the buttons you want for the new toolbar as described earlier, in the section "Adding a Button to a Toolbar."

5. When you're done, select Close to return to the workbook.

Using the Button Editor

Excel's Button Editor enables you to modify an existing button face or create your own. The following procedure shows you how it's done:

1. Display the toolbar containing the button you want to edit.

2. Select the **V**iew | **T**oolbars command to display the Toolbars dialog box.

3. Right-click on the button you want to edit, and select Edit Button Image from the shortcut menu. Excel displays the Button Editor dialog box, shown in Figure 8.14.

FIGURE 8.14.

The Button Editor enables you to design your own toolbar buttons.

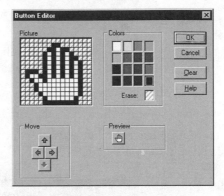

If you want to start a button from scratch, click the **C**lear button.

4. Select a color by clicking on one of the boxes in the Colors group.

5. Add the color to the image by clicking on one or more boxes in the Picture area. To clear a box, click on it again. The Preview area shows you what the button looks like at regular size.

6. Repeat steps 4 and 5 to draw the complete image.

7. Select OK.

Attaching a Toolbar to a Workbook

If you need a custom toolbar only for a specific workbook, you can attach the toolbar to the workbook by following these steps:

1. Open the workbook you want to use and activate a Visual Basic module.

2. Select the **T**ools | Attach **T**oolbars command. Excel displays the Attach Toolbars dialog box, shown in Figure 8.15.

3. In the C**u**stom Toolbars list, highlight the toolbar you want to attach.

4. Select the **C**opy >> button. Excel adds the name to the **T**oolbars in Workbook list.

FIGURE 8.15.

*Use the Attach Toolbars
dialog box to attach a
toolbar to a workbook.*

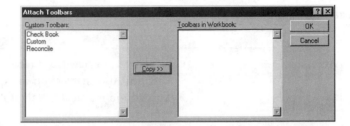

If you accidentally copy a toolbar, you can remove it by highlighting it in the **Toolbars**
in Workbook list and then selecting the **D**elete button.

5. Select OK.

After you've attached a toolbar, it's automatically copied into the Excel workspace whenever
you open the workbook.

Working with Excel's Add-Ins

Excel comes with more bells and whistles than most of us know what to do with. But despite
Excel's massive feature list, some optional components aren't loaded into Excel automatically.
These components, called *add-ins*, toss even more commands, functions, and features into the
Excel mix. You've already seen a few of these add-ins (such as the View Manager we looked at
in Chapter 5 and the Report Manager that was covered in Chapter 6, "Printing Your Work"),
but in this section I'll show you how to install and work with all the add-in files.

Loading Add-Ins

Why doesn't Excel just include its entire add-in library as part of the basic program? It's mostly
a question of speed and performance. Some of the add-ins are huge, and including them all
would slow Excel's startup time dramatically. It would also put a much larger burden on your
system's memory. So by keeping the add-ins as separate programs, you can choose to load only
those you need, when you need them. Table 8.2 describes the available Excel add-ins.

Table 8.2. Excel's add-in programs.

Add-In	Description
AccessLink	Enables you to view Excel table data using an Access form or report. Also enables you to export Excel data to Access. (This add-in is available only if Access is installed on your computer.)
Analysis Toolpak	Adds dozens of new functions and statistical features to Excel. I cover the Analysis Toolpak in detail in Chapter 18, "Working with the Analysis Toolpak."
Analysis Toolpak – VBA	Gives you access to the Analysis Toolpak from Visual Basic for Applications.
AutoSave	Automatically saves workbooks at regular intervals. Loading this add-in inserts an AutoSave command in the Tools menu; this command displays the AutoSave dialog box, shown in Figure 8.16.
MS Query	Enables you to access data in external databases. Microsoft Query can handle data sources in various formats, including Access, FoxPro, dBASE, and SQL Server. For full coverage of Query, see Chapter 15, "Using Microsoft Query" and Chapter 16, "Creating Advanced Queries."
ODBC	Adds functions for retrieving data from external databases using Microsoft's Open Database Connectivity (ODBC).
Report Manager	Prints reports consisting of one or more views and scenarios. I covered Report Manager in Chapter 6 (see the section called "Working with Reports").
Solver	Generates what-if scenarios based on linear and nonlinear optimization techniques. Head for Chapter 19, "Solving Complex Problems with Solver," to get details on Solver.
Template Utilities	Provides a collection of utilities used by the template worksheets that come with Excel.
Template Wizard with Data Tracking	Creates a template and a database from an existing worksheet. Whenever you enter data into the template, Excel copies it to the database automatically. I cover the Template Wizard in Chapter 12, "Working with Lists and Databases."

Add-In	Description
Update Add-In Links	Updates links to add-ins created for version 4.0 of Excel. This allows these older add-ins to take advantage of some of Excel's new functionality.
View Manager	Enables you to create different worksheet views (including window size and position, panes, display settings, and more). Chapter 5 explained how to use views.

FIGURE 8.16.

The AutoSave add-in saves your workbooks automatically at the time interval you specify.

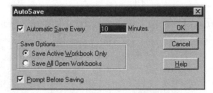

NOTE

You're not restricted to just the add-ins that come with the Excel package. Many third-party developers have created add-ins that are available free or at low cost. (The Excel forum on CompuServe is a good source for these files.) You can even create your own add-ins based on custom applications you create with Visual Basic for Applications. I'll tell you how in Chapter 21, "Getting Started with VBA."

Here are the steps to follow to load one or more add-in programs:

1. Select the **Tools | Add-Ins** command. Excel displays the Add-Ins dialog box, shown in Figure 8.17. The **A**dd-Ins Available list shows the add-ins that were installed when you installed Excel. Add-ins with a check mark beside them are currently loaded.

FIGURE 8.17.

Use the Add-Ins dialog box to select the add-ins you want to load.

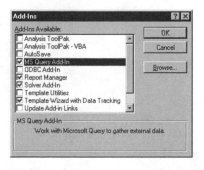

2. To activate an add-in, click on it, or highlight it and press the spacebar.

3. The displayed add-ins are those found in the \Excel\Library folder. If you've installed an add-in from a third-party developer, select the **B**rowse button, track down the add-in file in the Browse dialog box, and then select OK.

4. When you've activated all the add-ins you need, select OK to return to the worksheet. Excel loads the add-ins.

Installing Add-In Files

If one or more of Excel's add-ins didn't appear in the Add-Ins dialog box, it means they weren't installed when you set up Excel. To install these files, you must run the Setup program again. Here's how it's done:

1. Run the Setup program from the Start menu. (How you do this depends on how you installed Excel. For example, if you're using Office 95, you open the Start menu, open the **P**rograms folder, open the Microsoft Office folder, and then select Setup.)

2. In the Setup dialog box that appears, select the **A**dd/Remove button.

3. If you're using Microsoft Office Setup, the Maintenance dialog box appears. Highlight Microsoft Excel, and then select the Cha**n**ge Option button.

4. In the Microsoft Excel dialog box, highlight Add-Ins in the Options list, and then select Cha**n**ge Option. The Add-Ins dialog box appears, as shown in Figure 8.18.

FIGURE 8.18.

Use this Add-Ins dialog box to select the add-ins you want to install.

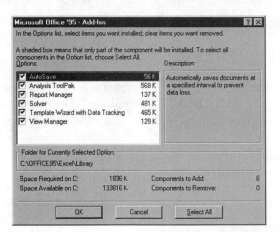

5. For each add-in you want to install, activate its check box by clicking on it or by highlighting it and pressing the spacebar.

6. When you're done, select OK to return to the Microsoft Excel dialog box. (If you're using Office Setup, select OK again to return to the Maintenance dialog box.)

7. Select **C**ontinue. Setup prompts you to insert one or more disks or the Office CD-ROM.

8. Insert the disks and follow the on-screen prompts.

Summary

This chapter gave you the grand tour of Excel's extensive customization options. We took a thorough look at the Options dialog box, and we saw how easy it is to customize Excel's menus and toolbars. Here are a few other chapters to read for related information:

■ I showed you how to create custom lists in Chapter 1, "Getting the Most Out of Ranges" (see the section titled "Creating a Custom AutoFill List").

■ For information on Excel's calculation modes, see Chapter 2, "Building Better Formulas."

■ I took you through the steps to customize Excel's default 56-color palette in Chapter 4, "Formatting Excel Worksheets," in the section titled "Using Color in Worksheets."

■ I covered automatic links in Chapter 7, "Exchanging Data with Other Applications."

■ To get lots of information on the options that make Excel easier for Lotus 1-2-3 users, read the section "Notes for Lotus 1-2-3 Users Switching to Excel" in Chapter 7.

■ To learn about default chart formats, see Chapter 9, "Working with Chart Types."

■ To find out more about iteration, circular reference formulas, and Goal Seek, head for Chapter 17, "Basic Analytic Methods."

■ To learn how to create macros that you can assign to custom menu commands and toolbar buttons, check out the chapters in Part V, "Unleashing Spreadsheet Applications with VBA."

■ You can also customize menus and toolbars with VBA macros. To find out the details, read Chapter 25, "Creating a Custom User Interface."

PART

Unleashing Excel's Charting and Graphics Capabilities

Working with Chart Types

9

One of the best ways to analyze your worksheet data—or get your point across to other people—is to display your data visually in a chart. Excel gives you tremendous flexibility when you're creating charts; it enables you to place charts in separate documents or directly on the worksheet itself. Not only that, but you have dozens of different chart formats to choose from, and if none of Excel's built-in formats is just right, you can further customize these charts to suit your needs.

This chapter takes an in-depth look at each of Excel's chart types. We'll also review the basics of creating charts, and I'll introduce you to Excel's new Data Map feature.

A Review of Chart Basics

Before getting down to the nitty-gritty of creating and working with charts, we'll take a look at some chart terminology that you need to become familiar with. Figure 9.1 points out the various parts of a typical chart. Each part is explained in Table 9.1.

FIGURE 9.1.

The elements of an Excel chart.

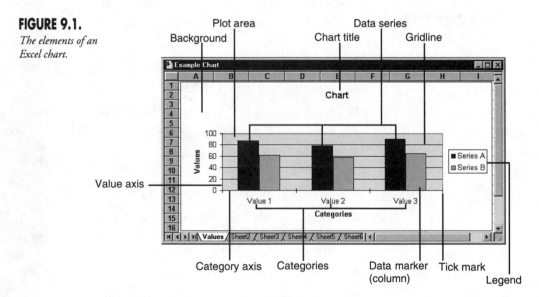

Table 9.1. The elements of an Excel chart.

Element	Description
Background	The area on which the chart is drawn. You can change the color and border of this area.
Category	A grouping of data values on the category axis. Figure 9.1 has three categories: Value 1, Value 2, and Value 3.
Category axis	The axis (usually the X axis) that contains the category groupings.

Element	Description
Data marker	A symbol that represents a specific data value. The symbol used depends on the chart type. In a column chart such as the one shown in Figure 9.1, each column is a marker.
Data series	A collection of related data values. Normally, the marker for each value in a series has the same pattern. Figure 9.1 has two series: Series A and Series B. These are identified in the legend.
Data value	A single piece of data. Also called a *data point*.
Gridlines	Optional horizontal and vertical extensions of the axis tick marks. These make data values easier to read.
Legend	A guide that shows the colors, patterns, and symbols used by the markers for each data series.
Plot area	The area bounded by the category and value axes. It contains the data points and gridlines.
Tick mark	A small line that intersects the category axis or the value axis. It marks divisions in the chart's categories or scales.
Title	The title of the chart.
Value axis	The axis (usually the Y axis) that contains the data values.

How Excel Converts Worksheet Data into a Chart

Creating an Excel chart usually is straightforward and often can be done in only a few keystrokes or mouse clicks. However, a bit of background on how Excel converts your worksheet data into a chart will help you avoid some charting pitfalls.

When Excel creates a chart, it examines both the shape and the contents of the range you've selected. From this data, the program makes various assumptions to determine what should be on the category axis, what should be on the value axis, how to label the categories, and which labels should show within the legend.

The first assumption Excel makes is that *there are more categories than data series*. This makes sense, because most graphs plot a small number of series over many different intervals. For example, a chart showing monthly sales and profit over a year has two data series (the sales and profit numbers) but 12 categories (the monthly intervals). Consequently, Excel assumes that the category axis (the X axis) of your chart runs along the longest side of the selected worksheet range.

The chart shown in Figure 9.2 is a plot of the range A1:D3 in the Column Categories worksheet. Because, in this case, the range has more columns than rows, Excel uses each column as a category. Conversely, Figure 9.3 shows the plot of the range A1:C4, which has more rows than columns. In this case, Excel uses each row as a category.

FIGURE 9.2.

A chart created from a range with more columns than rows.

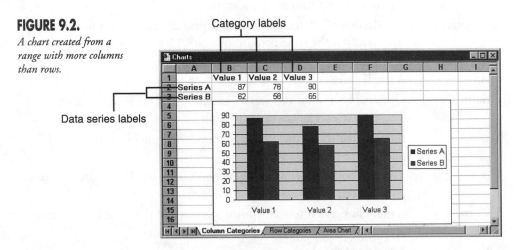

FIGURE 9.3.

A chart created from a range with more rows than columns.

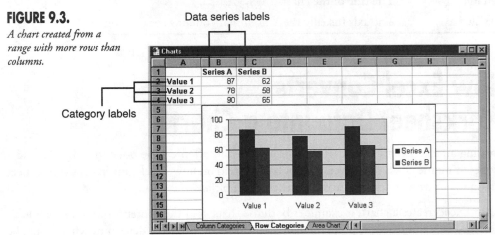

NOTE

If a range has the same number of rows and columns, Excel uses the columns as categories.

The second assumption Excel makes involves the location of labels for categories and data series:

■ For a range with more columns than rows (such as in Figure 9.2), Excel uses the contents of the top row (row 1 in Figure 9.2) as the category labels, and the far-left column (column A in Figure 9.2) as the data series labels.

■ For a range with more rows than columns (such as in Figure 9.3), Excel uses the contents of the far-left column (column A in Figure 9.3) as the category labels, and the top row (row 1 in Figure 9.3) as the data series labels.

> **NOTE**
>
> If a range has the same number of rows and columns, Excel uses the top row for the category labels and the far-left column for the data series labels.

Creating a Chart

When plotting your worksheet data, you have two basic options: you can create an *embedded chart*, which sits on top of your worksheet and can be moved, sized, and formatted, or you can create a separate *chart sheet* by using the automatic or cut-and-paste methods. Whether you choose to embed your charts or store them in separate sheets, the charts are linked with the worksheet data. Any changes you make to the data are automatically updated in the chart. The next few sections discuss each of these techniques.

Creating an Embedded Chart

When creating an embedded chart, you can use any of the following methods:

■ Use the Default Chart tool to create a default chart.

■ Use the ChartWizard to set chart options such as the chart type and axis titles.

■ Copy a chart from a separate chart sheet.

> **NOTE**
>
> Because you can print embedded charts along with your worksheet data, embedded charts are useful in presentations in which you need to show plotted data and worksheet information simultaneously.

Creating a Default Embedded Chart

Excel's default chart is a basic column chart. (See "Setting the Default Chart Type," later in this chapter, to learn how to customize the default chart.) Follow these steps to create an embedded chart using the default format:

1. Select the range you want to plot, including the row and column labels if there are any. Make sure that there are no blank rows between the column labels and the data.

2. Click on the Default Chart tool on the Chart toolbar. The mouse pointer changes to a crosshair with a chart icon.

    The Default Chart tool from the Chart toolbar.

3. Position the mouse pointer at the top-left corner of the area where you want to put the chart.

4. Drag the mouse pointer to the bottom-right corner of that area. Excel displays a box as you drag. When you release the mouse button, Excel draws the chart.

TIP

To create a square chart area, hold down the Shift key while dragging the mouse pointer. To align the chart with the worksheet gridlines, hold down the Alt key while dragging.

NOTE

If, when you release the mouse button, you see a ChartWizard dialog box, Excel doesn't have enough information to create the chart automatically. Follow the steps in the next section to create the chart.

Creating an Embedded Chart with the ChartWizard

If the default chart isn't what you want, Excel's ChartWizard tool takes you through the steps necessary for setting up an embedded chart and setting various customization options. The following steps show you how the ChartWizard works:

1. Select the cell range you want to plot. (This step is optional because you get a chance to select a range later in the process.)

2. Either click on the ChartWizard tool on the Standard toolbar (or the Chart toolbar) or select the **Insert | Chart | On** This Sheet command. The mouse pointer changes to a crosshair with a chart icon.

The ChartWizard tool from the Standard toolbar. (It's also on the Chart toolbar.)

3. Position the mouse pointer at the top-left corner of the area where you want to put the chart, and then drag the pointer to the bottom-right corner of the area. Excel displays a box as you drag. When you release the mouse button, Excel displays the ChartWizard - Step 1 of 5 dialog box, shown in Figure 9.4.

FIGURE 9.4.

Use the ChartWizard - Step 1 of 5 dialog box to select (or adjust) the range you want to plot.

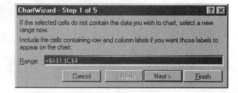

4. If you didn't do so earlier, select the cell range you want to chart, and then click the Next > button. The ChartWizard - Step 2 of 5 dialog box appears, as shown in Figure 9.5.

FIGURE 9.5.

Use the ChartWizard - Step 2 of 5 dialog box to select a chart type.

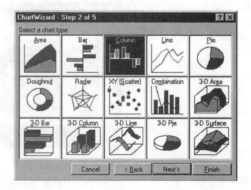

5. Select a chart type, and then click the Next > button. (I'll give you the details of each chart type later in this chapter.) Excel displays the ChartWizard - Step 3 of 5 dialog box, shown in Figure 9.6.

FIGURE 9.6.

Use the ChartWizard - Step 3 of 5 dialog box to pick out a format for the chart type you selected.

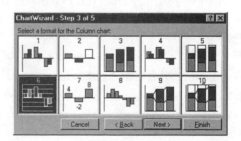

6. Select a chart format for the chart type you selected, and then click the Next > button. The ChartWizard - Step 4 of 5 dialog box appears, as shown in Figure 9.7.

FIGURE 9.7.

Use the ChartWizard - Step 4 of 5 dialog box to define the layout of the chart.

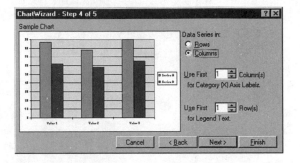

7. Select the options that define the layout of the data series and categories in your selected range. When you're done, click the Next > button. Excel displays the ChartWizard - Step 5 of 5 dialog box, shown in Figure 9.8.

FIGURE 9.8.

Use the ChartWizard - Step 5 of 5 dialog box to add explanatory text to your chart.

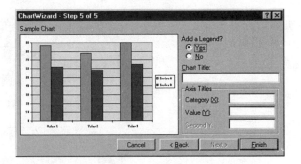

8. Select a legend option and add any titles you need. When you're done, select **F**inish. Excel draws the chart on the worksheet.

Embedding a Chart by Copying from a Chart Sheet

If you have a chart in a separate chart sheet (as explained in the next section), you can embed a copy in the current worksheet. This is a handy way to create an embedded chart if you don't have a mouse, because the normal Default Chart and ChartWizard methods require a mouse. Here are the steps to follow:

1. Activate the sheet that contains the chart you want to embed.

2. If you have a mouse, select the chart by clicking on the chart background. If you don't have a mouse, or if you prefer to use the keyboard, select the chart by first pressing the Esc key to clear any current selections and then pressing the up-arrow key. Excel puts black selection boxes around the chart and displays Chart in the formula bar's Name box, as shown in Figure 9.9.

FIGURE 9.9.

A selected chart displays selection handles around the background and Chart *in the Name box.*

Name box

Selection handles

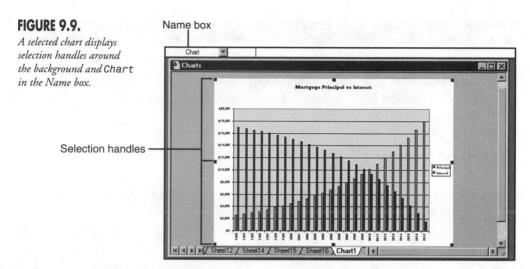

3. Select the **Edit** | **Copy** command.

4. Activate the worksheet in which you want to embed the chart.

5. Select the **Edit** | **Paste** command. Excel embeds the chart into the worksheet.

> **NOTE**
>
> You'll probably need to size the chart. See Chapter 10, "Enhancing Charts," for details.

Creating a Chart in a Separate Sheet

If you don't want a chart taking up space in a worksheet, or if you want to print a chart on its own, you can create a separate chart sheet. The following procedure outlines the steps:

1. Select the cell range you want to plot. (As before, this step is optional because you get a chance to select a range later in the process.)

2. Select the **Insert** | **Chart** | **As** New Sheet command. Excel displays the ChartWizard - Step 1 of 5 dialog box.

3. Follow steps 4 through 8 from the "Creating an Embedded Chart with the Chart-Wizard" section to use ChartWizard. When you finish, Excel inserts a new chart sheet and displays your chart.

> **TIP**
>
> To create a new chart sheet quickly, select the cell range and press F11 (if you have an extended keyboard) or Alt-F1.

> **TIP**
>
> To get a better view of the chart in a separate chart sheet, select the **View | Sized with Window** command. This command expands the chart to fill the entire window. It also means that the chart changes size when you change the size of the window.

Activating a Chart

Before you can work with chart types, you need to activate a chart. How you do this depends on the kind of chart you're dealing with:

- For an embedded chart, double-click inside the chart box. The box border changes to a thicker, broken line.
- For a chart sheet, select the sheet tab.

Selecting a Chart Type

After you've created a chart, you might decide that the existing chart type doesn't display your data the way you want. Or you might want to experiment with different chart types to find the one that best suits your data. Fortunately, the chart type isn't set in stone and can be changed at any time. Depending on the chart, you can use one of three methods to select a different chart type:

- Use the Chart Type dialog box.
- Use the Chart Type tool's palette of types.
- Use the chart AutoFormat feature.

Selecting a Chart Type from the Chart Type Dialog Box

Follow these steps to use the Chart Type dialog box to select a chart type:

1. Activate the chart you want to change.
2. Select the **Format | Chart Type** command. Excel displays the Chart Type dialog box, shown in Figure 9.10.

> **TIP**
>
> You also can display the Chart Type dialog box by right-clicking on the chart background and selecting the Chart Type command from the shortcut menu.

FIGURE 9.10.

The Chart Type dialog box.

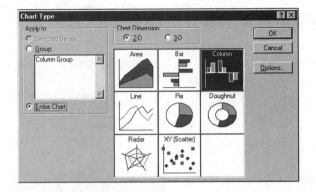

3. In the Apply to group, select **E**ntire Chart. (To learn about the other options in this group, see "Converting a Series to a Different Chart Type" and "Working with Chart Type Groups," later in this chapter.)

4. In the Chart Dimension group, select either **2**-D or **3**-D.

5. Select a chart type.

6. Chart subtypes are variations on the main chart type that display your data in slightly different ways. (For example, one of the column chart's subtypes is a stacked column chart. I explain many of the different subtypes later in this chapter.) To select a chart subtype, select the **O**ptions button, activate the Subtype tab from the dialog box that appears, and choose one of the **S**ubtype boxes.

7. Select OK.

Using the Chart Type Tool to Select a Chart Type

The following procedure shows you how to select a chart type using the Chart Type tool:

1. Activate the chart you want to change.

2. Display the Chart toolbar.

3. Drop down the Chart Type tool and select one of the chart types from the palette that appears. Using the selected chart type, Excel redraws the chart.

 The Chart Type tool from the Chart toolbar.

TIP

If you want to experiment with various chart types, you can "tear off" the Chart Type tool's palette. Drop the palette down, place the mouse pointer inside the palette, and drag the mouse until the palette separates. When you release the button, the Chart toolbar appears.

Selecting an AutoFormat Chart Type

To make your chart formatting chores easier, Excel comes with some built-in *AutoFormats*—predefined chart formats that you can apply easily. The following steps show you how to use the chart AutoFormat feature:

1. Activate the chart you want to change.
2. Select the Format | AutoFormat command. Excel displays the AutoFormat dialog box, shown in Figure 9.11.

FIGURE 9.11.

The chart AutoFormat dialog box.

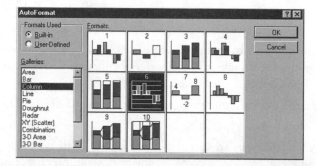

You also can display the AutoFormat dialog box by right-clicking on the chart background and selecting the shortcut menu's AutoFormat command.

3. Highlight a chart type from the **G**alleries list.
4. Pick out a chart format from the **F**ormats boxes.
5. Select OK.

In the AutoFormat dialog box, the Formats Used group has a **U**ser-Defined option. As the name implies, you can define your own chart AutoFormats. See the section titled "Working with User-Defined Chart AutoFormats" in Chapter 10.

Working with 2-D Area Charts

Area charts show the relative contributions over time that each data series makes to the whole picture. The smaller the area a data series takes up, the smaller its contribution to the whole.

For example, Figure 9.12 shows an area chart comparing yearly principal and interest over the 25-year term of a mortgage. The straight line across the top of the chart at about $19,000 indicates the total yearly mortgage payment. (The line is straight because the payments are constant over the term.) The two areas below this line show the relative contributions of principal and interest paid each year. As you can see, the area representing yearly principal increases over time, which means that the amount of principal in each payment increases as the term of the loan progresses. You can use area charts to show the relative contributions over time of things such as individual expense categories, sales regions, and production costs.

FIGURE 9.12.

An area chart that compares mortgage principal and interest.

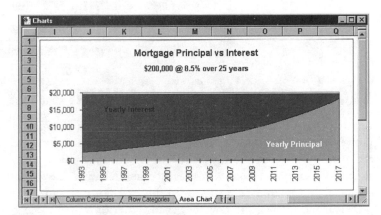

To select an area chart, display the AutoFormat dialog box, choose the Area item from the **G**alleries list, and select an area chart from the **F**ormats section.

Working with 2-D Bar Charts

Bar charts compare distinct items or show single items at distinct intervals. A bar chart is laid out with categories along the vertical axis and values along the horizontal axis. This format lends itself to competitive comparisons, because categories appear to be "ahead" or "behind." For example, Figure 9.13 shows a comparison of parking tickets written in a single month by four officers. You can easily see that the officer on top is the "winner," because the top bar extends farther to the right than anyone else's. You can use bar charts to show the results of sales contests, elections, sporting events, or any competitive activity.

To select a bar chart, display the AutoFormat dialog box, choose the Bar item from the **G**alleries list, and select a bar chart from the **F**ormats section.

> **TIP**
>
> Arrange bar charts with the longest bar on top and the others in descending order beneath it. This setup ensures that the chart looks "full," and it also emphasizes the competitive nature of this chart type.

FIGURE 9.13.
Bar charts are useful for competitive comparisons.

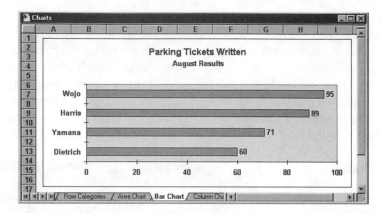

Working with 2-D Column Charts

Like bar charts, *column charts* compare distinct items or show single items at distinct intervals. However, a column chart is laid out with categories along the *horizontal* axis and values along the *vertical* axis (as are most Excel charts). This format is best suited for comparing items over time. For example, Figure 9.14 uses a column chart to show another view of the mortgage principal and interest comparison. In this case, it's easier to see the individual amounts for principal and interest and how they change over time.

FIGURE 9.14.
A column chart that shows the comparison of mortgage principal and interest.

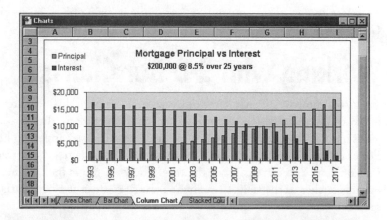

TIP

Try to keep the number of series in a column chart to a minimum. Having too many series causes the columns to become too narrow, making the chart confusing and difficult to read.

To select a column chart, display the AutoFormat dialog box, choose the Column item from the **G**alleries list, and select a column chart from the **F**ormats section.

Excel offers various column chart formats, including *stacked* columns. A *stacked column chart* is similar to an area chart; series values are stacked on top of each other to show the relative contributions of each series. Although an area chart is useful for showing the flow of the relative contributions over time, a stacked column chart is better for showing the contributions at discrete intervals. Figure 9.15 shows the mortgage principal and interest comparison as a stacked column chart.

FIGURE 9.15.

The mortgage principal and interest comparison as a stacked column chart.

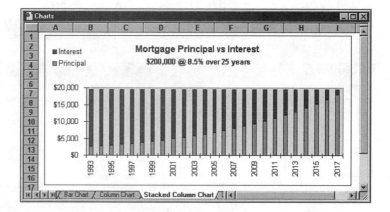

Working with 2-D Line Charts

Line charts show how a data series changes over time. The category (X) axis usually represents a progression of even increments (such as days or months), and the series points are plotted on the value (Y) axis. Figure 9.16 shows a simple line chart that displays a month of daily closing figures for a company's stock price. Use line charts when you're more concerned with the *trend* of a data series than with the actual quantities. For items such as interest rates, inflation, and profits, often it's just as important to know the *direction* of the data as it is to know the specific numbers.

To select a line chart, display the AutoFormat dialog box, choose the Line item from the **G**alleries list, and select a line chart from the **F**ormats section.

Excel offers several line chart formats, including a *High, Low, Close chart*, which is useful for plotting stock-market prices. To use this chart format, make sure that your data is in High, Low, Close order, and then select the format shown in Figure 9.17 from the collection of line chart formats in the AutoFormat dialog box.

FIGURE 9.16.
A line chart showing daily closes for a company's stock price.

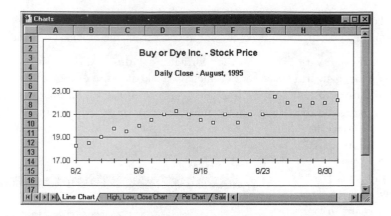

FIGURE 9.17.
A company's stock price plotted as a High, Low, Close chart.

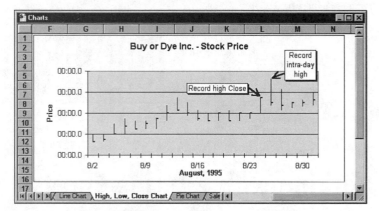

Working with 2-D Pie Charts

A *pie chart* shows the proportion of the whole that is contributed by each value in a single data series. The whole is represented as a circle (the "pie"), and each value is displayed as a proportional "slice" of the circle. Figure 9.18 shows a pie chart that plots the relative proportions of the Earth's most common elements. You can use pie charts to represent sales figures proportionally by region or by product, or to show population data such as age ranges or voting patterns.

To select a pie chart, display the AutoFormat dialog box, choose the Pie item from the **G**alleries list, and select a pie chart from the **F**ormats section.

> **TIP**
>
> For best effect, try to keep the number of pie slices to a minimum. Using too many slices makes each one hard to read and lessens the impact of this type of chart.

FIGURE 9.18.

Pie chart showing the proportions of terrestrial elements.

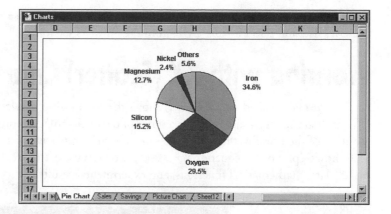

Working with Radar Charts

Radar charts make comparisons within a data series and between data series relative to a center point. Each category is shown with a value axis extending from the center point. To understand this concept, think of a radar screen in an airport control tower. The tower itself is the central point, and the radar radiates a beam (a value axis). When the radar makes contact with a plane, a blip appears on-screen. In a radar chart, this is a data point that's shown with a data marker.

One common use for a radar chart is to make comparisons between products. For example, suppose that you want to buy a new notebook computer. You decide to base your decision on six categories: price, weight, battery life, screen quality, keyboard quality, and service. To get a consistent scale, you rank each machine from 1 to 10 for each category. When you graph this data on a radar chart, the computer that covers the most area is the better machine. Figure 9.19 shows an example of this kind of analysis. In this case, Notebook "A" is a slightly better choice.

FIGURE 9.19.

Using a radar chart to compare products.

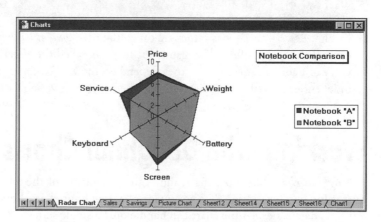

To select a radar chart, display the AutoFormat dialog box, choose the Radar item from the Galleries list, and select a radar chart from the Formats section.

Working with XY (Scatter) Charts

An *XY chart* (also called a *scatter chart*) shows the relationship between numeric values in two different data series. It also can plot a series of data pairs in XY coordinates. An XY chart is a variation of the line chart in which the category axis is replaced by a second value axis. Figure 9.20 shows a plot of the equation $Y = SIN(X)$. You can use XY charts for plotting items such as survey data, mathematical functions, and experimental results.

FIGURE 9.20.

An XY chart of the SIN( ) *function.*

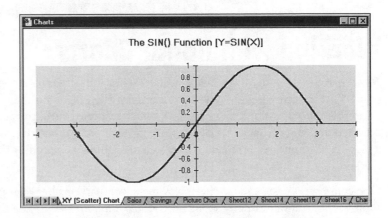

To select an XY chart, display the AutoFormat dialog box, choose the XY (Scatter) item from the Galleries list, and select an XY chart from the Formats section.

> **NOTE**
>
> In Figure 9.20, the X axis values are called the *independent variables* because you can control the series values. The result—SIN(X)—is called the *dependent variable* because you can't control these values; they depend on the X axis values. Excel always plots the independent variable on the X axis and the dependent variable on the Y axis.

Working with Doughnut Charts

A *doughnut chart*, like a pie chart, shows the proportion of the whole that is contributed by each value in a data series. The advantage of a doughnut chart, however, is that you can plot multiple data series. (A pie chart can handle only a single series.)

Figure 9.21 shows a doughnut chart that plots the percentage of total revenues contributed by each of three products. Notice how the chart plots two data series—one for 1993 and another for 1994.

FIGURE 9.21.

A doughnut chart that shows yearly revenue by product.

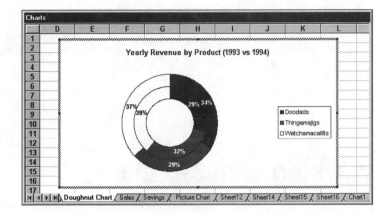

To select a doughnut chart, display the AutoFormat dialog box, choose the Doughnut item from the **G**alleries list, and select a doughnut chart from the **F**ormats section.

Setting the Default Chart Type

Many people use the same type of chart regularly. For example, stockbrokers use High, Low, Close line charts, and scientists use XY charts. If you prefer a specific chart type, you can tell Excel to use this type or format as the *default* for any new charts you create with the Default Chart tool. The following procedure lists the steps to work through:

1. Create a chart (or activate an existing chart) with the type you prefer.

2. Select the **T**ools | **O**ptions command, and then select the Chart tab in the Options dialog box.

3. Select the **U**se the Current Chart button. Excel displays the Add Custom AutoFormat dialog box, shown in Figure 9.22.

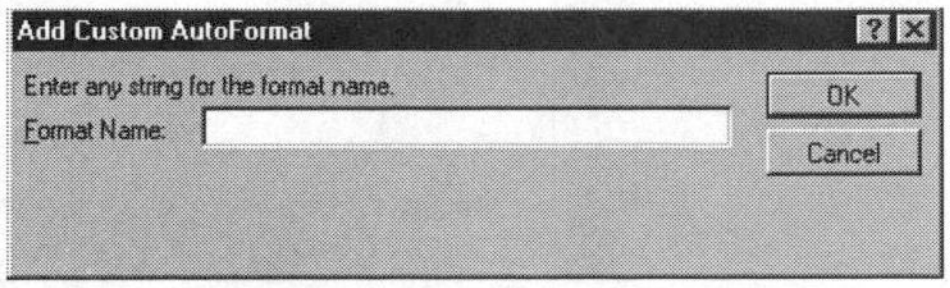

FIGURE 9.22.

Use the Add Custom AutoFormat dialog box to enter a name for your new default format.

4. Use the **F**ormat Name edit box to enter a name for the new default format.

5. Select OK. Excel returns to the Options dialog box and adds the new name to the **D**efault Chart Format list.

6. Select OK to return to the chart.

> **NOTE**
>
> The new default format appears in the AutoFormat dialog box when you select the **U**ser-Defined option. By selecting this default format, you can apply it to any active chart.

Working with 3-D Charts

In addition to the various 2-D chart types we've looked at so far, Excel also offers 3-D charts. Because they're striking, 3-D charts are suitable for presentations, flyers, and newsletters. (If you need a chart to help with data analysis, or if you just need a quick chart to help you visualize your data, you're probably better off with the simpler 2-D charts.) Excel has six 3-D chart types: area, bar, column, line, pie, and surface. You can select, format, and edit your 3-D charts using the same techniques you use with 2-D charts. (I'll discuss chart formatting and editing in the next chapter.) The next few sections introduce you to each 3-D chart type and show you how to manipulate the depth and perspective for each chart.

Working with 3-D Area Charts

Like their 2-D counterparts, 3-D area charts show the relative contributions of each data series over time. You can use 3-D charts in presentations to show the relative contributions of items such as individual expense categories, sales regions, and production costs. Figure 9.23 shows the 3-D version of the Mortgage Principal vs. Interest chart.

FIGURE 9.23.

3-D area chart comparing mortgage principal and interest.

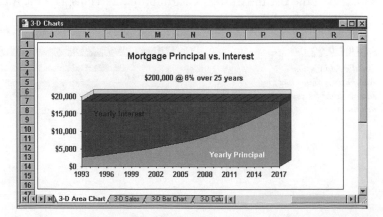

Excel offers seven 3-D area chart AutoFormats, three of which enable you to show separate area plots for each data series (something a 2-D area chart can't do). In this variation, the emphasis isn't on the relative contribution of each series to the whole; rather, it's on the relative differences among the series. Figure 9.24 shows an example.

FIGURE 9.24.

A 3-D area chart showing separate series areas.

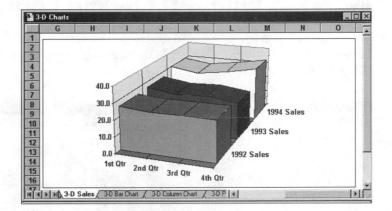

To select a 3-D area chart, select Format | AutoFormat to display the AutoFormat dialog box, choose the 3-D Area item from the Galleries list, and select a 3-D area chart from the Formats section.

Working with 3-D Bar Charts

Like 2-D bar charts, 3-D bar charts are useful for portraying competitive comparisons. You can use 3-D bar charts to present the results of sales contests, elections, or sporting events. For example, Figure 9.25 shows a comparison of a company's sales increases by region. In this format, it's clear that the West region is the "winner" because its bar extends farthest to the right.

FIGURE 9.25.

Use 3-D bar charts for competitive comparisons.

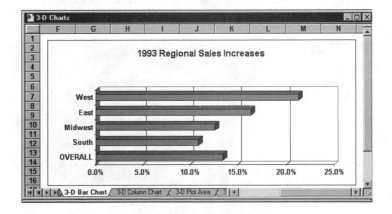

To select a 3-D bar chart, select Format | AutoFormat to display the AutoFormat dialog box, choose the 3-D Bar item from the Galleries list, and select a 3-D bar chart from the Formats section.

Working with 3-D Column Charts

You use 3-D column charts to compare multiple, distinct data items or to show individual data items over distinct intervals. Figure 9.26 shows a basic 3-D column chart that compares quarterly sales data over three years.

FIGURE 9.26.

3-D column charts compare multiple data series.

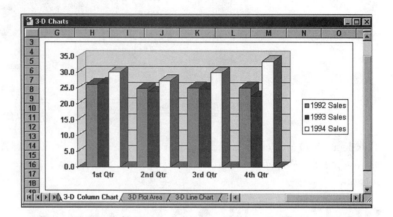

Excel has eight 3-D column AutoFormats, including three that use a three-dimensional plot area. These charts have three axes: the category axis remains the X axis, a new *series axis* becomes the Y axis, and the value axis becomes the Z axis. The advantage of this design is that it enables you to compare data both within a data series and among data series in the same chart. For example, Figure 9.27 updates the sales chart to the three-axis format. To see the quarterly progression for each year (that is, each data series), read the data markers left to right *across* the graph. To compare series, read the data markers from front to back *into* the graph.

FIGURE 9.27.

An Excel column chart with a three-dimensional plot area.

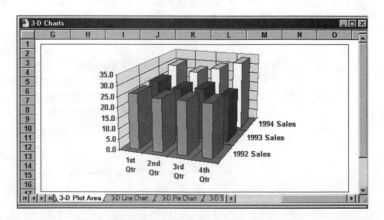

To select a 3-D column chart, select Format | AutoFormat to display the AutoFormat dialog box, choose the 3-D Column item from the Galleries list, and select a 3-D column chart from the Formats section.

Working with 3-D Line Charts

3-D line charts (they're also called *ribbon* charts) show how data series change over time using a three-dimensional plot area that incorporates the category (X) axis, the series (Y) axis, and the value (Z) axis. The individual lines are plotted as ribbons, which makes it easier to see each line and to distinguish each series when they intersect. Use 3-D line charts to see the trends underlying stock, bond, and futures prices. Also, economic indicators such as interest rates, the money supply, and inflation are best seen with this type of chart. Figure 9.28 shows a 3-D plot of a company's stock price and its 10-day moving average.

FIGURE 9.28.

3-D line charts plot series as ribbons.

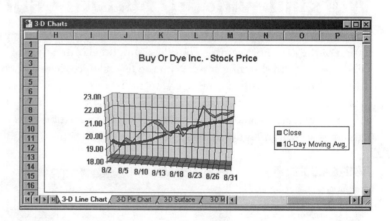

To select a 3-D line chart, select Format | AutoFormat to display the AutoFormat dialog box, choose the 3-D Line item from the Galleries list, and select a 3-D line chart from the Formats section.

Working with 3-D Pie Charts

Like 2-D pie charts, 3-D pie charts show the proportion of the whole that is contributed by each number in a single data series. A shallow cylinder (the "pie") represents the whole, and each "slice" represents an individual series value. Figure 9.29 shows a pie chart of the Earth's elements. As shown in the figure, you can highlight any of the pie slices by pulling them out from the pie. To move a slice, use the mouse pointer to drag the slice to the desired position. In Figure 9.29, the Iron slice has been moved out from the pie.

To select a 3-D pie chart, select Format | AutoFormat to display the AutoFormat dialog box, choose the 3-D Pie item from the Galleries list, and select a 3-D pie chart from the Formats section.

FIGURE 9.29.

A 3-D pie chart of the Earth's elements.

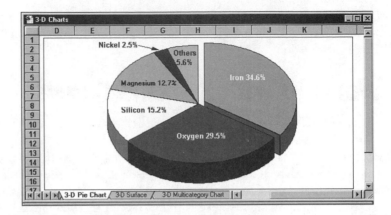

Working with 3-D Surface Charts

You use the 3-D surface chart to analyze two sets of data and determine the optimum combination of the two. For example, consider a simplified company in which profit is a function of sales expenses and shipping costs. With too few salespeople or sales materials, revenues would drop and so would profits. Conversely, spending too much on sales support also would reduce profit. Using a similar analysis, you can determine that spending too little or too much on shipping costs also would lead to lower profits. These relationships are summarized in the surface chart shown in Figure 9.30.

FIGURE 9.30.

A surface chart showing the relationship among sales, shipping costs, and profit.

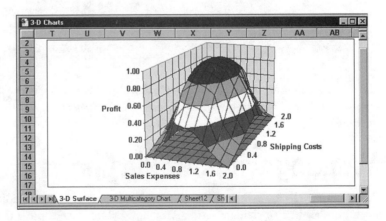

To select a 3-D surface chart, select Format | AutoFormat to display the AutoFormat dialog box, choose the 3-D Surface item from the Galleries list, and select a 3-D surface chart from the Formats section.

A surface chart is like a topographical map. The chart colors don't represent individual data series; instead, they represent points from both series that are at the same value (that is, the same height on the Z axis). In Figure 9.30, each color represents a correlation between sales expenses and shipping costs that produces a certain level of profit. The area defined by the highest color, and therefore the highest profit, is the optimum combination of sales and shipping costs.

Excel has four 3-D surface AutoFormats: a 3-D surface chart, a 3-D wireframe chart, a 2-D contour chart, and a 2-D wireframe contour chart.

> **NOTE**
>
> A contour chart shows you what the 3-D surface looks like from directly overhead. Use contour charts to help analyze the specific series combinations that produce an optimum result.

Changing the 3-D View

When you use 3-D charts, sometimes certain data points in the back of a chart get obscured behind taller data markers in the chart's foreground. This can mar the look of an otherwise attractive chart. Fortunately, Excel enables you to change a number of aspects of the 3-D view to try to get a better perspective on your data.

Excel's Format 3-D View dialog box, shown in Figure 9.31, handles these adjustments. (See the steps given later in this section for instructions on displaying this dialog box.)

FIGURE 9.31.

Use the Format 3-D View dialog box to change the view for a 3-D chart.

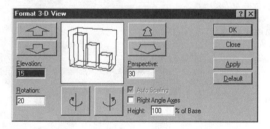

Within this dialog box you can set six options: **E**levation, **R**otation, **P**erspective, Auto **S**caling, Right Angle A**x**es, and H**e**ight.

Elevation, which is measured in degrees, controls the height from which you look at the chart. For most 3-D charts, you can enter an elevation value between –90 and 90. A 0-degree elevation puts you on the floor of the plot area, 90 degrees means that you're looking at the chart from directly overhead, and –90 degrees means that you're looking at the chart from directly underneath. Figure 9.32 shows a 3-D column chart from an elevation of 80 degrees. For 3-D bar charts, the allowable range of elevation is between 0 and 44 degrees. For pie charts, the range is from 10 to 80 degrees.

FIGURE 9.32.

A 3-D column chart from an elevation of 80 degrees.

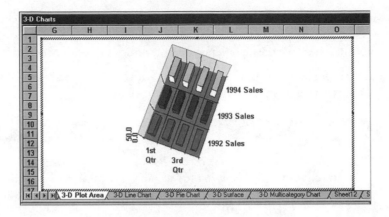

Rotation, also measured in degrees, controls the rotation of the chart around the vertical (Z) axis. For most 3-D charts, you can enter a value between 0 and 360 degrees. A 0-degree rotation puts you directly in front of the chart, 90 degrees brings you to the side of the chart, and 180 degrees shows you the back of the chart with the series in reverse order. For 3-D bar charts, the acceptable range of rotation is between 0 and 44 degrees. For pie charts, the rotation represents the angle of the first slice, in which 0 degrees puts the left edge of the slice at 12 o'clock, 90 degrees puts it at 3 o'clock, and so on. Figure 9.33 shows the 3-D pie chart of the Earth's elements (first shown in Figure 9.29) rotated to 300 degrees.

FIGURE 9.33.

Changing the rotation in a pie chart changes the angle of the first slice.

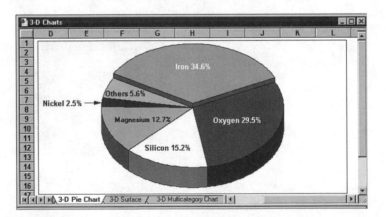

Perspective controls the sense of distance (or *perspective*) that a chart conveys. More perspective means that data markers at the back of the chart are shown relatively smaller than those at the front. (You can enter a value as high as 100 degrees.) Pie charts and 3-D bar charts don't have a perspective setting. Figure 9.34 shows a column chart with a high perspective value (80 degrees). This option is available only if the Right Angle Axes check box is deactivated.

FIGURE 9.34.

Use a high perspective value to add a sense of distance to a chart.

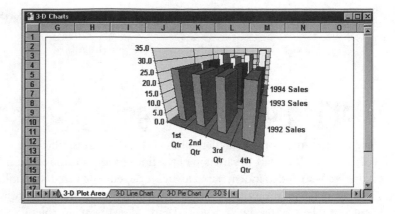

The Auto **S**caling option tells Excel to scale the chart automatically so that it always fills the entire chart window. This option is available only when the Right Angle A**x**es check box is selected.

The Right Angle A**x**es option controls the orientation of the chart axes. When you select this option, Excel draws the axes at right angles to each other and disables the **P**erspective option.

> **TIP**
>
> If your chart lines appear overly jagged, activate the Right Angle A**x**es option. The chart lines that define the walls and markers then run horizontally and vertically and should appear straight.

The H**e**ight option controls the height of the vertical (Z) axis. The height is measured as a percentage of the category (X) axis. This option is unavailable when you select Auto **S**caling.

Follow these steps to adjust the 3-D view of a chart:

1. Activate the 3-D chart you want to work with.
2. Select the F**o**rmat I 3-D **V**iew command. Excel displays the Format 3-D View dialog box.
3. Select the 3-D view options you want. The sample chart in the dialog box shows the effect of each change.
4. To see how your changes will look on the actual chart, select the **A**pply button. Excel changes the chart view but leaves the dialog box open.
5. To change the view permanently, select OK.

> **TIP**
>
> To return a chart to its default view, select the **D**efault button.

Plotting a Multicategory 3-D Chart

The three-dimensional equivalent of the 2-D XY chart is called the *multicategory* chart. You'll recall that an XY chart (a variation of the line chart) plots the relationship between two sets of numbers—an independent variable and a dependent variable. Similarly, the multicategory 3-D chart (a variation of the 3-D column chart) plots the relationship among *two* independent variables (that is, two categories) and a dependent variable. Excel plots the categories on the X and Y axes and plots the values on the Z axis.

As an illustration, consider the earlier example of the company profit that is a function of both sales expenses and shipping costs. In that example, both types of costs are independent variables, and the profit is the dependent variable. Figure 9.35 shows how you would set up a multicategory 3-D chart to analyze the relationship among these variables.

FIGURE 9.35.

A multicategory 3-D chart.

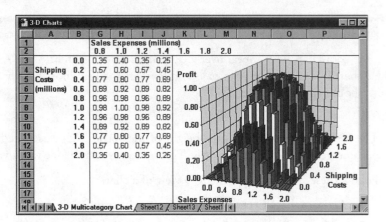

Creating a Data Map

One of the nifty new features you get with Excel for Windows 95 version 7 is called Data Map. Data Map is designed to plot geographical data by displaying, literally, a map. The values for each region (city, state, country, or whatever) are conveyed on the map using color-coded shading. Although Data Map is not strictly an Excel chart (Data Map is, in fact, a separate application that embeds a Data Map object in your worksheet), it is chartlike in that it plots values visually. Hence the coverage of Data Map in this chapter. This section shows you how to work with Data Map to plot geographical data.

Creating a Data Map

Data Map can handle all kinds of geographic data, including cities, states, provinces, countries, and even ZIP codes or postal codes. Before creating the map, make sure that the range you want to plot follows these guidelines:

- Arrange your data in columns, in which at least one column contains geographic data.

- Short forms (such as the standard two-letter state and province codes) are acceptable.

- If you're plotting postal codes, format them as text to avoid losing any leading zeros.

- When selecting the range to plot, be sure to include the column headings.

As an example, let's plot some of the data provided in the sample map information workbook. It's called Mapstats.xls and you'll find it in the \Windows\Msapps\Datamap\Data folder. Figure 9.36 shows part of the USA worksheet, which contains data by state for population, income, and other demographic information. We'll plot the total current population (the TOTPOPCUR column) by state. The steps to follow are outlined next.

FIGURE 9.36.

The Mapstats.xls workbook is full of demographic information for the United States, Canada, and many other countries.

	A	B	C	D	E	F
1	^ To select GEONAME and all DATA columns on this worksheet select "USA"					
2						
3	GEOABBR	GEONAME	TOTPOPHIS	TOTPOPCUR	TOTPOPPRO	FEMP0
4	AL	ALABAMA	4040587	4221932	4455517	
5	AK	ALASKA	550043	610350	679683	
6	AZ	ARIZONA	3665228	4000398	4452859	
7	AR	ARKANSAS	2350725	2441646	2566937	
8	CA	CALIFORNIA	29760022	31546602	33575312	14
9	CO	COLORADO	3294394	3630585	4079905	
10	CT	CONNECTICUT	3287116	3275195	3261723	
11	DE	DELAWARE	666168	707864	757702	
12	DC	DISTRICT OF COLUMBIA	606900	571592	530751	
13	FL	FLORIDA	12937926	13849741	14933526	6
14	GA	GEORGIA	6478216	7020384	7713623	
15	HI	HAWAII	1108229	1186692	1278719	
16	ID	IDAHO	1006749	1120679	1270278	
17	IL	ILLINOIS	11430602	11760900	12177648	5

Table of Contents / Data Vendors / World \ USA \ Ca

1. Select the geographic data you want to map. For our example, select the range B3:D54. (Note that this range includes the TOTPOPHIS column. This isn't strictly necessary—we could just select the noncontiguous ranges B3:B54 and D3:D54—but I want to show you how to switch between multiple columns of data and how to map multiple columns of data simultaneously.)

2. Either select the **I**nsert | **Map** command or click the Map button on the Standard toolbar. The mouse pointer changes to a crosshair.

    The Map button on the Standard toolbar.

3. Move the pointer into the worksheet where you want the map to appear, and drag the pointer to create a box that will hold the map.

4. If Data Map has more than one map available for your data, the Multiple Maps Available dialog box appears. For example, if you're plotting data by state, you see the dialog box shown in Figure 9.37. Highlight the map you want to use, and then select OK.

FIGURE 9.37.

This dialog box appears if Data Map has multiple maps that suit your data.

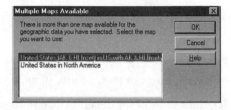

Data Map creates an initial version of the map and then displays the Data Map Control window, shown in Figure 9.38, which I'll discuss in the next section.

FIGURE 9.38.

Use the Data Map Control window to set the layout of the map.

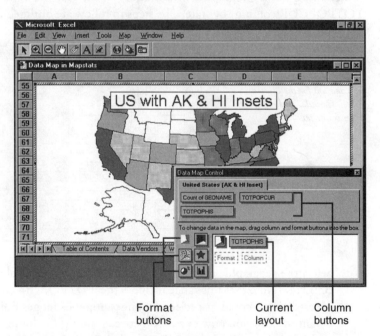

Working with the Data Map Control Window

The idea behind the Data Map Control window is to select the columns you want to map and to choose the format of the coding used to represent each value. The window is divided into three sections:

Column buttons: These buttons appear at the top of the window; you see one button for each column in the range you selected. For the column that contains the geographical data, you see Count of GEONAME (or whatever you named your column).

This button enables you to plot the number of times each geographical name appears in the column.

Format buttons: These buttons control how the data is plotted in the map. Here's a summary of what each button does:

Button	Name	Description
	Value Shading	Color-codes each region based on the number in the value axis (that is, the data column).
	Category Shading	Color-codes each region based on the entries in the category axis (that is, the column containing the geographic values). Groups similar geographic regions together.
	Dot Density	Conveys the data by means of dots (higher values are interpreted with a higher density of dots).
	Graduated Symbol	Conveys the data by means of a symbol that changes size with the data (a higher value generates a larger symbol).
	Pie Chart	Displays the data in a pie chart.
	Column Chart	Displays the data in a column chart.

Current layout: This area shows you the current map layout. The current format button is shown on the left (above the Format box), and the current data column is shown on the right (above the Column box). To change the current layout, use the following techniques:

■ To change the current column, drag one of the column buttons, and drop it on the current column. For example, we want to plot the TOTPOPCUR column, so drag it and drop it on the TOTPOPHIS button in the current layout area.

■ To change the current format, drag one of the format buttons, and drop it on the current format.

■ If you want to plot a second column, drag it and drop it *below* the current column.

When you've made your selections, you can toggle off the Data Map Control window either by selecting the **V**iew | Data Map **C**ontrol command or by clicking the Show/Hide Data Map Control button on the toolbar.

The Show/Hide Data Map Control button.

Formatting the Data Map

The basic data map might be all you need, but the Data Map program has quite a few formatting features you can use to get your map just so. Most of these features are straightforward, so I'll just run through them quickly:

- To zoom in on a section of the map, click the Zoom In button and then click on the area you want to magnify.

     The Zoom In button.

- To zoom out, click the Zoom Out button and then click on an area of the map.

     The Zoom Out button.

- To move the map within its box, click the Grabber button and then drag the map to the new location.

     The Grabber button.

- To change the map title, double-click on it and then edit the title text. You can also right-click on the title and select **F**ormat Font from the shortcut menu to change the title font. If you prefer to hide the title altogether, deactivate the **V**iew | **T**itle command.

- To add extra features to the map (such as cities, airports, and highways), select the **M**ap | **F**eatures command. In the Map Features dialog box, shown in Figure 9.39, activate the check box for each feature you want to see, and then select OK.

FIGURE 9.39.

Use the Map Features dialog box to add more features to the map.

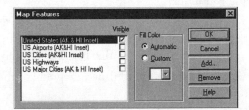

- If you're using the Value Shading format, you can set some options for this format by selecting the **M**ap | **V**alue Shading Options command. The dialog box that appears includes the following controls:

Number of value ranges: Use this control to specify the number of shading ranges that the values are divided into.

Equal number of items in each range of values: Select this option to group the same number of values into each range. For example, if you have 50 states and five value ranges, Data Map places 10 states in each range.

Equal spread of values in each range: Select this option to make each value range cover the same spread of values. For example, if your values range from 1 to 100 and you have five ranges, the first range covers 1 to 20, the second covers 21 to 40, and so on.

Color: Use this drop-down list to select the main color to use for the shading.

■ By default, Data Map displays the next-to-useless "compact" version of the legend. To get something more useful, right-click on the legend and select **E**dit. In the Edit Legend dialog box, deactivate the Use **C**ompact Format check box, edit the Legend Text boxes, and then select OK.

■ To see either the names of the map features or the underlying values for each feature, select the **T**ools | **L**abeler command, or click the Label button in the toolbar. In the dialog box that appears, select either **M**ap feature names or **V**alues from. (In the latter case, you also need to select a column from the drop-down list provided.) Select OK and then hover the mouse over a map feature to see the value, as shown in Figure 9.40.

FIGURE 9.40.

You can see the underlying values in your data map.

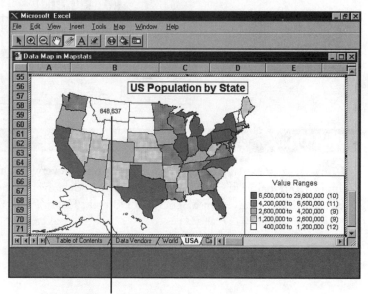

With the Label option turned on, point at a map feature to see its underlying value

Combining Multiple Chart Types in a Single Chart

All the charts you've seen so far (except XY charts) have used a single value axis and a single chart type. With Excel, you can *overlay* one chart on another to produce combination charts that display two different chart types simultaneously. The two types can even use different units and different value axes.

The next few sections show you how to use Excel's preformatted combination charts and how to add and format your own overlay charts.

Working with Excel's AutoFormat Combination Charts

The easiest way to create a combination chart is to select one of Excel's six *combination* AutoFormats. Select the Format | AutoFormat command, and in the AutoFormat dialog box, select Combination from the Galleries list. You see the formats shown in Figure 9.41.

FIGURE 9.41.

Excel's combination chart formats.

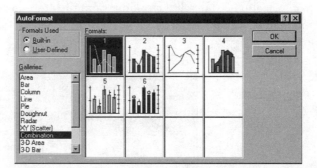

CAUTION

Converting an existing chart to a combination type overwrites any formatting you've applied. To maintain your formatting, add your own overlay. See the section in this chapter titled "Converting a Series to a Different Chart Type" for instructions.

Excel creates combination charts by overlaying one chart type on another. Table 9.2 outlines the chart types used in each of the combination chart formats.

Table 9.2. Excel's combination chart AutoFormats.

Combination	Description
1	A column chart overlaid by a line chart.
2	A column chart overlaid by a line chart that uses a separate value (Y) axis. The overlay axis appears on the right side of the plot area.
3	A line chart overlaid by a second line chart that uses a separate value (Y) axis. The overlay axis appears on the right side of the plot area.
4	An area chart overlaid by a column chart.
5	A column chart overlaid by a high, low, close line chart that uses a separate value (Y) axis. The overlay axis appears on the right side of the plot area.
6	A column chart overlaid by an open, high, low, close chart that uses a separate value (Y) axis. The overlay axis appears on the right side of the plot area.

Combination charts are useful for showing how distinct series are related. For example, Figure 9.42 shows a stock price high, low, close line chart overlaid on a column chart showing daily volume. The line chart value axis (showing units in dollars) is on the right, and the column chart value axis (showing units in shares) is on the left.

FIGURE 9.42.

A chart combining a high, low, close line chart type with a column chart type.

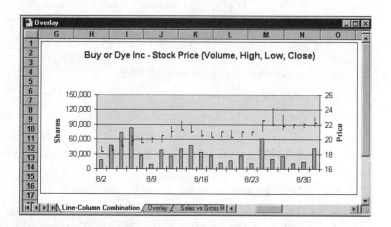

TIP

Scale the axes on your combination charts to prevent the series from interfering with each other. See Chapter 10 for information on formatting your chart axes.

Converting a Series to a Different Chart Type

If you want to create a combination chart not found among Excel's AutoFormat types, or if you have chart formatting you want to preserve, you can easily apply an overlay effect to an existing chart.

For example, Figure 9.43 shows a chart with three series: sales figures for 1993, sales figures for 1994, and a series that plots the growth from 1993 to 1994. The chart clearly shows that the growth series would make more sense as a line chart. Excel enables you to convert individual data series into chart types. To do so, follow these steps:

FIGURE 9.43.

The growth series would be better as a line chart.

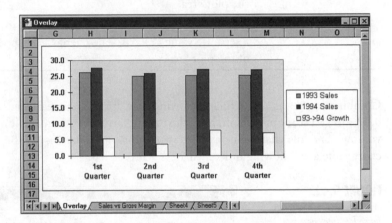

1. Activate the chart you want to work with.
2. Click on the series you want to convert.
3. Select the Format | Chart Type command (or right-click on the series and select Chart Type from the shortcut menu) to display the Chart Type dialog box.
4. In the Apply to group, activate the Selected Series option. (This option should already be selected.)
5. Select the chart type you want to use for the series.
6. Select OK. Excel converts the series to the chart type you selected. Figure 9.44 shows the preceding chart with the Growth series converted to a line chart.

FIGURE 9.44.

The revised chart with the Growth series converted to a line chart.

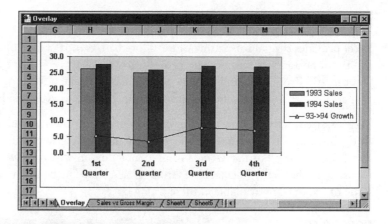

Working with Chart Type Groups

Excel divides a chart's data series into different *chart type groups.* Because most charts use only one chart type, usually there's only one chart group. When you convert one or more series to a different type, however, Excel creates a new chart type group for those series. For example, the combination chart shown in Figure 9.44 has two chart groups: column and line.

You can work with series individually or as a group. The next few sections show you how to work with groups.

Changing the Chart Type of a Chart Group

If you want to convert the series in an existing chart group to a different chart type, follow these steps:

1. Activate the chart you want to work with.
2. Select the Format | Chart **T**ype command (or right-click on one of the series, and select Chart Type) to display the Chart Type dialog box.
3. In the Apply to group, activate the **G**roup option.
4. Select the group you want to work with from the **G**roup list.
5. Select the chart type you want to use for the group.
6. Select OK. Excel converts the group to the chart type you selected.

Formatting Chart Groups

Excel provides several formatting options for chart groups. These options enable you to control the appearance of certain aspects of the group's chart type. For example, with a line chart you can add drop lines, and with a column chart you can adjust the gap between categories. You also can change the series order within the group and even display a second value axis.

To get started, activate the chart you want to work with, and then pull down the Format menu. At the bottom of the menu is a list of groups in the chart. When you select one of these groups, Excel displays the Format *Group* Group dialog box, in which *Group* is the group you chose. Figure 9.45 shows the Format Line Group dialog box. The next few sections take you through some of the options available in these dialog boxes.

FIGURE 9.45.

The Format Line Group dialog box.

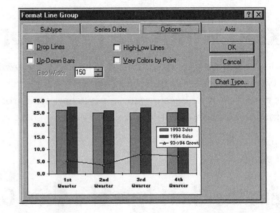

Setting Group Options

The Options tab of the Format Group dialog boxes contains various layout options specific to each chart type. In the Format Line Group dialog box, for example, you can add **D**rop Lines (I'll show you an example in the next chapter), **U**p-Down Bars, and High-**L**ow Lines (see Figure 9.42).

> **NOTE**
>
> Up-down bars are used mostly in stock charts. If the close is less than the open, the stock is "down" and a black bar joins the two values. If the stock is "up," a white bar joins them. Charts with up-down bars are called "candlestick" charts.

Changing the Series Order of a Group

To change the order of the series in a group, select the Series Order tab in the appropriate Format Group dialog box. To change the order, select a series from the **S**eries Order list, and then click either the Move **U**p or the Move **D**own button.

Adding a Second Value Axis

If your chart groups use different units or have data series with different value ranges, you can add a second value axis for one of the groups. For example, consider the combination chart shown in Figure 9.46. This chart attempts to compare yearly sales with gross margin. However, the numbers in each series use completely different ranges. The sales numbers range from 95.9 to 119.5, whereas the gross margin figures range from 0.275 to 0.311. Because Excel has to allow for the larger range, the gross-margin line is almost invisible. The solution is to add a second value axis for the line group. Figure 9.47 shows the result.

FIGURE 9.46.

Series with different ranges can produce ineffective charts.

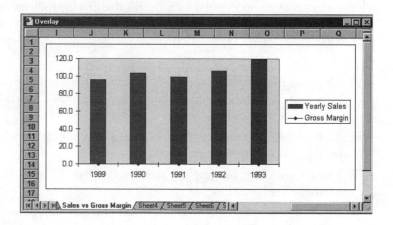

Follow the steps in this procedure to add a second value axis for a chart group:

1. Pull down the F**o**rmat menu, and select the group you want to work with from the list at the bottom of the menu.

2. Select the Axis tab from the dialog box that appears.

3. Activate the **S**econdary Axis option.

4. Select OK. Excel adds a new axis to the chart.

5. Scale each axis as needed (as described in the next chapter).

FIGURE 9.47.

Overlaying one series and adjusting the axes ranges leads to a better comparison.

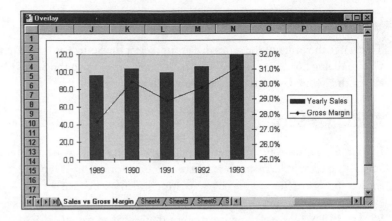

Summary

This chapter got you up to speed with Excel's charting capabilities. After some brief charting theory, we looked at the various ways you can create charts, and then we examined 2-D charts, 3-D charts, the Data Map applications, and combination charts. Here are a few more chapters to check out for related information:

- The Data Map application embeds its maps as objects in the current worksheet. To learn more about object linking and embedding, read Chapter 7, "Exchanging Data with Other Applications."

- To learn how to format charts, add objects to your charts, and edit chart data series, see Chapter 10, "Enhancing Charts."

- You can use charts for simple what-if data analysis. Chapter 17, "Basic Analytic Methods," tells you how.

- To learn how to manipulate charts under programmatic control, head for Chapter 24, "Manipulating Excel with VBA."

Enhancing Charts

10

After you've created a chart and selected the appropriate chart type, you can enhance the chart's appearance by formatting any of the various chart elements. This chapter shows you how to format chart axes, data markers, and gridlines; how to move and size an embedded chart; how to add graphic objects to a chart; and how to edit your chart's data series.

Selecting Chart Elements

An Excel chart is composed of elements such as axes, data markers, gridlines, and text, each with its own formatting options. Before you can format an element, however, you need to select it. Table 10.1 lists the mouse techniques for selecting various chart items. (Note that the chart must be activated before you try these techniques. See Chapter 9, "Working with Chart Types," to learn how to activate a chart.)

Table 10.1. Mouse techniques for selecting chart elements.

Action	Result
Click on the chart background.	The entire chart is selected.
Click on an empty part of the plot area.	The plot area is selected.
Click on an axis or an axis label.	The axis is selected.
Click on a gridline.	The gridline is selected.
Click on any marker in the series.	The data series is selected.
Click on a data marker once and then click on it a second time.	The data marker is selected.
Click on an object.	The chart object is selected.

If you don't have a mouse, or if you prefer to use the keyboard, you can navigate the chart elements using the arrow keys. To make navigating the chart easier, Excel groups related chart elements. For example, each data series is a group of individual data markers. Following is a list of the groups in a chart in their normal selection order:

Chart
Plot area
3-D floor
3-D walls
3-D corners
Legend

Axes
Titles
Gridlines
Data series
Other chart elements (such as high-low lines, trendlines, and error bars)
Other graphic objects (such as text and arrows)

NOTE

Excel provides no way to activate an embedded chart using the keyboard. To navigate an embedded chart using the keyboard, you must first activate the chart using the mouse.

You use the arrow keys to move between or within categories, as outlined in Table 10.2.

Table 10.2. Keyboard techniques for selecting chart elements.

Key to Press	Result
Up arrow	Selects the first element in the next chart group.
Down arrow	Selects the last element in the preceding group.
Right arrow	Selects the next element in the current group. If the last element in the current group is selected, pressing the right-arrow key selects the first element in the next group.
Left arrow	Selects the preceding element in the current group. If the first element in the current group is selected, pressing the left-arrow key selects the last element in the preceding group.

When you select a chart element, Excel displays the name of the element in the Name box of the formula bar, and it attaches *selection handles* to the element. Figure 10.1 shows a chart with the plot area selected.

FIGURE 10.1.

Excel surrounds selected chart elements with selection handles and displays the element's name in the Name box.

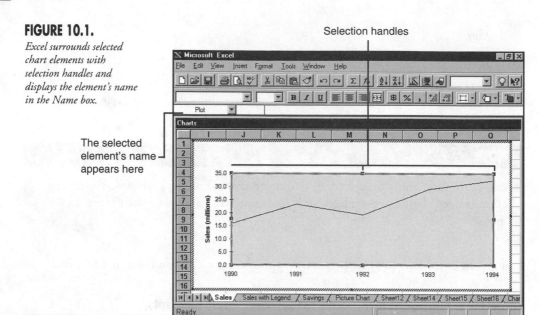

Selection handles

The selected element's name appears here

Formatting Chart Axes

Excel provides various options for controlling the appearance of your chart axes. You can hide axes; set the typeface, size, and style of axis labels; format the axis lines and tick marks; and adjust the axis scale. You can find most of the axis formatting options in the Format Axis dialog box, shown in Figure 10.2. To display this dialog box, select the axis you want to format, and then select the Format | Selected Axis command.

FIGURE 10.2.

Use the Format Axis dialog box to enhance the look of your chart axes.

TIP

To access the Format Axis dialog box quickly, you can either double-click on an axis, select the axis, and press Ctrl-1, or right-click on an axis and select Format Axis from the shortcut menu.

Formatting Axis Patterns

The Patterns tab in the Format Axis dialog box enables you to set various options for the axis line and tick marks. Here's a summary of the control groups in the Patterns tab:

Axis	These options format the axis line. Select **N**one to remove the line, or select Custom to adjust the **S**tyle, **C**olor, and **W**eight. The Sample box shows you how the line will look.
Tick Mark Type	These options control the position of the **Ma**jor and Mino**r** tick marks.
Tick-Mark Labels	These options control the position of the tick mark labels.

NOTE

The major tick marks are the tick marks that carry the axis labels. The minor tick marks are the tick marks that appear between the labels. See the next section to learn how to control the units of both the major and the minor tick marks.

Formatting an Axis Scale

You can format the scale of your chart axes to set things such as the range of numbers on an axis and where the category and value axes intersect.

To format the scale, select the Scale tab in the Format Axis dialog box. If you're formatting the value (Y) axis, you see the layout shown in Figure 10.3. These options format several scale characteristics, such as the range of values (Mi**n**imum and Ma**x**imum), the tick-mark units (Ma**j**or Unit and M**i**nor Unit), and where the category (X) axis crosses the value axis. For the last of these characteristics, you have three choices:

- Activate the Category (X) Axis **C**rosses at check box. This places the X axis at the bottom of the chart (that is, at the minimum value on the Y axis).
- Enter a value in the Category (X) Axis **C**rosses at text box.
- Activate the Category (X) Axis Crosses at **M**aximum Value check box (this places the X axis at the top of the chart).

Formatting the value axis scale properly can make a big difference in the impact of your charts. For example, Figure 10.4 shows a chart with a value axis scale ranging from 0 to 50. Figure 10.5 shows the same chart with the value axis scale between 18 and 23. As you can see, the trend of the data is much clearer and more dramatic in Figure 10.5.

FIGURE 10.3.

The Scale tab for the value (Y) axis.

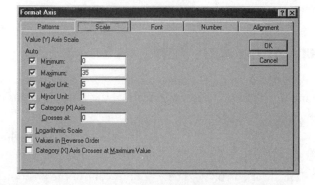

FIGURE 10.4.

A stock chart showing an apparently flat trend.

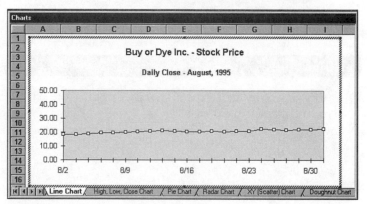

FIGURE 10.5.

The same stock chart with an adjusted scale shows an obvious up trend.

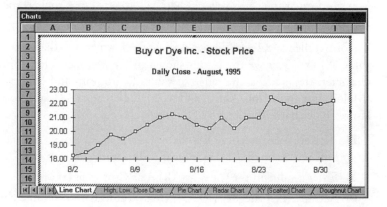

For the category (X) axis, the Scale tab appears as shown in Figure 10.6. These options mostly control where the value (Y) axis crosses the category (X) axis, and the frequency of categories:

■ Use the Value (Y) Axis **C**rosses at Category Number text box to control where the Y axis crosses the X axis. For example, an entry of 1 (the default) places the Y axis on the left side of the chart. If you prefer to see the Y axis on the right side of the chart, activate the Value (Y) Axis Crosses at **M**aximum Category check box.

■ The major tick-mark unit is controlled by the Number of Categories between Tick-Mark **L**abels text box. For example, an entry of 5 puts a tick mark label every five categories.

■ The total number of tick marks is controlled by the Number of Categories between Tick Mar**k**s text box. For example, an entry of 1 provides a tick mark for each category.

■ When the Value (Y) Axis Crosses **b**etween Categories check box is deactivated (the default), Excel plots the values on the tick marks. If you activate this check box, Excel plots the values between the tick marks.

■ Activating the Categories in **R**everse Order check box displays the categories along the X axis in reverse order.

FIGURE 10.6.

The Scale tab for the category (X) axis.

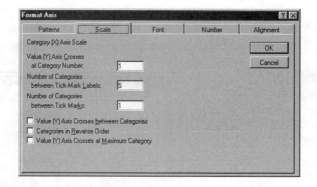

Formatting Axis Labels

You can change the font, numeric format, and alignment of the labels that appear along the axis. To change the label font, select the Font tab in the Format Axis dialog box, and then select the font options you want.

To change the numeric format of axis labels (assuming, of course, that the labels are numbers, dates, or times), you have two choices:

■ Format the worksheet data series that generated the labels. Excel uses this formatting automatically when it sets up the axis labels.

■ Select the Number tab in the Format Axis dialog box, and then select a numeric format from the options provided. (See the section "Numeric Display Formats" in

Chapter 4, "Formatting Excel Worksheets," for explanations of the various options in the Number tab.)

To format the alignment of the axis labels, select the Alignment tab in the Format Axis dialog box, and then select the option you want from the Orientation group.

TIP

You also can use the tools on the Formatting toolbar (such as Bold and Currency Style) to format the labels of a selected axis.

Hiding and Displaying Axes

In the "Working with Text Boxes" section of Chapter 4, I showed you how to add text boxes to your worksheets. You can use the same technique to add text boxes to your charts as well. Text boxes are useful for pointing out interesting results, adding explanatory notes, or for creating custom category or value labels.

If you're creating custom category or value labels, you'll want to avoid having the labels conflict with the chart's existing axis labels. The easiest way to do that is to hide the axis (which hides the labels too). For example, Figure 10.7 shows a line chart in which custom category labels have been added to the plot area, making the category axis unnecessary.

FIGURE 10.7.

Adding custom category labels often makes the category (X) axis unnecessary.

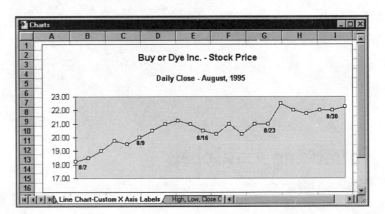

Follow these steps to hide an axis:

1. Select the Insert | Axes command. The Axes dialog box appears, as shown in Figure 10.8.

FIGURE 10.8.

*Use the Axes dialog box
to toggle the X or Y axis
on or off.*

To open the Axes dialog box quickly, right-click on an axis, and then choose Insert Axes from the shortcut menu.

2. Deactivate the check box for the axis you want to hide.
3. Select OK. Excel hides both the axis and the axis labels from the chart.

Formatting Chart Data Markers

A *data marker* is a symbol Excel uses to plot each value (data point). Examples of data markers are small circles or squares for line charts, rectangles for column and bar charts, and pie slices for pie charts. Depending on the type of marker you're dealing with, you can format the marker's color, pattern, style, or border.

To begin, select the data marker or markers you want to work with:

■ If you want to format the entire series, click on any data marker in the series, and then select the Format | Selected Series command. Excel displays the Format Data Series dialog box.

■ If you want to format a single data marker, click on the marker once to select the entire series, and then click on the marker a second time. (Note, however, that you don't double-click on the marker. If you do, you just get the Format Data Series dialog box. Click once on the marker, wait a couple of beats, and then click on it again.) Then choose the Format | Selected Data Point command to display the Format Data Point dialog box.

You also can display the Format Data Series dialog box either by double-clicking on an axis or by selecting the axis and pressing Ctrl-1. Displaying the Format Data Point is similar: select the data point and then either double-click on it or press Ctrl-1.

Whichever method you choose, select the Patterns tab to display the formatting options for the series markers. Figure 10.9 shows the Patterns tab for an area, bar, column, pie, or doughnut chart marker. (The corresponding Format Data Point dialog box has only the Patterns and Data Labels tabs.)

FIGURE 10.9.

The Patterns tab for area, bar, column, pie, and doughnut chart data series.

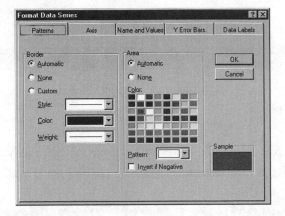

Use the Border group to either turn off the border or define the **S**tyle, **C**olor, and **W**eight of the marker border. Use the Area section to assign marker colors and patterns.

You get a different set of options when you format line, XY, or radar chart markers, as shown in Figure 10.10. Use the Line section to format the **S**tyle, **C**olor, and **W**eight of the data series line. The **S**moothed Line option (available only for line and XY charts) smoothes out some of a line's rough edges. Use the Marker section to format the marker Sty**l**e as well as the **F**oreground and **B**ackground colors.

FIGURE 10.10.

The Patterns dialog box for line, XY, and radar charts.

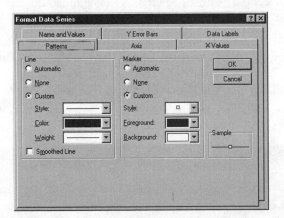

Displaying and Formatting Chart Gridlines

Adding horizontal or vertical gridlines can make your charts easier to read. For each axis, you can display a major gridline, a minor gridline, or both. The positioning of these gridlines is determined by the numbers you enter for the axis scales. For a value axis, major gridlines are governed by the Major Unit, and minor gridlines are governed by the Minor Unit. (The Major and Minor Units are properties of the value axis scale. To learn how to adjust these values, see the section earlier in this chapter titled "Formatting an Axis Scale.") For a category axis, major gridlines are governed by the number of categories between tick labels, and minor gridlines are governed by the number of categories between tick marks.

Displaying Gridlines

The following procedure shows you how to display gridlines:

1. Select the **I**nsert | **G**ridlines command. Excel displays the Gridlines dialog box, shown in Figure 10.11.

FIGURE 10.11.

The Gridlines dialog box.

TIP

To access the Gridlines dialog box quickly, right-click on the plot area, and select Insert Gridlines from the shortcut menu.

---

2. Activate the check boxes for the gridlines you want to display.
3. Select OK.

 Click on this tool on the Chart toolbar to display major value axis gridlines on your chart.

Formatting Gridlines

You can format the style, color, and weight of your gridlines by following these steps:

1. Select a gridline.
2. Select the **F**ormat | **S**elected Gridlines command to display the Format Gridline dialog box.

> **TIP**
>
> You also can display the Format Gridline dialog box by double-clicking on a gridline, by selecting a gridline and pressing Ctrl-1, or by right-clicking on a gridline and choosing Format Gridlines from the shortcut menu.

3. Use the Patterns tab to select the gridline options you want (**S**tyle, **C**olor, and **W**eight).
4. Select OK.

Formatting the Plot Area and Background

You can format borders, patterns, and colors for both the chart plot area and the background. To format either of these areas, follow this procedure:

1. Select the plot area or chart background.
2. Select either the Format | Selected Plot Area command or the Format | Selected Chart Area command to display the appropriate Format dialog box.

> **TIP**
>
> To quickly display the appropriate Format dialog box, you also can double-click on the plot area or background, you can select either one and press Ctrl-1, or you can right-click on either one and select either Format Plot Area or Format Chart Area from the shortcut menu.

3. In the Patterns tab, select the options you want in the Border and Area groups.
4. If you're in the Format Chart Area dialog box, you also can select the Font tab to format the chart font.
5. Select OK.

Working with User-Defined Chart AutoFormats

Excel has so many chart formatting options that you can spend more time making your charts look good than you spend making them in the first place. To save time down the road, you can store your favorite chart formats as *user-defined AutoFormats*. You later can quickly apply these formats using the AutoFormat dialog box (as described in the preceding chapter; see the section titled "Selecting an AutoFormat Chart Type").

Adding a User-Defined AutoFormat

The following procedure shows you the steps to follow to add a user-defined AutoFormat:

1. Apply the formatting options you want to save as an AutoFormat (or activate a chart that already uses the formatting).
2. Choose the Format | AutoFormat command to display the AutoFormat dialog box.
3. Activate the User-Defined option.
4. Select the Customize button. Excel displays the User-Defined AutoFormats dialog box.
5. Select the Add button. The Add Custom AutoFormat dialog box appears, shown in Figure 10.12.

FIGURE 10.12.

Use the Add Custom AutoFormat dialog box to name and describe your AutoFormat.

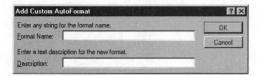

6. Use the Format Name text box to name your AutoFormat and the Description text box to enter a brief description (the maximum is 32 characters). When you're done, select OK. Excel returns you to the User-Defined AutoFormats dialog box and adds the new format to the Formats list.
7. Select Close to return to the chart.

Deleting a User-Defined AutoFormat

If you have some user-defined AutoFormats you no longer need, you should delete them. The following procedure takes you through the necessary steps:

1. Choose the Format | AutoFormat command to display the AutoFormat dialog box.
2. Activate the User-Defined option.
3. Select the Customize button to display the User-Defined AutoFormats dialog box.
4. Use the Formats list to highlight the AutoFormat you want to delete.
5. Select the Delete button. Excel asks you to confirm the deletion.
6. Select OK. Excel deletes the format.
7. Repeat steps 4 through 6 to delete other formats.
8. Select Close to return to the chart.

Sizing an Embedded Chart

You can size charts embedded in a worksheet to suit your needs. As with other Excel objects, when you select an embedded chart, a number of *selection handles* appear around the chart. You size the chart by dragging these handles with the mouse pointer. The following procedure outlines the steps to follow:

1. Click on the chart you want to size. Excel displays selection handles around the chart, as shown in Figure 10.13.

FIGURE 10.13.

Size a chart by dragging the selection handles.

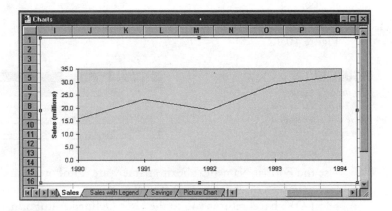

2. Position the mouse pointer over the handle you want to use for sizing. The pointer changes to a two-headed arrow.

3. Drag the handle to the position you want.

TIP

Hold down the Alt key while dragging the handle to make the chart border snap to the worksheet gridlines.

4. Release the mouse button. Excel changes the chart size.
5. Repeat steps 2 through 4 to adjust other sides of the chart.
6. Press the Esc key or click outside the chart to remove the selection handles.

Moving an Embedded Chart

As your worksheets grow, you might find that embedded charts are getting in the way of your data. You can move these charts by following these steps:

1. Click on the chart you want to move.

2. Position the mouse pointer inside the chart box.

3. Drag the mouse pointer to position the chart where you want it. Excel displays the new chart position with a dashed outline.

4. Release the mouse button. Excel moves the chart.

Adding Objects to a Chart

Using charts in a presentation is a great way to make a point or display important information. But even an attractively formatted chart can be difficult to interpret without some guidelines. The next few sections show you how to add text, legends, arrows, and other graphic objects to your charts to make them easier to understand.

> **NOTE**
>
> When you enhance your chart by adding text boxes or other elements such as arrows from Excel's drawing toolbar, these elements are not automatically resized or moved if you attempt to resize or move an embedded chart.

Adding and Formatting Chart Text

One of the best ways to make your charts more readable is to attach some descriptive text to various chart elements. Excel works with three types of text: titles, data labels, and text boxes. I covered text boxes in Chapter 4 (see the "Working with Text Boxes" section), so the next few sections show you how to use titles and data labels.

Adding Chart Titles

Excel enables you to add titles to the overall chart and to the chart axes, as shown in Figure 10.14. You use the Titles dialog box to add these titles (as described later in this section). Depending on the type of chart you're dealing with, the Titles dialog box provides you with some or all of the following options:

Chart **T**itle	Adds a title centered above the chart.
Value (Y) Axis	Adds a title beside the value axis.
Value (Z) Axis	Adds a title beside the value axis of a 3-D chart.
Category (X) Axis	Adds a title below the category axis.
Series (Y) Axis	Adds a title beside the series axis of a 3-D chart.

Second Value (**Y**) Axis	Adds a title to a second value axis (see the section called "Combining Multiple Chart Types in a Single Chart" in Chapter 9).
Second Category (**X**) Axis	Adds a title to a second category axis (see Chapter 9).

FIGURE 10.14.

A chart with sample text objects.

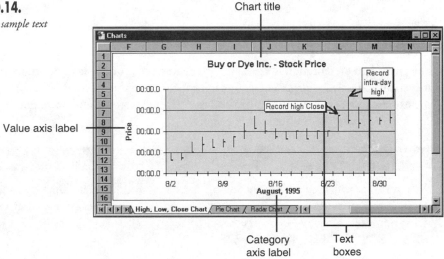

Work through the steps in the following procedure to add attached text to your chart. (If you're adding a label to a data point, select the appropriate data marker before beginning these steps.)

1. Activate the chart you want to work with.
2. Select the **Insert | Titles** command. Excel displays the Titles dialog box. Figure 10.15 shows the Titles dialog box for a 2-D chart.

FIGURE 10.15.

Use the Titles dialog box to select which title you want to appear on your chart.

3. Activate the check boxes for the titles you want to add to the chart.
4. Select OK. For each option you selected, Excel adds a temporary title to the chart.
5. Click on a title box to select it.
6. If you want to replace the existing text, type the title you want to use, and press Enter. If you prefer to edit the existing text, click on the title box again to place an insertion-point cursor inside the box.
7. Repeat steps 5 and 6 for the other titles you added.

TIP

To start a new line when entering attached text, press Ctrl-Enter. To enter a tab, press Ctrl-Tab.

Adding Data Marker Labels

You can add text to individual data markers by carrying out the steps in the following procedure:

1. Activate the chart you want to work with.
2. Select the **I**nsert | **D**ata Labels command. Excel displays the Data Labels dialog box. The available options depend on the type of chart. Figure 10.16 shows the options for a pie chart series.

FIGURE 10.16.

The Data Labels dialog box for a pie chart data series.

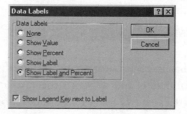

3. Select the label options you want to use.
4. Select OK.

Formatting Chart Text

You can format chart text to highlight the text or to make your chart conform to your presentation style. The following procedure shows you how it's done:

1. Activate the chart you want to work with.
2. Select the text box you want to format.
3. Select the F**o**rmat | S**e**lected *ChartText* command, in which *ChartText* is the type of text you selected (chart title, data label, and so on).

TIP

You also can press Ctrl-1 or right-click on the title and select Format *ChartText* from the shortcut menu (where, again, *ChartText* is the type of text you're working with).

4. Use the Patterns tab to format the box Border, as well as the Area colors and patterns.

5. Select the Font tab to format the text box's font.

6. Use the controls in the Alignment tab to format the Text Alignment and Orientation.

7. Select OK.

Using Worksheet Text in a Chart

You can add text to a chart by linking a text object to a cell in a worksheet. For example, you can link the title you use in a chart to the title of the underlying worksheet. That way, if you change the worksheet title, Excel updates the chart automatically. The following procedure shows you how to link chart text to a worksheet:

1. Select the chart text object you want to link.

2. Type = (an equals sign) to let Excel know that you want to enter a formula.

3. Activate the worksheet and select the cell containing the text you want.

4. Click on the Enter box or press Enter to confirm the formula. Excel adds the cell text to the chart edit box. The newly selected text replaces whatever text used to be in the object.

The reference that Excel uses for chart text has the form *worksheet!address*. Here, *worksheet* is the worksheet tab name, and *address* is the absolute cell address of the worksheet cell. For example, Figure 10.17 shows a chart title linked to a worksheet cell. The formula reference is `'High, Low, Close Chart'!$F$1`.

FIGURE 10.17.

A chart title linked to a worksheet cell.

Chart text formula

Worksheet text

Chart title

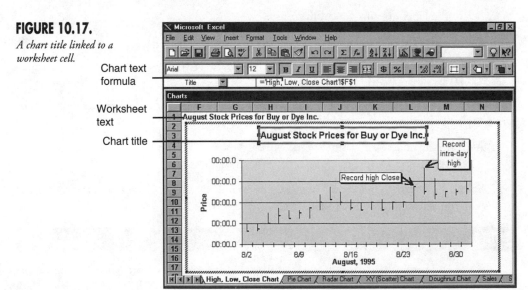

> **TIP**
>
> If you want the chart title to be the same as the worksheet name, first enter the following formula anywhere in the worksheet:
>
> ```
> =RIGHT(CELL("filename",A1),LEN(CELL("filename",A1))-FIND("]",
> ➥CELL("filename",A1)))
> ```
>
> Now activate the chart title and, in the formula bar, type an equals sign (=) and then click on the cell containing the formula.

Adding and Formatting a Chart Legend

If your chart includes multiple data series, you should add a legend to explain the series markers. This makes your chart more readable and makes it easier for others to distinguish each series.

To add a legend to a chart, simply select the Insert | Legend command. Excel creates the legend automatically from the worksheet data. To delete a legend, select it and press the Delete key.

 The Chart toolbar's Legend tool toggles the legend on and off.

You can format your legends with the same options you used to format chart text. Select the legend, and then select the Format | Selected Legend command to display the Format Legend dialog box. You can then use the Patterns and Font tabs to format the legend. You also can use the options in the Placement tab to change the position of the legend. (Alternatively, you can drag the legend to a different location.) Figure 10.18 shows a chart with a formatted legend.

FIGURE 10.18.

A chart with a formatted legend.

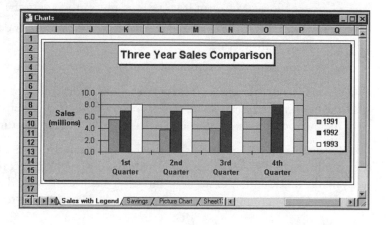

Adding and Formatting Chart Arrows

Even though you'll often use chart text for general remarks, it's common to use text to point out a significant result or a specific piece of data that needs explanation. When you do this, attach an arrow to the text that points at the appropriate data (see Figure 10.17 for an example). Follow these steps to add an arrow to a chart:

1. Display the Drawing toolbar and click on the Arrow tool.

     Click the Drawing button on the Standard toolbar to display the Drawing toolbar.

     The Arrow button from the Drawing toolbar.

2. Position the mouse pointer where you want the arrow to start.

3. Drag the pointer until the arrow has the length and direction you want, and then release the button.

To move an arrow, position the mouse pointer on the shaft of the arrow, and drag the arrow to the new position.

You can format an arrow by selecting it, executing the Format | Selected Object command, and then using the Patterns tab in the Format Object dialog box.

Creating Picture Charts

For a different twist to your column, line, or radar charts, you can replace the regular data markers with graphic images imported from programs such as Windows Paint or CorelDRAW!. The following procedure outlines the steps to follow:

1. Copy the image you want from your graphics program to the Windows Clipboard.

2. In Excel, activate the chart and then select the data series or data marker in which you want to use the picture.

3. Select the Edit | Paste command. Excel pastes the picture into the chart.

When you first paste the picture into the chart, Excel stretches the image according to the number that the marker represents. If you prefer, you can have Excel use stacks of the image to represent the number. Figure 10.19 shows an example of a stacked picture chart.

To change to a stacked picture, select the data series and then select the Format | Selected Series command to display the Format Data Series dialog box. Select the Patterns tab, and then activate the Stack option to stack the images. To adjust the scale that Excel uses, activate the Stack and Scale option, and enter a number in the Units/Picture text box.

FIGURE 10.19.

A stacked picture chart.

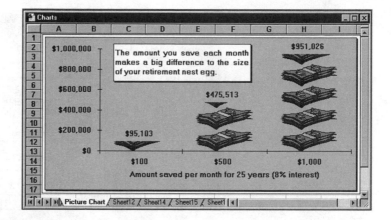

Data Series Editing

A chart is only as useful as the worksheet information on which it's based. If the chart data is out-of-date or erroneous, the chart itself is of little use and might even be misleading. Fortunately, Excel makes it easy to update your charts whenever you add or edit worksheet data.

The rest of this chapter shows you the ins and outs of the series formulas used by Excel charts. It also shows you how to use these formulas to edit your chart data series and even add new data series.

Changing Data Series Values

The easiest way to update a chart is to edit the individual data series numbers in the associated worksheet. Because Excel maintains a link between the worksheet and the chart, the chart is adjusted automatically. This provides you with an extra what-if analysis tool. By arranging your worksheet and chart so that you can see both windows, you can plug numbers into the worksheet and watch the results on the chart.

> **NOTE**
>
> See Chapter 17, "Basic Analytic Methods," for more information on using Excel for what-if analysis.

For example, Figure 10.20 shows a worksheet that computes the future value of regular deposits to a retirement account. The accompanying chart shows the cumulative savings over time. (The numbers shown in the chart for 15, 20, and 25 years are linked to the appropriate cells, as described earlier in this chapter.) By plugging in different numbers for the interest rate, annual deposit, or deposit type, you can watch the effect on the total savings. Figure 10.21 shows the result when you change the annual deposit from $5,000 to $10,000.

FIGURE 10.20.

Chart values are linked to the corresponding cells on the worksheet.

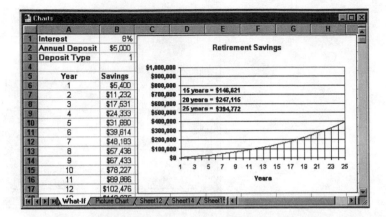

FIGURE 10.21.

When you change a variable in the worksheet, Excel updates the chart automatically.

Annual deposit changed to $10,000

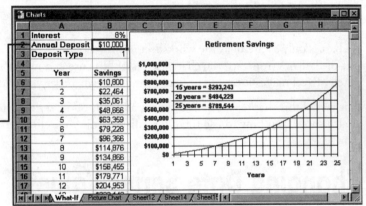

The process of editing numbers in a worksheet and watching a linked chart update automatically is relatively straightforward. Because the link extends both ways, however, it's possible to turn this process around. When you make changes to a chart data point, Excel updates the worksheet automatically. You can do this with 2-D bar, column, line, and XY charts by using the mouse to drag a data marker to a new position. If the data marker represents a worksheet value, Excel adjusts the contents of the corresponding cell. If the data marker represents a formula, Excel uses the Goal Seek tool to work backward and derive the appropriate formula input values.

NOTE

For an in-depth treatment of Goal Seek, see Chapter 17.

An example helps explain this process. Suppose that your goal is to retire in 25 years with $1,000,000 in savings. Assuming a constant interest rate, how much do you need to set aside annually to reach your goal? The idea is to adjust the chart data marker at 25 years so that it plots $1,000,000. The following procedure lists the steps required to do this:

1. Activate the chart and select the specific data marker you want to adjust by first selecting the series and then selecting the marker. Excel adds selection handles to the marker. For this example, you would select the data marker on the category axis that corresponds to 25 years.

2. Drag the black selection handle to the desired value. As you drag the handle, the current value appears in the formula bar's Name box. Figure 10.22 shows an example.

FIGURE 10.22.

You can use a chart to do what-if analysis by dragging a data marker to a new value.

The Name box displays the new value as you drag the data marker

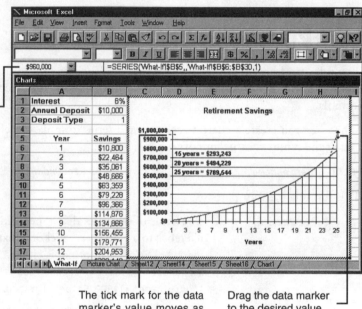

The tick mark for the data marker's value moves as you drag the data marker

Drag the data marker to the desired value

3. Release the mouse button. If the marker references a number in a cell, Excel changes the number and redraws the chart. If the marker references a formula, as in the example, Excel displays the Goal Seek dialog box, shown in Figure 10.23. The Set cell box shows the cell referenced by the data marker, the To value box shows the new number you selected, and the By changing cell box is the variable for the formula.

FIGURE 10.23.

If the data marker is derived from a formula, Excel runs Goal Seek.

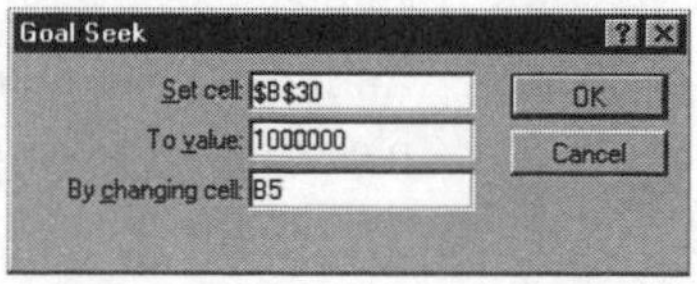

4. Enter the appropriate numbers. For the example, you would enter B5 in the By changing cell box to calculate the required annual deposit.

5. Select OK. Excel displays the Goal Seek Status dialog box as it calculates the new number.

6. When the iteration is complete, select OK.

> **NOTE**
>
> Use this technique to make visual adjustments to profit targets. You also can use Goal Seek to recalculate profit variables such as sales and expense budgets.

Working with Series Formulas

To understand how Excel links a worksheet and a chart, and to use the more complex series editing techniques presented in the rest of this chapter, you need to understand the series formula.

Whenever you create a chart, Excel sets up a series formula to define each chart data series. Here's the syntax for this formula:

```
=SERIES(SeriesName, XAxisLabels, YAxisValues, PlotOrder)
```

This formula has four parts:

SeriesName	The name of the series that appears in chart legends. It can be a reference to a worksheet label or a text string (in quotation marks). The general format is either *WorksheetName!CellReference* (Sales!$A$3, for example) or "*SeriesName*" ("1992 Sales", for example).
XAxisLabels	Appear as text on the category (X) axis (or as the X axis numbers in an XY chart). An X axis label can be a range or a range name. The general format is *WorksheetName!RangeReference* (Sales!$B$1:$E$1, for example).
YAxisValues	Plotted on the value (Y) axis. A Y axis value can be a range or a range name. The general format is *WorksheetName!RangeReference* (Sales!$B$3:$E$3, for example).
PlotOrder	An integer that represents the order in which each series is plotted on the chart.

As shown in Figure 10.24, the series formula appears in the formula bar whenever you select a chart data series.

FIGURE 10.24.

When you select a data series, the series formula appears in the formula bar.

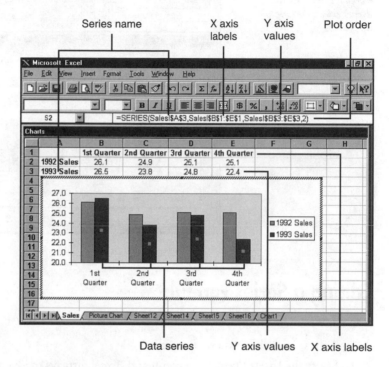

Editing a Data Series

When you make changes to an existing worksheet data series, Excel updates your charts automatically by referring to the series formula. If you make changes to an area of the worksheet not referenced by the series formula, however, Excel doesn't adjust the chart. If you extend or reduce a series on a worksheet, you have to tell Excel to extend or reduce the range in the series formula. For example, suppose that a new column showing yearly totals is added to the Sales worksheet, as shown in Figure 10.25. The formula for each series needs to be updated to include the new column.

FIGURE 10.25.

*When you extend a
worksheet series, Excel
doesn't extend the series on
the chart.*

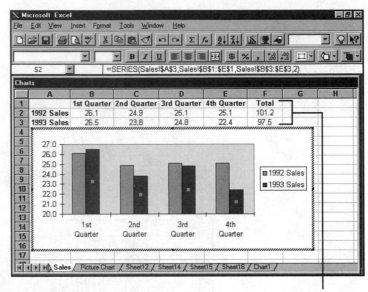

Series extension

Editing a Series Formula

Follow these steps to edit a series formula:

1. Activate the chart you want to edit.

2. Select the **I**nsert | **N**ew Data command. Excel displays the New Data dialog box, shown in Figure 10.26.

FIGURE 10.26.

*Enter a reference for the
new data in the New Data
dialog box.*

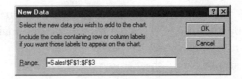

3. In the **R**ange edit box, enter a reference for the new data. You can either type the reference or select the range directly in the worksheet.

4. Select OK. Excel adjusts the series and adds the data to the chart.

TIP

Besides following the preceding steps, you also can edit the series formula in the formula bar. Select the series you want to edit, activate the formula bar, and adjust the appropriate worksheet references.

Figure 10.27 shows the Sales chart with the series extended.

FIGURE 10.27.

The Sales chart with the extended series.

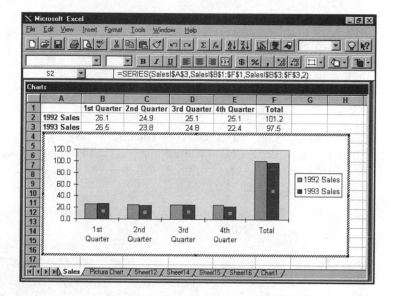

TIP

If you're extending a data series, Excel also supplies a simple drag-and-drop method for editing the series. Select the new data, drag the range over to the chart, and release the mouse button. Excel updates the appropriate data series automatically.

Editing a Data Series with the ChartWizard

If you extend or reduce a worksheet series, you can use the ChartWizard to update the chart series formulas. (See the section titled "Creating an Embedded Chart with the ChartWizard" in Chapter 9 for details on using the ChartWizard.) Here are the steps to follow:

1. Activate the chart you want to edit.

2. Select the ChartWizard tool from either the Chart toolbar or the Standard toolbar. Excel displays the ChartWizard - Step 1 of 2 dialog box. A moving line appears in the worksheet around the current chart range.

     The ChartWizard tool.

3. In the **R**ange box, enter the new range or select the new range on the worksheet. (Note that you must select the entire range, not just the extra data you're adding.)

4. Select Next >. Excel displays the ChartWizard - Step 2 of 2 dialog box.

5. Select any other adjustment options as needed.

6. Select OK.

Editing a Data Series by Copying

Another technique for editing a data series involves copying the new data points and then pasting the numbers onto the chart. Follow the steps in this procedure:

1. Activate the worksheet that contains the new data.

2. Select the range you want to copy (that is, the new data you want to add to the chart), and then select the **Edit | Copy** command. In this example, you would select the range F1:F3.

3. Activate the chart.

4. Select the **Edit | Paste Special** command. Excel displays the Paste Special dialog box, shown in Figure 10.28.

FIGURE 10.28.

The Paste Special dialog box, which appears when you paste new data onto a chart.

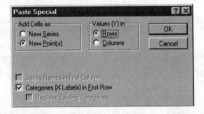

5. Select the appropriate options. In particular, be sure to activate the New **P**oint(s) option.

6. Select OK. Excel pastes the new data onto the chart.

Adding a Data Series

Besides editing existing data series, you'll often add new series to your worksheets. For example, Figure 10.29 shows the Sales worksheet with a new series added for 1994 sales. (This figure also shows the New Data dialog box, which you can use to add the new data series, as you'll see a little later.) To add this series to the chart, you need to define a new series formula.

To add a new series, you can use any of the methods outlined in the "Editing a Data Series" section, keeping these notes in mind:

■ If you use the **Insert | New** Data command, be sure to select the entire series when you enter the **R**ange reference, as shown in Figure 10.29.

■ If you copy the new series and paste it on the chart, make sure that you activate the New **S**eries option in the Paste Special dialog box.

Chapter 10

FIGURE 10.29.

To add a new data series to a chart, define a new data series formula.

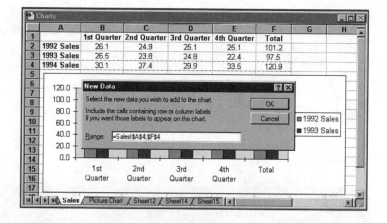

Excel also enables you to use drag-and-drop to add a data series. Select the range that includes the data for the new series, drag the range to the chart, and release the mouse button. Excel adds the new series automatically.

Merging Charts

Another way to add data series to a chart is to merge two similar charts. Follow the steps in this procedure to merge charts:

1. Activate the chart that contains the data series you want to add.
2. Select the **Edit | Copy** command.
3. Activate the chart that will receive the copy.
4. Select the **Edit | Paste** command. Excel adds the new series to the chart.

You can use this technique to combine charts from other departments for budget or sales presentations. For best results, the data in each chart should have the same layout.

When you paste the new series, Excel copies both the data series and their formats to the chart. To keep the formatting of the active chart, select the **Edit | Paste Special** command instead. In the Paste Special dialog box, activate the Formulas option, and then select OK.

Deleting a Data Series

To delete a data series from a chart, select the series and then select the Edit | Clear | Series command.

> **TIP**
>
> To delete a chart data series quickly, select it and press the Delete key.

> **CAUTION**
>
> After you delete a series, you can't retrieve it. As a precaution, save the chart before you perform any deletions. This way, if you accidentally delete a series, you can close the chart without saving changes and reopen it with the deleted series restored.

Summary

This chapter showed you how to enhance your charts. I took you through all kinds of formatting options for each of the chart elements, I showed you how to add graphic objects to your chart, and I showed you how to work with chart data series. Here are a few other chapters to read for related information:

- Many of the formatting options we discussed for the chart elements—such as numeric formats, fonts, and alignment—were discussed in detail in Chapter 4, "Formatting Excel Worksheets."

- Speaking of Chapter 4, that was also where I showed you how to create and edit text boxes (see the "Working with Text Boxes" section).

- Text boxes and arrows aren't the only graphic objects you can add to a chart. Chapter 11, "Working with Graphic Objects," gives you a complete rundown of Excel's drawing and graphics capabilities.

- Dragging data markers is only one example of what-if analysis. For lots more, head to Chapter 17, "Basic Analytic Methods."

Working with Graphic Objects

Excel gives you a powerful set of drawing tools to create and enhance graphic objects on your worksheets. You can add lines, circles, or polygons. You can import graphics from external sources, and you can even export pictures of your worksheets to use in other programs.

This chapter shows you how to add graphic objects to a worksheet, either by drawing them yourself using the Drawing toolbar or by importing graphics from outside Excel. It also shows you how to edit and enhance your graphics.

Using the Drawing Toolbar

The Drawing toolbar contains 11 tools you can use to create your own graphic objects. With these tools, you can add lines, rectangles, ovals, arcs, and polygons to your worksheets. Table 11.1 summarizes the 11 drawing tools.

 Click this button on the Standard toolbar to display the Drawing toolbar.

Table 11.1. Excel's drawing tools.

Button	Name	Description
	Line	Draws a straight line.
	Arrow	Draws an arrow.
	Freehand	Draws a freehand line.
	Rectangle	Draws a rectangle or square.
	Ellipse	Draws an ellipse or circle.
	Arc	Draws an arc or circle segment.
	Freeform Polygon	Draws a polygon from a combination of freehand and straight lines.
	Filled Rectangle	Draws a rectangle or square filled with a background pattern and color.
	Filled Ellipse	Draws an ellipse or circle filled with a background pattern and color.

Button	Name	Description
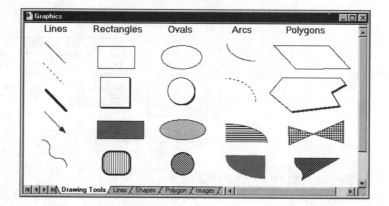	Filled Arc	Draws an arc or circle segment filled with a background pattern and color.
	Filled Freeform Polygon	Draws a freeform polygon filled with a background pattern and color.

The Drawing toolbar makes creating your own graphic objects easy. In most cases, you just select the button and then drag on the worksheet to create the object. Figure 11.1 shows several examples of objects you can create with the drawing tools.

FIGURE 11.1.

Excel's drawing tools enable you to create many graphic objects.

Drawing Lines

You can create three kinds of lines with Excel's drawing tools: straight lines, arrows, and freehand lines. Use lines to point out important worksheet information or to design a more complex graphic, such as a company logo. Follow these steps to create a line:

1. Select a line-drawing button. To draw multiple lines, double-click on the button. The mouse pointer changes to a crosshair.

2. Position the crosshair where you want to begin the line.

3. Press and hold down the left mouse button.

4. Drag the mouse pointer to where you want the line to end. If you're drawing a freehand line, drag the mouse pointer in the shape of the line you want.

5. Release the mouse button. Excel places black selection handles on each end of the line. If you're drawing an arrow, Excel adds an arrowhead.

6. If you're drawing multiple lines, repeat steps 2 through 5.

7. To finish drawing multiple lines, click on an empty part of the worksheet, or press the Esc key.

TIP

To restrict straight lines and arrows to horizontal, vertical, and 45-degree angles, hold down the Shift key while you draw. To create lines along the worksheet gridlines or diagonally between cell corners, hold down the Alt key while you draw.

Figure 11.2 demonstrates some ways to use lines in a worksheet.

FIGURE 11.2.

Examples of line objects in a worksheet.

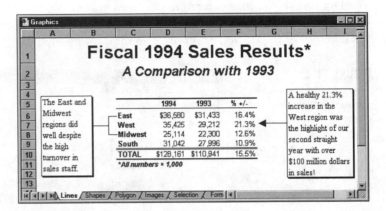

Drawing Shapes

You can create three kinds of predefined shapes with Excel's drawing tools: rectangles, ellipses, and arcs (a fourth shape—the polygon—is discussed in the next section). You'll use shapes often as part of complex graphics, such as a company logo. Follow the steps outlined here to create a shape:

1. Select a shape-drawing button. To draw multiple shapes, double-click on the button. The mouse pointer changes to a crosshair.

2. Position the crosshair where you want to begin drawing the shape.

3. Press and hold down the left mouse button.

4. Drag the mouse pointer until the shape has the size and form you want.

5. Release the mouse button. Excel places black selection handles around the shape.

6. If you're drawing multiple shapes, repeat steps 2 through 5.

7. To finish drawing multiple shapes, click on an empty part of the worksheet, or press the Esc key.

> **TIP**
>
> To make your rectangles square or your ellipses circular, hold down the Shift key while drawing. To align your shapes with the worksheet gridlines, hold down the Alt key while drawing.

You can use shapes to create your own custom worksheet formatting. For example, instead of using Excel's cell borders, create your own with the Rectangle button, as shown in Figure 11.3. This figure shows some examples of shapes used in a worksheet. The arrowhead on the end of the arc was accomplished by attaching an arrow with a very short shaft.

FIGURE 11.3.

Some sample shapes on a worksheet.

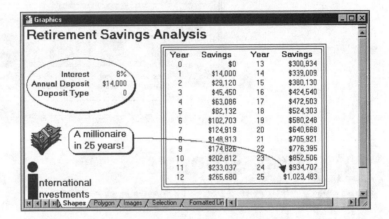

Drawing Polygons

The Freeform Polygon button enables you to combine freehand lines with straight lines to create a polygon of any shape or size. Here are the steps to follow to use this button:

1. Select the Freeform Polygon button. To draw multiple polygons, double-click on the button. The mouse pointer changes to a crosshair.

2. Position the crosshair where you want to begin the polygon.

3. To draw freehand, press and hold down the left mouse button. To draw a straight line, click the left mouse button.

4. Move the mouse pointer to draw the object you want.

5. To finish freehand drawing, release the mouse button. To finish drawing a straight line, click the left mouse button.

6. Repeat steps 2 through 5 to add other freehand or straight lines.

7. Double-click to finish drawing the polygon.

8. If you're drawing multiple polygons, repeat steps 2 through 7.

9. To finish drawing multiple polygons, click the Freeform Polygon button, or press the Esc key.

Polygons are useful for creating complex shapes. In Figure 11.4, a polygon has been added around the sales figures and shaded to create a 3-D effect.

FIGURE 11.4.

Use polygons for complex shapes.

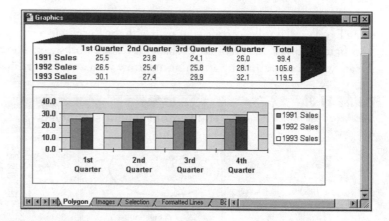

Importing Graphics from Other Applications

Although the drawing tools that come with Excel are handy for creating simple graphics effects, a more ambitious image requires a dedicated graphics program, such as Windows Paint or CorelDRAW!. With these programs, you can create professional-quality graphics and then import them into your Excel worksheet. If the application supports object linking and embedding (OLE), you can maintain a link between the object and the original program.

There are two basic methods for importing a graphic object into a worksheet:

■ You can use the Clipboard to copy and paste the object from the original application to the Excel worksheet. This method is useful if you need to use only part of a graphic image.

■ You can use the **I**nsert | **P**icture command to import an existing graphics file into the worksheet.

Follow these steps to use the Clipboard to import a graphic image from another application:

1. Activate the graphics application.

2. Select the graphic image you want to import.

3. Copy the image to the Windows Clipboard. (In most Windows applications, select the **E**dit | **C**opy command.)

4. Activate Excel and select the worksheet you want to receive the graphic.

5. Select the **Edit | P**aste command to copy the image to the worksheet.

TIP

If the graphics application supports OLE, use the **Edit | P**aste **S**pecial command to establish a link between the two applications, or select the **Edit | I**nsert **O**bject command to embed an object from the application. For more information on importing data into Excel, see Chapter 7, "Exchanging Data with Other Applications."

To insert an existing graphics file into your worksheet, follow these steps:

1. Activate the cell that you want to use as the upper-left corner of the image.

2. Choose the **Insert | P**icture command. Excel displays the Picture dialog box.

3. Highlight the graphics file you want to use.

4. Select OK. Excel inserts the file into the worksheet.

Use the images you import from dedicated graphics applications to enhance the appearance of your worksheets. Figure 11.3 displays a worksheet with an imported money-related graphic.

TIP

If you have access to a digital scanner, scan in your company logo, and import the file to use for presentations and reports. If your computer has a fax/modem, you also can capture your logo by faxing it to the computer and then using your fax software to save the image as a graphics file. You then can use a dedicated graphics program such as Paint to clean up the image before you import it into Excel.

If you don't have the time or the skill to create your own images, consider using a clip-art library. Clip art is professional-quality artwork that is commercially available in libraries of several hundred or more images. If you have Microsoft Office, you can use the ClipArt Gallery, which contains dozens of images. You can either use the **Insert | P**icture command, as described earlier (you'll find the ClipArt Gallery files in the \Clipart folder of your main MSOffice folder), or you can select the **Insert | O**bject command. In the Object dialog box that appears, select Microsoft ClipArt Gallery.

Also, some graphics programs, such as CorelDRAW! and Microsoft PowerPoint, include clip-art collections. If you find that you use certain images repeatedly, create a worksheet to hold copies of these images. This technique saves you from having to search through massive clip-art libraries every time you need an image. Figure 11.5 shows a worksheet containing several images imported from a clip-art library.

FIGURE 11.5.

Copy often-used images to a separate file for easy access.

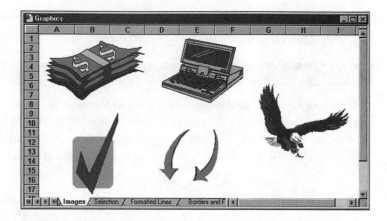

Selecting Graphic Objects

Before you can edit a graphic object, you must select it. The following procedure lists the steps to follow to select a graphic object:

1. Position the mouse pointer over the border of the graphic. The pointer changes to an arrow.

2. Click the mouse button. Excel displays selection handles around the object and shows the object identifier in the formula bar Name box (for example, Line 1 or Oval 5).

3. To select other objects, hold down the Shift key and repeat steps 1 and 2.

Every graphic object has an invisible rectangular *frame*. For a line or rectangle, the frame is the same as the object itself. For all other objects, the frame is a rectangle that completely encloses the shape or image. When you select an object, Excel displays black *selection handles* around the frame. Figure 11.6 shows several selected objects.

FIGURE 11.6.

Selected objects have handles around the object's frame.

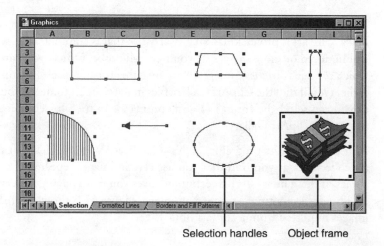

Selection handles   Object frame

Formatting Lines

If you select a line and then select the Format | Object command, Excel displays the Format Object dialog box for a line, shown in Figure 11.7. Using the options in this dialog box, you can control the Style, Color, and Weight of the line, and in the Arrowhead section, you can format the Style, Width, and Length of an arrow's head. You also can add an arrowhead to a plain line or remove an arrowhead from an arrow. Figure 11.8 shows some formatted lines and arrows.

FIGURE 11.7.

The Format Object dialog box for a drawn line.

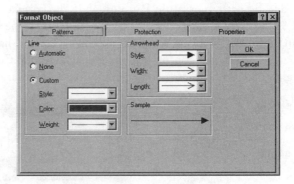

FIGURE 11.8.

Some formatted lines and arrows.

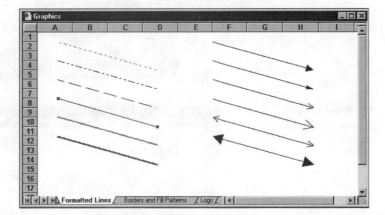

TIP

For all of Excel's graphic objects, you also can display the Format Object dialog box by double-clicking on the object, by selecting the object and pressing Ctrl-1, or by right-clicking on the object and selecting Format Object from the shortcut menu.

 Use the Pattern drop-down button on the Drawing toolbar to select a line style and color.

> **NOTE**
>
> To format a line drawn using the Freehand button, see the next section.

Formatting Borders and Fill Patterns

For all other types of Excel graphic objects—including freehand lines—you can format the border and fill pattern using the Patterns tab in the Format Object dialog box, shown in Figure 11.9. In this dialog box, you can set the fill **P**attern, the foreground and background colors, and the **S**tyle, **C**olor, and **W**eight of the border. You also have the option of adding a Sha**d**ow to a rectangle, oval, polygon, or freehand line. The **R**ound Corners option is available only for rectangles. Figure 11.10 shows some sample objects with various border styles and fill patterns.

FIGURE 11.9.

The Patterns tab dialog box for formatting object borders and fills.

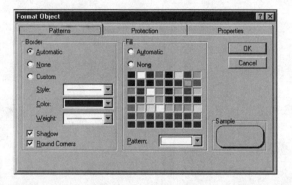

FIGURE 11.10.

Some sample objects with formatted borders and fill patterns.

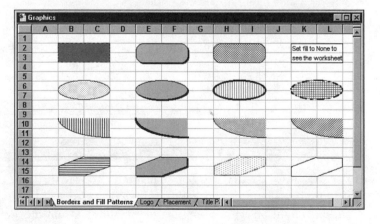

 Use the Pattern drop-down button on the Drawing toolbar to select a pattern and pattern color for the object.

Use the Drop Shadow button on the Drawing toolbar to add a shadow to a rectangle, oval, polygon, or freehand line.

Sizing Graphic Objects

You can resize any graphic object to change its shape or dimensions. The following procedure outlines the steps to work through:

1. Select the object you want to size. Excel displays black selection handles around the object's frame.
2. Position the mouse pointer over the handle you want to move. The pointer changes to a two-headed arrow. To change the size horizontally or vertically, use the appropriate handle on the middle of a side. To change the size in both directions at once, use the appropriate corner handle.
3. Drag the handle to the position you want. The pointer changes to a crosshair.
4. Release the mouse button. Excel redraws the object and adjusts the frame size.

TIP

To keep the same proportions when sizing an object, hold down the Shift key and drag a corner handle. To size an object using the worksheet gridlines, hold down the Alt key while dragging.

NOTE

When you scale an image such as a clip-art graphic, the scaling percentages for the height and width appear in the status bar at the bottom of the screen. The original graphic is 100% × 100%.

Editing Polygons

To change the size of a polygon, you can either use the procedure outlined in the preceding section or edit the polygon using the Reshape button. When you click the Reshape button, Excel displays *selection squares* at each vertex of the selected polygon. (Several vertices appear along each freehand line, and one vertex appears at the beginning and end of every straight line.) You can then move, add, or delete vertices to get the shape you want. The following procedure takes you through the appropriate steps:

1. Select the polygon you want to edit.

2. Select the Reshape button. Excel displays selection squares at each vertex of the polygon.

    The Drawing toolbar's Reshape button.

3. To move a vertex, position the mouse pointer over the vertex. The pointer changes to a crosshair, as shown in Figure 11.11. Drag the vertex to the position you want, and release the mouse button. Excel redraws the polygon with the new vertex position.

FIGURE 11.11.

The mouse pointer for moving a vertex.

4. To add a vertex, hold down the Ctrl key and position the mouse pointer over the appropriate polygon line. The pointer changes to a crosshair with a square in the middle, as shown in Figure 11.12. Drag the line to the new vertex point, and release the mouse button and the Ctrl key. Excel adds the vertex and redraws the polygon.

FIGURE 11.12.

The mouse pointer for adding a vertex.

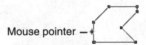

5. To delete a vertex, hold down the Ctrl key and position the mouse pointer over the vertex. The pointer changes to an ✕, as shown in Figure 11.13. Click once. Excel deletes the vertex and redraws the polygon.

FIGURE 11.13.

The mouse pointer for deleting a vertex.

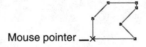

6. When you've finished editing the polygon, click the Reshape button or press Esc.

Moving Graphic Objects

You can move any graphic object to a different part of the worksheet by following these steps:

1. Select the object you want to move. Excel displays black selection handles around the object's frame.

2. Position the mouse pointer on any edge of the object. The pointer changes to an arrow.

3. Drag the object to the position you want. As you drag the object, a dashed outline shows you the new position.

4. Release the mouse button. Excel redraws the object in the new position.

TIP

To move an object using the worksheet gridlines, hold down the Alt key while dragging. To move an object only horizontally or vertically, hold down the Shift key while dragging.

You also can move graphic objects using the cut-and-paste method. The following procedure shows you how it's done:

1. Select the object you want to move. Excel displays black selection handles around the object's frame.

2. Choose the **Edit | Cut** command. Excel cuts the objects from the worksheet.

3. Move the cell selector to the new position.

4. Select **Edit | Paste**. Excel redraws the object in the new position.

TIP

Each graphic object's shortcut menu, which you can display by right-clicking on the object, includes Cut and Paste commands.

Copying Graphic Objects

If you want multiple copies of the same object, you don't have to draw each one. Instead, follow the steps outlined next to make as many copies of the object as you need:

1. Select the object you want to copy. Excel displays black selection handles around the object's frame.

2. Press the Ctrl key and position the mouse pointer on any edge of the object. The pointer changes to an arrow with a plus sign.

3. Drag the pointer to the position you want. As you do so, a dashed outline shows you the position of the copied object.

4. Release the mouse button. Excel copies the object to the new position.

You also can use the **Edit | Copy** command to copy graphic objects. The following procedure outlines the steps to follow:

1. Select the object you want to copy. Excel displays black selection handles around the object's frame.

2. Select the **Edit | Copy** command.

3. Position the cell selector at the approximate position at which you want the copy to appear.

4. Choose the **Edit | Paste** command. Excel pastes a copy of the object at the selected cell.

> **TIP**
>
> You also can right-click on the object and select the Copy command from the object's shortcut menu.

Deleting Graphic Objects

To delete a graphic object, select it and then select the **Edit | Clear | All** command. Excel deletes the object.

> **TIP**
>
> To delete an object quickly, select it and press the Delete key. Alternatively, you can right-click on the object and select Clear from the shortcut menu.

Selecting Multiple Graphic Objects

If you use graphics often, you could easily end up with a dozen or more objects in a worksheet. If you then want to rearrange or reformat a worksheet, it becomes time-consuming to move or format each object individually. To get around this problem, Excel enables you to select all the objects you want and work with them simultaneously.

Excel offers a couple of methods for selecting multiple objects. If you need just a few objects, or if the objects you need are scattered widely throughout the worksheet, hold down the Shift key and select each object individually. If the objects you want are grouped, you can use Excel's

Drawing Selection button to select them all together. The following procedure takes you through the necessary steps:

1. Select the Drawing Selection button.

      The Drawing Selection button from the Drawing toolbar.

2. Position the pointer at the top-left corner of the area you want to select.

3. Press and hold down the left mouse button. The mouse pointer changes to a crosshair.

4. Drag the pointer to the bottom-right corner of the area you want to select. As you drag the pointer, Excel indicates the selected area with a dashed border, as shown in Figure 11.14.

FIGURE 11.14.

Make sure that the selection area completely encloses each object you want to select.

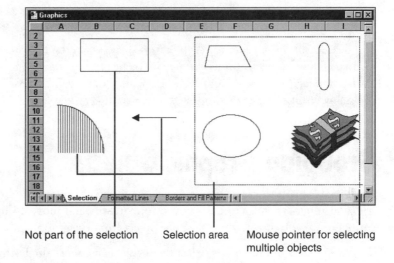

Not part of the selection   Selection area   Mouse pointer for selecting
                                                                                multiple objects

5. Release the mouse button. Excel places selection handles around each object in the selection area.

6. To end the selection, click the Drawing Selection button, or press the Esc key.

NOTE

The selection area must completely enclose an object to include it in the selection.

> **TIP**
>
> If you miss any objects, make sure that the Drawing Selection button is still active. Then, while holding down the Shift key, repeat steps 2 through 5 for the other objects you want to include.

After you've made a multiple selection, you can format, size, move, copy, or delete all the objects at once. Note, however, that you must format lines and shapes separately because they use different formatting options. To exclude an object from the selection, hold down the Shift key and click on the object's border. To exclude several objects from the selection, hold down Shift and use the Drawing Selection button to deselect the objects.

> **TIP**
>
> To select all the graphic objects in a worksheet, select the **E**dit | **G**o To command, and then click the **S**pecial button in the Go To dialog box. In the Go To Special dialog box that appears, activate the **Ob**jects option, and select OK. To deselect all objects, click on any empty part of the worksheet, or press the Esc key.

Grouping Graphic Objects

Excel enables you to create object *groups*. A group is a collection of objects you can format, size, and move—similar to the way you format, size, and move a single object. To select an entire group, you just need to select one object from the group.

To group two or more objects, select them and then choose the **F**ormat | **P**lacement | **G**roup command. Excel creates an invisible, rectangular frame around the objects.

 You also can use the Group Objects button on the Drawing toolbar to group selected objects.

> **NOTE**
>
> If you've combined multiple graphic objects into a design or logo, group the elements so that you can move or size them together.

Excel treats a group as a single graphic object with its own frame. In Figure 11.15, for example, a circle, a rectangle, and an edit box have been grouped. Any sizing, moving, or copying operations act on each member of the group.

FIGURE 11.15.

Excel treats a group of graphics as a single object.

Group frame ————

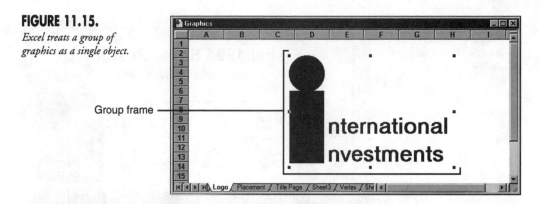

To ungroup objects, select the group and then select the Format | Placement | Ungroup command. Excel removes the group but leaves the individual objects selected.

 You can use the Ungroup Objects button on the Drawing toolbar to ungroup graphic objects.

Hiding Graphic Objects

One problem with graphic objects is that they take longer to display than regular worksheet elements. The more detailed the graphic or the more graphics on-screen, the longer Excel takes to redraw the screen. Even with today's powerful Pentium machines, redrawing can cause scrolling through a worksheet to be cumbersome and time-consuming.

To get around this problem, you can temporarily "hide" all the worksheet objects so that Excel doesn't redraw the objects every time you scroll past them. Follow these steps to hide graphic objects:

1. Select the Tools | Options command, and select the View tab in the Options dialog box.
2. Select the option you want from the Objects section. You have the following choices:

Show All   Displays all graphic objects normally.

Show Placeholders   Displays a gray rectangle in place of all embedded charts and pictures (see Figure 11.16). Lines, shapes, and polygons are still shown.

Hide All   Suppresses the display of all graphic objects.

3. Select OK.

FIGURE 11.16.

For faster screen redraws, you can hide objects with placeholders.

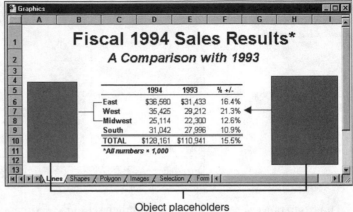

Object placeholders

TIP

Press Ctrl-6 to cycle through the Show **A**ll, Show **P**laceholders, and Hi**d**e All options without displaying the dialog box.

Controlling Object Placement

Most of your graphic objects are probably positioned relative to their specific worksheet cells. For example, you might have a text box with an arrow to explain the contents of a cell, or you might have a rectangle around a worksheet table. In either case, when you move or size the worksheet cells, you'll want the graphic to move or size along with the cells. You can control relative positioning with the options found in the Properties tab of the Format Object dialog box:

Move and **S**ize with Cells	Attaches the object to the cells underneath the object. When you move or size the cells, the object is moved or sized accordingly. This is the default option for drawn objects.
Move but Don't Size with Cells	Attaches the object only to the cell underneath its top-left corner. When you move this cell, the object moves with it but doesn't change size. This is the default option for embedded charts and pictures.
Don't Move or Size with Cells	The object isn't attached to the cell underneath it.

> **TIP**
>
> Use the **M**ove but Don't Size with Cells option for logos and designs that you want to remain the same size.

> **TIP**
>
> The Properties tab has a fourth option: **P**rint Object. Deactivate this option when you don't want the selected object to print with the worksheet.

Follow these steps to attach an object to its underlying cells:

1. Select the object.
2. Choose the F**o**rmat | Obj**e**ct command to display the Format Object dialog box.
3. Select the Properties tab.
4. Activate the placement option you want.
5. Select OK.

To illustrate object placement, Figure 11.17 shows three copies of a graphic image. Each copy has a different placement option, as described by the label above the object. Figure 11.18 shows the same graphics after one row has been inserted and another has had its height increased.

FIGURE 11.17.

Three objects with different placement options.

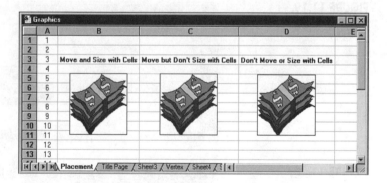

FIGURE 11.18.
The placement options determine how an object is affected by cell movement or sizing.

Row inserted here —

Row height increased —

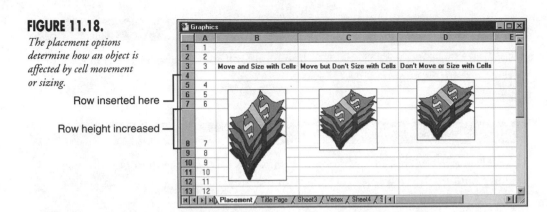

Ordering Overlapped Graphic Objects

When you have two graphic objects that overlap, the most recently created object covers part of the other object. The newer object is "in front" of the older one. You can change the order of the overlapped objects by selecting an object and then selecting either the Format | Placement | Bring to Front command or the Format | Placement | Send to Back command.

Figure 11.19 shows a filled rectangle in front of a text box. When you select the rectangle and then select Format | Placement | Send to Back, the rectangle creates an attractive shadow effect, as shown in Figure 11.20.

FIGURE 11.19.
The filled rectangle covers the edit box underneath.

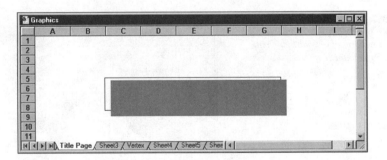

FIGURE 11.20.
Selecting Send to Back enables you to use the rectangle to create a shadow effect.

Chapter 11

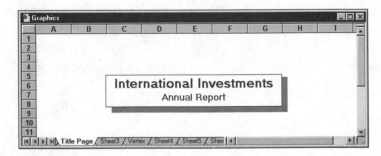

Select the Bring to Front button on the Drawing toolbar to bring an object to the front.

 Select the Send to Back button on the Drawing toolbar to send an object to the back.

Working with Cell Pictures

Excel enables you to take *pictures* of your worksheet cells, graphic objects, and charts. Similar to the way a photograph captures an image of a particular scene, an Excel picture captures an image of the selected range or object. You can treat the picture as you would any other graphic object: you can place it anywhere in the current sheet or even in another workbook, size it, copy it, and even format it to suit your needs. If you take a picture of a range of cells, you also have the option of linking the picture to the original cells. This way, if any of the range values change, Excel automatically updates the picture.

> **NOTE**
>
> Use an unlinked picture of a chart (rather than an embedded chart) in your worksheets when you want the displayed chart to remain static as the numbers in the worksheet change.

When you copy a picture, you set the copy options using the Copy Picture dialog box, shown in Figure 11.21. To set the appearance of the picture, you have two options:

As Shown on **S**creen	Copies the picture as it appears on-screen, including the row and column headings for cell ranges.
As Shown when **P**rinted	Copies the picture as it appears when printed but doesn't copy row and column headings for cell ranges.

FIGURE 11.21.

The Copy Picture dialog box.

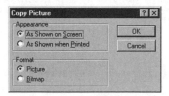

The option you choose depends on what you're copying and what kind of printer you have. The As Shown when **P**rinted option has the advantage of not copying row and column headers. If, however, you select this option and are using a black-and-white printer, Excel converts all colors in the selection to black and white. In general, the best choice is As Shown on **S**creen. If you use this option and you don't want the row and column headers copied, select the **T**ools

| Options command, select the View tab, and then deactivate the Row and Column Headers check box before copying the range.

Sometimes, the Copy Picture dialog box gives you the choice of either a Picture or a **B**itmap format. The Picture format, which is the default, copies a drawing of the image that scales proportionally when you size the picture. The **B**itmap format gives you a picture made of different colored pixels. Also, a graphic captured in Picture format is smaller and uses less memory than one captured in **B**itmap format.

Copying an Unlinked Picture

If you want to copy a picture of a cell range, graphic object, or chart, but you don't want Excel to update the picture every time the data changes, you need to copy an unlinked picture. The following procedure outlines the steps to follow:

1. Select the range, object, or chart you want to copy.
2. Hold down Shift and select the **E**dit | **C**opy Picture command. Excel displays the Copy Picture dialog box.
3. Select the copy options you want.
4. Select OK.
5. Activate the worksheet you want to receive the picture.
6. Select the cell at the upper-left corner of the area in which you want to copy the picture.
7. Hold down the Shift key and select the **E**dit | **P**aste Picture command. Excel pastes the picture onto the worksheet.

> **NOTE**
>
> Use Excel pictures when you need to view or print a range or chart on the same worksheet. Pictures are useful for performing worksheet analysis or data entry without having to set up separate windows or panes.

Copying a Linked Picture

If you want to copy a picture of a cell range, graphic object, or chart, and you want Excel to update the picture every time the data changes, you need to copy a linked picture. You can do this by following these steps:

1. Select the range you want to copy.
2. Select the **E**dit | **C**opy command to copy the range to the Clipboard.
3. Activate the worksheet you want to receive the picture.

4. Select the cell at the upper-left corner of the area in which you want to copy the picture.

5. Hold down the Shift key and select the **Edit | Paste Picture Link** command. Excel pastes the picture onto the worksheet and displays the linked range in the formula bar.

Excel updates linked pictures of ranges automatically, based on whether you change the numbers or the formatting of the original cells. For example, if you change the font or alignment in the original range, the picture, font, and alignment also change.

TIP

A quick way to make changes to a linked cell picture is by double-clicking on the picture. Excel activates the worksheet and automatically selects the range for you. When you change the cells, Excel updates the picture.

NOTE

Use Excel pictures to copy worksheet cells, objects, or charts to another Windows application. Copy the picture, activate the application, and choose its **Edit | Paste** command.

Summary

This chapter showed you how to work with graphic objects in Excel. I showed you how to add the various object types (lines, rectangles, and so on), and I showed you various methods for formatting and manipulating objects. Here's a list of some related chapters to check out:

- Graphic objects can turn a plain worksheet into a thing of beauty, but you shouldn't ignore Excel's other worksheet formatting options. You can learn all about them in Chapter 4, "Formatting Excel Worksheets."

- For more information about sharing data with other applications, Chapter 7, "Exchanging Data with Other Applications," is the place to be.

- Graphic objects add a nice touch to charts. For the full scoop on Excel's charting capabilities, see Chapter 9, "Working with Chart Types," and Chapter 10, "Enhancing Charts."

PART

Unleashing Excel's Databases and Lists

Working with Lists and Databases

12

These days, there's no shortage of dedicated database programs for the Windows market. There's the Access package that comes with Microsoft Office, of course, and there are also Windows versions of FoxPro, Paradox, and dBASE, to name a few. These high-end programs are full relational database management systems designed to handle complex, interrelated tables, queries, and reports.

If your database needs aren't quite so grandiose, however, these programs probably provide more than you need. If all you want is to store a few names and addresses, for example, it's overkill to fire up, say, Access every time you need to edit your data or find a name.

Fortunately, when it comes to simple tables of data, you don't have to bother with all the bells and whistles of the big-time database systems. Excel is more than capable of handling flat-file databases (or *lists,* as they're called in Excel) right in a worksheet. You can create simple data-entry forms with a few mouse clicks, and you can sort the data, summarize it, extract records based on criteria, and lots more. This chapter introduces you to Excel lists. You'll learn what lists are, how you can use them, how to create them in your Excel worksheets, and how to work with them.

What Is a List?

A *list* is a collection of related information with an organizational structure that makes it easy to find or extract data from its contents. Examples of lists are a phone book organized by name and a library card catalog organized by book title.

> **NOTE**
>
> If you're upgrading to Excel 7.0 from version 4.0 or earlier (or if you're converting to Excel 7.0 from another spreadsheet), a list is equivalent to what you used to call a *database.* Starting with version 5.0, Excel uses the term *list* so that you can differentiate between data on a worksheet and external data from a database management program (such as dBASE, Access, or SQL Server).

In Excel, the term *list* refers to a worksheet range that has the following properties:

Field	A single type of information, such as a name, an address, or a phone number. In Excel lists, each column is a field.
Field value	A single item in a field. In an Excel list, the field values are the individual cells.
Field name	A unique name you assign to every list field (worksheet column). These names are always found in the first row of the list.

Record	A collection of associated field values. In Excel lists, each row is a record.
List range	The worksheet range that includes all the records, fields, and field names of a list.

For example, suppose that you want to set up an accounts-receivable list. A simple system would include information such as the account name, account number, invoice number, invoice amount, due date, date paid, and calculation of the number of days overdue. Figure 12.1 shows how this system would be implemented as an Excel list.

FIGURE 12.1.

An accounts-receivable list.

Account Name	Account Number	Invoice Number	Invoice Amount	Due Date	Date Paid	Days Overdue
Emily's Sports Palace	0B-2255	117316	$ 1,584.20	12-Jan-95		55
Refco Office Solutions	14-5741	117317	$ 303.65	13-Jan-95		54
Chimera Illusions	02-0200	117318	$ 3,005.14	14-Jan-95	19-Jan-95	
Door Stoppers Ltd.	01-0045	117319	$ 78.85	16-Jan-95	16-Jan-95	
Meaghan Manufacturing	12-3456	117320	$ 4,347.21	19-Jan-95	14-Jan-95	
Brimson Furniture	10-0009	117321	$ 2,144.55	19-Jan-95		48
Katy's Paper Products	12-1212	117322	$ 234.69	20-Jan-95		47
Stephen Inc.	16-9734	117323	$ 157.25	22-Jan-95	21-Jan-94	
Door Stoppers Ltd.	01-0045	117324	$ 101.01	26-Jan-95		41
Voyatzis Designs	14-1882	117325	$ 1,985.25	26-Jan-95		41
Lone Wolf Software	07-4441	117326	$ 2,567.12	29-Jan-95	24-Jan-95	
Brimson Furniture	10-0009	117327	$ 1,847.25	1-Feb-95		35
Door Stoppers Ltd.	01-0045	117328	$ 58.50	2-Feb-95		34
O'Donoghue Inc.	09-2111	117329	$ 1,234.56	3-Feb-95		33

NOTE

You can use lists for just about anything you need to keep track of: inventory, accounts payable, books, CDs, and even household possessions.

Planning a List

You need to plan your list before you create it. What kind of information do you want to include? How much detail do you need for each record? What field names do you want to use? By asking yourself these questions in advance, you can save yourself the trouble of redesigning your list later.

The most important step in creating a list is determining the information you want it to contain. Although a list can be as large as the entire worksheet, in practice you should minimize the size of the range. This technique saves memory and makes managing the data easier. You therefore should strive to set up all your lists with only essential information.

For example, if you're building an accounts-receivable list, you should include only data that relates to the receivables. In such a list, you need two kinds of information: invoice data and customer data. The invoice data includes the invoice number, the amount, the due date, and the date paid. You also include a calculated field that determines the number of days the account is overdue. For the customer, you need at least a name and an account number. You don't need to include an address or a phone number, because this information isn't essential to the receivables data.

This last point brings up the idea of *data redundancy*. In many cases, you'll be setting up a list as part of a larger application. For example, you might have lists not only for accounts receivable, but also for accounts payable, customer information, part numbers, and so on. You don't need to include information such as addresses and phone numbers in the receivables list, because you should have that data in a more general customer-information list. To include this data in both places is redundant.

> **TIP**
>
> Different but related lists need to have a *key field* that is common to each. For example, the accounts-receivable and customer-information lists both could contain an account number field. This enables you to cross-reference entries in both lists.

After you decide what kind of information to include in your list, you need to determine the level of detail for each field. For example, if you're including address information, do you want separate fields for the street address, city, state, and ZIP code? For a phone number, do you need a separate field for the area code? In most cases, the best approach is to split the data into the smallest elements that make sense. This method gives you maximum flexibility when you sort and extract information.

The next stage in planning your list is to assign names to each field. Here are some guidelines to follow:

- Always use the top row of the list for the column labels.

- Although you can assign names as long as 255 characters, you should try to use short names to prevent your fields from becoming too wide.

> **TIP**
>
> If you need to use a long field name, turn on the Word Wrap alignment option to keep the field width small. Select the cell, select the Format | Cells command, choose the Alignment tab in the Format Cells dialog box, activate the **W**rap Text check box, and then select OK.

- Field names must be unique, and they must be text or text formulas. If you need to use numbers, format them as text.

- You should format the column labels to help differentiate them from the list data. You can use bold text, a different font color, a background color, and a border along the bottom of each cell.

The final step in setting up your list is to plan its position in the worksheet. Here are some points to keep in mind:

- Some Excel commands can automatically identify the size and shape of a list. To avoid confusing such commands, try to use only one list per worksheet. If you have multiple related lists, include them in other tabs in the same workbook.

- If you have any other nonlist data in a worksheet, leave at least one blank row or column between the data and the list. This technique helps Excel identify the list automatically.

- Excel has a command that enables you to filter your list data to show only records that match certain criteria. (See "Filtering List Data," later in this chapter, for details.) This command works by hiding rows of data. Therefore, if you have nonlist data you need to access, it's important not to place it to the left or right of a list.

Entering List Data

After you've set up your field names, you can start entering your list records. The following sections show you how to enter data directly on the worksheet or by using a data form.

Entering Data Directly on a Worksheet

The most straightforward way to enter information into a list is to directly type data in the worksheet cells. If you've formatted any of the fields (numeric formats, alignment, and so on), be sure to copy the formats to the new records.

> **TIP**
>
> Excel's Format Painter tool makes copying cell formatting easy. I covered the Format Painter in Chapter 4, "Formatting Excel Worksheets," in the "Copying Cell Formats with the Format Painter" section.

Entering and deleting records and fields within a list is analogous to inserting and deleting rows and columns in a regular worksheet model. Table 12.1 summarizes these list commands.

Table 12.1. Some basic list commands.

List Action	Excel Procedure
Add a record	Select a row, and then select **Insert	Rows**.
Add a field	Select a column, and then select **Insert	Columns**.
Delete a record	Select the entire row, and then select **Edit	Delete**.
Delete a field	Select the entire column, and then select **Edit	Delete**.

If you don't want to add or delete an entire row or column (for example, if other worksheet data is in the way), you can insert or delete data within the list range. If you're inserting or deleting a row, select a list record (be sure to include each field in the record). If you're inserting or deleting a column, select a list field (be sure to include each record in the field as well as the field name).

Entering list information can be tedious. Excel offers several shortcut keys to speed up the process, as summarized in Table 12.2.

Table 12.2. Excel data-entry shortcut keys.

Key	Action
Tab	Confirms the entry and moves to the field on the right.
Shift-Tab	Confirms the entry and moves to the field on the left.
Enter	Confirms the entry and moves to the next record.
Shift-Enter	Confirms the entry and moves to the preceding record.
Ctrl-"	Copies the number from the same field in the preceding record.
Ctrl-'	Copies the formula from the same field in the preceding record.
Ctrl-;	Enters the current date.
Ctrl-:	Enters the current time.

TIP

If pressing Enter or Shift-Enter doesn't move you to another record, select the **Tools | Options** command. Then select the Edit tab in the Options dialog box, and activate the **Move Selection after Enter** check box.

Entering Data Using a Data Form

Excel lists are powerful information-management tools, but creating and maintaining them can be tedious and time-consuming. To make data entry easier and more efficient, Excel offers the *data form* dialog box. You can use this form to add, edit, delete, and find list records quickly.

What Is a Data Form?

A *data form* is a dialog box that simplifies list management in the following ways:

- The dialog box shows only one record at a time, which makes data entry and editing easier.

- You can view many more fields in a form than you can see on-screen. In fact, depending on the size of your screen, you can view as many as 18 fields in a single form.

- When you add or delete records using the data form, Excel automatically adjusts the list range.

- You get an extra level of safety when you add or delete records. Excel prevents you from overwriting existing worksheet data when you add records, and it seeks confirmation for record deletions.

- Novice users or data-entry clerks are insulated from the normal list commands. Simple command buttons enable users to add, delete, and find data.

The good news about data forms is that Excel creates the form automatically based on the layout of your list. To view the form, you select any cell from within the list and then select the **Data | Form** command. (You also can select one of the field-name cells or a cell in a row or column immediately adjacent to the list.)

Figure 12.2 shows the data form for the Accounts Receivable list. When constructing the data form, Excel begins with the field names and adds a text box for each editable field. Excel includes fields that are the result of a formula or function (for example, the Days Overdue field in Figure 12.2) for display purposes only; you can't edit these fields. The scroll bar enables you to move quickly through the list. The record number indicator in the top-right corner of the dialog box keeps track of both the current list row and the total number of records in the list. The dialog box also includes several command buttons for adding, deleting, and finding records.

NOTE

The record-number indicator is unaffected by the list sort order. The first record below the field names is always record 1.

FIGURE 12.2.
An Excel data form.

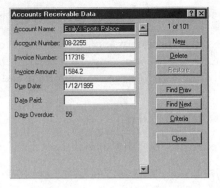

Editing Records

You can use the data form to edit any fields in your list records, with the exception of computed or protected fields. This procedure lists the steps to follow:

1. Display the data form.
2. Select the record you want to edit.
3. Edit the fields you want to change.
4. Repeat steps 2 and 3 for other records you want to edit.
5. Select Close to finish editing the list.

> **CAUTION**
>
> When you make changes to a record, Excel saves the changes permanently when you scroll to another record. Therefore, before leaving a record, check each field to ensure that it contains the data you want. To restore a record to its original data, select the data form's **R**estore button before you move to another record.

If you prefer to use the keyboard to navigate the data form, you can use Excel's shortcuts to speed up the process. These keyboard techniques are summarized in Table 12.3.

Table 12.3. Data-form keyboard techniques.

Key	Action
Alt-*underlined letter in a field name*	Selects the field if it's editable.
Alt-*underlined letter in a command button*	Selects the command button.
Tab	Moves to the next editable field.

Key	Action
Shift-Tab	Moves to the preceding editable field.
Enter	Moves to the next record.
Shift-Enter	Moves to the preceding record.
Down arrow	Moves to the same field in the next record.
Up arrow	Moves to the same field in the preceding record.
Page Down	Moves to the same field 10 records down.
Page Up	Moves to the same field 10 records up.
Ctrl-Page Down	Displays a blank record.
Ctrl-Page Up	Moves to the first record.

Adding Records

Adding records with the data form is fast and easy. Here are the steps to follow:

1. Display the data form.
2. Select the New button or press Ctrl-Page Down. Excel creates a blank record and displays New Record as the record-number indicator.
3. Fill in the fields for the new record.
4. Repeat steps 2 and 3 for other records you want to add.
5. Select Close to finish adding new records.

When you add records with the data form, Excel adds them to the bottom of the list without inserting a new row. If there is no room to extend the list range, Excel displays the warning message shown in Figure 12.3. To add new records, you must either move or delete the other data.

FIGURE 12.3.

Excel warns you when the list range runs out of room.

Deleting Records

Follow the steps in this procedure to delete records using the data form:

1. Display the data form.
2. Select the record you want to delete.
3. Select the **D**elete button. Excel warns you that the record will be deleted permanently.
4. Select OK to confirm the deletion. Excel returns you to the data form.
5. Repeat steps 2 through 4 to delete other records.
6. Select **C**lose to return to the worksheet.

> **NOTE**
>
> When you delete a record from the data form, Excel clears the data and shifts the records up to fill in the gap.

Finding Records

Although the data form enables you to scroll through a list, you might find that for larger lists you need to use the form's search capabilities to quickly locate what you want. You can find specific records in the list by first specifying the *criteria* that the search must match. Excel then compares each record with the criteria and displays the first record that matches. For example, you might want to find all invoices that are over $1,000 or those that are at least one day past due.

> **NOTE**
>
> You can perform only simple searches with the data form. For more complex search criteria, see "Filtering List Data," later in this chapter.

You construct the search criteria using text, numbers, and comparison operators such as equal to (=) and greater than (>). For example, to find all the invoices that are over $1,000, you type >1000 in the Invoice Amount field. To find an account named Read Inc., you type read inc. in the Account Name field. The following procedure takes you through the necessary steps:

1. Display the data form.
2. Select the **C**riteria button. Excel displays a blank record and replaces the record-number indicator with Criteria.

3. Select the field you want to use for the search.

4. Enter the criterion. Figure 12.4 shows the data form with a criterion entered for finding invoices on which the Invoice Amount is greater than 1,000.

FIGURE 12.4.

The Criteria data form with a sample criterion.

5. Repeat steps 3 and 4 if you want to use multiple criteria (see the following discussion).

6. Use the Find **N**ext and Find **P**rev buttons to move up or down to the next record that matches the criteria.

To refine your searches, you can use multiple criteria. For example, Figure 12.5 shows a form with three criteria entered. In this case, Excel will search for all invoices for companies that have the word *office* in their names, that are over $1,000, and that are past due. Note that all three criteria must be satisfied for Excel to find a match.

FIGURE 12.5.

You can enter multiple criteria to refine your searches.

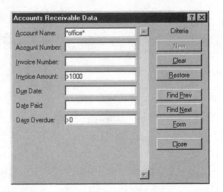

Another feature demonstrated in Figure 12.5 is the use of *wildcard characters*. Use the asterisk (*) to substitute for any number of characters. In Figure 12.5, *office* finds Refco Office Solutions or Wilson Office Supplies. You also can use the question mark (?) to substitute for a single character. For example, enter Re?d to find Read, Reid, or Reed.

Sorting a List

One of the advantages of a list is that you can rearrange the records so that they're sorted alphabetically or numerically. This feature enables you to view the data in order by customer name, account number, part number, or any other field. You even can sort on multiple fields, which would enable you, for example, to sort a client list by state and then by name within each state.

The sorting procedure is determined by the options in the Sort dialog box, shown in Figure 12.6, which gives you the following choices:

Sort By   This drop-down list box contains the list field names. Select a field from this list to determine the overall order for the sort. In Figure 12.6, the Due Date field is selected; therefore, the entire database will be sorted by Due Date.

FIGURE 12.6.

Use the Sort dialog box to change the sort order of your lists.

Then By   This drop-down list also contains the list field names. Select a field from this list to sort records that have the same data in the field specified in **S**ort By. In Figure 12.6, for example, all the records that have the same Due Date will be sorted by Account Name.

Then **B**y   Select a field name from this list to sort the records that have the same data in the fields specified by both **S**ort By and **T**hen By. Figure 12.6 shows that records that have the same Due Date and the same Account Name are sorted by the Invoice Amount field.

> **NOTE**
>
> Although Excel enables you to sort on as many as three fields, it isn't necessary to enter a field in all three lists. For most sorts, you'll need to choose a field in only the **S**ort By list.

My List Has   Excel usually can differentiate between field names (the header row) and data. If Excel finds what it thinks is a header row, it doesn't include it in the sort (and it activates the Header **R**ow option). If your list doesn't have a header row (or if you want the top row included in the sort), select the No Header Ro**w** option.

> **NOTE**
>
> Excel identifies the header row of a list by looking for differences in data type (most field names are text entries), capitalization, and formatting. If your list doesn't have a header row, you still can sort by using column headings (Column A, Column B, and so on).

> **CAUTION**
>
> Be careful when you sort list records that contain formulas. If the formulas use relative addresses that refer to cells outside their own record, the new sort order might change the references and produce erroneous results. If your list formulas must refer to cells outside the list, be sure to use absolute addresses.

For each sort field, you can specify whether the field is sorted in ascending or descending order. Table 12.4 summarizes Excel's ascending sort priorities.

Table 12.4. Excel's ascending sort order.

Type (in Order of Priority)	Order
Numbers	Largest negative to largest positive
Text	Space ! " # $ % & ' ( ) * + , − . / 0 through 9 (when formatted as text) : ; < = > ? @ A through Z (Excel ignores case) [\ ] ^ _ ' { | } ~
Logical	FALSE before TRUE
Error	All error values are equal
Blank	Always sorted last (ascending or descending)

The following procedure shows you how to sort a list:

1. Select a cell inside the list.

2. Select the **D**ata | **S**ort command. Excel displays the Sort dialog box.

3. Enter the sort options you want.

4. Select OK. Excel sorts the range.

Sort Options

If you select the **O**ptions button in the Sort dialog box, Excel displays the Sort Options dialog box (see Figure 12.7), which gives you the following choices:

First Key Sort Order   Sets a custom sort order for the field you chose in the **S**ort By list. For example, to sort by the days of the week, select the Sun, Mon, Tue,... option.

TIP

You might have noticed that the sort order options are the same as Excel's AutoFill lists. This means that you can create your own custom sort orders just by setting up custom AutoFill lists. I showed you how to do this in Chapter 1, "Getting the Most Out of Ranges," in the "Creating a Custom AutoFill List" section.

Case Sensitive   Select this option to have Excel differentiate between uppercase and lowercase during sorting. In an ascending sort, for example, lowercase letters are sorted before uppercase (for example, dBASE before DBASE).

Orientation   Excel normally sorts list rows (the Sort **T**op to Bottom option). To sort list columns, select Sort **L**eft to Right.

FIGURE 12.7.
Use the Sort Options dialog box to refine your sorting.

Using the Standard Toolbar's Sorting Buttons

Excel's Standard toolbar includes two buttons that enable you to quickly sort a list on a single field. Just select a cell in the field, and click either the Sort Ascending button (for an ascending sort) or the Sort Descending button (for a descending sort). Excel sorts the entire list (except the field names, of course) on the field you selected.

 The Sort Ascending button on the Standard toolbar.

 The Sort Descending button on the Standard toolbar.

> **NOTE**
>
> Both the Sort Ascending and the Sort Descending buttons use the currently selected options in the Sort Options dialog box.

Sorting on More Than Three Keys

You're not restricted to sorting on just three fields in an Excel list. By performing consecutive sorts, you can sort on any number of fields. For example, suppose that you want to sort a customer list by the following fields (in order of importance): Region, State, City, ZIP Code, and Name. To use five fields, you must perform two consecutive sorts. The first sort uses the three least important fields: City, ZIP Code, and Name. Of these three, City is the most important, so it is sorted by the Sort By field; ZIP Code is sorted by the Then By field, and Name is sorted by the Then By field. When this sort is complete, you must run a second sort using the remaining keys, Region and State. Select Region from the Sort By list and State from the Then By list.

By running multiple sorts and always using the least important fields first, you can sort on as many fields as you like.

Using a List in Natural Order

It's often convenient to see the order in which records were entered into a list, or the *natural order* of the data. Normally, you can restore a list to its natural order by selecting the Edit | Undo Sort command immediately after a sort.

Unfortunately, after several sort operations, it's no longer possible to restore the natural order. The solution is to create a new field, called, say, Record, in which you assign consecutive numbers as you enter the data. The first record is 1, the second is 2, and so on. To restore the list to its natural order, you sort on the Record field. Figure 12.8 shows the Accounts Receivable list with a Record field.

FIGURE 12.8.

The Record field tracks the order in which records are added to a list.

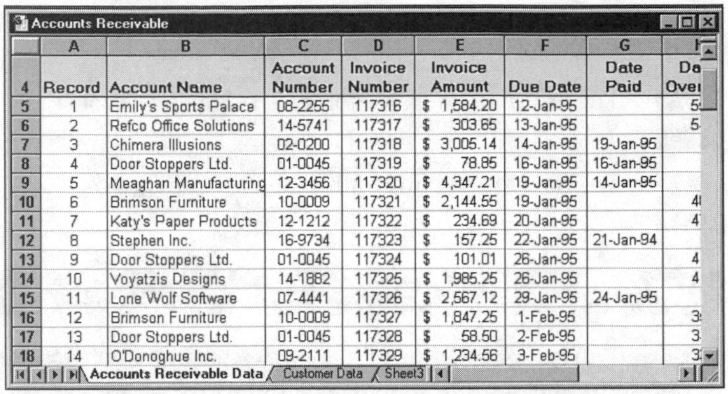

	A	B	C	D	E	F	G	H
4	Record	Account Name	Account Number	Invoice Number	Invoice Amount	Due Date	Date Paid	Da Ove
5	1	Emily's Sports Palace	08-2255	117316	$ 1,584.20	12-Jan-95		5
6	2	Refco Office Solutions	14-5741	117317	$ 303.65	13-Jan-95		5
7	3	Chimera Illusions	02-0200	117318	$ 3,005.14	14-Jan-95	19-Jan-95	
8	4	Door Stoppers Ltd.	01-0045	117319	$ 78.85	16-Jan-95	16-Jan-95	
9	5	Meaghan Manufacturing	12-3456	117320	$ 4,347.21	19-Jan-95	14-Jan-95	
10	6	Brimson Furniture	10-0009	117321	$ 2,144.55	19-Jan-95		4
11	7	Katy's Paper Products	12-1212	117322	$ 234.69	20-Jan-95		4
12	8	Stephen Inc.	16-9734	117323	$ 157.25	22-Jan-95	21-Jan-94	
13	9	Door Stoppers Ltd.	01-0045	117324	$ 101.01	26-Jan-95		4
14	10	Voyatzis Designs	14-1882	117325	$ 1,985.25	26-Jan-95		4
15	11	Lone Wolf Software	07-4441	117326	$ 2,567.12	29-Jan-95	24-Jan-95	
16	12	Brimson Furniture	10-0009	117327	$ 1,847.25	1-Feb-95		3
17	13	Door Stoppers Ltd.	01-0045	117328	$ 58.50	2-Feb-95		3
18	14	O'Donoghue Inc.	09-2111	117329	$ 1,234.56	3-Feb-95		3

Accounts Receivable Data / Customer Data / Sheet3

TIP

Use the Fill handle or the **E**dit | **F**ill | **S**eries command to quickly enter a sequence of numbers (such as the record numbers for a list). See Chapter 1 for more information.

TIP

If you're not sure how many records are in the list, and if the list isn't sorted in natural order, you might not know which record number to use next. To avoid guessing or searching through the entire Record field, you can generate the record numbers automatically with a formula and the MAX() function. For example, if the Record field is column A, and the new record is in row 100, you can calculate the next record number by entering the following formula in cell A100:

```
=MAX(A1:A99)+1
```

Sorting on Part of a Field

Excel performs its sorting chores based on the entire contents of each cell in the field. This method is fine for most sorting tasks, but occasionally you need to sort on only part of a field. For example, your list might have a Name field that contains a first name and then a last name. Sorting on this field will order the list by each person's first name, which is probably not what you want. To sort on the last name, you need to create a new column that extracts the last name from the field. You can then use this new column for the sort.

Excel's text functions (which we looked at in Chapter 3, "Harnessing the Power of Excel's Worksheet Functions") make it easy to extract substrings from a cell. In this case, we'll assume that each cell in the Name field has a first name, followed by a space, followed by a last name. Our task is to extract everything after the space, and the following formula does the job:

```
=RIGHT(C2, LEN(C2) - FIND(" ", C2, 1))
```

Here, I'm assuming that the field value is in cell C2. The `FIND(" ", C2, 1)` function returns the position of the first occurrence of a space in cell C2. Subtracting this value from the length (as given by the `LEN(C2)` function) returns the number of characters after the space. Because this is the number of characters in the last name, tossing the result into the `RIGHT()` function returns the last name.

Figure 12.9 shows this formula in action. Column C contains the names, and column D contains the formula to extract the last name. I sorted on column D to order the list by last name.

FIGURE 12.9.

To sort on part of a field, use Excel's text functions to extract the string you need for the sort.

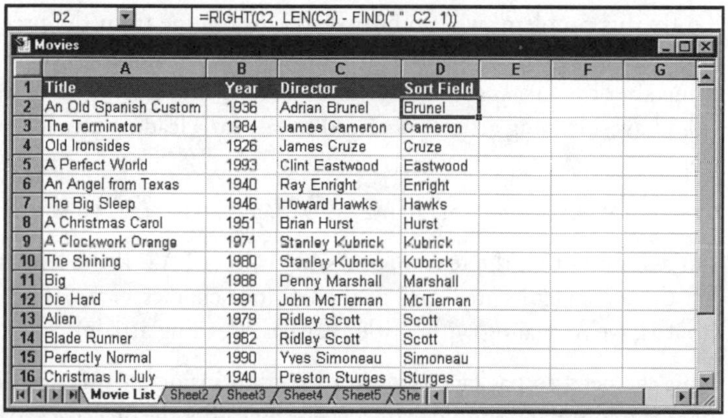

D2 =RIGHT(C2, LEN(C2) - FIND(" ", C2, 1))

Movies

	A	B	C	D	E	F	G
1	Title	Year	Director	Sort Field			
2	An Old Spanish Custom	1936	Adrian Brunel	Brunel			
3	The Terminator	1984	James Cameron	Cameron			
4	Old Ironsides	1926	James Cruze	Cruze			
5	A Perfect World	1993	Clint Eastwood	Eastwood			
6	An Angel from Texas	1940	Ray Enright	Enright			
7	The Big Sleep	1946	Howard Hawks	Hawks			
8	A Christmas Carol	1951	Brian Hurst	Hurst			
9	A Clockwork Orange	1971	Stanley Kubrick	Kubrick			
10	The Shining	1980	Stanley Kubrick	Kubrick			
11	Big	1988	Penny Marshall	Marshall			
12	Die Hard	1991	John McTiernan	McTiernan			
13	Alien	1979	Ridley Scott	Scott			
14	Blade Runner	1982	Ridley Scott	Scott			
15	Perfectly Normal	1990	Yves Simoneau	Simoneau			
16	Christmas In July	1940	Preston Sturges	Sturges			

Movie List / Sheet2 / Sheet3 / Sheet4 / Sheet5 / She

TIP

If you would rather not have the extra sort field (column D in Figure 12.9) cluttering the list, you can hide it by selecting a cell in the field and choosing the F**o**rmat | Column | **H**ide command. Fortunately, you don't have to unhide the field to sort on it because Excel still includes the field in the **S**ort By list.

Sorting Without Articles

Lists that contain field values starting with articles (*A*, *An*, and *The*) can throw off your sorting. For example, consider the Movies list we used as an example in the preceding section. Figure 12.10 shows the list sorted on the Title field. As you can see, records beginning with articles are erroneously sorted together.

434

FIGURE 12.10.

Leading articles can mess up your sorting.

To fix this problem, we can borrow the technique from the preceding section and sort on a new field in which the leading articles have been removed. As before, we want to extract everything after the first space, but we can't just use the same formula willy-nilly, because not all the titles have a leading article. We need to test for a leading article using the following OR() function:

```
OR(LEFT(A2,2) = "A ", LEFT(A2,3) = "An ", LEFT(A2,4) = "The ")
```

I'm assuming that the text we're testing is in cell A2. If the left two characters are "A " or the left three characters are "An " or the left four characters are "The ", this function returns TRUE (that is, we're dealing with a title that has a leading article).

Now we need to package this OR() function inside an IF() test. If the OR() function returns TRUE, the command should extract everything after the first space; otherwise, it should just return the entire title. Here it is, in all its glory:

```
=IF( OR(LEFT(A2,2) = "A ", LEFT(A2,3) = "An ", LEFT(A2,4) = "The "),
➥RIGHT(A2, LEN(A2) - FIND(" ", A2, 1)), A2)
```

Figure 12.11 shows this formula in action.

FIGURE 12.11.

A formula that removes leading articles.

Filtering List Data

One of the biggest problems with large lists is that it's often hard to find and extract the data you need. Sorting can help, but in the end you're still working with the entire list. What you need is a way to define the data you want to work with and then have Excel display only those records on-screen. This action is called *filtering* your data. Fortunately, Excel offers several techniques that get the job done.

Using AutoFilter to Filter a List

Excel's AutoFilter feature makes filtering out subsets of your data as easy as selecting an option from a drop-down list. In fact, that's literally what happens. If you select the **Data** | **Filter** | **AutoFilter** command, Excel adds drop-down arrows to the cells containing the list's column labels. Clicking one of these arrows displays a list of all the unique entries in the column. Figure 12.12 shows the drop-down list for the Account Name field in an Accounts Receivable database.

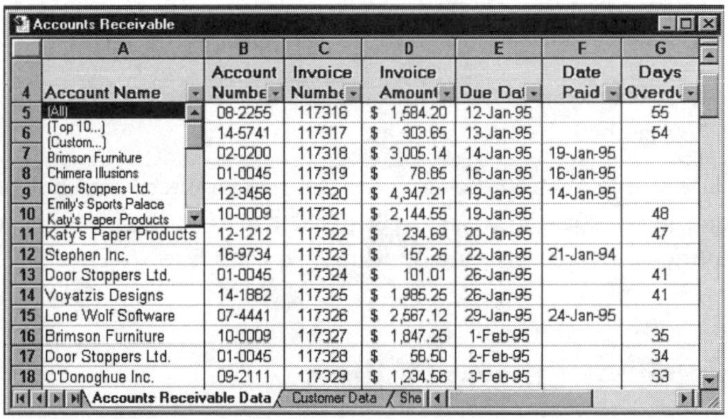

FIGURE 12.12.

For each list field, Auto-Filter adds drop-down lists that contain only the unique entries in the column.

TIP
If you want to use AutoFilter with only a single field, select that field's entire column before choosing the **Data**	**Filter**	**AutoFilter** command.

If you select an item from one of these lists, Excel takes the following actions:

■ It displays only those records that include the item in that field. For example, Figure 12.13 shows the resulting records when the item Refco Office Solutions is selected from the list attached to the Account Name column. The other records are hidden and can be retrieved whenever you need them.

FIGURE 12.13.

Selecting an item from a drop-down list displays only records that include the item in the field.

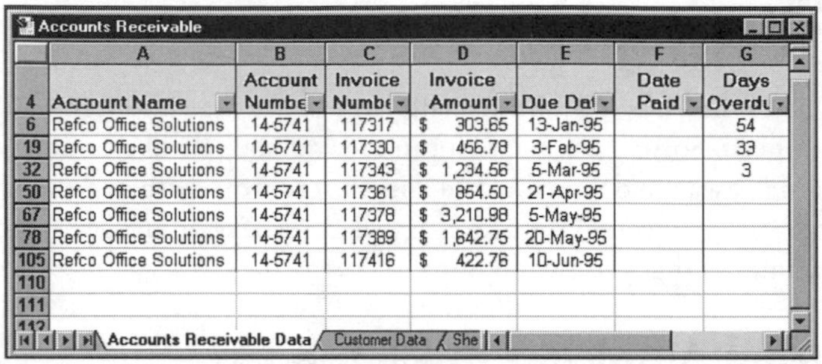

	A	B	C	D	E	F	G
4	Account Name	Account Number	Invoice Number	Invoice Amount	Due Date	Date Paid	Days Overdue
6	Refco Office Solutions	14-5741	117317	$ 303.65	13-Jan-95		54
19	Refco Office Solutions	14-5741	117330	$ 456.78	3-Feb-95		33
32	Refco Office Solutions	14-5741	117343	$ 1,234.56	5-Mar-95		3
50	Refco Office Solutions	14-5741	117361	$ 854.50	21-Apr-95		
67	Refco Office Solutions	14-5741	117378	$ 3,210.98	5-May-95		
78	Refco Office Solutions	14-5741	117389	$ 1,842.75	20-May-95		
105	Refco Office Solutions	14-5741	117416	$ 422.76	10-Jun-95		
110							
111							
112							

CAUTION

Because Excel hides the rows that don't meet the criteria, you shouldn't place any important data either to the left or to the right of the list.

- It changes the color of the column's drop-down arrow. This indicates which column you used to filter the list.
- It displays the row headings of the filtered records in a different color.
- It displays a message in the status bar telling you how many records it found that matched the selected item.

To continue filtering the data, you can select an item from one of the other lists. For example, you can select the nonblank cells in the Days Overdue column to see only those Refco Office Solutions invoices that are overdue. (To learn how to select nonblank fields, see the next section.)

AutoFilter Criteria Options

The items you see in each drop-down list are called the *filter criteria*. Besides selecting specific criteria (such as an account name), you also have the following choices in each drop-down list:

All	Removes the filter criterion for the column. If you've selected multiple criteria, you can remove all the filter criteria and display the entire list by selecting the **D**ata	**F**ilter	**S**how All command.
Top 10	Displays the Top 10 AutoFilter dialog box (new in Excel 7), shown in Figure 12.14. The left drop-down list has two choices, Top or Bottom; the center spinner enables you to choose a number; and the right drop-down list has two choices, Items and Percent. For example, if you choose the default choices (Top, 10, and Items), AutoFilter displays the records that have the 10 highest values in the current field.
Custom	Enables you to enter more sophisticated criteria. For details, see the next section.

Excel 7

FIGURE 12.14.

Use the Top 10 AutoFilter dialog box to filter your records based on values in the current field.

Blanks	Displays records that have no data in the field. In the Accounts Receivable list, for example, you could use this criterion to find all the unpaid invoices (that is, those with a blank Date Paid field).
NonBlanks	Displays records that have data in the field. Selecting this criterion in the Days Overdue field of the Accounts Receivable list, for example, finds invoices that are overdue.

Setting Up Custom AutoFilter Criteria

In its basic form, AutoFilter enables you to select only a single item from each column drop-down list. AutoFilter's *custom filter criteria,* however, give you a way to select multiple items. In the Accounts Receivable list, for example, you could use custom criteria to display all the invoices with

- an Account Number that begins with 07
- a Due Date in January
- an amount between $1,000 and $5,000
- an Account Name of either Refco Office Solutions or Brimson Furniture

When you select the Custom item from a column drop-down list, you see the Custom AutoFilter dialog box, shown in Figure 12.15. The group box shows the name of the field you're using, and it contains four drop-down lists and a couple of option buttons. You use the two drop-down lists across the top to set up the first part of your criterion. The list on the left contains a list of Excel's *comparison operators,* shown in Table 12.5. The combination text box drop-down list on the right enables you to select a unique item from the field or enter your own value.

Table 12.5. Excel's comparison operators.

Operator	Description
=	Equal to
>	Greater than
<	Less than
>=	Greater than or equal to
<=	Less than or equal to
<>	Not equal to

Unleashing Excel's Databases and Lists

FIGURE 12.15.

Use the Custom AutoFilter dialog box to enter your custom criteria.

For example, if you want to display invoices with an amount greater than or equal to $1,000, select the >= operator and enter 1000 in the text box.

For text fields, you also can use *wildcard characters* to substitute for one or more characters. Use the question mark (?) wildcard to substitute for a single character. For example, if you enter sm?th, Excel finds both Smith and Smyth. To substitute for groups of characters, use the asterisk (*). For example, if you enter *carolina, Excel finds all the entries that end with "carolina."

> **NOTE**
>
> If you enter a plain text criterion without any wildcards, Excel searches for items that begin with the text. Therefore, if you enter R, Excel matches all the entries that begin with R.

> **TIP**
>
> To include a wildcard as part of the criteria, precede the character with a tilde (~). For example, to find OVERDUE?, enter OVERDUE~?.

You can create *compound criteria* by activating the **And** or **Or** button and then entering another criterion in the bottom two drop-down lists. Use **And** when you want to display records that meet both criteria. Use **Or** when you want to display records that meet at least one of the two criteria.

For example, to display invoices with an amount greater than or equal to $1,000 and less than or equal to $5,000, you fill in the dialog box as shown in Figure 12.16.

FIGURE 12.16.

A compound criterion that displays the records with invoice amounts between $1,000 and $5,000.

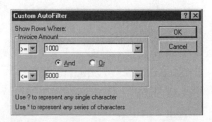

The following procedure takes you through the official steps to set up a custom AutoFilter criterion:

1. Select Custom from the drop-down list attached to the column you want to work with. Excel displays the Custom AutoFilter dialog box.

2. Select a comparison operator and enter a value for the first part of the criterion. If you don't want to create a compound criterion, skip to step 5.

3. Activate either the **And** or the **Or** option, as appropriate.

4. Select a comparison operator and enter a value for the second part of the criterion.

5. Select OK. Excel filters the list.

Showing Filtered Records

When you need to redisplay records that have been filtered via AutoFilter, use any of the following techniques:

- To display the entire list and remove AutoFilter's drop-down arrows, select the **Data** | **Filter** | AutoFilter command again.

- To display the entire list without removing the AutoFilter drop-down arrows, select the **Data** | **Filter** | **Show** All command.

- To remove the filter on a single field, display that field's AutoFilter drop-down list, and select the All option.

Using Complex Criteria to Filter a List

The AutoFilter should take care of most of your filtering needs, but it's not designed for heavy-duty work. For example, AutoFilter doesn't handle the following Accounts Receivable criteria:

- Invoice Amounts greater than $100, less than $1,000, or greater than $10,000
- Account Numbers that begin with 01, 05, or 12
- Days Overdue greater than the value in cell J1

To work with these more sophisticated requests, you need to use *complex criteria*.

Setting Up a Criteria Range

Before you can work with complex criteria, you must set up a *criteria range*. A criteria range has some or all of the list field names in the top row, with at least one blank row directly underneath. You enter your criteria in the blank row below the appropriate field name, and Excel searches the list for records with field values that satisfy the criteria. This setup gives you two major advantages over AutoFilter:

440

- By using either multiple rows or multiple columns for a single field, you can create compound criteria with as many terms as you like.

- Because you're entering your criteria in cells, you can use formulas to create *computed criteria.*

You can place the criteria range anywhere on the worksheet outside the list range. The most common position, however, is a couple of rows above the list range. Figure 12.17 shows the Accounts Receivable list with a criteria range. As you can see, the criteria are simply entered in the cell below the field name. In this case, the displayed criteria will find all Refco Office Solutions invoices that are greater than or equal to $1,000 and that are overdue (that is, invoices that have a value greater than zero in the Days Overdue field).

FIGURE 12.17.

Set up a separate criteria range (A1:C2, in this case) to enter complex criteria.

	A	B	C	D	E	F	G
1	Account Name	Invoice Amount	Days Overdue				
2	Refco Office Solutions	>=1000	>0				
3							
4	Account Name	Account Number	Invoice Number	Invoice Amount	Due Date	Date Paid	Days Overdue
5	Emily's Sports Palace	08-2255	117316	$ 1,584.20	12-Jan-95		55
6	Refco Office Solutions	14-5741	117317	$ 303.65	13-Jan-95		54
7	Chimera Illusions	02-0200	117318	$ 3,005.14	14-Jan-95	19-Jan-95	
8	Door Stoppers Ltd.	01-0045	117319	$ 78.85	16-Jan-95	16-Jan-95	
9	Meaghan Manufacturing	12-3456	117320	$ 4,347.21	19-Jan-95	14-Jan-95	
10	Brimson Furniture	10-0009	117321	$ 2,144.55	19-Jan-95		48
11	Katy's Paper Products	12-1212	117322	$ 234.69	20-Jan-95		47
12	Stephen Inc.	16-9734	117323	$ 157.25	22-Jan-95	21-Jan-94	
13	Door Stoppers Ltd.	01-0045	117324	$ 101.01	26-Jan-95		41
14	Voyatzis Designs	14-1882	117325	$ 1,985.25	26-Jan-95		41

Filtering a List with a Criteria Range

After you've set up your criteria range, you can use it to filter the list. The following procedure takes you through the basic steps:

1. Copy the list field names you want to use for the criteria, and paste them in the first row of the criteria range. If you'll be using different fields for different criteria, consider copying all your field names into the first row of the criteria range.

> **TIP**
>
> The only problem with copying the field names to the criteria range is that if you change a field name, you must change it in two places (that is, in the list and in the criteria). So instead of just copying the names, you can make the field names in the criteria range dynamic by using a formula to set each criteria field name equal to its corresponding list field name. For example, you could enter =A4 in cell A1 of Figure 12.17.

2. Below each field name in the criteria range, enter the criteria you want to use.

3. Select a cell in the list, and then select the **D**ata | **F**ilter | **Ad**vanced Filter command. Excel displays the Advanced Filter dialog box, shown in Figure 12.18.

FIGURE 12.18.

Use the Advanced Filter dialog box to select your list and criteria ranges.

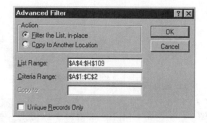

4. The **L**ist Range text box should contain the list range (if you selected a cell in the list beforehand). If it doesn't, activate the text box and select the list (including the field names).

5. In the **C**riteria Range text box, select the criteria range (again, including the field names you copied).

6. To avoid including duplicate records in the filter, activate the Unique **R**ecords Only check box.

7. Select OK. Excel filters the list to show only those records that match your criteria.

TIP

When you define specific names for list and criteria, Excel always selects the correct list and criteria ranges in the Advanced Filter dialog box. Use Database as the name for the list range and Criteria as the name for the criteria range. (In both cases, be sure to include the column labels in the named range.)

Entering Compound Criteria

To enter compound criteria in a criteria range, use the following guidelines:

- ■ To find records that match all the criteria, enter the criteria on a single row.

- ■ To find records that match one or more of the criteria, enter the criteria in separate rows.

Finding records that match all the criteria is equivalent to activating the **A**nd button in the Custom AutoFilter dialog box. The sample criteria shown in Figure 12.17 match records with the account name Refco Office Solutions *and* an invoice amount greater than $1,000 *and* a positive number in the Days Overdue field. To narrow the displayed records, you can enter criteria for as many fields as you like.

You also can use the same field name more than once. For example, suppose that you want to find all invoices with account names that begin with R and contain the strings "offic" and "sol." To do this, you include the Account Name column label three times in the criteria range and enter the appropriate criteria below each label. Figure 12.19 shows the criteria range and the resulting filter.

FIGURE 12.19.

You can construct compound criteria on the same field by using multiple instances of the field name in the criteria range.

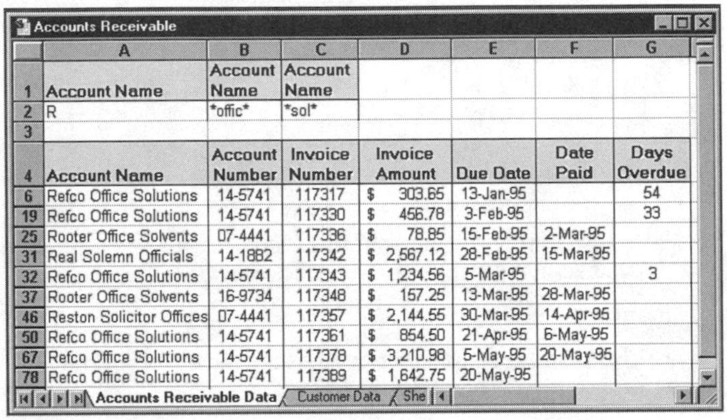

Accounts Receivable

	A	B	C	D	E	F	G
1	Account Name	Account Name	Account Name				
2	R	*offic*	*sol*				
3							
4	Account Name	Account Number	Invoice Number	Invoice Amount	Due Date	Date Paid	Days Overdue
6	Refco Office Solutions	14-5741	117317	$ 303.65	13-Jan-95		54
19	Refco Office Solutions	14-5741	117330	$ 456.78	3-Feb-95		33
25	Rooter Office Solvents	07-4441	117336	$ 78.85	15-Feb-95	2-Mar-95	
31	Real Solemn Officials	14-1882	117342	$ 2,567.12	28-Feb-95	15-Mar-95	
32	Refco Office Solutions	14-5741	117343	$ 1,234.56	5-Mar-95		3
37	Rooter Office Solvents	16-9734	117348	$ 157.25	13-Mar-95	28-Mar-95	
46	Reston Solicitor Offices	07-4441	117357	$ 2,144.55	30-Mar-95	14-Apr-95	
50	Refco Office Solutions	14-5741	117361	$ 854.50	21-Apr-95	6-May-95	
67	Refco Office Solutions	14-5741	117378	$ 3,210.98	5-May-95	20-May-95	
78	Refco Office Solutions	14-5741	117389	$ 1,642.75	20-May-95		

Accounts Receivable Data / Customer Data / She

Finding records that match at least one of several criteria is equivalent to activating the **Or** button in the Custom AutoFilter dialog box. In this case, you need to enter each criterion on a separate row. For example, to display all invoices with amounts greater than or equal to $10,000 or that are more than 45 days overdue, you would set up your criteria as shown in Figure 12.20.

FIGURE 12.20.

To display records that match one or more of the criteria, enter the criteria in separate rows.

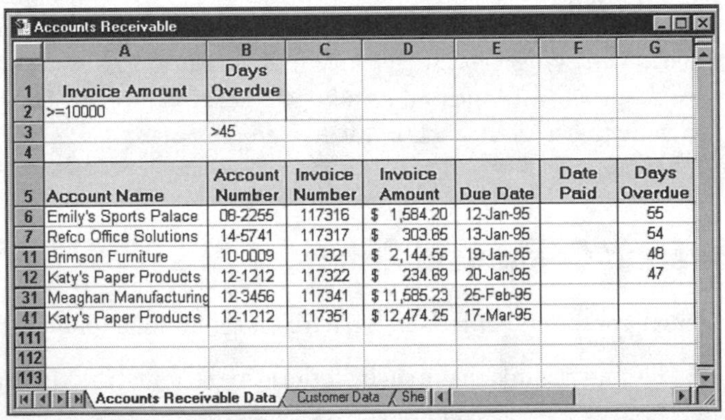

Accounts Receivable

	A	B	C	D	E	F	G
1	Invoice Amount	Days Overdue					
2	>=10000						
3		>45					
4							
5	Account Name	Account Number	Invoice Number	Invoice Amount	Due Date	Date Paid	Days Overdue
6	Emily's Sports Palace	08-2255	117316	$ 1,584.20	12-Jan-95		55
7	Refco Office Solutions	14-5741	117317	$ 303.65	13-Jan-95		54
11	Brimson Furniture	10-0009	117321	$ 2,144.55	19-Jan-95		48
12	Katy's Paper Products	12-1212	117322	$ 234.69	20-Jan-95		47
31	Meaghan Manufacturing	12-3456	117341	$ 11,585.23	25-Feb-95		
41	Katy's Paper Products	12-1212	117351	$ 12,474.25	17-Mar-95		
111							
112							
113							

Accounts Receivable Data / Customer Data / She

CAUTION

Don't include any blank rows in your criteria range, because blank rows throw off Excel when it tries to match the criteria.

Entering Computed Criteria

The fields in your criteria range aren't restricted to the list fields. You can create *computed criteria* that use a calculation to match records in the list. The calculation can refer to one or more list fields, or even to cells outside the list, and must return either TRUE or FALSE. Excel selects records that return TRUE.

To use computed criteria, add a column to the criteria range, and enter the formula in the new field. Make sure that the name you give the criteria field is different from any field name in the list. When referencing the list cells in the formula, use the first row of the list. For example, to select all records in which the Date Paid is equal to the Due Date in the accounts-receivable list, enter the following formula:

```
=F6=E6
```

Note the use of relative addressing. If you want to reference cells outside the list, use absolute addressing. See Chapter 2, "Building Better Formulas," to learn more about relative and absolute addressing.

TIP

Use Excel's AND, OR, and NOT functions to create compound computed criteria. For example, to select all records in which the Days Overdue value is less than 90 and greater than 31, type this:

```
=AND(G6<90, G6>31)
```

Figure 12.21 shows a more complex example. The goal is to select all records whose invoices were paid after the due date. The new criterion—named Late Payers—contains the following formula:

```
=IF(ISBLANK(F6),FALSE(),F6>E6)
```

If the Date Paid field (column F) is blank, the invoice hasn't been paid, and the formula returns FALSE. Otherwise, the logical expression F6>E6 is evaluated. If the Date Paid (column F) is greater than the Due Date field (column E), the expression returns TRUE, and Excel selects the record. In Figure 12.21, the Late Payers field displays FALSE, because the formula evaluates to FALSE for the first row in the list.

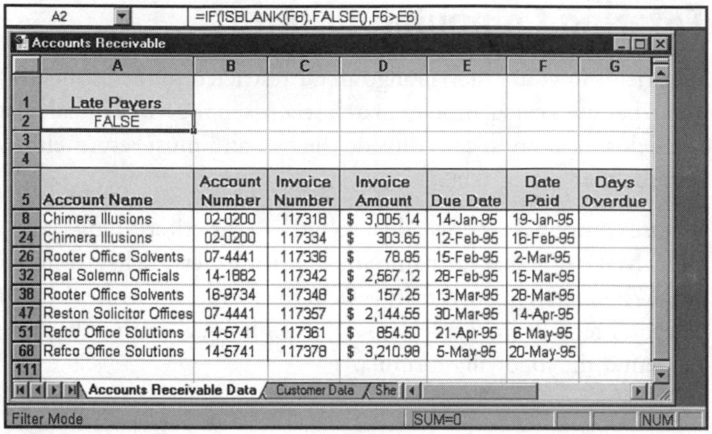

FIGURE 12.21.

Use a separate criteria range column for calculated criteria.

A2	▼	=IF(ISBLANK(F6),FALSE(),F6>E6)

Accounts Receivable

	A	B	C	D	E	F	G
1	Late Payers						
2	FALSE						
3							
4							
5	Account Name	Account Number	Invoice Number	Invoice Amount	Due Date	Date Paid	Days Overdue
8	Chimera Illusions	02-0200	117318	$ 3,005.14	14-Jan-95	19-Jan-95	
24	Chimera Illusions	02-0200	117334	$ 303.65	12-Feb-95	16-Feb-95	
26	Rooter Office Solvents	07-4441	117336	$ 78.85	15-Feb-95	2-Mar-95	
32	Real Solemn Officials	14-1882	117342	$ 2,567.12	28-Feb-95	15-Mar-95	
38	Rooter Office Solvents	16-9734	117348	$ 157.25	13-Mar-95	28-Mar-95	
47	Reston Solicitor Offices	07-4441	117357	$ 2,144.55	30-Mar-95	14-Apr-95	
51	Refco Office Solutions	14-5741	117361	$ 854.50	21-Apr-95	6-May-95	
68	Refco Office Solutions	14-5741	117378	$ 3,210.98	5-May-95	20-May-95	
111							

Accounts Receivable Data / Customer Data / She

Filter Mode | SUM=0 | | NUM

Copying Filtered Data to a Different Range

If you want to work with the filtered data separately, you can copy it (or *extract* it) to a new location. Follow the steps in this procedure:

1. Set up the criteria you want to use to filter the list.

2. If you want to copy only certain columns from the list, copy the appropriate field names to the range you'll be using for the copy.

3. Select the **D**ata | **F**ilter | **A**dvanced Filter command to display the Advanced Filter dialog box.

4. In the Action group, select the C**o**py to Another Location option.

5. Enter your list and criteria ranges, if necessary.

6. In the Copy **t**o text box, enter a reference for the copy location using the following guidelines (note that in each case you must select the cell or range in the same worksheet that contains the list):

   - To copy the entire filtered list, enter a single cell.

   - To copy only a specific number of rows, enter a range that contains the number of rows you want. If you have more data than fits in the range, Excel asks whether you want to paste the remaining data.

   - To copy only certain columns, select the column labels you copied in step 2.

CAUTION

If you select a single cell to paste the entire filtered list, make sure that you won't be overwriting any data. Otherwise, Excel will copy over the data without warning.

7. Select OK. Excel filters the list and copies the selected records to the location you specified.

Figure 12.22 shows the results of an extract in the Accounts Receivable list. I've hidden rows 9 through 106 to show all three ranges on-screen.

FIGURE 12.22.

The results of an extract in the Accounts Receivable list.

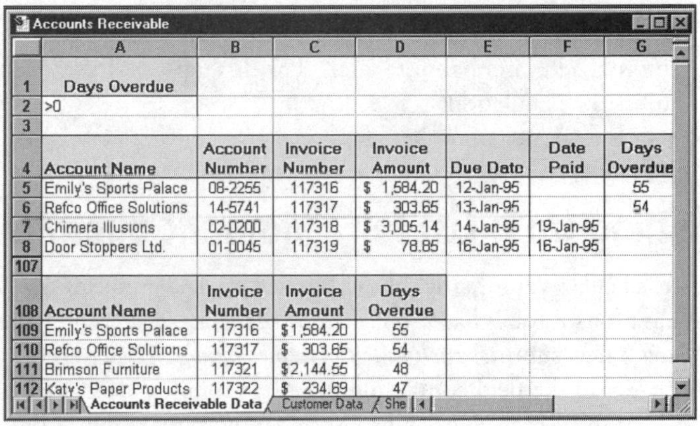

Summarizing List Data

Because a list is just a worksheet range, you can analyze list data using many of the same methods you use for regular worksheet cells. Typically, this task involves using formulas and functions to answer questions and produce results. To make your analysis chores easier, Excel enables you to create *automatic subtotals* that can give you instant subtotals, averages, and more. Excel goes one step further by also offering many list-specific functions. These functions work with entire lists or subsets defined by a criteria range. The rest of this chapter shows you how to use all these tools to analyze and summarize your data.

Creating Automatic Subtotals

Automatic subtotals enable you to summarize your sorted list data quickly. For example, if you have a list of invoices sorted by account name, you can use automatic subtotals to give you the following information for each account:

- The total number of invoices
- The sum of the invoice amounts
- The average invoice amount
- The maximum number of days an invoice is overdue

You can do all this and more without entering a single formula; Excel does the calculations and enters the results automatically. You also can just as easily create grand totals that apply to the entire list.

> **NOTE**
>
> As you can see, the term *automatic subtotal* is somewhat of a misnomer because you can summarize more than just totals. For this topic, at least, think of a subtotal as any summary calculation.

Setting Up a List for Automatic Subtotals

Excel calculates automatic subtotals based on data groupings in a selected field. For example, if you ask for subtotals based on account name, Excel runs down the account name column and creates a new subtotal *each time the name changes*. To get useful summaries, then, you need to sort a list on the field containing the data groupings you're interested in. Figure 12.23 shows the Accounts Receivable database sorted by account name. Subtotaling the Account Name field gives you summaries for Brimson Furniture, Chimera Illusions, Door Stoppers Ltd., and so on.

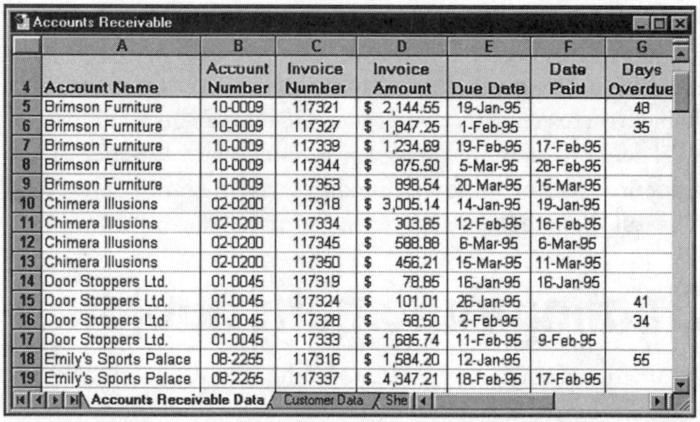

FIGURE 12.23.

A sorted list ready for displaying subtotals.

> **NOTE**
>
> If you want to display subtotals for a filtered list, be sure to filter the list before sorting it (as described earlier in this chapter).

Displaying Subtotals

When you subtotal your data, you use the Subtotal dialog box, shown in Figure 12.24. Before I take you through the steps necessary to display subtotals, take a look at the controls in this dialog box:

At Each Change in	This box contains the field names for your list. Select the field you want to use to group the subtotals.
Use Function	Select the function you want to use in the calculations. Excel gives you 11 choices, including Sum, Count, Average, Max, and Min.
Add Subtotal to	This is a list of check boxes for each field. Activate the appropriate check boxes for the fields you want to subtotal.
Replace **C**urrent Subtotals	Activate this check box to display new subtotal rows. To add to the existing rows, deactivate this option.
Page Break Between Groups	If you intend to print the summary, activate this check box to insert a page break between each grouping.
Summary Below Data	Deactivate this check box if you want the subtotal rows to appear above the groupings.

FIGURE 12.24.

You use the Subtotal dialog box to create subtotals for your list.

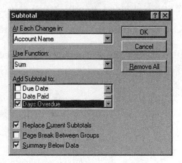

To subtotal a list, follow these steps:

1. If you haven't already done so, sort your list according to the groupings you want to use for the subtotals.
2. Select the **D**ata | Su**b**totals command to display the Subtotal dialog box.
3. Enter the options you want to use for the subtotals, as described earlier.
4. Select OK. Excel calculates the subtotals and enters them into the list.

Figure 12.25 shows the Accounts Receivable list with the Invoice Amount field subtotaled.

FIGURE 12.25.

A list showing Invoice Amount subtotals for each Account Name.

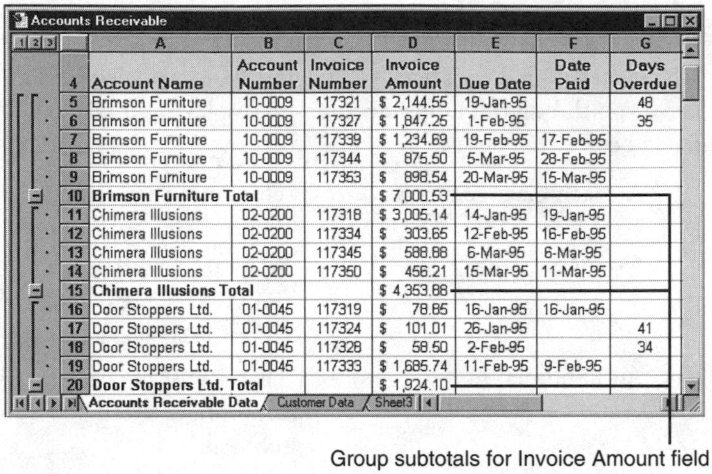

Group subtotals for Invoice Amount field

Adding More Subtotals

You can add any number of subtotals to the current summary. The following procedure shows you what to do:

1. Select the **D**ata | Su**b**totals command to display the Subtotal dialog box.

2. Enter the options you want to use for the new subtotal.

3. Deactivate the Replace **C**urrent Subtotals check box.

4. Select OK. Excel calculates the new subtotals and adds them to the list.

For example, Figure 12.26 shows the Accounts Receivable list with two new subtotals that count the invoices and display the maximum number of days overdue.

FIGURE 12.26.

You can use multiple subtotals in a list.

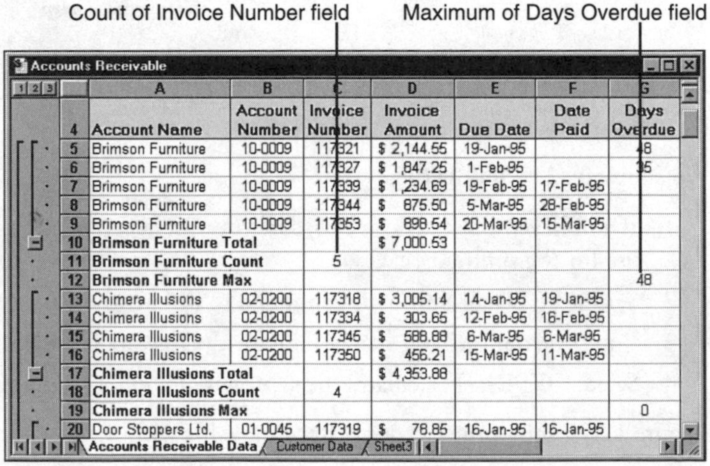

Count of Invoice Number field   Maximum of Days Overdue field

Nesting Subtotals

If the existing subtotal groups don't show enough detail, you can insert a subtotal within a subtotal group (this is called *nesting* subtotals). Follow the steps in this procedure:

1. Select the **D**ata | Su**b**totals command to display the Subtotal dialog box.

2. Select the field you want to use for the new subtotal grouping from the **A**t Each Change in list.

3. Enter any other options you want to use for the new subtotal.

4. Deactivate the Replace **C**urrent Subtotals check box.

5. Select OK. Excel calculates the new subtotals and adds them to the list.

Figure 12.27 shows the original Accounts Receivable subtotals (the ones shown in Figure 12.25) with nested subtotals for each month.

FIGURE 12.27.

You also can nest subtotals inside existing subtotal groups.

Nested subtotals

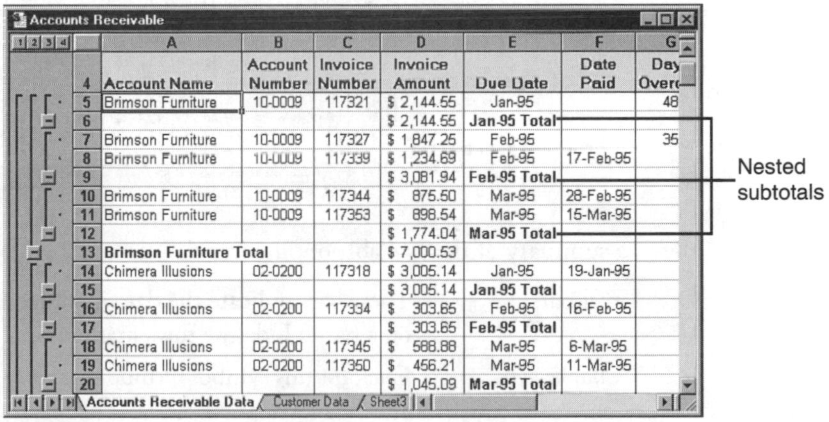

TIP

Because Excel uses the format of the data to decide on the subtotal groupings, you also can control the subtotals by formatting the data appropriately. In Figure 12.27, I formatted the Due Date field as *mmm-yy*. This changes, for example, 15-Dec-95 to Dec-95 and enables Excel to group the invoices by month.

Working with a Subtotal's Outline Symbols

When Excel creates a subtotal, it displays various *outline symbols* to the left of the worksheet. You can use these symbols to hide or show detail data in the subtotals. Although you can find a complete discussion of outlining in Chapter 5, "Advanced Worksheet Topics," this section gives you some basics to enable you to manipulate subtotals.

Outlines work by dividing your data into different *levels* that show different amounts of detail. The subtotaled data in Figure 12.28 has three levels:

Level 1	The list grand total, which appears at the bottom of the list. It can't be seen in Figure 12.28.
Level 2	The list subtotals.
Level 3	The entire list.

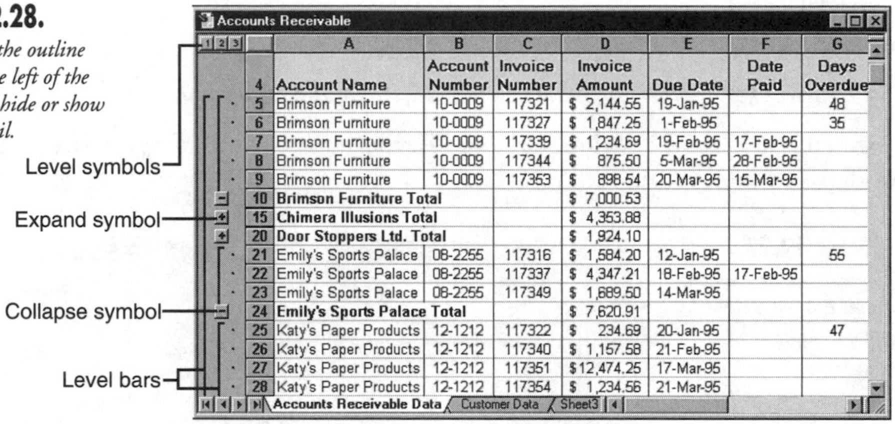

FIGURE 12.28.

You can use the outline symbols to the left of the worksheet to hide or show subtotal detail.

Level symbols

Expand symbol

Collapse symbol

Level bars

Here's a summary of the available outline tools:

Level bars	These bars indicate the data included in the current level. Click on a bar to hide the rows marked by a bar.
Collapse symbol	Click on this symbol to hide (or *collapse*) the rows marked by the attached level bar.
Expand symbol	When you collapse a level, the collapse symbol changes to an expand symbol (+). Click on an expand symbol to display the hidden rows.
Level symbols	These symbols tell you which level each level bar is on. Click on a level symbol to display all the detail data for that level.

In Figure 12.28, the detail data for Chimera Illusions and Door Stoppers Ltd. is collapsed, and the detail data for Brimson Furniture, Emily's Sports Palace, and Katy's Paper Products is expanded.

Removing Subtotals

To remove the subtotals from a list, select the **D**ata | Su**b**totals command to display the Subtotal dialog box, and then select the **R**emove All button.

Excel's List Functions

To get more control over your list analysis, you can use Excel's *list functions*. These functions are the same as those used in subtotals, but they have the following advantages:

- You can enter the functions into any cell in the worksheet.
- You can specify the range the function uses to perform its calculations.
- You can enter criteria or reference a criteria range to perform calculations on subsets of the list.

About List Functions

To illustrate the list functions, consider an example. If you want to, say, calculate the sum of a list field, you can enter SUM(*range*), and Excel produces the result. If you want to sum only a subset of the field, you must specify as arguments the particular cells to use. For lists containing hundreds of records, however, this process is impractical. (It's also illegal for two reasons: Excel allows a maximum of 30 arguments in the SUM() function, and it allows a maximum of 255 characters in a cell entry.)

The solution is to use DSUM(), which is the list equivalent of the SUM() function. The DSUM() function takes three arguments: a list range, a field name, and a criteria range. DSUM() looks at the specified field in the list and sums only records that match the criteria in the criteria range.

The list functions come in two varieties: those that don't require a criteria range and those that do.

List Functions That Don't Require a Criteria Range

Excel has two list functions that enable you to specify the criteria as an argument rather than a range: COUNTIF() and SUMIF().

Using *COUNTIF()*

The COUNTIF() function counts the number of cells in a range that meet a single criterion:

COUNTIF(*range*,*criteria*)

range	The range of cells to use for the count.
criteria	The criteria, entered as text, that determines which cells to count. Excel applies the criterion to *range*.

For example, Figure 12.29 shows a COUNTIF() function that calculates the total number of invoices that are more than 30 days overdue.

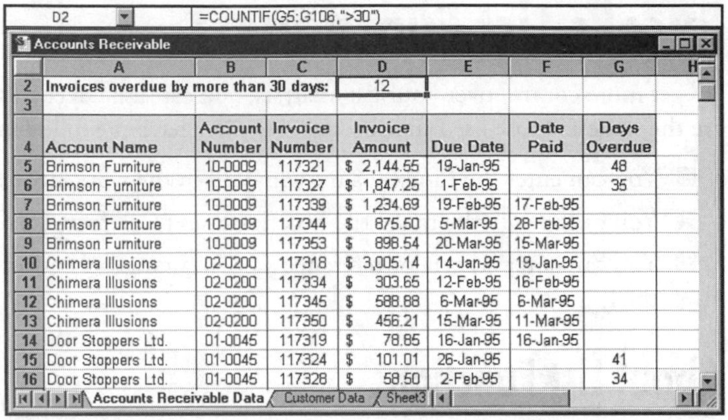

D2 =COUNTIF(G5:G106,">30")

Accounts Receivable

	A	B	C	D	E	F	G
2	Invoices overdue by more than 30 days:			12			
3							
4	Account Name	Account Number	Invoice Number	Invoice Amount	Due Date	Date Paid	Days Overdue
5	Brimson Furniture	10-0009	117321	$ 2,144.55	19-Jan-95		48
6	Brimson Furniture	10-0009	117327	$ 1,847.25	1-Feb-95		35
7	Brimson Furniture	10-0009	117339	$ 1,234.69	19-Feb-95	17-Feb-95	
8	Brimson Furniture	10-0009	117344	$ 875.50	5-Mar-95	28-Feb-95	
9	Brimson Furniture	10-0009	117353	$ 898.54	20-Mar-95	15-Mar-95	
10	Chimera Illusions	02-0200	117318	$ 3,005.14	14-Jan-95	19-Jan-95	
11	Chimera Illusions	02-0200	117334	$ 303.65	12-Feb-95	16-Feb-95	
12	Chimera Illusions	02-0200	117345	$ 588.88	6-Mar-95	6-Mar-95	
13	Chimera Illusions	02-0200	117350	$ 456.21	15-Mar-95	11-Mar-95	
14	Door Stoppers Ltd.	01-0045	117319	$ 78.85	16-Jan-95	16-Jan-95	
15	Door Stoppers Ltd.	01-0045	117324	$ 101.01	26-Jan-95		41
16	Door Stoppers Ltd.	01-0045	117328	$ 58.50	2-Feb-95		34

Accounts Receivable Data / Customer Data / Sheet3

FIGURE 12.29.

Use `COUNTIF()` *to count the cells that meet a criterion.*

Using *SUMIF()*

The `SUMIF()` function is similar to `COUNTIF()`, except that it sums the range cells that meet its criterion:

```
SUMIF(range,criteria,sum_range)
```

range The range of cells to use for the criterion.

criteria The criteria, entered as text, that determines which cells to sum. Excel applies the criteria to ***range***.

sum_range (Optional) The range from which the sum values are taken. Excel sums only those cells in *sum_range* that correspond to the cells in ***range*** and meet the criterion. If you omit *sum_range*, Excel uses ***range*** for the sum.

Figure 12.30 shows a Parts database. The `SUMIF()` function in cell F16 sums the Total Cost (F7:F14) for the parts in Division 3 (A7:A14).

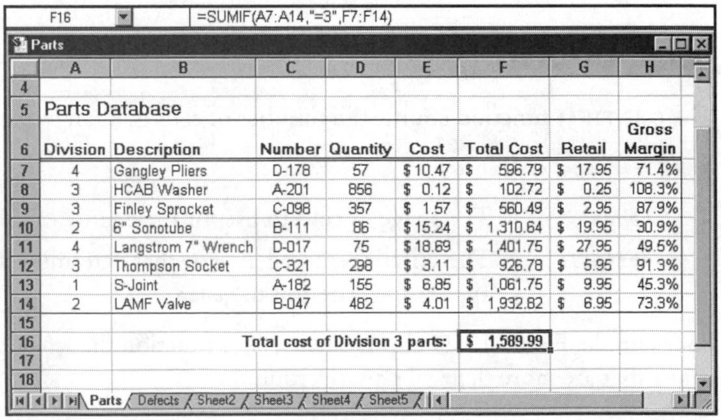

F16 =SUMIF(A7:A14,"=3",F7:F14)

Parts

	A	B	C	D	E	F	G	H
4								
5	Parts Database							
6	Division	Description	Number	Quantity	Cost	Total Cost	Retail	Gross Margin
7	4	Gangley Pliers	D-178	57	$ 10.47	$ 596.79	$ 17.95	71.4%
8	3	HCAB Washer	A-201	856	$ 0.12	$ 102.72	$ 0.25	108.3%
9	3	Finley Sprocket	C-098	357	$ 1.57	$ 560.49	$ 2.95	87.9%
10	2	6" Sonotube	B-111	86	$ 15.24	$ 1,310.64	$ 19.95	30.9%
11	4	Langstrom 7" Wrench	D-017	75	$ 18.69	$ 1,401.75	$ 27.95	49.5%
12	3	Thompson Socket	C-321	298	$ 3.11	$ 926.78	$ 5.95	91.3%
13	1	S-Joint	A-182	155	$ 6.85	$ 1,061.75	$ 9.95	45.3%
14	2	LAMF Valve	B-047	482	$ 4.01	$ 1,932.82	$ 6.95	73.3%
15								
16			Total cost of Division 3 parts:			$ 1,589.99		
17								
18								

Parts / Defects / Sheet2 / Sheet3 / Sheet4 / Sheet5

FIGURE 12.30.

Use `SUMIF()` *to sum cells that meet a criterion.*

List Functions That Require a Criteria Range

The remaining list functions require a criteria range. These functions take a little longer to set up, but the advantage is that you can enter compound and computed criteria.

All of these functions have the following format:

```
Dfunction(database,field,criteria)
```

`Dfunction`	The function name, such as DSUM or DAVERAGE.
`database`	The range of cells that make up the list you want to work with. You can use either a range name, if one is defined, or the range address.
`field`	The name of the field on which you want to perform the operation. You can use either the field name or the field number as the argument (in which the leftmost field is field number 1, the next field is field number 2, and so on). If you use the field name, enclose it in quotation marks (for example, `"Total Cost"`).
`criteria`	The range of cells that hold the criteria you want to work with. You can use either a range name, if one is defined, or the range address.

TIP

To perform an operation on every record in the list, leave all the *criteria* fields blank. This causes Excel to select every record in the list.

Table 12.6 summarizes the list functions.

Table 12.6. The list functions.

Function	Description
DAVERAGE()	Returns the average of the matching records in a specified field.
DCOUNT()	Returns the count of the matching records.
DCOUNTA()	Returns the count of the nonblank matching records.
DGET()	Returns the value of a specified field for a single matching record.
DMAX()	Returns the maximum value of a specified field for the matching records.
DMIN()	Returns the minimum value of a specified field for the matching records.
DPRODUCT()	Returns the product of the values of a specified field for the matching records.

continues

Table 12.6. continued

Function	Description
DSTDEV()	Returns the estimated standard deviation of the values in a specified field if the matching records are a sample of the population.
DSTDEVP()	Returns the standard deviation of the values of a specified field if the matching records are the entire population.
DSUM()	Returns the sum of the values of a specified field for the matching records.
DVAR()	Returns the estimated variance of the values of a specified field if the matching records are a sample of the population.
DVARP()	Returns the variance of the values of a specified field if the matching records are the entire population.

You enter list functions the same way you enter any other Excel function. You type an equals sign (=) and then enter the function—either by itself or combined with other Excel operators in a formula. The following examples all show valid list functions:

```
=DSUM(A6:H14, "Total Cost", A1:H3)
=DSUM(List, "Total Cost", Criteria)
=DSUM(AR_List, 3, Criteria)
=DSUM(1993_Sales, "Sales", A1:H13)
```

The next two sections provide examples of the DAVERAGE() and DGET() list functions.

Using *DAVERAGE()*

The DAVERAGE(*database,field,criteria*) function calculates the average *field* value in the *database* records that match the *criteria*. In the Parts database, for example, suppose that you want to calculate the average gross margin for all parts assigned to Division 2. You set up a criteria range for the Division field and enter 2, as shown in Figure 12.31. You then enter the following DAVERAGE() function (see cell H3):

```
=DAVERAGE(A6:H14, "Gross Margin", A2:A3)
```

> **TIP**
>
> As with all Excel formulas, your list functions will be much easier to read if you name your ranges.

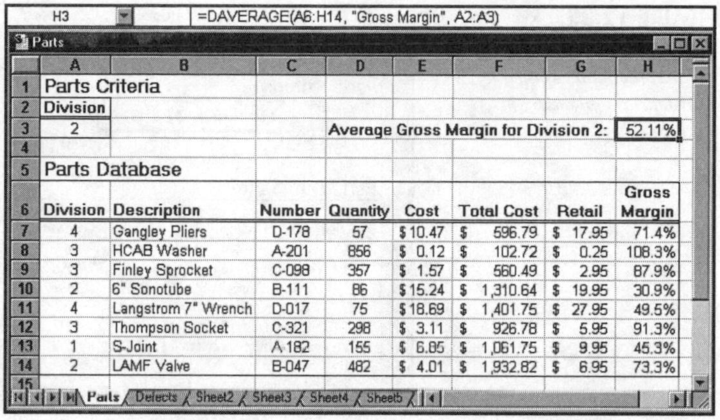

FIGURE 12.31.
Use DAVERAGE ( ) to calculate the field average in the matching records.

Using *DGET()*

The DGET(*database,field,criteria*) function extracts the value of a single *field* in the *database* records that match the *criteria*. If there are no matching records, DGET() returns #VALUE!. If there is more than one matching record, DGET() returns #NUM!.

DGET() typically is used to query the list for a specific piece of information. For example, in the Parts list, you might want to know the cost of the Finley Sprocket. To extract this information, you would first set up a criteria range with the Description field and enter Finley Sprocket. You would then extract the information with the following formula (assuming that the list and criteria ranges are named Database and Criteria, respectively):

```
=DGET(Database, "Cost", Criteria)
```

A more interesting application of this function would be to extract the name of a part that satisfies a certain condition. For example, you might want to know the name of the part that has the highest gross margin. Creating this model requires two steps:

1. Set up the criteria to match the highest value in the Gross Margin field.
2. Add a DGET() function to extract the Description of the matching record.

Figure 12.32 shows how this is done. For the criteria, a new field called Highest Margin is created. As the text box shows, this field uses the following computed criteria:

```
=H7=MAX($H$7:$H$14)
```

The range $H$7:$H$14 is the Gross Margin field. (Note the use of absolute references.) Excel matches only the record that has the highest Gross Margin. The DGET() function in cell H3 is straightforward:

```
=DGET(Database, "Description", Criteria)
```

This formula returns the Description of the part that has the highest Gross Margin.

	A	B	C	D	E	F	G	H
1	Parts Criteria							
2	Highest Margin	=H7=MAX($H$7:$H$14)						
3	FALSE					Part with Highest Gross Margin:		HCAB Washer
4								
5	Parts Database							
6	Division	Description	Number	Quantity	Cost	Total Cost	Retail	Gross Margin
7	4	Gangley Pliers	D-178	57	$10.47	$ 596.79	$ 17.95	71.4%
8	3	HCAB Washer	A-201	856	$ 0.12	$ 102.72	$ 0.25	108.3%
9	3	Finley Sprocket	C-098	357	$ 1.57	$ 560.49	$ 2.95	87.9%
10	2	6" Sonotube	B-111	86	$15.24	$1,310.64	$ 19.95	30.9%
11	4	Langstrom 7" Wrench	D-017	75	$18.69	$1,401.75	$ 27.95	49.5%
12	3	Thompson Socket	C-321	298	$ 3.11	$ 926.78	$ 5.95	91.3%
13	1	S-Joint	A-182	155	$ 6.85	$1,061.75	$ 9.95	45.3%
14	2	LAME Valve	B-047	482	$ 4.01	$1,932.82	$ 6.95	73.3%

Cell H3: =DGET(Database, "Description", Criteria)

Statistical List Functions

Many list functions are most often used to analyze statistical populations. Figure 12.33 shows a list of defects found among 12 work groups in a manufacturing process. In this example, the list (B3:D15) is named Defects, and two criteria ranges are used—one for each of the group leaders, Johnson (G3:G4 is Criteria1) and Perkins (H3:H4 is Criteria2).

Cell G10: =(DSUM(Defects,"Defects",Criteria1)-G6-G7)/(DCOUNT(Defects,,Criteria1)-2)

	B	C	D	...	F	G	H
1	Defects Database					Criteria	
2						1	2
3	Work group	Group Leader	Defects			Group Leader	Group Leader
4	A	Johnson	8			Johnson	Perkins
5	B	Perkins	10				
6	C	Perkins	0		Maximum	26	14
7	D	Johnson	11		Minimum	6	0
8	E	Johnson	9		Range	20	14
9	F	Johnson	6		Average	11.67	8.67
10	G	Perkins	11		Adjusted Avg	10	10
11	H	Perkins	10		Std Deviation (sample)	7.23	4.80
12	I	Perkins	7		Std. Deviation (pop.)	6.60	4.38
13	J	Perkins	14		Variance (sample)	52.27	23.07
14	K	Johnson	10		Variance (pop.)	43.56	19.22
15	L	Johnson	26				

The table shows several calculations. First, DMAX() and DMIN() are calculated for each criteria. The *range* (a statistic that represents the difference between the largest and smallest numbers in the sample; it's a crude measure of the sample's variance) is then calculated using the following formula (Johnson's groups):

```
=DMAX(Defects, "Defects", Criteria1) - DMIN(Defects, "Defects", Criteria1)
```

Of course, instead of using DMAX() and DMIN() explicitly, you can simply refer to the cells containing the DMAX() and DMIN() results.

The next line uses DAVERAGE() to find the average number of defects for each group leader. Notice that the average for Johnson's groups (11.67) is significantly higher than that for Perkins' groups (8.67). However, Johnson's average is skewed higher by one anomalously large number (26), and Perkins' average is skewed lower by one anomalously small number (0).

To allow for this situation, the Adjusted Avg line uses DSUM(), DCOUNT(), and the DMAX() and DMIN() results to compute a new average without the largest and smallest number for each sample. As you can see, without the anomalies, the two leaders have the same average.

> **NOTE**
>
> As shown in cell G10 of Figure 12.33, if you don't include a *field* argument in the DCOUNT() function, it returns the total number of records in the list.

The rest of the calculations use the DSTDEV(), DSTDEVP(), DVAR(), and DVARP() functions.

Summary

This chapter showed you how to work with lists (or databases, as they used to be called) in Excel. I showed you how to set up a list, how to use forms for data entry, how to sort and filter a list, how to work with automatic subtotals, and how to wield the list worksheet functions. For some list-related material, try these chapters on for size:

- If you need to fill in a list field with a series, the Fill handle or the **Edit | Fill | Series** command makes it easy. See Chapter 1, "Getting the Most Out of Ranges," for more information.

- Excel's lookup functions—VLOOKUP(), HLOOKUP(), MATCH(), and INDEX()—are handy for looking up values in a list. To find out their syntax and how they work, head for Chapter 3, "Harnessing the Power of Excel's Worksheet Functions."

- Excel uses formatting to differentiate list data from list headers. Everything you need to know is covered in Chapter 4, "Formatting Excel Worksheets."

- When Excel creates a subtotal, it displays various *outline symbols* to the left of the worksheet. You can find a complete discussion of outlining in Chapter 5, "Advanced Worksheet Topics."

- Automatic subtotals, filtering, and list functions are powerful tools for analyzing list data. But for large lists, they might not be enough to help you extract all the information you need. Pivot tables might be the answer, however. They're covered in depth in Chapter 13, "Creating Pivot Tables," and Chapter 14, "Customizing Pivot Tables."

■ If the data you want to work with is in an external database table (such as an Access file or a FoxPro file), you can use Microsoft Query to get at it. I explain this in Chapter 15, "Using Microsoft Query," and Chapter 16, "Creating Advanced Queries."

■ If you want to learn how to work with Excel lists via Visual Basic for Applications, read Chapter 26, "Database and Client/Server Programming."

Creating Pivot Tables

13

Lists and external databases can contain hundreds or even thousands of records. Analyzing that much data can be a nightmare without the right kinds of tools. To help you, Excel offers a powerful data-analysis tool called a *pivot table*. This tool enables you to summarize hundreds of records in a concise tabular format. You can then manipulate the table's layout to see different views of your data. This chapter introduces you to pivot tables and shows you various ways you can use them with your own data.

What Are Pivot Tables?

To understand pivot tables, you need to see how they fit in with Excel's other database-analysis features. Database analysis has several levels of complexity. The simplest level involves the basic lookup and retrieval of information. For example, if you have a database that lists the company sales reps and their territory sales, you could use a data form to search for a specific rep and to look up the sales in that rep's territory.

The next level of complexity involves more sophisticated lookup and retrieval systems in which the criteria and extract techniques discussed in Chapter 12, "Working with Lists and Databases," are used. You can then apply subtotals and the list functions (also described in Chapter 12) to find answers to your questions. For example, suppose that each sales territory is part of a larger region, and you want to know the total sales in the eastern region. You could either subtotal by region or set up your criteria to match all territories in the eastern region and use the DSUM() function to get the total. To get more specific information, such as total eastern region sales in the second quarter, you would just add the appropriate conditions to your criteria.

The next level of database analysis applies a single question to multiple variables. For example, if the company in the preceding example has four regions, you might want to see separate totals for each region broken down by quarter. One solution would be to set up four different criteria and four different DSUM() functions. But what if there were a dozen regions? Or a hundred? Ideally, you need some way of summarizing the database information into a "sales table" that has a row for each region and a column for each quarter. This is exactly what pivot tables do. With Excel's PivotTable Wizard, you can create your own tables with just a few mouse clicks.

How Pivot Tables Work

In the simplest case, pivot tables work by summarizing the data in one field (called a *data field*) and breaking it down according to the data in another field. The unique values in the second field (called the *row field*) become the row headings. For example, Figure 13.1 shows a database of sales by sales representatives. With a pivot table, you can summarize the numbers in the Sales field (the data field) and break them down by Region (the row field). Figure 13.2 shows the resulting pivot table. Notice how Excel uses the four unique items in the Region field (East, West, Midwest, and South) as row headings.

Chapter 13

FIGURE 13.1.

A database of sales by sales representatives.

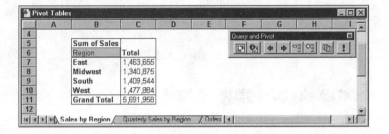

FIGURE 13.2.

A pivot table showing total sales by region.

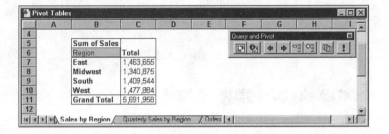

You can further break down your data by specifying a third field (called the *column field*) to use for column headings. Figure 13.3 shows the resulting pivot table with the four unique items in the Quarter field (1st, 2nd, 3rd, and 4th) used to create the columns.

FIGURE 13.3.

A pivot table showing sales by region for each quarter.

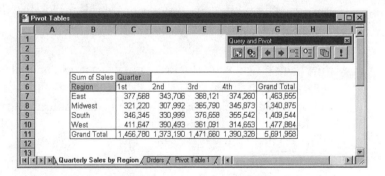

The big news with pivot tables is the "pivoting" feature. If you want to see different views of your data, you can, for example, drag the column field over to the row field area, as shown in Figure 13.4. The result, as you can see, is that the table shows each region as the main row category, with the quarters as regional subcategories.

FIGURE 13.4.

You can drag row or column fields to "pivot" the data and get a different view.

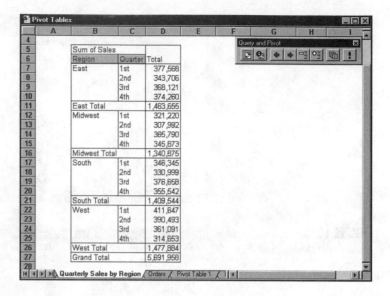

Some Pivot-Table Terms

Pivot tables have their own terminology, so here's a quick glossary of some terms you need to become familiar with:

Source list: The original data. You can use one or more Excel lists, an external database, an existing pivot table, or a crosstab table from Excel 4.0.

Field: A category of data, such as Region, Quarter, or Sales. Because most pivot tables are derived from lists or databases, a pivot-table field is directly analogous to a list or database field.

Item: An element in a field.

Row field: A field with a limited set of distinct text, numeric, or date values to use as row headings in the pivot table. In the preceding example, Region is the row field.

Column field: A field with a limited set of distinct text, numeric, or date values to use as column headings for the pivot table. In the second pivot table, shown in Figure 13.3, the Quarter field is the column field.

Page field: A field with a limited set of distinct text, numeric, or date values that you use to filter the pivot-table view. For example, you could use the Sales Rep field to create separate *pages* for each rep. Selecting a different sales rep filters the table to show data only for that person.

Pivot-table items: The items from the source list used as row, column, and page labels.

Data field: A field that contains the data you want to summarize in the table.

Data area: The interior section of the table in which the data summaries appear.

Layout: The overall arrangement of fields and items in the pivot table.

Building Pivot Tables

Excel provides the PivotTable Wizard to make creating and modifying your pivot tables easy. The PivotTable Wizard uses a four-step approach that enables you to build a pivot table from scratch. Here's a summary of the four steps:

1. Specify the type of source list to use for the pivot table.
2. Identify the location of the data.
3. Define the row, column, page, and data fields for the table.
4. Select a location, name, and other options for the table. Then create the table.

Throughout the rest of this chapter, I'll use the list shown in Figure 13.5 as an example. This is a list of orders placed in response to a three-month marketing campaign. Each record shows the date of the order, the product ordered (there are four types: Printer stand, Glare filter, Mouse pad, and Copy holder), the quantity and net dollars ordered, the promotional offer selected by the customer (1 Free with 10 or Extra Discount), and the advertisement to which the customer is responding (Direct mail, Magazine, or Newspaper).

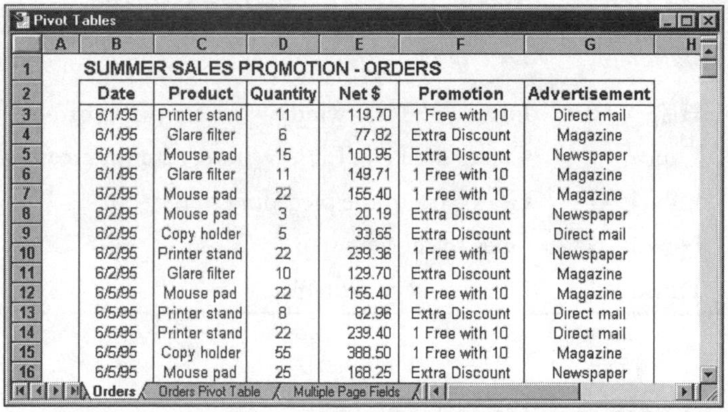

Pivot Tables

SUMMER SALES PROMOTION - ORDERS

Date	Product	Quantity	Net $	Promotion	Advertisement
6/1/95	Printer stand	11	119.70	1 Free with 10	Direct mail
6/1/95	Glare filter	6	77.82	Extra Discount	Magazine
6/1/95	Mouse pad	15	100.95	Extra Discount	Newspaper
6/1/95	Glare filter	11	149.71	1 Free with 10	Magazine
6/2/95	Mouse pad	22	155.40	1 Free with 10	Magazine
6/2/95	Mouse pad	3	20.19	Extra Discount	Newspaper
6/2/95	Copy holder	5	33.65	Extra Discount	Direct mail
6/2/95	Printer stand	22	239.36	1 Free with 10	Newspaper
6/2/95	Glare filter	10	129.70	Extra Discount	Magazine
6/5/95	Mouse pad	22	155.40	1 Free with 10	Magazine
6/5/95	Printer stand	8	82.96	Extra Discount	Direct mail
6/5/95	Printer stand	22	239.40	1 Free with 10	Direct mail
6/5/95	Copy holder	55	388.50	1 Free with 10	Magazine
6/5/95	Mouse pad	25	168.25	Extra Discount	Newspaper

Orders / Orders Pivot Table / Multiple Page Fields

FIGURE 13.5.
The Orders list that is used as an example throughout this chapter.

Figure 13.6 shows a simple pivot table for the Orders database. In this example, the quantity shipped is summarized by product and advertisement. The row headings were taken from the Product field, and the column headings were taken from the Advertisement field. The Promotion field is used as the page field to filter the data.

FIGURE 13.6.

A simple pivot table created from the Orders database.

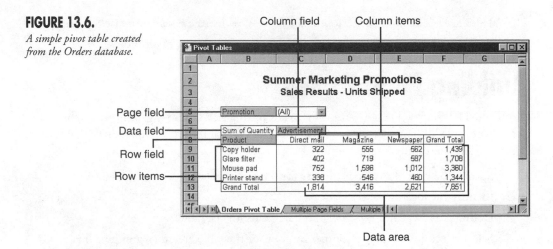

Navigating the PivotTable Wizard

The PivotTable Wizard dialog boxes, like other Excel Wizard tools, contain various buttons that enable you to navigate the PivotTable Wizard quickly. These buttons are summarized in Table 13.1.

Table 13.1. PivotTable Wizard navigation buttons.

Button	Description
Help	Displays a Help window for the current step
Cancel	Closes the PivotTable Wizard without creating the table
< Back	Goes back to the preceding step
Next >	Goes to the next step
Finish	Creates the pivot table

Creating a Pivot Table

The steps you use to create a pivot table vary depending on the source data you're using. You can use four types:

Microsoft Excel List or Database: A multicolumn list on a worksheet. The list must have labeled columns.

External Data Source: A separate database file in Access, dBASE, FoxPro, SQL Server, or some other format. You retrieve the data from Microsoft Query (as explained in the next chapter).

Multiple Consolidation Ranges: A collection of lists with row and column labels in one or more worksheets. Each range must have a similar layout and identical row and column labels.

Another Pivot Table: Another pivot table in the same workbook.

The next few sections show you how to create a pivot table for each type of source.

Creating a Pivot Table from an Excel List

The most common source for pivot tables is an Excel list. You can use just about any list to make up a pivot table (even, as you'll see, a list in an unopened workbook). But the best candidates for pivot tables exhibit two main characteristics:

- At least one of the fields contains "groupable" data. That is, the field contains data with a limited number of distinct text, numeric, or date values. In the Sales worksheet shown in Figure 13.1, the Region field is perfect for a pivot table because, despite having dozens of items, it has only four distinct values: East, West, Midwest, and South.

- Each field in the list must have a heading.

So given a list that fits these criteria, follow the steps in this procedure to create a pivot table:

1. Select a cell inside the list you want to use. (This isn't strictly necessary, but doing so saves you a step later.)

2. Select the **D**ata | **P**ivotTable command. Excel displays the PivotTable Wizard - Step 1 of 4 dialog box, shown in Figure 13.7.

    You also can start the PivotTable Wizard by clicking the PivotTable Wizard button on the Query and Pivot toolbar.

FIGURE 13.7.

The PivotTable Wizard - Step 1 of 4 dialog box, which appears when you start the PivotTable Wizard.

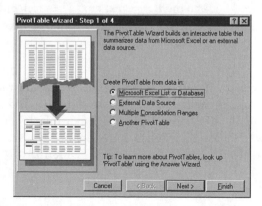

3. Make sure that the **M**icrosoft Excel List or Database option is activated, and then select Next >. You then see the PivotTable Wizard - Step 2 of 4 dialog box, shown in Figure 13.8.

FIGURE 13.8.

*The PivotTable Wizard -
Step 2 of 4 dialog box for
an Excel list.*

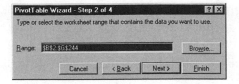

4. If you selected a cell in the list, the correct range coordinates should already be displayed in the **R**ange text box. If not, enter the range either by typing the address or by
   selecting the range directly on the worksheet. Select Next > to display the PivotTable
   Wizard - Step 3 of 4 dialog box, shown in Figure 13.9.

FIGURE 13.9.

*The layout used to create
the pivot table shown in
Figure 13.6.*

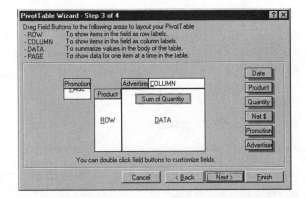

NOTE

If the workbook containing the list isn't open, select the Bro**w**se button, highlight the
workbook in the Browse dialog box, and then select OK. Excel adds the full pathname
of the workbook to the **R**ange text box. Then tack on the list's range coordinates to the
end of the pathname by pressing F2 (which puts Excel in Edit mode rather than Point
mode), pressing End, and then entering the address.

---

5. Specify the layout of the pivot table by dragging the field labels on the right to the
   appropriate areas. For example, to add a row field, drag a label and drop it anywhere
   inside the **R**OW box. Figure 13.9 shows the layout used to create the pivot table you
   saw in Figure 13.6. When you're done, select Next > to display the PivotTable Wizard
   - Step 4 of 4 dialog box, shown in Figure 13.10.

FIGURE 13.10.

Use the PivotTable Wizard - Step 4 of 4 dialog box to specify the table location and display options.

You can customize each field by double-clicking on the label. (You also can customize the fields after you've created the pivot table.) I'll explain each of the options in the PivotTable Field dialog box in Chapter 14, "Customizing Pivot Tables."

6. Use the PivotTable **S**tarting Cell text box to select the upper-left corner of the range you want to use for the table. You can type a reference or select it directly on the worksheet (or even on another sheet).

7. Enter a name for the table in the PivotTable **N**ame box.

8. Use the check boxes in the PivotTable Options group to refine the table's display:

   ■ Grand Totals For **C**olumns: Activate this check box to add an extra row at the bottom of the pivot table to show grand totals for each column.

   ■ Grand Totals For **R**ows: Activate this check box to add an extra column on the right of the pivot table to show grand totals for each row.

   ■ Save **D**ata With Table Layout: To make pivot table updating faster, Excel normally stores a hidden copy of the source data in a memory cache along with the table layout. If the source list contains a large amount of data, you might not want Excel to store a copy. In this case, deactivate the Save **D**ata With Table Layout check box. When you make changes to the pivot-table layout, Excel uses the source data directly to update the table.

   ■ **A**utoFormat Table: Activate this check box to format the pivot table using Excel's default AutoFormat.

NOTE

Should you save the source data with the table layout? The answer depends on several factors, including the size of the source data and its availability. On the up side, saving the data with the table means Excel can edit and refresh the pivot table faster (I'll talk about updating the pivot table a little later), and it means you don't have to keep a separate file for the source data. On the down side, if the source data is large, the size of your workbook (and the time it takes to save it) will increase accordingly. Also, you won't be able to use this pivot table to create another (as explained later in this chapter).

NOTE

It's a good idea to let Excel AutoFormat the pivot table. This way, when you pivot the data, the formatting pivots as well. (If you don't use AutoFormat, you must reformat the pivot table every time you pivot the data.)

9. Select the **F**inish button. Excel creates the pivot table in the location you specified and displays the Query and Pivot toolbar.

Creating a Pivot Table from an External Database

The PivotTable Wizard can still put together a pivot table even if your source data exists in an external database (for example, an Access, FoxPro, or SQL Server database). If you have Microsoft Query installed on your system, the PivotTable Wizard loads Query for you so that you can create a result set for the data you want to analyze. You then return this data to Excel so that the PivotTable Wizard can do its thing. (For details on using Microsoft Query, see Chapter 15, "Using Microsoft Query," and Chapter 16, "Creating Advanced Queries.") Here are the steps to follow:

1. Select the **D**ata | **P**ivotTable command (or click the PivotTable Wizard button in the Query and Pivot Toolbar) to display the PivotTable Wizard - Step 1 of 4 dialog box.

2. Activate the **E**xternal Data Source option, and then select Next >. Excel displays the version of the PivotTable Wizard - Step 2 of 4 dialog box that's shown in Figure 13.11.

FIGURE 13.11.

Use this version of the PivotTable Wizard - Step 2 of 4 dialog box to start Microsoft Query.

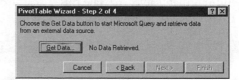

3. Select the **G**et Data button. Excel loads Microsoft Query.

4. Use Query to select a data source, filter the data, and display the result set you want to use for the pivot table.

5. Select Query's **File | R**eturn Data to Microsoft Excel command. The PivotTable Wizard stores the result set but doesn't display it in the worksheet. Select Next > to continue.

6. To finish the pivot table, follow steps 5 through 9 of the procedure outlined earlier, in the section called "Creating a Pivot Table from an Excel List."

TIP

If you think you'll be creating similar pivot tables with the same external data, you won't have to run the query again if you activate the Save **D**ata With Table Layout check box in the PivotTable Wizard - Step 4 of 4 dialog box. This option tells Excel to store a copy of the data in a memory cache with the table layout, so you can use this hidden data to build other pivot tables. (See the section later in this chapter titled "Creating a Pivot Table from Another Pivot Table.")

Using a Pivot Table to Consolidate Multiple Ranges

In Chapter 5, "Advanced Worksheet Topics," I showed you how to use the **D**ata | Co**n**solidate command to consolidate data from multiple worksheets. You'll recall that as long as each sheet used the same row and column labels (regardless of their position), Excel could easily gather the data and consolidate it to a new range.

As long as the ranges you're dealing with have row and column labels (and they use identical labels), you also can use pivot tables to consolidate multiple ranges of data. It takes a bit more work than using the **D**ata | Co**n**solidate command, but the resulting pivot table is much more flexible and customizable than the static table produced by the Consolidation feature.

As an example, we'll consolidate the sales budget data shown for the three divisional worksheets shown in Figure 13.12. The following procedure details the necessary steps.

1. Select the **D**ata | **P**ivotTable command (or click the PivotTable Wizard button in the Query and Pivot Toolbar) to display the PivotTable Wizard - Step 1 of 4 dialog box.

2. Activate the Multiple **C**onsolidation Ranges option, and then select Next > to display the PivotTable Wizard - Step 2a of 4 dialog, shown in Figure 13.13.

3. To have PivotTable Wizard create a page field for each range, activate the **C**reate a single page field for me option. To create your own page fields, choose the **I** will create the page field option (and then see the next section for details on how to create your own page field). Select Next > to display the PivotTable Wizard - Step 2b of 4 dialog box, shown in Figure 13.14.

FIGURE 13.12.

We'll use the PivotTable Wizard to consolidate the sales budget data from these three worksheets.

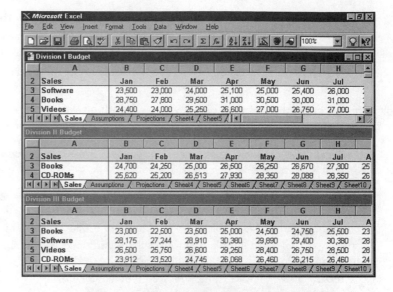

FIGURE 13.13.

Use the PivotTable Wizard - Step 2a of 4 dialog box to set up your page fields.

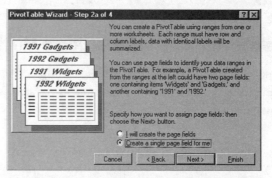

FIGURE 13.14.

You use the PivotTable Wizard - Step 2b of 4 dialog box to select the multiple ranges you want to use.

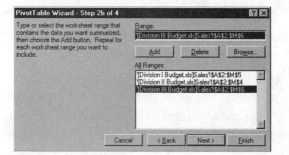

4. For each range you want to consolidate in the pivot table, enter a reference in the **R**ange text box (or select it on the sheet), and then select the **A**dd button. (Use Browse, as described earlier, to enter a range from an unopened workbook.) Select Next > when you're done.

5. To finish the pivot table, follow steps 5 through 9 of the procedure outlined earlier, in the section called "Creating a Pivot Table from an Excel List."

Figure 13.15 shows the resulting pivot table for our example. Notice how the PivotTable Wizard gives your pivot table generic names such as Row, Column, and Page1. (At least the **D**ata | Consolidate command, to give credit where credit is due, is smart enough to use the actual row and column labels from the source worksheets.) To change these names, see the section titled "Changing the Name of a Pivot-Table Field" in Chapter 14.

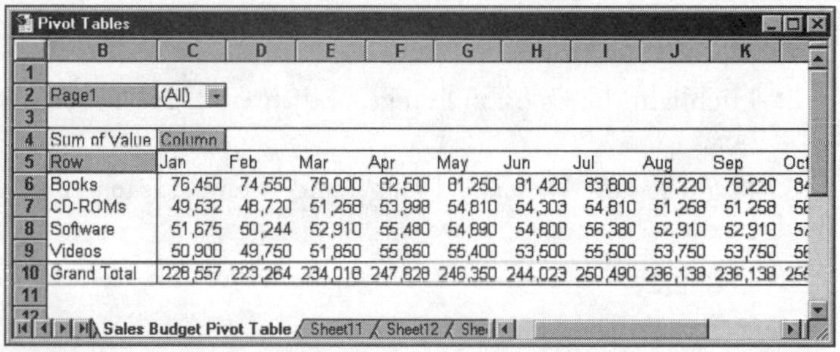

FIGURE 13.15.

When you consolidate multiple lists into a pivot table, Excel gives each field a generic name.

Creating Your Own Page Fields While Consolidating

As you saw in step 3 in the preceding section, the PivotTable Wizard can create page fields for each range in the consolidation, or you can create them yourself. (Creating page fields yourself is handy if you add to your data a new column that you want to use for the page field, for example.) If you choose the latter option, you'll see the PivotTable Wizard - Step 2b of 4 dialog box, shown in Figure 13.16.

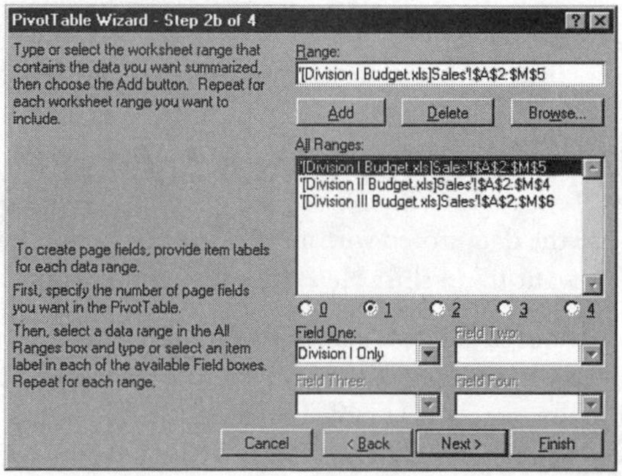

FIGURE 13.16.

You'll see this version of the PivotTable Wizard - Step 2b of 4 dialog box if you elect to create your own page fields.

To fill out this dialog box, first add the ranges you want to consolidate, as described in the preceding section. Then use the option buttons below the All Ranges list to specify how many page fields you want in the pivot table. Then select each range in the All Ranges list one at a time, and for each enter an item label in each of the available combo boxes below the option buttons. (One combo box is available for each page field you're creating.)

In our sales budget example, suppose that you want to create a single page field that shows a total of three pages (not including the default All page):

- Division I sales only
- Division II sales only
- Division III sales only

Setting this up requires four steps:

1. Activate the **1** option button.
2. Highlight the Division I range, and enter Division I Only in the Field **O**ne combo box.
3. Highlight the Division II range, and enter Division II Only in the Field **O**ne combo box.
4. Highlight the Division III range, and enter Division III Only in the Field **O**ne combo box.

Finish the pivot table normally, and you end up with the table shown in Figure 13.17. As you can see, the page field contains the items we just entered.

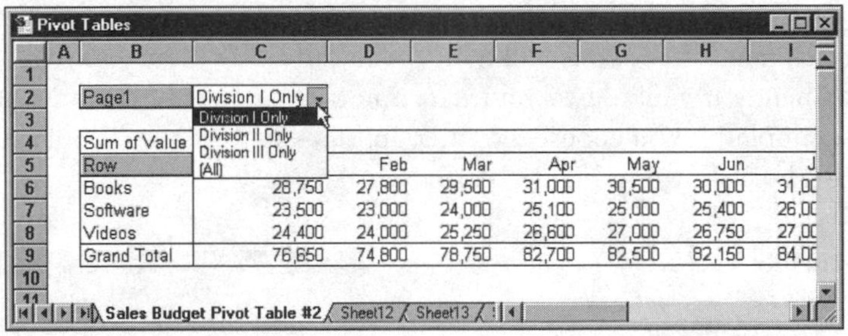

FIGURE 13.17.

The page field shows the items we entered in the preceding steps.

Creating a Pivot Table from Another Pivot Table

You can use the data stored with an existing pivot-table layout to create a new pivot table. Why would you want to do this? Here are some good reasons:

- If the source data isn't accessible for some reason (perhaps the file was deleted or is locked on your network), you can use the cached data stored with an existing pivot table to create a new table based on the same data. (Assuming, of course, that you didn't clear the Save **D**ata With Table Layout check box in the PivotTable Wizard - Step 4 of 4 dialog box.)

- If the source data was created with a query, you might not want to run the query again. External data is stored with the pivot table (again, assuming that the Save Data With Table Layout check box was activated), so there's no need to requery the source database.

- If the pivot table itself is large and complex, you can summarize the data even further by using the existing pivot table as the source data.

CAUTION

Both your new pivot table and the existing one will be linked to the same underlying data source. Therefore, when creating the new pivot table, make sure that you don't clear the Save Data With Table Layout check box in the PivotTable Wizard - Step 4 of 4 dialog box. If you do, the source data will be deleted for *both* pivot tables.

The following procedure shows you the necessary steps for creating a new pivot table from an existing one:

1. Select the **Data | Pivot**Table command (or click the PivotTable Wizard button in the Query and Pivot Toolbar) to display the PivotTable Wizard - Step 1 of 4 dialog box.

2. Activate the **A**nother PivotTable option, and then select Next > to display the PivotTable Wizard - Step 2 of 4 dialog box, shown in Figure 13.18.

FIGURE 13.18.

Use this version of the PivotTable Wizard - Step 2 of 4 dialog box to select the pivot table you want to use.

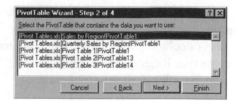

3. Highlight the pivot table that contains the data you want to use, and then select Next >.

4. To finish the pivot table, follow steps 5 through 9 of the procedure outlined earlier, in the section called "Creating a Pivot Table from an Excel List."

Updating a Pivot Table

Unfortunately, pivot tables aren't dynamic. That is, if the source data changes, you must update the pivot table to reflect the latest data. How you do this depends on how the data has changed:

- If any of the data used in a data field changes, or if any items in an existing row field or column field change, you need to refresh the pivot table.

474

- If you add new rows or columns to the source list, or if you delete existing rows or columns, you need to re-create the pivot table.

Refreshing a Pivot Table

If the data in the source list changes (in particular, if any of the items used in a data field, row field, or column field change), you can update the pivot table by refreshing it as explained here:

1. Activate the worksheet containing the pivot table.
2. Select a cell inside the pivot table.
3. Select the **Data** | **R**efresh Data command. Excel updates the table values.

> Click the Refresh Data button in the Query and Pivot toolbar to refresh your pivot-table data.

> **TIP**
>
> You also can refresh pivot-table data by right-clicking on a pivot-table cell and selecting Refresh Data from the shortcut menu.

Re-Creating a Pivot Table

When Excel refreshes a pivot table, it uses the same range for the source list that you specified when you created the pivot table originally. If you've made changes to that range—either by adding new rows or columns, or by deleting existing rows or columns—you need to tell Excel the new range so that it can re-create the pivot table. (This instruction also applies to pivot tables created from multiple consolidation ranges.)

Similarly, if you refresh a pivot table created from an external data source, Excel uses your original criteria to query the data source again. To use different criteria, or to adjust your criteria to allow for changes in the external source data, you need to re-create the pivot table.

Here are the steps to follow:

1. Activate the worksheet containing the pivot table.
2. Select a cell inside the pivot table.
3. Select the **Data** | **P**ivotTable command (or click the PivotTable Wizard button in the Query and Pivot Toolbar). Excel displays the PivotTable Wizard - Step 3 of 4 dialog box.
4. Select < **B**ack to return to the PivotTable Wizard - Step 2 of 4 dialog box. (If you created the pivot table from multiple consolidation ranges, you'll see the PivotTable Wizard - Step 2b of 4 dialog box instead.)

5. Adjust the range or, if you're dealing with an external data source, select the **G**et Data button, adjust the query, and return the data to Excel.

6. Work through the remaining PivotTable Wizard dialog boxes, if necessary.

TIP

These steps are also useful for converting an Excel version 4.0 crosstab table to a pivot table. Open the worksheet containing the crosstab table, select a cell within the table, and then choose the **D**ata I **P**ivotTable command.

TIP

If you find yourself constantly inserting or deleting rows or (less likely) columns in your source list, you can avoid re-creating the pivot table each time by assigning a range name to the source list. Then, when you create the pivot table, just enter the range name in the **R**ange text box. Excel adjusts the name with each insertion or deletion, so all you have to do is refresh the pivot table. (If you name the source list after you've created the pivot table, you'll need to re-create the table as described earlier and specify the range name in the **R**ange text box.)

Re-Creating a Pivot Table Without Saved Data

If you attempt to re-create a pivot table for which you didn't save the source data with the table layout, you'll see the dialog box shown in Figure 13.19. Specifically, you'll see this dialog box if you close and then reopen the workbook containing the pivot table. The problem is that because you didn't save the cached data, Excel discards the cache when you close the workbook. So before you can re-create the pivot table, you first must refresh the table so that Excel can rebuild the cache.

FIGURE 13.19.

If you didn't save the source data with the table layout, you must refresh the table before you can re-create it.

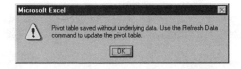

When you select OK to remove the dialog box, Excel displays the PivotTable Wizard - Step 2 of 4 dialog box. You might think that all you have to do is make sure that the correct range coordinates appear in the **R**ange text box and then select **F**inish to re-create the dialog box, but Excel will (annoyingly) just redisplay the error message shown in Figure 13.19. Instead, you must select Cancel in the PivotTable Wizard dialog box and then refresh your data as described earlier.

Creating a Chart from a Pivot Table

Pivot tables are certainly a powerful data-analysis tool, but as with all numerically intensive worksheet analysis, a picture is often worth a thousand numbers. In Excel, of course, the best way to get a picture of your data is to create a chart. (I covered charting in Chapter 9, "Working with Chart Types," and Chapter 10, "Enhancing Charts.")

Charting a pivot table isn't all that different from charting regular worksheet data. However, there are a few points you should keep in mind:

- Don't include grand totals in your charting range, because they can throw off the scale of the chart.

- Be sure to include the row field items and the column field items in your range. However, don't include either the top row of the pivot table or the page field in the range (see Figure 13.20).

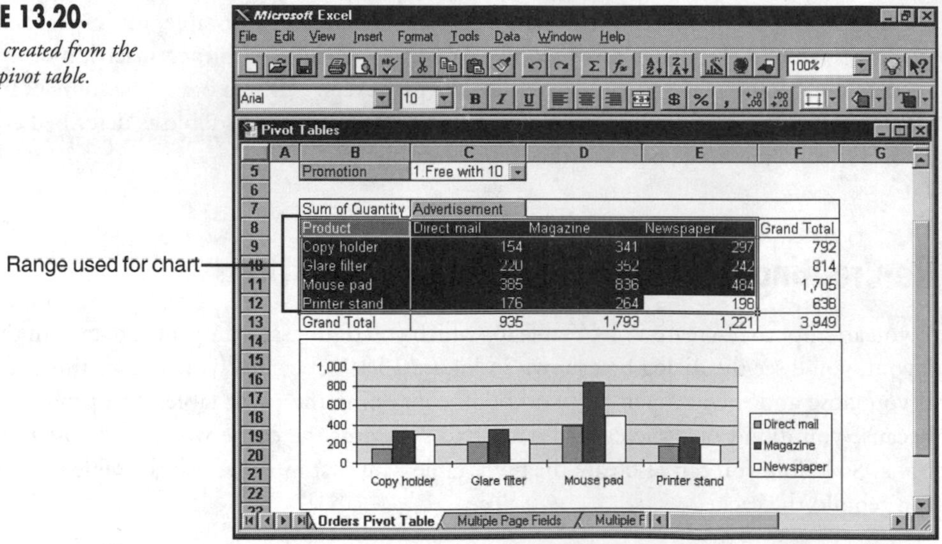

FIGURE 13.20.

A chart created from the Orders pivot table.

Range used for chart

TIP

If you're selecting the chart range with your mouse, always begin at the bottom-right corner of the range. If you start at the top-left corner, Excel thinks you're dragging the row field label to a new location.

- For best results, don't try to chart a pivot table that has more than two row fields or more than two column fields.

- Excel uses the field with the most items at the category (X) axis. In our Orders pivot table (see Figure 13.20), the row field has four items, whereas the column field has only three. Excel therefore will use the row field as the category axis. If you want to reverse this order, you can do so in step 4 of the ChartWizard.

- If your pivot table has a page field, when you select a different page, the chart is updated automatically. To take full advantage of this handy feature, try to embed your chart on the same page as the pivot table. This way, each time you select a different page, you can see the effect on the chart immediately.

Figure 13.20 shows a chart created from the Orders pivot table.

Summary

This chapter introduced you to pivot tables and showed you how to create them from Excel lists, external data sources, multiple consolidation ranges, and existing pivot tables. I also showed you how to update a pivot table and create a chart from the table. Here are some pointers to related information in this book:

- To compare pivot-table consolidation with the **Data | Consolidate** command, head back to Chapter 5, "Advanced Worksheet Topics."

- For full coverage of creating and working with charts, check out Chapter 9, "Working with Chart Types," and Chapter 10, "Enhancing Charts."

- We only scratched the surface of pivot-table potential in this chapter. You'll discover many more techniques for manipulating and customizing pivot tables in Chapter 14, "Customizing Pivot Tables."

- To get a complete explanation of querying external data sources, see Chapter 15, "Using Microsoft Query," and Chapter 16, "Creating Advanced Queries."

- Pivot tables are just one of Excel's many data-analysis features. To learn more about analysis with Excel, see the chapters in Part IV, "Unleashing Excel's Data Analysis Wizardry."

Customizing Pivot Tables

14

480

As you've seen, even a simple pivot table is a powerful tool for summarizing and consolidating large amounts of data. However, Excel doesn't stop there. After you've created a pivot table, myriad options are available for customizing the table to suit your needs. You can add and remove fields, group and sort field items, add field subtotals, and format the table. This chapter takes you through all of these analysis and customization options.

Displaying the PivotTable Field Dialog Box

Many of the field-related techniques you'll be working with in this chapter require you to display one of Excel's PivotTable Field dialog boxes. There are, in fact, two different dialog boxes, depending on the type of field you're dealing with. Figure 14.1 shows the PivotTable Field dialog box for a row, column, or page field, and Figure 14.2 shows the dialog box for a data field.

FIGURE 14.1.

The PivotTable Field dialog box for a row, column, or page field.

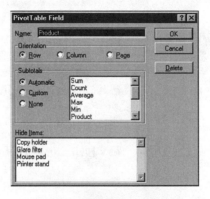

FIGURE 14.2.

The PivotTable Field dialog box for a data field.

Rather than repeating the instructions each time, I'll just summarize them in this section. To display the PivotTable Field dialog box, use any of the following methods:

- Select a cell in the field, and then select the **D**ata | PivotTable **F**ield command.
- Right-click on a cell in the pivot-table field, and select PivotTable Field from the shortcut menu.
- Double-click on a field label in the PivotTable Wizard - Step 3 of 4 dialog box.
- Select a cell in the pivot-table field, and click the PivotTable Field button on the Query and Pivot toolbar.

 The PivotTable Field button in the Query and Pivot toolbar.

Changing the Pivot-Table View

In their most basic form, pivot tables consolidate large amounts of complex data into a comprehensive, readable summary. But the real beauty of pivot tables is how they enable you to view your data from different angles. Simply by selecting a page from a page field's drop-down list, or by dragging fields to different table locations, you can see the numbers in an entirely different way. The next few sections show you how to use page fields and data pivoting to change the table view.

Working with Page Fields

Page fields filter your data the same way criteria do. (Criteria and filtering are covered in Chapter 12, "Working with Lists and Databases.") When you include a page field in your pivot table, Excel creates a drop-down list that contains the unique items from the field. You use these items to filter the list and display a different "page" of the table. (This is also known as *slicing* the data. Think of a scientist examining a cross section of some tissue or a mineral.)

Displaying a Different Page

To display a different pivot-table page, drop down the page field list and select one of the items. Excel filters the data to include only those records that match the page field item and then updates the table. When you want to remove the filter, select All from the list.

For example, in the Orders list pivot table (see Figure 13.6 in the preceding chapter), the page field is based on the Promotion column, which has two unique values: 1 Free with 10 and Extra Discount. To show only the totals for orders generated by the Extra Discount promotion, you would select Extra Discount from the page field drop-down list, as shown in Figure 14.3.

FIGURE 14.3.

Use the page field drop-down list to filter your data.

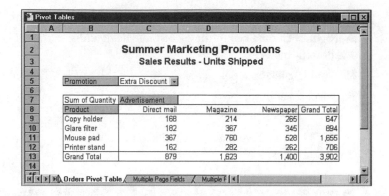

Displaying All Pages

If you want to include the various pivot-table pages in a report, you can tell Excel to create new worksheets for each page view. Here are the steps to follow:

1. Select All in the page field. (If you don't select All, Excel won't create a worksheet for the currently selected page.)

2. Click the Show Pages button on the Query and Pivot toolbar. Excel displays the Show Pages dialog box, shown in Figure 14.4.

 The Show Pages button from the Query and Pivot toolbar.

FIGURE 14.4.

Use the Show Pages dialog box to select the page field you want to use.

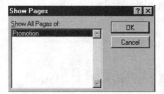

TIP

You also can display the Show Pages dialog box by right-clicking on the page field and selecting Show Pages from the shortcut menu.

---

3. If your pivot table has multiple page fields (I'll show you how to add fields to a pivot table later in this chapter), select the field you want to use from the **S**how All Pages of list box.

4. Select OK. For each page, Excel inserts a new worksheet, copies the pivot table to the sheet, displays the page, and names the worksheet after the page item.

Pivoting the Table

Pivot tables "pivot" because the data area acts as a kind of fulcrum around which you can move row, column, and page fields. You can perform two main pivoting actions:

- You can move a field to a different area of the pivot table. For example, you could move a page field into the row field area.
- You can change the field order within an area. If you have two row fields, for example, you could reverse their positions in the table.

> **NOTE**
>
> Pivoting the table is also known as *changing the table orientation* and *rotating the data.*

Moving a Field to a Different Area

Just because you created a pivot table with particular labels in the row, column, and page fields, that doesn't mean you have to leave these labels where they are. Keep in mind that the row, column, and page fields are only facets of your data. By their very nature (that is, fields with a limited set of distinct text, numeric, or date items), these fields can change places with each other to enable you to view your data in different ways. So if the pivot table doesn't show your data in quite the way you want, you can easily move any of the row, column, or page fields to a different area of the table.

For example, the basic Orders pivot table (see Figure 13.6) displays the sales for each product as a function of the advertisement the customer responded to. Suppose, instead, that you would rather see the sales for each product as a function of the sales promotion. In other words, you want to see the Promotion field as a column field rather than a page field.

To do this, use your mouse to drag the Promotion field label from the page field into the column field area, as shown in Figure 14.5. When you drop the field label, Excel adds it to the column area. It's perfectly OK to have multiple fields in one area, but in this case we'll take out the Advertisement field and move it to the page area. Again, just drag the field label and drop it in the new area. Figure 14.6 shows the final layout of the reorganized pivot table.

> **NOTE**
>
> Dragging the pivot-table fields is probably the easiest way to change the orientation of your data. There is, however, another way to go about it. Select a cell in the row, column, or page field you want to move, and then display the PivotTable Field dialog box (as described at the beginning of this chapter). Use the Orientation group to select a new area for the field (**R**ow, **C**olumn, or **P**age), and then select OK.

FIGURE 14.5.

You can move a field into a different area by dragging the field label and dropping it in the area.

To turn this field into a column field, drag it to the column area

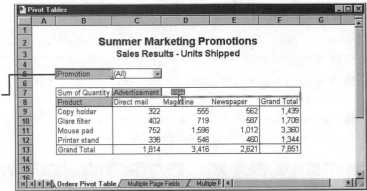

FIGURE 14.6.

The reorganized pivot table.

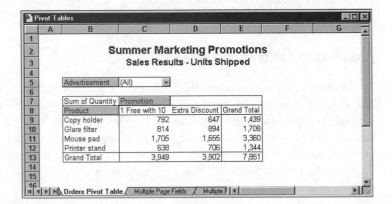

Multiple-Field Areas and Changing the Field Order

As you saw in the preceding section, when you move fields around, you often end up with a couple of fields in one area. This situation usually is temporary while you move fields to and fro, but it also can be handy for multidimensional analysis of your data.

Why multidimensional? The simplest pivot table would have a single row or column field that just shows the total for each item (see Figure 13.2 for an example). This would be a one-dimensional table.

Next on the pivot-table evolutionary scale would be a table with a row field and a column field (see Figure 13.3). The row and column provide two axes for the data summary, so this is a two-dimensional model.

To get a third dimension, you could add a page field to the table, as we did for the Orders pivot table (see Figure 13.6). As you saw earlier, however, the page field enables us to see only "slices" of this third dimension. To see the entire dimension at the same time, you need to change the page field into either a row field or a column field.

For example, consider the original Orders pivot table. Suppose that, instead of using a page field to see the effect of different promotions, we move the Promotion field into the row area. As you can see in Figure 14.7, the third dimension of our data—the breakdown of sales via product, advertisement, and promotion—becomes completely visible.

FIGURE 14.7.

By moving the Promotion label from the page area into the row area, we see the full third dimension of our data.

Sum of Quantity		Advertisement			
Product	Promotion	Direct mail	Magazine	Newspaper	Grand Total
Copy holder	1 Free with 10	154	341	297	792
	Extra Discount	168	214	265	647
Copy holder Total		322	555	562	1,439
Glare filter	1 Free with 10	220	352	242	814
	Extra Discount	182	367	345	894
Glare filter Total		402	719	587	1,708
Mouse pad	1 Free with 10	385	836	484	1,705
	Extra Discount	367	760	528	1,655
Mouse pad Total		752	1,596	1,012	3,360
Printer stand	1 Free with 10	176	264	198	638
	Extra Discount	162	282	262	706
Printer stand Total		338	546	460	1,344
Grand Total		1,814	3,416	2,621	7,851

In the same way that you can take a three-dimensional object and rotate it in space to see different sides and facets, so too can you rotate a three-dimensional pivot table to see different views of your data. In Figure 14.7, for example, the current layout breaks down each Product into its Promotion components. For the row area, you can think of the Product items as the main categories and the Promotion items as the subcategories. Suppose, instead, that you prefer to focus on the Promotion field and view the various Product items as subcategories. You can do this just by changing the order of the field labels within the row area. Use your mouse to drag the Promotion label and drop it on top of the Product label. (Or you could drag the Product label and drop it on the Promotion label.) As you can see in Figure 14.8, the table now breaks down each Promotion into its Product components.

FIGURE 14.8.

You can "rotate" the table by moving field labels within an area.

Sum of Quantity		Advertisement			
Promotion	Product	Direct mail	Magazine	Newspaper	Grand Total
1 Free with 10	Copy holder	154	341	297	792
	Glare filter	220	352	242	814
	Mouse pad	385	836	484	1,705
	Printer stand	176	264	198	638
1 Free with 10 Total		935	1,793	1,221	3,949
Extra Discount	Copy holder	168	214	265	647
	Glare filter	182	367	345	894
	Mouse pad	367	760	528	1,655
	Printer stand	162	282	262	706
Extra Discount Total		879	1,623	1,400	3,902
Grand Total		1,814	3,416	2,621	7,851

Adding Fields to a Pivot Table

A pivot table's fields aren't set in stone. If you create a pivot table and then need to add an extra field later, Excel is only too happy to oblige. You saw in the preceding chapter that you can pivot a field so that you end up with multiple fields in a single area. (For example, you can move a page field into the row area.) So as you might expect, you can also create multiple-field areas by adding new fields to the table. The next few sections discuss adding new row, column, page, and data fields.

Adding Row and Column Fields

Adding a row or column field creates subcategories for each row or column. For example, Figure 14.9 shows another pivot table for the Orders list (first introduced in Chapter 13, "Creating Pivot Tables"; see Figure 13.5). In this case, a new Date field has been added as a subcategory of the row field. As you can see, each Product is now broken down by month and given its own subtotal.

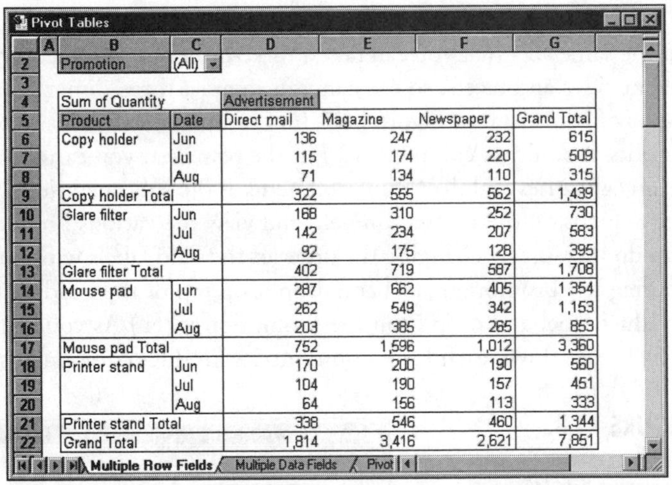

Promotion	(All)				
Sum of Quantity		Advertisement			
Product	Date	Direct mail	Magazine	Newspaper	Grand Total
Copy holder	Jun	136	247	232	615
	Jul	115	174	220	509
	Aug	71	134	110	315
Copy holder Total		322	555	562	1,439
Glare filter	Jun	168	310	252	730
	Jul	142	234	207	583
	Aug	92	175	128	395
Glare filter Total		402	719	587	1,708
Mouse pad	Jun	287	662	405	1,354
	Jul	262	549	342	1,153
	Aug	203	385	265	853
Mouse pad Total		752	1,596	1,012	3,360
Printer stand	Jun	170	200	190	560
	Jul	104	190	157	451
	Aug	64	156	113	333
Printer stand Total		338	546	460	1,344
Grand Total		1,814	3,416	2,621	7,851

FIGURE 14.9.
A pivot table with two row fields.

NOTE

In the pivot table in Figure 14.9, I had to *group* the date field to make it show only monthly totals. To learn how to group field data, see "Grouping Pivot-Table Items," later in this chapter.

Adding a Field Using the PivotTable Wizard

There are two ways to add a field to a pivot table: the PivotTable Wizard method and the shortcut menu method. This procedure shows you the steps to follow for the PivotTable Wizard method:

1. Select a cell inside the pivot table you want to work with.
2. Choose the **D**ata | **P**ivotTable command (or click the PivotTable Wizard button in the Query and Pivot Toolbar). Excel displays the PivotTable Wizard - Step 3 of 4 dialog box.

> **TIP**
>
> You also can display the PivotTable Wizard - Step 3 of 4 dialog box by right-clicking a pivot-table cell and selecting PivotTable from the shortcut menu.

3. Use your mouse to drag the field label you want to add and drop it on either the **R**OW area or the **C**OLUMN area (as appropriate).
4. Select the **F**inish button. Excel adds the new field and redisplays the pivot table.

Adding a Field Using the Shortcut Menu

The pivot-table shortcut menu offers you a quicker way to add a row or column field. To get started, use one of the following methods:

- If you're adding a row field, right-click on the row field label or on any row field item, and then select Add Row Field from the shortcut menu.
- If you're adding a column field, right-click on the column field label or on any column field item, and then select Add Column Field from the shortcut menu.

In the cascade menu of field names that appears (see Figure 14.10), click on the field you want to add.

FIGURE 14.10.

The pivot-table shortcut menu enables you to add a field quickly.

Adding Page Fields

Adding new row and column fields expands the pivot-table view to encompass more data. Adding a new page field, however, has just the opposite effect: it reduces the pivot-table view so that you see less data. In this sense, adding another page field is like adding a new filter to the list so that you're then using compound criteria to select the data. Compound criteria, you'll recall from Chapter 12, combine two or more criteria using either And (when only data that meets all the criteria is selected) or Or (when only data that meets at least one of the criteria is selected).

In the case of multiple page fields, each page item is a criterion. So with, say, two page fields, Excel displays only pivot-table data that meets *both* page criteria. For example, Figure 14.11 shows a pivot table based on the Orders list that shows products sold by month. There are two page fields: Promotion and Advertisement. The pivot-table data reflects only those products sold that meet the two criteria. In Figure 14.11, for example, the data displayed is for these products sold through the 1 Free with 10 promotion and the Magazine advertisement.

FIGURE 14.11.

A pivot table with two page fields.

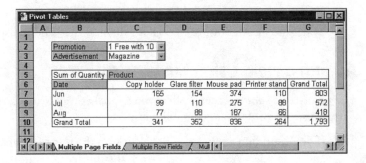

To add a new page field, you have two choices:

- Use the PivotTable Wizard to drag a second field into the **P**AGE area (as outlined earlier).

- Right-click inside the page area, click on Add Page Field in the shortcut menu, and then click on the field you want to add from the cascade menu that appears.

Adding Data Fields

If you have multiple numeric fields in your list, you can add as many of them as you like to the pivot table's data area. In the Orders list, for example, we have a Net $ field that shows the net dollars received for each order. In Figure 14.12, a second data field has been added to the pivot table to show the data for the Net $ field. In this case, I'm summarizing both data fields using Sum, but Excel has other summary functions you can use. (See the section "Changing the Data Field Summary Calculation," later in this chapter.)

FIGURE 14.12.
A pivot table with two data fields.

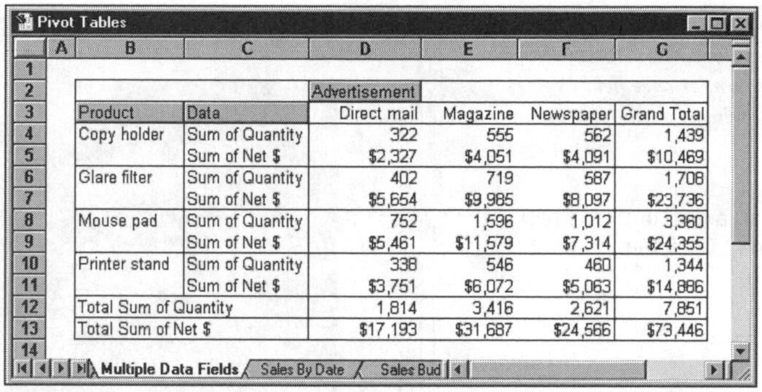

		Advertisement			
Product	Data	Direct mail	Magazine	Newspaper	Grand Total
Copy holder	Sum of Quantity	322	555	562	1,439
	Sum of Net $	$2,327	$4,051	$4,091	$10,469
Glare filter	Sum of Quantity	402	719	587	1,708
	Sum of Net $	$5,654	$9,985	$8,097	$23,736
Mouse pad	Sum of Quantity	752	1,596	1,012	3,360
	Sum of Net $	$5,461	$11,579	$7,314	$24,355
Printer stand	Sum of Quantity	338	546	460	1,344
	Sum of Net $	$3,751	$6,072	$5,063	$14,886
Total Sum of Quantity		1,814	3,416	2,621	7,851
Total Sum of Net $		$17,193	$31,687	$24,566	$73,446

As with row, column, and page fields, you have two choices when it comes to adding a new data field:

- Use the PivotTable Wizard to drag a second field into the DATA area (as outlined earlier).
- Right-click inside the data area, click on Add Data Field in the shortcut menu, and then click on the field you want to add from the cascade menu that appears.

Deleting Fields from a Pivot Table

If you want to simplify the pivot table, you can knock things down a dimension by removing a row, column, or page field. (You can also remove a data field if your pivot table has multiple data fields.) Excel gives you three methods for removing a field:

- Drag the field off the pivot table.
- Use the PivotTable Wizard.
- Delete the field from the PivotTable Field dialog box.

Deleting a Field by Dragging

To remove a row, column, or page field from the pivot table, you can use your mouse to drag the field out of the pivot area. (You can't use this method to delete a data field.) The *pivot area* is defined by two ranges:

- The rectangular range that holds the row fields, the column fields, and the data fields.
- The two rows of cells directly above the row fields (that is, the area where the page field normally appears).

To demonstrate this visually, Figure 14.13 shows the pivot area shaded dark gray. When you drag a row, column, or page field out of this area, the mouse pointer changes to a field icon with an X through it (as shown in Figure 14.13). When you release the mouse button, Excel deletes the field from the table.

FIGURE 14.13.

You can delete a row, column, or page field by dragging it outside the pivot area.

Drag a field outside the pivot area to delete it

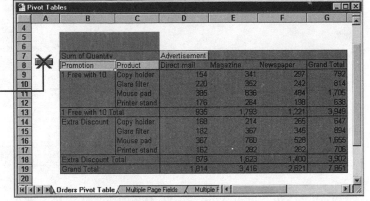

Deleting a Field Using the PivotTable Wizard

You can also use the PivotTable Wizard to remove a row, column, data, or page field from the pivot table. Follow the steps outlined here:

1. Select a cell inside the pivot table you want to work with.
2. Select the **D**ata | **P**ivotTable command (or click the PivotTable Wizard button in the Query and Pivot Toolbar) to display the PivotTable Wizard - Step 3 of 4 dialog box.

> **TIP**
>
> You also can display the PivotTable Wizard - Step 3 of 4 dialog box by right-clicking on a pivot-table cell and selecting PivotTable from the shortcut menu.

3. Use your mouse to drag the field label you want to remove and drop it off the table area.
4. Select the **F**inish button. Excel removes the new field and redisplays the pivot table.

Deleting a Field Using the PivotTable Field Dialog Box

The third and final method utilizes the PivotTable Field dialog box to delete a row, column, page, or data field. The following procedure takes you through the necessary steps:

1. Select a cell in the pivot-table field you want to delete.

2. Display the PivotTable Field dialog box (as described near the beginning of this chapter).

3. Select the **D**elete button. Excel deletes the field and returns you to the worksheet.

Hiding and Displaying Row or Column Items

You can reduce the clutter in your complex pivot tables by hiding individual items in the row or column fields. This technique reduces the number of rows or columns in the table and makes it easier to work with.

Hiding an Item

Next we'll use the pivot table shown in Figure 14.14 as an example by hiding the Newspaper item in the Advertisement column field. To hide an item in a row or column field, follow these steps:

1. Select any cell in the field that contains the item you want to hide.

2. Display the PivotTable Field dialog box (as described earlier in this chapter).

3. In the Hide **I**tems list, highlight the item you want to hide.

4. Select OK. Excel hides the item and adjusts the pivot-table totals, as shown in Figure 14.15.

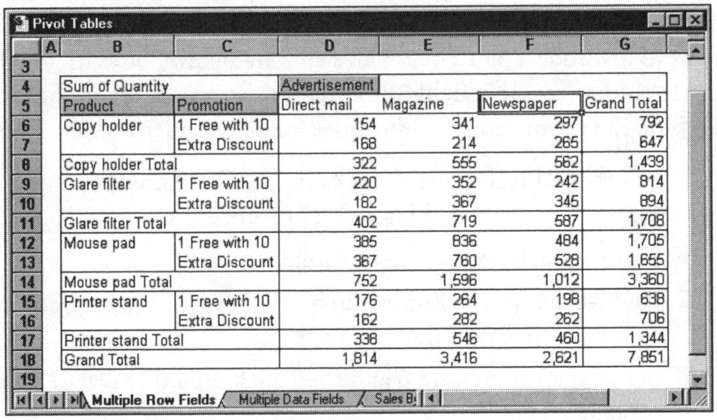

FIGURE 14.14.

The Newspaper item will be hidden in this pivot table.

Product	Promotion	Direct mail	Magazine	Newspaper	Grand Total
Sum of Quantity		Advertisement			
Copy holder	1 Free with 10	154	341	297	792
	Extra Discount	168	214	265	647
Copy holder Total		322	555	562	1,439
Glare filter	1 Free with 10	220	352	242	814
	Extra Discount	182	367	345	894
Glare filter Total		402	719	587	1,708
Mouse pad	1 Free with 10	385	836	484	1,705
	Extra Discount	367	760	528	1,655
Mouse pad Total		752	1,596	1,012	3,360
Printer stand	1 Free with 10	176	264	198	638
	Extra Discount	162	282	262	706
Printer stand Total		338	546	460	1,344
Grand Total		1,814	3,416	2,621	7,851

FIGURE 14.15.

The pivot table with the Newspaper item hidden.

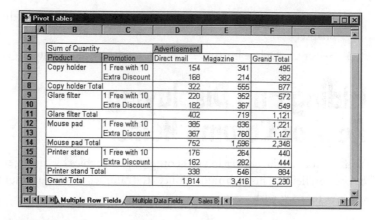

Sum of Quantity		Advertisement		
Product	Promotion	Direct mail	Magazine	Grand Total
Copy holder	1 Free with 10	154	341	495
	Extra Discount	168	214	382
Copy holder Total		322	555	877
Glare filter	1 Free with 10	220	352	572
	Extra Discount	182	367	549
Glare filter Total		402	719	1,121
Mouse pad	1 Free with 10	385	836	1,221
	Extra Discount	367	760	1,127
Mouse pad Total		752	1,596	2,348
Printer stand	1 Free with 10	176	264	440
	Extra Discount	162	282	444
Printer stand Total		338	546	884
Grand Total		1,814	3,416	5,230

Displaying a Hidden Item

Displaying a hidden item is just the opposite of hiding it:

1. Select any cell in the field that contains the item you want to display.
2. Display the PivotTable Field dialog box.
3. In the Hide Items list, remove the highlight from the item you want to display.
4. Select OK. Excel returns the item to the pivot table and adjusts the pivot-table totals.

Hiding and Displaying Subcategory Detail

A slightly different case is when your pivot table has multiple row or column fields. Instead of hiding a main category item (which you can do by following the steps given earlier), you might want to just hide a particular item's subcategories. For example, the pivot table shown in Figure 14.14 has two row fields: Product is the main category and Promotion is the subcategory. To hide the Promotion subcategories for a particular Product item, use any of these methods:

■ Select the Product item (for example, Copy holder), and then choose the **D**ata | **G**roup and Outline | **H**ide Detail command.

■ Double-click on the Product item.

■ Right-click on the Product item, click on Group and Outline in the shortcut menu, and then click on Hide Detail.

■ Select the Product item and then click the Hide Detail button on the Query and Pivot toolbar.

  The Hide Detail button on the Query and Pivot toolbar.

Figure 14.16 shows the pivot table with the subcategory detail hidden for the Copy holder and Glare filter items.

FIGURE 14.16.

The pivot table with the subcategory detail hidden for the Copy holder and Glare filter.

	Product	Promotion	Direct mail	Magazine	Newspaper	Grand Total
Sum of Quantity			Advertisement			
	Copy holder		322	555	562	1,439
	Glare filter		402	719	587	1,708
	Mouse pad	1 Free with 10	385	836	484	1,705
		Extra Discount	367	760	528	1,655
	Mouse pad Total		752	1,596	1,012	3,360
	Printer stand	1 Free with 10	176	264	198	638
		Extra Discount	162	282	262	706
	Printer stand Total		338	546	460	1,344
	Grand Total		1,814	3,416	2,621	7,851

To show the subcategory detail again, use any of these techniques:

- Select the Product item and then choose the **D**ata | **G**roup and Outline | **S**how Detail command.
- Double-click on the Product item.
- Right-click on the Product item, click on Group and Outline in the shortcut menu, and then click on Show Detail.
- Select the Product item and then click the Show Detail button on the Query and Pivot toolbar.

 The Show Detail button on the Query and Pivot toolbar.

Grouping Pivot-Table Items

The items that appear in a row or column field might have an underlying hierarchy. For example, if you have a row field in which the items are sales reps, each sales rep might belong to one of four regional offices. In our Orders example, one division of the company might manufacture the copy holder and mouse pad, whereas another division manufactures the glare filter and printer stand.

If these higher-level hierarchies aren't available in the source data, you can simulate them in the pivot table by *grouping* related items together. The next few sections explain everything.

Grouping by Item

The simplest way to create a pivot-table group is to use the labels for the various items in a particular field. For example, suppose that we want to group the Product field in the Orders list into two categories:

- The copy holder and mouse pad are grouped as Division I.
- The glare filter and printer stand are grouped as Division II.

Here are the steps to follow to use a field's items to create groupings:

1. Select the items you want to include in a group. In Figure 14.17, the Copy holder and Mouse pad items are selected.

FIGURE 14.17.

Select the items you want to group.

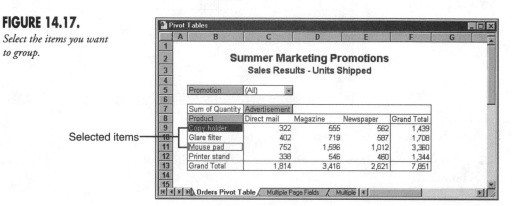

Selected items ─── [pointing to Copy holder and Mouse pad rows]

2. Select the **D**ata | **G**roup and Outline | **G**roup command, or click the Group button on the Query and Pivot toolbar.

 The Query and Pivot toolbar's Group button.

> **TIP**
>
> You also can group the selected items by right-clicking on them, clicking on Group and Outline in the shortcut menu, and then clicking on Group.

3. Repeat steps 1 and 2 to group the other items in the field.

As you can see in Figure 14.18, Excel adds a new row or column field for the groups and displays the items that compose the group as subcategories. Feel free to change Excel's generic Group1 and Group2 names to something more descriptive (such as Division I and Division II). You also can rename the new group field label (Product2 in Figure 14.18); see "Changing the Name of a Pivot-Table Field," later in this chapter.

> **NOTE**
>
> To ungroup the items, remove the new group field from the pivot table (as described earlier).

FIGURE 14.18.

Excel adds a new field for the group.

Pivot Tables						
A	B	C	D	E	F	G

Summer Marketing Promotions
Sales Results - Units Shipped

Promotion (All)

Sum of Quantity		Advertisement			
Product2	Product	Direct mail	Magazine	Newspaper	Grand Total
Group1	Copy holder	322	555	562	1,439
	Mouse pad	752	1,596	1,012	3,360
Group2	Glare filter	402	719	587	1,708
	Printer stand	338	546	460	1,344
Grand Total		1,814	3,416	2,621	7,851

Orders Pivot Table / Multiple Page Fields / Multiple

TIP

You can't group page fields directly, but there is a roundabout way to do it. You need to move the page field into either a row or a column orientation, group the field in its new position, and then move it back to the page area.

Grouping by Date or Time Ranges

All the pivot tables you've seen so far have used text values as items in their row and column fields. As I mentioned in the preceding chapter, however, it's OK to use fields that contain dates, times, and numbers. In this way, you can use pivot-table analysis on lists that contain birthdays, part numbers, test scores, elapsed times, and more.

The problem, though, is that your lists might not have a small number of distinct dates or numbers that Excel can use to set up categories in the row or column field. For example, consider the pivot table in Figure 14.19 that shows Product sales by Date. As you can see, Excel categorized the Date field by day, which means this pivot table has dozens of rows. We could reduce the clutter by using the technique from the preceding section to group, say, the June dates. However, Excel provides an easier way. This section shows you how to group dates and times, and we'll examine grouping numeric values in the next section.

Here are the steps to follow to group a date or time field:

1. Select a cell in the field you want to group.
2. Select the **D**ata | **G**roup and Outline | **G**roup command, or click the Group button on the Query and Pivot toolbar. Excel displays the Grouping dialog box, shown in Figure 14.20.

 The Query and Pivot toolbar's Group button.

FIGURE 14.19.

Row and column fields based on dates, times, or numbers often need to be grouped.

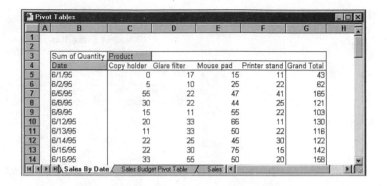

FIGURE 14.20.

Use the Grouping dialog box to select how you want the field grouped.

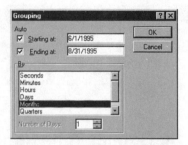

> **TIP**
>
> You also can display the Grouping dialog box by right-clicking on the field, clicking on Group and Outline in the shortcut menu, and then clicking on Group.

3. Use the **S**tarting at text box and the **E**nding at text box to enter the range of dates you want to group.

4. In the **B**y list, highlight the period you want to use for the group. If you select Days, you can also use the **N**umber of Days spinner to select the number of days to use for the grouping (for example, use 7 to group by week).

> **TIP**
>
> You can create both groups and subgroups by selecting multiple items in the **B**y list. For example, suppose that you select both Months and Quarters. Excel groups the field by months *and* adds a new field that groups the months by quarter.

5. Select OK. Excel groups the field and redisplays the pivot table. Figure 14.21 shows the Sales By Date pivot table grouped by month.

FIGURE 14.21.

The Sales By Date pivot table grouped by month.

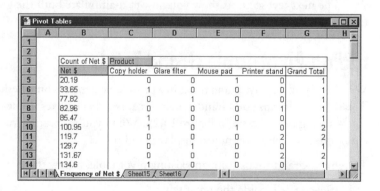

To ungroup the dates or times, Excel gives you three choices:

- Select a cell in the field, and choose the **D**ata | **G**roup and Outline | **U**ngroup command.
- Right-click on the field, click on Group and Outline, and then click on Ungroup.
- Click the Ungroup button on the Query and Pivot toolbar.

 The Query and Pivot toolbar's Ungroup button.

Grouping by Numeric Ranges

Grouping numeric fields is similar to grouping dates and times. For example, the pivot table in Figure 14.22 uses Net $ as the row field, Product as the column field, and Count of Net $ as the data field. (I'll tell you how to change the summary function used in the data field later in this chapter.) The idea behind this table is to get an idea of the frequency of different-sized orders. Were most of the orders small (say, under $500)? How many large orders (say, over $1,000) were there?

FIGURE 14.22.

A pivot table that displays the frequency of the order dollar amounts.

The problem, of course, is that the Net $ field just shows the individual dollar amounts for the various transactions. To make sense of this data, we need to group the Net $. You follow the

498

same steps as described in the preceding section. When you run the group command on the Net $ field, however, you see the version of the Grouping dialog box shown in Figure 14.23. Fill in the **S**tarting at and **E**nding at text boxes, use **B**y to specify an interval for the numbers, and then select OK. Figure 14.24 shows the Frequency of Net $ pivot table grouped with an interval of $500. (To ungroup the field, use any of the techniques outlined in the preceding section for dates and times.)

FIGURE 14.23.

Use this Grouping dialog box to select how you want your numbers grouped.

FIGURE 14.24.

The Frequency of Net $ pivot table grouped in $500 intervals.

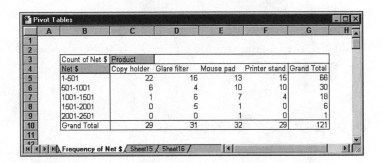

Count of Net $	Product				
Net $	Copy holder	Glare filter	Mouse pad	Printer stand	Grand Total
1-501	22	16	13	15	66
501-1001	6	4	10	10	30
1001-1501	1	6	7	4	18
1501-2001	0	5	1	0	6
2001-2501	0	0	1	0	1
Grand Total	29	31	32	29	121

Working with Pivot-Table Subtotals

As you've seen, Excel adds grand totals to the pivot table for each row and column item, and it adds subtotals for the outer layer of a pivot table with multiple fields in the row or column area. The next few sections show you how to manipulate both the grand totals and the subtotals.

Hiding Pivot-Table Grand Totals

Whether Excel displays grand totals in a pivot table depends on whether you activate the Grand Totals For **C**olumns and Grand Totals For **R**ows check boxes in the PivotTable Wizard - Step 4 of 4 dialog box, shown in Figure 14.25. When you're creating your tables, deactivate these check boxes to tell Excel not to display grand totals.

To remove grand totals from an existing pivot table, follow these steps:

1. Select a cell inside the pivot table.
2. Select the **D**ata | **P**ivotTable command (or click the PivotTable Wizard button in the Query and Pivot Toolbar). Excel displays the PivotTable Wizard - Step 3 of 4 dialog box.

3. Select Next > to display the PivotTable Wizard - Step 4 of 4 dialog box.

4. Deactivate the Grand Totals For **C**olumns and Grand Totals For **R**ows check boxes.

5. Select **F**inish.

FIGURE 14.25.

To hide grand totals, deactivate the first two check boxes in the Pivot-Table Wizard - Step 4 of 4 dialog box.

Hiding Pivot-Table Subtotals

Pivot tables with multiple row or column fields display subtotals for all fields except the inner-most field (that is, the field closest to the data area). To remove these subtotals, display the field's PivotTable Field dialog box (as described near the beginning of this chapter), activate the **N**one option in the Subtotals box, and then select OK.

Customizing the Subtotal Calculation

The subtotal calculation that Excel applies to a field is the same calculation it uses for the data area. (See the next section for details on how to change the data field calculation.) You can, however, change this calculation, add extra calculations, and even add a subtotal for the inner-most field. Display the PivotTable Field dialog box for the field, and then use any of these methods:

■ To change the subtotal calculation, highlight one of the 11 calculation functions (Sum, Count, Average, and so on) from the list in the Subtotals box, and then select OK.

■ To add extra subtotal calculations, highlight each of the calculation functions you want to use, and then select OK.

Changing the Data Field Summary Calculation

By default, Excel uses a Sum function for calculating the data field summaries. Although Sum is the most common summary function used in pivot tables, it's by no means the only one. In fact, Excel offers 11 summary functions, as outlined in Table 14.1.

Table 14.1. Excel's data field summary functions.

Function	Description
Sum	Totals the values for the underlying data.
Count	Counts the values for the underlying data.
Average	Computes the average of the values for the underlying data.
Max	Returns the largest value for the underlying data.
Min	Returns the smallest value for the underlying data.
Product	Computes the product of the values for the underlying data.
Count Nums	Totals the number of values in the underlying data that are numeric.
StdDev	Computes the standard deviation of the values for the underlying data, treated as a sample.
StdDevp	Computes the standard deviation of the values for the underlying data, treated as a population.
Var	Computes the variance of the values for the underlying data, treated as a sample.
Varp	Computes the variance of the values for the underlying data, treated as a population.

That's an impressive list, but you can also create your own custom calculations using Excel's numerous calculation types. To see these calculation types, select the **O**ptions >> button in the PivotTable Field dialog box to expand the dialog box as shown in Figure 14.26. In most cases, Excel takes the calculated result (using one of the preceding summary functions) and then modifies that result. I've listed the calculation types in Table 14.2.

FIGURE 14.26.

The expanded version of the data field PivotTable Field dialog box enables you select a custom calculation type.

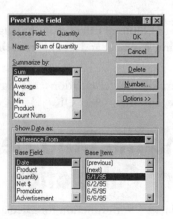

Table 14.2. Excel's pivot table calculation types.

Function	What It Displays the Data As
Difference From	The difference between the calculated result and the field and item you specify in the Base **F**ield and Base **I**tem lists.
% Of	The percentage that the calculated result is of the field and item you specify in the Base **F**ield and Base **I**tem lists.
% Difference From	The difference between the calculated result and the field and item you specify in the Base **F**ield and Base **I**tem lists, expressed as a percentage.
Running Total in	A running total for the field you specify in the Base **F**ield list.
% of row	The percentage that the calculated result is of the row's grand total.
% of column	The percentage that the calculated result is of the column's grand total.
% of total	The percentage that the calculated result is of the table's grand total.
Index	A function of the calculated result's row grand total and column grand total, and the pivot table's grand total (useful for ranking results). The formula used is (Result × Grand Total)/(Row Grand Total × Column Grand Total).

Figure 14.27 shows the Orders pivot table using the % of total calculation.

FIGURE 14.27.

The Orders pivot table using the % of total calculation.

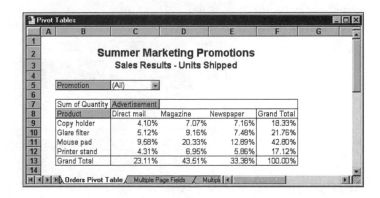

> **TIP**
>
> If you want to view the source values that a data field cell comprises, double-click on the cell. Excel extracts the values from the source data and displays them in a separate worksheet.

Formatting a Pivot Table

For our final pivot-table chore, we'll look at the various ways you can format the table to make it look its best for reports or presentations. The next three sections cover AutoFormatting the table, changing the name of a field, and changing the numeric format for the data field.

Using AutoFormat to Format a Pivot Table

As you might have found out the hard way, if you apply your own formatting to a table, Excel discards the formatting when you re-create or reorganize the table. To avoid having to reformat the table with each change, use the AutoFormat feature to format your pivot tables. Excel maintains the AutoFormat no matter how you alter the table.

To try this out, select a cell in the table, choose the Format | **A**utoFormat command, and then select a format from the **T**able Format list in the AutoFormat dialog box. Figure 14.28 shows the Orders pivot table formatted with the Colorful 2 AutoFormat.

FIGURE 14.28.

The Orders pivot table formatted with the Colorful 2 AutoFormat.

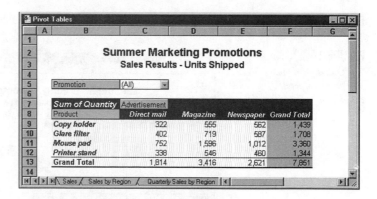

Changing the Data Field's Numeric Format

Numeric formatting applied to the data field with the Format | Cells command is also lost each time you reorganize your pivot tables. To maintain a permanent numeric format in the data field (or to change the existing numeric format), follow these steps:

1. Display the PivotTable Field dialog box for the data field.
2. Select the **N**umber button. Excel displays the Format Cells dialog box, shown in Figure 14.29.

FIGURE 14.29.

Use this version of the Format Cells dialog box to select a numeric format for your data field.

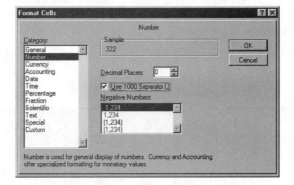

3. Select the numeric format you want to use. (See Chapter 4, "Formatting Excel Worksheets," for details.)
4. Select OK to return to the PivotTable Field dialog box.
5. Select OK to return to the worksheet.

Changing the Name of a Pivot-Table Field

Excel sometimes creates generic names for your pivot-table fields. For example, if your pivot table consolidates data from multiple ranges, Excel uses names such as Row, Column, and Page1 for the table fields. Similarly, if you group items based on their labels, Excel creates new fields with names like Product2 and Promotion3.

To change these generic names, or any row, column, or page field names, you can use either of the following techniques:

■ Select the cell containing the field label, and use the formula bar to edit the field name.

■ Display the PivotTable Field dialog box for the field, edit the field name that appears in the **N**ame text box, and then select OK.

Summary

This chapter showed you various techniques for customizing your pivot tables. You learned how to change the pivot-table view, add and delete fields, hide and group field items, work with subtotals and data field calculations, and format a pivot table. Here are some chapters that contain related information:

- For the basics of creating pivot tables, see Chapter 13, "Creating Pivot Tables."
- To get a complete explanation of querying external data sources, see Chapter 15, "Using Microsoft Query," and Chapter 16, "Creating Advanced Queries."
- Pivot tables are just one of Excel's many data-analysis features. To learn more about analysis with Excel, see the chapters in Part IV, "Unleashing Excel's Data Analysis Wizardry."

Using Microsoft Query

15

Chapter 12, "Working with Lists and Databases," showed you how to set up and work with data stored in a worksheet range. For the most part, the biggest problem with Excel lists is getting the data onto the worksheet in the first place. If the data doesn't exist in any other form, you have no choice but to enter it yourself. In many cases, though, the data you need already exists in a separate file elsewhere on your computer, or perhaps on a network server.

Excel provides several tools for accessing data files in non-Excel formats. Excel's **File | O**pen command can handle files in xBASE and Lotus 1-2-3 formats, and the TextImport Wizard can convert delimited or fixed-width text files into Excel (see Chapter 7, "Exchanging Data with Other Applications"). These methods, however, often fall short for three reasons:

- If you need only a small piece of a huge file, it's wasteful to import the entire file into Excel. Besides, databases with tens of thousands of records aren't all that uncommon, so a file import might choke on Excel's 16,384-row limit.

- Many databases contain related tables. For example, a database might include a table of customer data and a table of order data related by a common Customer ID field. If you need data from both tables, you're out of luck, because there's no way for Excel to honor the relationships between the two tables.

- The data you need might be in a file format not supported directly by Excel, such as SQL Server or Paradox.

To solve all of these problems, Excel comes with a separate program called Microsoft Query that you can use to access external database files from programs such as dBASE, Access, FoxPro, and SQL Server. This chapter shows you the basics of Microsoft Query and explains how to open external databases, extract the information you need, and return it to Excel. Chapter 16, "Creating Advanced Queries," shows you a few advanced tricks to help you get the most out of Microsoft Query.

About Microsoft Query

Microsoft Query is a small but powerful database application designed to provide you with easy access to various database formats. You can use Microsoft Query as a stand-alone program or via an Excel add-in.

A *query* is a request to a database for specific information. It combines criteria and extract conditions with functions to retrieve the data you want to work with. (As you'll soon see, the criteria you use to filter records in an external database table are similar to, but far more powerful than, those you used to filter Excel lists in Chapter 12.) Microsoft Query enables you to construct queries easily by using pull-down menu commands and drag-and-drop techniques. Query takes these actions and constructs SQL (Structured Query Language) statements that do the dirty work of retrieving and filtering the data. (If you're familiar with SQL, you can create these statements directly, as described in Chapter 16. SQL expertise, however, is by no means a prerequisite for working with Query.)

You also can use Microsoft Query to edit and maintain your database files. You can add and delete records, modify field contents, sort records, join databases, and even create new database files. The beauty of Microsoft Query is that you can do all this with many different database formats and maintain a consistent interface.

After you've queried, edited, and set up the data to your liking, you can copy the result into an Excel worksheet with a single command. And if the external data changes, you can refresh the worksheet data simply by running the same query again. (Microsoft Query enables you to save special query files, so you don't have to re-create your queries from scratch.)

Understanding ODBC

The data you can work with in Microsoft Query depends on the *Open Database Connectivity (ODBC) drivers* you installed with Excel. These drivers serve as intermediaries between Query and the external database. They take care of the messy problems of dealing with different database file structures and communicating between incompatible systems.

Each ODBC driver is a DLL (dynamic link library; a set of subroutines) that tells an ODBC-enabled application (such as Microsoft Query) how to interact (via SQL) with a specific data source. The go-between for the application and the driver is the ODBC Driver Manager, which keeps track of the location of the database, the database filename, and a few other options.

> **NOTE**
>
> Although you'll normally use Microsoft Query to work with external databases via ODBC, Excel itself is ODBC-enabled. This means you can access external databases directly from Excel using the VBA functions that come with the ODBC add-in. I'll show you how this is done in Chapter 26, "Database and Client/Server Programming."

Figure 15.1 shows how Excel, Microsoft Query, the ODBC Driver Manager, the ODBC device driver, and the database fit together.

Here are the basic steps you'll follow each time you need to access an external database:

1. Use the Microsoft Query add-in to start Query from Excel.
2. Use the ODBC Driver Manager to specify the database to use.
3. Use Microsoft Query to load tables, filter the data, and format the layout of the data (which is all done via the appropriate ODBC driver).
4. Return the query results to Excel.

Excel provides ODBC drivers for the sources listed in Table 15.1.

FIGURE 15.1.

The relationship between Excel, Query, the ODBC components, and the database.

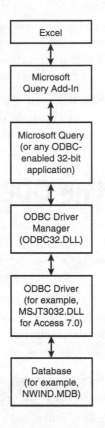

Table 15.1. Excel's ODBC device drivers.

Database	Versions	Driver DLL
Access	1.0, 1.5, 2.0	MSRD2X32.DLL
Access	7.0	MSJT3032.DLL
dBASE	III, IV, 5.0	MSXB3032.DLL
Excel (.XLS files)	3.0, 4.0, 5.0, 7.0	MSXL3032.DLL
FoxPro	2.0, 2.5, 2.6	MSXB3032.DLL
Paradox	3.x, 4.x, 5.x	MSPX3032.DLL
SQL Server	1.1, 4.2, NT, Sybase 4.2	SQLSRV32.DLL
Text		MSTX3032.DLL

Extra drivers for Btrieve (version 5.1), ODBC ODS Gateway, and other databases are available from Microsoft or from third-party vendors.

Some Notes About Databases and Tables

Although the terms "database" and "table" are often used interchangeably, they have distinct meanings in Microsoft Query (and, indeed, in relational database theory as a whole). To wit, a *table* is a collection of data organized into records and fields. It's directly analogous to an Excel list, in which a row is the equivalent of a record and a column is the equivalent of a field. A *database* is a collection of tables (and, like Access databases, can include other objects as well, such as forms and reports).

You'll often find that two or more of a database's tables are "joined" by a *relational key* field. For example, suppose that you have a table that contains data for your customers. This data includes the customer ID, the customer name, the customer address, and more. The same database might also have a table of orders placed by these customers. This table probably includes fields for the amount ordered and the date the order was placed, but it also needs to record which customer placed the order. You could enter the customer's name, address, phone number, and so on, but that would be wasteful because all that data already resides in the Customers table. A better approach is to include the CustomerID field and then relate the two tables using that field. For example, if an order is placed by a customer with ID 12-3456, you can find out, say, that customer's address simply by looking up 12-3456 in the Customers table. Figure 15.2 shows a graphical representation of this relationship (this figure was taken from a Microsoft Query screen).

FIGURE 15.2.

Two tables related via a common CustomerID field.

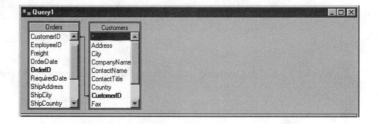

The last thing you need to know before we begin is that many tables include a field that contains only unique values. This so-called *primary key* field ensures that no two table records are alike and that there is an unambiguous way to reference each record in the table. For our Customers table, as long as we assign a unique ID number to each customer, we can use the CustomerID field as the primary key. Similarly, we can create an OrderID field in the Orders table, assign unique numbers to the field (such as invoice numbers), and use that as the primary key. As you'll see, Query displays primary key fields in bold (as shown in Figure 15.2).

Loading the Microsoft Query Add-In

As mentioned earlier, you can run Query either as a standalone program or via Excel's MS Query add-in. Our concern in this chapter is using Query as an adjunct to Excel, so I'll concentrate solely on working with Query via the MS Query add-in program. Assuming that Query is installed on your system, the following steps outline the procedure for loading the MS Query add-in.

> **NOTE**
>
> If you didn't install Query when you set up Excel, you can load it onto your system by running the Excel (or Microsoft Office) setup program and selecting the **Add/Remove** button. You need to add Microsoft Query, Excel's MS Query add-in, and the necessary ODBC drivers for the data you'll want to work with.

1. Select the **Tools | Add-Ins** command. Excel displays the Add-Ins dialog box, shown in Figure 15.3.

FIGURE 15.3.

Use the Add-Ins dialog box to select the add-ins you want to load.

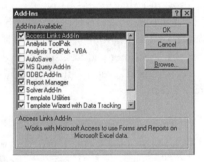

2. In the **Add**-Ins Available list, activate the check box beside the MS Query Add-In item.
3. Select OK to return to the worksheet.

When you load the MS Query add-in, Excel modifies the **D**ata menu by adding the Get External Data command. As you'll see in the next section, this command starts Microsoft Query so that you can work with an external database.

Starting Microsoft Query

To retrieve data from an external database file, you switch to Microsoft Query and specify the information you need. To display the Microsoft Query window, follow the steps given next.

NOTE

To run Microsoft Query as a standalone program, use Explorer or My Computer to display the \Program Files\Common Files\MSQuery folder, and double-click on the Msqry32 file.

1. Select the **D**ata | Get E**x**ternal Data command or click the Get External Data button in the Query and Pivot toolbar. Query loads and then displays the Select Data Source dialog box, shown in Figure 15.4. If you're starting Query for the first time, this dialog box is blank. Skip to the next section for instructions.

FIGURE 15.4.

Use the Select Data Source dialog box to choose the data source you want to work with.

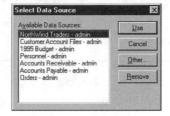

2. Highlight a data source in the A**v**ailable Data Sources list.
3. Select **U**se to open the source. Query displays the Add Tables dialog box, shown in Figure 15.5.

FIGURE 15.5.

Use the Add Tables dialog box to select the tables you want to include in your query.

4. For each database file you want to work with, highlight it in the **T**able list, and select the **A**dd button.
5. When you've finished adding tables, select **C**lose.

> **CAUTION**
>
> After you start Microsoft Query, Excel goes into a state of "suspended animation." This means you won't be able to work with Excel until you exit Query. If for some reason you lose your link with Query (Excel uses a DDE link to communicate with Query, and DDE is notoriously flaky), you might end up with both programs locked up. If this happens, try pressing Esc or Ctrl-Break to interrupt the macro that Excel uses to communicate with Query.

Working with Data Sources

A *data source* is a pointer that defines the data you want to work with. This includes the ODBC driver and the location of the file (or files). Data source locations generally fall into two categories:

- A single database file that includes multiple tables. For example, an Access database file would be a data source.
- A directory (or folder) of database files, each of which contains only a single table. For example, a directory of FoxPro or dBASE (versions III and IV) files would be a data source.

Defining a Data Source

Before you can work with Microsoft Query, you need to define at least one data source. As you saw in step 4 in the preceding section, you then use this data source to select which tables to include in the query. You'll usually define your data sources from within Query, but you also can use the Control Panel's 32bit ODBC utility. The next two sections explain both methods.

Defining a Data Source Using Query

This procedure outlines the steps you need to follow to define a data source:

1. If you're in the Select Data Source dialog box, select the **O**ther button. If you're in the Microsoft Query window, select the **F**ile | **N**ew Query command (or click the New Query button on the toolbar), and then select **O**ther. Query displays the ODBC Data Sources dialog box.

    The New Query button on the Query toolbar.

2. Select **N**ew. Query displays the Add Data Source dialog box, shown in Figure 15.6.

FIGURE 15.6.

Use the Add Data Source dialog box to select a driver for the database you want to work with.

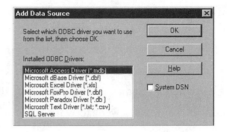

3. In the Installed ODBC **D**rivers list, highlight the driver for the database you want to work with, and then select OK. Query displays a Setup dialog box for the driver. The layout of the dialog box varies from driver to driver. Figure 15.7 shows the Setup dialog box for an Access source.

FIGURE 15.7.

The Setup dialog box for an ODBC Access data source.

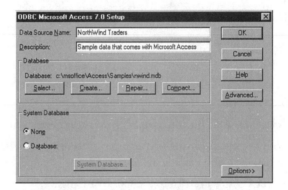

4. In the Data Source **N**ame text box, enter an identifier for the source. This is the name that will appear in the Select Data Source dialog box when you start Query.

5. Use the **D**escription text box to enter a description for the source.

6. Select the data source, using the appropriate method:

   - If you're defining an Access data source, choose the **S**elect button, highlight the database name in the Select Database dialog box that appears, and then select OK.

   - If you're defining a dBASE, FoxPro, or Paradox data source, use the **V**ersion drop-down list to select the version number of the program that created the files, and then choose **S**elect Directory to specify the directory (folder) where the files reside.

   - If you're defining an Excel data source, use the **V**ersion drop-down list to select the version number of Excel that created the files, and then choose **S**elect Workbook to specify the workbook file that contains the list or lists.

   - If you're defining a text data source, choose **S**elect Directory to specify the directory (folder) where the files can be found.

- If you're defining a SQL Server data source, use the **Server** combo box to enter the name of a SQL Server on your network.

7. Fill in the other dialog box options, as necessary.

8. Select OK to return to the ODBC Data Sources dialog box.

9. Select OK to return to the Select Data Source dialog box.

10. Highlight the source you want to work with, and then select **Use**. The Add Tables dialog box appears.

11. For each database file you want to work with, highlight it in the **Table** list and select the **Add** button. When you're done, select **Close**. Query displays a new query file.

Defining a Data Source Using the Control Panel

When you install Query, the setup program adds a new utility to the Control Panel: 32bit ODBC. You can use this utility as an alternative method for defining and working with data sources. The following steps show you how it works:

1. Select the Windows 95 Start button, select **Settings**, and then select **Control Panel**.

2. In the Control Panel window, select the 32bit ODBC icon. The Data Sources dialog box appears.

3. Select the **Add** button to display the Add Data Source dialog box.

4. Follow steps 3 through 8 from the preceding section. When you're done, you're returned to the Data Sources dialog box.

5. Select **Close** to return to the Control Panel.

Modifying a Data Source

If a data source changes in any way—for example, by being moved to a different location, by the file being renamed, or by the files being updated to a new version—you need to modify the data source accordingly. The only way to modify a data source is to use the Control Panel's 32bit ODBC utility, as detailed here:

1. Open the Control Panel window and select the 32bit ODBC icon.

2. In the Data Sources dialog box, use the User **D**ata Sources (Driver) list to highlight the data source you want to modify.

3. Select the **Setup** button. The Setup dialog box for the data source's driver appears.

4. Make your changes and select OK.

5. Select **Close** to return to the Control Panel.

> **NOTE**
>
> You can't change the ODBC driver for a data source directly. Instead, you need to delete the existing data source (as explained in the next section) and then redefine it for the new ODBC driver.

Deleting a Data Source

There are many reasons why you might no longer need a particular data source:

- The database file or directory that a data source points to might get removed from the system or network.
- You've defined a new data source that uses a different ODBC driver.
- You have no further use for the data referenced by the data source.

Whatever the reason, you should delete unneeded data sources to keep the Available Data Sources list uncluttered and to prevent errors (for example, by trying to access a database that no longer exists). Deleting a data source requires two separate procedures: you first remove the data source from Query and then delete the data source in the 32bit ODBC utility. Here are the complete steps:

1. In Query, select the **File | Table** Definition command to display the Select Data Sources dialog box.
2. In the Available Data Sources list, highlight the data source you want to remove.
3. Select the **Remove** button.
4. Select Cancel to return to Query.
5. Open the Control Panel window and select the 32bit ODBC icon.
6. In the User **D**ata Sources (Driver) list, highlight the data source you want to delete.
7. Select the De**l**ete button. A dialog box appears asking whether you're sure you want to delete the data source.
8. Select **Yes**.
9. Select **C**lose to return to the Control Panel.

A Tour of the Microsoft Query Window

After you've added one or more tables, Microsoft Query creates a new query file and displays it in a window, as shown in Figure 15.8. To get you comfortable with the layout of this window, here's a rundown of the various features (not all of which might be currently visible on your screen):

FIGURE 15.8.

The Microsoft Query window.

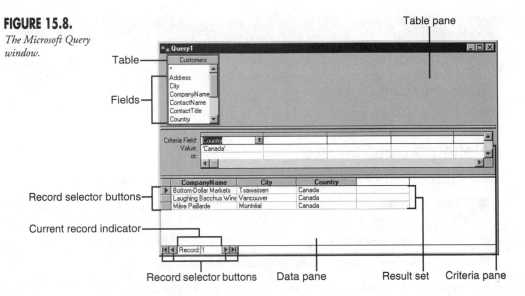

Table pane

Table — [Customers] Fields — [Address, City, CompanyName, ContactName, ContactTitle, Country]

Record selector buttons

Current record indicator

Record selector buttons   Data pane   Result set   Criteria pane

Table pane

The query file's window is divided into three panes. The top pane is the *table pane*. It displays one or more boxes that represent the tables you added to the query from the Add Tables dialog box. Each box displays the name of the table at the top, followed by a list of the database field names. You can toggle the table pane on and off by selecting the **View | Tables** command or by clicking the Show/Hide Tables toolbar button.

 The Show/Hide Tables button on the Query toolbar.

Criteria pane

This is the middle pane, and it's where you define the criteria for your query. Note that the criteria pane isn't displayed when you begin a new query. To toggle the criteria pane on and off, select the **View | Criteria** command or click the Show/Hide Criteria button on the toolbar.

 The Show/Hide Criteria button on the Query toolbar.

Data pane

The bottom pane displays the results of the query (called, appropriately enough, the *result set*). This area is empty initially, so you have to add fields from the databases included in the query. Skip to the section titled "Adding Fields to the Data Pane" for details.

Navigation buttons

You use these buttons to move from record to record in the result set. To learn how these buttons work, see "Navigating Records and Columns," later in this chapter.

To move from pane to pane, either use your mouse to click on the pane you want to work with, or press F6 to cycle through the panes. (You can also press Shift-F6 to cycle backward through the panes.) To change the size of a pane, use your mouse to drag the bar that separates each pane from its neighbor.

Adding Fields to the Data Pane

To get the information you want from an external database, you need to add one or more table fields to the query window's data pane. After you've added fields, you can move them around, edit them, change their headings, and more. This section shows you various methods for adding fields to the data pane. The next section takes you through the basics of working with table fields.

Excel seems to delight in providing umpteen methods for performing basic tasks, and Query is no different. For example, you can use three separate techniques to add fields to the data pane, as described next.

Adding a Field with the Add Column Command

The basic method for adding a field involves Query's Add Column command. (In Query parlance, a *column* is a field in the result set.) Here are the steps to follow:

1. Select the **R**ecords | Add **C**olumn command. Query displays the Add Column dialog box, shown in Figure 15.9.

FIGURE 15.9.

Use the Add Column dialog box to add a field to the data pane.

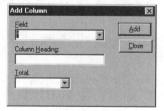

2. In the **F**ield list, select the table field you want to add. To add all the fields, select the asterisk (*).

NOTE

If you have more than one table in the query, the field names use the format *table.field*. Here, *table* is the name of the table, and *field* is the name of the field (for example, Customers.Address).

3. By default, Query uses the field name as the column heading. To specify a different heading, enter it in the Column **H**eading text box.

4. To display summary data (that is, the field's sum, average, count, minimum, or maximum) rather than the field values, select the appropriate option from the **T**otal drop-down list.

5. Select the **A**dd button. Query adds the field to the data pane.

6. Repeat steps 2 through 5 to add more fields.

7. When you're done, select **C**lose.

Adding a Field with the Mouse

You might find that your mouse provides the most convenient method for adding fields to the data pane. You can try two basic techniques:

■ Double-click on a field name. Query adds the fields to the next available column in the data pane.

■ Drag the field from the field list and drop it inside the data pane. Drop the name on an existing field to position the new field to the left of the existing field.

If you want to add multiple fields at once, hold down Ctrl and click on each field. (If the fields are contiguous, you can select them by clicking on the first field, holding down Shift, and then clicking on the last field.) Then drag the selection into the data pane.

If you want to place all the fields inside the data pane, you have two ways to proceed. If you want the fields to appear in the order in which they appear in the table, either double-click on the asterisk (*) field or drag the asterisk field and drop it inside the data pane. If you want the fields to appear in alphabetical order, double-click on the table name, and then drag any of the fields into the data pane.

Adding a Field from Within the Data Pane

You also can add a field directly from the data pane. Either click on the header of the data pane's empty column or press F6 until you're inside the data pane. In either case, Query adds a drop-down arrow to the column header. Then click on the drop-down arrow or press Alt-down arrow to display a list of the available fields, as shown in Figure 15.10. Select the field you want.

FIGURE 15.10.

The data pane's columns hold a list of the available fields.

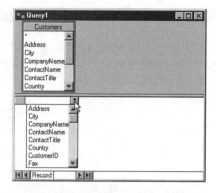

Working with the Data Pane

After you've added a field or two to the data pane, Query gives you plenty of ways to adjust the pane so that the data appears just the way you want it. The next few sections fill you in on the details.

Navigating Records and Columns

Getting around in the data pane is fairly simple. With your mouse, you can just click anywhere inside the record or column you want to move to. For data that doesn't appear inside the data pane, use the scroll bars to maneuver to the correct location. With your keyboard, use the keys outlined in Table 15.2.

Table 15.2. Data pane navigation keys.

Press This	To Move to This
Tab	The next column
Shift-Tab	The preceding column
End	The last column
Home	The first column
Down arrow	The next record
Up arrow	The preceding record
Ctrl-End	The last column of the last record
Ctrl-Home	The first column of the first record

Navigating with Go To

To head for a specific record number, select the **Records | Go To** command. Query displays the Go To dialog box, shown in Figure 15.11. Enter the record number you want in the **Go To Record** text box, and then select OK.

FIGURE 15.11.

Use the Go To dialog box to navigate to a specific record number.

Using the Navigation Buttons

Each query file also has a set of navigation buttons at the bottom of its window. Table 15.3 displays each button and explains how to use it.

Table 15.3. Query file window navigation buttons.

Button	Description
⏮	Takes you to the first record.
◀	Takes you to the preceding record.
Record: 1	Displays the current record number. To move to a different record, click on the number, enter the new record number, and press Enter.
▶	Takes you to the next record.
⏭	Takes you to the last record.

Selecting Records and Columns

Many Query operations require you to select an entire record or column. For example, if you want to delete a record or edit a column, you have to select the record or column beforehand. Here are the techniques you can use:

■ To select a column, either click on the column heading or move to any cell in the column and press Ctrl-Spacebar.

■ To select a row, either click the row-selector button to the left of the row or press Shift-Spacebar.

NOTE

You also can select multiple records or columns, as long as they're contiguous. With your mouse, select the first record or column, hold down the Shift key, and then select the last record or column. With your keyboard, select the first record or column, hold down Shift, and then use the arrow keys to select adjacent records or columns.

Changing a Field

If you add a field by mistake, if you want to replace an existing field with a different one, or if you want to change the field's column heading, use either of these techniques to display the Edit Column dialog box (which is identical to the Add Column dialog box you saw earlier):

- Select the column you want to edit, and then select the **R**ecords | **E**dit Column command.
- Double-click on the column heading.

Make your changes and then select OK to return to the query.

Editing Field Data

The fields you add to the data pane are normally read-only. If you want to make changes to the data before retrieving it into Excel, activate the **R**ecords | **A**llow Editing command. This command removes the read-only status so that you can make changes. You edit a field in a specific record the same as you do a worksheet cell: by pressing F2 or by double-clicking on the field. I'll discuss result-set editing—including adding new records, copying records, and deleting records—in the next chapter.

NOTE

Query doesn't write your changes to the source data until you move to a different record. If you make a mistake when editing data, select the **E**dit | **U**ndo Current Record command *before* moving to another record.

Moving a Column

If you're not happy with the order in which the columns appear in the data pane, it's easy to change that order. All you do is select the column (or columns) you want to move and then drag the column header left or right, as appropriate. Query inserts the column to the left of whichever column you drop it on.

Sorting the Data

Microsoft Query displays the records in the table's natural order (that is, the order in which the records were entered into the table). To change the sort order, follow the steps in this procedure:

1. Move to the column you want to use for the sort (this method saves you a step later).

2. Select the **R**ecords | **S**ort command. Query displays the Sort dialog box, shown in Figure 15.12.

FIGURE 15.12.

Use the Sort dialog box to sort the query.

3. Use the **C**olumn list to select a field to use for the sort (if you didn't already select the field in step 1).

4. Activate either **A**scending or **D**escending.

5. Select the **A**dd button. Query adds the sort to the Sorts in **Q**uery list and sorts the data.

6. Repeat steps 2 through 4 to refine the sort order with other fields. If you want to remove a sort from the query, highlight it in the Sorts in **Q**uery list, and select the **R**emove button.

7. Select **C**lose to return to the query.

Sorting with the Toolbar Buttons

For quicker sorts, try the Query toolbar's two sorting buttons: Sort Ascending and Sort Descending.

    The Sort Ascending button.

    The Sort Descending button.

Query gives you three ways to use these buttons for sorting:

■ For a single-column sort, select any cell in the column you want to use as the basis of the sort, and then click the appropriate sorting button.

- To refine the sort using another column, select any cell in the column, hold down Ctrl, and then click a sorting button.

- To sort on multiple columns at the same time, arrange the columns in the sort priority you want, with the most important columns to the left. (For example, suppose that you want to sort by country and then by city within each country. In this case, put the Country field to the left of the City field.) Select each column and then click a sorting button.

TIP

Query has a *grouping* feature that sorts your result set automatically. To try it, select the **View** | Query **P**roperties command, activate the **G**roup Records check box in the Query Properties dialog box that appears, and then select OK. With grouping turned on, Query sorts the result set automatically, starting with the far-left column and working to the right. There is one caveat, however: you can't edit the result set while grouping is turned on.

Removing a Column

The table pane has only enough room to show a few fields at once. To make the table pane easier to navigate, you should remove any fields you don't need. To remove a field, select it and then either select the **R**ecords | **R**emove Column command or press Delete.

Hiding and Showing Columns

Instead of removing a column entirely from the data pane, you might prefer to hide it temporarily. This is also handy if one of the data-pane columns contains sensitive information, such as payroll data.

To hide a column, select any cell in the column (if you want to hide multiple columns, select each column), and then select the Forma**t** | **H**ide Columns command.

To display hidden columns, select the Forma**t** | **S**how Columns command to display the Show Columns dialog box, shown in Figure 15.13. For each column you want to show, highlight it in the Co**l**umns list, and then select the **S**how button. When you're done, select **C**lose.

FIGURE 15.13.

Use the Show Columns dialog box to display one or more of your hidden columns.

Formatting the Data Pane

Query gives you several methods for formatting the data pane. You can change the font, adjust the width of the columns, and adjust the height of the record rows. I won't go into detail about each of these operations because they're virtually identical to the methods you would use in Excel. Here's a summary of what you can do:

- To change the font, select the Format | Font command, make your selections in the Font dialog box, and then select OK.

- To change the column width, select the Format | Column Width command, enter the new width in the Column Width dialog box, and then select OK. (You also can choose **S**tandard Width to revert the columns to their default widths, or **B**est Fit to make the columns as wide as the widest entry.)

- To change the row height, select the Format | **R**ow Height command, enter the new height in the Row Height dialog box, and then select OK. (You also can choose **S**tandard Height to revert the rows to their default heights.)

> **TIP**
>
> As in Excel, you also can use your mouse to adjust column widths and row heights. To change a column's width, move the mouse pointer to the right edge of the column header, and drag the pointer to the left or right. To change a row's height, move the mouse pointer to the bottom of the row's selector button, and then drag the pointer up or down.

As mentioned earlier, a query is actually a separate file in Microsoft Query format. This section looks at a few techniques related to the query and the query file.

Controlling Query Calculation

When you add fields or criteria (as discussed in the next section), Microsoft Query normally calculates the query results automatically. If you're working with large tables or complicated criteria, it might take some time for Query to display the result set. To prevent Microsoft Query from updating the results every time you make a change, you can turn off the Automatic Query feature by using either of the following methods:

- Pull down the **R**ecords menu and deactivate the Automatic **Q**uery command.

- Click the Auto Query button on the Query toolbar to return the button to its normal (that is, unpressed) state.

    The Auto Query button.

With Automatic Query turned off, you must tell Query when you want to update the result set. Again, you can choose from two methods:

- Select the **Records** | Query **N**ow command.
- Click the Query Now button on the Query toolbar.

 The Query Now button.

Filtering Records with Criteria

Chapter 12 showed you how to filter records in an Excel list by setting up criteria. You also can filter the records in an external database; the process is similar to the one you learned for lists. This section leads you through the basics of filtering records with criteria. (We'll explore more advanced criteria in the next chapter.)

Creating Simple Criteria

Excel's AutoFilter enables you to set up simple criteria such as showing only records in which the State field is CA or in which the Account Number field is 12-3456 (see Chapter 12). Query enables you to create similar filters, and the process is almost as easy, as you'll see in these steps:

1. Move to the column that contains the field you want to use to filter the records.
2. Select the value in the field you want to use as a criterion.
3. Click the Criteria Equals button on the Query toolbar. Query filters the data based on the selected field value.

 The Criteria Equals button.

4. Repeat steps 1 through 3 to filter the records even further.

Entering Simple Criteria in the Criteria Pane

As you learned in Chapter 12, you can set up a criteria range in a worksheet to use when filtering your records. The equivalent in Microsoft Query is the *criteria pane*. You can add field names to this pane and then set up criteria that range from simple field values to complex expressions for compound and computed criteria.

If you use the technique described in the preceding section for entering simple criteria, you'll see that Query displays the criteria pane automatically and adds the field names and values to the criteria pane.

You also can enter simple criteria directly in the criteria pane (this is handy, for instance, if you don't have a mouse and can't use the Criteria Equals tool). The following procedure shows the necessary steps:

1. Display the criteria pane, if necessary, and move the cursor into the first header of the Criteria Field row.

2. Use the drop-down list to select a field to use for the criterion. (Alternatively, you can drag a field from the table pane and drop it on the criteria pane.)

3. Select the cell below the field name (that is, on the Value row) and enter the field value you want to use for the criterion. Enclose text in single quotation marks (for example, 'CA') and dates in number signs (for example, #1995-01-15#). For more information, see the next section.

4. To run the query, move the cursor to a different cell, select a different pane, or press Enter. (This is assuming, of course, that the Automatic Query feature is activated. If it's not, you need to run the query by hand, as described earlier.)

Figure 15.14 shows a sample query that filters the Customers table to show only those records in which the Country field contains Canada.

FIGURE 15.14.

A query that uses a criterion to filter data from the Customers table.

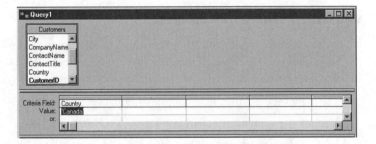

Entering Criteria Expressions in Microsoft Query

Entering criteria expressions in Microsoft Query is similar to entering them in Excel (see Chapter 12 for details). You should, however, be aware of the following differences:

■ Enclose text in single quotation marks (for example, 'CA') rather than double quotation marks. In most cases, Query adds the single quotation marks for you.

■ Enclose dates in number signs (for example, #1994-01-15#). Again, Query usually recognizes a date and adds the number signs for you.

■ If you're working with numbers, you can use the normal comparison operators such as equal to (=), not equal to (<>), greater than (>), and less than (<). For example, suppose that you have an Invoices table with an Amount field. To filter the table to show only those invoices on which the amount is greater than or equal to $1,000, you add the Amount field to the criteria pane and enter the following criterion: >=1000.

■ To use wildcard characters, you must include the keyword Like and then use an underscore to substitute for a single character, or a percent sign to substitute for a group of characters. For example, to find all records in which the NAME field includes the word Office, you type Like '%Office%' in the criteria pane's NAME field.

- Depending on the ODBC driver you're using, your text criteria might or might not be case-sensitive in Microsoft Query. (For example, the Access driver isn't case-sensitive, but the FoxPro driver is.) You therefore should either test the driver with some sample data or just assume that the driver is case-sensitive. For the latter case, you'll need to use the same uppercase and lowercase formats found in the table. For example, suppose that you're setting criteria for a table with a REGION field that contains only two-letter state abbreviations in uppercase. To ensure that you match these field entries properly, enter your REGION criteria in uppercase.

Creating Complex Criteria

As you learned in Chapter 12, *complex criteria* come in two flavors: *compound criteria*, which combine two or more criteria expressions, and *computed criteria,* which use formulas to filter data. I'll show you how to enter compound criteria in this section, and I'll leave computed criteria to the next chapter.

You enter compound criteria in the criteria pane the same way you do in a criteria range on an Excel worksheet:

- You can add either multiple fields or multiple instances of a single field to the criteria pane.

- If you enter criteria expressions in multiple columns in the same row, Query selects the records that match *all* the criteria.

- If you enter criteria expressions on different rows either in multiple columns or in a single column, Query selects the records that match *at least one* of the rows.

For example, Figure 15.15 shows a result set from the compound criteria shown in the criteria pane. This query selects records in which the Country field is Brazil *and* the City field starts with Rio (the first Value row in the criteria pane), *or* the Country field is Spain (the second row).

FIGURE 15.15.

The result set from a compound criterion.

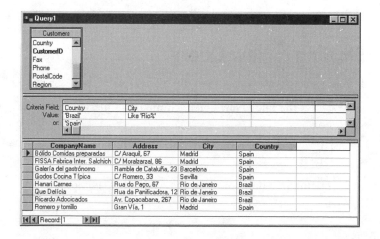

Editing Criteria

If your criteria need some adjustments, Query gives you a couple of ways to edit each criterion:

- If you want to change a field in the criteria pane, move to the field's header and use the drop-down list to select a different field.
- To edit a criterion, move to the cell containing the criterion, and then either double-click on the cell or press F2. An insertion-point cursor appears inside the cell so that you can add or edit text.

Removing Criteria

To remove a criterion from the query, use any of the following techniques:

- In the criteria pane, select the column containing the criterion you want to delete, and then press the Delete key.
- To leave the criteria-pane column in place, move to the cell containing the criterion and press Delete.
- To delete all the criteria, select the **Criteria | Remove** All Criteria command.

Saving the Query

If you think you'll be using the query again in the future, you can save it by following these steps:

1. Select the **File | Save** Query command. If you're saving the query for the first time, the Save As dialog box appears.

    You also can click the Save Query button to save a query.

2. Enter a name and location for the query.
3. Select OK.

Starting a New Query

If you want to start with a fresh query file, follow these steps:

1. Select the **File | New** Query command. Query displays the Select Data Source dialog box.

    You also can click the New Query button to start a new query.

2. Highlight a data source in the Available Data Sources list.

3. Select **U**se to open the source. Query displays the Add Tables dialog box.

4. For each table you want to work with, highlight the table in the Table **N**ame list and select the **A**dd button.

5. Select **C**lose to display the new query.

Returning the Query Results to Excel

When you have the result set you want, you can import the data into Excel by following this procedure:

1. Select the **F**ile | **R**eturn Data to Microsoft Excel command. Query switches to Excel and displays the Get External Data dialog box, shown in Figure 15.16.

 You also can click the Return Data to Excel button to return the query results.

FIGURE 15.16.

Use the Get External Data dialog box to set a few options for the external data you're returning.

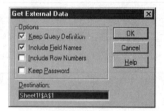

2. Select the options you want to use for the returned data:

■ **K**eep Query Definition: Activate this check box to keep a copy of the query definition in the worksheet. This way, you can refresh the data at any time.

■ Include **F**ield Names: Activate this check box to add the result set's field names as column headers in the returned data.

■ **I**nclude Row Numbers: Activate this check box to include the result set's record numbers as the first column in the returned data.

■ Keep **P**assword: If the data source requires a password, activate this check box to save the password with the data. This way, you can access the same data source (say, to refresh the data) without having to reenter the password.

3. Use the **D**estination box to select the top-left corner of the range you want to use for the data.

4. Select OK. Excel pastes the result set into the worksheet.

Working with the Result Set

After you've retrieved the result set, you can work with the data as you would any Excel list. You also can refresh the data and edit the query, as explained in the next two sections.

Refreshing the Result Set

If the data in the external database changes (or if you want to see whether it has changed), you can update the result set in your worksheet to reflect those changes. To refresh the data, select a cell in the result set, and then select the **D**ata | **R**efresh Data command (or click the Refresh Data button on the Query and Pivot toolbar). Excel runs the query again and then retrieves the new results.

 The Refresh Data button on the Query and Pivot toolbar.

> **NOTE**
>
> Excel refreshes the query results automatically only if you saved the query definition when you retrieved the result set.

> **CAUTION**
>
> When Excel retrieves the updated result set, it overwrites your existing data. Any sorting or rearranging of the data you've done will be lost.

Displaying Only Unique Field Values

Depending on the data you're working with, your result set might contain one or more fields with duplicate values. If this isn't what you want (for instance, if all you need to see is a list of the states where you have customers), you can tell Query to display only unique values.

You do this by selecting the **V**iew | Query **P**roperties command, activating the **U**nique Values Only check box in the Query Properties dialog box that appears, and then selecting OK.

Editing the Query

To make changes to the query, follow the steps in this procedure:

1. Select a cell in the result set.
2. Select the **D**ata | Get **E**xternal Data command. The Get External Data dialog box appears.
3. Select the **E**dit Query button. Excel switches to Microsoft Query and loads the query file.

NOTE

Excel loads the query file automatically only if you saved the query definition when you originally retrieved the result set.

4. Make your changes to the query.

5. Select the **F**ile | **R**eturn Data to Microsoft Excel command. Query switches to Excel and displays the Get External Data dialog box.

6. Select OK. Excel pastes the result set into the worksheet.

Summary

This chapter introduced you to Microsoft Query, the tool that enables Excel users to access external data. I gave you an overview of Query and the ODBC drivers that are the nuts and bolts of the whole process. You then learned how to start Query, set up a data source, add tables, create a result set using fields and criteria, and then return the results to Excel. If you're looking for some related information, here are a few chapters to check out:

■ For certain types of data (especially Access databases), you might be better off using some of Excel's other features for exchanging data with applications. Chapter 7, "Exchanging Data with Other Applications," outlines each of these features in detail.

■ After you get your external data into Excel, it's treated just like any other Excel list. To learn all about creating, editing, and filtering Excel lists, see Chapter 12, "Working with Lists and Databases."

■ You can create pivot tables directly from external data sources. The full instructions for doing so can be found in Chapter 13, "Creating Pivot Tables."

■ We really only scratched the surface of Query's criteria features. In Chapter 16, "Creating Advanced Queries," we'll look at the complete list of Query's criteria operators, computed criteria, using multiple tables, SQL, and more.

■ To learn how to control and work with external data in your VBA programs, head for Chapter 26, "Database and Client/Server Programming."

Creating Advanced Queries

16

Chapter 15, "Using Microsoft Query," gave you a basic introduction to Query and showed you how to set up simple and compound criteria using the criteria pane. If all you need is to import some raw data—possibly filtered by a criterion or two—into a worksheet, the techniques you learned in Chapter 15 are sufficient. If, however, you're after more sophisticated game—such as criteria that perform calculations and queries that use related tables—you'll need to learn about Query's more advanced features. This chapter will help you do just that. We'll investigate various advanced Query topics, such as calculated criteria, multiple-table queries, and SQL.

A Closer Look at Query Criteria

In the preceding chapter I showed you some basic features of Query criteria, including how to enter text, dates, and numbers, and how to use the criteria pane to construct compound criteria. In this section we'll examine criteria in more depth so that you'll be able to harness the full power of Query's filtering features.

Building Criteria Expressions

The queries you saw in Chapter 15 were simple filters that used literal values to select matching table records. To create more advanced queries, however, you have to go beyond literals and construct full-fledged *expressions* that combine operators, functions, and field names with literal values. Query uses the result of the expression to filter the table.

Most criteria expressions are logical formulas that, when applied to each record in the table, return either TRUE or FALSE. The result set contains only those records for which the expression returned TRUE. In fact, we can see that even criteria that use simple literal values are also expressions (albeit not very sophisticated ones). For example, suppose that you have a CustomerName field in the criteria pane and you enter Barney's Beanery as the criterion. This entry is equivalent to the following logical formula:

```
CustomerName = 'Barney's Beanery'
```

Query constructs the result set by applying this formula to each record in the table and selecting only those records for which it returns TRUE (that is, those records in which the CustomerName field contains Barney's Beanery).

Criteria Identifiers

In Query, an *identifier* is a field name from the query's underlying table. For example, suppose that you have an Order Details table that includes a ProductID field and a Quantity field. If you want to see all the records in which the quantity ordered equals the product ID, you add the Quantity field to the criteria pane and enter ProductID as the criterion.

Using Operators in Criteria

Query has a few dozen operators you can include in your expressions. The five types of operators—comparison, logical, arithmetic, Like, and miscellaneous—are covered in the next few sections.

Comparison Operators

You use comparison operators to compare field values to a literal, a function result, or a value in another field. Table 16.1 lists Query's comparison operators.

Table 16.1. Comparison operators for criteria expressions.

Operator	General Form	Matches Records in Which the Field Value Is...
=	= Value	Equal to Value
<>	<> Value	Not equal to Value
>	> Value	Greater than Value
>=	>= Value	Greater than or equal to Value
<	< Value	Less than Value
<=	<= Value	Less than or equal to Value

You'll mostly use operators on numeric or date fields, but you also can use them on text fields. For example, the expression `< 'D'` matches field values that begin with the letters A, B, or C.

Logical Operators

You use the logical operators to combine or modify true/false expressions. Table 16.2 summarizes Query's three logical operators.

Table 16.2. Logical operators for criteria expressions.

Operator	General Form	Matches Records in Which...
And	Expr1 And Expr2	Both Expr1 and Expr2 are TRUE
Or	Expr1 Or Expr2	At least one of Expr1 and Expr2 is TRUE
Not	Not Expr	Expr is not TRUE

The And and Or operators enable you to create compound criteria using a single expression. For example, suppose that you want to match all the records in your Customers table in which the CustomerName field contains both quicky and mart. As shown in Figure 16.1, the following expression does the job:

```
Like '%quicky%' And Like '%mart%'
```

FIGURE 16.1.

You can use And to build compound criteria in a single cell.

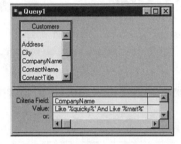

Similarly, suppose that you want to find all the customers from either New York state or California. You would add the Region field to the criteria pane and enter the following expression:

```
'NY' Or 'CA'
```

The Not operator looks for records that *don't* match a particular logical expression. For example, if you want to find all non-North American customers, you add the Country field to the criteria pane and enter the following expression:

```
Not 'USA' and Not 'Canada' And Not 'Mexico'
```

Arithmetic Operators

You use the arithmetic operators shown in Table 16.3 to perform various math operations on a field. For example, suppose that you have a sales history table with UnitSales1994 and UnitSales1995 fields. To find all the records in which the unit sales in 1995 were at least 10 percent higher than those in 1994, you would add the UnitSales1995 field to the criteria pane and enter the following expression:

```
>=UnitSales1994*1.1
```

Table 16.3. Arithmetic operators for criteria expressions.

Operator	General Form	Description
+	Value1 + Value2	Adds Value1 and Value2
−	Value1 − Value2	Subtracts Value2 from Value1
*	Value1 * Value2	Multiplies Value1 and Value2
/	Value1 / Value2	Divides Value1 by Value2

The *Like* Operator

As you learned in Chapter 15, you can use the Like operator in conjunction with Query's wildcard characters (_ for a single character and % for multiple characters) to perform inexact matching. As shown in Table 16.4, there are six possible variations on the Like operator theme that you can use in your criteria expression.

Table 16.4. The Like operator for criteria expressions.

Example	*Matches Records in Which the Field Value...*
Like 'string%'	Begins with string
Not Like 'string%'	Does not begin with string
Like '%string'	Ends with string
Not Like '%string'	Does not end with string
Like '%string%'	Contains string
Not Like '%string%'	Does not contain string

Miscellaneous Operators

To finish our look at criteria operators, Table 16.5 presents a few miscellaneous operators that you should find useful when constructing your expressions.

Table 16.5. Miscellaneous operators for criteria expressions.

Operator	*General Form*	*Selects the Records in Which the Field Value...*
In	In(Value1,Value2,...)	Equals Value1 or Value2 or ...
Between	Between Value1 And Value2	Is between Value1 and Value2
Is Null		Is empty
Is Not Null		Is not empty

The In operator is a useful replacement for multiple Or criteria. For example, suppose that you want to filter a table to show only those records in which the Region field equals NY, CA, TX, IN, or ME. You *could* do this by using several Or operators, like so:

```
'NY' Or 'CA' Or 'TX' Or 'IN' Or 'ME'
```

The following expression, however, is more efficient:

```
In('NY','CA','TX','IN','ME')
```

The Between operator matches records in which the field value falls between the two specified values. Note that Query will also match records in which the field value *equals* the two specified values. For example, the following expression matches records in which the Region field is between or equal to CA and NY:

```
Between 'CA' And 'NY'
```

Entering Complex Criteria in the Add Criteria Dialog Box

The examples so far have focused on entering criteria in the criteria pane, but you also can enter complex criteria using the Add Criteria dialog box shown in Figure 16.2. This dialog box contains the following features:

And/**O**r	Use these options to create compound criteria. (When you add your first criterion, these options are disabled.) Select **A**nd when you want the records to match all the criteria; select **O**r when you want the records to match at least one of the criteria.
Total	A list of summary functions (Sum, Avg, Count, Min, and Max). See "Using Calculations in Queries," later in this chapter, for instructions on how to use these summary functions.
Field	A list of the table fields.
Operator	A list of operators. Rather than comparison operators (=, >, <=, and so on), Query uses English-language equivalents of the SQL (Structured Query Language) operators (equals, is greater than, is less than or equal to, and so on).
Value	The field value to use in the criterion. You can enter your own values or use the Values button to select from a list of the unique values in the field.

FIGURE 16.2.

You also can use the Add Criteria dialog box to add complex criteria to the query.

Follow the steps in the next procedure to add criteria using the Add Criteria dialog box:

1. Select the **C**riteria | **A**dd Criteria command to display the Add Criteria dialog box.

2. Select the options you want to use in the criterion.

3. Select the **A**dd button. Query adds the criterion and updates the result set.

4. If you want to add another criterion, select **A**nd or **O**r, as appropriate.

5. Repeat steps 2 through 4 to define more criteria.

6. When you're done, select **C**lose to return to the query.

Using Calculations in Queries

Most queries just display the raw data for the fields included in the data pane, possibly filtered by some criteria. If you need to analyze the result set, however, you need to introduce calculations into your query. (I'm assuming here that you don't want or need to perform the calculations in Excel.) Query lets you set up three kinds of calculations:

A summary column: A column in the result set that uses one of several predefined functions for calculating a value (or values) based on the entries in a particular field. A summary column derives either a single value for the entire result set or several values for the grouped records in the result set.

A calculated column: A column in the result set in which the "field" is an expression. The field values are derived using an expression based on one or more fields in the table.

A calculated criteria column: A column in the criteria pane where the "field" is an expression.

Working with Summary Columns

The easiest way to analyze the data in a table is to use a summary column and one of Query's predefined "totals." There are five totals in all: Sum, Avg, Count, Max, and Min. The idea is that you add a single field to the data pane and then convert that column into a summary column using one of these totals. Table 16.6 outlines the available totals you can use for your summary columns.

Table 16.6. Types of totals available for summary columns.

Total	What It Calculates
Sum	The sum of the values in the field (numeric fields only)
Avg	The average of the values in the field (numeric fields only)
Count	The number of values in the field (all field types)
Min	The smallest value in the field (all field types except memo fields)
Max	The largest value in the field (all field types except memo fields)

Here are the steps required to create a summary column:

1. Clear all columns from the data pane except the column you want to use for the calculation, as shown in Figure 16.3.

FIGURE 16.3.

To create a summary column, empty the data pane except for the field you'll be using for the calculation.

2. Select a cell inside the column.
3. Select the **R**ecords | **E**dit Column command to display the Edit Column dialog box.
4. Use the **T**otal drop-down list to select the total you want to use. Query updates the Column **H**eading text box to reflect the total you selected. For example, if the field is named Quantity and the total you selected is Sum, the Column **H**eading text changes to Sum of Quantity, as shown in Figure 16.4.

FIGURE 16.4.

Use the Edit Column dialog box to select the type of total you want to calculate.

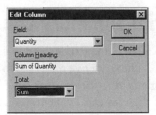

5. Select OK. Query performs the calculation and replaces the column with a summary column showing the result.

Figure 16.5 shows the result of the Sum calculation on the Quantity field.

NOTE

To remove the total and change the column back to its normal state, select the **R**ecords | **E**dit Column command, and select the blank item in the **T**otal drop-down list.

FIGURE 16.5.

Query replaces the original column with a summary column showing the result of the calculation.

Cycling Through the Totals

Query has a Cycle thru Totals button on the toolbar that makes it easy to see a variety of calculations on the same field. To try it out, follow these steps:

1. Clear all columns from the data pane except the column you want to use for the calculation.

2. Select a cell inside the column.

3. Click the Cycle thru Totals button. Query changes the column into a summary column showing the sum of the field values.

 The Cycle thru Totals button.

4. Continue clicking the Cycle thru Totals button to run through the totals in the following order: Sum, Avg, Count, Min, Max.

5. After displaying the Max total, click the Cycle thru Totals button again to return the column to its normal state.

Creating a Summary Column for Groups of Records

In its basic guise, a summary column shows a total for all the records in a table. Suppose, however, that you prefer to see that total broken out into subtotals. For example, rather than a simple sum on the Order Details table's Quantity field, how about seeing the sum of the orders grouped by supplier?

To group your totals, all you have to do is add the appropriate field to the data pane to the left of the column you're using for the calculation. For example, Figure 16.6 shows the data pane with the CompanyName field from the Suppliers table to the left of the Quantity field. (I'll show you how to work with multiple tables in a single query later in this chapter.) Converting the Quantity column into a Sum of Quantity summary column gives us the result set shown in Figure 16.7. As you can see, Query groups the entries in the CompanyName column and displays a subtotal for each group.

FIGURE 16.6.

To group your totals, add the field used for the grouping to the left of the field used for the calculation.

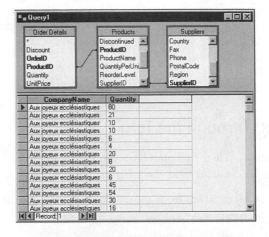

FIGURE 16.7.

Query uses the columns to the left of the summary column to set up its groupings.

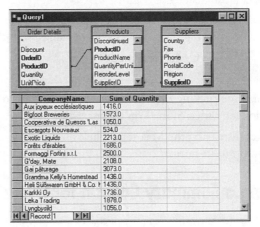

You can extend this technique to derive totals for more specific groups. For example, suppose that you want to see subtotals for each product made by the suppliers. All you must do is add the ProductName field to the data pane to the left of the Quantity column, but to the right of the CompanyName column, as shown in Figure 16.8. Query creates the groups from left to right, so the records are first grouped by CompanyName and then by ProductName.

FIGURE 16.8.

You can refine your groupings by adding more columns to the left of the summary column.

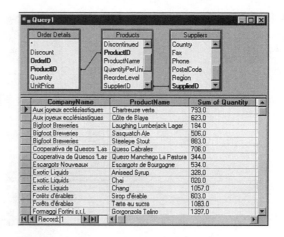

Setting Up a Calculated Column

The five types of totals available for summary columns are handy, but they might not be what you need. If you want to create columns that use more sophisticated expressions, you need to set up a calculated column.

A calculated column is a result-set column that gets its values from an expression rather than a field. The expression you use can be any combination of operator, identifier, and literal value, and there are even a few built-in functions you can use.

Building a calculated column is simple: instead of specifying a field name when adding a column to the result set, you enter an expression instead. (You type the expression either directly into the column header or in the **F**ield text box in the Add Column dialog box.) For example, the Order Details table contains both a Quantity field and a UnitPrice field. The *extended price* is just the quantity ordered multiplied by the price of the item. We can set up a calculated column to show the extended price by entering the following expression as the header of a new column in the data pane:

```
Quantity*UnitPrice
```

Figure 16.9 shows the results.

> **NOTE**
>
> If you want to use a field name that contains a space (such as Unit Price), you need to enclose the field name in quotation marks, like this:
>
> ```
> Quantity*"Unit Price"
> ```

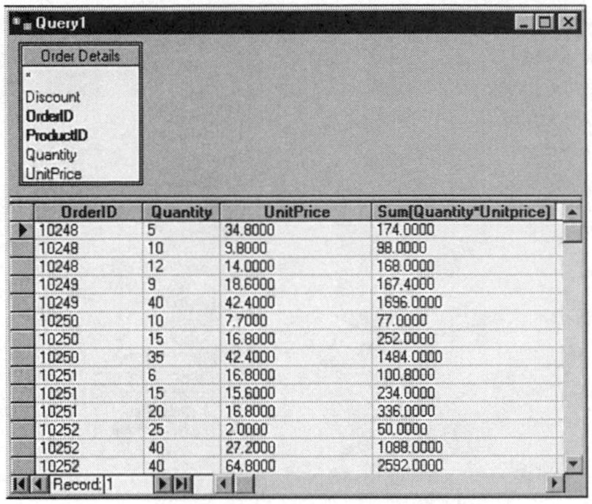

FIGURE 16.9.

A result set with a calculated column.

You also can use any of Query's five built-in summary functions in your calculated columns: Sum, Avg, Count, Max, and Min. Note that if you use one of these functions in your expression—even as part of a larger expression—Query turns the column into a summary column and groups the data accordingly.

For example, instead of seeing the extended price for each item, it might be more useful to see the total extended price for each order. To do that, we need to remove the Quantity and UnitPrice columns from the result set, leaving only the OrderID column to the left of the calculated column. We then enter the following expression in the calculated column:

```
Sum(Quantity*UnitPrice)
```

Again, if you want to use a field name that contains a space, enclose the name in quotation marks.

As you can see in Figure 16.10, Query has grouped the records on the OrderID field and displayed extended price subtotals for each group.

Generating Calculated Criteria

Calculated criteria are similar to calculated columns. The only difference is that the calculation appears in the criteria pane and is used to filter the underlying table. You use a criteria pane column heading to enter an expression for the calculation you want to use.

For example, suppose that you want to see all the items ordered for which the extended price is greater than $1,000. Here's the full expression you need to use:

```
Quantity*UnitPrice>1000
```

The calculation (`Quantity*UnitPrice`) is entered into the column head, and the criterion (`>1000`) is entered into the Value line below it, as shown in Figure 16.11.

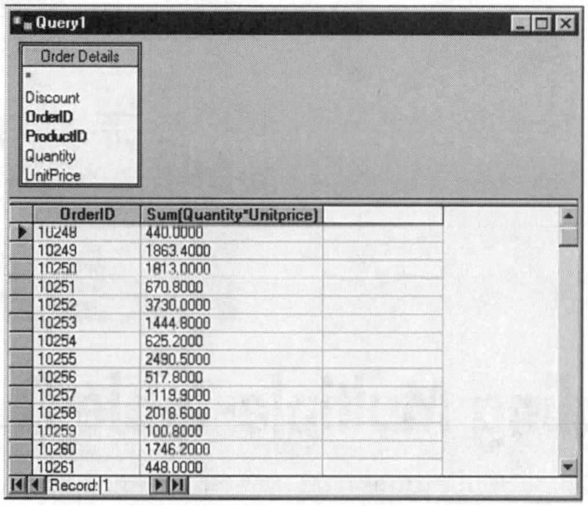

FIGURE 16.10.

If you use one of the summary functions in a calculated column, Query groups the records.

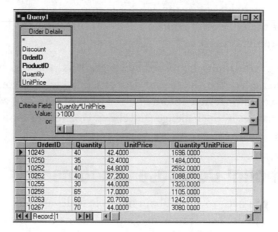

FIGURE 16.11.

A calculated criterion entered into the criteria pane.

As with calculated columns, you also can use any of the five summary functions in your calculated criteria. As before, if you use a summary function, Query groups the records based on the fields in the data pane, from left to right. Figure 16.12 shows a calculated criteria that uses the Sum function. Notice how Query grouped the result set on the OrderID column.

FIGURE 16.12.

Query groups the result set if you use a summary function as part of the calculated criteria.

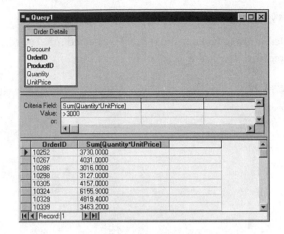

Juggling Multiple-Table Queries

Most database applications (and *all* well-designed database applications) store their information in multiple tables. And while most of these tables will have nothing to do with each other (such as, say, tables of customer information and employee payroll data), it's likely that at least some of the tables will contain related information (such as tables of customer information and customer orders).

Working with multiple, related tables presents you with two challenges: you need to design your queries so that the related data is accessible, and you need to set up links between the tables so that the related information can be retrieved and worked with quickly and easily. This section tackles both challenges and shows you how to exploit the full multiple-table powers of Query.

Relational Database Fundamentals

Why do you need to worry about multiple tables anyway? Isn't it easier to work with one large table than to use two or three medium-sized ones? To answer these questions and demonstrate the problems that arise when you ignore relational database models, take a look at a simple example: a table of sales leads.

The Pitfalls of a Nonrelational Design

Table 16.7 outlines a structure for a simple table (named Leads) that stores data on sales leads.

Table 16.7. A structure for a simple sales-leads table (Leads).

Field	Description
LeadID	The primary key
FirstName	The contact's first name
LastName	The contact's last name
Company	The company that the contact works for
Address	The company's address
City	The company's city
State	The company's state
ZIP	The company's ZIP code
Phone	The contact's phone number
Fax	The contact's fax number
Source	Where the lead came from
Notes	Notes or comments related to the sales lead

This structure works fine until you need to add two or more leads from the same company (a not uncommon occurrence). In this case, you'll end up with repeated information in the Company, Address, City, and State fields. (The ZIP field will also repeat, as will, in some cases, the Phone, Fax, and Source fields.)

All this repetition makes the table unnecessarily large, which is bad enough, but it also creates two major problems:

- The data-entry clerk must enter the repeated information for each lead from the same company.
- If any of the repeated information changes (such as the company's name or address), each corresponding record must be changed.

One way to eliminate the repetition and solve the data-entry and maintenance inefficiencies is to change the focus of the table. As it stands, each record in the table identifies a specific contact in a company. But the company information is what repeats, so it makes some sense to allow only one record per company. You could then include separate fields for each sales lead within the company. The new structure might look something like the one shown in Table 16.8.

Table 16.8. A revised, company-centered structure for the sales-leads table.

Field	Description
LeadID	The primary key
Company	The company name
Address	The company's address
City	The company's city
State	The company's state
ZIP	The company's ZIP code
Phone	The company's phone number
Fax	The company's fax number
First_1	The first name of contact #1
Last_1	The last name of contact #1
Source_1	Where the lead for contact #1 came from
Notes_1	Notes or comments related to contact #1
First_2	The first name of contact #2
Last_2	The last name of contact #2
Source_2	Where the lead for contact #2 came from
Notes_2	Notes or comments related to contact #2
First_3	The first name of contact #3
Last_3	The last name of contact #3
Source_3	Where the lead for contact #3 came from
Notes_3	Notes or comments related to contact #3

In this setup, the company information appears only once, and the contact-specific data (I'm assuming that this involves only the first name, last name, source, and notes) appears in separate field groups (for example, First_1, Last_1, Source_1, and Notes_1). This method solves the earlier problems, but at the cost of a new dilemma: the structure as it stands holds only three sales leads per company. It is, of course, entirely conceivable that a large firm might have more than three contacts and perhaps even dozens. This situation raises two unpleasant difficulties:

■ If you run out of the repeating groups of contact fields, new ones must be added. Although this might not be a problem for the database designer, most data-entry clerks generally don't have access to the table design (nor should they).

■ In dBASE files, empty fields take up as much disk real estate as full ones, so making room for, say, a dozen contacts from one company means that all the records with only one or two contacts have huge amounts of wasted space.

How a Relational Design Can Help

To solve the twin problems of repetition between records and repeated field groups within records, you need to turn to the relational database model. This model was developed by Dr. Edgar Codd of IBM in the early 1970s. It was based on a complex relational algebra theory, so the pure form of the rules and requirements for a true relational database setup is quite complicated and decidedly impractical for real-world applications. The next few sections look at a simplified version of the model.

Step 1: Separate the Data

After you know which fields you need to include in your database application, the first step in setting up a relational database is to divide these fields into separate tables in which the "theme" of each table is unique. In technical terms, each table must be composed only of entities (that is, records) from a single *entity class.*

For example, the table of sales leads you saw earlier dealt with data that had two entity classes: the contacts and the companies they worked for. Every one of the problems encountered with that table can be traced to the fact that we were trying to combine two entity classes into a single table. So the first step toward a relational solution is to create separate tables for each class of data. Table 16.9 shows the table structure for the contact data (the Contacts table), and Table 16.10 shows the structure for the company information (the Company table). Note, in particular, that both tables include a primary key field.

Table 16.9. The structure for the Contacts table.

Field	Description
ContactID	The primary key
FirstName	The contact's first name
LastName	The contact's last name
Phone	The contact's phone number
Fax	The contact's fax number
Source	Where the lead came from
Notes	Notes or comments related to the sales lead

Table 16.10. The structure for the Company table.

Field	Description
CompanyID	The primary key
CompanyName	The company name
Address	The company address
City	The company city
State	The company state
ZIP	The company ZIP code
Phone	The company phone number (main switchboard)

Step 2: Add Foreign Keys to the Tables

At first glance, separating the tables seems self-defeating because, if you've done the job properly, the two tables have nothing in common. So the second step in relational design is to define the commonality between the tables.

In the sales-leads example, what is the common ground between the Contacts and Company tables? It's that every one of the leads in the Contacts table works for a specific firm in the Company table. So what's needed is some way of relating the appropriate information in Company to each record in Contacts (without, of course, the inefficiency of simply cramming all the data into a single table, as we tried earlier).

The way you do this in relational database design is to establish a field that is common to both tables. You then can use this common field to set up a link between the two tables. The field you use must satisfy three conditions:

- It must not have the same name as an existing field in the other table.
- It must uniquely identify each record in the other table.
- To save space and reduce data-entry errors, it should be the smallest field that satisfies the preceding two conditions.

In the sales-leads example, a field needs to be added to the Contacts table that establishes a link to the appropriate record in the Company table. The CompanyName field uniquely identifies each firm, but it's too large to be of use. The Phone field is also a unique identifier and is smaller, but the Contacts table already has a Phone field. The best solution is to use CompanyID, the Company table's primary key field. Table 16.11 shows the revised structure for the Contacts table that includes the CompanyID field.

Table 16.11. The final structure for the Contacts table.

Field	Description
ContactID	The primary key
CompanyID	The Company table foreign key
FirstName	The contact's first name
LastName	The contact's last name
Phone	The contact's phone number
Fax	The contact's fax number
Source	Where the lead came from
Notes	Notes or comments related to the sales lead

When a table includes a primary key field from a related database, the field is called a *foreign key*. Foreign keys are the secret to successful relational database design.

Step 3: Establish a Link Between the Related Tables

After you've inserted your foreign keys into your tables, the final step in designing your relational model is to establish a link between the two tables. This step is covered in detail later in this chapter.

Types of Relational Models

Depending on the data you're working with, you can set up one of several different relational database models. In each of these models, however, you need to differentiate between a *child* table (also called a *dependent* table or a *controlled* table) and a *parent* table (also called a *primary* table or a *controlling* table). The child table is the one that is dependent on the parent table to fill in the definition of its records. The Contacts table, for example, is a child table because it is dependent on the Company table for the company information associated with each person.

The One-to-Many Model

The most common relational model is one in which a single record in the parent table relates to multiple records in the child table. This is called a *one-to-many* relationship. The sales-leads example is a one-to-many relationship because one record in the Company table can relate to many records in the Contacts table (that is, you can have multiple sales contacts from the same firm). In these models, the "many" table is the one to which you add the foreign key.

Another example of a one-to-many relationship is an application that tracks accounts-receivable invoices. You need one table for the invoice data (Invoices) and another for the customer data (Customer). In this case, one customer can place many orders, so Customer is the parent table, Invoices is the child table, and the common field is the Customer table's primary key.

The One-to-One Model

If your data requires that one record in the parent table be related to only one record in the child table, you have a *one-to-one* model. The most common use for one-to-one relations is to create separate entity classes to enhance security. In a hospital, for example, each patient's data is a single entity class, but it makes sense to create separate tables for the patient's basic information (such as name, address, and so on) and medical history. This setup enables you to add extra levels of security to the confidential medical data (such as a password). The two tables then are related based on a common PatientID key field.

Another example of a one-to-one model is employee data. You can separate the less-sensitive information, such as job title and startup date, into one table, and put restricted information, such as salary and commissions, into a second table. If each employee has a unique identification number, you can use that number to set up a relation between the two tables.

Note that in a one-to-one model the concepts of *child* and *parent* tables are interchangeable. Each table relies on the other to form the complete picture of each patient or employee.

The Many-to-Many Model

In some cases, you might have data such that many records in one table can relate to many records in another table. This is called a *many-to-many* relationship. In this case, there is no direct way to establish a common field between the two tables. To see why, look at an example from a pared-down accounts-receivable application.

Table 16.12 shows a simplified structure for an Invoices table. It includes a primary key—InvoiceID—as well as a foreign key—CustID—from a separate table of customer information (which we'll ignore in this example).

Table 16.12. The structure for an Invoices table.

Field	Description
InvoiceID	The primary key
CustID	The foreign key from a table of customer data

Table 16.13 shows a stripped-down structure for a table of product information. It includes a primary key field—ProductID—and a description field—Product.

Table 16.13. The structure for a Products table.

Field	Description
ProductID	The primary key
Product	The product description

The idea here is that a given product can appear in many invoices, and any given invoice can contain many products. This is a many-to-many relation, and it implies that *both* tables are parents (or to put it another way, neither table is directly dependent on the other). But relational theory says that a child table is needed to establish a common field. In this case, the solution is to set up a third table—called a *relation table*—that is the child of both of the original tables. In our example, the relation table would contain the detail data for each invoice. Table 16.14 shows the structure for such a table. As you can see, the table includes foreign keys from both Invoices (InvoiceID) and Products (ProductID), as well as a Quantity field.

Table 16.14. The structure for a table of invoice detail data.

Field	Description
InvoiceID	The foreign key from the Invoices table
ProductID	The foreign key from the Products table
Quantity	The quantity ordered

Working with Tables

Now that you know why multiple-table queries are necessary, we can turn our attention to creating and working with them. A multiple-table query is, to state the obvious, a query that uses two or more tables. So the first order of business is to show you how to work with tables in a query, and the next couple of sections do just that.

Adding Tables to the Query

When you start a new query and have selected your data source, Query displays the Add Tables dialog box so that you can select the tables to use. You can add all the tables you need at this beginning stage of the query, or you can add new tables to an existing query by following the steps outlined next:

1. Select the Ta**b**le | **A**dd Tables command, or click the Add Table(s) button on the toolbar. Query displays the Add Tables dialog box.

The Add Table(s) button.

2. Highlight the table you want to add.

3. Select the **A**dd button. Query adds the table to the query.

4. Repeat steps 2 and 3 to add more tables.

5. Select the **C**lose button to return to the query.

Understanding Join Lines

Figure 16.13 shows a query with a single table—Orders—and a result set that includes the OrderID, the OrderDate, and the RequiredDate.

FIGURE 16.13.

A single-table query showing data from the Orders table.

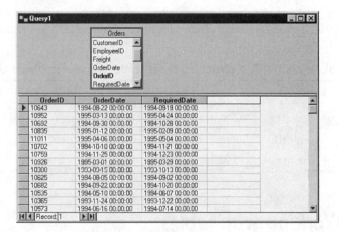

What if we want to see the name of the customer who placed each order? The Orders table contains a CustomerID field, so that tells us we might be able to link this table with the Customers table. Adding the Customers table to the query produces the display shown in Figure 16.14.

If you add related tables that have already been linked as described earlier, Query displays the relationship between them using a *join line*. As you can see in Figure 16.14, the join line connects the two fields that contain the related information. In this case, CustomerID is the primary key field for the Customers table, and it appears as a foreign key in the Orders table. This enables you to relate any order with its corresponding customer information. For example, to show the name of the company that placed each order, all you have to do is add the Customers table's CompanyName field to the data pane, as shown in Figure 16.15.

FIGURE 16.14.

A multiple-table query showing a join line between the two tables.

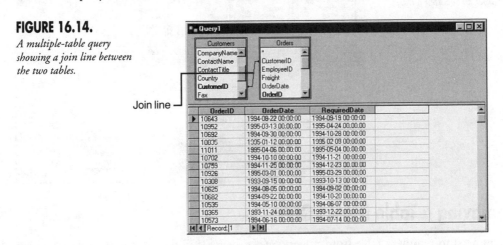

FIGURE 16.15.

When two tables are linked, Query automatically displays the related data for each record.

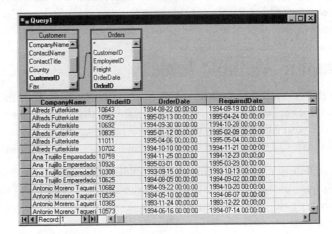

This process can be extended quite easily to several tables. In Figure 16.16, for example, two new tables have been added to the query: Order Details and Products. As the join lines show, the Orders and Order Details tables are related via the OrderID field, and the Order Details and Products tables are related via the ProductID field. The result set shows data from all four tables.

FIGURE 16.16.

A four-table query showing join lines and related data.

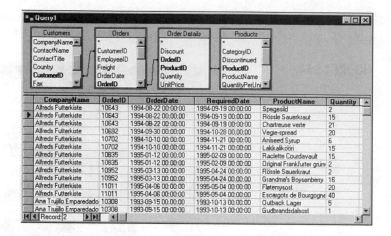

Removing a Table from a Query

If you need to remove a table from a query, select the table in the table pane and then either select the Ta**b**le | **R**emove Table command or press Delete. Query removes the table and also removes any of the table's fields from the result set.

Joining Multiple Tables

In the examples we looked at in the preceding section, the tables were already linked, so the join lines appeared automatically. Certain database management systems—such as Microsoft Access and dBASE for Windows—enable you to set up relationships between the tables in a database. Query can read these links, and it uses them to set up its join lines.

In other cases, however, the tables you'll be working with will have no predefined relationship. For example, older dBASE files and the sample FoxPro files that come with Query contain only a single table in their DBF files, so there's no way to predefine a relationship between these separate files.

However, Query has a powerful feature—called *joining*—that enables you to establish a relationship between two or more tables within Query itself. To take advantage of this feature, your tables must have at least one field in common. The fields don't need to have the same name, but the data within each field must be of a common type.

For example, consider two DBF files that come with Microsoft Query: CUSTOMER.DBF and ORDERS.DBF. These two tables have a CUSTMR_ID field in common, so we can use this common field to join the two tables.

Types of Joins

Query enables you to set up three kinds of joins: an inner join, an outer join, and a self-join.

Inner join: An inner join includes only those records in which the related fields in the two tables match each other exactly. This is the most common type of join.

Outer join: An outer join includes every record from one of the tables and only those records from the other table in which the related fields match each other exactly. For example, suppose that you have a PRODUCT table and an ORDDTAIL (order details) table with a common PRODUCT_ID field. Creating an inner join shows you the products that have been ordered and the quantities ordered. But what if you want to see which products have *not* been ordered? In this case, you set up an outer join that displays every record in the PRODUCT table, as shown in Figure 16.17. Query shows the QUANTITY ordered for each matching record and displays a blank for records for which there is no match.

FIGURE 16.17.

An outer join that tells you which products haven't been ordered.

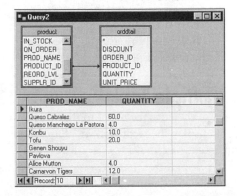

NOTE

Notice that the join line for an outer join is terminated with an arrowhead rather than a second dot. The arrowhead points to the table that contributes only the matching records (or blanks).

NOTE

Outer join queries are limited to two tables.

Self-join: A self-join is a join on a second copy of the same table. Self-joins are handy for tables that include different fields with the same type of information. For example, the sample table EMPLOYEE.DBF that comes with Query has an EMPLOY_ID field that lists the identification number of each employee. The same table also includes a REPORTS_TO field that lists the identification number of the employee's manager. To display the name of each employee's manager, you add a second copy of the EMPLOYEE table (which Query names EMPLOYEE_1) and join the REPORTS_TO and EMPLOY_ID fields, as shown in Figure 16.18.

FIGURE 16.18.

An example of a self-join.

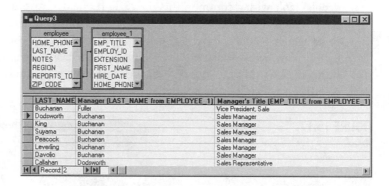

You also can distinguish joins by the operator used to match the related fields. Most joins are *equi-joins* because they use the equal to (=) operator to match the fields. In an inner join, for example, if you display the records in which the values in one field equal the values in another, you've set up an equi-join. *Theta joins* are joins that use an operator other than equal to, such as not equal to (<>), greater than (>) or less than (<).

Creating an Inner Join by Dragging

The easiest way to create an inner join between two tables (or a self-join between two copies of the same table) is to use your mouse to drag one of the related fields and drop it on the other. Here are the explicit steps required:

1. Add the tables you want to join.

2. Arrange the table boxes so that you can see the fields you want to use for the join in each box.

3. Drag the related field from one table, and drop it on the related field in the other table, as shown in Figure 16.19. Query sets up an inner join line between the two fields.

FIGURE 16.19.

Query lets you use drag-and-drop to join two tables.

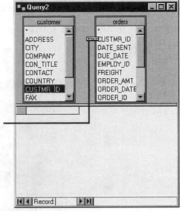

Drag the related field from the table and
drop it on the related field in the other table

Joining Tables with the Joins Dialog Box

If you want to create an outer join or a theta join, you need to use the Joins dialog box, shown in Figure 16.20. It includes the following features:

Left	A list of fields in the first table.
Right	A list of fields in the second table.
Operator	The operator to use for the join. Use equal to (=) for an equi-join, or any other operator for a theta join.
Join Includes	This group gives a selection of options for the join. (The available options depend on the operator you select.) Here's a summary:

1   Select this option to create an inner join.

2   Select this option to create a *left outer join* that displays all the records from the table listed in the **Left** box and only matching records from the table in the **Right** box.

3   Select this option to create a *right outer join* that displays all the records from the table listed in the **Right** box and only matching records from the table listed in the **Left** box.

Joins in Query   Lists the current joins in the query (written in SQL).

Follow these steps to add a join using the Joins dialog box:

1. Add the tables you want to join.
2. Select the Ta**b**le | **J**oins command to display the Joins dialog box.
3. Select the join options you want to use.

4. Select the **Add** button. Query adds the join to the query.

5. Repeat steps 3 and 4 to add other joins.

6. Select the **Close** button to return to the query. Query adds the appropriate join lines.

FIGURE 16.20.

Use the Joins dialog box to join two tables.

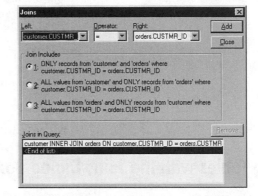

After you have your joins set up, you can add the appropriate fields to the data pane and even filter the data using criteria.

Removing a Join

If you no longer need a join, you can remove it by using either of the following techniques:

- Click on the join line and press Delete.

- Select the Table | Joins command to display the Joins dialog box, highlight the join in the Joins in Query list, and then select the **Remove** button.

Adding and Editing Data Within Query

Although you'll mostly use Query to display, join, and filter existing data, you also can use it to create new tables and records and to edit records in the result set. The next couple of sections give you the details.

Creating a New Table

If you don't have access to a database management program, you still can create new tables by using Query in association with the ODBC driver for the type of table you need. The following procedure takes you through the necessary steps:

1. Select the **File** | **Table Definition** command to display the Select Data Source dialog box.

2. If you want to create the table in the same location and using the same format as one of the existing data sources, highlight the data source and then select **U**se.

   If you want to use a different data source, select **O**ther and then define the data source, as described in Chapter 16, "Creating Advanced Queries."

3. In the Select Table dialog box that appears, use one of the following techniques:

   ■ If you want to create your table from scratch, select the **N**ew button. Query displays the New Table Definition dialog box, shown in Figure 16.21.

FIGURE 16.21.

Use the New Table Definition dialog box to create a new table from scratch.

   ■ If you want to use an existing table as a model, highlight the table in the **T**able list, and then select Vie**w**. The View Table Definition dialog box appears. This dialog box is similar to the New Table Definition dialog box, except that the fields from the existing table are listed in the **F**ields box.

4. Enter the name for the new table in the **T**able Name text box.

5. To define a field to include in the table, fill in the following options:

   ■ **F**ield Name: The name of the field.

   ■ **T**ype: The type of data that the field will contain. (The available options depend on the type of data source you're using.)

   ■ **L**ength: The size of the field.

   ■ **D**ecimal: The number of decimal places in numeric data.

   ■ **R**equired: Activate this check box to require that a value be entered into the field.

6. Select the **A**dd button to add the field to the **F**ields list.

7. Repeat steps 5 and 6 to define the other fields you want to include in the table.

8. When you've added all the fields you need, select Creat**e**. A dialog box appears to let you know that the table was created.

9. Select OK to return to the Select Table dialog box.

10. Select **C**lose.

> **NOTE**
>
> You also can create a new table by saving the current result set as a table. To do this, select the **F**ile | **S**ave As command to display the Select Data Source dialog box. Highlight a data source (which tells Query where to save the table and which format to use), and then select **S**ave. In the Save As dialog box that appears, enter a name for the table, and then select OK. Excel might ask you if you want to create an index for this table. If you do, select **Y**es and then enter an index name and the field on which to index the table.

Editing Data in the Result Set

The data that appears in the result set is normally read-only; therefore, you can't change any of the fields, and you can't add or delete records. If you need to make changes to the data, however, you can do so by activating the **R**ecords | **A**llow Editing command. (Note that this command works only for single-table queries. You can't edit records in a multiple-table query.) With this command active, you can perform the following editing chores on your data:

Add a record. If you move to the end of the result set, you see a new, blank record, as shown in Figure 16.22. You can use this record to add new records to the table.

FIGURE 16.22.

When you activate the Records | Allow Editing command, a new, blank record appears at the bottom of the table.

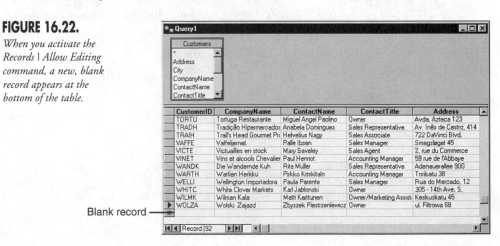

Blank record

Delete a record. To delete a record, select it and then either select the **E**dit | **D**elete command or press the Delete key. A dialog box appears to ask whether you want to delete the record. Select OK.

Edit a record. To make changes to a field in a particular record, either double-click on the cell or select the cell and then press F2.

Working with Query's SQL Statements

When you work with Query—whether you're adding columns to the data pane, sorting the records, adding criteria, or joining tables—what you're really doing is building a Structured Query Language (SQL) statement. When you run the query, the SQL statement is sent to the ODBC driver, which translates the statement into the appropriate SQL syntax for the underlying tables.

Although you'll rarely need to edit the SQL statement, it's a valuable troubleshooting tool if your query isn't returning the result set you expected. The next couple of sections give a basic SQL primer and show you how to view and edit Query's SQL statement.

Understanding the SQL *SELECT* Statement

SQL is a rather complex language with many different "verbs" and keywords. Fortunately, Query deals with only a subset of SQL: the SQL SELECT statement. The SELECT statement is used to create a result set based on the tables, fields, criteria, and other clauses specified in the statement. Here's the syntax of SELECT:

```
SELECT [DISTINCT] select_list
    FROM table_names
    [LEFT¦RIGHT OUTER JOIN table_names ON clause]
    WHERE criteria¦inner_join_clause
    ORDER BY field_list [DESC] ¦ GROUP BY field_list
```

Let's examine each element in this statement and see how it relates to Query's features:

SELECT	The SELECT statement always begins with the SELECT keyword.
DISTINCT	This optional keyword appears when you activate the **U**nique Values Only check box in the Query Properties dialog box.
select list	This is a list of field names. They correspond to the field names included in the data pane.
FROM table_names	This is a list of the query's tables. They correspond to the tables added to the table pane.
LEFT¦RIGHT OUTER JOIN	This clause appears when you set up a left or right outer join. It also includes a *table_names* element that specifies the tables used in the join, and a *clause* element that defines the join (that is, the fields used and the operator).

WHERE	This keyword filters the data. It is followed either by *criteria*, if you entered criteria in the criteria pane, or by *inner join clause*, if you set up an inner join.
ORDER BY *field_list* [DESC]	This clause appears if you sort the result set. The optional DESC keyword appears if the sort is descending.
GROUP BY *field_list*	This clause appears if you activate the **G**roup Records check box in the Query Properties dialog box.

Viewing the SQL Statement

To view the current SQL statement, select the **View** | **S**QL command to display the SQL dialog box. For example, Figure 16.23 shows the SQL statement that corresponds to the query shown in Figure 16.1.

FIGURE 16.23.

An SQL statement.

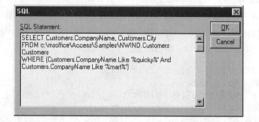

As another example, Figure 16.24 shows the SQL statement that corresponds to the query shown in Figure 16.15. Notice how the inner join clause appears as part of the WHERE clause.

FIGURE 16.24.

An SQL statement for an inner join.

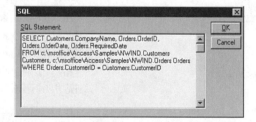

Summary

This chapter took you through a few advanced query techniques. We examined query criteria—including operators, identifiers, and functions—in greater depth. I showed you how to use calculations in your queries, how to work with multiple tables, how to edit query data, and how to work with Query's SQL statements. If you want more information, here are a few other places to check:

- To learn more about using criteria and filtering in an Excel list, see Chapter 12, "Working with Lists and Databases."
- The basics of using Query were covered in Chapter 15, "Using Microsoft Query."
- To learn how to control and work with external data in your VBA programs, read Chapter 26, "Database and Client/Server Programming."

Summary

PART

IN THIS PART

Unleashing Excel's Data Analysis Wizardry

Basic Analytic Methods

17

At times it's not enough to simply enter data in a worksheet, build a few formulas, and add a little formatting to make things presentable. We're often called on to divine some inner meaning from the jumble of numbers and formula results that litter our workbooks. In other words, we need to *analyze* our data to see what nuggets of understanding we can unearth.

This chapter looks at a few simple analytic techniques that have many uses. You'll learn how to use Excel's numerous methods for what-if analysis, how to use iteration to solve problems, how to use trend analysis, and how to wield Excel's useful Goal Seek tool.

Using What-If Analysis

What-if analysis is perhaps the most basic method for interrogating your worksheet data. In fact, it's probably safe to say that most spreadsheet work involves what-if analysis of one form or another.

With what-if analysis, you first calculate a formula D, based on the input from variables A, B, and C. You then say, "What if I change variable A? Or B or C? What happens to the result?"

For example, Figure 17.1 shows a worksheet that calculates the future value of an investment based on five variables: the interest rate, period, annual deposit, initial deposit, and deposit type. Cell C9 shows the result of the FV() function. Now the questions begin. What if the interest rate were 7 percent? What if you deposited $8,000 per year? Or $12,000? What if you reduced the initial deposit? Answering these questions is a simple matter of changing the appropriate variables and watching the effect on the result.

FIGURE 17.1.

The simplest what-if analysis involves changing worksheet variables and watching the result.

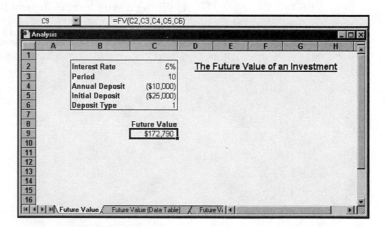

Setting Up a One-Input Data Table

The problem with modifying formula variables is that you see only a single result at one time. If you're interested in studying the effect a range of values has on the formula, you need to set up a *data table*. In the investment analysis worksheet, for example, suppose that you want to see the future value of the investment with the annual deposit varying between $7,000 and $13,000. You could just enter these values in a row or column and then create the appropriate formulas. Setting up a data table, however, is much easier, as the following procedure shows:

1. Add to the worksheet the values you want to input into the formula. You have two choices for the placement of these values:

    ■ If you want to enter the values in a row, start the row one cell up and one cell to the right of the formula.

    ■ If you want to enter the values in a column, start the column one cell down and one cell to the left of the cell containing the formula (see Figure 17.2).

FIGURE 17.2.

Enter the values you want to input into the formula.

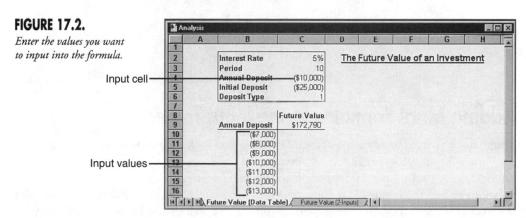

2. Select the range that includes the input values and the formula. (In Figure 17.2, this would be B9:C16.)

3. Select the **D**ata | **T**able command. Excel displays the Table dialog box.

4. If you entered the input values in a row, select the **R**ow Input Cell text box, and enter the cell address of the input cell. If the input values are in a column, enter the input cell's address in the **C**olumn Input Cell text box instead. In the investment analysis example, you enter C4 in the **C**olumn Input Cell, as shown in Figure 17.3.

FIGURE 17.3.

In the Table dialog box, enter the input cell where you want Excel to substitute the input values.

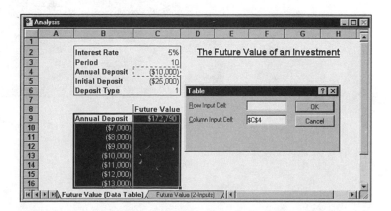

5. Select OK. Excel takes each of the input values and places them in the input cell; Excel then displays the results in the data table, as shown in Figure 17.4.

FIGURE 17.4.

Excel substitutes each input value into the input cell and displays the results in the data table.

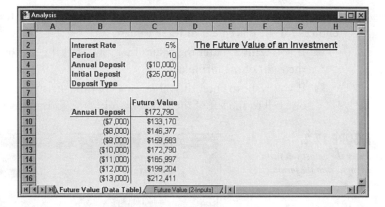

Adding More Formulas to the Input Table

You're not restricted to just a single formula in your data tables. If you want to see the effect of the various input values on different formulas, you can easily add them to the data table. For example, in our future value worksheet, it would be interesting to factor inflation into the calculations so that the user could see how the investment appears in today's dollars. Figure 17.5 shows the revised worksheet with a new Inflation variable (cell C8) and a formula that converts the calculated future value into today's dollars (cell D9).

FIGURE 17.5.

To add a formula to a data table, enter the new formula next to the existing one.

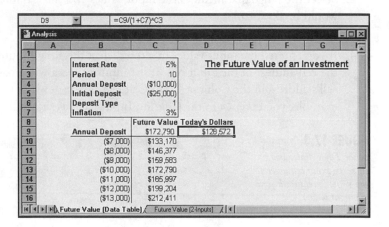

NOTE

This is the formula for converting a future value into today's dollars:

```
Future Value / (1 + Inflation Rate) ^ Period
```

Here, `Period` is the number of years from now that the future value exists.

To create the new data table, follow the steps outlined earlier. However, make sure that the range you select in step 2 includes the input values and *both* formulas (that is, the range B9:D16 in Figure 17.5). Figure 17.6 shows the results.

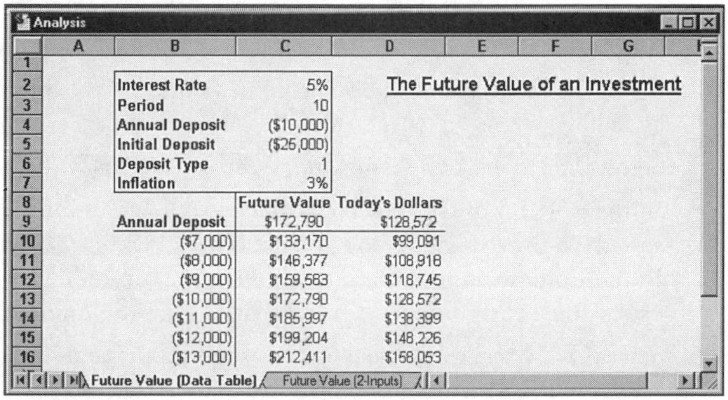

FIGURE 17.6.

The results of the data table with multiple formulas.

	A	B	C	D	E	F	G	
1								
2		Interest Rate	5%		The Future Value of an Investment			
3		Period	10					
4		Annual Deposit	($10,000)					
5		Initial Deposit	($25,000)					
6		Deposit Type	1					
7		Inflation	3%					
8			Future Value	Today's Dollars				
9		Annual Deposit	$172,790	$128,572				
10		($7,000)	$133,170	$99,091				
11		($8,000)	$146,377	$108,918				
12		($9,000)	$159,583	$118,745				
13		($10,000)	$172,790	$128,572				
14		($11,000)	$185,997	$138,399				
15		($12,000)	$199,204	$148,226				
16		($13,000)	$212,411	$158,053				

Future Value [Data Table] / Future Value (2-Inputs)

NOTE

After you have a data table set up, you can do regular what-if analysis by adjusting the other worksheet variables. Each time you make a change, Excel recalculates every formula in the table.

Setting Up a Two-Input Table

You also can set up data tables that take two input variables. This option enables you to see the effect on an investment's future value when you enter different values for, say, the annual deposit and the interest rate. This procedure shows how to set up a two-input data table:

1. Enter one set of values in a column below the formula and the second set of values in the row beside the formula, as shown in Figure 17.7.

FIGURE 17.7.

Enter the two sets of values you want to input into the formula.

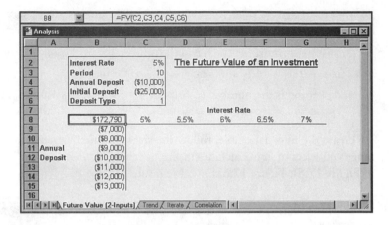

2. Select the range that includes the input values and the formula (B8:G15 in Figure 17.7).

3. Select the **D**ata | **T**able command to display the Table dialog box.

4. In the **R**ow Input Cell text box, enter the cell address of the input cell that corresponds to the row values you entered (C2 in Figure 17.7—the Interest Rate variable). In the **C**olumn Input Cell text box, enter the cell address of the input cell you want to use for the column values (C4 in Figure 17.7—the Annual Deposit variable).

5. Select OK. Excel runs through the various input combinations and then displays the results in the data table, as shown in Figure 17.8.

FIGURE 17.8.

Excel substitutes each input value into the input cell and displays the results in the data table.

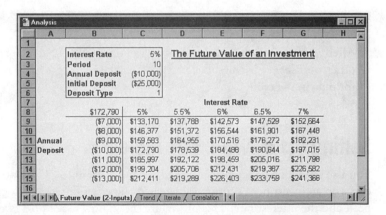

TIP

As mentioned earlier, if you make changes to any of the variables in a table formula, Excel recalculates the entire table. This isn't a problem in small tables, but large ones can take a very long time to calculate. If you prefer to control the table recalculation, choose the **T**ools | **O**ptions command, select the Calculation tab, and then activate the Automatic Except **T**ables check box. To recalculate a table, press F9 (or Shift-F9 to recalculate the current worksheet only).

Editing a Data Table

When you select the **D**ata | **T**able command, Excel enters an *array formula* in the interior of the data table. This formula is a TABLE() function with the following syntax:

```
{=TABLE(row_input_ref, column_input_ref)}
```

Here, *row_input_ref* and *column_input_ref* are the cell references you entered in the Table dialog box. The braces ({ }) indicate that this is an array, which means you can't change or delete individual elements of the table. (To learn more about arrays, see Chapter 2, "Building Better Formulas.") If you want to delete or move the data table, you first must select the entire table.

Working with Goal Seek

Here's a what-if question for you: what if you already know the result you want? For example, you might know that you want to have $50,000 in a college fund 18 years from now, or that you have to achieve a 30 percent gross margin in your next budget. If you need to manipulate only a single variable to achieve these results, you can use Excel's Goal Seek feature. You tell Goal Seek the final value you need and which variable to change, and it finds a solution for you (if one exists).

NOTE

For more complicated scenarios with multiple variables and constraints, you need to use Excel's Solver feature. See Chapter 19, "Solving Complex Problems with Solver," for details.

How Does Goal Seek Work?

When you set up a worksheet to use Goal Seek, you usually have a formula in one cell and the formula's variable—with an initial value—in another. (Your formula can have multiple variables, but Goal Seek enables you to manipulate only one variable at a time.) Goal Seek operates by using an *iterative method* to find a solution. That is, Goal Seek first tries the variable's initial value to see whether that produces the result you want. If it doesn't, Goal Seek tries different values until it converges on a solution. (To learn more about iterative methods, see "Using Iteration," later in this chapter.)

Running Goal Seek

Suppose that you want to set up a college fund for your newborn child. Your goal is to have $50,000 in the fund 18 years from now. Assuming 5 percent interest, how much will you need to deposit into the fund every year? The following procedure shows how to use Goal Seek to calculate the answer:

1. Set up your worksheet to use Goal Seek. Figure 17.9 shows the College worksheet, which I've set up the following way:

    ■ Cell C8 contains the FV() function that calculates the future value of the college fund. When we're done, this cell's value should be $50,000.

    ■ Cell C6 contains the annual deposit into the fund (with an initial value of $0). This is the value Goal Seek adjusts to find a solution.

    ■ The other cells (C4 and C5) are used in the FV() function; however, for this exercise we'll assume that they're constants.

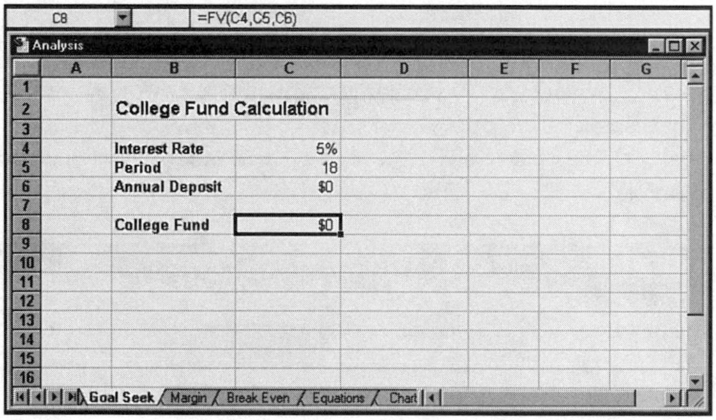

FIGURE 17.9.

A worksheet set up to use Goal Seek.

2. Select the **T**ools | **G**oal Seek command. Excel displays the Goal Seek dialog box.

3. In the **S**et cell text box, enter a reference to the cell that contains your goal. For this example, enter C8.

4. In the To **v**alue text box, enter the final value you want for the goal cell. The example's value is 50000.

5. Use the By **c**hanging cell text box to enter a reference to the variable cell. In the example, enter C6. Figure 17.10 shows the completed dialog box.

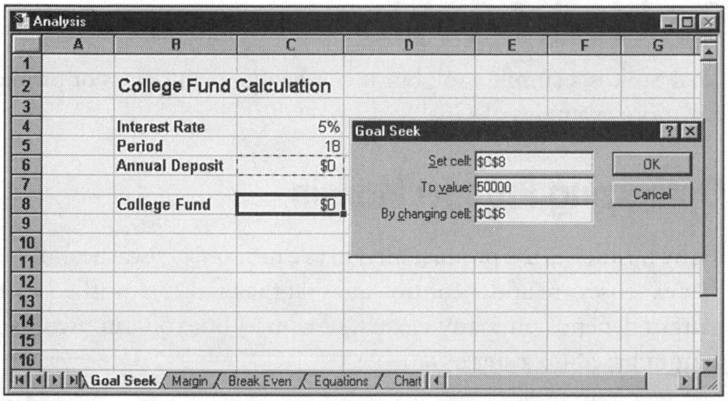

FIGURE 17.10.

The completed Goal Seek dialog box.

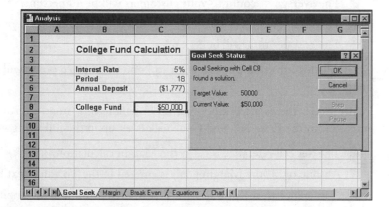

6. Select OK. Excel begins the iteration and displays the Goal Seek Status dialog box. When finished, the dialog box tells you whether Goal Seek found a solution, as shown in Figure 17.11.

FIGURE 17.11.

The Goal Seek Status dialog box shows you the solution (if one was found).

NOTE

Most of the time, Goal Seek finds a solution relatively quickly. For longer operations, you can select the **P**ause button in the Goal Seek Status dialog box to stop Goal Seek. To walk through the process one iteration at a time, select the **S**tep button. To resume Goal Seek, select **C**ontinue.

7. If Goal Seek found a solution, you can accept the solution by selecting OK. To ignore the solution, select Cancel.

Goal Seek Examples

Goal Seek is a simple tool, but it can handle many types of problems. This section looks at a few more examples of Goal Seek.

Optimizing Product Margin

Many businesses use product margin as a measure of fiscal health. A strong margin usually means that expenses are under control and that the market is satisfied with your price points. Product margin depends on many factors, of course, but you can use Goal Seek to find the optimum margin based on a single variable.

For example, suppose that you want to introduce a new product line, and you want the product to return a margin of 30 percent during the first year. You're making the following assumptions:

- The sales during the year will be 100,000 units.
- The average discount to your customers will be 40 percent.
- The total fixed costs will be $750,000.
- The cost per unit will be $12.63.

Given all this information, you want to know what price point will produce the 30 percent margin.

Figure 17.12 shows a worksheet set up to handle this situation. An initial value of $1.00 is entered into the Price cell, and Goal Seek is set up in the following way:

- The **S**et cell reference is C14, the Margin calculation.
- A value of .3 (the Margin goal) is entered in the To **v**alue text box.
- A reference to the Price cell (C4) is entered into the By **c**hanging cell text box.

FIGURE 17.12.

A worksheet set up to calculate a price point that will optimize gross margin.

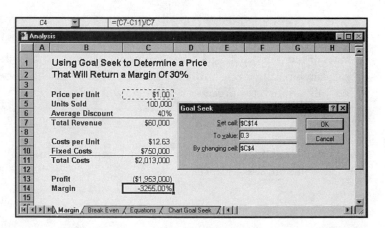

When you run Goal Seek, it produces a solution of $47.87 for the price, as shown in Figure 17.13. This solution can be rounded up to $47.95.

FIGURE 17.13.

The result of Goal Seek's labors.

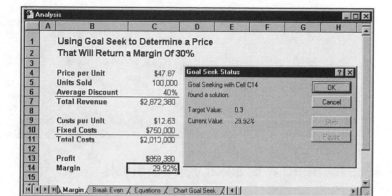

A Note About Goal Seek's Approximations

Notice that the solution in Figure 17.13 is an approximate figure. That is, the margin value is 29.92%, not the 30% we were looking for. That's pretty close (it's off by only 0.0008), but it's not exact. Why didn't Goal Seek find the exact solution?

The answer lies in one of the options Excel uses to control iterative calculations. Some iterations can take an extremely long time to find an exact solution, so Excel compromises by setting certain limits on iterative processes. To see these limits, select the **T**ools | **O**ptions command and select the Calculation tab in the Options dialog box that appears (see Figure 17.14). These two options control iterative processes:

Maximum It**e**rations   The value in this text box controls the maximum number of iterations. In Goal Seek, this value represents the maximum number of values that Excel plugs into the variable cell.

Maximum **C**hange   The value in this text box is the threshold Excel uses to determine whether it has converged on a solution. If the difference between the current solution and the desired goal is within this value, Excel stops iterating.

It was the Maximum **C**hange value that prevented us from getting an exact solution for the profit margin calculation. On a particular iteration, Goal Seek hit the solution .2992, which put us within 0.0008 of our goal of 0.3. 0.0008 is less than the default value of 0.001 in the Maximum **C**hange text box, so Excel called a halt to the procedure.

To get an exact solution, you must adjust the Maximum **C**hange value to 0.0001.

FIGURE 17.14.

*The text boxes in the
Iteration group place limits
on iterative calculations.*

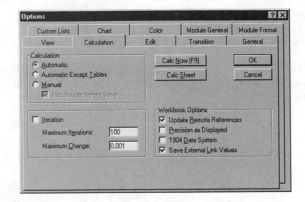

Performing a Break-Even Analysis

In a *break-even analysis,* you determine the number of units you have to sell of a product so
that your total profits are 0 (that is, the product revenue equals the product costs). Setting up
a profit equation with a goal of 0 and varying the units sold is perfect for Goal Seek.

To try this, we'll extend the example used in the "Optimizing Product Margin" section. In this
case, assume a unit price of $47.95 (the solution found to optimize product margin, rounded
up to the nearest 95 cents). Figure 17.15 shows the Goal Seek dialog box filled out as detailed
here:

- The **S**et cell reference is set to C13, the Profit calculation.
- A value of 0 (the Profit goal) is entered in the To **v**alue text box.
- A reference to the Units Sold cell (C5) is entered into the By **c**hanging cell text box.

FIGURE 17.15.

*The Goal Seek dialog box
set up to calculate a break-
even analysis.*

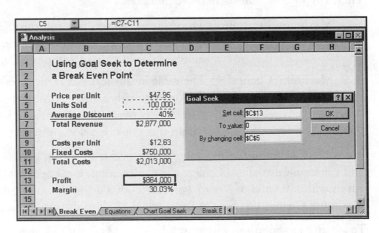

Figure 17.16 shows the solution: 46,468 units must be sold to break even.

FIGURE 17.16.

The break-even solution.

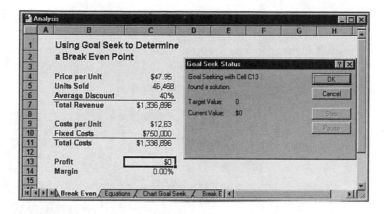

Solving Algebraic Equations

Goal Seek also is useful for solving complex algebraic equations of one variable. For example, suppose that you need to find the value of *x* to solve the following rather nasty equation:

$$\frac{(3x - 8)^2 (x - 1)}{4x^2 - 5} = 1$$

This equation, although too complex for the quadratic formula, can be easily rendered in Excel. The left side of the equation can be represented with the following formula:

`=(((3*A2-8)^2)*(A2-1))/(4*A2^2-5)`

Cell A2 represents the variable *x*. You can solve this equation in Goal Seek by setting the goal for this equation to 1 (the right side of the equation) and by varying cell A2. Figure 17.17 shows a worksheet and the completed Goal Seek dialog box.

FIGURE 17.17.

Solving an algebraic equation with Goal Seek.

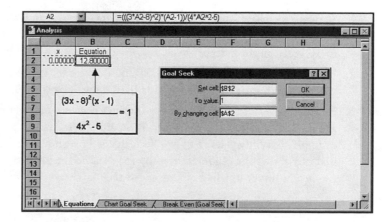

Figure 17.18 shows the result. The value in cell A2 is the solution *x* that satisfies the equation. Notice that the equation result (cell B2) is not quite 1. As mentioned earlier in this chapter, if you need higher accuracy, you must change Excel's convergence threshold. In this example, select the **Tools | Options** command, and in the Calculation tab, type `0.000001` in the Maximum **C**hange text box.

FIGURE 17.18.

Cell A2 holds the solution for the equation in cell A1.

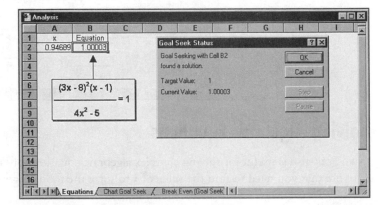

Goal Seeking with Charts

If you have your data graphed in a 2-D bar, column, line, or XY chart, you can run Goal Seek by using the mouse to drag a data marker to a new position. If the data marker represents a formula, Excel uses Goal Seek to work backward and derive the appropriate formula input values.

The following example helps explain this process. Suppose that you want to invest some money every year so that in 10 years, you'll have $150,000. Assuming a constant interest rate, how much do you need to set aside annually to reach your goal? The solution is to adjust the chart data marker at 10 years so that it has the value $150,000. The following procedure shows you the steps to follow:

1. Activate the chart and select the specific data marker you want to adjust. Excel adds selection handles to the marker. For the example, select the data marker corresponding to 10 years on the category axis.

2. Drag the black selection handle to the desired value. As you drag the handle, the current value appears in the formula bar's Name box, shown in Figure 17.19.

3. Release the mouse button. If the marker references a number in a cell, Excel changes the number and redraws the chart. If the marker references a formula, as in the example, Excel displays the Goal Seek dialog box, shown in Figure 17.20. The **S**et cell text box shows the cell referenced by the data marker, and the To **v**alue text box shows the new number to which you dragged the marker.

FIGURE 17.19.

Drag the data marker to the desired value.

Current value

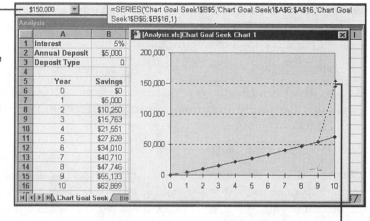

Drag the chart data
marker to the value
you want

FIGURE 17.20.

If the data marker is derived from a formula, Excel runs Goal Seek.

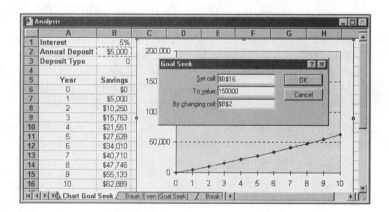

4. Enter the appropriate reference in the By changing cell text box. For the example, you enter B2 to calculate the required annual deposit.

5. Select OK. The Goal Seek Status dialog box appears while Excel derives the solution for the new number.

6. When the iteration is complete, select OK and Excel redraws the chart.

Using Iteration

A common business problem involves calculating a profit-sharing plan contribution as a percentage of a company's net profits. This isn't a simple multiplication problem, because the net profit is determined, in part, by the profit-sharing figure. For example, suppose that a company has a gross margin of $1,000,000 and expenses of $900,000, which leaves a gross profit of $100,000. The company also sets aside 10 percent of net profits for profit sharing. The net profit is calculated with the following formula:

```
Net Profit = Gross Profit - Profit Sharing Contribution
```

This is called a *circular reference formula* because there are terms on the left and right side of the equals sign that depend on each other. Specifically, the `Profit Sharing Contribution` is derived with the following formula:

```
Profit Sharing Contribution = (Net Profit)*0.1
```

One way to solve such a formula is to guess at an answer and see how close you come. For example, because profit sharing should be 10 percent of net profits, a good first guess might be 10 percent of *gross* profits, or $10,000. If you plug this number into the formula, you end up with a net profit of $90,000. This isn't right, however, because 10 percent of $90,000 is $9,000. Therefore, the profit-sharing guess is off by $1,000.

So you can try again. This time, use $9,000 as the profit-sharing number. Plugging this new value into the formula gives a net profit of $91,000. This number translates into a profit-sharing contribution of $9,100—which is off by only $100.

If you continue this process, your profit-sharing guesses will get closer to the calculated value (this process is called *convergence*). When the guesses are close enough (for example, within a dollar), you can stop and pat yourself on the back for finding the solution. This process is called *iteration*.

Of course, you didn't spend your (or your company's) hard-earned money on a computer so that you could do this sort of thing by hand. Excel makes iterative calculations a breeze, as you'll see in the following procedure:

1. Set up your worksheet and enter your circular reference formula. Figure 17.21 shows a worksheet for the example used earlier. If Excel displays a dialog box telling you it can't resolve circular references, select OK.

FIGURE 17.21.

A worksheet with a circular reference formula.

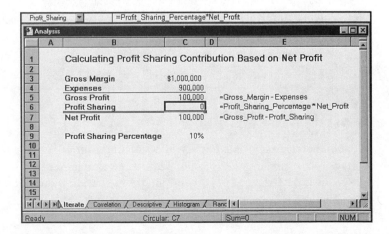

2. Select the **T**ools | **O**ptions command, and then select the Calculation tab in the Options dialog box.

3. Activate the **It**eration check box.

4. Use the Maximum It**e**rations text box to specify the number of iterations you need. In most cases, the default figure of 100 is more than enough.

5. Use the Maximum **C**hange text box to tell Excel how accurate you want your results to be. The smaller the number, the longer the iteration takes and the more accurate the calculation will be. Again, the default value is probably a reasonable compromise.

6. Select OK. Excel begins the iteration and stops when it has found a solution, as shown in Figure 17.22.

FIGURE 17.22.

The solution to the iterative profit-sharing problem.

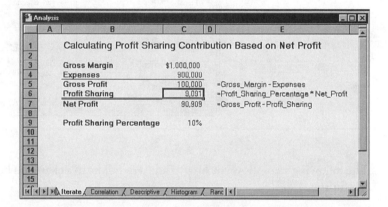

TIP

If you want to watch the progress of the iteration, turn on the **M**anual check box in the Calculation tab, and enter 1 in the Maximum It**e**rations text box. When you return to your worksheet, each time you press F9, Excel performs a single pass of the iteration.

NOTE

Excel's Solver utility is a powerful iterative method. See Chapter 19 for details.

Trend Analysis with Best-Fit Lines

Whether you're looking at stock prices, putting together a business plan, or setting up a budget, you need to analyze the overall trend of your data to get the big picture and to make short-term predictions.

Excel offers various tools for trend analysis, and this section explains a few of them. Specifically, you'll look at two methods that calculate the trend based on the *line of best-fit*. This is a straight line through the data points in which the differences between the points above and below the line cancel each other out (more or less). For example, in Figure 17.23, I've charted the worksheet sales figures, inserted a trendline, and extended the line into the next fiscal year. This line clearly shows the trend of the data and enables you to estimate future sales.

FIGURE 17.23.

A best-fit trendline.

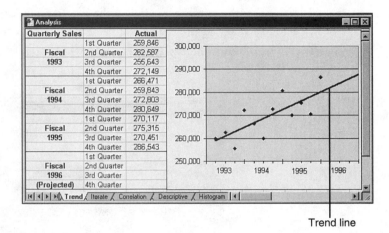

Trend line

The following steps show you how to add a trendline to a chart and how to extend the line into the future:

1. Activate the chart and select the data series you want to work with.

2. Either select the Insert | Trendline command or right-click on the series and choose Insert Trendline from the shortcut menu. Excel displays the Trendline dialog box.

3. In the Type tab, highlight the Trend type you want to use.

4. In the Options tab, use the Forward spinner to select the number of units you want to project the trendline into the future. (In the preceding example, I entered 4 to extend the trendline by four quarters.)

5. Select OK. Excel inserts the trendline and extends it into the future.

How accurate is such a prediction? A linear projection based on historical data assumes that the factors influencing the data over the historical period will remain constant. If this is a reasonable assumption in your case, the projection will be a reasonable one. Of course, the longer you extend the line, the more likely it is that some of the factors will change or that new ones will arise. As a result, best-fit extensions should be used only for short-term projections.

Extending a Series with the Fill Handle

If you prefer to see exact data points in your forecast, you can use the fill handle to project a best-fit line into the future. All you do is highlight the historical data and then drag the fill handle to extend the selection. Excel calculates the best-fit line from the existing data, projects this line into the new data, and calculates the appropriate values.

Figure 17.24 shows an example. Here, I've used the fill handle to project the quarterly sales figures over the next fiscal year. The accompanying chart clearly shows the extended best-fit line.

FIGURE 17.24.

Using the fill handle to project historical data into the future.

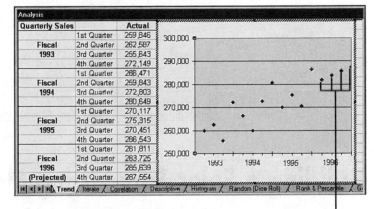

Projected values

Using the Series Command

You also can use the Series command to project a best-fit line. The following steps show you how it's done:

1. Select the range that includes both the historical data and the cells that will contain the projections (make sure that the projection cells are blank).
2. Select the **Edit | Fill | Series** command. Excel displays the Series dialog box.
3. Activate the AutoFill check box.
4. Select OK. Excel fills in the blank cells with the best-fit projection.

The Series command is also useful for producing the data that defines the full best-fit line so that you can see the trend. Follow the steps in this procedure:

1. Copy the historical data onto an adjacent row or column.
2. Select the range that includes both the copied historical data and the cells that will contain the projections (again, make sure that the projection cells are blank).
3. Select the **Edit | Fill | Series** command. Excel displays the Series dialog box.
4. Activate the **Trend** check box, and make sure that the **Linear** check box is also activated.
5. Select OK. Excel replaces the copied historical data with the best-fit numbers and projects the trend onto the blank cells.

Figure 17.25 shows a chart with the best-fit line on top of the historical data.

FIGURE 17.25.

A best-fit trend line created with the Series command.

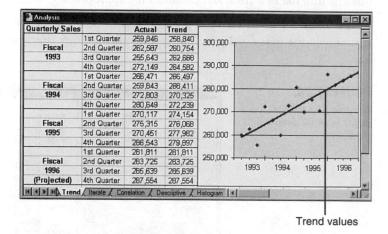

Quarterly Sales		Actual	Trend
	1st Quarter	259,846	258,840
Fiscal	2nd Quarter	262,587	260,754
1993	3rd Quarter	255,643	262,668
	4th Quarter	272,149	264,582
	1st Quarter	266,471	266,497
Fiscal	2nd Quarter	259,843	268,411
1994	3rd Quarter	272,803	270,325
	4th Quarter	280,649	272,239
	1st Quarter	270,117	274,154
Fiscal	2nd Quarter	275,315	276,068
1995	3rd Quarter	270,451	277,982
	4th Quarter	286,543	279,897
	1st Quarter	281,811	281,811
Fiscal	2nd Quarter	283,725	283,725
1996	3rd Quarter	285,639	285,639
(Projected)	4th Quarter	287,554	287,554

Trend values

Building a Sales Forecasting Model

In these complex and uncertain times, forecasting business performance is increasingly important. Today, more than ever, managers at all levels need to make intelligent predictions of future sales and profit trends as part of their overall business strategy. By forecasting sales six months, a year, or even three years down the road, managers can anticipate related needs such as employee acquisitions, warehouse space, and raw material requirements. Similarly, a profit forecast enables the planning of the future expansion of a company.

Business forecasting has been around for many years, and various methods have been developed—some more successful than others. The most common forecasting method is the qualitative "seat of the pants" approach, in which a manager (or a group of managers) estimates future trends based on experience and knowledge of the market. This method, however, suffers from an inherent subjectivity and a short-term focus, because many managers tend to extrapolate from recent experience and ignore the long-term trend. Other methods (such as averaging past results) are more objective but generally are useful for forecasting only a few months in advance.

This section presents a technique called *linear regression analysis*. Regression is a powerful statistical procedure that has become a popular business tool. In its general form, you use regression analysis to determine the relationship between a dependent variable (car sales, for example) and one or more independent variables (such as interest rates or disposable income). The worksheets we'll look at explore two relatively simple cases:

■ Sales as a function of time. Essentially, this case determines the trend over time of past sales and extrapolates the trend in a straight line to determine future sales.

■ Sales as a function of the season (in a business sense). Many businesses are seasonal; that is, their sales are traditionally higher or lower during certain periods of the fiscal year. Retailers, for example, usually have higher sales in the fall leading up to Christmas. If the sales for your business are a function of the season, you need to remove these seasonal biases to calculate the true underlying trend.

This section uses sales as an example; however, you can use this application to forecast expenses, profits, or any other quantity for which you have historical data.

About the Forecast Workbook

The Forecast workbook (which is available on the CD that comes with this book) contains the following eight worksheets:

Monthly Data: Use this worksheet to enter up to 10 years of monthly historical data. This worksheet also calculates the 12-month moving averages used by the Monthly Seasonal Index worksheet.

Monthly Seasonal Index: Calculates the seasonal adjustment factors (the seasonal indexes) for the monthly data.

Monthly Trend: Calculates the trend of the monthly historical data. Both a normal trend and a seasonally adjusted trend are computed.

Monthly Forecast: Derives a three-year monthly forecast based on both the normal trend and the seasonally adjusted trend.

Quarterly Data: Consolidates the monthly actuals into quarterly data and calculates the four-quarter moving average (used by the Quarterly Seasonal Index worksheet).

Quarterly Seasonal Index: Calculates the seasonal indexes for the quarterly data.

Quarterly Trend: Calculates the trend of the quarterly historical data. Both a normal trend and a seasonally adjusted trend are computed.

Quarterly Forecast: Derives a three-year quarterly forecast based on both the normal trend and the seasonally adjusted trend.

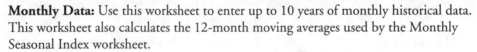

TIP

The Forecast workbook contains dozens of formulas. You'll probably want to switch to manual calculation mode when working with this file.

Entering Historical Data

The sales forecast workbook is driven entirely by the historical data you enter into the Monthly Data worksheet, shown in Figure 17.26. Use the Actual column to enter the data in the appropriate rows for each month.

FIGURE 17.26.

Use the Monthly Data worksheet to enter your historical data.

	A	B	C	D
1	Monthly Sales - Data		Actual	12-Month Moving Avg
2		January, 1985	90.0	-
3		February, 1985	95.0	-
4		March, 1985	110.0	-
5		April, 1985	105.0	-
6		May, 1985	100.0	-
7	1985	June, 1985	100.0	-
8		July, 1985	105.0	-
9		August, 1985	105.0	-
10		September, 1985	110.0	-
11		October, 1985	120.0	-
12		November, 1985	130.0	-
13		December, 1985	140.0	109.2
14		January, 1986	90.0	109.2
15		February, 1986	95.0	109.2

Monthly Data / Monthly Seasonal Index / Monthly Tre

NOTE

The worksheet shown in Figure 17.26 contains dummy data for illustration purposes. The version that comes on the CD has 1s in all the Actual cells.

Keep the following points in mind when working with this table:

- All cells are locked except for those in the Actual column. If you need to work with any other part of the sheet, you must unprotect it (by selecting the **T**ools | **P**rotection | Un**p**rotect Sheet command).

- The worksheet is set up to handle 10 years of data—from 1985 to 1994. If you'll be starting with a different year, begin with row two and change the year in cell A7. The other years (cells A19, A31, and so on) are derived from formulas. You therefore have to make only one change.

- The years displayed in column A are linked to various other cells in the workbook (including the cells in column B), so their format shouldn't be changed.

- If you'll be entering less than 10 years of data, you have to delete the moving average formulas that you don't need. If you don't, your seasonal index calculations will be wrong.

- If you add new historical data later, you can insert the corresponding moving average formulas by using the fill handle to fill down from one of the existing formulas.

Calculating a Normal Trend

As mentioned earlier, you can use FORECAST.XLS to calculate either a normal trend that treats all sales as a simple function of time or a deseasoned trend that takes seasonal factors into account. This section covers the normal trend.

All the trend calculations in FORECAST.XLS use a variation of Excel's TREND() function. TREND() calculates the best-fit line through your data; that is, the differences between the line and the actual data are minimized. The line takes the following general form:

y = mx + b

y is the dependent variable, *x* is the independent variable, and *m* and *b* represent the line's slope and y-intercept, respectively. In our case, the dependent variable is sales, and the independent variable is time.

Here's the syntax of the TREND() function:

TREND(***known_y's***, *known_x's, new_x's, const*)

known_y's	The range representing the known dependent variables. You'll be using the actual monthly sales you entered in the Monthly Data worksheet.
known_x's	The range or array representing the known independent variables. If you omit *known_x's,* Excel uses the array {1,2,3,...,*n*}, in which *n* is the number of cells in the ***known_y's*** range. You use this array when the independent variable is time. Our formulas therefore will omit the *known_x's.*
new_x's	A range or array representing the new independent variable values for which you want TREND() to calculate the corresponding dependent variable values. If you omit *new_x's,* Excel uses the same values as *known_x's.*
const	A logical value that determines whether the constant *b* is forced to equal 0. If *const* is True or omitted, *b* is calculated normally. If it's False, *b* is set to 0.

For example, suppose that you have a range named Actual that contains 12 months of sales data, and you're assuming that sales is dependent on time. You use the following formula to calculate a forecast value for the 13th month:

=TREND(Actual,,13)

Similarly, to calculate the trend of the existing data, you enter the following array formula in a range of 12 cells:

{=TREND(Actual)}

This formula is equivalent to the following formula:

{=TREND(Actual,,{1;2;3;4;5;6;7;8;9;10;11;12})}

Calculating the Monthly Trend

The preceding example is the basis for the Normal Trend calculation in the Monthly Trend worksheet, shown in Figure 17.27. This worksheet displays (in column B) a linked copy of the sales you entered in Monthly Data. Because the data is linked, you easily can update the Monthly Trend values whenever you make changes to the Monthly Data worksheet.

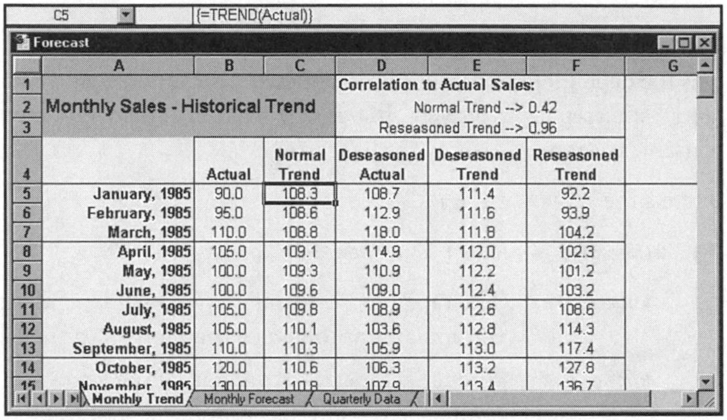

FIGURE 17.27.

The Monthly Trend worksheet.

		C5		{=TREND(Actual)}			
Forecast							
	A	B	C	D	E	F	G
1				Correlation to Actual Sales:			
2	Monthly Sales - Historical Trend			Normal Trend --> 0.42			
3				Reseasoned Trend --> 0.96			
4		Actual	Normal Trend	Deseasoned Actual	Deseasoned Trend	Reseasoned Trend	
5	January, 1985	90.0	108.3	108.7	111.4	92.2	
6	February, 1985	95.0	108.6	112.9	111.6	93.9	
7	March, 1985	110.0	108.8	118.0	111.8	104.2	
8	April, 1985	105.0	109.1	114.9	112.0	102.3	
9	May, 1985	100.0	109.3	110.9	112.2	101.2	
10	June, 1985	100.0	109.6	109.0	112.4	103.2	
11	July, 1985	105.0	109.8	108.9	112.6	108.6	
12	August, 1985	105.0	110.1	103.6	112.8	114.3	
13	September, 1985	110.0	110.3	105.9	113.0	117.4	
14	October, 1985	120.0	110.6	106.3	113.2	127.8	
15	November, 1985	130.0	110.8	107.9	113.4	136.7	

Monthly Trend / Monthly Forecast / Quarterly Data /

NOTE

You'll be using the values in the Monthly Data worksheet to calculate the trend, so technically you don't need the figures in column B. I included them, however, to make it easier to compare the trend and the actuals. Including the Actual values is also handy if you want to create a chart that includes these values.

To avoid entering dozens of linking formulas, I used a named range and an array. I defined the name Actual for the range of historical sales figures in the Monthly Data worksheet. I then selected the corresponding range in Monthly Trend and made the following entry as an array formula:

```
=Actual
```

Recall that you enter a formula as an array by pressing Ctrl-Shift-Enter; see Chapter 2 for more information.

NOTE

If you don't have enough data to fill in the entire 10-year range, you first must remove the existing array in Monthly Trend (because you can't change part of an existing array). To do this quickly, select a cell within the array, press Ctrl-/ to select the entire array, activate the formula bar, and then press Ctrl-Enter. Note that later you'll also have to use this method to remove the array in the Normal Trend column.

NOTE

If you make changes to the values in the Monthly Data worksheet, Excel won't automatically update the corresponding values in the Monthly Trend worksheet's Actual column (because you can't change part of an array). To update these values, select a cell within the array, press Ctrl-/ to select the entire array, activate the formula bar, and then press Ctrl-Shift-Enter to reenter the array.

After the data is in place, calculating the trend line for the historical sales requires three steps:

1. In the Normal Trend column, select the entire range that corresponds to the number of months of historical sales figures you've entered (C5:C124 if you filled in the entire 10-year range in the Monthly Data worksheet).

2. Type the following formula, but don't press Enter:

   `=TREND(Actual)`

3. Press Ctrl-Shift-Enter to enter the formula as an array.

To get some idea whether the trend is close to your data, cell F2 calculates the *correlation* between the trend values and the actual sales figures. (See Chapter 18, "Working with the Analysis Toolpak," to learn more about correlation.) A positive number signifies that the trend line approximates the sales direction; the closer the number is to 1, the better the approximation.

Calculating the Forecast Trend

As you saw earlier in this chapter, to get a sales forecast, you extend the historical trend line into the future. This is the job of the Monthly Forecast worksheet, shown in Figure 17.28.

FIGURE 17.28.

The Monthly Forecast worksheet.

		Normal Trend Forecast	Deseasoned Trend Forecast	Reseasoned Trend Forecast
	Monthly Sales - Forecast			
	January, 1995	138.2	134.8	111.6
	February, 1995	138.4	135.0	113.6
	March, 1995	138.7	135.2	126.0
	April, 1995	138.9	135.4	123.7
	May, 1995	139.2	135.6	122.3
1995	June, 1995	139.4	135.8	124.6
	July, 1995	139.7	136.0	131.1
	August, 1995	139.9	136.2	138.0
	September, 1995	140.2	136.4	141.7
	October, 1995	140.4	136.6	154.2
	November, 1995	140.7	136.8	164.8
	December, 1995	140.9	136.9	180.1
	January, 1996	141.2	137.1	113.5
	February, 1996	141.4	137.3	115.6

C2 =TREND(Actual,,ROWS(Actual)+ROW()-1)

Calculating a forecast trend is a little different from calculating a historical trend, because you have to specify the *new_x's* argument for the TREND() function. In this case, the *new_x's* are the sales periods in the forecast interval. For example, suppose that you have a 10-year period of monthly data from January 1985 to December 1994. This involves 120 periods of data. Therefore, to calculate the trend for January 1995 (the 121st period), you use the following formula:

```
=TREND(Actual,,121)
```

You use 122 as the *new_x's* argument for February 1995, 123 for March 1995, and so on.

The Monthly Forecast worksheet uses the following formula to calculate these *new_x's* values:

```
ROWS(Actual)+ROW()-1
```

ROWS(Actual) returns the number of sales periods in the Actual range in the Monthly Data worksheet. ROW()-1 is a trick that returns the number you need to add to get the forecast sales period. For example, the January 1995 forecast is in cell C2; therefore, ROW()-1 returns 1.

Calculating the Seasonal Trend

Many businesses experience predictable fluctuations in sales throughout their fiscal year. Resort operators see most of their sales during the summer months; retailers look forward to the Christmas season for the revenue that will carry them through the rest of the year. Figure 17.29 shows a sales chart for a company that experiences a large increase in sales during the fall.

FIGURE 17.29.

A sales chart for a company showing seasonal variations.

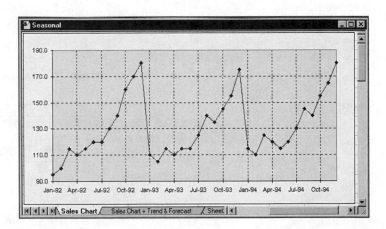

Because of the nonlinear nature of the sales in companies that see seasonal fluctuations, the normal trend calculation won't give an accurate forecast. You need to include seasonal variations in your analysis, which involves four steps:

1. For each month (or quarter), calculate a *seasonal index* that identifies seasonal influences.

2. Use these indexes to calculate seasonally adjusted (or *deseasoned*) values for each month.

3. Calculate the trend based on these deseasoned values.

4. Compute the true trend by adding the seasonal indexes to the calculated trend (from step 3).

The next few sections show how the Forecast workbook implements each step.

Computing the Monthly Seasonal Indexes

A *seasonal index* is a measure of how the average sales in a given month compare to a "normal" value. For example, if January has an index of 90, January's sales are (on average) only 90 percent of what they are in a normal month.

Therefore, you first must define what "normal" signifies. Because you're dealing with monthly data, you define normal as the 12-month moving average. (An *n*-month moving average is the average taken over the past *n* months.) The 12-Month Moving Avg column in the Monthly Data sheet uses a formula named `TwelveMonthMovingAvg` to handle this calculation. This is a relative range name, so its definition changes with each cell in the column. Figure 17.30 shows how the formula appears in the Define Name dialog box when cell D13 is selected. As you would expect, the formula calculates the average for the range C2:C13, or for the preceding 12 months.

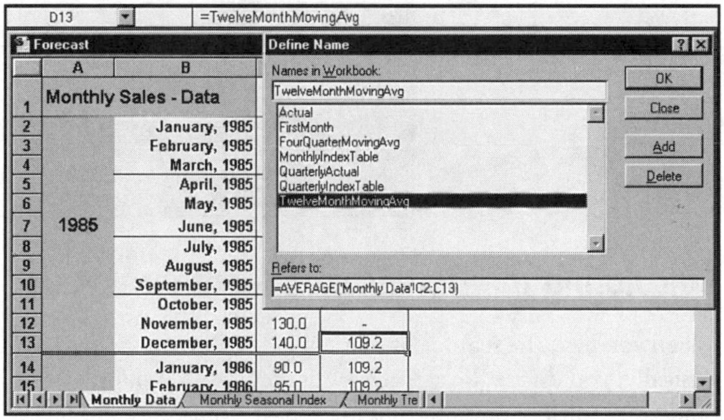

FIGURE 17.30.

The
`TwelveMonthMovingAvg`
named formula.

This moving average defines the "normal" value for any given month. The next step is to compare each month to the moving average. Do this by dividing each monthly sales figure by its corresponding moving-average calculation and multiplying by 100—which equals the sales *ratio* for the month. For example, the sales in December 1985 (cell C13) were 140.0, and the moving average is 109.2 (D13). Dividing C13 by D13 and multiplying by 100 returns a ratio of about 128. You can loosely interpret this to mean that the sales in December were 28 percent higher than the sales in a normal month.

To get an accurate seasonal index for December (or any month), however, you must calculate ratios for every December that you have historical data. Take an average of all these ratios to reach a true seasonal index (except for a slight adjustment, as you'll see).

The purpose of the Monthly Seasonal Index worksheet, shown in Figure 17.31, is to derive a seasonal index for each month. The worksheet's table calculates the ratios for every month over the span of the historical data. The Avg Ratio column then calculates the average for each month. To get the final values for the seasonal indexes, however, you need to make a small adjustment. The indexes should add up to 1200 (100 per month, on average) to be true percentages. As you can see in cell B15, however, the sum is 1214.0. This means that you have to reduce each average by a factor of 1.0116 (1214/1200). The Seasonal Index column does that, thereby producing the true seasonal indexes for each month.

FIGURE 17.31.

The Monthly Seasonal Index worksheet.

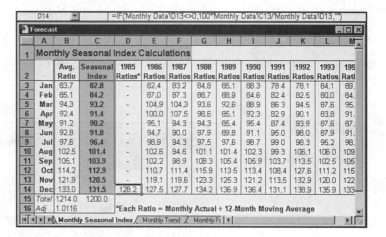

Calculating the Deseasoned Monthly Values

When you have the seasonal indexes, you need to put them to work to "level the playing field." Basically, you divide the actual sales figures for each month by the appropriate monthly index (and also multiply them by 100 to keep the units the same). This effectively removes the seasonal factors from the data (this process is called *deseasoning* or *seasonally adjusting* the data).

The Deseasoned Actual column in the Monthly Trend worksheet performs these calculations, as shown in Figure 17.32. Following is a typical formula (from cell D5):

```
=100*B5/INDEX(MonthlyIndexTable,MONTH(A5),3)
```

B5 refers to the sales figure in the Actual column, and `MonthlyIndexTable` is the range A3:C14 in the Monthly Seasonal Index worksheet. The `INDEX()` function finds the appropriate seasonal index for the month (given by the `MONTH(A5)` function).

FIGURE 17.32.

A calculation from the Monthly Trend worksheet.

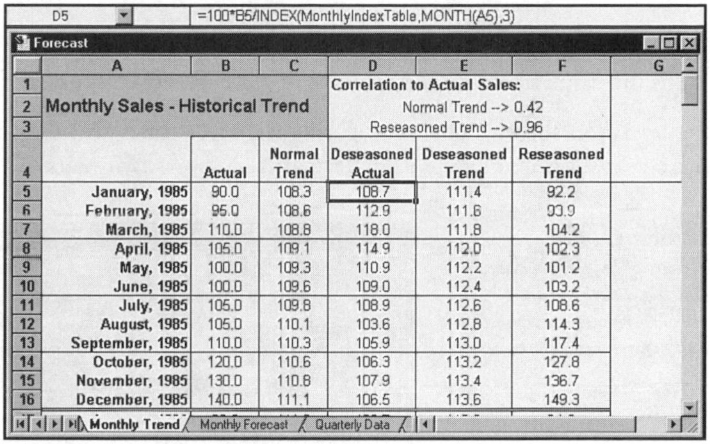

D5			=100*B5/INDEX(MonthlyIndexTable,MONTH(A5),3)			

Forecast

	A	B	C	D	E	F	G
1				Correlation to Actual Sales:			
2	Monthly Sales - Historical Trend			Normal Trend --> 0.42			
3				Reseasoned Trend --> 0.96			
4		Actual	Normal Trend	Deseasoned Actual	Deseasoned Trend	Reseasoned Trend	
5	January, 1985	90.0	108.3	108.7	111.4	92.2	
6	February, 1985	95.0	108.6	112.9	111.6	93.9	
7	March, 1985	110.0	108.8	118.0	111.8	104.2	
8	April, 1985	105.0	109.1	114.9	112.0	102.3	
9	May, 1985	100.0	109.3	110.9	112.2	101.2	
10	June, 1985	100.0	109.6	109.0	112.4	103.2	
11	July, 1985	105.0	109.8	108.9	112.6	108.6	
12	August, 1985	105.0	110.1	103.6	112.8	114.3	
13	September, 1985	110.0	110.3	105.9	113.0	117.4	
14	October, 1985	120.0	110.6	106.3	113.2	127.8	
15	November, 1985	130.0	110.8	107.9	113.4	136.7	
16	December, 1985	140.0	111.1	106.5	113.6	149.3	

Monthly Trend / Monthly Forecast / Quarterly Data

Calculating the Deseasoned Trend

The next step is to calculate the historical trend based on the new deseasoned values. The Deseasoned Trend column uses the following array formula to accomplish this task:

```
{=TREND('Monthly Trend'!DeseasonedActual)}
```

The name `DeseasonedActual` refers to the values in the Deseasoned Actual column.

Calculating the Reseasoned Trend

By itself, the deseasoned trend doesn't amount to much. To get the true historical trend, you need to add the seasonal factor back in to the deseasoned trend (this process is called *reseasoning* the data). The Reseasoned Trend column does the job with a formula similar to the one used in the Deseasoned Actual column:

```
=E5*INDEX(MonthlyIndexTable,MONTH(A5),3)/100
```

Calculating the Seasonal Forecast

To derive a forecast based on seasonal factors, combine the techniques you used to calculate a normal trend forecast and a reseasoned historical trend. In the Monthly Forecast worksheet (see Figure 17.28), the Deseasoned Trend Forecast column computes the forecast for the deseasoned trend:

```
=TREND('Monthly Trend'!DeseasonedTrend,,ROWS('Monthly Trend'!Deseasoned Trend)+
➥ROW()-1)
```

The Reseasoned Trend Forecast column adds the seasonal factors back in to the deseasoned trend forecast:

```
=D2*Index(MonthlyIndexTable,MONTH(B2),3)/100
```

D2 is the value from the Deseasoned Trend Forecast column, and B2 is the forecast month.

Figure 17.33 shows a chart comparing the actual sales and the reseasoned trend for the last three years of the sample data. The chart also shows two years of the reseasoned forecast.

FIGURE 17.33.

A chart of the sample data, which compares actual sales, the reseasoned trend, and the reseasoned forecast.

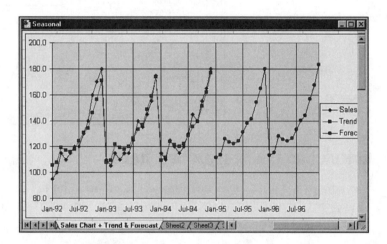

Working with Quarterly Data

If you prefer to work with quarterly data, the Quarterly Data, Quarterly Seasonal Index, Quarterly Trend, and Quarterly Forecast worksheets perform the same functions as their monthly counterparts. You don't have to reenter your data, because the Quarterly Data worksheet consolidates the monthly numbers by quarter.

Summary

This chapter showed you various Excel techniques for performing data analysis. You learned how to use data tables for what-if analysis, how to use Goal Seek and iteration, how to perform trend analysis with best-fit lines, and how to build a sales forecasting model using the TREND() function. Here are some related chapters to investigate:

- To learn more about entering and working with arrays and array formulas, read Chapter 2, "Building Better Formulas."

■ For more information on Excel's charting capabilities, check out Chapter 9, "Working with Chart Types," and Chapter 10, "Enhancing Charts."

■ Excel's Analysis Toolpak is chock-full of powerful analytic features. I'll tell you about them in Chapter 18, "Working with the Analysis Toolpak."

■ Solver is Excel's most sophisticated goal-seeking what-if tool. I'll show you how to use it in Chapter 19, "Solving Complex Problems with Solver."

■ You can store different combinations of worksheet variables as *scenarios* and then display these combinations with the click of a mouse. I'll show you how to get the most out of scenarios in Chapter 20, "Working with Scenarios."

Working with the Analysis Toolpak

18

Excel's Analysis Toolpak is a large collection of powerful statistical functions and commands. Most of these tools use advanced statistical techniques and were designed with only a limited number of technical users in mind. However, in this chapter, I'll discuss a few tools that do have general applications.

Loading the Analysis Toolpak

To use the tools and functions in the Analysis Toolpak, you need to load the add-in macro that makes them available to Excel. The following procedure takes you through the steps:

1. Select the **Tools | Add-Ins** command. Excel displays the Add-Ins dialog box.
2. Activate the Analysis Toolpak check box in the **Add-Ins Available** list.

> **NOTE**
>
> If you don't see an Analysis Toolpak check box in the **Add-Ins Available** list, you didn't install the Analysis Toolpak when you installed Excel. You need to run the Excel setup program and use it to install the Analysis Toolpak.

3. Select OK.

New Analysis Toolpak Functions

The Analysis Toolpak adds over 90 new functions to Excel's already impressive function list. The next few sections give you a rundown of each new function's name and arguments as well as a brief description of what the function does.

New Date Functions

The Analysis Toolpak features a half dozen new date functions, which I describe in a moment. The following is a summary of the various arguments used in the date functions:

basis   The day-count basis you want Excel to use. You have four options:

basis	*Day Count Basis*
0 (or omitted)	30 days per month and 360 days per year (U.S.).
1	The actual number of days per month and per year.
2	The actual number of days per month and 360 days per year.

3	The actual number of days per month and 365 days per year.
4	30 days per month and 360 days per year (European).

date	A date serial number.
days	The number of working days before or after *start_date*. Use a positive number to get a later date or a negative number to get an earlier date.
end_date	The ending date used in the calculation.
holidays	An array or a reference to a range of dates to exclude as work days (such as federal or state holidays).
months	The number of months from *start_date*. Use a positive number to get a date after *start_date* or a negative number to get a date before *start_date*.
return_type	A number that determines on what day the week begins:

return_type	*Week Begins On*
1	Sunday
2	Monday

start_date	The date from which you want to start the calculation.

EDATE(***start_date,months***)

Returns a date that is a given number of months before or after a specified date.

EOMONTH(***start_date,months***)

Returns a date for the last day of the month that is a given number of months before or after a specified date.

WORKDAY(***start_date,days***,*holidays*)

Returns a date that is a specified number of working days before or after a given date (excluding weekends).

NETWORKDAYS(***start_date,end_date***,*holidays*)

Returns the number of whole working days between two dates (weekends are excluded).

WEEKNUM(***date***,*return_type*)

Returns a number indicating where the specified date's week falls numerically during the year.

```
YEARFRAC(start_date,end_date,basis)
```

Calculates the fraction of a year represented by the number of days between two dates.

New Financial Functions

The Analysis Toolpak gives you access to over three dozen new financial functions, as outlined in the following list. Here's a summary of a few of the most common arguments used in these financial functions. (For another list of financial functions arguments, see Chapter 3, "Harnessing the Power of Excel's Worksheet Functions.")

basis	The day-count basis you want Excel to use. You have four options:

basis	Day Count Basis
0 (or omitted)	30 days per month and 360 days per year (U.S.).
1	The actual number of days per month and per year.
2	The actual number of days per month and 360 days per year.
3	The actual number of days per month and 365 days per year.
4	30 days per month and 360 days per year (European).

discount	The security's discount rate.
effect_rate	The effective annual interest rate.
first_coupon	The security's first coupon date.
first_interest	The security's first interest date.
frequency	The number of coupon payments per year.
guess	A number you guess is close to the result of XIRR. If omitted, *guess* is assumed to be 0.1 (10%).
investment	The amount invested in the security.
issue	The security's issue date.
last_interest	The security's last interest date.
maturity	The security's maturity date.
nominal_rate	The nominal annual interest rate.
npery	The number of compounding periods per year.
par	The security's par value.
pr	The security's price per $100 face value.

rate	The security's annual coupon rate or the interest rate on a loan.
redemption	The security's redemption value per $100 face value.
settlement	The security's settlement date.
yld	The security's annual yield.

ACCRINT(*issue,first_interest,settlement,rate*,par,*frequency*,basis)

Returns the accrued interest for a security that pays periodic interest.

ACCRINTM(*issue*,maturity,*rate*,par,basis)

Returns the accrued interest for a security that pays interest at maturity.

AMORDEGRC(*cost,date_purchased,first_period,salvage,period,rate,basis*)

Returns the depreciation for each accounting period (using the French accounting system). This function is the same as AMORLINC() (described forthwith), except that a depreciation coefficient is applied depending on the life of the assets.

AMORLINC(*cost,date_purchased,first_period,salvage,period,rate,basis*)

Returns the depreciation for each accounting period (using the French accounting system).

COUPDAYBS(*settlement,maturity,frequency*,basis)

Returns the number of days from the beginning of the coupon period to the settlement date.

COUPDAYS(*settlement,maturity,frequency*,basis)

Returns the number of days in the coupon period that includes the settlement date.

COUPDAYSNC(*settlement,maturity,frequency*,basis)

Returns the number of days from the settlement date to the next coupon date (that is, the difference between COUPDAYS() and COUPDAYSBS()).

COUPNCD(*settlement,maturity,frequency*,basis)

Returns the next coupon date after the settlement date.

COUPNUM(*settlement,maturity,frequency*,basis)

Returns the number of coupons payable between the settlement date and the maturity date, rounded up to the nearest whole coupon.

COUPPCD(*settlement,maturity,frequency*,basis)

Returns the previous coupon date before the settlement date.

CUMIPMT(*rate,nper,pv,start_period,end_period,type*)

Returns the cumulative interest paid on a loan between two periods.

CUMPRINC(*rate,nper,pv,start_period,end_period,type*)

Returns the cumulative principal paid on a loan between two periods.

DISC(*settlement,maturity,pr,redemption,basis*)

Returns the discount rate for a security.

DOLLARDE(*fractional_dollar,fraction*)

Converts a fractional dollar price (such as a stock quote) to a decimal dollar price.

DOLLARFR(*decimal_dollar,fraction*)

Converts a decimal dollar price to a fractional dollar price (such as a stock quote).

DURATION(*settlement,maturity,rate,yld,frequency,basis*)

Returns the Macauley annual duration of a security with periodic interest payments.

EFFECT(*nominal_rate,npery*)

Returns the effective annual interest rate for a loan, given the nominal annual interest rate and the number of compounding periods.

FVSCHEDULE(*principal,schedule*)

Returns the future value of an initial principal after applying a series of compound interest rates.

INTRATE(*settlement,maturity,investment,redemption,basis*)

Returns the interest rate for a fully invested security.

MDURATION(*settlement,maturity,rate,yld,frequency,basis*)

Returns the modified Macauley duration for a security with an assumed par value of $100.

NOMINAL(*effect_rate,npery*)

Returns the nominal annual interest rate given the effective annual interest rate and the number of compounding periods.

ODDFPRICE(*settlement,maturity,issue,first_coupon,rate,yld,redemption,frequency,*
➥*basis*)

Returns the price per $100 face value of a security with an odd (short or long) first period.

ODDFYIELD(*settlement,maturity,issue,first_coupon,rate,pr,redemption,frequency,*
➥*basis*)

Returns the yield of a security that has an odd (short or long) first period.

ODDLPRICE(*settlement,maturity,last_interest,rate,yld,redemption,frequency,basis*)

Returns the price per $100 face value of a security that has an odd (short or long) last period.

ODDLYIELD(*settlement,maturity,last_interest,rate,pr,redemption,frequency,basis*)

Returns the yield of a security that has an odd (short or long) last period.

PRICE(*settlement,maturity,rate,yld,redemption,frequency,basis*)

Returns the price per $100 face value of a security that pays periodic interest.

PRICEDISC(*settlement,maturity,discount,redemption,basis*)

Returns the price per $100 face value of a discounted security.

PRICEMAT(*settlement,maturity,issue,rate,yld,basis*)

Returns the price per $100 face value of a security that pays interest at maturity.

RECEIVED(*settlement,maturity,investment,discount,basis*)

Returns the amount received at maturity for a fully invested security.

TBILLEQ(*settlement,maturity,discount*)

Returns the bond-equivalent yield for a treasury bill.

TBILLPRICE(*settlement,maturity,discount*)

Returns the price per $100 face value for a treasury bill.

TBILLYIELD(*settlement,maturity,pr*)

Returns the yield for a treasury bill.

XIRR(*values,dates,guess*)

Returns the internal rate of return for a schedule of cash flows that is not necessarily periodic.

XNPV(*rate,values,dates*)

Returns the net present value for a schedule of cash flows that is not necessarily periodic.

YIELD(*settlement,maturity,rate,pr,redemption,frequency,basis*)

Returns the yield on a security that pays periodic interest.

YIELDDISC(*settlement,maturity,pr,redemption,basis*)

Returns the annual yield for a discounted security.

YEILDMAT(*settlement,maturity,issue,rate,pr,basis*)

Returns the annual yield of a security that pays interest at maturity.

New Math and Engineering Functions

The Analysis Toolpak adds a fistful of new math functions (over 50 in all), as detailed in the following list. Here's a summary of the arguments used in these functions:

from_unit	A measurement unit (for example, "mi" for mile).
i_num	The imaginary coefficient of a complex number.
inumber	A complex number expressed as text in $x + y$i or $x + y$j format.
n	An integer that specifies the order of a Bessel function.
number	A numeric value.
places	The number of characters to use.
real_num	The real coefficient of a complex number.
suffix	The suffix for the imaginary component of a complex number.
to_unit	A measurement unit (for example, "mi" for mile).
x	A numeric value.

BESSELI(***x***,***n***)

Returns the modified Bessel function $I_n(x)$, which is equivalent to the Bessel function J_n evaluated for purely imaginary arguments.

BESSELJ(***x***,***n***)

Returns the Bessel function $J_n(x)$.

BESSELK(***x***,***n***)

Returns the modified Bessel function $K_n(x)$, which is equivalent to the Bessel functions J_n and Y_n evaluated for purely imaginary arguments.

BESSELY(***x***,***n***)

Returns the Bessel function $Y_n(x)$ (also known as the Weber function or the Neumann function).

BIN2DEC(***number***)

Converts a binary number to its decimal equivalent.

BIN2HEX(***number***,*places*)

Converts a binary number to its hexadecimal equivalent.

BIN2OCT(***number***,*places*)

Converts a binary number to its octal equivalent.

COMPLEX(***real_num***,***i_num***,*suffix*)

Converts real and imaginary coefficients into a complex number of the form $x + y$i or $x + y$j.

`CONVERT(`***`number,from_unit,to_unit`***`)`

Converts a number from one measurement system (such as imperial) to a different system (such as metric). See the Excel Help system for a complete list of the strings you can use for the ***from_unit*** and ***to_unit*** arguments.

`DEC2BIN(`***`number`***`,places)`

Converts a decimal integer to its binary equivalent.

`DEC2HEX(`***`number`***`,places)`

Converts a decimal integer to its hexadecimal equivalent.

`DEC2OCT(`***`number`***`,places)`

Converts a decimal integer to its octal equivalent.

`DELTA(`***`number1`***`,number2)`

Checks two values to see if they are equal. Returns 1 if they're equal, 0 if they're not.

`ERF(`***`lower_limit`***`,upper_limit)`

Returns the error function integrated between a lower limit and an upper limit.

`ERFC(`***`x`***`)`

Returns the complementary error function integrated between *x* and infinity.

`FACTDOUBLE(`***`number`***`)`

Returns the double factorial of a number.

`GCD(`***`number1`***`,number2,...)`

Returns the greatest common divisor of two or more integers.

`GESTEP(`***`number`***`,step)`

Returns 1 if a number is greater than or equal to a specified step value; returns 0 otherwise.

`HEX2BIN(`***`number`***`,places)`

Converts a hexadecimal number to its binary equivalent.

`HEX2DEC(`***`number`***`,places)`

Converts a hexadecimal number to its decimal equivalent.

`HEX2OCT(`***`number`***`,places)`

Converts a hexadecimal number to its octal equivalent.

`IMABS(`***`inumber`***`)`

Returns the absolute value (modulus) of a complex number.

IMAGINARY(*inumber*)

Returns the imaginary coefficient of a complex number.

IMARGUMENT(*inumber*)

Returns the argument Φ, an angle expressed in radians, such that

IMCONJUGATE(*inumber*)

Returns the complex conjugate of a complex number.

IMCOS(*inumber*)

Returns the cosine of a complex number.

IMDIV(*inumber1,inumber2*)

Returns the quotient of two complex numbers.

IMEXP(*inumber*)

Returns the exponential of a complex number.

IMLN(*inumber*)

Returns the natural logarithm of a complex number.

IMLOG10(*inumber*)

Returns the common logarithm (base 10) of a complex number.

IMLOG2(*inumber*)

Returns the base-2 logarithm of a complex number.

IMPOWER(*inumber,number*)

Returns a complex number, raised to a power.

IMPRODUCT(*inumber1,inumber2,...*)

Returns the product of two or more complex numbers.

IMREAL(*inumber*)

Returns the real coefficient of a complex number.

IMSIN(*inumber*)

Returns the sine of a complex number.

IMSQRT(*inumber*)

Returns the square root of a complex number.

IMSUB(*inumber1*,*inumber2*)

Returns the difference between two complex numbers.

IMSUM(*inumber1*,*inumber2*,...)

Returns the sum of two or more complex numbers.

ISEVEN(*number*)

Returns TRUE if the number is even, FALSE if it's odd.

ISODD(*number*)

Returns TRUE if the number is odd, FALSE if it's even.

LCM(*number1*,number2,...)

Returns the least common multiple of two or more integers.

MROUND(*number*,*multiple*)

Returns a number rounded to the specified multiple.

MULTINOMIAL(*number1*,number2,...)

Returns the ratio of the factorial of a sum of numbers to the product of factorials.

OCT2BIN(*number*,places)

Converts an octal number to its binary equivalent.

OCT2DEC(*number*,places)

Converts an octal number to its decimal equivalent.

OCT2HEX(*number*,places)

Converts an octal number to its hexadecimal equivalent.

QUOTIENT(*numerator*,*denominator*)

Returns the integer portion of a division.

RANDBETWEEN(*bottom*,*top*)

Returns a random number between two specified numbers.

SERIESSUM(*x*,*n*,*m*,*coefficients*)

Returns the sum of a power series.

SQRTPI(*number*)

Returns the square root of *number**pi.

612

Analysis Toolpak Statistical Tools

When you load the Analysis Toolpak, the add-in inserts a new **D**ata Analysis command to Excel's **T**ools menu. This command displays the Data Analysis dialog box, shown in Figure 18.1. This dialog box gives you access to 19 new statistical tools that handle everything from an analysis of variance (anova) to a z-test.

FIGURE 18.1.

The Data Analysis dialog box contains 19 powerful statistical-analysis features.

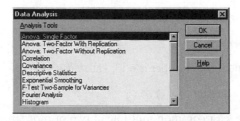

Here's a summary of what each statistical tool can do for your data:

Anova: Single Factor	A simple (that is, single-factor) analysis of variance. An analysis of variance (anova) tests the hypothesis that the means from several samples are equal. Excel 4.0 macro function equivalent: ANOVA1().
Anova: Two-Factor With Replication	An extension of the single-factor anova to include more than one sample for each group of data. Excel 4.0 macro function equivalent: ANOVA2().
Anova: Two-Factor Without Replication	A two-factor anova that doesn't include more than one sampling per group. Excel 4.0 macro function equivalent: ANOVA3().
Correlation	Returns the correlation coefficient: a measure of the relationship between two sets of data. Worksheet function equivalent: CORREL().
Covariance	Returns the average of the products of deviations for each data point pair. Covariance is a measure of the relationship between two sets of data. Worksheet function equivalent: COVAR().
Descriptive Statistics	Generates a report showing various statistics (such as median, mode, and standard deviation) for a set of data. Excel 4.0 macro function equivalent: DESCR().
Exponential Smoothing	Returns a predicted value based on the forecast for the prior period, adjusted for the error in that period. Excel 4.0 macro function equivalent: EXPON().

F-Test Two-Sample for Variances	Performs a two-sample F-test to compare two population variances. This tool returns the one-tailed probability that the variances in the two sets are not significantly different. Worksheet function equivalent: `FTEST()`.
Fourier Analysis	Performs a Fast Fourier Transform. You use Fourier Analysis to solve problems in linear systems and to analyze periodic data. Excel 4.0 macro function equivalent: `FOURIER()`.
Histogram	Calculates individual and cumulative frequencies for a range of data and a set of data bins. Excel 4.0 macro function equivalent: `HISTOGRAM()`.
Moving Average	Smoothes a data series by averaging the series values over a specified number of preceding periods. Excel 4.0 macro function equivalent: `MOVEAVG()`.
Random Number Generation	Fills a range with independent random numbers. Excel 4.0 macro function equivalent: `RANDOM()`.
Rank and Percentile	Creates a table containing the ordinal and percentage rank of each value in a set. Excel 4.0 macro function equivalent: `RANKPERC()`.
Regression	Performs a linear regression analysis that fits a line through a set of values using the least-squares method. Excel 4.0 macro function equivalent: `REGRESS()`.
Sampling	Creates a sample from a population by treating the input range as a population. Excel 4.0 macro function equivalent: `SAMPLE()`.
t-Test: Paired Two-Sample for Means	Performs a paired two-sample student's t-test to determine whether a sample's means are distinct. Excel 4.0 macro function equivalent: `PTTESTM()`.
t-test: Two-Sample Assuming Equal Variances	Performs a paired two-sample student's t-test, assuming the variances of both data sets are equal. Excel 4.0 macro function equivalent: `TTESTM()`.
t-test: Two-Sample Assuming Unequal Variances	Performs a paired two-sample student's t-test, assuming the variances of both data sets are unequal. Excel 4.0 macro function equivalent: `PTTESTV()`.
z-Test: Two-Sample Means	Performs a two-sample z-test for means with known for variances. Excel 4.0 macro function equivalent: `ZTESTM()`.

The next few sections look at five of these tools in more depth: Correlation, Descriptive Statistics, Histograms, Random Number Generation, and Rank and Percentile.

Determining the Correlation Between Data

Correlation is a measure of the relationship between two or more sets of data. For example, if you have monthly figures for advertising expenses and sales, you might wonder if they're related. That is, do higher advertising expenses lead to more sales?

To determine this, you need to calculate the *correlation coefficient.* The coefficient is a number between −1 and 1 that has the following properties:

Correlation Coefficient	Interpretation
1	The two sets of data are perfectly and positively correlated. For example, a 10 percent increase in advertising produces a 10 percent increase in sales.
Between 0 and 1	The two sets of data are positively correlated (an increase in advertising leads to an increase in sales). The higher the number the higher the correlation between the data.
0	There is no correlation between the data.
Between 0 and −1	The two sets of data are negatively correlated (an increase in advertising leads to a *decrease* in sales). The lower the number, the more negatively correlated the data.
−1	The data sets have a perfect negative correlation. For example, a 10 percent increase in advertising leads to a 10 percent decrease in sales (and, presumably, a new advertising department).

To calculate the correlation between data sets, follow these steps:

1. Select the **T**ools | **D**ata Analysis command. Excel displays the Data Analysis dialog box.

2. Highlight the Correlation option and then select OK. The Correlation dialog box, shown in Figure 18.2, appears.

FIGURE 18.2.

Use the Correlation dialog box to set up the correlation analysis.

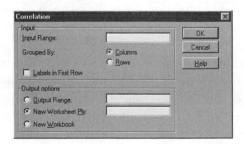

3. In the Input group, select the data range you want to analyze, including the row or column headings.

4. If you included labels in your range, make sure **L**abels In First Row is checked. (If your data is arranged in rows, this check box will say **L**abels In First Column.)

5. Excel displays the correlation coefficients in a table, so use the **O**utput Range box to enter a reference to the upper-left corner of the table. (If you're comparing two sets of data, the output range is three columns wide by three rows high.) You also can select a different sheet or workbook.

6. Select OK. Excel calculates the correlation and displays the table.

Figure 18.3 shows a worksheet that compares advertising expenses with sales. For a control, I've also included a column of random numbers. The Correlation table lists the various correlation coefficients. In this case, the high correlation between advertising and sales (0.74) means that these two factors are strongly (and positively) correlated. As you can see, there is (as you might expect) almost no correlation among the advertising, sales data, and the random numbers.

FIGURE 18.3.

The correlation between advertising expenses, sales, and a set of randomly generated numbers.

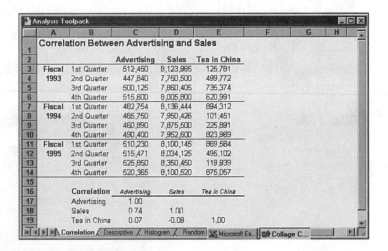

NOTE

The 1.00 values that run diagonally through the Correlation table signify that any set of data is always perfectly correlated to itself.

NOTE

To calculate a correlation without going through the Data Analysis dialog box, use the CORREL(*range1,range2*) function. This function returns the correlation coefficient for the data in the two ranges given by *range1* and *range2*. (You can use references, range names, numbers, or an array for the function arguments.)

Generating Descriptive Statistics

Excel has separate statistical functions for calculating values such as the mean, standard deviation, and maximum and minimum values of a sample. If you need to derive all of these basic analysis stats, entering all those functions can be a pain. Instead, use the Analysis Toolpak's Descriptive Statistics tool. This tool automatically calculates 16 of the most common statistical functions and lays them all out in a table. Follow the steps outlined forthwith.

> **NOTE**
>
> Keep in mind that the Descriptive Statistics tool outputs only numbers, not formulas. Therefore, if your data changes, you'll have to repeat the following steps to run the tool again.

1. Select the range that includes the data you want to analyze (including the row and column headings, if any).

2. Select the **T**ools | **D**ata Analysis command to display the Data Analysis dialog box.

3. Highlight the Descriptive Statistics option and select OK. Excel displays the Descriptive Statistics dialog box. Figure 18.4 shows the completed dialog box.

FIGURE 18.4.

Use the Descriptive Statistics dialog box to select the options you want to use for the analysis.

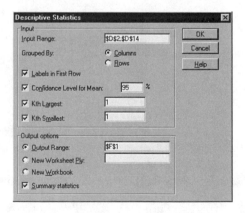

4. Use the Output options group to select a location for the output. For each set of data included in the input range, Excel creates a table that is two columns wide and up to 18 rows high.

5. Select the statistics you want to include in the output.

   ■ **S**ummary Statistics: Select this option to include statistics such as the mean, median, mode, standard deviation, and more.

- Kth Largest: Select this option to add a row to the output that specifies the *k*th largest value in the sample. The default value for *k* is 1 (that is, the largest value), but if you want to see any other number, enter a value for *k* in the text box.

- Kth Smallest: Select this option to include the sample's *k*th smallest value in the output. Again, if you want *k* to be something other than 1 (that is, the smallest value), enter a number in the text box.

- Confidence Level for Mean: Select this option if your data set is a sample of a larger population and you want Excel to calculate the confidence interval for the population mean. A confidence level of 95 percent means that you can be 95 percent confident that the population mean will fall within the confidence interval. For example, if the sample mean is 10 and Excel calculates a confidence interval of 1.5, you can be 95 percent sure that the population mean will fall between 8.5 and 11.5.

6. Select OK. Excel calculates the various statistics and displays the output table. See Figure 18.5 for an example.

FIGURE 18.5.

Use the Analysis Toolpak's Descriptive Statistics tool to generate the most common statistical measures for a sample.

	A	B	C	D	E	F	G	H
1		Defects Database					Defects	
2		Workgroup	Group Leader	Defects				
3		A	Johnson	8		Mean	10.17	
4		B	Perkins	10		Standard Error	1.75	
5		C	Perkins	0		Median	10.00	
6		D	Johnson	11		Mode	10.00	
7		E	Johnson	9		Standard Deviation	6.06	
8		F	Johnson	8		Sample Variance	36.70	
9		G	Perkins	11		Kurtosis	4.65	
10		H	Perkins	10		Skewness	1.40	
11		I	Perkins	7		Range	26.00	
12		J	Perkins	14		Minimum	0.00	
13		K	Johnson	10		Maximum	26.00	
14		L	Johnson	26		Sum	122.00	
15						Count	12.00	
16						Largest(1)	26.00	
17						Smallest(1)	0.00	
18						Confidence Level(95.0%)	3.85	
19								

Descriptive / Histogram / Random (Dice Roll) / Rank

Working with Histograms

The Analysis Toolpak's Histogram tool calculates the frequency distribution of a range of data. It also calculates cumulative frequencies for your data and produces a bar chart that shows the distribution graphically.

Before you use the Histogram tool, you need to decide which groupings (or *bins*) you want Excel to use for the output. These bins are numeric ranges, and the Histogram tool works by counting the number of observations that fall into each bin. You enter the bins as a range of numbers, where each number defines a boundary of the bin.

For example, Figure 18.6 shows a worksheet with two ranges. One is a list of student grades. The second range is the bin range. For each number in the bin range, Histogram counts the number of observations that are greater than or equal to the bin value, and less than (but *not* equal to) the next higher bin value. Therefore, in Figure 18.6, the six bin values correspond to the following ranges:

```
 0 <= Grade < 50
50 <= Grade < 60
60 <= Grade < 70
70 <= Grade < 80
80 <= Grade < 90
90 <= Grade < 100
```

FIGURE 18.6.

A worksheet set up to use the Histogram tool. Notice that you have to enter the bin range in ascending order.

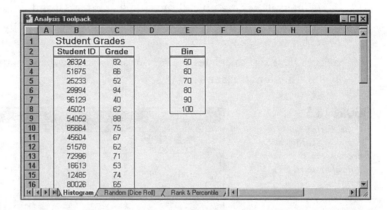

CAUTION

Make sure you enter your bin values in ascending order.

NOTE

How many bins should you use? The answer usually depends on the data. If you want to calculate the frequency distribution for a set of student grades, for example, you would probably set up six bin values (50, 60, 70, 80, 90, and 100). For less obvious distributions, you can use the following rule:

If n is the number of cells in the input range, enclose n between two successive powers of 2 and take the higher exponent to be the number of bins.

For example, if n is 100, you would use 7 bins, because 100 lies between 2^6 (64) and 2^7 (128). You also can use the following formula to calculate the number of bins:

```
=CEILING(LOG(COUNT(input_range),2),1)
```

Follow these steps to use the Histogram tool:

1. Select the **Tools** | **D**ata Analysis command. Excel displays the Data Analysis dialog box.

2. Highlight the Histogram option and then select OK. Excel displays the Histogram dialog box. Figure 18.7 shows the dialog box already filled in.

FIGURE 18.7.

Use the Histogram dialog box to select the options you want to use for the Histogram analysis.

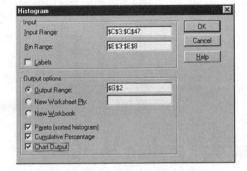

3. Use the **Input** Range and **B**in Range text boxes to enter the ranges holding your data and bin values, respectively.

4. Use the Output options group to select a location for the output. The output range will be one row taller than the bin range, and it could be up to six columns wide (depending on which of the following options you choose).

5. Select the other options you want to use for the frequency distribution:

   ■ **Pareto:** If you activate this check box, Excel displays a second output range with the bins sorted in order of descending frequency. (This is called a *Pareto distribution.*)

   ■ **Cum**ulative Percentage: If you activate this option, Excel adds a new column to the output that tracks the cumulative percentage for each bin.

   ■ **Chart Output:** If you select this option, Excel automatically generates a chart for the frequency distribution.

6. Select OK. Excel displays the histogram data, as shown in Figure 18.8.

NOTE

The problem with the Histogram tool's output is that there are no formulas linking the output to your data. If the data changes, you have to run the Histogram tool again. For simple frequency distributions, use the FREQUENCY(*data_range,bin_range*) function to set up a link between your data and the distribution output.

FIGURE 18.8.

The output of the Histogram tool.

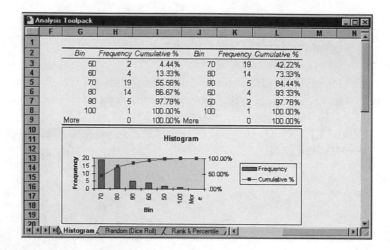

Generating Random Numbers

If you're using a worksheet to set up a simulation, you'll need realistic data on which to do your testing. You could make up the numbers, but it's possible you might skew the data unconsciously. A better approach is to use the Analysis Toolpak's Random Number Generation tool to generate the data for you.

Unlike the RAND() function, which generates only real numbers between 0 and 1, the Random Number Generation tool can produce numbers in any range and can generate different distributions, depending on the application. Table 18.1 summarizes the seven available distribution types.

Table 18.1. The distributions available with the Random Number Generation tool.

Distribution	Description
Uniform	Generates numbers with equal probability from the range of values you provide. Using the range 0 to 1 produces the same distribution as the RAND() function.
Normal	Produces numbers in a bell curve (normal) distribution based on the mean and standard deviation you enter. This is good for generating samples of things such as test scores and population heights.
Bernoulli	Generates a random series of 1's and 0's based on the probability of success on a single trial. A common example of a Bernoulli distribution is a coin toss (in which the probability of success is 50 percent; in this case, as in all Bernoulli distributions, you would have to assign either heads or tails to be 1 or 0).

Binomial	Generates random numbers characterized by the probability of success over a number of trials. For example, you could use this type of distribution to model the number of responses received for a direct mail campaign. The probability of success would be the average (or projected) response rate, and the number of trials would be the number of mailings in the campaign.
Poisson	Generates random numbers based on the probability of a designated number of events occurring in a time frame. The distribution is governed by a value, **Lambda**, that represents the mean number of events known to occur over the time frame.
Patterned	Generates random numbers according to a pattern that's characterized by a lower and upper bound, a step value, and a repetition rate for each number and the entire sequence.
Discrete	Generates random numbers from a series of values and probabilities for these values (in which the sum of the probabilities equals 1). You could use this distribution to simulate the rolling of dice (where the values would be 1 through 6, each with a probability of 1/6; see the following example).

Follow the steps outlined in the following procedure to use the Random Number Generation tool.

NOTE

If you'll be using a Discrete distribution, be sure to enter the appropriate values and probabilities before starting the Random Number Generation tool.

1. Select the **T**ools | **D**ata Analysis command to display the Data Analysis dialog box.
2. Highlight the Random Number Generation option and then select OK. The Random Number Generation dialog box appears, as shown in Figure 18.9.
3. If you want to generate more than one set of random numbers, enter the number of sets (or variables) you need in the Number Of **V**ariables box. Excel enters each set in a separate column. If you leave this box blank, Excel uses the number of columns in the **O**utput Range.
4. Use the Number Of Random Num**b**ers text box to enter how many random numbers you need. Excel enters each number in a separate row. If you leave this box blank, Excel fills the **O**utput Range.
5. Use the **D**istribution drop-down list to select the distribution you want to use.

FIGURE 18.9.

Use the Random Number Generation dialog box to set up the options for your random numbers.

6. In the Parameters group, enter the appropriate parameters for the distribution you selected.

7. The **R**andom Seed number is the value Excel uses to generate the random numbers. If you leave this box blank, Excel generates a different set each time. If you enter a value (which must be an integer between 1 and 32,767), you can reuse the value later to reproduce the same set of numbers.

8. Use the Output options group to select a location for the output.

9. Select OK. Excel calculates the random numbers and displays them in the worksheet.

NOTE

You also can use the Excel 4.0 macro function RANDOM() to generate random numbers from a macro. The function arguments are the same as those you enter into the Random Number Generation dialog box.

As an example, Figure 18.10 shows a worksheet that is set up to simulate rolling two dice. The Probabilities box shows the values (the numbers 1 through 6) and their probabilities (=1/6 for each). A Discrete distribution is used to generate the two numbers in cells H2 and H3. The Discrete distribution's Value and Probability Input Range parameter is the range $D$2:$E$7. Figure 18.11 shows the formulas used to display Die #1. (The formulas for Die #2 are similar, except that $H$2 is replaced with $H$3.)

NOTE

The die markers in Figure 18.10 were generated using a 24-point Wingdings font.

FIGURE 18.10.

A worksheet that simulates the rolling a pair of dice.

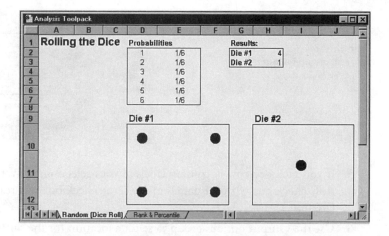

FIGURE 18.11.

The formulas used to display Die #1.

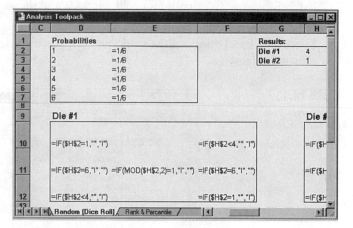

Working with Rank and Percentile

If you need to rank data, use the Analysis Toolpak's Rank And Percentile tool. This command not only ranks your data from first to last, but it also calculates the percentile—the percentage of items in the sample that are at the same or a lower level than a given value. Follow the steps in the following procedure to use the Rank and Percentile tool:

1. Select the Tools | Data Analysis command to display the Data Analysis dialog box.
2. Highlight the Rank and Percentile option and then select OK. Excel displays the Rank and Percentile dialog box, shown in Figure 18.12.
3. Use the Input Range text box to enter a reference for the data you want to rank.
4. Select the appropriate Grouped By option (Columns or Rows).

FIGURE 18.12.

*Use the Rank and
Percentile dialog box to
select the options you want
to use for the analysis.*

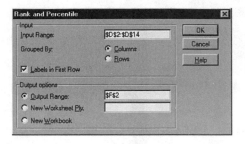

5. If you included row or column labels in your selection, activate the **L**abels in First Row check box. (If your data is in rows, the check box will read **L**abels in First Column.)

6. Use the Output options group to select a location for the output. For each sample, Excel displays a table that is four columns wide and the same height as the number of values in the sample.

7. Select OK. Excel calculates the results and displays them in a table similar to the one shown in Figure 18.13.

FIGURE 18.13.

*Sample output from the
Rank and Percentile tool.*

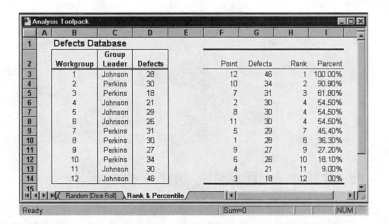

NOTE

Use the RANK(*number*,*ref*,*order*) function to calculate the rank of a *number* in the range *ref*. If *order* is 0 or omitted, Excel ranks *number* as though *ref* was sorted in descending order. If *order* is any nonzero value, Excel ranks *number* as though *ref* was sorted in ascending order.

For the percentile, use the PERCENTRANK(*range*,*x*,*significance*) function, where *range* is a range or array of values, *x* is the value of which you want to know the percentile, and *significance* is the number of significant digits in the returned percentage. (The default is 3.)

Summary

This chapter took you on a tour of Excel's Analysis Toolpak add-in. We looked at the impressive array of date, financial, math, and engineering functions that the Analysis Toolpak brings to Excel's table, and we also examined the statistical tools that let you perform powerful data-analysis operations. Here are some references to chapters that provide related information:

- To learn more about entering and working with arrays and array formulas, read Chapter 2, "Building Better Formulas."

- When you load the Analysis Toolpak, the add-in makes all the new functions available to the Function Wizard. For details on using the Function Wizard to construct functions, see Chapter 3, "Harnessing the Power of Excel's Worksheet Functions."

- I examined a number of other analytical techniques in Chapter 17, "Basic Analytic Methods."

Solving Complex Problems with Solver

19

IN THIS CHAPTER

In Chapter 17, "Basic Analytic Methods," you learned how to use Goal Seek to find solutions to formulas by changing a single variable. Unfortunately, most problems in business and science aren't so easy. You'll usually face formulas with at least two and sometimes dozens of variables. Often a problem will have more than one solution, and your challenge will be to find the *optimal* solution (that is, the one that maximizes profit, or minimizes costs, or matches another criteria). For these bigger challenges, you need a more muscular tool. Excel has just the answer: Solver. Solver is a sophisticated optimization program that enables you to find the solutions to complex problems that would otherwise require high-level mathematical analysis. This chapter introduces you to Solver (a complete discussion would require a book in itself) and takes you through a few examples.

Some Background on Solver

Problems such as "What product mix will maximize profit?" or "What transportation routes will minimize shipping costs while meeting demand?" traditionally have been solved by numerical methods such as *linear programming* and *nonlinear programming*. An entire mathematical field—*operations research*—has been developed to handle such problems, which are found in all kinds of disciplines. The drawback to linear and nonlinear programming is that solving even the simplest problem by hand is a complicated, arcane, and time-consuming business. In other words, it's a perfect job to slough off on a computer.

This is where Solver comes in. Solver incorporates many of the algorithms from operations research, but it keeps the sordid details in the background. All you do is fill out a dialog box or two, and Solver does the rest (the hard part).

The Advantages of Solver

Solver, like Goal Seek, uses an iterative method to perform its magic. This means that Solver tries a solution, analyzes the results, tries another solution, and so on. However, this cyclic iteration isn't just guesswork on Solver's part. The program looks at how the results change with each new iteration and, through some sophisticated mathematical trickery, it can tell (usually) in what direction it should head for the solution.

However, the fact that Goal Seek and Solver are both iterative doesn't make them equal. In fact, Solver brings a number of advantages to the table:

■ Solver enables you to specify multiple adjustable cells. You can use up to 200 adjustable cells in all.

■ Solver enables you to set up *constraints* on the adjustable cells. For example, you can tell Solver to find a solution that not only maximizes profit, but that also satisfies certain conditions, such as achieving a gross margin between 20 percent and 30 percent or keeping expenses under $100,000. These conditions are said to be *constraints* on the solution.

■ Solver seeks not only a desired result (the "goal" in Goal Seek) but also the optimum one. This means you can find a solution that is the maximum or minimum possible.

■ For complex problems, Solver can generate multiple solutions. You then can save these different solutions under different scenarios. (See Chapter 20, "Working with Scenarios," to learn how to use Excel's scenarios.)

When Do You Use Solver?

Solver is a powerful tool that isn't needed by most Excel users. It would be overkill, for example, to use Solver to compute net profit given fixed revenue and cost figures. Many problems, however, require nothing less than the Solver approach. These problems cover many different fields and situations, but they all have the following characteristics in common:

■ They have a single *target cell* that contains a formula you want to maximize, minimize, or set to a specific value. This formula could be a calculation, such as total transportation expenses or net profit.

■ The target cell formula contains references to one or more *changing cells* (also called *unknowns* or *decision variables*). Solver adjusts these cells to find the optimal solution for the target cell formula. These changing cells might include items such as units sold, shipping costs, or advertising expenses.

■ Optionally, there are one or more *constraint cells* that must satisfy certain criteria. For example, you might require that advertising be less than 10 percent of total expenses, or that the discount to customers be a number between 40 percent and 60 percent.

What types of problems exhibit these kinds of characteristics? A surprisingly broad range, as the following list shows:

The transportation problem: This problem involves minimizing shipping costs from multiple manufacturing plants to multiple warehouses while meeting demand.

The allocation problem: This problem requires minimizing employee costs while maintaining appropriate staffing requirements.

The product mix problem: This problem requires generating the maximum profit with a mix of products, while still meeting customer requirements. You solve this problem when you sell multiple products with different cost structures, profit margins, and demand curves.

The blending problem: This problem involves manipulating the materials used for one or more products to minimize production costs, meet consumer demand, and maintain a minimum level of quality.

Linear algebra: This problem involves solving sets of linear equations.

Loading Solver

Solver is an add-in to Microsoft Excel, so you'll need to load Solver before you can use it. The following procedure takes you through the steps necessary to load Solver:

1. Select the **Tools | Add-Ins** command. Excel displays the Add-Ins dialog box.
2. Activate the Solver Add-In check box in the **Add-Ins** Available list.

> **NOTE**
>
> If you don't see a Solver Add-In check box in the **Add-ins** Available list, you didn't install Solver when you installed Excel. You need to run the Excel setup program and use it to install the Solver add-in.

3. Select OK. Excel adds a Solver command to the **Tools** menu.

Using Solver

So that you can see how Solver works, I'll show you an example. In Chapter 17, you used Goal Seek to compute the break even point for a new product. (Recall that the break even point is the number of units that need to be sold to produce a profit of 0). I'll extend this analysis by computing the break even for two products: a Finley sprocket and a Langstrom wrench. The goal is to compute the number of units to sell for both products so that the total profit is 0.

The most obvious way to proceed is to use Goal Seek to determine the break even points for each product separately. Figure 19.1 shows the results.

FIGURE 19.1.

The break even points for two products (using separate Goal Seek calculations on the Product Profit cells).

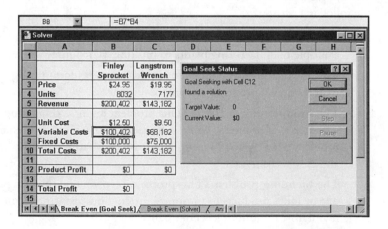

This method works, but the problem is that the two products don't exist in a vacuum. For example, there will be cost savings associated with each product because of joint advertising campaigns, combined shipments to customers (larger shipments usually mean better freight rates), and so on. To allow for this, you need to reduce the cost for each product by a factor related to the number of units sold by the other product. In practice, this would be difficult to estimate, but to keep things simple, I'll use the following assumption: the costs for each product are reduced by one dollar for every unit sold of the other product. For instance, if the Langstrom wrench sells 10,000 units, the costs for the Finley sprocket are reduced by $10,000. I'll make this adjustment in the Variable Costs formula. For example, the formula that calculates Variable Costs for the Finley sprocket (cell B8) becomes the following:

```
=B4*B7 - C4
```

Similarly, the formula that calculates Variable Costs for the Langstrom wrench (cell C8) becomes the following:

```
=C4*C7 - B4
```

By making this change, you move out of Goal Seek's territory. The Variable Costs formulas now have two variables: the units sold for the Finley sprocket and the units sold for the Langstrom wrench. I've changed the problem from one of two single-variable formulas, which are easily handled (individually) by Goal Seek, to a single formula with two variables—which is the terrain of Solver.

To see how Solver handles such a problem, follow the steps outlined in the following procedure:

1. Select the **Tools** | Solver command. Excel displays the Solver Parameters dialog box.
2. In the Set Target Cell text box, enter a reference to the target cell—that is, the cell with the formula you want to optimize. In the example, you would enter B14.
3. In the Equal to section, activate the appropriate option button. Select **Max** to maximize the target cell, **Min** to minimize it, or **Value** of to solve for a particular value (in which case you also need to enter the value in the text box provided). In the example, you would activate **Value** of and enter 0 in the text box.
4. Use the **B**y Changing Cells box to enter the cells you want Solver to change while it looks for a solution. In the example, you would enter B4,C4. See Figure 19.2.

TIP

The **G**uess button enters into the **B**y Changing Cells text box all the nonformula cells referenced by the target cell's formula.

NOTE

You can enter a maximum of 200 changing cells.

FIGURE 19.2.

Use the Solver Parameters dialog box to set up the problem for Solver.

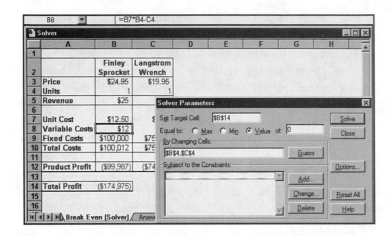

5. Select **S**olve. (I discuss constraints and other Solver options in the next few sections.) Solver works on the problem and then displays the Solver Results dialog box, which tells you whether or not it found a solution. (See the section later in this chapter titled "Making Sense of Solver's Messages.")

6. If Solver found a solution that you want to use, activate the **K**eep Solver Solution option and then select OK. If you don't want to accept the new numbers, select Restore **O**riginal Values and select OK or just click Cancel. (To learn how to save a solution as a scenario, see the section later in this chapter titled "Saving a Solution as a Scenario.")

Figure 19.3 shows the results for the example. As you can see, Solver has produced a Total Profit of 0 by running one product (the Langstrom wrench) at a slight loss and the other at a slight profit. While this is certainly a solution, it's not really the one you want. Ideally, for a true break even analysis, both products should end up with a Product Profit of 0. The problem is that we didn't tell Solver that was the way you wanted the problem solved. In other words, we didn't set up any *constraints*.

FIGURE 19.3.

When Solver finishes its calculations, it displays a completion message and enters the solution (if it found one) into the worksheet cells.

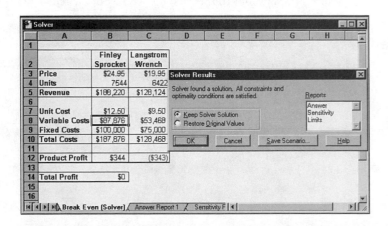

Adding Constraints

The real world puts restrictions and conditions on formulas. A factory might have a maximum capacity of 10,000 units a day; the number of employees in a company might have to be a number greater than or equal to zero (negative employees would really reduce staff costs, but nobody has been able to figure out how to do it yet); your advertising costs might be restricted to 10 percent of total expenses. All these are examples of what Solver calls *constraints*. Adding constraints tells Solver to find a solution so that these conditions are not violated.

To find the best solution for the break even analysis, you need to tell Solver to optimize both Product Profit formulas to 0. The following steps show you how to do this:

> **NOTE**
>
> If Solver's completion message is still on-screen from the last section, select Cancel to return to the worksheet without saving the solution.

1. Select the **T**ools | Solver command to display the Solver Parameters dialog box. Solver reinstates the options you entered the last time you used Solver.

2. To add a constraint, select the **A**dd button. Excel displays the Add Constraint dialog box.

3. In the Cell **R**eference box, enter the cell you want to constrain. For the example, you would enter cell B12 (the Product Profit formula for the Finley sprocket).

4. The drop-down list in the middle of the dialog box contains several comparison operators for the constraint. The available operators are less than or equal to (<=), equal to (=), greater than or equal to (>=), and integer (int). (Use the integer operator when you need a constraint, such as total employees, to be an integer value instead of a real number.) Select the appropriate operator for your constraint. For the example, select the equal to operator (=).

5. In the **C**onstraint box, enter the value by which you want to restrict the cell. For the example, enter 0. See Figure 19.4.

FIGURE 19.4.

Use the Add Constraint dialog box to specify the constraints you want to place on the solution.

6. If you want to enter more constraints, select the **A**dd button and repeat steps 3 through 5. For the example, you also need to constrain cell C12 (the Product Profit formula for the Langstrom wrench) so that it, too, equals 0. When you're done, select

OK to return to the Solver Parameters dialog box. Excel displays your constraints in the Subject to the Constraints list box.

NOTE

You can add a maximum of 100 constraints.

---

7. Select **S**olve. Solver again tries to find a solution, but this time it uses your constraints as guidelines.

TIP

If you need to make a change to a constraint before you begin solving, highlight the constraint in the Subject to the Constraints list box, select the **C**hange button, and then make your adjustments in the Change Constraint dialog box that appears. If you want to delete a constraint you no longer need, highlight it and select the **D**elete button.

Figure 19.5 shows the results of the break even analysis after adding the constraints. As you can see, Solver was able to find a solution in which both Product Margins are 0.

FIGURE 19.5.

The solution to the break even analysis after adding the constraints.

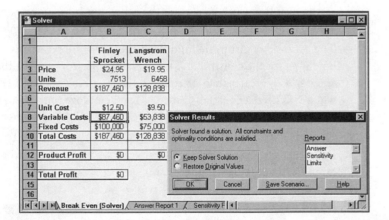

Saving a Solution as a Scenario

If Solver finds a solution, you can save the changing cells as a scenario that you can display at any time. (See Chapter 20 to learn how to work with Excel's scenarios.) Use the steps in the following procedure to save a solution as a scenario:

1. Select the **T**ools | Sol**v**er command to display the Solver Parameters dialog box.

2. Enter the appropriate target cell, changing cells, and constraints, if necessary.

3. Select **S**olve to begin solving.

4. If Solver finds a solution, select the **S**ave Scenario button in the Solver Results dialog box. Excel displays the Save Scenario dialog box, shown in Figure 19.6.

FIGURE 19.6.

Use the Save Scenario dialog box to save the current Solver solution as a scenario.

5. Use the Scenario Name text box to enter a name for the scenario.

6. Select OK. Excel returns you to the Solver Results dialog box.

7. Keep or discard the solution, as appropriate.

Setting Other Solver Options

Most Solver problems should respond to the basic target cell/changing cell/constraint cell model you've looked at so far. However, if you're having trouble getting a solution for a particular model, Solver has a number of options that might help. Start Solver and, in the Solver Parameters dialog box, select the **O**ptions button to display the Solver Options dialog box, shown in Figure 19.7.

FIGURE 19.7.

The Solver Options dialog box controls how Solver solves a problem.

Controlling Solver

The following options control how Solver works:

Max **T**ime	The amount of time Solver takes is a function of the size and complexity of the model, the number of changing cells and constraint cells, and the other Solver options you've chosen. If you find that Solver runs out of time before finding a solution, increase the number in this text box.

CAUTION

Integer programming (where you have integer constraints) can take a long time because of the complexity involved in finding solutions that satisfy exact integer constraints. If you find your models taking an abnormally long time to solve, increase the value in the Tolerance box to get an approximate solution. (See "Tolerance" in the following list.)

Iterations	This box controls the number of iterations Solver tries before giving up on a problem. Increasing this number gives Solver more of a chance to solve the problem, but it will take correspondingly longer.
Precision	This number determines how close a constraint cell must be to the constraint value you entered before Solver declares the constraint satisfied. The higher the precision (that is, the lower the number), the more accurate the solution (and the longer it takes Solver to find it).
Tolerance	If you have integer constraints, this box determines what percentage of the integer Solver has to be within before declaring the constraint satisfied. For example, if the integer tolerance is set to 0.05 percent, Solver will declare a cell with the value 99.95, to be close enough to 100 to declare it an integer.
Assume Linear Model	In the simplest possible terms, a *linear model* is one in which the variables are not raised to any powers and none of the so-called *transcendent* functions—such as SIN() and COS()—are used. They're called linear models because they can be charted as straight lines. If your formulas are linear, make sure that this check box is activated, because this will greatly speed up the solution process.
Show Iteration Results	Select this option to have Solver pause and show you its trial solutions. To resume, select Continue from the Show Trial Solution dialog box that appears.
Use Automatic Scaling	Select this check box if your model has changing cells that are significantly different in magnitude. For example, you might have a changing cell that controls customer discount (a number between 0 and 1) and sales (a number that might be in the millions).

Selecting the Method Used by Solver

The options in the Estimates, Derivatives, and Search groups at the bottom of the dialog box control the method used by Solver. The default options perform the job in the vast majority of cases. However, here is a quick rundown of the options, in case you need them:

Estimates	These two options determine how Solver obtains its initial estimates of the model variables. The Tangent option is the default, and you need to select **Q**uadratic only if your model is highly nonlinear.
Derivatives	Some models require Solver to calculate partial derivatives. These two options specify the method Solver uses to do this. **F**orward differencing is the default method. The **C**entral differencing method takes longer than forward differencing, but you might want to try it when Solver reports that it can't improve a solution. (See the section later in this chapter titled "Making Sense of Solver's Messages.")
Search	When finding a solution, Solver starts with the initial values in the model and then must decide which direction to take to adjust the variables. These options determine the method Solver uses to make this decision. The default **N**ewton option tells Solver to use a quasi-Newton search method. This method uses more memory, but it's faster than the Conjugate method, which uses a conjugate gradient search. Usually you'll need to select **C**onjugate only for large models in which memory is at a premium.

Working with Solver Models

Excel attaches your most recent Solver parameters to the worksheet when you save it. If you would like to save different sets of parameters, you can do so by following these steps:

1. Select the **T**ools | Sol**v**er command to display the Solver Parameters dialog box.
2. Enter the parameters you want to save.
3. Select the **O**ptions button to display the Solver Options dialog box.
4. Enter the options you want to save.
5. Select the **S**ave Model button. Solver displays the Save Model dialog box to prompt you to enter a range in which to store the model. See Figure 19.8.

FIGURE 19.8.

Enter a location for the model.

6. You don't need to specify the entire area, just the first cell. Keep in mind that Solver displays the data in a column, so pick a cell with enough empty space below it to hold all the data. You'll need one cell for the target cell reference, one for the changing cells, one for each constraint, and one to hold the array of Solver options.

7. Select OK. Solver gathers the data, enters it into your selected range, and then returns you to the Solver Options dialog box.

Figure 19.9 shows an example of a saved model (the range F3:F7). I've changed the worksheet view to show formulas and added some explanatory text so you can see exactly how Solver saves the model. Notice how the formula for the target cell (F3) includes both the target (B14) and the target value (=0).

FIGURE 19.9.

A saved Solver model.

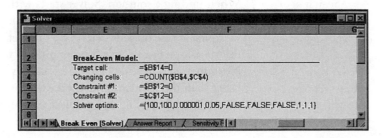

To use your saved settings, select the **Load Model** button from the Solver Options dialog box, enter the range containing the settings in the Load Model dialog box, and then select OK.

Making Sense of Solver's Messages

When Solver finishes its calculations, it displays the Solver dialog box and a message that tells you what happened. Some of these messages are straightforward, but others are more than a little cryptic. This section looks at the most common messages and gives their translations.

If Solver found a solution successfully, you'll see one of the following messages:

> `Solver found a solution. All constraints and optimality conditions are satisfied.`
> This is the message you hope to see. It means that the value you wanted for the target cell has been found, and Solver was able to find the solution while meeting your constraints within the precision and integer tolerance levels you set.

`Solver has converged to the current solution. All constraints are satisfied.`
Solver normally assumes it has a solution if the value of the target cell formula remains virtually unchanged during a few iterations. This is called *converging to a solution.* Such is the case with this message, but it doesn't necessarily mean that Solver has found a solution. It may be that the iterative process is just taking a long time or that the initial values in the changing cells were set too far from the solution. You should try re-running Solver with different values. You also can try using a higher precision setting (that is, entering a smaller number in the **P**recision text box).

If Solver didn't find a solution, you'll see one of the following messages telling you why:

`Solver cannot improve the current solution. All constraints are satisfied.` This message tells you that Solver has found a solution, but it may not be the optimal one. Try setting the precision to a smaller number or using the central differencing method for partial derivatives.

`The Set Cell values do not converge.` This means that the value of the target cell formula has no finite limit. For example, if you're trying to maximize profit based on product price and unit costs, Solver won't find a solution; the reason is that continually higher prices and lower costs lead to higher profit. You need to add (or change) constraints in your model, such as setting a maximum price or minimum cost level (for example, the amount of fixed costs).

`Solver could not find a feasible solution.` Solver couldn't find a solution that satisfied all your constraints. Check your constraints to make sure that they're realistic and consistent.

`Stop chosen when the maximum` x `limit was reached.` This message appears when Solver bumps up against either the maximum time limit or the maximum iteration limit. If it appears that Solver is heading toward a solution, select the **K**eep Solver Solution button and try again.

`The conditions for Assume Linear Model are not satisfied.` Solver based its iterative process on a linear model, but when the results are put into the worksheet, they don't conform to the linear model. You need to clear the Assume Linear **M**odel check box and try again.

A Solver Example

The best way to learn how to use a complex tool such as Solver is to get your hands dirty with some examples. Luckily, Excel comes with several sample worksheets that use simplified models to demonstrate the various problems Solver can handle. I look at one of these worksheets in detail in this section.

The Transportation Problem

The *transportation problem* is the classic model for solving linear programming problems. The basic goal is to minimize the costs of shipping goods from several production plants to various warehouses scattered around the country. Your constraints are as follows:

1. The amount shipped to each warehouse must meet the warehouse's demand for goods.

2. The amount shipped from each plant must be greater than or equal to 0.

3. The amount shipped from each plant can't exceed the plant's supply of goods.

Figure 19.10 shows the model for solving the transportation problem.

FIGURE 19.10.

A worksheet for solving the transportation problem.

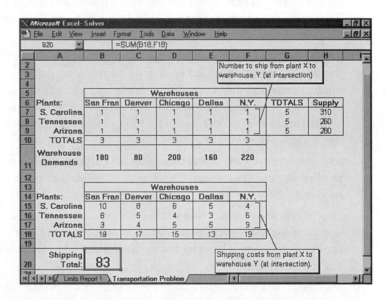

The top table (A6:F10) lists the three plants (A7:A9) and the five warehouses (B6:F6). This table will hold the number of units shipped from each plant to each warehouse. In the Solver model, these will be the changing cells. The total shipped to each warehouse (B10:F10) must match the warehouse demands (B11:F11) to satisfy constraint #1. The amount shipped from each plant (B7:F9) must be greater than or equal to 0 to satisfy constraint #2. The total shipped from each plant (G7:G9) must be less than or equal to the available supply for each plant (H7:H9) to satisfy constraint #3.

> **NOTE**
>
> When you need to use a range of values in a constraint, you don't need to set up a separate constraint for each cell. Instead, you can compare entire ranges. For example, the constraint that the total shipped from each plant be less than or equal to the plant supply can be entered as follows:
>
> `G7:G9<=H7:H9`

The bottom table (A14:F18) holds the corresponding shipping costs from each plant to each warehouse. The total shipping cost (cell B20) is the target cell you want to minimize.

Figure 19.11 shows the final Solver Parameters dialog box that you'll use to solve this problem. (Note that I also activated the Assume Linear **M**odel check box in the Solver Options dialog box.) Figure 19.12 shows the solution that Solver found.

FIGURE 19.11.

The Solver Parameters dialog box filled in for the transportation problem.

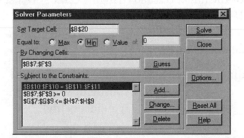

FIGURE 19.12.

The optimal solution for the transportation problem.

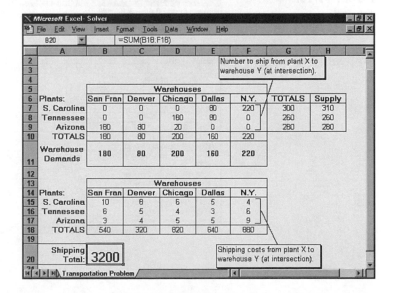

Displaying Solver's Reports

When Solver finds a solution, the Solver dialog box gives you the option of generating three reports: the Answer report, the Sensitivity report, and the Limits report. Highlight the reports you want to see from the **R**eports list box and then select OK. Excel displays each report on its own worksheet.

> **TIP**
>
> If you've named the cells in your model, Solver uses these names to make its reports easier to read. If you haven't already done so, you should define names for the target cell, changing cells, and constraint cells before creating a report.

The Answer Report

The Answer report displays information about the model's target cell, changing cells, and constraints. For the target cell and changing cells, Solver shows original and final values, as shown in Figure 19.13. For the constraints, the report shows the address and name for each cell, their final values formulas, and two values called the *status* and the *slack* (see Figure 19.14). The status can take one of three values:

Binding — Signifies that the final value in the constraint cell equals the constraint value (or the constraint boundary, if the constraint is an inequality).

FIGURE 19.13.

Solver's Answer report.

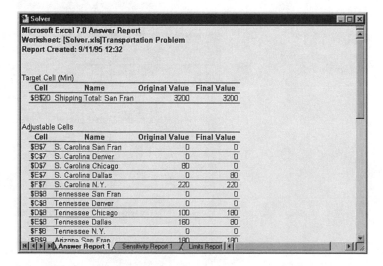

FIGURE 19.14.

The Constraints section of Solver's Answer report.

Cell	Name	Cell Value	Formula	Status	Slack
$G$7	S. Carolina TOTALS	300	$G$7<=$H$7	Not Binding	10
$G$8	Tennessee TOTALS	260	$G$8<=$H$8	Binding	0
$G$9	Arizona TOTALS	280	$G$9<=$H$9	Binding	0
$B$10	TOTALS San Fran	180	$B$10=$B$11	Binding	0
$C$10	TOTALS Denver	80	$C$10=$C$11	Binding	0
$D$10	TOTALS Chicago	200	$D$10=$D$11	Binding	0
$E$10	TOTALS Dallas	160	$E$10=$E$11	Binding	0
$F$10	TOTALS N.Y.	220	$F$10=$F$11	Binding	0
$B$7	S. Carolina San Fran	0	$B$7>=0	Binding	0
$C$7	S. Carolina Denver	0	$C$7>=0	Binding	0
$D$7	S. Carolina Chicago	0	$D$7>=0	Binding	0
$E$7	S. Carolina Dallas	80	$E$7>=0	Not Binding	80
$F$7	S. Carolina N.Y.	220	$F$7>=0	Not Binding	220
$B$8	Tennessee San Fran	0	$B$8>=0	Binding	0
$C$8	Tennessee Denver	0	$C$8>=0	Binding	0
$D$8	Tennessee Chicago	180	$D$8>=0	Not Binding	180
$E$8	Tennessee Dallas	80	$E$8>=0	Not Binding	80
$F$8	Tennessee N.Y.	0	$F$8>=0	Binding	0
$B$9	Arizona San Fran	180	$B$9>=0	Not Binding	180
$C$9	Arizona Denver	80	$C$9>=0	Not Binding	80
$D$9	Arizona Chicago	20	$D$9>=0	Not Binding	20

Not Binding	This value tells you that the constraint cell value satisfied the constraint, but it doesn't equal the constraint boundary.
Not Satisfied	Signifies that the constraint was not satisfied.

The slack is the difference between the final constraint cell value and the value of the original constraint (or its boundary). In the optimal solution for the transportation problem, for example, the total shipped from the South Carolina plant is 300, but the constraint on this total is 310 (the total supply). Therefore, the slack value is 10. If the status is binding, the slack value is always 0.

The Sensitivity Report

The Sensitivity report attempts to show how sensitive a solution is to changes in the model's formulas. The layout of the Sensitivity report depends on the type of model you're using. For a linear model (that is, a model in which you activated the Assume Linear Model check box in the Solver Options dialog box), you'll see the report shown in Figure 19.15. Actually, this report is divided into two sections: Changing Cells (see Figure 19.15) and Constraints (see Figure 19.16).

The Changing Cells section shows, for each cell, the address and name of the cell, its final value, and the following measures:

Reduced Cost	The corresponding increase in the target cell given a one-unit increase in the changing cell.

Objective Coefficient	The relative relationship between the changing cell and the target cell.
Allowable Increase	The change in the objective coefficient before there would be an increase in the optimal value of the changing cell.
Allowable Decrease	The change in the objective coefficient before there would be a decrease in the optimal value of the changing cell.

FIGURE 19.15.

The Changing Cells section of Solver's Sensitivity report.

Microsoft Excel 7.0 Sensitivity Report
Worksheet: [Solver.xls]Transportation Problem
Report Created: 9/11/95 12:33

Changing Cells

Cell	Name	Final Value	Reduced Cost	Objective Coefficient	Allowable Increase	Allowable Decrease
$B$7	S. Carolina San Fran	0	6	10	1E+30	6
$C$7	S. Carolina Denver	0	3.000000002	8.000000003	1E+30	3.000000002
$D$7	S. Carolina Chicago	0	0	6	1E+30	0
$E$7	S. Carolina Dallas	80	0	5	0	1
$F$7	S. Carolina N.Y.	220	0	4	4	1E+30
$B$8	Tennessee San Fran	0	4	6	1E+30	4
$C$8	Tennessee Denver	0	2.000000001	5.000000001	1E+30	2.000000001
$D$8	Tennessee Chicago	180	0	4	0	1
$E$8	Tennessee Dallas	80	0	3	1	0
$F$8	Tennessee N.Y.	0	4	6	1E+30	4
$B$9	Arizona San Fran	180	0	3	4	1E+30
$C$9	Arizona Denver	80	0	4	2.000000001	1E+30
$D$9	Arizona Chicago	20	0	5	1	2.000000001
$E$9	Arizona Dallas	0	1	5	1E+30	1
$F$9	Arizona N.Y.	0	6	9	1E+30	6

FIGURE 19.16.

The Constraints section of Solver's Sensitivity report.

Constraints

Cell	Name	Final Value	Shadow Price	Constraint R.H. Side	Allowable Increase	Allowable Decrease
$G$7	S. Carolina TOTALS	300	0	310	1E+30	10
$G$8	Tennessee TOTALS	260	-2	260	80	10
$G$9	Arizona TOTALS	280	-1	280	80	10
$B$10	TOTALS San Fran	160	4	180	10	80
$C$10	TOTALS Denver	80	5	80	10	80
$D$10	TOTALS Chicago	200	6	200	10	80
$E$10	TOTALS Dallas	160	5	160	10	80
$F$10	TOTALS N.Y.	220	4	220	10	220

The Constraints section shows, for each constraint cell, the address and name of the cell, its final value, and the following values:

Shadow Price	The corresponding increase in the target cell given a one-unit increase in the constraint value.
Constraint R.H. Side	The constraint value you specified (that is, the right-hand side of the constraint equation).

Allowable Increase   The change in the constraint value before there would be an increase in the optimal value of the changing cell.

Allowable Decrease   The change in the constraint value before there would be a decrease in the optimal value of the changing cell.

The Sensitivity report for a nonlinear model shows the changing cells and the constraint cells. For each cell, the report displays the address, the name, and the final value. The Changing Cells section also shows the Reduced Gradient value, which measures the corresponding increase in the target cell given a one-unit increase in the changing cell (similar to the Reduced Cost measure for a linear model). The Constraints section also shows the Lagrange Multiplier value, which measures the corresponding increase in the target cell given a one-unit increase in the constraint value (similar to the Shadow Price in the linear report).

The Limits Report

The Limits report, shown in Figure 19.17, displays the target cell and its value, as well as the changing cells and their addresses, names, values, and the following measures:

Lower Limit   The minimum value that the changing cell can assume while keeping the other changing cells fixed and still satisfy the constraints.

Upper Limit   The maximum value that the changing cell can assume while keeping the other changing cells fixed and still satisfy the constraints.

Target Value   The target cell's value when the changing cell is at the lower limit or upper limit.

FIGURE 19.17.

Solver's Limits report.

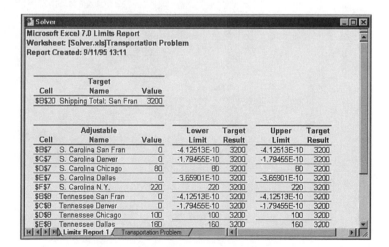

Summary

This chapter showed you how to solve complex problems by using Excel's powerful Solver tool. I gave you some background about Solver's operations research underpinnings and the types of problems Solver was designed to work with. I then showed you how to use Solver, add constraints, save scenarios and models, and display Solver's reports. We closed the chapter by looking at the classic transportation problem. Here's a short list of chapters that contain related information:

- I examined a number of other analytical techniques (including Goal Seek, Solver's simpler cousin) in Chapter 17, "Basic Analytic Methods."

- Excel's Analysis Toolpak is loaded with powerful analytic features. I told you all about them in Chapter 18, "Working with the Analysis Toolpak."

- To learn more about scenarios, read Chapter 20, "Working with Scenarios."

Working with Scenarios

20

648

By definition, what-if analysis is not an exact science. All what-if models make guesses and assumptions based on history, expected events, or whatever voodoo comes to mind. A particular set of guesses and assumptions that you plug into a model is called a *scenario*. Because most what-if worksheets can take a wide range of input values, you usually end up with a large number of scenarios to examine. Instead of going through the tedious chore of inserting all these values into the appropriate cells, Excel has a Scenario Manager feature that can handle the process for you. This chapter completes our look at Excel's data-analysis features by examining this useful tool.

How Scenarios Work

As you've seen in the last few chapters, Excel has powerful features that enable you to build sophisticated models that can answer complex questions. The problem, though, isn't in *answering* questions but in *asking* them. For example, Figure 20.1 shows a worksheet model that analyzes a mortgage. You use this model to decide how much of a down payment to make, how long the term should be, and whether to include an extra principal paydown every month. The Results section compares the monthly payment and total paid for the regular mortgage and for the mortgage with a paydown. It also shows the savings and reduced term that result from the paydown.

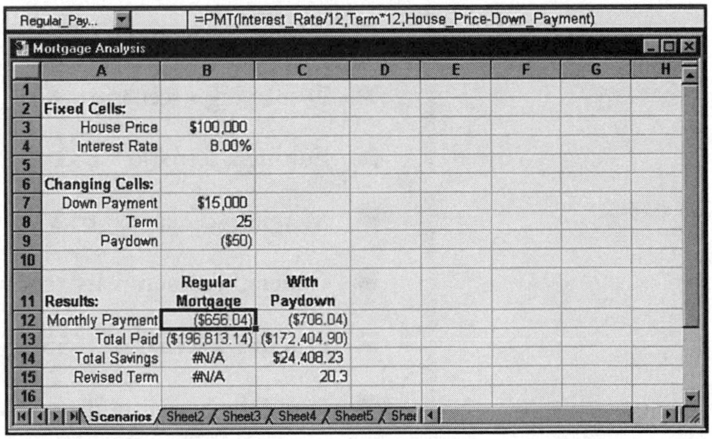

FIGURE 20.1.

A mortgage-analysis worksheet.

Here are some possible questions to ask this model:

- How much will I save over the term of the mortgage if I use a shorter term and a larger down payment and include a monthly paydown?

- How much more will I end up paying if I extend the term, reduce the down payment, and forego the paydown?

These are examples of *scenarios* that you would plug into the appropriate cells in the model. Excel's Scenario Manager helps by letting you define a scenario separately from the worksheet. You can save specific values for any or all of the model's input cells, give the scenario a name, and then recall the name (and all the input values it contains) from a list.

Setting Up Your Worksheet for Scenarios

Before creating a scenario, you need to decide which cells in your model will be the input cells. These will be the worksheet variables—the cells that, when you change them, change the results of the model. (Not surprisingly, Excel calls these the *changing cells*.) You can have as many as 32 changing cells in a scenario. For best results, follow these guidelines when setting up your worksheet for scenarios:

- The changing cells should be constants. Formulas can be affected by other cells, and that can throw off the entire scenario.
- To make it easier to set up each scenario and to make your worksheet easier to understand, group the changing cells and label them. (See Figure 20.1.)
- For even greater clarity, assign a range name to each changing cell.

Adding a Scenario

To work with scenarios, you use Excel's Scenario Manager tool. This feature enables you to add, edit, display, and delete scenarios as well as create summary scenario reports.

Once your worksheet is set up the way you want, you can add a scenario to the sheet by following these steps:

1. Select the **Tools | Scenarios** command. Excel displays the Scenario Manager dialog box, shown in Figure 20.2.

FIGURE 20.2.

Excel's Scenario Manager.

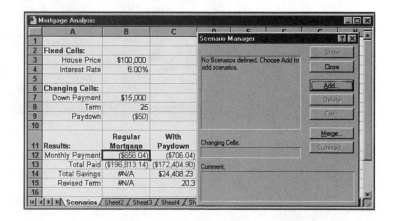

2. Select the **A**dd button. The Add Scenario dialog box, shown in Figure 20.3, appears.

FIGURE 20.3.

Use the Add Scenario dialog box to add scenarios to a workbook.

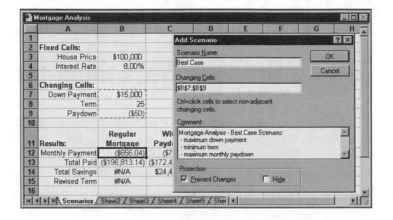

3. In the Scenario **N**ame text box, enter a name for the scenario.

4. In the Changing **C**ells box, enter references to your worksheet's changing cells. You can type in the references (be sure to separate noncontiguous cells with commas) or select the cells directly on the worksheet.

5. In the **C**omment box, enter a description for the scenario. This will appear in the Comment section of the Scenario Manager dialog box.

6. Select OK. Excel displays the Scenario Values dialog box, shown in Figure 20.4.

FIGURE 20.4.

Use the Scenario Values dialog box to enter the values you want to use for the scenario's changing cells.

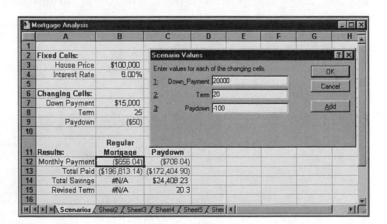

7. Use the text boxes to enter values for the changing cells.

NOTE

To learn about protecting and hiding scenarios, see Chapter 5, "Advanced Worksheet Topics."

NOTE

You'll notice in Figure 20.4 that Excel displays the range name for each changing cell, which makes it easier to enter your numbers correctly. If your changing cells aren't named, Excel just displays the cell addresses instead.

8. To add more scenarios, select the **A**dd button to return to the Add Scenario dialog box and repeat steps 3 through 7. Otherwise, select OK to return to the Scenario Manager dialog box.

9. Select the Close button to return to the worksheet.

Displaying a Scenario

After you define a scenario, you can enter its values into the changing cells simply by selecting the scenario from the Scenario Manager dialog box. The following steps give you the details:

1. Select the **T**ools | Scenarios command to display the Scenario Manager.

2. In the S**c**enarios list, highlight the scenario you want to display.

3. Select the **S**how button. Excel enters the scenario values into the changing cells, as shown in Figure 20.5.

FIGURE 20.5.

When you select Show, Excel enters the values for the highlighted scenario into the changing cells.

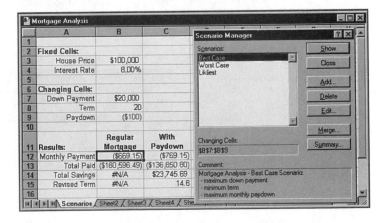

4. Repeat steps 2 and 3 to display other scenarios.

5. Select the Close button to return to the worksheet.

Editing a Scenario

If you need to make changes to a scenario—whether changing the scenario's name, selecting different changing cells, or entering new values—follow these steps:

1. Select the **T**ools | **S**cenarios command to display the Scenario Manager.

2. In the Scenarios list, highlight the scenario you want to edit.

3. Select the **E**dit button. Excel displays the Edit Scenario dialog box (which is identical to the Add Scenario dialog box, shown in Figure 20.3).

4. Make your changes, if necessary, and select OK. The Scenario Values dialog box appears (see Figure 20.4).

5. Enter the new values if necessary and then select OK to return to the Scenario Manager dialog box.

6. Repeat steps 2 through 5 to edit other scenarios.

7. Select the Close button to return to the worksheet.

Merging Scenarios

The scenarios you create are stored with each worksheet in a workbook. If you have similar models in different sheets (for example, budget models for different divisions), you can create separate scenarios for each sheet and then merge them later on. Here are the steps to follow:

1. Activate the worksheet you want to contain the merged scenarios.

2. Select the **T**ools | **S**cenarios command to display the Scenario Manager.

3. Select the **M**erge button. Excel displays the Merge Scenarios dialog box, shown in Figure 20.6.

FIGURE 20.6.

Use the Merge Scenarios dialog box to select the scenarios you want to merge.

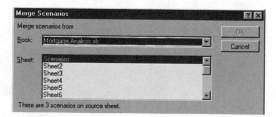

4. In the **B**ook drop-down list, select the workbook that contains the scenario sheet.

5. In the **S**heet list, select the worksheet that contains the scenario.

6. Select OK. Excel returns you to the Scenario Manager.

7. Repeat steps 3 through 6 to merge other scenarios.

8. Select Close to return to the worksheet.

Generating a Summary Report

You can create a summary report that shows the changing cells in each of your scenarios along with selected result cells. This is a handy way to compare different scenarios. You can try it by following the procedure that is outlined forthwith.

> **NOTE**
>
> When Excel sets up the scenario summary, it uses either the cell addresses or defined names of the individual changing cells and results cells, as well as the entire range of changing cells. Your reports will be more readable if you name in advance the cells you'll be using.

1. Select the **T**ools | **S**cenarios command to display the Scenario Manager.

2. Select the **S**ummary button. Excel displays the Scenario Summary dialog box.

3. In the Report Type group, select either Scenario **S**ummary or Scenario **P**ivotTable.

4. In the **R**esult Cells box, enter references to the result cells you want to appear in the report, as shown in Figure 20.7. You can select the cells directly on the sheet or type in the references. (Remember to separate noncontiguous cells with commas.)

FIGURE 20.7.

Use the Scenario Summary dialog box to select the report type and result cells.

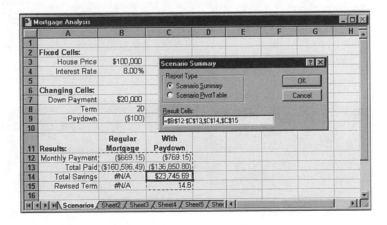

5. Select OK. Excel displays the report.

Figure 20.8 shows the Scenario Summary report for the Mortgage Analysis worksheet. The names shown in column C (Down_Payment, Term, and so on) are the names I assigned to each of the changing cells and result cells.

FIGURE 20.8.

The Scenario Summary report for the Mortgage Analysis worksheet.

Cell names —

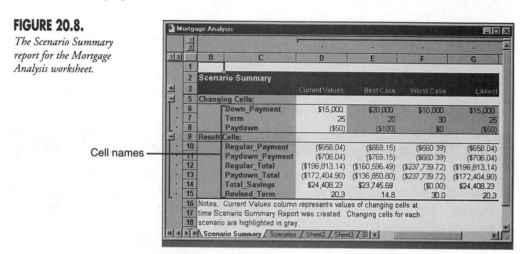

Figure 20.9 shows the Scenario PivotTable report for the Mortgage Analysis worksheet. (By the way, the pivot table's page field enables you to switch between scenarios created by different users.)

FIGURE 20.9.

The Scenario PivotTable report for the Mortgage Analysis worksheet.

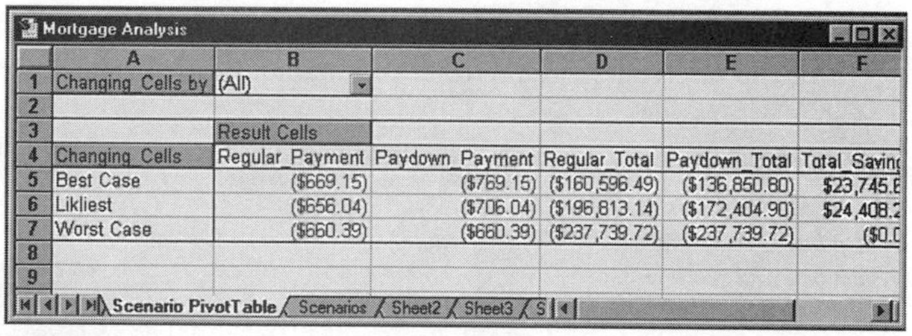

> **NOTE**
>
> To learn how to work with the outline that Excel creates for the Scenario Summary worksheet, see Chapter 5. If you created a Summary PivotTable report, you can find out how to work with pivot tables in Chapter 13, "Creating Pivot Tables," and Chapter 14, "Customizing Pivot Tables."

Deleting a Scenario

If you have scenarios you no longer need, you can delete them by following the steps in this procedure:

1. Select the **Tools | Scenarios** command to display the Scenario Manager.
2. In the Scenarios list, highlight the scenario you want to delete.

> **CAUTION**
>
> Excel doesn't warn you when it's about to delete a scenario, and there's no way to retrieve a scenario deleted accidentally, so be sure the scenario you highlighted is one you can live without.

3. Select the **D**elete button. Excel deletes the scenario.
4. Select Close to return to the worksheet.

Using the Scenarios Drop-Down List

The Scenarios drop-down list box on the WorkGroup toolbar, shown in Figure 20.10, offers an easy way to add, display, and edit scenarios. The next three sections fill you in on the details.

FIGURE 20.10.

The Scenarios drop-down list on the WorkGroup toolbar.

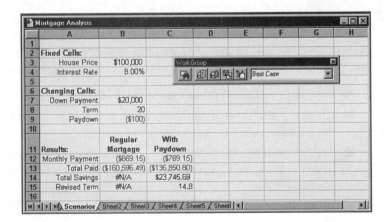

Adding a Scenario

To add a scenario with the Scenarios list, follow these steps:

1. Enter the values into the changing cells that you want to use for the scenario.
2. Select the changing cells.
3. In the Scenarios list, enter a name for the scenario and press Enter.

Displaying a Scenario

Displaying a scenario with the Scenarios list is simplicity itself: Just pull down the list and select the scenario you want to display. One caveat, though: If you select the same scenario twice in succession, Excel asks whether you want to redefine the scenario. Select **No** to keep the current scenario definition. (If you *do* want to make changes to a scenario, see the next section.)

Editing a Scenario

To revise the values in the changing cells of a scenario, work through the steps in the following procedure:

1. Use the Scenarios list to display the scenario you want to edit.
2. Make your changes to the changing cells.
3. Select the scenario again. Excel asks whether you want to redefine the scenario.
4. Select **Yes**. Excel changes the scenario.

Summary

This chapter showed you how to work with Excel's scenarios. I gave you some background on how scenarios work, and then I showed you how to add, display, edit, and merge scenarios. You also learned how to generate a summary report and how to use the Scenarios drop-down list. Here are a few other chapters to turn to for related information:

- I showed you how to protect scenarios in Chapter 5, "Advanced Worksheet Topics."
- Chapter 5 also covered outlining, which you need to know if you want to work with the Scenario Summary worksheets.
- The Scenario Summary feature can create a pivot table. If you need a refresher course in pivot tables, see Chapter 13, "Creating Pivot Tables," and Chapter 14, "Customizing Pivot Tables."
- I examined a number of what-if analytical techniques in Chapter 17, "Basic Analytic Methods."
- Excel's Analysis Toolpak is loaded with powerful analytic features. I told you all about them in Chapter 18, "Working with the Analysis Toolpak."
- You can save a Solver solution as a scenario. To find out how it's done, head to Chapter 19, "Solving Complex Problems with Solver."

V

PART

Unleashing Spreadsheet Applications with VBA

Getting Started with VBA

21

Excel includes Microsoft's long-awaited common macro language: Visual Basic for Applications (which I'll refer to simply as "VBA" from now on). This chapter introduces you to this powerful tool and shows you how to use VBA to record simple macros that help automate routine tasks. To get the most out of VBA, however, you need to do some programming. This chapter gets you started by showing you how to use VBA variables and operators and how to write simple command macros and user-defined functions.

What Is a Macro?

A *macro* is a small program that contains a list of instructions that you want Excel to perform. Like DOS batch files, macros combine several operations into a single procedure that you can invoke quickly. This list of instructions is composed mostly of *macro statements* that are closely related to Excel commands. Some of these statements perform specific macro-related tasks, but most just correspond to Excel's menu commands and dialog box options. For example, VBA's `ActiveWindow.Close` function works just like the **F**ile | **C**lose command.

How Does VBA Fit In?

VBA is a programming environment designed specifically for application macros. Excel was the first program to include VBA, but now other Microsoft applications (such as Project and Access) feature VBA as well. It's also possible that Microsoft will license the technology to other vendors so they can incorporate VBA in their applications. At the very least, you're likely to see other macro programming languages that are "VBA-compatible."

This all means that VBA likely will become the de facto standard for macro programming. The advantage of this is obvious: a standard language means that, no matter which program you use, you have to learn only one set of statements and techniques. And it also means that applications will get along better than they ever have, because VBA "knows" the functions and commands used by every program. Eventually, you'll be able to use VBA to design your own applications that consist of bits and pieces from other programs.

The power of VBA is clear, but perhaps its biggest advantage is that it's just plain easier to use than most programming languages (including the old Excel 4.0 macro language). If you don't want to do any programming, VBA enables you to record macros and attach them to buttons either on the worksheet or on a toolbar. You also can create dialog boxes by simply drawing the appropriate controls onto a worksheet or onto a separate dialog sheet. Other visual tools enable you to customize menus and toolbars as well, so you have everything you need to create simple applications without writing a line of code.

Of course, if you want to get the most out of VBA, you'll need to augment your interface with programming code. Unlike the Excel 4.0 macro language, VBA is a full-blown programming environment that includes most high-level programming constructs as well as every Excel function. Add the powerful debugging tool and the ability to create a Help system into the mix, and you have everything you need to create professional-level spreadsheet applications.

The Three Types of Macros

VBA macros come in three flavors: *command macros, user-defined functions,* and *subroutine macros.* Here's a summary of the differences:

- Command macros (which also are known as Sub procedures for reasons that will become clear later in this chapter) are the most common type of macro, and they usually contain statements that are the equivalent of menu options and other Excel commands. The distinguishing feature of a command macro is that, like regular Excel commands, they have an effect on their surroundings (the worksheet, workspace, and so on). Whether it's formatting a range, printing a worksheet, or creating custom menus, command macros *change* things. I show you how to create command macros in the section called "Writing Your Own Command Macro."

- User-defined functions (also called Function procedures) work just like Excel's built-in functions. Their distinguishing characteristic is that they accept arguments, manipulate those arguments, and then return a result. A properly designed function macro has no effect on the current environment. I show you how to create these functions in the section titled "Creating User-Defined Functions with VBA."

- Subroutine macros are a combination of command and function macros. They can take arguments and return values like a function macro, but they also can affect their surroundings like a command macro. You invoke subroutines from within other macros, and their usual purpose is to streamline macro code. If you have a task that you need to run several times in a macro, you'll typically split off the task into a subroutine instead of cluttering up your macro.

Recording a VBA Macro

By far the easiest way to create a command macro is to use the Macro Recorder. With this method, you just run through the task you want to automate (including selecting ranges, menu commands, and dialog box options), and Excel translates everything into the appropriate VBA statements. These are copied to a separate sheet called a *module* where you can then replay the entire procedure any time you like. The following procedure takes you through the steps required to record a command macro:

1. Either select the **Tools** | **Record** Macro | **Record** New Macro command or click the Record Macro button on the Visual Basic toolbar. Excel displays the Record New Macro dialog box, shown in Figure 21.1.

    The Record Macro button.

2. Excel proposes a name for the macro (such as Macro1), but you can change the name to anything you like. (You must follow Excel's usual naming conventions: no more than 255 characters, the first character must be a letter or an underscore (_), and no spaces or periods are allowed.)

FIGURE 21.1.

Use the Record New Macro dialog box to name and describe your macro.

3. Enter a description of the macro in the **D**escription text box.

4. Select OK. Excel returns you to the worksheet, displays `Recording` in the status bar, and displays the Stop Recording Macro toolbar.

5. Perform the tasks you want to include in the macro.

6. When you finish the tasks, select the **T**ools | **R**ecord Macro | **S**top Recording command or click the Stop Macro button.

 The Stop Macro button.

Viewing the Resulting Module

Excel stores your recorded macros in a special sheet called a *module*. By default, Excel uses a sheet named Module1 for recorded macros, and it places this sheet at the end of the current workbook. To see your macro, move to the last sheet in the workbook and select the tab labeled Module1.

If you've renamed the module or you're not sure where the macro is stored, follow these steps to display the macro:

1. Select the **T**ools | **M**acro command. Excel displays the Macro dialog box.

2. In the **M**acro Name/Reference list, highlight the macro you want to display.

3. Select the **E**dit button. Excel opens the module and displays the macro.

As you can see in Figure 21.2, Excel translates your actions into VBA code and combines everything into a single macro.

FIGURE 21.2.

A sample recorded macro.

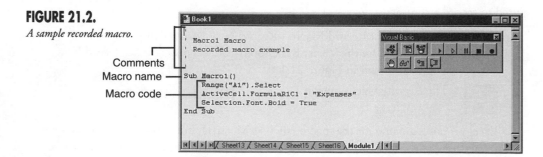

A typical macro has the following features:

Comments: The first few lines begin with an apostrophe ('), which tells Excel that these lines are *comments* that aren't processed when you run the macro. In each recorded macro, the comments display the name of the macro and the description you entered in the Record New Macro dialog box.

Sub/End Sub: These keywords mark the beginning (Sub) and end (End Sub) of a macro. The Sub keyword is the reason why command macros also are called Sub procedures.

Macro Name: After the Sub keyword, Excel enters the name of the macro followed by a left and right parenthesis (the parentheses are used for *arguments,* as you'll see later).

Macro code: The main body of the macro (in other words, the lines between the Sub and End Sub lines) consists of a series of statements. These are Excel's interpretations of the actions you performed during the recording. In the example, three actions were performed:

1. Cell A1 was selected.
2. The string Expenses was typed into the cell and the Enter button on the formula bar was clicked.
3. The cell was formatted as boldface.

> **NOTE**
>
> If your recorded macro doesn't have the preceding features, you might have recorded an Excel 4.0 macro instead. To make sure you record in VBA, click the **O**ptions button in the Record New Macro dialog box and activate the **V**isual Basic option from the expanded dialog box.

Setting Recording Options

Excel provides you with several options for recording macros. To check them out, display the Record New Macro dialog box, then select the **O**ptions button. The dialog box expands to the one shown in Figure 21.3.

> **NOTE**
>
> By default, Excel uses absolute references during recording. If you prefer to use relative references, select the **T**ools | **R**ecord Macro | **U**se Relative References command before you start recording.

FIGURE 21.3.

Use the Record New Macro dialog box to name your macro and assign a shortcut key and storage location.

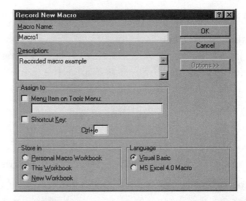

NOTE

If you want to adjust the options for a macro you've already recorded, select the **Tools |
M**acro command, highlight the macro you want to work with from the list that
appears, and then click the **O**ptions button.

Here's a rundown of the available options:

- If you think you'll run the macro often, you can add a command that automatically
  runs the macro to the **T**ools menu. Activate the Men**u** Item on Tools Menu check
  box, and then enter the command name you want to use in the text box. To make one
  of the letters an accelerator key, place an ampersand (&) before the letter (for example,
  E&xpenses Macro). Make sure, however, that you don't use the same accelerator key as
  an existing **T**ools menu command.

- To assign a shortcut key to the macro, activate the Shortcut **K**ey check box and use
  the C**t**rl- text box to enter the letter you want to use with Ctrl for the key combination. For example, if you enter e, you can run the macro by pressing Ctrl-E. Note that
  Excel shortcut keys are case-sensitive. That is, if you enter E in the Ctrl- text box, you
  would have to press Ctrl-Shift-E to run the macro.

CAUTION

The shortcut keys Excel suggests are ones that don't conflict with Excel's built-in
shortcuts (such as Ctrl-B for Bold or Ctrl-C for Copy). If you use a key that clashes
with an Excel shortcut, Excel will override its own shortcut and run your macro
instead. (Provided, that is, that the workbook containing the macro is open.)

There are only eight letters not assigned to Excel commands that you can use with
your macros: *e, j, k, l, m, q, t,* and *y.* You can get an extra 26 shortcut keys by using

uppercase letters. For example, Excel differentiates between Ctrl-a and Ctrl-A (or, more explicitly, Ctrl-Shift-a). You also can use the OnKey method to trigger a macro when the user presses a specific key combination. See Chapter 27, "VBA Procedures That Respond to Events," for details.

■ As you've seen, Excel normally stores your recorded macros in a separate sheet at the end of the current workbook. These macros are available only when the workbook is open; if you close it, you can't use the macros. Although this is often desirable behavior, you'll no doubt have some macros you want available all the time. To ensure this, you can store the macros in the Personal Macro Workbook. This is a hidden workbook (its filename is Personal.xls) that is opened automatically when you start Excel. To store a macro in the Personal Macro Workbook, activate the **P**ersonal Macro Workbook option.

NOTE

If you used the Global macro sheet (GLOBAL.XLM) in Excel 4.0, you still can use it in version 7.0. Note, however, that all global macros in version 7.0, regardless of the language you use, are stored in the Personal Macro Workbook.

■ If you want to store your macro in a new workbook, activate the **N**ew Workbook option.

Editing a Recorded Macro

As you're learning VBA, you'll often end up with recorded macros that don't turn out quite right the first time. Whether the macro runs a command it shouldn't or is missing a command altogether, you'll often have to patch things up after the fact.

A VBA module is more like a word-processing document than a worksheet, so you make changes the same way you would in a word processor or text editor. If your macro contains statements that you want to remove, just delete the offending lines from the module.

If you left out a step or two, follow these instructions to insert new recorded actions into an existing macro:

1. Activate the module that contains the macro you want to change.

> **NOTE**
>
> If you need to make changes to a macro stored in the Personal Macro Workbook (Personal.xls), you must first unhide it by selecting the **W**indow | **U**nhide command.

2. Position the insertion point where you want the new statements recorded.
3. Select the **T**ools | **R**ecord Macro | **M**ark Position for Recording command. This tells Excel where you want the new actions recorded.
4. Activate the worksheet or chart you want to use for the recording.
5. Select **T**ools | **R**ecord Macro | **R**ecord at Mark to resume the recording.
6. Perform the actions you want added to the macro.
7. When you finish, select **T**ools | **R**ecord Macro | **S**top Recording.

Writing Your Own Command Macro

Although the Macro Recorder makes it easy to create your own homegrown macros, there are plenty of macro features that you can't access with mouse or keyboard actions or by selecting menu options. For example, VBA has a couple of dozen information macro functions that return data about cells, worksheets, workspaces, and more. Also, the control functions enable you to add true programming constructs such as looping, branching, and decision-making.

To access these macro elements, you need to write your own VBA routines from scratch. This is easier than it sounds, because all you really need to do is enter a series of statements in a module. The next two sections take you through the various steps.

> **NOTE**
>
> Although the next two sections tell you how to create VBA macros, I realize there's an inherent paradox here: How can you write your own macros when you haven't learned anything about them yet? Making you familiar with VBA's statements and functions is the job of the last half of this chapter and the other nine chapters in Part V. The next couple of sections will get you started, and you can use this knowledge as a base on which to build your VBA skills in subsequent chapters.

Creating a New Module

If you want to enter your macro in an existing module, just display the sheet as described in the section in this chapter called "Viewing the Resulting Module." If you want to start a new module sheet, follow these steps:

1. Open the workbook you want to use for the macros.

2. Select the sheet before which you want to insert the module.

3. Select the **Insert | Macro | Module** command or click the Insert Module button on the Visual Basic toolbar. Excel adds a new module to the workbook.

 The Insert Module button on the Visual Basic toolbar.

Writing a Command Macro

With a module open and active, follow these steps to write your own command macro:

1. Place the insertion point where you want to start the macro.

2. If you want to begin your macro with a few comments that describe what the macro does, type an apostrophe (') at the beginning of each comment line.

3. To start the macro, type Sub followed by a space and the name of the macro. When you press Enter at the end of this line, Excel automatically adds a pair of parentheses at the end of the macro name.

4. Enter the VBA statements you want to include in the macro. For clarity, indent each line by pressing the Tab key at the beginning of the line.

5. When you're finished, start a new line and type End Sub to mark the end of the macro.

When you press Enter to start a new line, VBA analyzes the line you just entered and performs three chores:

- It formats the colors of each word in the line: VBA keywords are blue, comments are green, and all other text is black.

- VBA keywords are converted to their proper case. For example, if you type end sub, VBA converts this to End Sub when you press Enter.

- It checks for syntax errors. VBA signifies a syntax error either by displaying a dialog box to let you know what the problem is or by not converting a word to its proper case or color.

TIP

By always entering VBA keywords in lowercase letters, you'll be able to catch typing errors by looking for those keywords that VBA doesn't recognize (that is, the ones that remain in lowercase).

Running a VBA Macro

Excel offers several methods for running your VBA macros. Here's a quick rundown:

- From any sheet in a workbook, select the **Tools | M**acro command to display the Macro dialog box. Highlight the macro you want to run in the **M**acro Name/Reference list, and then select the **R**un button.

- In a module, place the insertion point anywhere inside the macro, and then either select the **R**un | **S**tart command, press the F5 key, or click on the Run Macro tool on the Visual Basic toolbar.

 The Run Macro tool on the Visual Basic toolbar.

CAUTION

Before you run a macro directly from a module, check to see if the macro includes statements that make changes to a worksheet (such as entering data and formatting cells). If it does, you need to do one of two things:

- Activate the worksheet and then run the macro using the **T**ools | **M**acro command.

- Make sure the macro includes a command to select a worksheet. For example, the command `Worksheets("Sheet1").Select` selects the worksheet named Sheet1. See Chapter 22, "Understanding Objects," for more information on working with objects such as a worksheet.

- If you assigned a shortcut key to the macro, press the key combination.

- If you added a new command to the **T**ools menu for the macro, select the command.

NOTE

You also can assign macros to custom menus and toolbars. I show you how in Chapter 25, "Creating a Custom User Interface." In addition, you should check out Chapter 27 to learn about a few techniques that you can use to run macros automatically.

Assigning a Procedure to a Macro Button

If you're constructing macros for someone else to use, there's an easy way to give the user quick access to the macro: a *macro button*. A macro button is an object you draw on the worksheet (similar to the dialog box objects—such as check boxes and option buttons—that I talked about in Chapter 5, "Advanced Worksheet Topics"). As you can see from Figure 21.4, macro buttons look just like dialog box command buttons. When the user clicks a button, the procedure that you've assigned to the button executes.

FIGURE 21.4.

You draw macro buttons on the worksheet to give the user quick access to macros.

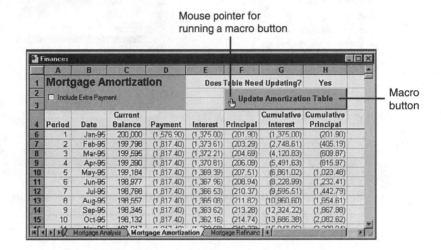

Mouse pointer for running a macro button

Macro button

Follow these steps to assign a procedure to a macro button:

1. Open the workbook that contains the procedure and activate the worksheet on which you want to draw the button.

2. Display the Drawing toolbar and click the Create Button button. The mouse pointer changes to a crosshair.

    The Create Button button from the Drawing toolbar.

3. Move the mouse pointer to where you want one corner of the button to appear.

4. Drag the mouse pointer until the button is the size and shape you want. (Hold down the Shift key while dragging to make the button a square, or hold down the Alt key to align the button with the worksheet gridlines.) When you release the mouse button, Excel displays the Assign Macro dialog box, shown in Figure 21.5.

5. Highlight the procedure in the **M**acro Name/Reference list.

   or

   To record the procedure, select the **R**ecord button and record the procedure as described earlier.

6. If you selected a procedure from the list, select OK.

7. To change the button text, first place the insertion point inside the button by using one of the following techniques:

   ■ If the button is currently selected, click it.

■ If the button isn't currently selected, hold down the Ctrl key and double-click the button.

FIGURE 21.5.

*Use the Assign Macro
dialog box to assign a
procedure to the macro
button.*

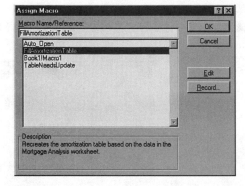

8. Delete the existing text and type in the text you want. You also can use any of Excel's text formatting options to alter the look of the button text.

9. Exit the button by clicking on the worksheet.

To run the procedure, position the mouse pointer over the button (which will change to a hand, as shown in Figure 21.4) and click.

TIP

You can assign procedures to worksheet graphic objects (such as pictures, charts, and drawings). Just select the object, select the Tools | Assign Macro command, and then select the procedure from the Assign Macro dialog box.

NOTE

If you need to move, size, or format a button, refer to Chapter 11, "Working with Graphic Objects," for instructions. When selecting a button, however, you need to hold down the Ctrl key before you click on it to prevent Excel from running the procedure.

Creating User-Defined Functions with VBA

Excel comes with hundreds of built-in functions—one of the largest function libraries of any spreadsheet package. However, even with this vast collection, you'll still find that plenty of applications are not covered. For example, you might need to calculate the area of a circle of a given radius or the gravitational force between two objects. You could, of course, easily calculate these things on a worksheet, but if you need them frequently, it makes sense to define your own functions that you can use anytime. The next four sections show you how it's done.

Understanding User-Defined Functions

As I mentioned earlier in this chapter, the defining characteristic of user-defined functions is that they return a result. They can perform any number of calculations on numbers, text, logical values, or whatever, but they're not allowed to affect their surroundings. They can't move the active cell, format a range, or change the workspace settings. In fact, anything you can access using the menus is off-limits in a user-defined function.

So, what *can* you put in a user-defined function? All of Excel's built-in worksheet functions are fair game, and you can use any VBA function that isn't the equivalent of a menu command or desktop action.

All user-defined functions have the same basic structure, as shown in Figure 21.6. This is a procedure named HypotenuseLength that calculates the length of a right triangle's hypotenuse given the other two sides.

FIGURE 21.6.

A user-defined function that calculates the length of a right triangle's hypotenuse.

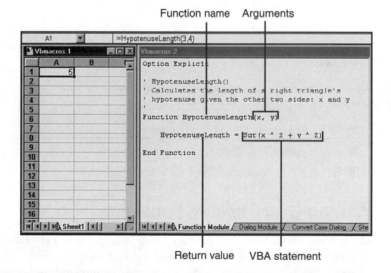

Function name   Arguments

Return value   VBA statement

NOTE

You'll find the code for the HypotenuseLength function, as well as all the other procedures in this chapter, on this book's CD. Look for a file named Chap21.xls.

Here's a summary of the various parts of a user-defined function:

The `Function` statement: This keyword identifies the procedure as a user-defined function. The `Function` keyword is the reason that user-defined functions also are called `Function` procedures.

The function name: This is a unique name for the function. Names must begin with an alphabetic character, they can't include a space or a period, and they can't be any longer than 255 characters.

The function arguments: Just as many of Excel's built-in worksheet functions accept arguments, so do user-defined functions. Arguments are typically one or more values that the function uses as the raw materials for its calculations. You always enter arguments between parentheses after the function name, and you separate multiple arguments with commas.

The VBA statements: This is the code that actually performs the calculations. Each expression is a combination of values, operators, variables, and VBA or Excel functions that produce a result.

The return value: User-defined functions usually return a value. To do this, include a statement where you set the name of the function equal to an expression. For example, in the `HypotenuseLength` function, the following statement defines the return value:

```
HypotenuseLength = Sqr(x ^ 2 + y ^ 2)
```

The `End Function` keywords: These keywords indicate the end of the function procedure.

All your user-defined functions will have this basic structure, so you need to keep three things in mind when designing these kinds of macros:

- What arguments will the macro take?
- What formulas will you use within the macro?
- What value or values will be returned?

Writing User-Defined Functions

User-defined functions can't contain menu commands or mouse and keyboard actions. This means, of course, that there is no way to record user-defined functions. You have to write them by hand; the process is very similar to creating a command macro from scratch. Here are the general steps to follow to write a user-defined function:

NOTE

As with command macros, I don't expect you to sit down and start cranking out user-defined functions right away. The knowledge of what statements to include in a user-defined function will come only after you've read more of the upcoming VBA chapters.

1. Activate the module you want to use for the function.

2. Place the insertion point where you want to start the macro.

3. If you like, enter one or more comments that describe what the macro does. Be sure to type an apostrophe (') at the beginning of each comment line.

4. Start the macro by typing Function followed by a space and the name of the macro. If your function uses arguments, enclose them in parentheses after the function name (be sure to separate each argument with a comma).

5. Enter the VBA statements that you want to include in the function. As with Sub procedures, you should indent each line for clarity by pressing the Tab key at the beginning of the line.

6. When you finish, start a new line and type End Function to mark the end of the procedure.

Employing User-Defined Functions

You can employ user-defined functions only within worksheet formulas or in other VBA statements. After you make sure that the sheet containing the module is open (unless, of course, the macro is stored in the Personal Macro Workbook), you have two choices:

- In the cell, enter the function the same way you would any of Excel's built-in functions. That is, enter the name of the function and then the necessary arguments enclosed in parentheses. In Figure 21.6, the window on the right shows the HypotenuseLength function in action. Cell A1 contains the following formula:

  =HypotenuseLength(3,4)

- Select the Insert | Function command, highlight User Defined in the Function Category list, and then select the macro from the Function Name list. Select Next and enter the arguments. When you're done, select Finish.

Assigning User-Defined Functions to Function Categories

By default, Excel places user-defined functions in the User Defined category. If you would like to see your function in one of Excel's other function categories (for example, the HypotenuseLength function would fit nicely in the Math & Trig category), follow these steps:

1. Activate the module that contains the user-defined function.

674

2. Select the **V**iew | **O**bject Browser command or click the Object Browser button on the Visual Basic toolbar. Excel displays the Object Browser dialog box.

 The Object Browser button.

3. If necessary, use the **L**ibraries/Workbooks drop-down list to select the appropriate workbook and the **O**bjects/Modules list to select the appropriate module.

4. In the **M**ethods/Properties list, highlight the user-defined function you want to work with.

5. Select the **O**ptions button. Excel displays the Macro Options dialog box.

6. Use the **F**unction Category drop-down list to select a category for the user-defined function.

7. Select OK to return to the Object Browser, and then select Close.

An Introduction to VBA Programming

Although it's possible to create useful VBA applications without programming, most macro developers occasionally have to write at least a little bit of code. And it goes without saying that if you hope to build anything even remotely complex or powerful, a knowledge of VBA programming is a must. The rest of this chapter gets you started with some programming fundamentals. If you combine these with the objects I discuss in Chapter 22 and the control structures I talk about in Chapter 23, "Controlling VBA Code and Interacting with the User," you'll have a solid base from which to explore further programming topics.

VBA Procedures

The basic unit of VBA programming is the *procedure,* which is a block of code in a module that you refer to as a unit. Earlier in this chapter you learned about the two most common types of procedures: command macros (also known as Sub procedures) and user-defined functions (or Function procedures).

The Structure of a Procedure

To recap what you learned earlier, a Sub procedure is allowed to modify its environment, but it can't return a value. Here is the basic structure of a Sub procedure:

```
Sub ProcedureName (argument1, argument2, ...)
    [VBA statements]
End Sub
```

For example, Listing 21.1 presents a Sub procedure that enters some values for a loan in various ranges and then adds a formula to calculate the loan payment.

Listing 21.1. A sample Sub procedure.

```
Sub EnterLoanData()
    Range("IntRate").Value = .08
    Range("Term").Value = 10
    Range("Principal").Value = 10000
    Range("Payment").Formula = "=PMT(IntRate/12, Term*12, Principal)"
End Sub
```

A Function procedure, on the other hand, can't modify its environment, but it does return a value. Here is its structure:

```
Function ProcedureName (argument1, argument2, ...)
    [VBA statements]
    ProcedureName = returnValue
End Function
```

For example, Listing 21.2 is a Function procedure that sums two ranges, stores the results in variables named totalSales and totalExpenses (see the section in this chapter titled "Working with Variables"), and then uses these values and the fixedCosts argument to calculate the net margin:

Listing 21.2. A sample Function procedure.

```
Function CalcNetMargin(fixedCosts)
    totalSales = Application.Sum(Range("Sales"))
    totalExpenses = Application.Sum(Range("Expenses"))
    CalcNetMargin = (totalSales-totalExpenses-fixedCosts)/totalSales
End Function
```

Calling a Procedure

Once you've written a procedure, you can use it either in a worksheet formula or in another procedure. This is known as *calling* the procedure.

Calling a Unique Procedure Name in the Same Workbook

If a procedure has a unique name in a workbook, you call it by entering the procedure name and then including any necessary arguments. For example, as you learned in the preceding chapter, you called the HypotenuseLength procedure from a worksheet cell by entering a formula such as the following:

```
=HypotenuseLength(3,4)
```

If you like, you also can call a procedure from another procedure. For example, the following VBA statement sets a variable named TotalPerimeter equal to the total perimeter of a right triangle that has two sides of length X and Y:

```
TotalPerimeter = X + Y + HypotenuseLength(X,Y)
```

Calling a Nonunique Procedure Name in the Same Workbook

Every procedure in a module must have a unique name, but you can have multiple modules in a workbook. Although you should try to give all your procedures unique names, that may not always be convenient. If you have a workbook with two or more procedures that have the same name, you can differentiate between them by calling each procedure with the following general format:

```
ModuleName.ProcedureName
```

For example, to call a procedure named NetMargin in a module named Financial, you would use the following form:

```
Financial.NetMargin
```

If the module name contains more than one word, enclose the name in square brackets, like this:

```
[Financial Functions].NetMargin
```

> **TIP**
>
> Some procedures are used only inside their own modules and shouldn't be called from another module or from a worksheet. To make sure of this, you can declare the procedure to be *private*. This means that no other module or worksheet can access the procedure. To declare a procedure as private, include the keyword Private before

either Sub or Function. For example, the following statement declares the SupportCode procedure as private:

```
Private Sub SupportCode()
```

Calling a Procedure in Another Workbook

If you have a VBA statement that needs to call a procedure in another workbook, you first need to set up a *reference* to the workbook. Doing this gives you access to all the workbook's procedures. The following procedure shows you what to do:

1. Activate the module containing the procedure that must access the other workbook.
2. Select the **T**ools | **R**eferences command. The References dialog box appears, as shown in Figure 21.7.

FIGURE 21.7.

Use the References dialog box to set up a reference between VBA and a workbook.

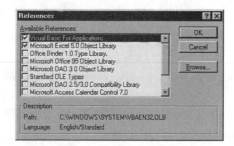

3. If the workbook is open, it will appear in the **A**vailable References list. Highlight the workbook and activate the check box. If the workbook isn't open, click the **B**rowse button, choose the workbook you want from the Browse dialog box that appears and then select OK to return to the References dialog box.
4. Select OK to return to the module.

Once you have the reference established, you call the procedure the same way you call the procedures in the current workbook. If the two workbooks have procedures with the same names, you need to add the workbook name and module name to the call:

```
[WorkbookName].ModuleName.ProcedureName
```

For example, the following statement calls the NetMargin procedure in the Financial module of the Budget.xls workbook:

```
[Budget.xls].Financial.NetMargin
```

Again, if the module name uses multiple words, enclose it in square brackets.

> **TIP**
>
> In the same way that you can make an individual procedure private, you also can make an entire module private. This prevents any other module or workbook from accessing the module's procedures. To declare a module as private, include the following statement near the top of the module (that is, before you define any procedures):
>
> ```
> Option Private Module
> ```

Working with Variables

Your VBA procedures often will need to store temporary values for use in later statements and calculations. For example, you might want to store values for total sales and total expenses to use later in a gross margin calculation. In VBA, as in most programming languages, you store temporary values in *variables*. This section explains this important topic and shows you how to use variables in your VBA procedures.

Declaring Variables

Declaring a variable tells VBA the name of the variable you're going to use. You declare variables by including Dim statements (Dim is short for *dimension*) at the beginning of each Sub or Function procedure. A Dim statement has the following syntax:

```
Dim variableName
```

variableName is the name of the variable. The name must begin with an alphabetic character, it can't be longer than 255 characters, it can't be a VBA keyword, and it can't contain a space or any of the following characters:

. ! # $ % & @

For example, the following statement declares a variable named totalSales:

```
Dim totalSales
```

> **NOTE**
>
> To avoid confusing variables with the names of objects, properties, or methods, many macro programmers begin their variable names with a lowercase letter. This is the style used in this book.

Most programmers set up a declaration section at the beginning of each procedure and use it to hold all their Dim statements. Then, once the variables have been declared, you can use them throughout the procedure. Figure 21.8 shows a Function procedure that declares two variables—totalSales and totalExpenses—and then uses Excel's Sum function to store a range sum in each variable. Finally, the CalcGrossMargin calculation uses each variable to return the function result.

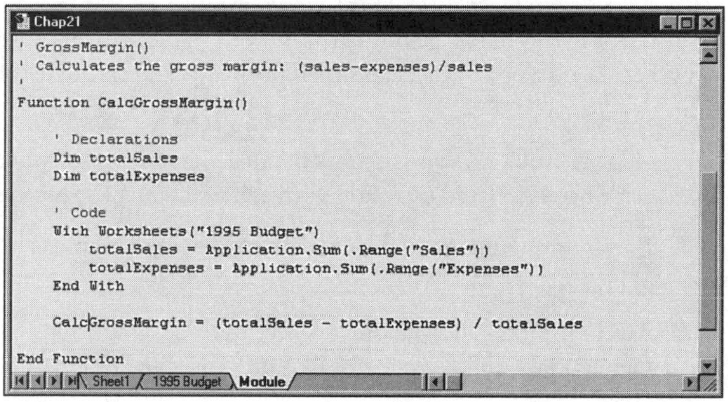

FIGURE 21.8.

A function that uses variables to store the intermediate values of a calculation.

```
' GrossMargin()
' Calculates the gross margin: (sales-expenses)/sales
'
Function CalcGrossMargin()

    ' Declarations
    Dim totalSales
    Dim totalExpenses

    ' Code
    With Worksheets("1995 Budget")
        totalSales = Application.Sum(.Range("Sales"))
        totalExpenses = Application.Sum(.Range("Expenses"))
    End With

    CalcGrossMargin = (totalSales - totalExpenses) / totalSales

End Function
```

In the CalcGrossMargin function, notice that you store a value in a variable with a simple assignment statement of the following form:

variableName = value

TIP

To conserve space, you can declare multiple variables on a single line. In the CalcGrossMargin function, for example, you could declare totalSales and totalExpenses using the following statement:

```
Dim totalSales, totalExpenses
```

NOTE

If you want to use a variable in all the procedures in a module, place the declaration at the top of the module before your first procedure. This is called a *global* declaration.

Avoiding Variable Errors

One of the most common errors in VBA procedures is to declare a variable and then later misspell the name. For example, suppose I had entered the following statement in the `GrossMargin` procedure from the preceding section:

```
totlExpenses = Application.Sum(.Range("Expenses"))
```

VBA supports *implicit declarations,* which means that if it sees a name it doesn't recognize, it assumes that the name belongs to a new variable. In this case, VBA would assume that `totlExpenses` is a new variable, proceed normally, and calculate the wrong answer for the function.

To avoid this problem, you can tell VBA to generate an error whenever it comes across a name that hasn't been declared explicitly with a `Dim` statement. There are two ways to do this:

- For an individual module, enter the following statement before the first procedure:

  `Option Explicit`

- To do it for all your modules, select the **T**ools | **O**ptions command, select the Module General tab, and activate the **R**equire Variable Declaration check box.

> **NOTE**
>
> Activating the **R**equire Variable Declaration check box forces VBA to add the `Option Explicit` statement at the beginning of each new module. However, it *doesn't* add this statement to any existing modules; you need to do that by hand.

Variable Data Types

The *data type* of a variable determines the kind of data the variable can hold. Table 21.1 lists all the VBA data types.

Table 21.1. The VBA data types.

Data Type	Description	Storage Size	Type-Declaration Character
Array	A set of variables where each element in the set is referenced by an index number.	Depends on the size of the array.	
Boolean	Takes one of two logical values: TRUE or FALSE.	2 bytes	

Data Type	Description	Storage Size	Type-Declaration Character
Currency	Used for monetary or fixed-decimal calculations where accuracy is important. The value range is from –922,337,203,685,477.5808 to 922,337,203,685,477.5807.	8 bytes	@
Date	Used for holding date data. The range is from January 1, 0100 to December 31, 9999.	8 bytes	
Double	Double-precision floating point. Negative numbers range from –1.79769313486232E308 to –4.94065645841247E–324. Positive numbers range from 4.94065645841247E–324 to 1.79769313486232E308.	8 bytes	#
Integer	Small integer values only. The range is from –32,768 to 32,767.	2 bytes	%
Long	Large integer values. The range is from –2,147,483,648 to 2,147,483,647.	4 bytes	&
Object	Refers to objects only.	4 bytes	
Single	Single-precision floating point. Negative numbers range from –3.402823E38 to –1.401298E–45. Positive numbers range from 1.401298E–45 to 3.402823E38.	4 bytes	!
String	Holds string values. The strings can be up to 64KB.	1 byte per character	$
Variant	Can take any kind of data.		

You specify a data type by including the As keyword in a Dim statement. Here is the general syntax:

```
Dim variableName As DataType
```

variableName	The name of the variable.
DataType	One of the data types from Table 21.1.

For example, the following statement declares a variable named `textString` to be of type `String`:

```
Dim textString As String
```

Here are a few notes to keep in mind when using data types:

- If you don't include a data type when declaring a variable, VBA assigns the `Variant` data type. This enables you to store any kind of data in the variable.

- If you declare a variable to be one data type and then try to store a value of a different data type in the variable, VBA displays an error. To help avoid this, many programmers like to use the *type-declaration characters*. (See Table 21.1.) By appending one of these characters to the end of a variable name, you automatically declare the variable to be of the type represented by the character. For example, `$` is the type-declaration character for a string, so the variable `textString$` is automatically a `String` data type variable. Having the `$` (or whatever) at the end of the variable name also reminds you of the data type, so you'll be less likely to store the wrong type of data.

- To specify the data type of a procedure argument, use the `As` keyword in the argument list. For example, the following `Function` statement declares variables x and y to be `Single`:

```
Function HypotenuseLength(x As Single, y As Single)
```

- To specify the data type of the return value in a `Function` procedure, use the `As` keyword at the end of the `Function` statement:

```
Function HypotenuseLength(x, y) As Single
```

Using Array Variables

In Chapter 2, "Building Better Formulas," I told you about Excel arrays, which I defined as a group of cells or values that Excel treats as a unit. VBA, too, has arrays. In this case, though, an array is a group of variables of the same data type.

Why would you need to use an array? Well, suppose you wanted to store 20 employee names in variables to use in a procedure. One way to do this would be to create 20 variables named, say, `employee1`, `employee2`, and so on. It's much more efficient to create a single `employee` array variable that can hold up to 20 names. Here's how you would do so:

```
Dim employee(19) As String
```

As you can see, this declaration is very similar to one you would use for a regular variable. The difference is the 19 enclosed in parentheses. The parentheses tell VBA that you're declaring an array, and the number tells VBA how many elements you'll need in the array. Why 19 instead of 20? Well, each element in the array is assigned a *subscript*, where the first element's subscript is 0, the second is 1, and so on up to, in this case, 19. So the total number of elements in this array is 20.

You use the subscripts to refer to any element simply by enclosing its index number in the parentheses, like so:

```
employee(0) = "Ponsonby"
```

By default, the subscripts of VBA arrays start at 0 (this is called the *lower bound* of the array) and run up to the number you specify in the Dim statement (this is called the *upper bound* of the array). If you would prefer your array index numbers to start at 1, include the following statement at the top of the module (that is, before declaring your first array and before your first procedure):

```
Option Base 1
```

Another way to specify a specific lower bound is to add the To keyword to your array declaration. Here's the syntax:

```
Dim arrayName(LowerBound To UpperBound) As DataType
```

arrayName	The name of the array variable.
LowerBound	A long integer specifying the lower bound of the array.
UpperBound	A long integer specifying the upper bound of the array.
DataType	One of the data types from Table 21.1.

For example, here's a declaration that creates an array variable with subscripts running from 50 to 100:

```
Dim myArray(50 To 100) As Currency
```

Dynamic Arrays

What do you do if you're not sure how many subscripts you'll need in an array? You could guess at the correct number, but that might leave you with one of the following problems:

- If you guess too low and try to access a subscript higher than the array's upper bound, VBA will generate an error message.
- If you guess too high, VBA will still allocate memory to the unused portions of the array, so you'll waste precious system resources.

To avoid both of these problems, you can declare a *dynamic* array by leaving the parentheses blank in the Dim statement:

```
Dim myArray() As Double
```

Then, when you know the number of elements you need, you can use a ReDim statement to allocate the correct number of subscripts (notice that you don't specify a data type in the ReDim statement):

```
ReDim myArray(52)
```

A partial listing of a procedure named `PerformCalculations` follows. The procedure declares `calcValues` as a dynamic array and `totalValues` as an integer. Later in the procedure, `totalValues` is set to the result of a function procedure named `GetTotalValues`. The `ReDim` statement then uses `totalValues` to allocate the appropriate number of subscripts to the `calcValues` array.

```
Sub PerformCalculations()
    Dim calcValues() As Double, totalValues as Integer
.
.
.
    totalValues = GetTotalValues()
    ReDim calcValues(totalValues)
.
.
.
End Sub
```

Multidimensional Arrays

If you enter a single number between the parentheses in an array's `Dim` statement, VBA creates a *one-dimensional* array. But you also can create arrays with two or more dimensions (60 is the maximum). For example, suppose you wanted to store both a first name and a last name in your `employees` array. To store two sets of data with each element, you would declare a two-dimensional array, like so:

```
Dim employees(19,1) As String
```

The subscripts for the second number work like the subscripts you've seen already. That is, they begin at 0 and run up to the number you specify. So this *Dim* statement sets up a "table" (or a *matrix*, as it's usually called) with 20 "rows" (one for each employee) and two "columns" (one for the first name and one for the last name). Here are two statements that initialize the data for the first employee:

```
employees(0,0) = "Biff"
employees(0,1) = "Ponsonby"
```

Working with Constants

Constants are values that don't change. They can be numbers, strings, or other values, but, unlike variables, they keep their value throughout your code. VBA recognizes two types of constants: built-in and user-defined.

Using Built-In Constants

Many properties and methods have their own predefined constants. For Excel objects, these constants begin with the letters `xl`. For VBA objects, the constants begin with `vb`.

For example, the Window object's `WindowState` property recognizes three built-in constants: `xlNormal` (to set a window in its normal state), `xlMaximized` (to maximize a window), and `xlMinimized` (to minimize a window). To maximize the active window, for example, you would use the following statement:

```
ActiveWindow.WindowState = xlMaximized
```

You can see a list of the Excel and VBA built-in constants by following these steps:

1. Activate a module in any open workbook.
2. Select the **View | O**bject Browser command to display the Object Browser dialog box.
3. In the **Libraries/Workbooks** list, select either VBA or Excel.
4. In the **Ob**jects/Modules list, select Constants. A list of built-in constants appears in the **Methods/Properties** list, as shown in Figure 21.9.

FIGURE 21.9.

You can use the Object Browser to display a list of the Excel and VBA built-in constants.

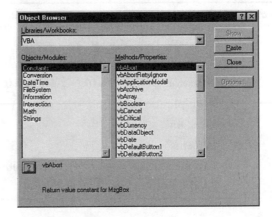

5. If you want to use the constant in your code, highlight it and then select the **P**aste button. Otherwise, select Close to return to the module.

Creating User-Defined Constants

To create your own constants, use the `Const` statement:

```
Const CONSTANTNAME = expression
```

CONSTANTNAME	The name of the constant. Most programmers use all-uppercase names for constants.
expression	The value (or a formula that returns a value) that you want to use for the constant.

For example, the following statement creates a constant named `DISCOUNT` and assigns it the value `0.4`:

```
Const DISCOUNT = 0.4
```

VBA Operators

Just as you use operators such as addition (+) and multiplication (*) to build formulas in Excel worksheets, so too do you use operators to combine functions, variables, and values in a VBA statement. VBA operators fall into four general categories: arithmetic, comparison, logical, and miscellaneous.

Arithmetic Operators

VBA's arithmetic operators are similar to those you've been using in your worksheets. Table 21.2 lists each of the arithmetic operators you can use in your VBA statements.

Table 21.2. The VBA arithmetic operators.

Operator	Name	Example	Result
+	Addition	10+5	15
–	Subtraction	10–5	5
–	Negation	–10	–10
*	Multiplication	10*5	50
/	Division	10/5	2
%	Percentage	10%	0.1
^	Exponentiation	10^5	100000
Mod	Modulus	10 Mod 5	0

The Mod operator works like Excel's MOD() worksheet function. That is, it divides one number by another and returns the remainder. Here's the general form to use:

```
result = dividend Mod divisor
```

    dividend   The number being divided.

    divisor   The number being divided into *dividend*.

    result   The remainder of the division.

For example, 16 Mod 5 returns 1 because 5 goes into 16 three times with 1 remainder.

Comparison Operators

You use the comparison operators in a statement that compares two or more numbers, text strings, cell contents, or function results. If the statement is true, the result of the formula is given the logical value True (which is equivalent to any nonzero value). If the statement is false, the formula returns the logical value False (which is equivalent to 0). Table 21.3 summarizes VBA's comparison operators.

Table 21.3. The VBA comparison operators.

Operator	Name	Example	Result
=	Equal to	=10=5	False
>	Greater than	=10>5	True
<	Less than	=10<5	False
>=	Greater than or equal to	="a">="b"	False
<=	Less than or equal to	="a"<="b"	True
<>	Not equal to	="a"<>"b"	True

Logical Operators

You use the logical operators to combine or modify true/false expressions. Table 21.4 summarizes VBA's logical operators.

Table 21.4. The VBA logical operators.

Operator	General Form	What It Returns
And	*Expr1* And *Expr2*	True if both *Expr1* and *Expr2* are True; False otherwise.
Eqv	*Expr1* Eqv *Expr2*	True if both *Expr1* and *Expr2* are True or if both *Expr1* and *Expr2* are False; False otherwise.
Imp	*Expr1* Imp *Expr2*	False if *Expr1* is True and *Expr2* is False; True otherwise.
Or	*Expr1* Or *Expr2*	True if at least one of *Expr1* and *Expr2* are True; False otherwise.
Xor	*Expr1* Xor *Expr2*	False if both *Expr1* and *Expr2* are True or if both *Expr1* and *Expr2* are False; True otherwise.
Not	Not *Expr*	True if *Expr* is False; False if *Expr* is True.

Miscellaneous Operators

Besides the operators just mentioned, VBA also recognizes three other operators: concatenation (&), similarity (Like), and Equivalence (Is).

Like Excel's & operator, you use VBA's concatenation operator (&) to combine strings, cell contents, string variables, or the results of string functions. For example, the following listing shows a simple Function procedure that accepts two strings as arguments and returns the two strings combined, separated by a space:

```
Function Concatenate(firstWord, secondWord) As String

    Concatenate = firstWord & " " & secondWord

End Function
```

The similarity operator (Like) compares two strings using the following syntax:

```
result = string Like pattern
```

string	A string, string variable, cell value, or string function result.
pattern	The string or pattern that you want to compare with *string*. You can use a string, string variable, cell value, or string function result. If you use a string, you can include the following wildcard characters:

Character	What It Matches
?	Any single character
*	A group of characters
#	A single digit
[charlist]	Any single character in charlist
[!charlist]	Any single character not in charlist
result	True if pattern is contained in string; False otherwise.

Here are a few examples of the Like operator in action:

Expression	Result
"Reed" Like "Reid"	False
"Reed" Like "R*d"	True
"1234.95" Like "1234.9#"	True
"Reed" Like "Re[aei]d"	True
"Reed" Like "Re[!ae]d"	False

> **NOTE**
>
> VBA string comparisons are case-sensitive by default. If you would prefer to use case-

insensitive comparisons, add the following statement to the top of the module:

```
Option Compare Text
```

You use the equivalence operator (Is) to see if two object variables refer to the same object. (You'll be learning about Excel and VBA objects in the next chapter.) Here's the syntax:

```
result = object1 Is object2
```

> object1   An object variable.
>
> object2   An object variable.
>
> result   True if both *object1* and *object2* refer to the same object; False otherwise.

Summary

This chapter introduced you to VBA, Excel's powerful macro and development language. I showed you how to record, write, and run a macro, how to create procedures and user-defined functions, and how to work with variables and operators. You'll find related information in the following chapters:

- Excel has a number of options you can use to customize VBA. I outlined each option in Chapter 8, "Customizing Excel."

- You can create worksheet-level dialog boxes using macro buttons combined with the check boxes, list boxes, option buttons and other dialog box controls. I showed you how to add dialog box controls to a worksheet in Chapter 5, "Advanced Worksheet Topics."

- Objects are one of the most important concepts in VBA. To learn how they work, see Chapter 22, "Understanding Objects."

- You can run macros from custom menus and toolbars. I show you how in Chapter 26, "Database and Client/Server Programming."

- VBA boasts a number of methods for running macros automatically (such as when the user opens a workbook, presses a key, or enters data in a cell). See Chapter 27, "VBA Procedures That Respond to Events," for details.

- You'll find a summary of every VBA statement in Appendix B, "VBA Statements."

- Appendix C, "VBA Functions," presents a brief look at all the VBA functions.

Understanding Objects

22

Many of your VBA procedures will perform calculations using simple combinations of numbers, operators, and Excel's built-in functions. You'll probably find, however, that most of your code manipulates the Excel environment in some way, whether it's entering data in a range, formatting a chart, or setting Excel workspace options. Each of these items—the range, the chart, the Excel workspace—is called an *object* in VBA. Objects are perhaps the most crucial concept in VBA programming, and I explain them in detail in this chapter.

What Is an Object?

The dictionary definition of an object is "anything perceptible by one or more of the senses, especially something that can be seen and felt." Of course, you can't feel anything in Excel, but you can see all kinds of things. To VBA, an object is anything in Excel that you can see *and* manipulate in some way. For example, a range is something you can see, and you can manipulate it by entering data, changing colors, setting fonts, and so on. A range, therefore, is an object.

What isn't an object? Excel 7.0 is so customizable that most things you can see qualify as objects, but not everything does. For example, the Maximize and Minimize buttons in workbook windows are not objects. Yes, you can operate them, but you can't change them. Instead, the window itself is the object, and you manipulate it so that it is maximized or minimized.

You can manipulate objects in VBA in one of two ways:

- You can make changes to the object's *properties*.
- You can make the object perform a task by activating a *method* associated with the object.

To help you understand properties, methods, and objects, I'll put things in real-world terms. Specifically, let's look at your computer as though it were an Excel object. For starters, you can think of your computer in one of two ways: as a single object and as a *collection* of objects (such as the monitor, the keyboard, the system unit, and so on).

If you wanted to describe your computer as a whole, you would mention things like the name of the manufacturer, the price, the color, and so on. Each of these items is a *property* of the computer. You also can use your computer to perform tasks, such as writing letters, crunching numbers, and playing games. These are the *methods* associated with your computer. The sum total of all these properties and methods gives you an overall description of your computer.

But your computer is also a collection of objects, each with its own properties and methods. The system unit, for example, has all kinds of properties: the height, width, and weight, the type of processor, the size of the hard disk, and so on. Its methods would be things such as turning the computer on and off and inserting and removing disks.

If you like, you can extend this analysis to lower levels. For example, the system unit is also a collection of objects (the hard disk, the motherboard, the power supply).

In the end, you have a complete description of the computer, both in terms of what it looks like (its properties) and in terms of how it behaves (its methods).

The Object Hierarchy

As we've seen, your computer's objects are arranged in a hierarchy with the most general object (the computer as a whole) at the top. Lower levels progress through more specific objects (such as the system unit, the motherboard, and the processor).

Excel's objects are arranged in a hierarchy also. The most general object—the Application object—refers to Excel itself. Beneath the Application object, Excel has nine objects, as outlined in Table 22.1. Notice that, in most cases, each object is part of a *collection* of similar objects.

Table 22.1. Excel objects beneath the Application object.

Object	Collection	Description
AddIn	AddIns	An Excel add-in file. The AddIns collection refers to all the add-ins available to Excel (that is, all the add-ins that are listed in the Add-Ins dialog box).
AutoCorrect	None	Contains the settings for the AutoCorrect feature.
Debug	None	The VBA Debug window.
Dialog	Dialogs	A built-in Excel dialog box. The Dialogs object is a collection of all the Excel built-in dialog boxes.
Name	Names	A defined name. The Names collection is a list of all the defined names available to Excel, including built-in names such as Database and Print_Area.
MenuBar	MenuBars	A menu bar. The MenuBars object is the collection of Excel menu bars, both built-in and custom.
Toolbar	Toolbars	A toolbar. The Toolbars collection is a list of all the built-in and custom toolbars that are available.
Window	Windows	An open window. The Windows object is the collection of all the open windows.
Workbook	Workbooks	An open workbook. The Workbooks object is the collection of all the open workbooks.

> **NOTE**
>
> I won't discuss any of these objects in detail in this chapter. For the Application, AutoCorrect, Name, AddIn, Window, and Workbook objects (as well as many others, including ranges and charts), see Chapter 24, "Manipulating Excel with VBA." For the Dialog, MenuBar, and Toolbar objects, see Chapter 25, "Creating a Custom User Interface." For the Debug object, see Chapter 29, "Debugging VBA Procedures."

Most of the objects in Table 22.1 have objects beneath them in the hierarchy. A Workbook object, for example, contains Worksheet objects and possibly Chart objects and Module objects. Similarly, a Worksheet object contains many objects of its own, such as Range objects and an Outline object.

To specify an object in the hierarchy, you usually start with the uppermost object and add the lower objects, separated by periods. For example, here's one way you could specify the range B2:B5 on the worksheet named Sheet1 in the workbook named Book1:

```
Application.Workbooks("Book1").Worksheets("Sheet1").Range("B2:B5")
```

As you'll see, there are ways to shorten such long-winded "hierarchical paths."

Working with Object Properties

Every Excel object has a defining set of characteristics. These characteristics are called the object's *properties,* and they control the appearance and position of the object. For example, each Window object has a WindowState property you can use to display a window as maximized, minimized, or normal. Similarly, a Range object has a Font property that defines the range font, a Formula property for the range formula, a Name property to hold the range name, and many more.

When you refer to a property, you use the following syntax:

```
Object.Property
```

For example, the following expression refers to the ActiveWindow property of the Application object:

```
Application.ActiveWindow
```

One of the most confusing aspects of objects and properties is that some properties do double duty as objects. Figure 22.1 illustrates this. The Application object has an ActiveWindow property that tells you the name of the active window. However, ActiveWindow is also a Window object. Similarly, the Window object has an ActiveCell property, but ActiveCell is also a Range object. Finally, a Range object has a Font property, but a font is also an object with its own properties (Italic, Name, Size, and so on).

FIGURE 22.1.

Some Excel properties also can be objects.

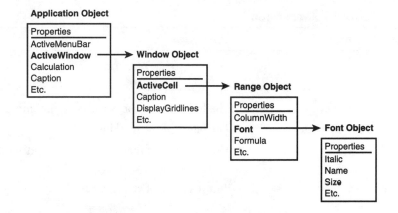

In other words, lower-level objects in the object hierarchy are really just properties of their parent objects. This idea will often help you to reduce the length of a hierarchical path (and thus save wear and tear on your typing fingers). For example, consider the following object path:

```
Application.ActiveWindow.ActiveCell.Font.Italic
```

Here, an object such as `ActiveCell` implicitly refers to the `ActiveWindow` and `Application` objects, so you can knock the path down to size as follows:

```
ActiveCell.Font.Italic
```

Common Object Properties

Each Excel object has a number of properties. Table 22.2 is a list of frequently used properties associated with the some of the common objects I mentioned earlier.

Table 22.2. Frequently used properties of some common Excel objects.

Property	Description
	Application
ActiveWindow	The active window
ActiveWorkbook	The active workbook
Calculation	The calculation mode
Caption	The name that appears in the title bar of the main Excel window
ScreenUpdating	Turns screen updating on or off
StandardFont	The standard font name for new worksheets

continues

Table 22.2. continued

Property	Description
	Workbook
ActiveSheet	The active sheet
FullName	The full name of the workbook, including the path
Name	The name of the workbook
Path	The full path of the workbook, excluding the name of the workbook
Saved	Returns False if changes have been made to the workbook
	Worksheet
Name	The name of the worksheet
ProtectContents	Protects the worksheet cell contents
Visible	Hides or unhides the worksheet
	Window
ActiveCell	The active cell
Caption	The name that appears in the window's title bar
DisplayGridlines	Turns the grid lines on or off
DisplayHeadings	Turns the row and column headings on or off
Visible	Hides or unhides the window
WindowState	Sets the window view to maximized, minimized, or normal
	Range
Column	The first column of the range
Font	The font of the range
Formula	The range formula
Name	The range name
Row	The first row of the range
Style	The range style
Value	The value of a cell
Worksheet	The worksheet that contains the range

NOTE

To learn how to refer to individual workbooks, worksheets, and windows, see the section in this chapter titled "Working with Object Collections."

Setting the Value of a Property

To set a property to a certain value, you use the following syntax:

```
Object.Property=value
```

Here, `value` is the value you want to use. `value` can be either a constant or a formula that returns a constant, and it can be any one of the following types:

- A numeric value. For example, the following statement sets the size of the font in the active cell to 14:

  ```
  ActiveCell.Font.Size = 14
  ```

- A string value. You denote a string by surrounding it with double quotation marks. The following example sets the font name in the active cell to Times New Roman:

  ```
  ActiveCell.Font.Name = "Times New Roman"
  ```

- A logical value (that is, `True` or `False`). The following statement turns on the `Italic` property in the active cell:

  ```
  ActiveCell.Font.Italic = True
  ```

Returning the Value of a Property

Sometimes you need to know the current setting of a property before changing the property or performing some other action. You can find out the current value of a property by using the following syntax:

```
variable=Object.Property
```

Here, `variable` is a variable or another property. For example, the following statement stores the contents of the active cell in a variable named `cellContents`:

```
cellContents = ActiveCell.Value
```

Working with Object Methods

An object's properties describe what the object is, whereas its *methods* describe what the object *does*. For example, a Worksheet object can recalculate its formulas using the `Calculate` method. Similarly, a Range object can sort its cells by using the `Sort` method.

How you refer to a method depends on whether or not the method uses any arguments. If it doesn't, the syntax is similar to that of properties:

```
Object.Method
```

For example, the following statement saves the active workbook:

```
ActiveWorkbook.Save
```

If the method requires arguments, you use the following syntax:

```
Object.Method (argument1, argument2, ...)
```

> **NOTE**
>
> Technically, the parentheses around the argument list are necessary only if you'll be storing the result of the method in a variable or object property.

For example, the Range object has an `Offset` method that returns a range offset from the specified range. Here's the syntax:

```
Object.Offset(rowOffset, columnOffset)
```

Object	The Range object.
rowOffset	The number of rows to offset.
columnOffset	The number of columns to offset.

For example, the following expression returns a cell offset five rows and three columns from the active cell:

```
ActiveCell.Offset(5, 3)
```

To make your methods clearer to read, you can use VBA's predefined *named arguments*. For example, the syntax of the `Offset` method has two named arguments: *rowOffset* and *columnOffset*. Here's how you would use them in the previous example:

```
ActiveCell.Offset(rowOffset:=5, columnOffset:=3)
```

Notice how the named arguments are assigned values by using the := operator.

> **TIP**
>
> Another advantage to using named arguments is that you can enter the arguments in any order you like, and you can ignore any arguments you don't need (except necessary arguments, of course).

> **NOTE**
>
> In this example, the `Offset` method returns a Range object. It is quite common for methods to return objects, and it's perfectly acceptable to change the properties or use a method of the returned object.

Common Object Methods

Each Excel object has several methods you can use. Table 22.3 summarizes a few of the most frequently used methods associated with the common objects discussed earlier.

> **NOTE**
>
> You can find more detailed descriptions of most of these methods in Chapter 24, "Manipulating Excel with VBA."

Table 22.3. Frequently used methods for common Excel objects.

Method	Description
	Application
FindFile	Displays the Find File dialog box.
Quit	Exits Excel.
Undo	Cancels the last action.
	Workbook
Activate	Activates a workbook.
Close	Closes a workbook.
Protect	Protects a workbook.
Save	Saves a workbook.
Save As	Saves a workbook under a different name.
Unprotect	Unprotects a workbook.
	Worksheet
Activate	Activates a worksheet.
Calculate	Recalculates a worksheet.
Copy	Copies a worksheet.
Delete	Deletes a worksheet.
Move	Moves a worksheet.
Protect	Protects a worksheet.
Unprotect	Unprotects a worksheet.
	Window
Activate	Activates a window.
Close	Closes a window.

continues

Table 22.3. continued

Method	Description
	Range
Clear	Clears everything from the range.
ClearContents	Clears the contents of each cell in the range.
ClearFormats	Clears the formatting of every cell in the range.
Copy	Copies the range.
Cut	Cuts the range.
Offset	Returns a range that is offset from the specified range.
Paste	Pastes the Clipboard contents into the range.
Select	Selects a range.
Sort	Sorts the range.

Working with Object Collections

A *collection* is a set of similar objects. For example, the Workbooks collection is the set of all the open Workbook objects. Similarly, the Worksheets collection is the set of all Worksheet objects in a workbook. Collections are objects, so they have their own properties and methods, and you can use the properties and methods to manipulate one or more objects in the collection.

The members of a collection are called the *elements* of the collection. You can refer to individual elements using either the object's name or by using an *index*. For example, the following statement closes a workbook named Budget.xls:

```
Workbooks("Budget.xls").Close
```

On the other hand, the following statement uses an index to make a copy of the first picture object in the active worksheet:

```
ActiveSheet.Pictures(1).Copy
```

If you don't specify an element, VBA assumes you want to work with the entire collection.

> **NOTE**
>
> It's important here to reiterate that you can't refer to many Excel objects by themselves. Instead, you must refer to the object as an element in a collection. For example,

when referring to the Budget.xls workbook, you can't just use `Budget.xls`. You have to use `Workbooks("Budget.xls")` so that VBA knows you're talking about a currently open workbook.

Common Object Collections

Here's a list of collections that you are likely to use most frequently:

`Sheets`	Contains all the sheets in a workbook. This includes not only worksheets, but also modules, charts, and dialog sheets. The available methods include `Add` (to create a new sheet), `Copy`, `Delete`, `Move`, and `Select`.
`Workbooks`	Contains all the open workbooks. Use this collection's `Open` method to open a workbook. The `Add` method creates a new workbook.
`Worksheets`	Contains all the worksheets in a workbook. The `Visible` property enables you to hide or unhide the collection. The methods are the same as for `Sheets`.
`Windows`	Contains all the open windows. The `Arrange` method enables you to arrange the collection on-screen (for example, tile or cascade).

Using the Object Browser

The Object Browser is a handy tool that shows you the objects available for your procedures as well as the properties and methods of each object. You also can use it to move quickly between procedures and to paste code templates into a module. To display the Object Browser, activate a module and then either select the **View | O**bject Browser command or click on the Object Browser button on the Visual Basic toolbar. You'll see the Object Browser dialog box, shown in Figure 22.2.

 The Object Browser button on the Visual Basic toolbar.

TIP

You also can press F2 to display the Object Browser.

FIGURE 22.2.

VBA's Object Browser.

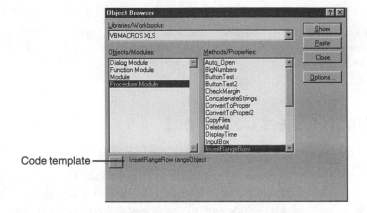

Code template

Here's a rundown of the Object Browser's features:

- ■ **Libraries/Workbooks:** This drop-down list contains all the libraries and workbooks referenced by any module in the current workbook. A *library* is a file that contains information about the objects in an application. You'll always see at least two libraries in this list: The Excel library lists the Excel objects you can use in your code, and the VBA (Visual Basic for Applications) library lists the functions and language constructs specific to VBA.

- ■ **Objects/Modules:** When you highlight a library in **Libraries/Workbooks**, the **Ob**jects/ Modules list shows the available objects in the library. When you highlight a workbook, **Ob**jects/Modules shows the modules in the workbook.

- ■ **Methods/Properties:** When you highlight an object in the **Ob**jects/Modules list, **M**ethods/Properties shows the methods and properties available for that object. When you highlight a module, **M**ethods/Properties shows the procedures contained in the module. To move to one of these procedures, highlight it, and then click on the **S**how button.

- ■ Code template: This section displays code templates you can paste into your modules. These templates list the method, property, or function name followed by the appropriate named arguments, if there are any. (See Figure 22.3.) You can paste this template into a procedure and then edit the template. Follow the next steps to paste code templates.

    1. In a VBA module, place the insertion point where you want the code template to appear.

    2. Display the Object Browser, as described earlier.

    3. Select a library from the **Libraries/Workbooks** list and then select an object from the Objects/Modules list.

4. Use the **Methods/Properties** list to highlight the method or property you want to use.

5. If you would like to display a Help screen for the selected method or property, select the **?** button, read the Help screen that appears, and then return to the Object Browser.

6. Select the **Paste** button. VBA returns you to the module and pastes the code template into the procedure.

FIGURE 22.3.

The Object Browser displays code templates that you can paste into your procedures.

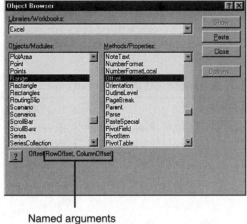

Named arguments

Assigning an Object to a Variable

As you learned in the preceding chapter, you can declare a variable as an Object data type by using the following form of the Dim statement:

```
Dim variableName As Object
```

Once you've set up your object variable, you can assign an object to it by using the Set statement. Set has the following syntax:

```
Set variableName = ObjectName
```

variableName   The name of the variable.

ObjectName   The object you want to assign to the variable.

For example, the following statements declare a variable named budgetSheet to be an Object and then assign it to the 1995 Budget worksheet in the Budget.xls workbook:

```
Dim budgetSheet As Object
Set budgetSheet = Workbooks("Budget.xls").Worksheets("1995 Budget")
```

Working with Multiple Properties or Methods

Because most Excel objects have many different properties and methods, you'll often need to perform multiple actions on a single object. This is accomplished easily with multiple statements that set the appropriate properties or run the necessary methods. However, this can be a pain if you have a long object name.

For example, take a look at the `FormatRange` procedure shown in Listing 22.1. This procedure formats a range in the Sales worksheet with six statements. The Range object name—`Worksheets("Sales").Range("B2:B5")`—is quite long and is repeated in all six statements.

Listing 22.1. A procedure that formats a range.

```
Sub FormatRange()

    Worksheets("Sales").Range("B2:B5").Style = "Currency"
    Worksheets("Sales").Range("B2:B5").WrapText = True
    Worksheets("Sales").Range("B2:B5").Font.Size = 16
    Worksheets("Sales").Range("B2:B5").Font.Bold = True
    Worksheets("Sales").Range("B2:B5").Font.Color = RGB(255, 0, 0) ' Red
    Worksheets("Sales").Range("B2:B5").Font.Name = "Times New Roman"

End Sub
```

> **NOTE**
>
> You'll find the code for the `FormatRange` procedure, as well as all the other procedures in this chapter, on this book's CD. Look for the file named Chap22.xls.

To shorten this procedure, VBA provides the `With` statement. Here's the syntax:

```
With object
    [statements]
End With
```

`object`	The name of the object.
`statements`	The statements you want to execute on *object*.

The idea is that you strip out the common object and place it on the `With` line. Then all the statements between `With` and `End With` need only reference a specific method or property of that object. In the `FormatRange` procedure, the common object in all six statements is `Worksheets("Sales").Range("B2:B5")`. Listing 22.2 shows the `FormatRange2` procedure that uses the `With` statement to strip out this common object and make the previous macro more efficient:

Listing 22.2. A more efficient version of `FormatRange()`.

```
Sub FormatRange2()

    With Worksheets("Sales").Range("B2:B5")
        .Style = "Currency"
        .WrapText = True
        .Font.Size = 16
        .Font.Bold = True
        .Font.Color = RGB(255, 0, 0) 'Red
        .Font.Name = "Times New Roman"
    End With

End Sub
```

NOTE

You can make the `FormatRange2` procedure even more efficient when you realize that the Font object also is repeated several times. In this case, you can *nest* another `With` statement inside the original one. The new `With` statement would look like this:

```
With .Font
    .Size = 16
    .Bold = True
    .Color = RGB(255, 0, 0)
    .Name = "Times New Roman"
End With
```

Summary

This chapter introduced you to the all-important subject of objects. I told you what an object is and I showed you how Excel's objects are arranged in a hierarchy, with the `Application` object at the top. We then examined object properties, methods, collections, and variables, and I also showed you how to use the Object Browser.

- VBA's `For Each...Next` loop provides you with an easy way to cycle through all the elements in an object collection. I'll tell you how to use this loop in Chapter 23, "Controlling VBA Code and Interacting with the User."

- For more detailed discussions of many of Excel's objects (including the `Application`, Window, Workbook, Range, and Chart objects, see Chapter 24, "Manipulating Excel with VBA."

- For the Dialog, MenuBar, and Toolbar objects, see Chapter 25, "Creating a Custom User Interface."

- To learn how to use the `Debug` object, see Chapter 29, "Debugging VBA Procedures."

- You'll find a summary of every VBA statement in Appendix B, "VBA Statements."

- Appendix C, "VBA Functions," presents a brief look at all the VBA functions.

Controlling VBA Code and Interacting with the User

23

One of the advantages of writing your own VBA procedures instead of simply recording them is that you end up with much more control over what your code does and how it performs its tasks. In particular, you can create procedures that make decisions based on certain conditions and that can perform *loops*—the running of several statements repeatedly. The statements that handle this kind of processing—*control structures*—are the subject of this chapter.

Code That Makes Decisions

A smart procedure performs tests on its environment and then decides what to do next based on the results of each test. For example, suppose you've written a `Function` procedure that uses one of its arguments as a divisor in a formula. You should test the argument before using it in the formula to make sure that it isn't 0 (to avoid producing a `Division by zero` error). If it is, you could then display a message that alerts the user of the illegal argument.

Using *If...Then* to Make True/False Decisions

Simple true/false decisions are handled by the `If...Then` statement. You can use either the single-line syntax or the *block* syntax:

```
If condition Then statement
```

or

```
If condition Then
    [statements]
End If
```

`condition`	You can either use a logical expression that returns `True` or `False` or you can use any expression that returns a numeric value. In the latter case, a return value of zero is functionally equivalent to `False`, and any nonzero value is equivalent to `True`.
`statement(s)`	The VBA statement or statements to run if `condition` returns `True`. If `condition` returns `False`, VBA skips over the `statements`.

Whether you use the single-line or block syntax depends on the statements you want to run if the `condition` returns a `True` result. If you have only one statement, you can use either syntax. If you have multiple statements, you must use the block syntax.

Listing 23.1 shows a revised version of the `CalcGrossMargin` procedure from Chapter 21, "Getting Started with VBA." This version—called `CalcGrossMargin2`—uses `If...Then` to check the `totalSales` variable. The procedure calculates the gross margin only if `totalSales` is not zero.

Listing 23.1. An `If...Then` example.

```
Function CalcGrossMargin2()

    Dim totalSales
    Dim totalExpenses

    With Worksheets("1995 Budget")
        totalSales = Application.Sum(.Range("Sales"))
        totalExpenses = Application.Sum(.Range("Expenses"))
    End With

    If totalSales <> 0 Then
        CalcGrossMargin2 = (totalSales - totalExpenses) / totalSales
    End If

End Function
```

NOTE

You'll find the `CalcGrossMargin2` procedure, and all the procedures listed in this chapter, in the file Chap23.xls on the CD that is included with this book.

TIP

You can make the `If...Then` statement in the `CalcGrossMargin2` procedure slightly more efficient by taking advantage of the fact that in the condition, zero is equivalent to `False` and any other number is equivalent to `True`. This means you don't have to explicitly test the `totalSales` variable to see whether it is zero. Instead, you can use the following statements:

```
If totalSales Then
    GrossMargin = (totalSales-totalExpenses)/totalSales
End If
```

On the other hand, many programmers feel that including the explicit test for a nonzero value (`totalSales <> 0`) makes the procedure easier to read and more intuitive. Since, in this case, the efficiency gained is only minor, you're probably better off leaving in the full expression.

Using *If...Then...Else* to Handle a *False* Result

Using the `If...Then` statement to make decisions adds a powerful new weapon to your VBA arsenal. However, this technique suffers from an important drawback: A `False` result only avoids one or more statements; it doesn't execute any of its own. This is fine in many cases, but there will be times when you need to run one group of statements if the condition returns `True` and a different group if the result is `False`. To handle this, you need to use an `If...Then...Else` statement:

```
If condition Then
    [TrueStatements]
Else
    [FalseStatements]
End If
```

`condition`	The test that returns `True` or `False`.
`TrueStatements`	The statements to run if `condition` returns `True`.
`FalseStatements`	The statements to run if `condition` returns `False`.

If the `condition` returns `True`, VBA runs the group of statements between `If...Then` and `Else`. If it returns `False`, VBA runs the group of statements between the `Else` and the `End If`.

Let's look at an example. Suppose you want to calculate the future value of a series of regular deposits, but you want to differentiate between monthly deposits and quarterly deposits. Listing 23.2 shows a `Function` procedure called `FutureValue` that does the job.

Listing 23.2. A procedure that uses *If...Then...Else*.

```
Function FutureValue(Rate, Nper, Pmt, Frequency)

    If Frequency = "Monthly" Then
        FutureValue = Application.Fv(Rate / 12, Nper * 12, Pmt / 12)
    Else
        FutureValue = Application.Fv(Rate / 4, Nper * 4, Pmt / 4)
    End If

End Function
```

The first three arguments—`Rate`, `Nper`, and `Pmt`—are, respectively, the annual interest rate, the number of years in the term of the investment, and the total deposit available annually. The fourth argument—`Frequency`—is either `"Monthly"` or `"Quarterly"`. The idea is to adjust the first three arguments based on the `Frequency`. For example, if `Frequency` is `"Monthly"`, you need to divide the interest rate by 12, multiply the term by 12, and divide the annual deposit by 12. The `If...Then...Else` statement runs a test on the `Frequency` argument:

```
If Frequency = "Monthly" Then
```

If this is `True`, the function adjusts `Rate`, `Nper`, and `Pmt` accordingly and returns the future value. Otherwise, a quarterly calculation is assumed, and different adjustments are made to the arguments.

> **TIP**
>
> `If...Then...Else` statements are much easier to read when you indent the expressions between `If...Then`, `Else`, and `End If`, as I've done in Listing 23.2. This enables you to easily identify which group of statements will be run if there is a `True` result and which group will be run if the result is `False`. Pressing the Tab key once at the beginning of each line does the job.

> **NOTE**
>
> Notice in Listing 23.2 that to use a built-in Excel function, you precede the function name with the `Application` object (for example, `Application.Fv`). To find out more about this, see Chapter 24, "Manipulating Excel with VBA."

Using *Select Case* to Make Multiple Decisions

The problem with `If...Then...Else` is that normally you can make only a single decision. The statement calculates a single logical result and performs one of two actions. But there are plenty of situations that require multiple decisions before you can decide which action to take.

One solution is to use the `And` and `Or` operators to evaluate a series of logical tests. For example, the `FutureValue` procedure probably should test the `Frequency` argument to make sure it's either `"Monthly"` or `"Quarterly"` and not something else. The following `If...Then` statement uses the `Or` operator to accomplish this:

```
If Frequency = "Monthly" Or Frequency = "Quarterly" Then
```

If `Frequency` doesn't equal either of these values, the entire condition returns `False` and the procedure can return a message to the user.

This approach works, but you're really only performing multiple logical tests; in the end, you're still making a single decision. A better approach is to use VBA's `Select Case` statement, as follows:

```
Select Case TestExpression
   Case FirstExpressionList
       [FirstStatements]
```

```
    Case SecondExpressionList
        [SecondStatements]...
    Case Else
        [ElseStatements]
End Select
```

`TestExpression`	This expression is evaluated at the beginning of the structure. It must return a value (logical, numeric, string, and so on).
`ExpressionList`	A list of one or more expressions in which each expression is separated by a comma. VBA examines each element in the list to see whether one matches the `TestExpression`. These expressions can take any one of the following forms:

`Expression`

`Expression To Expression`

`Is LogicalOperator Expression`

The `To` keyword defines a range of values (for example, `1 To 10`). The `Is` keyword defines an open-ended range of values (for example, `Is >= 100`).

`Statements`	These are the statements VBA runs if any part of the associated `ExpressionList` matches the `TestExpression`. VBA runs the optional `ElseStatements` if no `ExpressionList` matches the `TestExpression`.

NOTE

If more than one `ExpressionList` contains an element that matches the `TestExpression`, VBA runs only the statements associated with the `ExpressionList` that appears first in the `Select Case` structure.

For example, suppose you want to write a procedure that converts a raw score into a letter grade according to the following table:

Raw Score	Letter Grade
80 and over	A
Between 70 and 79	B
Between 60 and 69	C
Between 50 and 59	D
Less than 50	F

Listing 23.3 shows the `LetterGrade` procedure, which uses a `Select Case` statement to make the conversion.

Listing 23.3. A procedure that makes multiple decisions using a `Select Case` statement.

```
Function LetterGrade(rawScore)

    Select Case rawScore
        Case Is < 50
            LetterGrade = "F"
        Case Is < 60
            LetterGrade = "D"
        Case Is < 70
            LetterGrade = "C"
        Case Is < 80
            LetterGrade = "B"
        Case Else
            LetterGrade = "A"
    End Select

End Function
```

Code That Loops

If your procedure needs to repeat a section of code, you can set up a loop that tells VBA how many times to run through the code. The next few sections look at VBA's three different types of loops.

Using *Do...Loop* Structures

What do you do when you need to loop but you don't know in advance how many times to repeat the loop? This could happen if, for example, you want to loop only until a certain condition is met, such as encountering a blank cell. The solution is to use a `Do...Loop`.

The `Do...Loop` has four different syntaxes:

`Do While` *condition*
    `[statements]`
`Loop`
	Checks *condition* before entering the loop. Executes the *statements* only while *condition* is `True`.

`Do`
    `[statements]`
`Loop While` *condition*
	Checks *condition* after running through the loop once. Executes the *statements* only while *condition* is `True`. Use this form when you want the loop to be processed at least once.

`Do Until` *condition*
    `[statements]`
`Loop`
	Checks *condition* before entering the loop. Executes the *statements* only while *condition* is `False`.

`Do`	Checks *condition* after running through the loop once.
`    [statements]`	Executes the *statements* only while *condition* is `False`.
`Loop Until condition`	Again, use this form when you want the loop to be processed at least once.

Listing 23.4 shows a procedure called `BigNumbers` that runs down a worksheet column and changes the font color to magenta whenever a cell contains a number greater than or equal to 1,000.

Listing 23.4. A procedure that uses a `Do...Loop` to process cells until it encounters a blank cell.

```
Sub BigNumbers()

    Dim rowNum As Integer, colNum As Integer, currCell As Range
    rowNum = ActiveCell.Row                              'Initialize row #
    colNum = ActiveCell.Column                           'Initialize column #
    Set currCell = ActiveSheet.Cells(rowNum, colNum)     'Get first cell

    Do While currCell.Value <> ""                        'Do while not empty
        If IsNumeric(currCell.Value) Then                'If it's a number,
            If currCell.Value >= 1000 Then               'and it's a big one,
                currCell.Font.Color = RGB(255, 0, 255)   'color font magenta
            End If
        End If
        rowNum = rowNum + 1                              'Increment row #
        Set currCell = ActiveSheet.Cells(rowNum, colNum) 'Get next cell
    Loop

End Sub
```

The idea is to loop until the procedure encounters a blank cell. This is controlled by the following `Do While` statement:

```
Do While currCell.Value <> ""
```

`currCell` is an object variable that is `Set` using the `Cells` method (which I'll describe in the next chapter). Next, the first `If...Then` uses the `IsNumeric` function to check if the cell contains a number, and the second `If...Then` checks to see if the number is greater than or equal to 1,000. If both conditions are `True`, the font color is set to magenta—`RGB(255,0,255)`.

> **NOTE**
>
> Use the `RGB(red,green,blue)` VBA function anytime you need to specify a color for a property. Each of the three named arguments (*red*, *green*, and *blue*) are integers between 0 and 255 that determine how much of each component color is mixed into the final color. In the *red* component, for example, 0 means no red is present and 255

means that pure red is present. Here are some sample values for each component that produce common colors:

red	green	blue	Result
0	0	0	Black
0	0	255	Blue
0	255	0	Green
0	255	255	Cyan
255	0	0	Red
255	0	255	Magenta
255	255	0	Yellow
255	255	255	White

Using *For...Next* Loops

The most common type of loop is the `For...Next` loop. Use this loop when you know exactly how many times you want to repeat a group of statements. The structure of a `For...Next` loop looks like this:

```
For counter = start To end [Step increment]
    [statements]
Next [counter]
```

`counter`	A numeric variable used as a *loop counter*. The loop counter is a number that counts how many times the procedure has gone through the loop.
`start`	The initial value of `counter`. This is usually 1, but you can enter any value.
`end`	The final value of `counter`.
`increment`	This optional value defines an increment for the loop counter. If you leave this out, the default value is 1. Use a negative value to decrement `counter`.
`statements`	The statements to execute each time through the loop.

The basic idea is simple. When Excel encounters the `For...Next` statement, it follows this five-step process:

1. Set `counter` equal to `start`.
2. Test `counter`. If it's greater than `end`, exit the loop (that is, process the first statement after the `Next` statement). Otherwise, continue. If `increment` is negative, VBA checks to see whether `counter` is less than `end`.

3. Execute each statement between the For and Next statements.

4. Add *increment* to *counter*. Add 1 to *counter* if *increment* is not specified.

5. Repeat steps 2 through 4 until done.

Listing 23.5 shows a simple Sub procedure—LoopTest—that uses a For...Next statement. Each time through the loop, the procedure uses the StatusBar property to display the value of Counter (the loop counter) in the status bar. (See the section "Using VBA to Get and Display Information," later in this chapter, to learn more about the StatusBar property.) When you run this procedure, Counter gets incremented by one each time through the loop, and the new value gets displayed in the status line.

Listing 23.5. A simple For...Next loop.

```
Sub LoopTest()

    Dim counter

    For counter = 1 To 10
    'Display the message
        Application.StatusBar = "Counter value: " & counter
    ' Wait for 1 second
        Application.Wait Now + TimeValue("00:00:01")
    Next counter

    Application.StatusBar = False

End Sub
```

> **NOTE**
>
> The LoopTest procedure also uses the Wait method to slow things down a bit. The argument Now + TimeValue("00:00:01") pauses the procedure for one second before continuing.

Following are some notes on For...Next loops.

- If you use a positive number for *increment* (or if you omit *increment*), *end* must be greater than or equal to *start*. If you use a negative number for *increment*, *end* must be less than or equal to *start*.

- If *start* equals *end*, the loop will execute once.

- As with If...Then...Else structures, indent the statements inside a For...Next loop for increased readability.

- To keep the number of variables defined in a procedure to a minimum, always try to use the same name for all your For...Next loop counters. The letters *i* through *n* traditionally are used for counters in programming. For greater clarity, you might want to use names such as counter.

- If you need to break out of a For...Next loop before the defined number of repetitions is completed, use the Exit For statement, described in the section of this chapter called "Using Exit For or Exit Do to Exit a Loop."

Using *For Each...Next* Loops

A useful variation of the For...Next loop is the For Each...Next loop, which operates on a collection of objects. You don't need a loop counter, because VBA just loops through the individual elements in the collection and performs on each element whatever operations are inside the loop. Here's the structure of the basic For Each...Next loop:

```
For Each element In group
    [statements]
Next [element]
```

element	A variable used to hold the name of each element in the collection.
group	The name of the collection.
statements	The statements to be executed for each element in the collection.

As an example, let's create a command procedure that converts a range of text into proper case (that is, the first letter of each word is capitalized). This function can come in handy if you import mainframe text into your worksheets, because mainframe reports usually appear entirely in uppercase. This process involves three steps:

1. Loop through the selected range with For Each...Next.

2. Convert each cell's text to proper case. Use Excel's PROPER() function to handle this:

   PROPER(*text*)

text	The text to convert to proper case.

3. Enter the converted text into the selected cell. This is the job of the Range object's Formula method:

   Object.Formula = *Expression*

Object	The Range object in which you want to enter *Expression*.
Expression	The data you want to enter into *Object*.

Listing 23.6 shows the resulting procedure, ConvertToProper. Note that this procedure uses the Selection object to represent the currently selected range.

Listing 23.6. A Sub procedure that uses For Each...Next to loop through a selection and convert each cell to proper text.

```
Sub ConvertToProper()

    Dim cellObject As Object

    For Each cellObject In Selection
        cellObject.Formula = Application.Proper(cellObject)
    Next

End Sub
```

Using *Exit For* or *Exit Do* to Exit a Loop

Most loops run their natural course and then the procedure moves on. There might be times, however, when you want to exit a loop prematurely. For example, you might come across a certain type of cell, or an error might occur, or the user might enter an unexpected value. To exit a For...Next loop or a For Each...Next loop, use the Exit For statement. To exit a Do...Loop, use the Exit Do statement.

Listing 23.7 shows a revised version of the BigNumbers procedure, which exits the Do...Loop if it comes across a cell that isn't a number.

Listing 23.7. In this version of the BigNumbers procedure, the Do...Loop is terminated with the Exit Do statement if the current cell isn't a number.

```
Sub BigNumbers2()

    Dim rowNum As Integer, colNum As Integer, currCell As Range
    rowNum = ActiveCell.Row                          'Initialize row #
    colNum = ActiveCell.Column                       'Initialize column #
    Set currCell = ActiveSheet.Cells(rowNum, colNum) 'Get first cell

    Do While currCell.Value <> ""                    'Do while not empty

        If IsNumeric(currCell.Value) Then            'If it's a number,
            If currCell.Value >= 1000 Then           'and it's a big one,
                currCell.Font.Color = RGB(255, 0, 255) 'color font magenta
            End If
        Else                                         'If it's not,
            Exit Do                                  'exit the loop
        End If
        rowNum = rowNum + 1                          'Increment row #
        Set currCell = ActiveSheet.Cells(rowNum, colNum) 'Get next cell

    Loop

End Sub
```

NOTE

If you want to exit a procedure before reaching `End Sub` or `End Function`, use `Exit Sub` or `Exit Function`.

Using VBA to Get and Display Information

A well-designed application not only makes intelligent decisions and streamlines code with loops but also keeps the user involved. It should display messages at appropriate times and ask the user for input. When interacting with the application, the user feels that he or she is a part of the process and has some control over what the program does—which means that the user won't lose interest in the program and will be less likely to make careless mistakes. The rest of this chapter takes you through various methods for giving and receiving user feedback.

Displaying Information to the User

Displaying information is one of the best (and easiest) ways to keep your users involved. If an operation is going to take a long time, keep the user informed of the operation's time and progress. If the user makes an error (for example, if he enters the wrong argument in a user-defined function), he should be gently admonished so that he will be less likely to repeat the error.

VBA gives you four main ways to display information: the `Beep` statement, the `SoundNote` property, the `StatusBar` property, and the `MsgBox` function.

Beeping the Speaker

VBA's most rudimentary form of communication is the simple, attention-getting beep. It's Excel's way of saying "Ahem!" or "Excuse me!" and it's handled, appropriately enough, by the `Beep` statement.

For example, Listing 23.8 shows the `RecalcAll` procedure that recalculates all the open workbooks and then sounds three beeps to mark the end of the process:

Listing 23.8. A procedure that recalculates all open workbooks and then sounds two beeps.

```
Sub RecalcAll()

    Dim i As Integer
```

continues

Listing 23.8. continued

```
Application.Calculate
For i = 1 To 3
    Beep
    ' Pause for 2 seconds between beeps
    Application.Wait Now + TimeValue("00:00:02")
Next i

End Sub
```

CAUTION

Avoid overusing the Beep statement. You need to get the user's attention, but constant beeping only defeats that purpose; most users get annoyed at any program that barks at them incessantly. Good uses for the Beep statement are signaling errors and signaling the end of long operations.

Using Other Sounds

The Beep statement is useful, but it's primitive. If you have the necessary hardware, you can get your procedures to play much more sophisticated sounds, including your own recorded voice.

Chapter 4, "Formatting Excel Worksheets," showed you how to add a sound note to a cell. You also can work with sound notes in VBA. A SoundNote is a Range object property that is also an object in its own right. SoundNote objects have methods that enable you to import sound files, record sounds, and play a cell's sound note.

NOTE

To record and play sound notes, you (or the user's system) must have the appropriate sound hardware installed.

Importing a Sound File

The SoundNote object includes an Import method that imports a sound file directly into a sound note. Here's the proper syntax:

object.SoundNote.Import(***file,resource***)

object	The cell that will contain the SoundNote object.
file	The full pathname of the sound file.
resource	An argument used only in Excel for the Macintosh.

For example, the following statement imports a sound file called Dogbark.wav into the active cell:

```
ActiveCell.SoundNote.Import "C:\Sounds\Dogbark.wav"
```

Recording a Sound Note

If you prefer to record your own sounds, the SoundNote object also includes a Record method:

```
object.SoundNote.Record
```

>   object   The cell that will contain the SoundNote object.

If you use the Record method to record a sound, you'll see the Record dialog box when you run the procedure. Choose **R**ecord, record your note, choose **S**top when you're done, and then select OK. The following statement records a sound note and stores it in the active cell:

```
ActiveCell.SoundNote.Record
```

Playing a Sound

After you've inserted a sound note, you can use the Play method to play it (again, assuming that the user's computer has the appropriate hardware):

```
object.SoundNote.Play
```

>   object   The cell that contains the SoundNote object.

For example, the following statement plays a message recorded in a cell named ErrorMessage in the active worksheet:

```
Range("ErrorMessage").SoundNote.Play
```

Adding Sound Checks to Your Procedures

As you've seen, using sounds in your procedures requires special hardware and software. A well-written procedure should check that a computer is capable of playing or recording sounds before trying to use them. You do this by testing the Application object's CanPlaySounds or CanRecordSounds properties. If these properties return True, you can play and record sounds, respectively.

In the following example, the code first checks the CanPlaySounds property before playing a sound:

```
If Application.CanPlaySounds Then
    Range("ErrorMessage").SoundNote.Play
End If
```

Displaying a Message in the Status Bar

You can use the `Application` object's `StatusBar` property to display text messages in the status bar at the bottom of the screen. This provides you with an easy way to keep the user informed about what a procedure is doing or how much is left to process.

Listing 23.9, an example of the `StatusBar` property, shows a revised version of the `ConvertToProper` procedure. The goal is to display a status bar message of the form `Converting cell x of y`, in which *x* is the number of cells converted so far and *y* is the total number of cells to be converted.

> **NOTE**
>
> In Listing 23.9, note the use of an underscore (_) at the end of two of the lines. This is VBA's *line continuation character,* and it's used to spread a single VBA statement over more than one line. This is handy if you have a lengthy statement that would otherwise extend past the right side of the window. When you use the line-continuation character, make sure you insert a space before the underscore.

Listing 23.9. A procedure that uses the `StatusBar` property to inform the user of the progress of the operation.

```
Sub ConvertToProper2()

    Dim cellVar As Object
    Dim cellsConverted As Integer, totalCells As Integer

    ' Initialize some variables
    cellsConverted = 0
    totalCells = Selection.Count

    For Each cellVar In Selection
        cellVar.Formula = Application.Proper(cellVar)
        cellsConverted = cellsConverted + 1
        Application.StatusBar = "Converting cell " & _
                                cellsConverted & " of " & _
                                totalCells
    Next

    Application.StatusBar = False

End Sub
```

The `cellsConverted` variable tracks the number of cells converted, and the `totalsCells` variable stores the total number of cells in the selection (given by `Selection.Count`).

The `For Each...Next` loop does three things:

- It converts one cell at a time to proper case.
- It increments the `cellsConverted` variable.
- It sets the `StatusBar` property to display the progress of the operation. (Note the use of the concatenation operator to combine text and variable values.)

When the loop is done, the procedure sets the `StatusBar` property to `False` to clear the status bar.

Displaying a Message Using *MsgBox*

The problem with using the `StatusBar` property to display messages is that it's often a bit too subtle. Unless the user knows to look in the status bar, he or she might miss your messages altogether. When the user really needs to see a message, you can use the `MsgBox` function:

`MsgBox(`***prompt***`,buttons,title,helpFile,context)`

prompt	The message you want to display in the dialog box.
buttons	A number or constant that specifies, among other things, the command buttons that appear in the dialog. (See the next section.) The default value is `0`.
title	The text that appears in the dialog box title bar. If you omit the title, VBA uses "Microsoft Excel."
helpFile	The text that specifies the Help file that contains the custom help topic. If you enter *helpFile*, you also have to include *context*. If you include *helpFile*, a **H**elp button appears in the dialog box.
context	A number that identifies the help topic in *helpFile*.

For example, the following statement displays the message dialog box shown in Figure 23.1:

`MsgBox "You must enter a number between 1 and 100",,"Warning"`

FIGURE 23.1.

A simple message dialog box produced by the `MsgBox` *function.*

NOTE

The `MsgBox` function, like all VBA functions, needs parentheses around its arguments only when you use the function's return value. See the section later in this chapter called "Getting Return Values from the Message Dialog Box."

> **TIP**
>
> For long prompts, VBA wraps the text inside the dialog box. If you would like to create your own line breaks, use VBA's `Chr` function and the carriage-return character (ASCII 13) between each line:
>
> ```
> MsgBox "First line" & Chr(13) & "Second line"
> ```

Setting the Style of the Message

The default message dialog box displays only an OK button. You can include other buttons and icons in the dialog box by using different values for the *buttons* parameter. Table 23.1 lists the available options.

Table 23.1. The `MsgBox` buttons parameter options.

Constant	Value	Description
		Buttons
vbOKOnly	0	Displays only an OK button (the default).
vbOKCancel	1	Displays the OK and Cancel buttons.
vbAbortRetryIgnore	2	Displays the **A**bort, **R**etry, and **I**gnore buttons.
vbYesNoCancel	3	Displays the **Y**es, **N**o, and Cancel buttons.
vbYesNo	4	Displays the **Y**es and **N**o buttons.
vbRetryCancel	5	Displays the **R**etry and Cancel buttons.
		Icons
vbCritical	16	Displays the Critical Message icon.
vbQuestion	32	Displays the Warning Query icon.
vbExclamation	48	Displays the Warning Message icon.
vbInformation	64	Displays the Information Message icon.
		Defaults
vbDefaultButton1	0	The first button is the default.
vbDefaultButton2	256	The second button is the default.
vbDefaultButton3	512	The third button is the default.

Constant	Value	Description
		Modality
vbApplicationModal	0	The user must respond to the message box before continuing work in the current application.
vbSystemModal	4096	All applications are suspended until the user responds to the message box.

You derive the *buttons* argument in one of two ways:

- By adding up the values for each option
- By using the VBA constants separated by plus signs (+)

For example, Listing 23.10 shows a procedure named ButtonTest, and Figure 23.2 shows the resulting dialog box. Here, three variables—*msgPrompt, msgButtons,* and *msgTitle*—store the values for the MsgBox function's ***prompt***, *buttons,* and *title* arguments. In particular, the following statement derives the *buttons* argument:

```
msgButtons = vbYesNoCancel + vbQuestion + vbDefaultButton2
```

You also could derive the *buttons* argument by adding up the values that these constants represent (3, 32, and 256, respectively), although the procedure becomes less readable that way.

Listing 23.10. A procedure that creates a message dialog box.

```
Sub ButtonTest()

    Dim msgPrompt As String, msgTitle As String
    Dim msgButtons As Integer, msgResult As Integer

    msgPrompt = "Are you sure you want to copy" & Chr(13) & _
                "the selected files to drive A?"
    msgButtons = vbYesNoCancel + vbQuestion + vbDefaultButton2
    msgTitle = "Copy Files"

    msgResult = MsgBox(msgPrompt, msgButtons, msgTitle)

End Sub
```

FIGURE 23.2.

The dialog box that is displayed when you run the code shown in Listing 23.10.

Getting Return Values from the Message Dialog Box

A message dialog box that displays only an OK button is straightforward. The user either clicks on OK or presses Enter to remove the dialog from the screen. The multi-button styles are a little different, however; the user has a choice of buttons to select, and your procedure should have a way to find out what the user chose.

You do this by storing the MsgBox function's return value in a variable. Table 23.2 lists the seven possibilities.

Table 23.2. The MsgBox function's return values.

Constant	Value	Button Selected
vbOK	1	OK
vbCancel	2	Cancel
vbAbort	3	Abort
vbRetry	4	Retry
vbIgnore	5	Ignore
vbYes	6	Yes
vbNo	7	No

To process the return value, you can use an If...Then...Else or Select Case structure to test for the appropriate values. For example, the ButtonTest procedure shown earlier used a variable called *msgResult* to store the return value of the MsgBox function. Listing 23.11 shows a revised version of ButtonTest that uses a Select Case statement to test for the three possible return values. (Note that the vbYes case runs a procedure named CopyFiles. The ButtonTest procedure assumes that the CopyFiles procedure already exists elsewhere in the module.)

Listing 23.11. This example uses Select Case to test the return values of the MsgBox function.

```
Sub ButtonTest2()

    Dim msgPrompt As String, msgTitle As String
    Dim msgButtons As Integer, msgResult As Integer

    msgPrompt = "Are you sure you want to copy" & Chr(13) & _
                "the selected files to drive A?"
    msgButtons = vbYesNoCancel + vbQuestion + vbDefaultButton2
    msgTitle = "Copy Files"

    msgResult = MsgBox(msgPrompt, msgButtons, msgTitle)
```

```
    Select Case msgResult
        Case vbYes
            CopyFiles
        Case vbNo
            Exit Sub
        Case vbCancel
            Application.Quit
    End Select

End Sub
```

Getting Input from the User

As you've seen, the MsgBox function enables your procedures to interact with the user and get some feedback. Unfortunately, this method limits you to simple command-button responses. For more varied user input, you need to use more sophisticated techniques.

Prompting the User for Input

The InputBox function displays a dialog box with a message that prompts the user to enter data, and it provides a text box for the data itself. The syntax for this method appears as the following:

```
Application.InputBox(prompt,title,default,xpos,ypos,helpFile,context,type)
```

prompt	The message you want to display in the dialog box.
title	Text that appears in the dialog box title bar. The default value is the null string (nothing).
default	The default value displayed in the text box. If you omit *default*, the text box is displayed empty.
xpos	The horizontal position of the dialog box from the left edge of the screen. The value is measured in points (there are 72 points in an inch). If you omit *xpos*, the dialog box is centered horizontally.
ypos	The vertical position, in points, from the top of the screen. If you omit *ypos*, the dialog is centered vertically in the current window.
helpFile	Text specifying the Help file that contains the custom help topic. If you enter *helpFile*, you also have to include *context*. If you include *helpFile*, a **H**elp button appears in the dialog box.
context	A number that identifies the help topic in *helpFile*.

type	A number that specifies the data type of the return value, as follows:

type	Data Type
0	Formula
1	Number
2	Text (the default)
4	Boolean (True or False)
8	Reference (a Range object)
16	Error value
32	An array of values

For example, Listing 23.12 shows a procedure called GetInterestRate that uses the InputBox method to prompt the user for an interest rate value. Figure 23.3 shows the dialog box that appears.

Listing 23.12. A procedure that prompts the user for an interest rate value.

```
Function GetInterestRate()

    Dim done As Boolean

    ' Initialize the loop variable
    done = False

    While Not done
        ' Get the interest rate
        GetInterestRate = Application.InputBox( _
                        prompt:="Enter an interest rate between 0 and 1:", _
                        title:="Enter Interest Rate", _
                        type:=1)

        ' First, check to see if the user cancelled
        If GetInterestRate = "" Then
            Exit Function
        Else
            ' Make sure the entered rate is betwen 0 and 1
            If GetInterestRate >= 0 And GetInterestRate <= 1 Then
                done = True
            End If
        End If
    Wend

End Function
```

FIGURE 23.3.

A dialog box generated by the InputBox function.

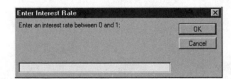

The InputBox method returns one of the following values:

- The value entered into the text box, if the user selects OK.
- An empty string, if the user selects Cancel.

In Listing 23.12, the result of the InputBox method is stored in the GetInterestRate function. The procedure first checks to see if InputBox returned the empty string (""). If so, the Exit Function statement bails out of the procedure. Otherwise, an If...Then statement checks to make sure that the number is between 0 and 1. If it is, the done variable is set to True so the While...Wend loop will exit; if the number isn't between 0 and 1, the procedure loops and the dialog box is redisplayed.

Accessing Excel's Built-In Dialog Boxes

Many VBA methods are known as *dialog box equivalents* because they enable you to select the same options that are available in Excel's built-in dialog boxes. Using dialog box equivalents works fine if your procedure knows which options to select, but there are times when you might want the user to specify some of the dialog box options.

For example, if your procedure will print a document (using the PrintOut method), you might need to know how many copies the user wants or how many pages to print. You could use the InputBox method to get this data, but it's usually easier just to display the Print dialog box.

The built-in dialog boxes are Dialog objects, and Dialogs is the collection of all the built-in dialog boxes. To reference a particular dialog box, use one of the predefined Excel constants. Table 23.3 lists a few of the more common ones.

Table 23.3. Some of Excel's built-in dialog box constants.

Constant	Dialog Box
xlDialogChartWizard	ChartWizard
xlDialogColumnWidth	Column Width
xlDialogDefineName	Define Name
xlDialogFindFile	Find File
xlDialogFont	Font
xlDialogFormatAuto	AutoFormat
xlDialogFormulaFind	Find
xlDialogFormulaGoto	Go To
xlDialogFormulaReplace	Replace
xlDialogFunctionWizard	FunctionWizard

continues

Table 23.3. continued

Constant	Dialog Box
xlDialogGoalSeek	Goal Seek
xlDialogNew	New
xlDialogNote	Cell Note
xlDialogOpen	Open
xlDialogOptionsCalculation	Options (Calculation tab)
xlDialogOptionsEdit	Options (Edit tab)
xlDialogOptionsGeneral	Options (General tab)
xlDialogOptionsView	Options (View tab)
xlDialogPageSetup	Page Setup
xlDialogPasteSpecial	Paste Special
xlDialogPivotTableWizard	PivotTable Wizard
xlDialogPrint	Print
xlDialogPrinterSetup	Printer Setup
xlDialogPrintPreview	Print Preview
xlDialogRowHeight	Row Height
xlDialogSaveAs	Save As
xlDialogSort	Sort

NOTE

To see a complete list of constants for Excel's built-in dialog boxes, select the **View |
Object Browser** command from any module. In the Object Browser dialog box, select
Excel from the **Libraries/Workbooks** list and then choose Constants in the **Objects/
Modules** list. You'll find the dialog constants in the **Methods/Properties** list. (They all
begin with xlDialog.)

To display any of these dialog boxes, use the Dialog object's Show method. For example, the
following statement displays the Print dialog box:

```
Application.Dialogs(xlDialogPrint).Show
```

If the user selects Cancel to exit the dialog box, the Show method returns False. This means
you can use Show inside an If statement to determine what the user did:

```
If Not Application.Dialogs(xlDialogPrint).Show Then
    MsgBox "File was not printed"
End If
```

Summary

This chapter showed you how to take command of your VBA code by using control structures and user interaction. To make logical (true/false) decisions, use `If...Then` or `If...Then...Else`. To make multiple decisions, use `Select Case`. To loop through a section of code, use `Do...Loop`, `For...Next`, or `For Each...Next` loops. If you need to exit a loop, use either the `Exit For` or `Exit Do` statement. User interaction is handled by the `Beep` function, the `SoundNote` object, the `MsgBox` function, and the `InputBox` method.

To get some related information, tune in to the following chapters:

- For more information on properties and methods of objects such as `Application` and `Range`, read Chapter 24, "Manipulating Excel with VBA."

- To get maximum control over your code's user interaction, you'll need to build your own custom dialog boxes. To find out how, see Chapter 25, "Creating a Custom User Interface."

- You also can control your code using "events" such as opening a workbook, entering data into a cell, and recalculating a worksheet. For details, see Chapter 27, "VBA Procedures That Respond to Events."

Manipulating Excel with VBA

24

Most VBA procedures eventually do *something* to the Excel environment. They might select a cell or range, enter a formula, copy and move data, or even set some of Excel's options. Therefore, knowing how VBA interacts with Excel is crucial if you ever hope to write useful routines. This chapter looks closely at that interaction. I'll show you how to set Excel's options and how to work with all of the most common Excel objects, including the `Application`, Workbook, Worksheet, and Range objects.

Reading and Setting Excel's Options

Chapter 8, "Customizing Excel," took you through each of the tabs in the Options dialog box (which you can display by selecting the **Tools | O**ptions command). All of the controls in this dialog box are accessible through the properties of various Excel objects. The next few sections take you through the equivalent properties for the options in the View, Calculation, Edit, and General tabs. If you need more information about each option, turn to Chapter 8.

> **NOTE**
>
> Keep in mind that you can use any property to either read the current state of the property or to change the value of the property. For example, you can store the current setting of the `Application.DisplayFormulaBar` property in a variable named `currFormulaBar` with the following statement:
>
> ```
> currFormulaBar = Application.DisplayFormulaBar
> ```
>
> To set the property, use a statement such as the following:
>
> ```
> Application.DisplayFormulaBar = False
> ```

The View Tab

Table 24.1 lists the available options in the View tab and their equivalent object properties.

Table 24.1. Object property equivalents for the View tab options.

Option	Property and Description

Formula Bar	`Application.DisplayFormulaBar`
	Toggles the formula bar on and off. For example, the following statement hides the formula bar:
	`Application.DisplayFormulaBar = False`

Status Bar	`Application.DisplayStatusBar` Toggles the status bar on and off.
Note Indicator	`Application.DisplayNoteIndicator` Toggles the note indicators on and off.

Option	Property and Description
Info **W**indow	`Application.DisplayInfoWindow` Toggles the Info window on and off.

Show	`Workbook.DisplayDrawingObjects`
	Returns or sets how graphics are displayed in the specified *Workbook*. The three possible values are `xlAll` (equivalent to activating the Show **A**ll option), `xlPlaceholders` (the Show **P**laceholders option), and `xlHide` (the Hi**d**e All option). For example, the following statement displays the active workbook's graphics as placeholders:
	`ActiveWorkbook.DisplayDrawingObjects =`
	`xlPlaceholders`

Automatic Page Breaks	`Worksheet.Display.AutomaticPageBreaks` Toggles the *Worksheet* object's automatic page breaks on and off.
Formulas	`Window.DisplayFormulas` Toggles the *Window* object's formulas on and off.
Gridlines	`Window.DisplayGridlines` Toggles the *Window* object's gridlines on and off.
Row & Column H**e**aders	`Window.DisplayHeadings` Toggles the *Window* object's row and column headers on and off.
Outline Symbols	`Window.DisplayOutline` Toggles the *Window* object's outline symbols on and off.
Zero Values	`Window.DisplayZeros` Toggles the *Window* object's zero values on and off.
Horizo**n**tal Scroll Bar	`Window.DisplayHorizontalScrollBar` Toggles the *Window* object's horizontal scroll bar on and off.
Vertical Scroll Bar	`Window.DisplayVerticalScrollBar` Toggles the *Window* object's vertical scroll bar on and off.
Sheet Ta**b**s	`Window.DisplayWorkbookTabs` Toggles the *Window* object's worksheet tabs on and off.

If you find yourself consistently toggling one of these features on or off, it's a hassle to constantly crank up the Options dialog box. To make your life easier, it's no problem to set up a procedure to do the toggling for you. For example, I often toggle gridlines on and off, so I created the `ToggleGridlines` procedure shown in Listing 24.1.

Listing 24.1. A procedure that toggles the active window's gridlines on and off.

```
Sub ToggleGridlines()

    With ActiveWindow.
        DisplayGridlines = Not .DisplayGridlines
    End With

End Sub
```

NOTE

ToggleGridlines and all the listings in this chapter can be found in the workbook Chap24.xls, which you'll find on the CD that comes with this book.

The Calculation Tab

Table 24.2 lists the available options in the Calculation tab and their equivalent object properties.

Table 24.2. Object property equivalents for the Calculation tab options.

Option	Property and Description
Calculation	Application.Calculation Returns or sets the calculation mode using three values: xlAutomatic (equivalent to activating the **A**utomatic option), xlSemiautomatic (the Automatic Except **T**ables option), and xlManual (the **M**anual option). For example, the following statement sets the calculation mode to manual: Application.Calculation = xlManual.
Recalculate Before Save	Application.CalculateBeforeSave If the Calculation property is set to xlManual, this property returns or sets whether or not Excel recalculates before a workbook is saved.
Iteration	Application.Iteration Returns or sets whether or not Excel uses iteration to resolve circular references.
Maximum Iterations	Application.MaxIterations Returns or sets the maximum number of iterations.

Option	Property and Description
Maximum **C**hange	`Application.MaxChange` Returns or sets the maximum amount of change used in each iteration.
Update **R**emote References	`Workbook.UpdateRemoteReferences` Returns or sets whether or not Excel updates remote references for the specified *Workbook* object.
Precision as Displayed	`Workbook.PrecisionAsDisplayed` Returns or sets whether or not calculations in the specified *Workbook* object use only the precision of the numbers as they are displayed.
1904 **D**ate System	`Workbook.Date1904` Returns or sets whether or not the specified *Workbook* object uses the 1904 date system.
Save External **L**ink Values	`Workbook.SaveLinkValues` Returns or sets whether or not Excel will save link values for the specified *Workbook* object.

The Edit Tab

Table 24.3 lists the available options in the Edit tab and their equivalent object properties.

Table 24.3. Object property equivalents for the Edit tab options.

Option	Property and Description
Edit Directly in Cell	`Application.EditDirectlyInCell` Returns or sets whether or not Excel allows editing directly in cells.
Allow Cell **D**rag and Drop	`Application.CellDragAndDrop` Toggles cell drag-and-drop editing on and off.
Alert Before Overwriting Cells	`AlertBeforeOverwriting` If the `CellDragAndDrop` property is set to `True`, this property returns or sets whether or not Excel displays a warning before overwriting nonempty cells during a drag-and-drop operation.

continues

Table 24.3. continued

Option	Property and Description
Move Selection After Enter	`Application.MoveAfterReturn` Returns or sets whether or not Excel moves the active cell after the user presses Enter.
Direction	`Application.MoveAfterReturnDirection` If the `MoveAfterReturn` property is set to `True`, this property returns or sets the direction in which the active cell is moved. You have four choices: `xlToLeft`, `xlToRight`, `xlUp`, and `xlDown`.
Fixed Decimal	`Application.FixedDecimal` Returns or sets whether or not Excel formats entered numbers with the number of decimal places specified by the `FixedDecimalPlaces` property.

Places	`Application.FixedDecimalPlaces`
	If the `FixedDecimal` property is set to `True`, this property returns or sets the number of decimal places. For example, to enter all numbers with two decimal places, you would use the following two statements:
	`Application.FixedDecimal = True`
	`Application.FixedDecimalPlaces = 2`

Cut, Copy, and Sort **O**bjects with Cells	`Application.CopyObjectsWithCells` Returns or sets whether or not graphic objects move with cells that are cut, copied, or sorted.
Ask to **U**pdate Automatic Links	`Application.AskToUpdateLinks` Returns or sets whether or not Excel asks to update links when you open workbooks that contain links.
Animate Insertion and Deletion	`Application.EnableAnimations` Toggles animated inserting and deleting on and off.
Enable Auto**C**omplete for Cell Values	`Application.EnableAutoComplete` Toggles `AutoComplete` on and off.

The General Tab

Table 24.4 lists the available options in the General tab and their equivalent object properties.

Table 24.4. Object property equivalents for the General tab options.

Option	Property and Description
Reference Style	`Application.ReferenceStyle` Returns or sets the reference style used by Excel. Set this property to `xlA1` to use A1-style references or `xlR1C1` to use R1C1-style references.
Recently Used File List	`Application.DisplayRecentFiles` Toggles on and off the **File** menu's list of the last four files you used.
Microsoft Excel 4.0 Menus	`Application.Excel4Menus` Toggles the Excel 4.0 menu structure on and off.
Ignore Other Applications	`Application.IgnoreRemoteRequests` Returns or sets whether or not Excel ignores Dynamic Data Exchange (DDE) requests from other applications.
Prompt for File Properties	`Application.PromptForSummaryInfo` Returns or sets whether or not Excel displays the Properties dialog box whenever you save a new workbook.
Sheets in New Workbook	`Application.SheetsInNewWorkBook` Returns or sets the default number of sheets in new workbooks. You can use a number between 1 and 255.
Standard Font	`Application.StandardFont` Returns or sets the standard Excel font. When setting this property, use a string that corresponds to a typeface available on the system.

Size	`Application.StandardFontSize`
	Returns or sets the default font size. For example, the following two statements set the default font to 12-point Arial:
	`Application.StandardFont = "Arial"`
	`Application.StandardFontSize = 12`

continues

Table 24.4. continued

Option	Property and Description
Default File Location	`Application.DefaultFilePath` Returns or sets the initial folder that appears when you first display the Open or Save As dialog boxes.
Alternate Startup File **L**ocation	`Application.AltStartupPath` Returns or sets a startup directory in addition to \Excel\XLStart.
User **N**ame	`Application.UserName` Returns or sets the user name you want displayed in the Properties dialog box and in scenarios, views, and file sharing.

> **NOTE**
>
> The Reset TipWizard check box is a bit of an anomaly in that, when you activate it, Excel resets the TipWizard toolbar when you exit the dialog box. In other words, activating Reset TipWizard tells Excel to perform an *action*. In VBA, though, actions correspond to methods, so the VBA equivalent of the Reset TipWizard option is a method: `Application.ResetTipWizard`. Including this statement in your code will reset the TipWizard.

The *Application* Object

As mentioned in Chapter 22, "Understanding Objects," the `Application` object represents Excel as a whole. The `Application` object enables you to use VBA to control Excel options (as you saw in the preceding section), worksheet functions, and more.

Accessing Worksheet Functions

VBA has a few dozen functions of its own, but its collection is downright meager compared to the hundreds of worksheet functions available with Excel. If you need to access one of these worksheet functions, VBA makes them available via the `Application` object. Each function works exactly as it does on a worksheet, the only difference being that you have to append `Application.` to the name of the function.

For example, to run the SUM() worksheet function on the range named Sales and store the result in a variable named salesTotal, you would use the following statement:

```
salesTotal = Application.Sum(Range("Sales"))
```

CAUTION

The Application object includes only those worksheet functions that don't duplicate an existing VBA function. For example, VBA has a UCase function that's equivalent to Excel's UPPER() worksheet function (both convert a string into uppercase). In this case, you must use VBA's UCase function in your code. If you try to use Application.Upper, you'll receive the error message Object doesn't support this property or method.

NOTE

For a complete list of VBA functions, see Appendix C, "VBA Functions."

Other Properties of the *Application* Object

Besides the properties you saw earlier that control many of Excel's workspace options, the Application object has dozens of other properties that affect a number of aspects of the Excel environment. Here's a rundown of some Application object properties you'll use most often in your VBA code:

CanPlaySounds: This read-only property returns True if the system can play sound notes. (See Chapter 23, "Controlling VBA Code and Interacting with the User," for a complete description of the CanPlaySounds and CanRecordSounds properties.)

CanRecordSounds: This read-only property returns True if the system can record sound notes.

Caption: Returns or sets the name that appears in the title bar of the main Excel window. For example, to change the title bar caption from "Microsoft Excel" to "ACME Coyote Supplies," you would use the following statement:

```
Application.Caption = "ACME Coyote Supplies"
```

CutCopyMode: Returns of sets Excel's Cut or Copy mode status. If your code copies a Range object and then pastes it (as described later in this chapter), Excel stays in Copy mode after the paste. This means that it displays a moving border around the range and displays Select destination and press ENTER or choose Paste in the status bar. If you would prefer not to confuse the user with these Copy mode indicators, you can take Excel out of Copy mode (or Cut mode, if you cut the range) by running the following statement:

```
Application.CutCopyMode = False
```

`DisplayAlerts`: Determines whether or not Excel displays alert dialog boxes. For example, if your code deletes a worksheet, Excel normally displays an alert box asking you to confirm the deletion. To suppress this alert box and force Excel to accept the default action (which is, in this case, deleting the sheet), set the `DisplayAlerts` property to `False`.

> **NOTE**
>
> Excel restores the `DisplayAlerts` property to its default state (`True`) when your procedure finishes. If you would prefer to turn the alerts back on before then, set the `DisplayAlerts` property to `True`.

`EnableCancelKey`: This property controls what Excel does when the user presses Esc (or Ctrl-Break). As you know, pressing Esc interrupts the running procedure and displays the Macro Error dialog box. If you don't want the user to interrupt a critical section of code, you can disable the Esc key (and Ctrl-Break) by setting the `EnableCancelKey` property to `xlDisabled`. To restore interrupts to their default state, set the `EnableCancelKey` property to `xlInterrupt`. You also can set `EnableCancelKey` to `xlErrorHandler` to run an error handler routine established by the `On Error Go To` statement. For details on the `On Error Go To` statement, see Chapter 27, "VBA Procedures That Respond to Events."

> **CAUTION**
>
> Wield the `EnableCancelKey` property with care. If you disable the Esc key and your code ends up in an infinite loop, there's no way to shut down the procedure short of shutting down Excel itself.

`OperatingSystem`: Returns the name and version number of the current operating system. This is a useful way of determining whether or not your procedure should run a feature specific to Windows 95 or to the Macintosh version of Excel.

`Path`: Returns the path of the `Application` object. That is, it tells you the drive and folder where the Excel executable file resides (such as C:\MSOFFICE\EXCEL).

`ScreenUpdating`: Returns or sets Excel's screen updating. When `ScreenUpdating` is set to `True` (the default), the user sees the results of all your code actions: cut-and-paste operations, drawing objects added or deleted, range formatting, and so on. Applications look more professional (and are noticeably faster) if the user just sees the end result of all these actions. To do this, turn off screen updating (by setting the ScreenUpdating property to False), perform the actions, and then turn screen updating back on.

Version: Returns the Excel version number.

WindowState: Returns or sets the state of the main Excel window. This property is controlled via three built-in constants:

xlMaximized	The window is maximized.
xlMinimized	The window is minimized.
xlNormal	The window is neither maximized nor minimized.

Methods of the *Application* Object

The Application object features a few dozen methods that perform actions on the Excel environment. Here's a summary of the most common methods:

Calculate: Calculates all the open workbooks. Note that you don't need to specify the Application object. You can just enter Calculate by itself.

CheckSpelling: When used with the Application object, the CheckSpelling method checks the spelling of a single word using the following syntax:

Application.CheckSpelling(*word*, *customDictionary*, *ignoreUppercase*)

word	The word you want to check.
customDictionary	The filename of a custom dictionary that Excel can search if *word* wasn't found in the main dictionary.
ignoreUppercase	Set to True to tell Excel to ignore words entirely in uppercase.

For example, the code shown in Listing 24.2 gets a word from the user, checks the spelling, and then tells the user whether or not the word is spelled correctly. (You also can use this property with a Worksheet or Range object, as described later in this chapter.)

Listing 24.2. A procedure that checks the spelling of an entered word.

```
Sub SpellCheckTest()

    Dim word2Check As String, result As Boolean

    word2Check = InputBox("Enter a word:")

    result = Application.CheckSpelling(word2Check)
    If result = True Then
        MsgBox "'" & word2Check & "' is spelled correctly!"
    Else
        MsgBox "Oops! '" & word2Check & "' is spelled incorrectly."
    End If

End Sub
```

`Quit`: Quits Excel without running any `Auto_Close` procedures. (See Chapter 27 to learn about `Auto_Close` procedures.) If there are any open workbooks with unsaved changes, Excel will ask if you want to save the changes. To prevent this, either save the workbooks before running the `Quit` method (I'll tell you how in the next section) or set the `DisplayAlerts` property to `False`. (In the latter case, note that Excel will *not* save changes to the workbooks.)

`Save`: Saves the current workspace. Here's the syntax:

`Application.Save(`*`filename`*`)`

>   *`filename`*   The name of the workspace file.

`Volatile`: When inserted inside a user-defined function, the `Volatile` method tells Excel to recalculate the function every time the worksheet is recalculated. (If you don't include the `Volatile` method, Excel only recalculates the function whenever its input cells change.)

`Wait`: Pauses a running macro until a specified time is reached. Here's the syntax:

`Application.Wait(`*`time`*`)`

>   *`time`*   The time you want the macro to resume running.

For example, if you wanted your procedure to delay for about five seconds, you would use the following statement:

`Application.Wait Now + TimeValue("00:00:05")`

Manipulating Workbook Objects

Workbook objects appear directly below the `Application` object in Excel's object hierarchy. You can use VBA to create new workbooks, open or delete existing workbooks, save and close open workbooks, and much more. The next section takes you through various techniques for specifying workbooks in your VBA code, and then we'll look at some Workbook object properties and methods.

Specifying a Workbook Object

If you need to do something with a workbook, or if you need to work with an object contained in a specific workbook (such as a worksheet), you need to tell Excel which workbook you want to use. VBA gives you no less than three ways to do this:

>   **Use the `Workbooks` collection.** The Workbooks object is the collection of all open workbook files. To specify a particular workbook, either use its index number (where 1 represents the first workbook opened) or enclose the workbook name in quotation marks. For example, if the Budget.xls workbook were the first workbook opened, the following two statements would be equivalent:

```
Workbooks("Budget.xls")
Workbooks(1)
```

Use the ActiveWorkbook object. The ActiveWorkbook object represents the currently active workbook.

Use the ThisWorkbook object. The ThisWorkbook object represents the workbook where the VBA code is executing. If your code deals only with objects residing in the same workbook as the code itself, you can use the ActiveWorkbook object. However, if your code deals with other workbooks, use ThisWorkbook whenever you need to make sure that the code affects only the workbook containing the procedure.

Opening a Workbook

To open a workbook file, use the Open method of the Workbooks collection. The Open method has a dozen arguments you can use to fine tune your workbook openings, but only one of these is mandatory. Here's the simplified syntax showing the one required argument (for the rest of the arguments, look up the Open method in the VBA Help file):

```
Workbooks.Open(fileName)
```

fileName   The full name of the workbook file, including the drive and folder that contain the file.

For example, to open a workbook named Data.xls in the current drive and folder, you would use the following statement:

```
Workbooks.Open "Data.xls"
```

> **NOTE**
>
> You can use VBA to change the default drive and directory. To change the drive, use the ChDrive function. For example, the statement ChDrive "D" changes the current drive to drive D. To change the current folder (directory), use the ChDir function. For example, the statement ChDir "\My Documents\Worksheets" changes the default folder to \My Documents\Worksheets on the current drive. If you need to know the name of the current directory, use the CurDir function.

Creating a New Workbook

If you need to create a new workbook, use the Workbooks collection's Add method:

```
Workbooks.Open(template)
```

template	This optional argument determines how the workbook is created. If *template* is a string specifying an Excel file, VBA uses the file as a template for the new workbook. You also can specify one of the following constants:

xlWorksheet	Creates a workbook with a single worksheet.
xlChart	Creates a workbook with a single chart sheet.
xlExcel4MacroSheet	Creates a workbook with a single Excel 4 macro sheet.
xlExcel4IntlMacroSheet	Creates a workbook with a single Excel 4 international macro sheet.

Workbook Object Properties

Here's a rundown of some common properties associated with Workbook objects:

FullName: Returns the full pathname of the workbook. The full pathname includes the workbook's drive, folder, and filename.

Name: Returns the filename of the workbook.

Path: Returns the path of the workbook file.

> **NOTE**
>
> A new, unsaved workbook's path property returns an empty string (`""`).

ProtectStructure: Returns True if the workbook's structure is protected. (See Chapter 5, "Advanced Worksheet Topics," to learn about workbook protection.)

ProtectWindows: Returns True if the workbook's window size and position are protected.

Saved: Determines whether or not changes have been made to a workbook since it was last saved.

> **TIP**
>
> To close a workbook without saving changes and without Excel asking if you want to save changes, set the workbook's Saved property to True.

Workbook Object Methods

Workbook objects have dozens of methods that enable you to do everything from saving a workbook to closing a workbook. Here are a few methods that you'll use most often:

`Activate`: Activates the specified open workbook. For example, the following statement activates the Finances.xls workbook:

```
Workbooks("Finances.xls").Activate
```

`Close`: Closes the specified workbook. This method uses the following syntax:

Object `.Close(` *saveChanges,fileName,routeWorkbook* `)`

Object	The Workbook object you want to close.
saveChanges	If the workbook has been modified, this argument determines whether or not Excel saves those changes:

saveChanges	*Action*
True	Saves changes before closing.
False	Doesn't save changes.
Omitted	Asks the user if he wants to save changes.

fileName	Saves the workbook under this filename.
routeWorkbook	Routes the workbook according to the following values:

routeWorkbook	*Action*
True	Sends the workbook to the next recipient.
False	Doesn't send the workbook.
Omitted	Asks the user if he wants to send the workbook.

`PrintOut`: Prints the specified workbook using the following syntax:

Object `.PrintOut(` *from,to,copies,preview,activePrinter,printToFile,collate* `)`

Object	The Workbook object you want to print.
from	The page number from which to start printing.
to	The page number of the last page to print.
copies	The number of copies to print. The default value is 1.
preview	If `True`, Excel displays the Print Preview window before printing. The default value is `False`.
activePrinter	Specifies the printer to use.

printToFile	If True, Excel prints the workbook to a file and prompts the user for a filename.
collate	If True and *copies* is greater than 1, collates the copies.

PrintPreview: Displays the specified workbook in the Print Preview window.

Protect: Protects the specified workbook. The Protect method uses the syntax outlined in the following list:

Object.Protect(*password,structure,windows*)

Object	The Workbook object you want to protect.
password	A text string that specifies the (case-sensitive) password to use with the protection.
structure	If True, Excel protects the workbook's structure.
windows	If True, Excel protects the workbook's windows.

Save: Saves the specified workbook. If the workbook is new, use the SaveAs method instead.

SaveAs: Saves the specified workbook to a different file. Here's the simplified syntax for the SaveAs method (to see all eight arguments in the full syntax, look up the SaveAs method in the VBA Help file):

Object.SaveAs(*fileName*)

Object	The Workbook object you want to save to a different file.
fileName	The full name of the new workbook file, including the drive and folder where you want the file to reside.

Unprotect: Unprotects the specified workbook. Here's the syntax:

Object.Unprotect(*password*)

Object	The Workbook object you want to unprotect.
password	The protection password.

Dealing with Worksheet Objects

Worksheet objects contain a number of properties and methods you can exploit in your code. These include options for activating and hiding worksheets, adding new worksheets to a workbook, and moving, copying, and deleting worksheets. The next few sections discuss each worksheet operation.

Creating a New Worksheet

The `Worksheets` collection, which consists of all the worksheets in a specified workbook, has an `Add` method you can use to insert new sheets into the workbook. Here's the syntax for this method:

```
Worksheets.Add(before,after,count,type)
```

before	The sheet before which the new sheet is added. If you omit both *before* and *after*, the new worksheet is added before the active sheet.
after	The sheet after which the new sheet is added. You can't specify both the *before* and *after* arguments.
count	The number of new worksheets to add. VBA adds one worksheet if you omit *count*.
type	The type of worksheet. You have three choices: `xlWorksheet` (the default), `xlExcel4MacroSheet`, or `xlExcel4IntlMacroSheet`.

In the following statement, a new worksheet is added to the active workbook before the Sales sheet:

```
Worksheets.Add before:=Worksheets("Sales")
```

Properties of the Worksheet Object

Let's take a tour through some of the most useful properties associated with Worksheet objects:

`Name`: Renames the specified worksheet. For example, the following statement renames the Sheet1 worksheet to 1994 Budget:

```
Worksheets("Sheet1").Name = "1994 Budget"
```

`Outline`: Returns an `Outline` object that represents the outline for the specified worksheet.

NOTE

Once you have the `Outline` object, use the `ShowLevels` method to select an outline level. For example, the following statement displays the second outline level for the Net Worth worksheet:

```
Worksheets("Net Worth").Outline.ShowLevels 2
```

Here are some other outline-related properties and methods you can use:

Range*.AutoOutline**: Automatically creates an outline for the specified ***Range object.

> *Window*`.DisplayOutline`: Set this property to `True` to display the outline for the specified *Window* object.
>
> *Range*`.ClearOutline`: Clears the outline for the specified *Range* object.

`ProtectContents`: Returns `True` if the specified worksheet is protected.

`ProtectDrawingObjects`: Returns `True` if the drawing objects on the specified worksheet are protected.

`ProtectionMode`: Returns `True` if user-interface-only protection is activated for the specified worksheet.

`ProtectScenarios`: Returns `True` if the scenarios in the specified worksheet are protected.

`StandardHeight`: Returns the standard height of all the rows in the specified worksheet.

`StandardWidth`: Returns the standard width of all the columns in the specified worksheet.

`UsedRange`: Returns a Range object that represents the used range in the specified worksheet.

`Visible`: Controls whether or not the user can see the specified worksheet. Setting this property to `False` is equivalent to selecting the **F**ormat | **S**heet | **H**ide command. For example, to hide a worksheet named Expenses, you would use the following statement:

```
Worksheets("Expenses").Visible = False
```

To unhide the sheet, set its `Visible` property to `True`.

Methods of the Worksheet Object

Here's a list of some common Worksheet object methods:

`Activate`: Makes the specified worksheet active (so that it becomes the `ActiveSheet` property of the workbook. For example, the following statement activates the Sales worksheet in the Finance.xls workbook:

```
Workbooks("Finance.xls").Worksheets("Sales").Activate
```

`Calculate`: Calculates the specified worksheet. For example, the following statement recalculates the Budget 1995 worksheet:

```
Worksheets("Budget 1995").Calculate
```

`CheckSpelling`: Displays the Spelling dialog box to check the spelling on the specified worksheet. Here is the syntax of this version of the `CheckSpelling` method:

```
object.CheckSpelling(customDictionary,ignoreUppercase,alwaysSuggest)
```

object	The worksheet you want to check.
customDictionary	The filename of a custom dictionary that Excel can search if a word can't be found in the main dictionary.
ignoreUppercase	Set to True to tell Excel to ignore words entirely in uppercase.
alwaysSuggest	Set to True to tell Excel to display a list of suggestions for each misspelled word.

Copy: Copies the specified worksheet using the following syntax:

```
object.Copy(before,after)
```

object	The worksheet you want to copy.
before	The sheet before which the sheet will be copied. If you omit both *before* and *after*, VBA creates a new workbook for the copied sheet.
after	The sheet after which the new sheet is added. You can't specify both the *before* and *after* arguments.

In the following statement, the Budget 1994 worksheet is copied to a new workbook:

```
Worksheets("Budget 1994").Copy
```

Delete: Deletes the specified worksheet.

For example, the following statement deletes the active worksheet:

```
ActiveSheet.Delete
```

Move: Moves the specified worksheet using the following syntax:

```
object.Move(before,after)
```

object	The worksheet you want to move.
before	The sheet before which the sheet will be moved. If you omit both *before* and *after*, VBA creates a new workbook for the moved sheet.
after	The sheet after which the new sheet is added. You can't specify both the *before* and *after* arguments.

In the following statement, the Budget 1994 worksheet is moved before the Budget 1995 worksheet:

```
Worksheets("Budget 1994").Move Before:=Worksheets("1995 Budget")
```

`Protect`: Sets up protection for the specified worksheet. Here's the syntax to use:

object`.Protect(`*password,drawingObjects,contents,scenarios,userInterfaceOnly*`)`

object	The worksheet you want to protect.
password	A text string that specifies the (case-sensitive) password to use with the protection.
drawingObjects	Set to `True` to protect the worksheet's drawing objects.
contents	Set to `True` to protect the worksheet's cell contents.
scenarios	Set to `True` to protect the worksheet's scenarios.
userInterfaceOnly	Set to `True` to protect the worksheet's user interface, but not its macros.

For example, the following statement protects the Payroll worksheet's contents and scenarios and sets up a password for the protection:

```
Worksheets("Payroll").Protect _
    password:="cheapskate", _
    contents:=True, _
    scenarios:=True
```

`Select`: Selects the specified worksheet.

`SetBackgroundPicture`: Adds a bitmap image to the background of the specified worksheet. Here is the syntax:

object`.SetBackgroundPicture(`***fileName***`)`

object	The worksheet you want to use.
fileName	The filename of the bitmap image you want to use.

For example, the following statement sets the background image of Sheet1 to C:\Windows\Clouds.bmp, as shown in Figure 24.1:

```
Worksheets("Sheet1").SetBackgroundPicture "C:\Windows\Clouds.bmp"
```

FIGURE 24.1.

Use the SetBackgroundPicture method to specify a bitmap image as a worksheet's background.

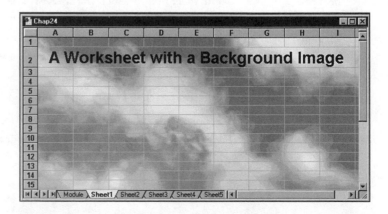

`Unprotect`: Unprotects the specified worksheet. Here's the syntax:

`Object``.Unprotect(`*`password`*`)`

`Object`	The Worksheet object you want to unprotect.
`password`	The protection password.

Working with Range Objects

Mastering cell and range references is perhaps the most fundamental skill to learn when working with spreadsheets. After all, most worksheet chores involve cells, ranges, and range names. However, this skill takes on added importance when dealing with VBA procedures. When you're working on a worksheet, you can easily select cells and ranges with the mouse or the keyboard, or you can paste range names into formulas. In a procedure, though, you always have to describe—or even calculate—the range with which you want to work.

What you describe is the most common of all VBA objects: the Range object. A Range object can be a single cell, a row or column, a selection of cells, or a 3-D range. The following sections look at various techniques that return a Range object, as well as a number of Range object properties and methods.

Returning a Range Object

Much of your VBA code will concern itself with Range objects of one kind or another. So you need to be well-versed in the various techniques that are available for returning range objects, be they single cells, rectangular ranges, or entire rows and columns. This section takes you through each of these techniques.

Using the *Range* Method

The `Range` method is the most straightforward way to identify a cell or range. It has two syntaxes. The first requires only a single argument:

`object``.Range(`*`name`*`)`

`object`	The Worksheet object to which the `Range` method applies. If you omit *`object`*, VBA assumes the method applies to the `ActiveSheet` object.
`name`	A range reference or name entered as text.

For example, the following statements enter a date in cell B2 and then create a data series in the range B2:E10 of the active worksheet (I'll discuss the `Formula` and `DataSeries` methods in more detail later):

```
Range("B2").Formula = "01/01/95"
Range("B2:B13").DataSeries Type:=xlDate, Date:=xlMonth
```

The Range method also works with named ranges. For example, the following statement clears the contents of a range named *Criteria* in the Data worksheet:

```
Worksheets("Data").Range("Criteria").ClearContents
```

The second syntax for the Range method requires two arguments:

```
object.Range(cell1,cell2)
```

object	The Worksheet object to which the Range method applies. If you omit object, VBA assumes that the method applies to the ActiveSheet object.
cell1, cell2	The cells that define the upper-left corner (cell1) and lower-right corner (cell2) of the range. Each can be a cell address as text, a Range object consisting of a single cell, or an entire column or row.

The advantage of this syntax is that it separates the range corners into separate arguments. This enables you to modify each corner under procedural control. For example, you could set up variables named upperLeft and lowerRight and then return Range objects of different sizes:

```
Range(upperLeft,lowerRight)
```

Working with Cells

The Cells method returns a single cell as a Range object. Here's the syntax:

```
object.Cells(rowIndex,columnIndex)
```

object	A Worksheet or Range object. If you omit object, the method applies to the ActiveSheet object.
rowIndex	The row number of the cell. If object is a worksheet, a rowIndex of 1 refers to row 1 on the sheet. If object is a range, rowIndex 1 refers to the first row of the range.
columnIndex	The column of the cell. You can enter a letter as text or a number. If object is a worksheet, a columnIndex of "A" or 1 refers to column A on the sheet. If object is a range, columnIndex "A" or 1 refers to the first column of the range.

For example, the following procedure fragment loops five times and enters the values Field1 through Field5 in cells A1 through E1:

```
For colNumber = 1 To 5
    Cells(1, colNumber).Value = "Field" & colNumber
Next colNumber
```

TIP

You also can refer to a cell by enclosing an A1-style reference in square brackets ([]). For example, the following statement checks the spelling of the text in cell C4 of the active worksheet:

```
ActiveSheet.[C4].CheckSpelling
```

NOTE

The `Cells` method has a second syntax that doesn't require arguments: `object.Cells`. When `object` is a worksheet, this method returns a collection of all the cells in the sheet.

Returning a Row

If you need to work with entire rows or columns, VBA has several methods and properties you can use. In each case, the object returned is a Range.

The most common way to refer to a row in VBA is to use the `Rows` method. This method uses the following syntax:

```
object.Rows(index)
```

object	The Worksheet or Range object to which the method applies. If you omit *object,* VBA uses the `ActiveSheet` object.
index	The row number. If *object* is a worksheet, an *index* of 1 refers to row 1 on the sheet. If *object* is a range, an *index* of 1 refers to the first row of the range. If you omit *index,* the method returns a collection of all the rows in *object.*

For example, Listing 24.3 shows a procedure named `InsertRangeRow`. This procedure inserts a new row before the last row of whatever range is passed as an argument (`rangeObject`). This would be a useful subroutine in programs that need to maintain ranges (such as a database).

Listing 24.3. A procedure that uses the `Rows` method to insert a row.

```
Sub InsertRangeRow(rangeObject As Range)

    Dim totalRows As Integer, lastRow As Integer
```

continues

Listing 24.3. continued

```
With rangeObject
    totalRows = .Rows.Count           ' Total rows in the range
    lastRow = .Rows(totalRows).Row    ' Last row number
    .Rows(lastRow).Insert             ' Insert before last row
End With

End Sub
```

After declaring the variables, the first statement uses the Rows method without the *index* argument to return a collection of all the rows in rangeObject and uses the Count property to get the total number of rangeObject rows:

```
totalRows = rangeObject.Rows.Count
```

The second statement uses the totalRows variable as an argument in the Rows method to return the last row of rangeObject, and then the Row property returns the row number:

```
lastRow = rangeObject.Rows(totalRows).Row
```

Finally, the last statement uses the Insert method to insert a row before lastRow. (Insert has three different syntaxes. See the Help system for details.)

To use InsertRangeRow, you need to pass the procedure a Range object. For example, to insert a row into a range named Test, you would use the following statement:

```
InsertRangeRow Range("Test")
```

> **NOTE**
>
> You also can use the EntireRow property to return a row. The syntax *object*.EntireRow returns the entire row or rows that contain the Range object. This is most often used to mimic the Shift-Spacebar shortcut key that selects the entire row of the active cell. To do this, you use the following statement:
>
> ```
> ActiveCell.EntireRow.Select
> ```

Returning a Column

To return a column, use the Columns method. The syntax for this method is almost identical to the Rows method:

```
object.Columns(index)
```

object	The Worksheet or Range object to which the method applies. If you omit *object*, VBA uses the ActiveSheet object.
index	The column number. If *object* is a worksheet, an *index* of "A" or 1 refers to column A on the sheet. If *object* is a range, *index* "A" or 1 refers to the first column of the range. If you omit *index*, the method returns a collection of all the columns in *object*.

For example, the following statement sets the width of column B on the active worksheet to 20:

```
Columns("B").ColumnWidth = 20
```

NOTE

The syntax *object*.EntireColumn returns the entire column or columns that contain the Range object.

Using the Offset Method

When defining your Range objects, you often won't know the specific range address to use. For example, you may need to refer to the cell that is two rows down and one column to the right of the active cell. You could find out the address of the active cell and then calculate the address of the other cell, but VBA gives you an easier (and more flexible) way: the Offset method. Offset returns a Range object that is offset from a specified range by a certain number of rows and columns. Here is its syntax:

object.Offset(*rowOffset,columnOffset*)

object	The original Range object.
rowOffset	The number of rows to offset *object*. You can use a positive number (to move down), a negative number (to move up), or 0 (to use the same rows). If you omit *rowOffset*, VBA uses 0.
columnOffset	The number of columns to offset *object*. Again, you can use a positive number (to move right), a negative number (to move left), or 0 (to use the same columns). If you omit *columnOffset*, VBA uses 0.

For example, the following statement formats the range B2:D6 as bold:

```
Range("A1:C5").Offset(1,1).Font.Bold = True
```

Listing 24.4 shows a procedure called ConcatenateStrings that concatenates two text strings. This is handy, for instance, if you have a list with separate first and last name fields and you want to combine them.

Listing 24.4. A procedure that uses the Offset method to concatenate two text strings.

```
Sub ConcatenateStrings()

    Dim string1$, string2$

    ' Store the contents of the cell 2 to the left of the active cell
    string1$ = ActiveCell.Offset(0, -2)

    ' Store the contents of the cell 1 to the left of the active cell
    string2$ = ActiveCell.Offset(0, -1)

    ' Enter combined strings (separated by a space) into active cell
    ActiveCell.Value = string1$ & " " & string2$

End Sub
```

The procedure begins by declaring String1$ and String2$. (The $ type declaration characters automatically declare these variables as string types; see Chapter 21, "Getting Started with VBA," for details.) The next statement stores in String1$ the contents of the cell two columns to the left of the active cell by using the Offset method as follows:

```
String1$ = ActiveCell.Offset(0, -2)
```

Similarly, the next statement stores in String2$ the contents of the cell one column to the left of the active cell. Finally, the last statement combines String1$ and String2$ (with a space in between) and enters the new string in the active cell.

Selecting a Cell or Range

If you've used the Excel 4.0 macro language, you know that most of its range operations require you to first select the range and then do something to it. For example, changing the font to Times New Roman in the range B1 to B10 of the active sheet requires two commands:

```
=SELECT(!$B$1:$B$10)
=FORMAT.FONT("Times New Roman")
```

VBA, however, enables you to access objects directly without having to select them first. This means that your VBA procedures rarely have to select a range. The preceding example can be performed with a single (and faster) VBA statement:

```
Range("B1:B10").Font.Name = "Times New Roman"
```

However, there are times when you do need to select a range. For example, to create a chart with VBA, you first select a range and then run the `Charts.Add` method. To select a range, use the `Select` method:

object`.Select`

> *object*   The Range object you want to select.

For example, the following statement selects the range A1:E10 in the Sales worksheet:

```
Worksheets("Sales").Range("A1:E10").Select
```

> **TIP**
>
> To return the currently selected range, use the `Selection` property. For example, the following statement applies the Times New Roman font to the currently selected range:
>
> ```
> Selection.Font.Name = "Times New Roman"
> ```

Defining a Range Name

Range names in VBA are Name objects. To define them, you use the `Add` method for the `Names` collection (which is usually the collection of defined names in a workbook). Here is an abbreviated syntax for the `Names` collection's `Add` method (this method has nine arguments; see the VBA Reference in the Help system):

```
Names.Add(text,refersTo)
```

> *text*   The text you want to use as the range name.
>
> *refersToR1C1* The item to which you want the name to refer. You can enter a
>   constant, a formula as text (such as `"=Sales-Expenses"`), or a
>   worksheet reference (such as `"Sales!A1:C6"`).

For example, the following statement adds the range name `SalesRange` to the `Names` collection of the active workbook:

```
ActiveWorkbook.Names.Add _
    Text:="SalesRange", _
    RefersToR1C1:="=Sales!$A$1$C$6"
```

More Range Object Properties

Some of the examples you've seen in the last few sections have used various Range object properties. Here's a summary of the properties you're likely to use most often in your VBA code:

Column: Returns the number of the first column in the specified range.

Count: Returns the number of cells in the specified range.

CurrentArray: Returns a Range object that represents the entire array in which the specified range resides.

CAUTION

If the specified range isn't part of an array, the CurrentArray property generates a No cell found error message. To prevent this error, use the HasArray property to test whether or not the range is part of an array. If the range is part of an array, HasArray returns True.

CurrentRegion: Returns a Range object that represents the entire region in which the specified range resides. A range's "region" is the area surrounding the range that is bounded by at least one empty row above and below, and at least one empty column to the left and right.

Formula: Returns or sets a formula for the specified range.

FormulaArray: Returns or sets an array formula for the specified range.

NumberFormat: Returns or sets the numeric format in the specified range. Enter the format you want to use as a string, as shown in the following statement:

```
Worksheets("Analysis").Range("Sales").NumberFormat = _
    "$#,##0.00_);[Red]($#,##0.00)"
```

Row: Returns the number of the first row in the specified range.

Value: Returns or sets the value in the specified cell.

More Range Object Methods

Here's a look at a few more methods that should come in handy in your VBA procedures:

Address: Returns the address, as text, of the specified range.

Clear: Removes everything from the specified range (contents, formats, and notes).

ClearContents: Removes the contents of the specified range.

ClearFormats: Removes the formatting for the specified range.

ClearNotes: Removes the cell notes for the specified range.

Copy: Copies the specified range to the Clipboard or to a new destination. Copying a range is similar to cutting a range. Here is the syntax for the Copy method:

```
object.Copy(destination)
```

object	The range to copy.
destination	The cell or range where you want the copied range to be pasted.

Cut: Cuts the specified range to the Clipboard or to a new destination. The Cut method uses the following syntax:

```
object.Cut(destination)
```

object	The Range object to cut.
destination	The cell or range where you want the cut range to be pasted.

For example, the following statement cuts the range A1:B3 and moves it to the range B4:C6:

```
Range("A1:B3").Cut Destination:=Range("B4")
```

DataSeries: Creates a data series in the specified range. The DataSeries method uses the following syntax:

```
object.DataSeries(rowcol,type,date,step,stop,trend)
```

object	The range to use for the data series.
rowcol	Use xlRows to enter the series in rows or xlColumns to enter the data in columns. If you omit *rowcol*, Excel uses the size and shape of the range.
type	The type of series. Enter xlLinear (the default), xlGrowth, xlChronological, or xlAutoFill.
date	The type f date series, if you used xlChronological for the *type* argument. Your choices are xlDay (the default), xlWeekday, xlMonth, or xlYear.
step	The step value for the series (the default value is 1).
stop	The stop value for the series. If you omit *stop*, Excel fills the range.
trend	Use True to create a linear or growth trend series. Use False (the default) to create a standard series.

FillDown: Uses the contents and formatting from the top row of the specified range to fill down into the rest of the range.

FillLeft: Uses the contents and formatting from the rightmost column of the specified range to fill left into the rest of the range.

FillRight: Uses the contents and formatting from the leftmost column of the specified range to fill right into the rest of the range.

`FillUp`: Uses the contents and formatting from the bottom row of the specified range to fill up into the rest of the range.

`Insert`: Inserts cells into the specified range using the following syntax:

***object*.Insert(*shift*)**

object	The range into which you want to insert the cells.
shift	The direction you want to shift the existing cells. Use either `xlToRight` or `xlDown`.

`Resize`: Resizes the specified range. Here is the syntax for this method:

***object*.Resize(*rowSize*,*colSize*)**

object	The range to resize.
rowSize	The number of rows in the new range.
colSize	The number of columns in the new range.

For example, suppose you use the `InsertRangeRow` procedure from Listing 24.3 to insert a row into a named range. In most cases, you'll want to redefine the range name so that it includes the extra row you added. Listing 24.5 shows a procedure that calls `InsertRangeRow` and then uses the `Resize` method to adjust the named range.

Listing 24.5. A procedure that uses `Resize` to adjust a named range.

```
Sub InsertAndRedefineName()

    InsertRangeRow(Range("Test"))

    With Range("Test")
        Names.Add _
            Name:="Test", _
            RefersToR1C1:=.Resize(.Rows.Count + 1)
    End With

End Sub
```

In the `Names.Add` method, the new range is given by the expression `.Resize(.Rows.Count + 1)`. Here, the `Resize` method returns a range that has one more row than the Test range.

Tips for Faster Procedures

Short procedures usually are over in the blink of an eye. However, the longer your procedures get, and the more they interact with Excel objects, the more time they take to complete their tasks. For these more complex routines, you need to start thinking not only about *what* the procedure does, but *how* it does it. The more efficient you can make your code, the faster the procedure will execute. This section gives a few tips for writing efficient code that runs quickly.

Turn Off Screen Updating

One of the biggest drags on procedure performance is the constant screen updating that occurs. If your procedure uses many statements that format ranges, enter formulas, or cut and copy cells, the procedure will spend most of its time updating the screen to show the results of these operations. This not only slows everything down, but it also looks unprofessional. It's much nicer when the procedure performs all its chores "behind the scenes" and then presents the user with the finished product at the end of the procedure.

You can do this with the Application object's ScreenUpdating property. Set ScreenUpdating to False to turn off screen updates and set it back to True to resume updating.

Hide Your Worksheets

If your procedure does a lot of switching between worksheets, you can speed things by hiding the worksheets while you work with them. To do this, set the worksheet's Visible property to False. You can work with hidden worksheets normally, and when your procedure is done, you can set Visible to True to display the results to the user.

> **CAUTION**
>
> As soon as you've hidden an active worksheet, VBA deactivates it. Therefore, if your procedures reference the active sheet, you need to activate the worksheet (using the Activate method) right after hiding it.

Don't Select Worksheets or Ranges Unless You Have To

Two of VBA's slowest methods are Activate and Select, so they should be used sparingly. In the majority of cases, you can indirectly work with ranges and worksheets by referencing them as arguments in the Range method (or any other VBA statement that returns a Range object) and the Worksheets collection.

Don't Recalculate Until You Have To

As you know, manual calculation mode prevents Excel from recalculating a worksheet until you say so. This saves you time when using sheets with complicated models—models in which you don't necessarily want to see a recalculation every time you change a variable.

You can get the same benefits in your procedures by using the `Application` object's `Calculation` property. Place Excel in manual calculation mode (as described earlier in this chapter) and then, when you need to update your formula results, use the `Calculate` method.

Optimize Your Loops

One of the cornerstones of efficient programming is loop optimization. Because a procedure might run the code inside a loop hundreds or even thousands of times, a minor improvement in loop efficiency can result in considerably reduced execution times.

When analyzing your loops, make sure that you're particularly ruthless about applying the previous tips. One `Select` method is slow; a thousand will drive you crazy.

Also, weed out from your loops any statements that return the same value each time. For example, consider the following procedure fragment:

```
For i = 1 To 5000
    Application.StatusBar = "The value is " & Worksheets("Sheet1").[A1].Value
Next i
```

The idea of this somewhat useless code is to loop 5,000 times, each time displaying in the status bar the contents of cell A1 in the Sheet1 worksheet. The value in cell A1 never changes, but it takes time for Excel to get the value, slowing the loop considerably. A better approach would be the following:

```
currCell = Worksheets("Sheet1").[A1].Value
For i = 1 To 5000
    Application.StatusBar = "The value is: " & currCell
Next I
```

Transferring the unchanging `CurCell` calculation outside the loop, and assigning it to a variable, means that the procedure has to call the function only once.

To test the difference, Listing 24.6 shows the `TimingTest` procedure. This procedure uses the `Timer` function (which returns the number of seconds since midnight) to time two `For...Next` loops. The first loop is unoptimized and the second loop is optimized. On my system, the unoptimized loop takes about 45 seconds, while the optimized loop takes only 22 seconds—less than half the time.

Listing 24.6. A procedure that tests the difference between an optimized and an unoptimized loop.

```
Sub TimingTest()

    Dim i As Integer, currCell As Variant
    Dim start1 As Long, finish1 As Long
    Dim start2 As Long, finish2 As Long

    ' Start timing the unoptimized loop
    start1 = Timer
    For i = 1 To 5000
```

```
        Application.StatusBar = "The value is " & Worksheets("Sheet1").[A1].Value
    Next i
    finish1 = Timer

    ' Start timing the optimized loop
    start2 = Timer
    currCell = Worksheets("Sheet1").[A1].Value
    For i = 1 To 5000
        Application.StatusBar = "The value is " & currCell
    Next i
    finish2 = Timer

    MsgBox "The first loop took " & finish1 - start1 & " seconds." & _
        Chr(13) & _
        "The second loop took " & finish2 - start2 & " seconds."

    Application.StatusBar = False

End Sub
```

Working with Add-In Applications

If you've used any of Excel's add-in applications, you know they're handy because they add extra functions and commands and look as though they were built right into the program. For your own applications, you can convert your workbooks to add-ins and gain the following advantages:

- Your Function procedures appear in the Function Wizard dialog box in the User Defined category.
- Your Sub procedures do *not* appear in the Macro dialog box. This means users must access your add-in procedures entirely by shortcut keys, menu commands, toolbar buttons, or other indirect means (such as the event handlers discussed in Chapter 27).
- Add-ins execute faster than normal files.
- The code is compiled into a compressed format that no one else can read or modify.

It's important to keep in mind that add-in applications are *demand-loaded.* This means that, when you install your application, it gets read into memory in two stages:

1. The application's functions are added to the Function Wizard, its shortcut keys are enabled, its menus and menu commands are added to the appropriate menu bar, and its toolbars are displayed.
2. The rest of the application is loaded into memory when the user either chooses one of the add-in functions, presses an add-in shortcut key, selects an add-in menu item, or clicks an add-in toolbar button.

The exception to this is when the add-in file contains an Auto_Open procedure. (See Chapter 27 for more information.) In this case, the entire add-in is loaded at the start.

766

Creating an Add-In Application

When you've fully debugged and tested your code and are ready to distribute the application to your users, follow these steps to convert the workbook into the add-in format:

1. Activate a module in the workbook you want to save as an add-in.
2. Select the **Tools | Make** Add-In command to display the Make Add-In dialog box.
3. Enter a new name, drive, and folder (if required) for the file.
4. Make sure that Microsoft Excel Add-In is selected in the Save File as **Type** drop-down list.
5. Select OK.

> **NOTE**
>
> Be sure to fill in both the **Title** and **Comments** boxes on the Summary tab of the Properties dialog box (select the **File | Properties** command; see Figure 24.2) before converting the workbook to an add-in. The **Title** text will be the name of the add-in and the comments will appear at the bottom of the Add-Ins dialog box when you highlight your add-in.

FIGURE 24.2.

Use the Summary tab of the Properties dialog box to describe the file before converting it to an add-in.

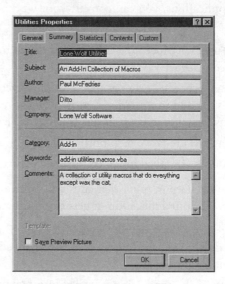

CAUTION

Don't save the add-in using the same name as the original workbook. As I've said, you can't edit an add-in file, so if you lose the original, the add-in can never be changed.

Controlling Add-Ins with VBA

VBA provides you with several methods and properties that enable you to control add-in applications at the procedural level. From a VBA point of view, an AddIn object is an individual add-in application, and AddIns is the collection of all the add-in applications available to Excel. The AddIns collection is identical to the list of add-ins you see when you display the Add-Ins dialog box (by selecting the **Tools | Add-Ins** command).

To refer to an AddIn object, use the AddIns method:

```
Addins(index)
```

index	This argument can be any one of the following:
	A number representing the add-in you want to use, where 1 signifies the first add-in that appears in the Add-Ins dialog box, 2 is the second add-in that appears, and so on.
	The name, as text, of the add-in you want to use. For the add-ins that come with Excel, the name of the add-in is the name that appears in the Add-Ins dialog box. For your own add-ins, the name is either the file name (minus the extension) or the text you entered into the **T**itle edit box of the Summary Info dialog.
	An array of numbers or names.

For example, the following statement refers to the Solver add-in application:

```
AddIns("Solver Add-In")
```

Before you can work with your own add-ins, you need to add them to the AddIns collection. VBA provides the Add method to do just that:

```
Addins.Add(fileName, copyFile)
```

fileName	A string containing the full pathname of the add-in file.
copyFile	An optional logical argument to use when the add-in file is stored on a floppy disk, CD-ROM, or network drive. If *copyFile* is True, Excel copies

the add-in file to your hard disk. If it's `False`, Excel leaves the file where it is. If you omit *copyFile*, Excel displays a dialog box that asks what you want to do. The *copyFile* argument is ignored if *fileName* references a file on your hard disk.

The `Add` method's only purpose in life is to tell Excel that the add-in is available. To actually use the file (in order to make its commands and functions available to the user), you need to install it by setting its `Installed` property to `True`. (This is the equivalent of activating the add-in's check box in the Add-Ins dialog box.) This does two things:

■ It performs the first part of the demand-loading sequence (in other words, the add-in's functions, shortcut keys, menus, and toolbars become available).

■ The add-in's `Auto_Add` procedure (if it has one) is executed. This is another of the automatic procedures discussed earlier. It's useful for things such as initializing the add-in and telling the user that the add-in is loaded.

Listing 24.7 shows you how to work with add-ins from a VBA procedure.

Listing 24.7. Working with add-in applications.

```
Sub InstallBudgetTools()

    AddIns.Add FileName:="C:\Budget\Tools.xla"
    With AddIns("Budget Tools")
        .Installed = True
        MsgBox "The " & .Title & _
            " add-in is now installed.", _
            vbInformation
    End With

End Sub
```

The `InstallBudgetTools` procedure adds and installs an add-in named "Budget Tools." First, the `Add` method makes the add-in available to Excel. Then a `With` statement takes the Budget Tools add-in and installs it and then displays a message telling the user the add-in has been installed.

Note, in particular, the use of the `Title` property in the `MsgBox` statement. AddIn objects share many of the same properties found in Workbook objects. These properties include `Author`, `Comments`, `FullName`, `Name`, `Path`, `Subject`, and `Title`.

When you no longer need to work with an add-in, you can remove it by setting its `Installed` property to `False`.

Summary

This chapter showed you how to use VBA to manipulate Excel. We examined various properties and methods for common objects, including the `Application`, Workbook, Worksheet, and Range objects. Here are some chapters to check out for related information:

- For a general discussion of Excel objects, see Chapter 22, "Understanding Objects."

- To learn about loops and other VBA control structures (and, in particular, the `For Each...Next` structure that lets you cycle through the elements in a collection), see Chapter 23, "Controlling VBA Code and Interacting with the User."

- I'll show you how to use VBA to work with both Excel databases and external databases in Chapter 26, "Database and Client/Server Programming."

- You can use VBA to manipulate other applications and, in some cases, you can even work with other application's objects. See Chapter 28, "Working with Other Applications: OLE, DDE, and More," to find out how it's done.

- For a complete list of VBA functions, see Appendix C, "VBA Functions."

Creating a Custom User Interface

25

VBA procedures are only as useful as they are convenient. There isn't much point in creating a procedure that saves you (or your users) a few keystrokes if you (or they) have to expend a lot of energy hunting down a routine. The Personal Macro Library helps, but overloading it can make navigating the Macro dialog box a nightmare. Shortcut keys are true time-savers, but Excel has only so many (and our brains can memorize only so many Ctrl-*key* combinations).

Instead of these quick-and-dirty solutions, you need to give some thought to the type of user interface you want to create for your spreadsheet application. The interface includes not only the design of the worksheets, but also three other factors that let the user interact with the model: dialog boxes, menus, and toolbars. And while you certainly can give the user access to Excel's built-in dialogs, menus, and toolbars, you'll find that you often need to create your own interface elements from scratch. This chapter shows you how to do just that. We'll look at building custom dialog boxes, menus, and toolbars.

Creating a Custom Dialog Box

The InputBox method you learned about in Chapter 23, "Controlling VBA Code and Interacting with the User," works fine if you need just a single item of information, but what if you need four or five? Or what if you want the user to choose from a list of items? In some cases, you can use Excel's built-in dialog boxes, but these might not have the exact controls you need, or they might have controls you don't want the user to have access to.

The solution is to build your own dialog boxes. You can add as many controls as you need (including list boxes, option buttons, and check boxes), and your procedures have complete access to all the results. Best of all, VBA makes constructing even the most sophisticated dialog boxes as easy as dragging the mouse pointer. The next few sections show you how to create dialog boxes and integrate them into your applications.

Inserting a New Dialog Sheet

You create a custom dialog box in a separate dialog sheet. A *dialog sheet* is a special sheet that has a *dialog frame*—an empty dialog box—and a grid to which you add the controls. The first thing you need to do is to insert a dialog sheet into the workbook, as described in the following steps:

1. Select the workbook you want to use to store the dialog box.

2. Excel inserts the dialog sheet before the active sheet, so you need to activate the sheet that you want the dialog sheet to appear before. For example, to have the dialog sheet appear before Sheet1, activate Sheet1.

3. Select the **I**nsert | **M**acro | **D**ialog command. Excel inserts a new sheet and displays the Forms toolbar, as shown in Figure 25.1.

FIGURE 25.1.

The Insert \ Macro \ Dialog command adds a new dialog sheet to the workbook.

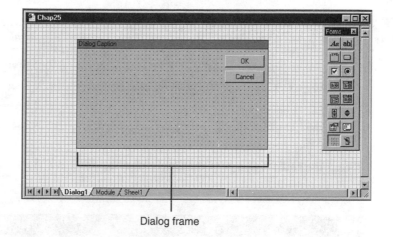

Dialog frame

Changing the Name of the Dialog Box

When you create a new dialog sheet, the displayed dialog frame is given the somewhat uninspiring name Dialog Caption. To change this name, first activate the title bar by double-clicking on it. Then just delete the existing name and type the name you want to use. When you're done, click anywhere outside the title bar.

Adding Controls to a Dialog Sheet

The new dialog sheet displays a default dialog box frame with the OK and Cancel buttons already added. The idea is that you use this frame to "draw" the controls you need. Later, you can either link the controls directly to worksheet cells or create procedures to handle the selections.

The Forms toolbar contains tools for all the controls you can add to a dialog box. Here are the basic steps to follow to add any control to the dialog box:

1. Click the button you want to use.
2. Move the mouse pointer into the dialog box and position it where you want the top-left corner of the control to appear.
3. Drag the mouse pointer. VBA displays a gray border indicating the outline of the control.
4. Release the mouse button. VBA creates the control and gives it a default name (such as Check Box *n,* where *n* signifies that this is the *n*th control you've created on this dialog box).

As soon as you've added a control, you can move it around, size it, or delete it. Table 25.1 summarizes the techniques for these actions.

Table 25.1. Mouse techniques for working with controls.

Action	Result
Click on the control	Selects the control
Hold down the Shift key and click on each control	Selects multiple controls
Drag the control	Moves the control
Select the control and drag any of the selection handles that appear	Sizes a control
Select the control and press the Delete key	Deletes a control

NOTE

To size the dialog box itself, click on the title bar and then drag the selection handles that appear around the dialog frame.

Setting the Tab Order

As you know, you can navigate a dialog box by pressing the Tab key. The order in which the controls are selected is called the *tab order* (or the *z-order*). VBA sets the tab order according to the order you create the controls on the dialog sheet. In most cases, this order isn't what you want to end up with, so VBA enables you to control the tab order yourself. The following procedure shows you how it's done:

1. Select the **Tools | T**ab Order command. Excel displays the Tab Order dialog box, shown in Figure 25.2.

FIGURE 25.2.

Use the Tab Order dialog box to set the order in which the user navigates the dialog box when pressing the Tab key.

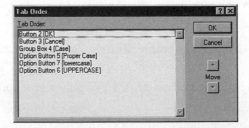

TIP

You can also display the Tab Order dialog box by right-clicking on an empty part of the dialog box and selecting Tab Order from the shortcut menu.

2. In the **T**ab Order list, highlight the control you want to move.

3. Use the Move control to move the item up (by clicking the up arrow) or down (by clicking the down arrow).

4. Repeat steps 2 and 3 for other controls you want to move.

5. Click OK or press Enter.

Setting Control Properties

Dialog box controls are objects with their own set of properties and methods. A check box, for example, is a CheckBox object, and it has properties that control the name of the check box, whether or not it is initially checked, its accelerator key, and more. There are also collections of control objects. `CheckBoxes`, for example, is a collection of all the check boxes on a dialog sheet.

NOTE

You can reference each control in a collection in one of two ways:

- You can use a number that corresponds to the control's position in the tab order among similar controls. For example, `CheckBoxes(2)` refers to the second check box in the tab order, not the second control in the tab order.

- You can use the unique name Excel defines for each control. These names take the form *Control Type n,* where *Control Type* is the type of control (`Check Box` or `Button`, for example) and *n* means that the control was the *n*th control added to the dialog box. For example, if a check box was the third item added to a dialog box, you could reference the check box as `CheckBoxes("Check Box 3")`. The name of a control appears in the formula bar's Name box whenever you select a control.

You can manipulate control properties at runtime, before you display the dialog box, while displaying it, or after. However, you can set some control properties at design time (that is, in the dialog sheet) by following these steps:

1. Select the control with which you want to work.

2. Select the Format | Object command or click the Control Properties button on the Forms toolbar. Excel displays the Format Object dialog box.

 The Control Properties button on the Forms toolbar.

TIP

You can also display the Format Object dialog box either by selecting the control and pressing Ctrl-1 or by right-clicking the control and selecting Format Object from the shortcut menu.

---

3. Select the Control tab.

4. Enter your options.

5. Select OK to return to the dialog sheet.

Figure 25.3 shows the Control tab for a check box. Each type of control has its own unique options (which I discuss later), but you'll see two for most objects:

Accelerator Key   Defines which letter in the control's name (or *caption,* as it's called in VBA) will be the accelerator key. This letter appears underlined in the caption, and the user can select the control by holding down the Alt key and pressing the letter.

Cell **L**ink   A worksheet cell that holds the value of the control when the user exits the dialog box. If a check box is activated, for example, its linked cell will contain the value TRUE.

FIGURE 25.3.

The Control tab for a check box.

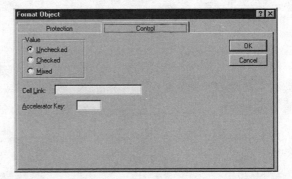

CAUTION

A cell linked to a control changes value if the control changes, even when the user clicks Cancel to exit the dialog box. It's usually better (and safer) to assign the value of a control to a variable and then, if appropriate, place the value in the cell under program control.

Creating a Dialog Box Using VBA Code

Although you'll normally create your custom dialog boxes by hand on a dialog sheet, you can also create them using VBA code. The next few sections take you through each step that your procedure will have to go through to create a dialog box.

Step 1: Create a New Dialog Sheet

Use the `Add` method of the `DialogSheets` collection to create the new dialog sheet. Here is the proper syntax for this method:

```
DialogSheets.Add(before)
```

> `before`   The sheet before which you want the dialog sheet created.

For example, the following procedure fragment creates a new dialog sheet before Sheet1, activates the sheet, and then renames it:

```
dim dlgSheet As DialogSheet
DialogSheets.Add before:=Worksheets("Sheet1")
Set dlgSheet = Worksheets("Sheet1").Previous
dlgSheet.Activate
dlgSheet.Name = "Convert Case Dialog"
```

Step 2: Set Some Dialog Frame Properties

The new sheet is a DialogSheet object with a `DialogFrame` property that represents the dialog frame which is, in turn, a DialogFrame object. Use this object to set the following properties:

> `Caption`: The dialog frame's title bar text.

> `Height`: The height of the dialog frame.

> `Width`: The width of the dialog frame.

Here's a procedure fragment that sets these properties for the dialog frame created in the last section:

```
With dlgSheet.DialogFrame
    .Caption = "Convert Case"
    .Height = 90
    .Width = 215
End Width
```

Step 3: Add the Controls

Each type of control has its own collection object, which is a property of the DialogSheet object. For example, the check box control has a `CheckBoxes` collection. In each case, you can use the collection's `Add` method to add the control to the frame using the following syntax:

object.Add(*left,top,width,height*)

> *object*   The collection object for the control you want to add.

> *left*   The control's horizontal position, as measured in points (1/72 of an inch), from the left edge of the dialog sheet.

> *top*   The control's vertical position, in points, from the top edge of the dialog sheet.

width	The control's width in points.
height	The control's height in points.

Because it's difficult to judge the appropriate coordinates for the *left* and *top* arguments relative to the dialog sheet, most programmers position their controls relative to the upper-left corner of the dialog frame. To do this, set these arguments equal to values that are offset from the dialog frame's Left and Top properties, as shown here:

```
With dlgSheet.DialogFrame
    dlgSheet.GroupBoxes.Add _
        left:=.Left + 10, _
        top:=.Top + 22, _
        height:=60, _
        width:=120
End With
```

Step 4: Set the Control Properties

Each control you add to the dialog frame is an object in its own right and with its own properties and methods. For example, a check box is a CheckBox object. I discuss the unique properties for each type of control in the next section, but here are seven that are common to all control objects (see the next section for some examples):

Accelerator: The accelerator key.

Caption: Returns or sets the control's caption.

Enabled: Set this property to False to disable a control.

LinkedCell: Returns or sets the cell that's linked to the control's value.

Name: Returns or sets the name of the control.

Visible: Set this property to False whenever you need to hide a control.

ZOrder: Returns the control's tab order position. Note that this property is read-only, so make sure you add the controls in the correct tab order.

An Example

Let's combine these four steps into a working example. The CreateDialog procedure in Listing 25.1 creates the dialog sheet and dialog box shown in Figure 25.4.

Listing 25.1. A procedure that creates a dialog box.

```
Sub CreateDialog()

    Dim dlgSheet As DialogSheet
    Dim currSheet As String
    Dim objectVar As Object
    Dim i As Integer

    ' Save the name of the current sheet
```

```
currSheet = ActiveSheet.Name

' Add a new dialog sheet
DialogSheets.Add before:=Worksheets("Sheet1")
Set dlgSheet = Worksheets("Sheet1").Previous
dlgSheet.Name = "Convert Case Dialog"

With dlgSheet.DialogFrame
    ' Adjust the frame's properties
    .Caption = "Convert Case"
    .Height = 90
    .Width = 215

    ' Adjust the position of the OK and Cancel buttons
    ' to match the new width of the dialog frame
    Set objectVar = dlgSheet.Buttons(1)
    objectVar.Left = .Left + (.Width - objectVar.Width - 5)
    Set objectVar = dlgSheet.Buttons(2)
    objectVar.Left = .Left + (.Width - objectVar.Width - 5)

    ' Add the group box
    dlgSheet.GroupBoxes.Add _
        Left:=.Left + 10, _
        Top:=.Top + 22, _
        Height:=60, _
        Width:=120

    ' Add the option buttons
    dlgSheet.OptionButtons.Add _
        Left:=.Left + 20, _
        Top:=.Top + 27, _
        Height:=17, _
        Width:=100
    dlgSheet.OptionButtons.Add _
        Left:=.Left + 20, _
        Top:=.Top + 44, _
        Height:=17, _
        Width:=100
    dlgSheet.OptionButtons.Add _
        Left:=.Left + 20, _
        Top:=.Top + 61, _
        Height:=17, _
        Width:=100
End With

With dlgSheet

    ' Set the properties for the Group Box
    .GroupBoxes(1).Caption = "Case"

    ' Set the properties for the Option Buttons
    With .OptionButtons(1)
        .Caption = "Proper Case"
        .Accelerator = "P"
        .Value = xlOn
    End With

    With .OptionButtons(2)
```

continues

Listing 25.1. continued

```
            .Caption = "UPPERCASE"
            .Accelerator = "U"
            .Value = xlOff
       End With

       With .OptionButtons(3)
            .Caption = "lowercase"
            .Accelerator = "L"
            .Value = xlOff
       End With
    End With

    ' Activate the sheet where we started
    Sheets(currSheet).Activate

End Sub
```

FIGURE 25.4.

The dialog sheet and dialog box created from the procedure in Listing 25.1.

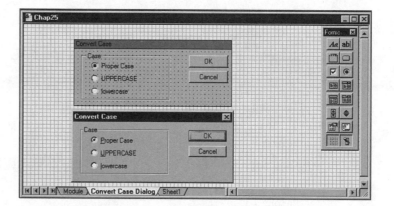

Types of Controls

VBA offers a dozen different controls for your custom dialog boxes. The next few sections introduce you to each type of control and show you the various options and properties associated with each control.

Command Buttons

Most dialog boxes include command buttons to enable the user to carry out a command at the click of the mouse. The default dialog sheet, in fact, starts with the two most common command buttons: OK and Cancel.

To create other buttons, use the Create Button tool on the Forms toolbar. Once you've added a button, you can change its name by double-clicking the button and entering the text.

The Create Button tool.

The Format Object dialog box for command buttons includes the following options:

Default The button appears surrounded by a thin black border, and it is selected automatically when the user presses Enter. The default OK button has this option activated.

Cancel The button is selected if the user presses the Esc key. The default Cancel button has this option activated.

Dismiss The dialog box exits if the user selects the button. The default OK button has this option activated.

Help The button is selected if the user presses F1. Use this option if you plan to include context-sensitive help in your application.

A command button is a Button object, and Buttons is the collection of all the buttons on a dialog sheet. Button objects have the following properties (among others):

AutoSize: If this property is set to True, the button resizes automatically to fit the text on its face (as given by the Caption property).

CancelButton: If this property is set to True, the button is selected when the user presses Esc.

Caption: Returns or sets the button text.

DefaultButton: If this property is set to True, the button is selected when the user presses Enter.

DismissButton: If this property is set to True, the dialog box exits when the user selects the button.

HelpButton: If this property is set to True, the button is selected when the user presses F1.

Labels

You use labels to add text to the dialog box. To create labels, use the Label button on the Forms toolbar. Once you've added a label, you can change its caption by double-clicking on the label and entering the text.

 The Label button.

Although labels are mostly used to display text, you can also use them to name controls—such as edit boxes, list boxes, scroll bars, and spinners—that don't have their own captions. You can even add accelerator keys to the text so the user has a shortcut to access these controls. The following procedure shows you the steps to follow:

1. Before creating the control you want to name, add a label and change the text to the name of the control.
2. In the label's Format Object dialog box, select the Control tab, enter a letter in the **A**ccelerator Key box, and then select OK.
3. Add the control and position it just below the label.

TIP

To assign a label and accelerator key to an existing control, add the label and then adjust the tab order so the label comes immediately before the control.

A label is a Label object, and Labels is the collection of all the labels on a dialog sheet. Use the Label object's Caption property to return or set the label text.

Edit Boxes

Edit boxes (also known as text boxes) are versatile controls that enable the user to enter text, numbers, cell references, and formulas. To create an edit box, use the Edit Box button on the Forms toolbar.

 The Edit Box button.

The Format Object dialog box for an edit box includes the following options:

Edit Validation	These option buttons determine the type of data the user enters into the text box (such as **T**ext, **I**nteger, or **R**eference).
Multiline Edit	Enables the user to enter multiple lines of text. The text wraps automatically.
Vertical Scrollbar	Adds a scroll bar to the side of the text box to enable the user to navigate the text.
Password Edit	Text entered into the edit box appears as asterisks (which is useful for entering passwords and other confidential data).

An edit box is an EditBox object, and EditBoxes is the collection of all edit boxes on a dialog sheet. Here are a few useful properties of the EditBox object:

DisplayVerticalScrollBar: If this property is set to True, a scroll bar appears in the edit box.

InputType: Returns or sets the type of data the user can enter into the edit box. The possible choices are xlFormula, xlInteger, xlNumber, xlReference, and xlText.

MultiLine: Set this property to True to enable the user to enter multiple lines of text.

PasswordEdit: If this property is set to True, the edit box displays the user's entry as asterisks.

Text: Returns or sets the text inside the edit box.

Group Boxes

You use group boxes to create a group of two or more option buttons. The user can then select only one option from the group. Use the Group Box button to create a group box. You can change its caption by double-clicking on the default caption and then entering your text.

> **NOTE**
>
> To group two or more option buttons together, create the group box and then create the option buttons in it.

 The Group Box tool.

A group box is a GroupBox object, and GroupBoxes is the collection of all group boxes on a dialog sheet. Use the GroupBox object's Caption property to change the caption that appears at the top of the box.

Option Buttons

Option buttons are controls that usually appear in groups of two or more, and the user can select only one of the options. To create an option button, use the Option Button tool. As usual, you can change the caption by double-clicking the option button.

 The Option Button tool.

The Format Object dialog box for an option button enables you to determine which of the buttons is initially selected. Display the Format Object dialog box for that button and activate the **C**hecked option.

> **NOTE**
>
> If you don't surround the option buttons with a group box, VBA treats all the option buttons in a dialog box as one group.

An option button is an OptionButton object, and OptionButtons is the collection of all option buttons on a dialog sheet. You can set the option button text with the Caption property. To activate an option button, set its `Value` property to `xlOn`; to deactivate an option button, set the `Value` property to `xlOff`.

Check Boxes

Check boxes enable you to include options that the user can toggle on or off. To create a check box, use the Check Box button on the Forms toolbar and then double-click on the caption to change it.

 The Check Box button.

As with option buttons, you can also control whether or not a check box is initially activated (checked). In the Control tab of a check box's Format Object dialog box, activate either **Un**-checked, **C**hecked, or **M**ixed (to indicate the option is only partially selected).

A check box is a CheckBox object, and `CheckBoxes` is the collection of all the check boxes on a dialog sheet. You can set the check box text with the `Caption` property. To set the check box status, set its `Value` property to `xlOn` (to activate the check box), `xlOff` (to deactivate it), or `xlMixed`.

List Boxes

VBA offers two different list boxes you can use to present the user with a list of choices.

List box: A simple list of items from which the user selects an item (or items). Use the List Box button to create a list box.

 The List Box button.

The Format Object dialog box for a list box includes the following options:

Input Range	A worksheet range that includes the items that will appear inside the list box.
Cell Link	The cell that will contain the user's selection.
Selection Type	Controls how the user selects items from the list. Activate **S**ingle to enable the user to select only one item, **M**ulti to enable the user to select multiple items by clicking each item, or **E**xtend to enable the user to select multiple items by holding down Ctrl and clicking each item.

Combination list-edit box: A control that combines an edit box with a list box. The user either selects an item from the list or enters an item in the edit box. Use the Combination List-Edit button to create this control. Because the combination list-edit box is actually two separate controls, you'll need to format each control separately. The edit box options are the same for the edit box control discussed earlier, and the list box options include only the **I**nput Range and **C**ell Link text boxes.

 The Combination List-Edit button.

Both of these controls are ListBox objects, and `ListBoxes` is the collection of all list boxes on a dialog sheet. Here is a summary of the properties you can set for a ListBox object:

`List`: Returns or sets the list items as an array of strings. You can use this property with or without an *index* argument. Without the argument, `List` returns or sets the entire list. For example, the following statement uses VBA's `Array` function to set the items for the `Stooges` list box:

```
DialogSheets("Dialog1").ListBoxes("Stooges").List = _
    Array("Curly","Larry","Moe")
```

Use the *index* argument to return or set the text for a single item. For example, after running the previous statement, the statement `DialogSheets("Dialog1").ListBoxes("Stooges").List(2)` returns the string "Larry".

`ListCount`: Returns the number of items in the specified list box.

`ListFillRange`: Returns or sets the worksheet range used to fill the specified list box.

`ListIndex`: Returns or sets the index number of the currently selected item in the specified list.

`MultiSelect`: Determines how the user selects multiple items in the specified list box. Your choices are `xlNone` (multiple selections are not allowed), `xlSimple` (user selects multiple items by clicking each item), and `xlExtended` (user selects multiple items by holding down Ctrl and clicking each item).

`Selected`: In a multi-select list box, this property returns or sets the selected items in the list using an array of Boolean values (that is, `TRUE` and `FALSE`).

`Value`: In a single-select list box, this property returns the number of the selected item in this list. To return the text of the selected item, use a code fragment similar to the following:

```
With DialogSheets("Dialog1").ListBoxes(1)
    selectedItem = .List(.Value)
End With
```

List boxes also have a few useful methods for controlling the items that appear in a list box from your VBA code:

`AddItem`: Adds an item to the specified list box. Here's the syntax:

object.AddItem(**text**,index)

object	The ListBox object to which you want to add the item.
text	The item's text.
index	The new item's position in the list. If you omit this argument, Excel adds the item to the end of the list.

`RemoveAllItems`: Removes all the items from the specified list box.

`RemoveItem`: Removes one or more items from the specified list box using the following syntax:

`object.RemoveItem(index,count)`

object   The ListBox object from which you want to remove the item.

index   The index number of the first item you want to remove.

count   The number of items you want to remove. If you omit *count*, Excel removes only the item specified by *index*.

Drop-Down Lists

A drop-down list box is similar to a list box, except that normally only a single item is shown at a time. Dropping down the box displays a list of items for the user to select. VBA gives you a choice of two different drop-down lists:

Drop-down list: A noneditable list of items. Use the Drop-Down button to create a drop-down list.

 The Drop-Down button.

Combination drop-down edit list: A control that combines an edit box with a drop-down list. The user either selects an item from the list or enters an item in the edit box. Use the Combination Drop-Down Edit button to create this control.

 The Combination Drop-Down Edit button.

As with list boxes, the Format Object dialog box includes an **I**nput Range text box that you can use to enter a range containing the list items. There's also a **D**rop Down Lines text box that you can use to specify how many items appear when the user drops down the list.

Both of these controls are DropDown objects, and `DropDowns` is the collection of all list boxes on a dialog sheet. The available properties and methods are the same as those for the ListBox object, with two exceptions: There's no `MultiSelect` property (and, hence, no `Selected` property), and you can use the `DropDownLines` property to specify the number of items that appear when the list is dropped down.

Scroll Bars

Scroll bars are normally used to navigate windows, but by themselves you can use them to enter values between a predefined maximum and minimum. Use the Scroll Bar button to create either a vertical or horizontal scroll bar.

The Scroll Bar button.

The Format Object dialog box for a scroll bar includes the following options:

Current Value	The initial value of the scroll bar.
Minimum Value	The value of the scroll bar when the scroll box is at its leftmost position (for a horizontal scroll bar) or its topmost position (for a vertical scroll bar).
Ma**x**imum Value	The value of the scroll bar when the scroll box is at its rightmost position (for a horizontal scroll bar) or its bottommost position (for a vertical scroll bar).
Incremental Change	The amount the scroll bar's value changes when the user clicks on a scroll arrow.
Page Change	The amount the scroll bar's value changes when the user clicks between the scroll box and a scroll arrow.

A scroll bar is a ScrollBar object, and ScrollBars is the collection of all scroll bars on a dialog sheet. Here's a rundown of the ScrollBar object properties you'll use most often in your VBA code:

LargeChange: Returns or sets the amount the scroll bar value changes when the user clicks between the scroll box and one of the scroll arrows.

Max: Returns or sets the maximum value for the scroll bar.

Min: Returns or sets the minimum value for the scroll bar.

SmallChange: Returns or sets the amount the scroll bar value changes when the user clicks one of the scroll arrows.

Value: Returns or sets the current value of the scroll bar.

Spinners

A spinner is similar to a scroll bar in that the user can click the spinner arrows to increment or decrement a value. To create a spinner, use the Spinner button on the Forms toolbar.

 The Spinner button.

The options in a spinner's Format Object dialog box are the same as those for a scroll bar (except you can't enter a **P**age Change value).

A spinner is a Spinner object, and Spinners is the collection of all the spinners on a dialog sheet. You can control a Spinner object using the same properties outlined for a ScrollBar object (except that there is no LargeChange property for a Spinner object).

Most spinners have an edit box control beside them (set up to handle integer input) to give the user the choice of entering the number directly or selecting the number by using the spinner arrows. You have to use VBA code to make sure the values in the edit box and the spinner stay in sync. (That is, if you increment the spinner, the value shown in the edit box increments as well, and vice versa.)

To do this, you have to add *event handler code* for both controls. (This is described in detail in the section "Creating Event Handler Code.") For example, suppose you have an edit box named Edit Box 10 and a spinner named Spinner 11. Here's the basic event handler code that will keep the values of the two controls synchronized:

```
Sub EditBox10_Change()
    DialogSheets("Dialog1").Spinners("Spinner 11").Value = _
        DialogSheets("Dialog1").EditBoxes("Edit Box 10").Text
End Sub

Sub Spinner11_Change()
    DialogSheets("Dialog1").EditBoxes("Edit Box 10").Text _
        DialogSheets("Dialog1").Spinners("Spinner 11").Value =
End Sub
```

Using a Custom Dialog Box in a Procedure

After you've created your dialog box, the next step is to incorporate your handiwork into some VBA code. This involves two separate techniques:

■ Displaying the dialog box
■ Processing the dialog box results

Displaying the Dialog Box

The DialogSheet object has a Show method you use to display the dialog box to the user. For example, to display the dialog box created from the procedure in Listing 25.1, you use the following statement:

```
DialogSheets("Convert Case Dialog").Show
```

> **TIP**
>
> Before getting to the code stage, you might want to try out your dialog box in the dialog sheet to make sure it looks okay. To do this, either select the Tools | Run Dialog command or click the Run Dialog button on the Forms toolbar.
>
> The Run Dialog button.

Processing the Dialog Box Results

When the user clicks OK or Cancel (or any other button for which the **D**ismiss option is activated), you usually need to examine the dialog box results and process them.

In most cases, the first thing to find out is whether the user has clicked OK or Cancel because usually this determines whether or not the other dialog box selections should be ignored. If OK is clicked, the Show method returns the value True; if Cancel is clicked, Show returns False. A simple If...Then...Else usually does the job. Here is an example:

```
If DialogSheets(1).Show Then
    (process the other results)
Else
    Exit Sub (or whatever)
End If
```

If the results of the other dialog box controls need to be processed, you can use the control's object to get the current value of the control. Table 25.2 lists some control objects, the properties that return the controls' current state, and a description of what kind of data gets returned.

Table 25.2. Return value properties for some dialog box controls.

Object	Property	What It Returns
CheckBox	Value	xlOn, xlOff, or xlMixed
DropDown	Value	The position of the selected item in the list (where 1 is the first item)
EditBox	Text	The value entered in the box
ListBox	Value	The position of the selected item in the list (where 1 is the first item)
OptionButton	Value	Either xlOn or xlOff
ScrollBar	Value	A number between the scroll bar's minimum and maximum values
Spinner	Value	A number between the spinner's minimum and maximum values

For example, Listing 25.2 shows a procedure that displays the Convert Case dialog box and then, if OK was selected, examines the state of each option button to see if it was selected (and therefore set to xlOn).

Listing 25.2. A procedure that shows and processes the Convert Case custom dialog box.

```
Sub ConvertCase()

    Dim s As DialogSheet, sheetExists As Boolean, c As Range

    ' First check to see if the dialog sheet exists
    sheetExists = False
    For Each s In DialogSheets
        If s.Name = "Convert Case Dialog" Then sheetExists = True
    Next s

    ' If the dialog box doesn't exist, create it
    If Not sheetExists Then CreateDialog

    With DialogSheets("Convert Case Dialog")
        If .Show Then
            For Each c in Selection
                If .OptionButtons(1).Value = xlOn Then
                    c.Value = Application.Proper(c)
                ElseIf .OptionButtons(2).Value = xlOn Then
                    c.Value = UCase(c)
                Else
                    c.Value = LCase(c)
                End If
            Next c
        End If
    End With

End Sub
```

Creating Event Handler Code

VBA is, more or less, an *event-driven* language, which means that your code can respond to specific events, such as a user clicking a command button or selecting an item from a list. The procedure can then take appropriate action, whether it's validating the user's input or asking for confirmation of the requested action.

> **NOTE**
>
> VBA has only a limited number of events to which it can respond. Conversely, in Visual Basic (Microsoft's standalone programming environment), procedures can respond to dozens of different events, such as a dialog box control receiving the focus and the user placing the mouse pointer over an object.

The procedures that perform these tasks are called *event handlers;* you create them by following these steps:

1. Select the control for which you want to create an event handler.

2. Click the Edit Code button on the Forms toolbar. Excel displays a VBA module and enters the appropriate Sub and End Sub statements.

 The Edit Code button.

3. Enter the rest of the procedure code between the Sub and End Sub statements.

TIP

If you want to assign an existing procedure to a control event, select the control and then select the **Tools | Assign** Macro command. In the Assign Macro dialog box, select the procedure you want to use.

To assign a macro using VBA code, use the OnAction property. For example, the following statement assigns the procedure named ProcessData to the command button named process:

```
Dialogsheets("Dialog1").Buttons("Process").OnAction = "ProcessData"
```

For example, the following event handler gets processed whenever the user selects the Option Button 5 control:

```
Sub OptionButton5_Click()
    DialogSheets(1).ListBoxes(1).Enabled = True
    DialogSheets(1).Focus = DialogSheets(1).ListBoxes(1)
End Sub
```

A list box is enabled, and the dialog box focus is switched to this list box.

Using VBA to Modify Menus

You can use VBA objects, properties, and methods to make modifications to Excel's menus within procedures. This includes adding menus and entire menu bars, renaming commands, and disabling or enabling commands. This section takes you on a brief tour of some of these techniques.

NOTE

Excel's Menu Editor makes it easy to customize menus. See Chapter 8, "Customizing Excel," for details.

792

Working with Menu Bars

When working with menu bars, you can either use a custom menu bar you have created or one of the built-in menu bars listed in Table 25.3.

Table 25.3. Excel's built-in menu bars.

Menu Bar	Description
Worksheet	Appears when a worksheet is active.
Chart	Appears when a chart is active.
No Documents Open	Appears when no workbooks are open.
Module	Appears when a VBA module is active.
Shortcut Menus 1	Appears when the user right-clicks on a toolbar, tool, cell, row or column header, workbook tab, window title bar, or desktop.
Shortcut Menus 2	Appears when the user right-clicks on a drawn object, macro button, or text box.
Shortcut Menus 3	Appears when the user right-clicks on a chart element (for example, data series, text, arrow, plot area, gridline, floor, legend, or the entire chart).

NOTE

Excel stores your customized menus in the current workbook. If you close the workbook, Excel reverts to the default menus. If you want your custom menus to appear all the time, unhide the Personal Macro Workbook (Personal.xls) and use it to customize your menus.

Menu bars are MenuBar objects, and `MenuBars` is the collection of all menu bars. Use the MenuBars object's `Add` method to create a new, custom menu bar. For example, the following statement creates a custom menu bar named `CustomBar`:

```
MenuBars.Add("CustomBar")
```

You can refer to a menu bar in one of three ways:

- Use `ActiveMenuBar` to refer to the currently displayed menu bar.
- Use the name of a custom menu bar.
- Use the Excel constants listed in Table 25.4.

Table 25.4. Excel menu bar constants.

Constant	Menu Bar
xlWorksheet	Worksheet
xlChart	Chart
xlNoDocuments	No Documents Open
xlInfo	Info Window
xlModule	VBA Module

For example, `MenuBars("CustomBar")` refers to a custom menu bar named *CustomBar*, and `MenuBars(xlWorksheet)` refers to the Worksheet menu bar.

Here are a few common methods used with menu bars:

Activate: Displays the specified menu bar.

Delete: Deletes the specified custom menu bar.

Reset: Restores the specified built-in menu bar to its default state.

Working with Menus

Menus are Menu objects, and `Menus` is the collection of all menus on a menu bar. You can refer to a menu in one of two ways:

- ■ Use the name of the menu.
- ■ Use the position of the menu on the menu bar, where the leftmost menu is 1.

For example, `MenuBars(xlWorksheet).Menus("File")` and `MenuBars(xlWorksheet).Menus(1)` both refer to the Worksheet menu bar's **F**ile menu.

Adding a Menu

To add a menu to a menu bar, use the `Add` method for the `Menus` collection:

object.Menus.Add(*caption*,*before*,*restore*)

object	The MenuBar object to which you're adding the menu.
caption	The menu name. Include an ampersand before a letter to make that letter the menu's accelerator key.
before	The menu to the left of which you want the new menu added. You can use either the menu's name or its position in the menu bar. If you omit *before*, the menu is added to the left of the **H**elp menu.
restore	If *restore* is True, Excel restores the previously deleted built-in menu named ***caption***. If *restore* is False or omitted, Excel adds the menu.

For example, the following statement adds a **Procedures** menu to the end of the Worksheet menu bar:

```
MenuBars(xlWorksheet).Menus.Add caption:="&Procedures"
```

Deleting a Menu

To delete a built-in or custom menu, use the `Delete` method:

object`.Delete`

> *object*   The Menu object you want to delete.

The following statement deletes the **Procedures** menu from the active menu bar:

```
ActiveMenuBar.Menus("Procedures").Delete
```

Working with Menu Commands

Menu commands are MenuItem objects, and `MenuItems` is the collection of all commands on a menu. As with menus, a menu command can be referred to in one of two ways:

- Use the name of the command.
- Use the position of the command on the menu, where the top command is 1.

Adding a Command

To add a command to a menu, use the `Add` method for the `MenuItems` collection:

object`.MenuItems.Add(`*caption*`,`*onAction*`,`*shortcutKey*`,`*before*`,`*restore*`,`*statusBar*`,`
↪*helpContextID*`,`*helpFile*`)`

object	The Menu object to which you're adding the command.
caption	The command name. Include an ampersand before a letter to make that letter the command's accelerator key. To create a separator bar, use a hyphen (-).
onAction	The procedure to run when the user selects the command.
shortcutKey	Used only on Macintosh systems.
before	The command above which you want the new command added. You can use either the command's name or its position in the menu. If you omit *before*, the command is added to the bottom of the menu.
restore	If *restore* is `True`, Excel restores the previously deleted built-in command named *caption*. If *restore* is `False` or omitted, Excel adds the command.

statusBar	Text that appears in Excel's status bar whenever the menu item is highlighted.
helpContextID	The context ID for the custom Help topic associated with the command.
helpFile	The Help file containing the custom Help topic specified by *helpContextID*.

For example, the following statement adds a command named **H**ide Gridlines to the **T**ools menu:

```
MenuBars(xlWorksheet).Menus("Tools").MenuItems.Add _
    caption:="&Hide Gridlines", _
    onAction:="Personal.xls!HideGridlines", _
    statusBar:="Turns off the worksheet gridlines"
```

Adding a Cascade Menu

Some menu commands (such as Excel's **I**nsert | **N**ame command) display a cascade menu. To create this kind of command, use the AddMenu method:

object.MenuItems.AddMenu(*caption*,*before*,*restore*)

object	The Menu object to which you're adding the cascade menu.
caption	The command name. Include an ampersand before a letter to make that letter the menu's accelerator key.
before	The command above which you want the new command added. You can use either the command's name or its position in the menu. If you omit *before*, the command is added to the bottom of the menu.
restore	If *restore* is True, Excel restores the previously deleted built-in command named *caption*. If *restore* is False or omitted, Excel adds the command.

For example, the following statements add a **P**rocedures cascade menu to the **T**ools menu and then add several commands to the new menu:

```
With MenuBars(xlWorksheet).Menus("Tools")
    .MenuItems.AddMenu Caption:="&Procedures"
    .MenuItems("Procedures").MenuItems.Add _
        caption:="&Hide Gridlines", _
        onAction:="ToggleGridlines"
    .MenuItems("Procedures").MenuItems.Add _
        caption = "&Convert Case", _
        onAction:="ConvertCase"
End With
```

Adding a Check Mark to a Command

Some menu commands toggle settings on and off. When a setting is on, Excel indicates it by placing a check mark beside the command. You can do the same thing for your custom commands by setting the Checked property to True for a MenuItem object. (To remove the check mark, set Checked to False.)

For example, the following statements add a check mark beside the **H**ide Gridlines command (I'm using the *menuVar* variable to save space, but it isn't necessary for setting the property):

```
Set menuVar = MenuBars(xlWorksheet).Menus("Tools").MenuItems("Procedures")
menuVar.MenuItems("Hide Gridlines").Checked = True
```

Disabling and Enabling a Command

Excel dims menu commands to show you when a command has been disabled. When set to False, the Enabled MenuItem property allows you to disable commands in your procedures; when set to True, the Enabled MenuItem property allows you to enable commands in your procedures.

To disable the **H**ide Gridlines command, for example, use the following code:

```
Set menuVar = MenuBars(xlWorksheet).Menus("Tools").MenuItems("Procedures")
menuVar.MenuItems("Hide Gridlines").Enabled = False
```

Renaming a Command

To change the name of a command, you can alter its Caption property. The most common use for renaming commands is to reflect a different workspace state. For example, instead of placing a check mark beside the **H**ide Gridlines command, you could rename it to **S**how Gridlines as follows:

```
Set menuVar = MenuBars(xlWorksheet).Menus("Tools").MenuItems("Procedures")
menuVar.MenuItems("Hide Gridlines").Caption = "S&how Gridlines"
menuVar.MenuItems("Show Gridlines").StatusBar = "Shows worksheet gridlines"
```

> **TIP**
>
> To avoid confusing your users, try to keep the same accelerator key when you rename a command.

Deleting a Command

When you no longer need a command, or when you want to remove a command that might be dangerous for novice users, use the Delete method:

object.Delete

  object The MenuItem object you want to delete.

The following statement deletes the **H**ide Gridlines command:

```
Set menuVar = MenuBars(xlWorksheet).Menus("Tools")
menuVar.MenuItems("Hide Gridlines").Delete
```

Using VBA to Customize Excel's Toolbars

Excel's built-in toolbars give you easy access to many of the program's most-used features. You can add the same point-and-shoot functionality to your VBA procedures by adding new buttons and assigning procedures to them. Then, when a user clicks on the button, the procedure runs. You can even design your own button icons and create entire toolbars for your macros. This section shows you how to do all of these things and more.

Working with Toolbars

Toolbars are Toolbar objects, and `Toolbars` is the collection of all the toolbars in the workspace. You can refer to a toolbar in one of two ways:

- Use the name of the toolbar.
- Use the toolbar number shown in Table 25.5.

Table 25.5. Excel's toolbar names and numbers.

Name	Number
Standard	1
Formatting	2
Query and Pivot	3
Chart	4
Drawing	5
TipWizard	6
Forms	7
Stop Recording	8
VBA	9
Auditing	10
Workgroup	11
Microsoft	12
Full Screen	13

Displaying a Toolbar

To display a toolbar, set the Toolbar object's `Visible` property to `True`. For example, the following statement displays the Drawing toolbar:

```
Toolbars("Drawing").Visible = True
```

When you want to hide the toolbar again, set the `Visible` property to `False`.

Changing the Position of a Toolbar

Toolbars can be *docked* at the top or bottom of the screen or on the left or right side of the screen. They can also *float* in the desktop area. You can use the `Position` property to control these attributes. Table 25.6 lists the constants to use with the `Position` property.

Table 25.6. Excel constants to use with the `Position` property.

Constant	Where It Positions the Toolbar
xlTop	In the top docking area
xlBottom	In the bottom docking area
xlLeft	In the left docking area
xlRight	In the right docking area
xlFloating	Floating

You can also use the `Width` and `Height` properties to change the dimensions of a floating toolbar. You specify a value in *points*; one point equals 1/72 of an inch.

In the following statement, the Drawing toolbar is displayed in the floating position with a width of 100 points:

```
With Toolbars("Drawing")
    .Position = xlFloating
    .Width = 100
End With
```

Adding a Toolbar

Many macro programmers prefer to leave Excel's built-in toolbars intact and create their own custom toolbars. This is handy for giving easy access to large numbers of procedures; it also can add a nice touch to an application.

You add a toolbar with the `Add` method of the `Toolbars` collection:

```
Toolbars.Add(name)
```

name   The name you want to use for the toolbar. If you omit *name*, VBA assigns a default name of Toolbar *n*, where *n* signifies the *n*th unnamed toolbar.

For example, the following statement creates a new toolbar named Custom Tools:

```
Toolbars.Add Name:="Custom Tools"
```

Deleting a Toolbar

To delete a toolbar, use the Delete method:

object.Delete

  object   The Toolbar object you want to delete.

The following statement deletes the Custom Tools toolbar:

```
Toolbars("Custom Tools").Delete
```

Restoring a Built-In Toolbar

If you make changes to one of Excel's built-in toolbars, you can revert the toolbar to its default state by using the Reset method:

object.Reset

  object   The built-in Toolbar object you want to reset.

For example, the following code fragment loops through the Toolbars collection and resets the toolbar if it's built-in or deletes it if it isn't built-in:

```
For Each toolbarVar In Toolbars
    If toolbarVar.BuiltIn Then
        toolbarVar.Reset
    Else
        toolbarVar.Delete
    End If
Next toolbarVar
```

> **NOTE**
>
> The BuiltIn property returns True if the toolbar is built-in; otherwise, it returns False.

> **NOTE**
>
> Note that once you create a toolbar, you need to attach it to the workbook. See Chapter 8 to learn how to attach a toolbar to a workbook.

Working with Toolbar Buttons

You can customize toolbar buttons by assigning procedures to them, adding new buttons, disabling and enabling buttons, and deleting buttons you don't need. A button is a ToolbarButton object, and `ToolbarButtons` is a collection of the buttons on a toolbar.

To reference a toolbar button, you can use one of the following three methods (depending on the context):

- The button's name
- The button's ID number
- The button's position on the toolbar

NOTE

To see a complete list of button names and ID numbers, press F1 to open Excel's Help Topics dialog box, select the Index tab, and look up ToolbarButton objects. Select the subitem Available Buttons and Button IDs.

Adding a Button to a Toolbar

To add a button to a toolbar, use the `Add` method of the `ToolbarButtons` collection:

object`.ToolbarButtons.Add(button,before,onAction,pushed,enabled,statusBar,`
➡`helpContextID,helpFile)`

object	The Toolbar object to which you want to add the button.
button	The button's ID number or name. If you want to enter a space, set *button* to 0.
before	The position of the button before which you want to position the new button. If you omit *before,* the button appears at the end of the toolbar. If the toolbar is empty, set *before* to 1.
onAction	The procedure to run when the user clicks the button.
pushed	If `True`, the button appears pressed. If `False` or omitted, the button appears normal.
enabled	If `True` or omitted, the button is enabled. If `False`, the button is disabled.
statusBar	Text that appears in Excel's status bar whenever the mouse pointer lingers over the button.
helpContextID	The context ID for the custom Help topic associated with the button.
helpFile	The Help file containing the custom Help topic specified by *helpContextID.*

For example, the following statement adds a happy face button (ID 211) to the beginning of a custom toolbar named Custom Tools:

```
Toolbars("Custom Tools").ToolbarButtons.Add _
    button:= 211, _
    before:= 1, _
    onAction:="Personal.xls!HideGridlines"
```

> **NOTE**
>
> You can create your own toolbar button faces with the Button Image Editor. See Chapter 8 for more information.

Setting a Button's Tooltip

When you create a new button, Excel gives the button a default tooltip of "Custom." To give the tooltip a more descriptive name, set the button's Name property. For example, the following statement changes the tooltip for the first button in the Custom Tools toolbar to Toggles gridlines:

```
Toolbars("Custom Tools").ToolbarButtons(1).Name = "Toggles gridlines"
```

Making a Button Appear Pressed

The Add method enables you to initialize a button to appear either pressed or normal; you can also control this attribute during runtime. To make a button appear pressed, set the button's Pushed property to True. To revert the button to its normal appearance, set Pushed to False.

For example, the following statements toggle the Pushed property of the first button on the Custom Tools toolbar between True and False:

```
With Toolbars("Custom Tools").ToolbarButtons(1)
    .Pushed = Not .Pushed
End With
```

Disabling and Enabling a Button

You can control the enabling and disabling of buttons at runtime. To disable a button, set the Enabled property to False. When a button is disabled, the computer will beep if the user tries to select it. To enable a button, set the Enabled property to True.

Deleting a Button

To delete a toolbar button, use the Delete method:

object.Delete

    object   The ToolbarButton object you want to delete.

The following statement deletes the first tool in the Custom Tools toolbar:

```
Toolbars("Custom Tools").ToolbarButtons(1).Delete
```

Summary

This chapter showed you how to use VBA to create a custom user interface. I showed you how to work with dialog boxes, menus, and toolbars. Here are some places to go for related material:

- I showed you how to create custom menus and toolbars by hand in Chapter 8, "Customizing Excel."

- For the basics of VBA and Excel objects, see Chapter 22, "Understanding Objects."

- For a good example of a custom user interface (including a dialog box for data entry, custom menus, and toolbars), see Chapter 26, "Database and Client/Server Programming."

- You can create event handler code for other types of Excel events (such as opening and closing a workbook, pressing a key, and entering data). Chapter 27, "VBA Procedures That Respond to Events," gives you the details.

- For another example of an application that uses custom dialog boxes, menus, and toolbars, see Chapter 30, "Check Book: A Sample Application."

Database and Client/Server Programming

26

Increasingly, many people are using Excel as a front end for database work, either as a standalone application or as part of a client/server system. In Part III, "Unleashing Excel's Databases and Lists," I showed you a number of Excel techniques for setting up, maintaining, and manipulating lists and external databases. These techniques give you powerful ways to work with both native Excel data and external data in various formats. However, what if you need to set up Excel so that other, less experienced users can work with data? In this case, you need to set up a custom user interface that shields these users from the intricacies of Excel databases and lists. This chapter shows you how to do just that. We'll look at using VBA to work with Excel lists (including entering, editing, filtering, deleting, sorting, and subtotaling data), external databases, and client/server considerations.

Working with List Data

If the data you want to work with exists on an Excel worksheet, VBA offers a number of list-related properties and methods for both Range objects and Worksheet objects. To demonstrate these VBA techniques, I'll take you through an example: a simple database application that stores information about customers.

The application's workbook is called Customer.xls, and you'll find it on the CD that comes with this book. When you open Customer.xls, you'll see the screen shown in Figure 26.1. The workbook contains three sheets:

Customer Database: The worksheet on which you enter data and work with data. There are two sections: Customer Database is where you enter your data, and Customer Criteria is where you enter your advanced filter criteria. The Customer Database section includes fields for the customer's title (Mr., Ms., and so on), first name, last name, position, company name, and more.

Module: A collection of Visual Basic procedures. I describe each procedure in this chapter.

Dialog: A custom dialog box you can use to add, edit, and delete customer records (see Figure 26.2). This dialog box is a fairly simple affair with its two command buttons and 14 edit boxes (one for each field in the database). The dialog box shown in Figure 26.2 is used for adding customers, but as you'll soon see, it's quite simple to customize the dialog box for use with other procedures.

> **NOTE**
>
> When setting up a database application, it's important to make data entry easy for the user. For example, the Customer Database section includes four features that simplify data entry:
>
> ■ The ZIP Code field has been formatted to accept both the normal five-digit ZIP codes and the newer nine-digit ZIP codes. Note that a dash is added

automatically whenever you enter a nine-digit ZIP code. For example, if you enter 123456789, the data appears as 12345-6789.

■ The Phone Num and Fax Num fields have been formatted to accept a number with or without the area code and to enter the dash automatically. For example, if you enter 1234567, the number appears as 123-4567. If you enter 12345678901, the number appears as 1-234-567-8901.

■ The Memo field is used for miscellaneous comments about the customer (for example, birth date, names of children, favorite color). The field is formatted as word wrap, so you can enter as much information as you need.

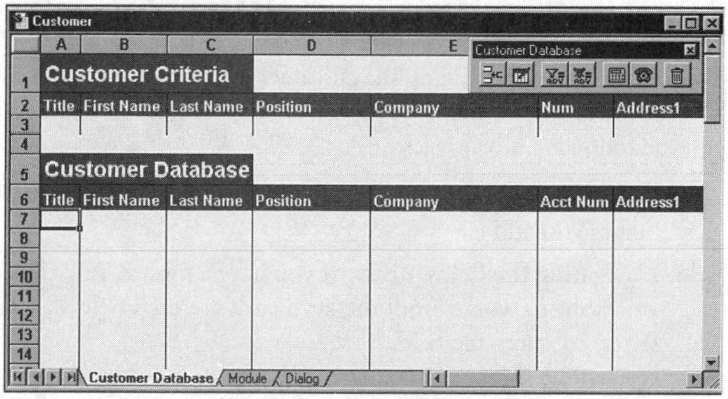

FIGURE 26.1.

The Customer Database worksheet.

FIGURE 26.2.

The custom dialog box used in the customer database application.

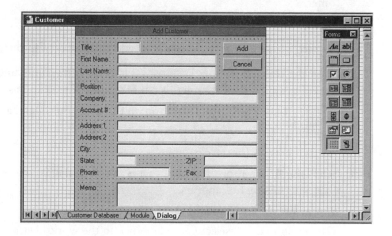

Entering Data

As mentioned in Chapter 12, "Working with Lists and Databases," you can use two basic methods to enter database records on a worksheet: enter the data directly, or use an Excel form.

However, there are a few reasons why neither method is ideal for a database application:

- Entering data directly on the worksheet becomes a problem for a database that's wider than the screen (as is the customer database). Not all the fields appear on-screen at once, which means you can never see the entire record you're adding, and it can be a chore to navigate between fields at either end of the database.

- As you'll see, if you want to control a database using VBA, it simplifies your code immeasurably if the database range has a defined name (such as "Database"). If you add new records at the end of the list manually, you have to redefine the database range name.

- The Form dialog box solves the aforementioned problems, but there's no way to manipulate the form's fields from VBA.

Entering Data Using a Custom Dialog Box

To overcome these problems, the customer database application comes with the custom dialog box shown in Figure 26.2. Using this dialog box to enter your customers' information gives you the following advantages:

- There is an edit box for every field in the database, so you always see the entire record before you add it.

- Navigating the fields is easy. If you have a mouse, just click on the field with which you want to work. From the keyboard, use each field's accelerator key (the underlined letter) to select the field.

- When you select **Add**, the dialog box stays on-screen so you can add another customer.

- The Database range name is updated automatically.

The following procedure shows you how to add customers with the custom dialog box:

1. Select the **D**ata | Customer **D**atabase | **A**dd Customers command or click the Add Customer button on the Customer Database toolbar. The Add Customer dialog box appears.

   The Add Customer button on the Customer Database toolbar.

2. Fill in the fields for the customer.

3. Select the **A**dd button. The customer is added to the database and a fresh Add Customer dialog box appears.

4. Repeat steps 2 and 3 to add more customers.

5. When you're done, select Close to return to the worksheet.

NOTE

The **Data** | Customer **D**atabase submenu and the Customer Database toolbar are set up and displayed when you first open the Customer.xls workbook. The procedure that handles this automatically is called Auto_Open, and you'll find it near the top of the Module sheet. For more information about Auto_Open macros that run automatically when you open a workbook, see Chapter 27, "VBA Procedures That Respond to Events."

Handling Data Entry with VBA

The commands for adding a customer are in the AddCustomer procedure in the Module sheet shown in Listing 26.1.

Listing 26.1. The AddCustomer procedure.

```
Sub AddCustomer()
    '
    ' Set up dialog box
    '
    Set dbDialog = DialogSheets("Dialog")
    With dbDialog
        .DialogFrame.Caption = "Add Customer"    ' Set dialog title
        .EditBoxes.Caption = ""                  ' Clear edit boxes
        .EditBoxes.Enabled = True                ' Enable edit boxes
        .Buttons(1).Caption = "Add"          ' Make sure first button is Add
        .Buttons(2).Caption = "Cancel"       ' Start second button as Cancel
    End With
    '
    ' Display dialog and loop until done
    '
    Do While dbDialog.Show
        WriteNewData                             ' Write the new record
        dbDialog.Buttons(2).Caption = "Close"    ' Change button to Close
        dbDialog.EditBoxes.Caption = ""          ' Clear edit boxes
    Loop

End Sub
```

This procedure first sets up the dbDialog variable to refer to DialogSheets("Dialog") and then uses a With statement to set up the dialog box as follows:

- The dialog box title is changed to Add Customer. (You need to do this because, as you'll see, this dialog box is also used in the procedures for editing and deleting customers, so the title might have been changed by one of these procedures.)
- The edit boxes are cleared and enabled. (The DeleteCustomer procedure disables the edit boxes, so you have to enable them here just in case.)

- The caption for the first command button is set to Add.
- The caption for the second button is set to Cancel.

A Do...Loop is set up to display (dbDialog.Show) and process the dialog box. If you click the second command button, the loop ends and the procedure is done. Otherwise, the loop statements are executed. The first statement calls a procedure named WriteNewData to create the new customer record, as shown in Listing 26.2 (and discussed thereafter). The next line changes the name of the second command button to Close. (Because you're adding a customer, it's too late to cancel the procedure. Therefore, it's normal programming practice to rename a Cancel button "Close" in this situation.) The last line clears the edit boxes for the next record.

Listing 26.2. The WriteNewData procedure.

```
Sub WriteNewData()
    Dim i As Integer, dbTopRow As Integer, dbNewRow As Integer
    Dim dbRows As Integer, dbColumns As Integer
    '
    ' Get Database range data
    '
    With Range("Database")
        dbRows = .Rows.Count
        dbColumns = .Columns.Count
        dbTopRow = .Row
        dbNewRow = dbTopRow + dbRows
    End With
    '
    ' Enter new data in fields
    '
    For i = 1 To dbColumns
        Cells(dbNewRow, i).Value = dbDialog.EditBoxes(i).Caption
    Next i
    '
    ' Define new Database range name
    '
    Range("Database").Select
    Selection.Resize(RowSize:=dbRows + 1, ColumnSize:=dbColumns).Select
    Names.Add Name:="Database", RefersToR1C1:=Selection

    Cells(dbNewRow, 1).Select    ' Select first cell in new record
End Sub
```

The `WriteNewData` procedure is used to add the new data to the worksheet cells and redefine the Database range name. The `With` statement sets several variables that define the boundaries of the Database range. In particular, the `dbNewRow` variable points to the first row below the database.

Then a `For...Next` loop adds the new data. The `Cells` method is used to return the individual cells in the new row. In each case, the cell value is assigned the appropriate edit box caption.

> **TIP**
>
> In this `For...Next` loop, column *i* corresponds to edit box *i*. To get this correspondence, you need to add the edit boxes to the dialog frame in the same order they appear in the worksheet (working from left to right).

The next three statements redefine the Database named range. The existing range is selected and the `Resize` method adds one row. With this new range selected, the `Names.Add` method redefines Database to refer to the selection.

The last line selects the first cell of the new record.

Editing Data

If you need to make changes to a record, you can just edit the worksheet cells directly. However, the Customer Database application enables you to edit the data using the convenience of the custom dialog box.

Editing Data Using the Custom Dialog Box

To see how data editing works, follow these steps to edit a record:

1. Select any cell within the record you want to edit.
2. Select the **D**ata | Customer **D**atabase | **E**dit Customer command or click the Edit Customer button on the Customer Database toolbar. The Edit Customer dialog box appears, as shown in Figure 26.3.

    The Edit Customer button on the Customer Database toolbar.

> **CAUTION**
>
> Be sure to select a cell within the database when you select the **E**dit Customer command. If you don't, the application displays a warning message. If you get this message and you've selected a record, you may have to redefine the Database range name to include the entire list.

FIGURE 26.3.

The Edit Customer dialog box.

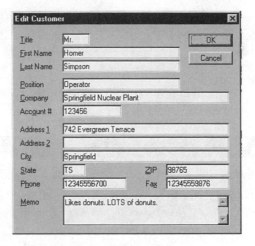

3. Make your changes to the record.
4. Select OK. The application writes the changes to the worksheet.

Handling Data Editing with VBA Code

When you select the **E**dit Customer command, the application runs the `EditCustomer` procedure, shown in Listing 26.3.

Listing 26.3. The `EditCustomer` procedure.

```
Sub EditCustomer()
    Dim i As Integer, currRow As Integer, lastCol As Integer
    '
    ' Make sure selection is inside database
    '
    currRow = ActiveCell.Row
    If Not InsideDatabase(currRow) Then
        Exit Sub
    End If
    '
    ' Store last column number
    '
    lastCol = Range("Database").Columns.Count
    '
    ' Set up dialog box
    '
    Set dbDialog = DialogSheets("Dialog")
    For i = 1 To lastCol
        dbDialog.EditBoxes(i).Caption = Cells(currRow, i) ' Fill edit boxes
    Next i
    With dbDialog
        .DialogFrame.Caption = "Edit Customer"    ' Set dialog box title
        .EditBoxes.Enabled = True                 ' Enable edit boxes
        .Buttons(1).Caption = "OK"        ' Make sure first button is OK
```

```
        .Buttons(2).Caption = "Cancel"   ' Start second button as Cancel
    End With
    '
    ' Display the dialog box
    '
    If Not dbDialog.Show Then
        Exit Sub
    End If
    '
    ' Enter edited data in fields
    '
    For i = 1 To lastCol
        Cells(currRow, i).Value = dbDialog.EditBoxes(i).Caption
    Next i

End Sub
```

The first part of this procedure runs the InsideDatabase function to make sure the active cell is within the Database range (see Listing 26.4). The next section performs the dialog box setup. A For...Next loop reads the record into the edit boxes, and then a With statement sets the dialog title, enables the edit boxes, and sets the captions for the two command buttons.

Then, the procedure displays the dialog box and, if you click Cancel, exits the procedure. Otherwise, the For...Next loop enters the new data into the record.

Here's the listing for the InsideDatabase function.

Listing 26.4. The InsideDatabase function tests whether or not the active cell is inside the Database range.

```
Function InsideDatabase(currRow As Integer)

    With Range("Database")
        If currRow <= .Row Or currRow >= (.Row + .Rows.Count) Then
            MsgBox Prompt:="You must select a record inside the database.", _
                    Title:="Customer Database", _
                    Buttons:=vbExclamation
            InsideDatabase = False
        Else
            InsideDatabase = True
        End If
    End With

End Function
```

The variable currRow holds the row number of the active cell. If this number is less than or equal to the first row of the database (as given by the Row property) or below the database (that is, greater than or equal to the sum of Row and Rows.Count), a MsgBox function displays a warning message.

Filtering Data

Chapter 12 showed you how to filter a list to see only certain records. You can use the same techniques to filter the customer database. If you have simple criteria, the AutoFilter feature is probably your best bet.

Filtering the Customer Database

For more complex filtering, use the Customer Criteria range to enter your compound or computed criteria. When you're ready to filter the list, you can do it in one step by clicking the Advanced Filter button on the Customer Database toolbar. When you want to exit filter mode and return to the normal view, click the Show All button.

  The Advanced Filter button on the Customer Database toolbar.

  The Show All button on the Customer Database toolbar.

If you don't have a mouse, you can use Excel's regular menu commands:

■ Select the **D**ata | **F**ilter | **A**dvanced Filter command to run the advanced filter.

■ Select the **D**ata | **F**ilter | **S**how All command to exit filter mode.

> **CAUTION**
>
> The Advanced Filter button uses a range named Criteria to filter the records. By default, this range consists of the Customer Criteria column headings and the first row beneath them (A2:N3). If you use multiline criteria to display records that match one criterion or another, you'll need to redefine the Criteria range appropriately.

Filtering Data with VBA

The Advanced Filter and Show All buttons in the Customer Database toolbar are attached to the `FilterCustomers` and `ShowAllCustomers` procedures shown in Listing 26.5.

Listing 26.5. The `FilterCustomers` and `ShowAllCustomers` procedures.

```
Sub FilterCustomers()
    Range("Database").AdvancedFilter _
        Action:=xlFilterInPlace, _
        CriteriaRange:=Range("Criteria")
End Sub

Sub ShowAllCustomers()
```

```
    ActiveSheet.ShowAllData
End Sub
```

FilterCustomers runs the AdvancedFilter method on the Database range object:

object.AdvancedFilter(*action*,*criteriaRange*,*copyToRange*,*unique*)

object	The Range object you want to filter.
action	A constant that specifies where you want the data filtered. You can use either xlFilterInPlace or xlFilterCopy.
criteriaRange	A Range object that specifies the criteria range to use for the filter. (In the application, the *criteriaRange* argument uses the Criteria named range. Here is why: If you use multiple lines for your criteria, you have to redefine the Criteria name before running this procedure.)
copyToRange	If *action* is xlFilterCopy, use *copyToRange* to specify the destination for the copied rows.
unique	If you set this argument to True, Excel filters only unique records. If set to False (the default), Excel filters all records that meet the criteria.

The ShowAllCustomers procedure runs the ShowAllData method for the active sheet.

AutoFiltering a Worksheet

If you need to place a worksheet in AutoFilter mode from within a VBA, use the Range object's AutoFilter method. If you just want to add the AutoFilter drop-down arrows to each field, run the AutoFilter method without any arguments. For example, the following statement adds AutoFilter drop-down arrows to the Database range:

```
Range("Database").AutoFilter
```

To remove the AutoFilter arrows, run the AutoFilter method again.

As an alternative, you can use the AutoFilter method to filter a list. Here's the syntax:

object.AutoFilter(*field*,*criteria1*,*operator*,*criteria2*)

object	The Range object you want to filter.
field	An integer that specifies the offset of the field to use for the filter (where the leftmost field is 1).
criteria1	The criterion for filter, entered as a string (for example, "CA"). If you omit *criteria1*, VBA uses All. If *operator* is xlTop10Items, use *criteria1* to specify the number of items to return (for example, "20").

operator	If you specify both *criteria1* and *criteria2*, use *operator* to build compound criteria. In this case, you can use either xlAnd (the default) or xlOr. You also can use xlTop10Items to use the Top 10 AutoFilter.
criteria2	A second criteria string to use for compound criteria.

For example, the following statement filters the Database range to show only those customers where the State field (Field 10) is "CA" or "NY":

```
Range("Database").AutoFilter _
    field:=10, _
    criteria1:="CA", _
    operator:=xlOr, _
    criteria2:="NY"
```

> **NOTE**
>
> Use the Worksheet object's AutoFilterMode property to determine whether or not the AutoFilter drop-down arrows are currently displayed on the worksheet. (The AutoFilterMode property returns True if the sheet is currently in AutoFilter mode.) If you want to know whether or not a worksheet contains filtered data, use the Worksheet object's FilterMode property. (The FilterMode property returns True if the sheet is currently filtered.)

Getting a Count of the Database Records

As your database grows, you might need to know how many records it contains. You can find out by selecting the **D**ata | Customer **D**atabase | **C**ount Customers command or by clicking the Count Customers button in the Customer Database toolbar. A dialog box appears with the current count.

 The Count Customers button in the Customer Database toolbar.

The **C**ount Customers command and the Count Customers button are attached to the CountCustomers procedure shown in Listing 26.6. The totalRows variable holds the count, which is given by the Rows.Count property, minus 1 (because you don't want to count the column headings). Then, the variables alertMsg, alertButtons, and alertTitle are assigned values, and the MsgBox function displays the count message.

Listing 26.6. The CountCustomers procedure.

```
Sub CountCustomers()
    Dim totalRows As Integer
    Dim alertMsg As String, alertButtons As Integer, alertTitle As String
```

```
'
' Customer count is total rows in Database minus 1
'
    totalRows = Range("Database").Rows.Count - 1

    alertMsg = "There are currently " & _
        totalRows & _
        " customers in the database."
    alertButtons = vbInformation
    alertTitle = "Customer Database"
    MsgBox alertMsg, alertButtons, alertTitle
End Sub
```

Deleting Records

To save memory and make the database easier to manage, you should delete customer records you no longer need. As usual, the next two sections show you the interface and the underlying code.

Deleting a Customer Database Record

Here are the steps to follow for deleting a customer from the Customer Database application:

1. Select any cell within the record of the customer you want to delete.
2. Select the **Data | Customer Database | Delete** Customer command or click the Delete Customer button in the Customer Database toolbar. The Delete Customer dialog box appears.

    The Delete Customer button in the Customer Database toolbar.

3. If you're sure you want to delete this customer, select the Delete button. The application deletes the record and returns you to the worksheet.

Handling Record Deletion with VBA

The `DeleteCustomer` procedure, shown in Listing 26.7, handles the customer deletions. This procedure is almost identical to the `EditCustomer` procedure discussed earlier. The major difference is that if you select the Delete button, the procedure runs the following statement:

```
ActiveCell.EntireRow.Delete
```

The `EntireRow` property returns the entire row of, in this case, the selected customer. The `Delete` method deletes the row.

Listing 26.7. The `DeleteCustomer` procedure.

```
Sub DeleteCustomer()
    Dim i As Integer, currRow As Integer, lastCol As Integer
    currRow = ActiveCell.Row
    '
    ' Make sure selection is inside database
    '
    If Not InsideDatabase(currRow) Then
        Exit Sub
    End If

    lastCol = Range("Database").Columns.Count
    '
    ' Set up dialog box
    '
    Set dbDialog = DialogSheets("Dialog")
    For i = 1 To lastCol
        dbDialog.EditBoxes(i).Caption = Cells(currRow, i) ' Fill edit boxes
    Next i
    With dbDialog
        .EditBoxes.Enabled = False
        .DialogFrame.Caption = "Delete Customer"  ' Set dialog box title
        .Buttons(1).Caption = "Delete"   ' Make sure first button is Delete
        .Buttons(2).Caption = "Cancel"   ' Make sure second button is Cancel
    End With
    '
    ' Display the dialog box
    '
    If Not dbDialog.Show Then
        Exit Sub
    End If
    '
    ' Delete customer
    '
    ActiveCell.EntireRow.Delete
End Sub
```

Sorting Data

The Customer Database application doesn't include any code for sorting data, but it's easy enough to handle using VBA. The mechanism is the Range object's Sort method, which uses the following syntax:

object.Sort(key1,order1,key2,order2,key3,order3,header,orderCustom,matchCase,
➥orientation)

object	The Range object you want to sort. If *object* is a single cell, Excel sorts the cell's current region.
key1	The first key field. You can enter either a range name or a Range object.
order1	The order for *key1*. Use either xlAscending (the default) or xlDescending.

key2	The second key field. You can enter either a range name or a Range object.
order2	The order for *key2* (xlAscending or xlDescending).
key3	The third key field. You can enter either a range name or a Range object.
order3	The order for *key3* (xlAscending or xlDescending).
header	Tells Excel whether or not the sort range contains a header in the first row. Use xlYes (the default), xlNo, or xlGuess (to let Excel try and figure out if the range contains a header row).
orderCustom	An integer value that specifies which of Excel's custom sort orders to use. The default value is 1 (which corresponds to the Normal sort order).
matchCase	Specifies whether or not the sort is case-sensitive. If True, the sort is case-sensitive; if False (the default), the sort is not case-sensitive.
orientation	Specifies whether Excel sorts by rows (top to bottom) or columns (left to right). Use either xlTopToBottom (the default) or xlLeftToRight.

For example, the following statement sorts the Database range by State and then in descending order by City:

```
Range("Database").Sort _
    key1:=Worksheets("Customer Database").Range("J7"), _
    key2:=Worksheets("Customer Database").Range("I7"), _
    order2:=xlDescending, _
    header:=xlYes
```

Subtotaling Data

If your list contains numeric data, you can use VBA code to add automatic subtotals to the list. The Range object has a Subtotal method that does the job:

object.Subtotal(*groupBy,function,totalList*,replace,pageBreaks,summaryBelowData)

object	The Range object you want to subtotal. If *object* is a single cell, Excel applies the subtotals to the cell's current region.
groupBy	An integer that represents the field to use for the subtotal groupings (where the first field in *object* is 1).
function	The function to use for these subtotals: xlAverage, xlCount, xlCountNums, xlMax, xlMin, xlProduct, xlStDev, xlStDevP, xlSum, xlVar, or xlVarP.
totalList	The fields to which the subtotals are added. Use an array of integers, where each integer represents a field (where the first field in *object* is 1).

replace	Set this argument to True to replace the existing subtotals. The default value is False.
pageBreaks	Set this argument to True to add page breaks after each grouping. The default value is False.
summaryBelowData	Specifies where Excel places the subtotals in relation to the detail. Use either xlBelow (the default) or xlAbove.

The following statement sets up subtotals for a range named Invoices. The records are grouped by the values in the first field, and the subtotals are added to Fields 5 and 6.

```
Range("Invoices").Subtotal _
    groupBy:=1, _
    function:=xlSum, _
    totalList:=Array(5,6), _
    replace:=True
```

> **NOTE**
>
> To remove subtotals from a range, use the Range object's RemoveSubtotals method. For example, the following statement removes the subtotals from the Invoices range:
>
> ```
> Range("Invoices").RemoveSubtotals
> ```

Working with Data Access Objects

In Chapter 15, "Using Microsoft Query," and Chapter 16, "Creating Advanced Queries," you learn how to use Microsoft Query to open and query external databases and to return the resultant records to Excel. *Data access objects* (DAO) enable you to do the same thing from within VBA procedures, *without* having to load Microsoft Query or the Query add-in file. This section takes you through the basics of using DAO to access and work with external databases.

About Data Access Objects

DAO is a separate library of objects and their associated properties and methods. These objects expose the full functionality of the Microsoft Jet database engine—the engine used in Access, which is Microsoft's relational database system.

Setting Up a Reference to the DAO Library

To make the DAO library available to your VBA applications, you need to set up a reference to the library in the workbook that contains your code. The following steps show you how it's done:

1. Activate or create the module in the workbook you'll be using to access external databases.

2. Select the **T**ools | **R**eferences command to display the References dialog box.

3. In the **A**vailable References list, activate Microsoft DAO 3.0 Object Library, shown in Figure 26.4.

FIGURE 26.4.

To use data access objects in the current workbook, you need to establish a reference to the DAO library.

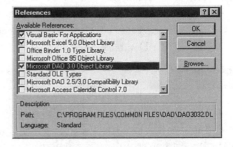

4. Select OK. Excel sets up the reference and returns you to the module.

The Data Access Objects Hierarchy

Once you've set up a reference to the DAO library, the full DAO hierarchy becomes available to your VBA code. Figure 26.5 shows a simplified version of the DAO hierarchy.

FIGURE 26.5.

A simplified version of the DAO hierarchy.

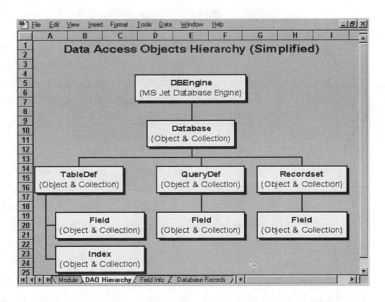

Here's a rundown of the various objects in this hierarchy:

DBEngine   This top-level object represents the Microsoft Jet database engine as a whole. A particular session of the DBEngine object is called a *Workspace*, but you'll rarely have to deal with a Workspace object directly.

Database A Database object represents an open database (such as an Access .MDB database or a FoxPro .DBF file). The Databases collection refers to all the open Database objects.

TableDef A TableDef object represents the definition of a table in a Database object. A TableDef is a container for the table's Field and Index objects. The TableDefs collection refers to all the table definitions in a Database object.

> **NOTE**
>
> DAO distinguishes between two kinds of tables: a *base table* and an *attached table*. A base table is a table in a Microsoft Jet (.MDB) database. Attached tables are tables from another database that are linked to a Microsoft Jet database. (This is why attached tables are also called *linked tables*.) As you'll see a bit later, the most efficient way to work with a non-Jet database (such as a FoxPro or dBASE file) is to link it to an existing Jet database.

QueryDef A QueryDef object represents the definition of a query in a Database object. A QueryDef is a container for the query's Field objects. The QueryDefs collection refers to all the query definitions in a Database object.

Recordset A Recordset object represents either the records in a base table from a Database object or the records that result from a query. Most of your DAO labors will involve manipulating Recordset objects in one way or another. The Recordsets collection refers to all the open Recordset objects in a Database object.

Field A Field object represents a column of data. For a TableDef or QueryDef object, a Field object contains the specifications for a field used in a table or query. For a Recordset object, a Field object represents the value in a particular field for the current record. The Fields collection refers to all the fields in a TableDef, QueryDef, or Recordset object.

Index An Index object specifies an order for the records in a TableDef object. The Indexes collection refers to all the Index objects stored in a TableDef object. Note that each Index object has an associated Fields collection that contains the fields used for the index.

We'll now turn our attention to using these objects to connect to external databases.

Accessing Data in an External Database

Accessing the data contained in an external database from a VBA procedure takes three or four steps, depending on the type of database:

1. Declare variables for the objects you'll be using (you'll usually need variables for at least a Database and a Recordset object).

2. Open the database. If you're using a non-Jet external database (such as a FoxPro, Paradox, dBASE, or SQL Server database), open a Jet database to use for attaching the external database.

3. For a non-Jet external database, attach the database to the open Jet database.

4. Open the Recordset for the table with which you want to work.

The next two sections supply the details for these steps.

Connecting to a Jet Database

As you might expect, the Jet database engine has the easiest time connecting to databases in its native Jet format (the .MDB files, such as those created with Access). Listing 26.8 shows an example.

Listing 26.8. A procedure that connects to a Jet database.

```
Sub Jand so ononnection()

    Dim db As Database
    Dim rs As Recordset

    ' Open the Jet database
    Set db = OpenDatabase("C:\MSOffice\Access\Samples\NWind.MDB")

    ' Open the Recordset
    Set rs = db.OpenRecordset("Customers", dbOpenTable)

    ' Display confirmation message
    MsgBox "Opened " & db.Name & " Successfully!" & _
           Chr(13) & Chr(13) & _
           "The open Recordset is " & rs.Name

    ' Close the database
    db.Close

End Sub
```

First, the Database and Recordset object variables are declared (db and rs, respectively). Then the OpenDatabase method is invoked to open the database. OpenDatabase is a method of the Workspace object (which, you'll recall, is an instance of the DBEngine object). Here's the syntax:

object.OpenDatabase(***dbname***,*exclusive,read-only,source*)

    object   The Workspace object in which you want to open the database. If you omit *object*, VBA uses the current workspace.

dbname	For a Jet database, *dbname* is the full pathname (including the drive and directory) of the database file. For a non-Jet database, use an ODBC source name or a directory name (such as a directory of FoxPro files).
exclusive	Set this argument to True to open the database with exclusive access. The default value is False.
read-only	Set this argument to True to open the database with read-only access. The default value is False.
source	A string that specifies extra parameters for opening the database (see the next section for details).

Once the database is open, the procedure then opens a Recordset object using the Database object's OpenRecordset method:

object.OpenRecordset(*source,type,options*)

object	The Database object that contains the *source* to use for the Recordset. (You can also use a TableDef or QueryDef object.)
source	A string specifying the source for the Recordset. You can use a table name, a query name, or a SQL statement.
type	The type of Recordset you want to create. Use dbOpenTable (the default) for a table Recordset; use dbOpenDynaset for a dynaset Recordset; use dbOpenSnapshot for a snapshot Recordset. (For an explanation of each type of Recordset, see the section "Understanding the Recordset Types," later in this chapter.)
options	One or more (integer) constants that specify the characteristics of the new Recordset:

dbAppendOnly	You can append only new records. (Used only with dynaset types.)
dbForwardOnly	A forward-scrolling snapshot. Use this option for faster performance if you're just making a single pass through the records.
dbSQLPassThrough	Enables you to pass SQL statements through to an ODBC database. See the section "Client/Server Query Considerations," later in this chapter.
dbSeeChanges	Generates an error if another user changes a record you're editing.
dbDenyWrite	Prevents others from editing and adding records.

dbDenyRead	Prevents others from viewing records. (Used only with table types.)
dbReadOnly	You can't make changes to the records.
dbInconsistent	You can update all fields in a multiple-table query Recordset. (Used only with dynaset types.)
dbConsistent	You can only make changes to a field in a multiple-table query Recordset that keep the records consistent with each other. (Used only with dynaset types.)

Finally, a MsgBox statement displays the name of the open database (using the Database object's Name property) and the name of the open Recordset (using the Recordset object's Name property).

Connecting to a Non-Jet Database

If the data you want to work with exists in a non-Jet database, you need to attach the data source to an existing Jet database as a new TableDef object. (It's possible to run the OpenDatabase method directly on a non-Jet database, but it's more efficient—and your Recordset operations will perform faster—if you link the database to a Jet database.)

> **NOTE**
>
> What do you do if you don't have access to a Jet database? The answer is easy: create your own using the CreateDatabase method. For example, the following statement creates a Jet database named MyJetDB.mdb and assigns it to a Database object variable (the dbLangGeneral argument specifies the collating order used for string comparisons):
>
> ```
> Dim db As Database
> Set db = CreateDatabase("MyJetDB.mdb", dbLangGeneral)
> ```

Listing 26.9 shows the NonJand so ononnection procedure that connects to a FoxPro database.

Listing 26.9. A procedure that connects to a non-Jet database.

```
Sub NonJand so ononnection()
    Dim db As Database
    Dim tdFox As TableDef
    Dim rs As recordset

    ' Open the Jet database
    Set db = OpenDatabase("C:\MSOffice\Access\Samples\NWind.MDB")

    ' Create TableDef and set the connection information.
    Set tdFox = db.CreateTableDef("Linked FoxPro Table")
    tdFox.Connect = "FoxPro 2.6;DATABASE=C:\Progra~1\Common~1\Msquery"
```

continues

Listing 26.9. continued

```
tdFox.SourceTableName = "Customer"

' Append the TableDef to create the link
 db.TableDefs.Append tdFox

 ' Open the Recordset
Set rs = db.OpenRecordset("Linked FoxPro Table", dbOpenSnapshot)

 ' Display confirmation message
MsgBox "Opened " & db.Name & " Successfully!" & _
        Chr(13) & Chr(13) & _
        "The open Recordset is " & rs.Name & _
        Chr(13) & _
        "The source table is   " & tdFox.SourceTableName

 ' Close the database
 db.Close

End Sub
```

A TableDef object variable named `tdFox` is declared to hold the new TableDef. A Jet database is opened and then the new TableDef is created using the Database object's `CreateTableDef` method. This method has a number of arguments, but your code will be easier to read if you use the TableDef object's properties to set up the TableDef. In most cases, all you need to include in the `CreateTableDef` method is a name for the new TableDef (Linked FoxPro Table in Listing 26.9).

The next two lines set the `Connect` and `SourceTableName` properties. Here's a simplified syntax for the `Connect` property:

object.Connect=*databasetype*;DATABASE=*path*

object	The TableDef object.
databasetype	A string indicating the type of database you're attaching. Here are your choices:

dBASE III	Paradox 5.x	Excel 3.0
dBASE IV	Btrieve	Excel 4.0
dBASE 5	FoxPro 2.0	Excel 5.0
Paradox 3.x	FoxPro 2.5	Excel 7.0
Paradox 4.x	FoxPro 2.6	Text

path	The drive and directory (folder) containing the table you want to use (such as a FoxPro .DBF file). Note that you'll usually have to specify directory names using MS-DOS eight-character names.

The `SourceTableName` property specifies the table you want to use. In Listing 26.9, setting this property to `Customer` tells DAO that you want to work with the Customer.dbf table.

Once the new TableDef object is ready, you add it to the Database object's `TableDefs` collection by using the `Append` method. When that's done, you can use the TableDef as though it were a Jet table (including opening a new Recordset on the table, as I've done in Listing 26.9).

Connecting in a Client/Server Environment

In client/server environments, the `Connect` property usually requires a few more parameters. When linking to a SQL Server data source, for example, you'll need to specify not only a database but also a user name, a password, and a data source name (DSN). For these kinds of ODBC databases, the *databasetype* argument is `ODBC`; you specify the other parameters using the `UID` (user ID), `PWD` (password), and `DSN` (data source name) keywords. Here's the general form:

object`.Connect = "ODBC;DATABASE=`*dbname*`;UID=`*userID*`;PWD=`*password*`;DSN=`*datasource*`"`

For example, the following statement connects a linked TableDef object named `tdSQLServer` to a SQL Server data source named Publishers, specifies the database named Pubs as the default database, and also specifies a user ID and password:

```
tdSQLServer.Connect = "ODBC;DATABASE=pubs;UID=bwana;PWD=nottelling;DSN=Publishers"
```

> **TIP**
>
> If the `Connect` string is only `ODBC;` (for example, `tdWhatever="ODBC;"`), VBA displays the SQL Data Source dialog box with a list of all the defined data sources so the user can choose (or even create) the one he or she wants. See Chapter 15 to learn how to define data sources. Note that if the user cancels this dialog box, a trappable runtime error occurs (error number 3059—see Chapter 27 to learn more about trapping errors).

> **NOTE**
>
> As mentioned earlier, it's possible to use the `OpenDatabase` method to connect to a non-Jet database directly. This also holds, naturally, for ODBC databases located on servers; you simply use the `OpenDatabase` method's *source* argument to specify the appropriate connection string (the user ID, password, and so on).
>
> However, you'll find your work with the resultant Recordset (and especially your queries) will be noticeably faster if, instead, you link the server data to a Jet database on the client machine. That's because the Jet database engine caches information (such as the field and index data) locally, which greatly improves performance. Note, however, that if you change any fields or indexes on the server, you need to update the cached data by running the TableDef object's `RefreshLink` method.

Working with Recordsets

As I mentioned earlier, once you've opened a database, attached an external table (if necessary), and created a new Recordset, you'll spend most of your time manipulating the Recordset in some way. This section gives you more information about Recordsets and takes you through a few useful properties and methods.

Understanding the Recordset Types

As you know from the discussion of the `OpenRecordset` method, you can specify one of three different Recordset types. Here's a rundown of what each type of Recordset means:

Table type   This type refers to a base table or attached table in an open Database object. Certain actions, such as sorting and indexing, can be performed only on table-type Recordsets.

Dynaset type   This type refers to a dynamic, virtual table that is (usually) the result of a query. Dynasets can include fields from multiple tables, and they are dynamic because you can update the records by adding, editing, or deleting.

Snapshot type   This type is similar to a dynaset, except that the records are static; you can't make changes, add records, or delete records. This is the fastest type, and it's the one you should use if you only want to view the data.

Getting Field Information

Before working with a Recordset, you might need to find out some information about the fields in the Recordset. For example, you might want to find out the names of all the fields, their sizes, whether or not a field requires a value, and the type of data each field uses. Each Recordset object is a container for all the Field objects in the Recordset. Therefore, you can get information on each field by running through the `Fields` collection. Listing 26.10 shows a procedure that does this.

Listing 26.10. A procedure that displays information on all the fields in a Recordset.

```
Sub DisplayFieldInfo()

    Dim db As Database
    Dim rs As recordset
    Dim fld As Field
    Dim i As Integer

    ' Open the Jet database
    Set db = OpenDatabase("C:\MSOffice\Access\Samples\NWind.MDB")
```

```
    ' Open the Recordset
    Set rs = db.OpenRecordset("Customers", dbOpenSnapshot)

    ' Head for Field Info to monitor the action
    Worksheets("Field Info").Activate

    With Worksheets("Field Info").[B1]
        ' Clear the current data
        .Clear
        .Offset(1).Clear
        .Offset(3, -1).CurrentRegion.Offset(0, 1).Clear

        ' Display Recordset name
        .Offset(1).Value = rs.Name

        ' Enumerate all fields in the Recordset
        For i = 0 To rs.fields.Count - 1
            Application.StatusBar = _
                "Enumerating field " & _
                i + 1 & " of " & _
                rs.fields.Count

            ' Set the Field variable and then run through the properties
            Set fld = rs.Fields(i)
            .Offset(3, i).Value = fld.Name
            .Offset(4, i).Value = fld.AllowZeroLength
            .Offset(5, i).Value = fld.Attributes
            .Offset(6, i).Value = fld.CollatingOrder
            .Offset(7, i).Value = fld.DefaultValue
            .Offset(8, i).Value = fld.OrdinalPosition
            .Offset(9, i).Value = fld.Required
            .Offset(10, i).Value = fld.Size
            .Offset(11, i).Value = fld.SourceField
            .Offset(12, i).Value = fld.SourceTable
            .Offset(13, i).Value = TypeOfField(fld.Type)
            .Offset(14, i).Value = fld.ValidationRule
            .Offset(15, i).Value = fld.ValidationText
            .Offset(1, i).EntireColumn.AutoFit
        Next i

        ' Display database name
        .Value = db.Name
    End With

    ' Close the database
    db.Close

    Application.StatusBar = False
End Sub

Function TypeOfField(fldConstant As Integer) As String
    Select Case fldConstant
        Case 1    ' dbBoolean
            TypeOfField = "Boolean"
        Case 2    ' dbByte
            TypeOfField = "Byte"
        Case 3    ' dbInteger
            TypeOfField = "Integer"
```

continues

Listing 26.10. continued

```
        Case 4    ' dbLong
            TypeOfField = "Long Integer"
        Case 5    ' dbCurrency
            TypeOfField = "Currency"
        Case 6    ' dbSingle
            TypeOfField = "Single"
        Case 7    ' dbDouble
            TypeOfField = "Double"
        Case 8    ' dbDate
            TypeOfField = "Date"
        Case 10   ' dbText
            TypeOfField = "Text"
        Case 11   'dbLongBinary
            TypeOfField = "OLE Object"
        Case 12   ' dbMemo
            TypeOfField = "Memo"
        Case 15   ' dbGUID
            TypeOfField = "GUID"
    End Select
End Function
```

The `For...Next` loop runs from 0 (the first field number) to one less than the number of fields in the Recordset `rs` (the number of fields is given by `rs.Fields.Count`). In each pass through the loop, the `fld` variable is set to `rs.Fields(i)`, and then the properties of this Field object are enumerated (such as `Name`, `AllowZeroLength`, `Size`, and `Type`.) Note that the procedure doesn't return the `Type` property directly. Instead, the constant is translated into a string by the `TypeOfField` function. (You can, if you like, create similar functions that translate the constants returned by the Attributes and CollatingOrder fields.)

Recordset Properties

Here's a look at some Recordset properties you'll use most often:

`AbsolutePosition`: Returns or sets the relative record number in the Recordset. (Note that the relative position of a particular record might change each time you create the Recordset, so you can't use this property as a substitute for the xBASE `RECNO()` function.)

`BOF`: Returns `True` if the current record position is before the first record.

`Bookmark`: Sets or returns a `Variant` value that uniquely identifies the current record. For example, the following code saves the current position to a `Variant` variable named `CurrRecord`, moves to the end of the Recordset (using the `MoveLast` method), and then returns to the previous position:

```
currRecord = rs.Bookmark
rs.MoveLast
rs.Bookmark = currRecord
```

`Bookmarkable`: Returns `True` if the Recordset supports bookmarks. You should always test your Recordset's `Bookmarkable` property before attempting to set a bookmark.

`DateCreated`: The date and time the Recordset was created.

`EOF`: Returns `True` if the current record position is after the last record.

`Filter`: Returns or sets the criteria that determines which records are included in the Recordset. For example, the following statements set the variable `rsCustomers` to the Customers tables and the `Filter` property to include only those records in which the Country field is "Canada" and then open a new Recordset (`rsCanada`) based on the filtered records:

```
Set rsCustomer = OpenRecordset("Customers")
rs.Filter = "Country = 'Canada'"
Set rsCanada = rsCustomer.OpenRecordset()
```

`Index`: Returns or sets the current Index object for a table-type Recordset. Use the TableDef's `Indexes` collection to find out the available indexes for a table.

`LastModified`: Returns a bookmark that identifies the most recently added or modified record.

`LastUpdated`: The date and time of the most recent change made to the Recordset.

`NoMatch`: Returns `True` if the `Seek` method or one of the `Find` methods failed to find the desired record. Returns `False`, otherwise.

`RecordCount`: The number of records in the Recordset.

> **NOTE**
>
> The `RecordCount` property works only for base tables (attached tables always return 1). To find the number of records in an attached table, you could use the following code fragment (assuming that `rs` represents a Recordset for an attached table):
>
> ```
> rs.MoveLast
> TotalRecords = rs.AbsolutePosition + 1
> ```
>
> (The `MoveLast` method moves to the end of the Recordset, as described in the next section.) In the Chap26.xls workbook that comes on this book's CD, you'll find a `TotalAttachedRecords` function that uses this code to return the total number of records in an attached table. Note that this is only an approximate number in a multiuser environment (because other users might be in the process of adding or deleting records.)

`Sort`: Returns or sets the sort order for a dynaset-type or snapshot-type Recordset. (Use the `Index` property to sort a table-type Recordset.) To set the sort order, set this property equal to a field name, followed by either `Asc` (the default) or `Desc`. Here are a couple of examples (where `rs` is a Recordset variable):

```
rs.Sort = "Country"
```

```
rs.Sort = "LastName Desc"
```

Recordset Methods

Here are a few methods you can use to manipulate a Recordset:

AddNew: Adds a new record to a table-type or dynaset-type Recordset.

CancelUpdate: Cancels any pending changes made by the AddNew or Edit methods. (Changes aren't written to the Recordset until you run the Update method.)

Close: Closes the Recordset.

Delete: Deletes the current record in a table-type or dynaset-type Recordset.

Edit: Copies the current record in a table-type or dynaset-type Recordset to the copy buffer for editing. For example, the following code uses the FindFirst method to find the first record where the Country field equals "Czechoslovakia." The record is opened for editing using the Edit method, the Country field is modified, and then Recordset is updated with the Update method. The FindNext method looks for more instances of "Czechoslovakia." Here is the code:

```
findString = "Country = 'Czechoslovakia'"
replaceString = "Czech Republic"
rs.FindFirst findString              ' Find first occurrence
Do While rs.NoMatch                  ' Loop until no more matches
    rs.Edit                          ' Open record for editing
    rs.Fields("Country") = replaceString  ' Modify Country field
    rs.Update                        ' Update the Recordset
    rs.FindNext findString           ' Find the next match
Loop
```

FindFirst, FindLast, FindNext, FindPrevious: Searches the Recordset for the first, last, next, or previous records that meet the specified criteria. If no record matches the criteria, the NoMatch property returns True.

GetRows: Retrieves multiple records into an array. See the section "Retrieving Data into Excel" for details on this method.

Move: Moves the current record pointer by a specified number of records. Here's the syntax:

object.Move(*rows,start*)

object	The Recordset object.
rows	A long integer specifying the number of records to move. Use a negative number to move backwards.
start	A variable name that identifies a bookmark from which to start the move. If you omit *start*, the move occurs from the current record.

MoveFirst, MoveLast, MoveNext, MovePrevious: Moves the current record to the first, last, next, or previous record in the Recordset. Use the BOF property to determine if MovePrevious moves the record pointer before the first record; use EOF to determine if MoveNext moves the record pointer past the last record.

Seek: Searches an indexed table-type Recordset for a record that meets the specified criteria. Here's the syntax for the Seek method:

object.Seek(*comparison,key1,key2...*)

object	The indexed table-type Recordset object.
comparison	A comparison operator: =, >, >=, <, <=, or <>.
key1,key2...	One or more values that correspond to the fields in the current index.

Note that you need to set the current index for the Recordset before you use the Seek method. For example, the following code sets a Recordset's Index property and then uses Seek to find a matching record:

```
Set rs = db.OpenRecordset("Customers")
rs.Index = "Country"
rs.Seek "=", "Czechoslovakia"
```

TIP

Index-based Seek searches are much faster than any of the Find methods, so you should always use Seek if an appropriate Index object is available.

Update: Writes changes made by AddNew or Edit to a table-type or dynaset-type Recordset.

Querying a Recordset

In general, the Recordsets you open will contain all the records in the underlying table. If you want to filter the records, however, DAO gives you three choices:

- Specify the Recordset's Filter property and then run the OpenRecordset method on the filtered records. (The Filter property was described earlier in this chapter.)
- Run the OpenRecordset method and specify a SQL expression instead of a table name.
- Run the OpenRecordset method on a QueryDef object.

Opening a Recordset Using a SQL Expression

In Chapter 16, I showed you the syntax for the SQL SELECT statement. You can use the same syntax to construct SELECT expressions that open a Recordset as a filtered dynaset. For example, Listing 26.11 shows a procedure that opens a Recordset based on the Customers table in the Nwind.mdb database. However, selectStr variable holds a SELECT statement that filters the data as follows:

- Only the CompanyName, Region, and Country fields are used.
- The records are restricted to those where the Country field is Canada.
- The Recordset is ordered by the CompanyName field.

Listing 26.11. A procedure that opens a Recordset using a SQL SELECT expression.

```
Sub QueryCustomers()

    Dim db As Database
    Dim selectStr As String
    Dim rs As Recordset

    ' Open the Jet database
    Set db = OpenDatabase("C:\MSOffice\Access\Samples\NWind.MDB")

    ' Store the SELECT statement in a string variable
    selectStr = "SELECT CompanyName,Region,Country " & _
                "FROM Customers " & _
                "WHERE Country = 'Canada' " & _
                "ORDER BY CompanyName"

    ' Open the Recordset
    Set rs = db.OpenRecordset(selectStr)

    ' Display confirmation message
    MsgBox "The filtered Recordset contains " & _
           rs.RecordCount & " records."

    ' Close the database
    db.Close

End Sub
```

Opening a Recordset from a QueryDef Object

If the Database object already contains one or more queries in the form of QueryDef objects, you can open a Recordset by using the QueryDef object's OpenRecordset method. For example, Listing 26.12 opens a database, assigns the variable qd to the "Products Above Average Price" QueryDef object, and then creates the Recordset from the QueryDef.

Listing 26.12. A procedure that creates a Recordset from a QueryDef object.

```
Sub QueryDefExample()

    Dim db As Database
    Dim qd As QueryDef
    Dim rs As Recordset

    ' Open the Jet database
```

```
    Set db = OpenDatabase("C:\MSOffice\Access\Samples\NWind.MDB")

    ' Assign the QueryDef object
    qd = db.QueryDefs("Products Above Average Price")

    ' Open the Recordset
    Set rs = qd.OpenRecordset()

    ' Display confirmation message
    MsgBox "The filtered Recordset contains " & _
           rs.RecordCount & " records."

    ' Close the database
    db.Close

End Sub
```

NOTE

You can create new QueryDef objects by using the Database object's `CreateQueryDef` method. This method takes two arguments: the name of the new QueryDef object and the SQL expression that defines the query. For example, the following statement creates a new QueryDef object called "Canadian Customers" based on the SQL expression used in Listing 26.11.

```
Dim db As Database, qd As QueryDef
Set db = OpenDatabase("NWind.MDB")
selectStr = "SELECT CompanyName,Region,Country " & _
            "FROM Customers " & _
            "WHERE Country = 'Canada' " & _
            "ORDER BY CompanyName"
Set qd = db.CreateQueryDef("Canadian Customers",selectStr)
```

Client/Server Query Considerations

For client/server applications, you have two choices when it comes to querying the server:

- You can construct ordinary Jet queries based on the linked server data.
- You can construct a *pass-through* query that the Jet engine sends directly to the server for processing.

Which type of query you use depends on the application, but there are a few general guidelines you can follow:

Use a pass-through query if

- you would prefer to off-load some of the query processing to the server.
- you need to take advantage of some server-specific features that have no equivalent in VBA (such as stored procedures and security functionality).

- you need to use some server-specific SQL features that aren't supported by the Jet SQL standard.
- you want to create a new database or table on the server.
- you would like to perform some System Administrator chores (such as updating user accounts).

Use an ordinary Jet query if

- you want to update the resultant Recordset. A pass-through query always returns a snapshot-type Recordset, which is not updatable.
- you're not sure about the exact syntax that the server database uses. By creating the query in the Jet syntax, the Jet engine will translate your query into the SQL statement that's appropriate for the server.
- you need to include a user-defined function as part of your query.

If you decide that a pass-though query is the way to go, you can execute a SQL pass-through query by specifying the dbSQLPassThrough constant as the *options* argument in the OpenRecordset method.

Retrieving Data into Excel

To get data from an external database into an Excel worksheet, you have three choices:

- Retrieving an individual field value
- Retrieving one or more entire rows
- Retrieving an entire Recordset

Retrieving an Individual Field Value

For individual field values, move to the record you want to work with and then use the Field object's Value property. For example, the following statement returns the value of the current record's Country field in the Recordset named rs and stores it in cell A1 of the active worksheet:

```
ActiveSheet.[a1] = rs.Fields("Country").Value
```

Retrieving One or More Entire Rows

To get full records, use the Recordset object's GetRows method. The GetRows(*n*) method returns *n* records in a two-dimensional array, where the first subscript is a number that represents the field (the first field is 0) and the second subscript represents the record number (where the first record is 0). Listing 26.13 shows a procedure that opens a Recordset from a QueryDef and enters the first 100 rows into a worksheet named Database Records.

Listing 26.13. A procedure that reads 100 rows from a Recordset into a worksheet.

```
Sub ReadDataIntoExcel()

    Dim db As Database, qd As QueryDef, rs As Recordset
    Dim selectStr As String, recArray As Variant
    Dim i As Integer, j As Integer

    ' Open the Jet database, QueryDef, and Recordset
    Set db = OpenDatabase("C:\MSOffice\Access\Samples\NWind.MDB")
    Set qd = db.QueryDefs("Canadian Customers")
    Set rs = qd.OpenRecordset()

    ' Head for Database Records and clear the sheet
    Worksheets("Database Records").Activate
    With Worksheets("Database Records").[a1]
        .CurrentRegion.Clear

        ' Read the data using GetRows
        recArray = rs.GetRows(100)
        For i = 0 To UBound(recArray, 1)
            For j = 0 To UBound(recArray, 2)
                .Offset(i + 1, j) = recArray(i, j)
            Next j
        Next i

        ' Enter the field names and format the cells
        For j = 0 To rs.fields.Count - 1
            .Offset(0, j) = rs.fields(j).Name
            .Offset(0, j).Font.Bold = True
            .Offset(0, j).EntireColumn.AutoFit
        Next j

    End With

    ' Close the database
    db.Close

End Sub
```

Retrieving an Entire Recordset

If you need to retrieve an entire Recordset into a worksheet, you can do so easily with the Range object's CopyFromRecordset method:

object.CopyFromRecordset(*data*,*maxRows*,*maxColumns*)

>   *object*   A Range object that specifies the upper-left corner of the destination range.
>
>   *data*   The Recordset containing the data you want to retrieve.

maxRows	The maximum number of records to retrieve. If you omit *maxRows*, Excel copies every record.
maxColumns	The maximum number of fields to retrieve. If you omit *maxColumns*, Excel copies every field.

Here are a few notes to bear in mind when working with `CopyFromRecordset`:

- Excel begins the copying from the current record. If you want to retrieve every record, make sure you run the `MoveFirst` method to move to the first record.

- When the `CopyFromRecordset` method is done, the Recordset object's `EOF` property is `True`.

- `CopyFromRecordset` will choke if the Recordset object has a field that contains OLE objects.

Listing 26.14 shows the `RetrieveCategories` procedure that uses the `CopyFromRecordset` method.

Listing 26.14. A procedure that filters out OLE Object fields before retrieving a Recordset.

```
Sub RetrieveCategories()

    Dim db As Database, rs As Recordset, fld As Field
    Dim selectStr As String, i As Integer

    ' Open the Jet database
    Set db = OpenDatabase("C:\MSOffice\Access\Samples\NWind.MDB")

    ' Open the full Categories table
    Set rs = db.OpenRecordset("Categories")

    ' The selectStr variable will hold the SQL SELECT statement
    ' that filters the Recordset to remove OLE Object fields
    selectStr = "SELECT "

    ' Run through the Recordset fields
    For Each fld In rs.fields
        ' Check for OLE Object fields
        If fld.Type <> dbLongBinary Then
            ' If it's not an OLE Object field, add it to the SELECT statement
            selectStr = selectStr & fld.Name & ","
        End If
    Next fld

    ' Remove the trailing comma
    selectStr = Left(selectStr, Len(selectStr) - 1)

    ' Add the FROM clause
    selectStr = selectStr & " FROM Categories"

    ' Open the filtered Recordset
    Set rs = db.OpenRecordset(selectStr)

    ' Retrieve the records
    Worksheets("Database Records").Activate
```

```
With Worksheets("Database Records").[a1]
    .CurrentRegion.Clear

    ' Retrieve the records
    .Offset(1).CopyFromRecordset rs

    ' Enter the field names and format the cells
    For i = 0 To rs.fields.Count - 1
        .Offset(0, i) = rs.fields(i).Name
        .Offset(0, i).Font.Bold = True
        .Offset(0, i).EntireColumn.AutoFit
    Next i

End With

' Close the database
db.Close

End Sub
```

RetrieveCategories connects to a Jet database and opens the Categories table as the rs Recordset variable. You want to make sure that you don't try to copy any OLE Object fields, so the procedure constructs a SQL SELECT statement that excludes any fields that contain OLE objects. The selectStr variable will hold the SELECT statement; therefore, it's initialized to "SELECT ". Then a For...Next loop runs through each field in rs and looks for OLE Object fields (where the Type property is dbLongBinary; see the DAO Help listing for the constants that correspond to the other field types). If a field isn't an OLE Object type, its name (and a comma separator) is appended to the SELECT statement.

Next, the trailing comma is removed and the FROM clause is concatenated to the SELECT statement. A new Recordset is opened based on selectStr, and then the CopyFromRecordset method retrieves the records.

Summary

This chapter showed you how to program Excel lists and external databases. We looked at using VBA to perform a number of basic list chores, including entering and editing data, filtering, deleting, and sorting records, and subtotaling data. I also showed you how to access and work with external databases and client/server environments. Here are a few chapters that contain related information:

- I discussed Excel lists in detail in Chapter 12, "Working with Lists and Databases."
- You'll find the details for accessing external databases through using Microsoft Query in Chapter 15, "Using Microsoft Query," and Chapter 16, "Creating Advanced Queries."
- For a general discussion of objects, see Chapter 22, "Understanding Objects." For some Excel-specific objects (including Range and Worksheet objects), see Chapter 24, "Manipulating Excel with VBA."

■ You can use VBA to manipulate other applications and, in some cases, you can even work with other applications' objects. See Chapter 28, "Working with Other Applications: OLE, DDE, and More," to find out how it's done.

VBA Procedures That Respond to Events

27

You have learned how to start your procedures from the Macro dialog box, with a shortcut key, with a macro button, or with a customized menu command or toolbar button. In each case, you had to do something to get the procedure up and running. However, Excel also enables you to create procedures that automatically run, for example, when a workbook is opened, when the user enters data, or when a worksheet recalculates. This chapter shows you how to create such procedures.

Running a Procedure When You Open a Workbook

Excel can automatically run a procedure when you open a workbook. This is useful for setting up the workbook environment (the calculation mode, view settings, custom menus and toolbars) or displaying a dialog box of options.

You set up this automatic routine by creating a Sub procedure named Auto_Open in any VBA module in the workbook. When Excel is opening a workbook and sees an Auto_Open procedure, it automatically runs the code. Listing 27.1 shows the Auto_Open procedure from the Customer.xls workbook we looked at in Chapter 26, "Database and Client/Server Programming." This procedure does four things:

■ It creates a custom submenu on the **D**ata menu.

■ It sets up OnSheetActivate and OnSheetDeactivate procedures (discussed later in this chapter).

■ It initializes and displays a custom toolbar.

■ It takes the user to the Customer Database worksheet.

Listing 27.1. The Auto_Open procedure automatically runs when the workbook is opened.

```
Sub Auto_Open()
    '
    ' Set up Customer Database submenu on the Data menu
    '
    Application.StatusBar = "Setting up the Customer Database submenu..."
    With MenuBars(xlWorksheet).Menus("Data")
        '
        ' Add submenu and submenu items
        '
        .MenuItems.Add Caption:="-"
        .MenuItems.AddMenu Caption:="Customer &Database"
        With .MenuItems("Customer Database")
            .MenuItems.Add Caption:="&Add Customer...", _
                        OnAction:="AddCustomer"
            .MenuItems.Add Caption:="&Edit Customer...", _
                        OnAction:="EditCustomer"
            .MenuItems.Add Caption:="-"
```

```
                .MenuItems.Add Caption:="&Count Customers...", _
                              OnAction:="CountCustomers"
                .MenuItems.Add Caption:="&Phone Customer...", _
                              OnAction:="PhoneCustomer"
                .MenuItems.Add Caption:="-"
                .MenuItems.Add Caption:="&Delete Customer...", _
                              OnAction:="DeleteCustomer"
        End With
    End With
'
' Set up macros to run automatically when Customer Database
' worksheet is activated and deactivated
'
Application.StatusBar = "Setting up automatic macros..."
With Workbooks("CUSTOMER.XLS").Worksheets("Customer Database")
    .OnSheetActivate = "ActivateCustomerDatabase"
    .OnSheetDeactivate = "DeactivateCustomerDatabase"
End With
'
' Display Customer Database toolbar
' If you customize the Customer Database toolbar, you
' may have to modify the ToolbarButtons statements
'
Application.StatusBar = "Setting up the toolbar..."
With Toolbars("Customer Database")
    .Visible = True
    .Position = xlFloating
    .Width = 300
    .Left = 412
    .Top = 25
    With .ToolbarButtons(1)
        .OnAction = "AddCustomer"
        .Name = "Add Customer"
        .StatusBar = "Adds a customer to the database"
    End With
    With .ToolbarButtons(2)
        .OnAction = "EditCustomer"
        .Name = "Edit Customer"
        .StatusBar = "Edits the current customer"
    End With
    With .ToolbarButtons(4)
        .OnAction = "FilterCustomers"
        .Name = "Filter Customers"
        .StatusBar = "Filters the database using the current value"
    End With
    With .ToolbarButtons(5)
        .OnAction = "ShowAllCustomers"
        .Name = "Show All Customers"
        .StatusBar = "Removes the filter and displays all records"
    End With
    With .ToolbarButtons(7)
        .OnAction = "CountCustomers"
        .Name = "Count Customers"
        .StatusBar = "Displays a count of the database records"
    End With
    With .ToolbarButtons(8)
        .OnAction = "PhoneCustomer"
        .Name = "Phone Customer"
```

continues

Listing 27.1. continued

```
                .StatusBar = "Uses Phone Dialer to call the current customer"
            End With
            With .ToolbarButtons(10)
                .OnAction = "DeleteCustomer"
                .ToolbarButtons(10).Name = "Delete Customer"
                .StatusBar = "Deletes the current customer"
            End With
        End With
    End With
    '
    ' Activate the Customer Database sheet and select the first record
    '
    Application.StatusBar = "Activating the database..."
    Worksheets("Customer Database").Activate
    ActiveSheet.Cells(Range("Database").Row + 1, 1).Select
    '
    'Reset the status bar
    '
    Application.StatusBar = False

End Sub

Sub ActivateCustomerDatabase()
    Dim subMenu As Menu
    '
    ' Display Customer Database toolbar
    '
    Toolbars("Customer Database").Visible = True
    '
    ' Activate Customer Database submenu commands
    '
    Set subMenu = MenuBars(xlWorksheet).Menus("Data").MenuItems("Customer
    ➥Database")
    subMenu.MenuItems("Add Customer...").Enabled = True
    subMenu.MenuItems("Edit Customer...").Enabled = True
    subMenu.MenuItems("Count Customers...").Enabled = True
    subMenu.MenuItems("Phone Customer...").Enabled = True
    subMenu.MenuItems("Delete Customer...").Enabled = True

End Sub

Sub DeactivateCustomerDatabase()
    Dim subMenu As Menu
    '
    ' Hide Customer Database toolbar
    '
    Toolbars("Customer Database").Visible = False
    '
    ' Deactivate Customer Database submenu commands
    '
    Set subMenu = MenuBars(xlWorksheet).Menus("Data").MenuItems("Customer
    ➥Database")
    subMenu.MenuItems("Add Customer...").Enabled = False
    subMenu.MenuItems("Edit Customer...").Enabled = False
    subMenu.MenuItems("Count Customers...").Enabled = False
    subMenu.MenuItems("Phone Customer...").Enabled = False
    subMenu.MenuItems("Delete Customer...").Enabled = False

End Sub
```

> **TIP**
>
> To prevent an `Auto_Open` procedure from running, hold down the Shift key while opening the workbook.

> **CAUTION**
>
> You can't have more than one `Auto_Open` procedure in a workbook. If you do, Excel won't run any of them.

Running a Procedure When You Close a Workbook

Because most `Auto_Open` procedures change the Excel environment in some way, you usually need to reset everything when you close the worksheet. To reset the environment automatically, include a procedure named `Auto_Close` in the workbook. Listing 27.2 shows the `Auto_Close` procedure from the Customer.xls workbook. This procedure deletes the submenu that was added to the **D**ata menu and hides the custom toolbar.

Listing 27.2. The `Auto_Close` procedure from the Customer.xls workbook.

```
Sub Auto_Close()
    Dim i As Integer
    '
    ' Delete Customer Database submenu
    '
    With MenuBars(xlWorksheet).Menus("Data")
        For i = 1 To .MenuItems.Count
            If .MenuItems(i).Caption = "Customer &Database" Then
                If .MenuItems(i - 1).Caption = "-" Then
                    '
                    ' Delete the separator bar
                    '
                    .MenuItems(i - 1).Delete
                End If
                '
                ' Delete the menu
                '
                .MenuItems(i - 1).Delete
            End If
        Next
    End With
    '
    ' Hide the Customer Database toolbar
    '
```

continues

Listing 27.2. continued

```
    Toolbars("Customer Database").Visible = False

End Sub
```

> **CAUTION**
>
> As with `Auto_Open`, you can't have more than one `Auto_Close` procedure in a workbook.

A Note About the *Open* and *Close* Methods

As you learned back in Chapter 24, "Manipulating Excel with VBA," you can open workbooks from within a VBA procedure by running the `Workbooks` collection's `Open` method. Bear in mind, however, that when you open a workbook using the `Open` method, VBA does *not* run the workbook's `Auto_Open` procedure (if it has one).

Similarly, if you close a workbook using the `Close` method, the workbook's `Auto_Close` procedure won't run.

To make sure that a workbook's `Auto_Open` or `Auto_Close` procedures execute, use the `RunAutoMacros` method:

object.RunAutoMacros(*which*)

  object   The Workbook object containing the `Auto_Open` or `Auto_Close` procedure.

  which   A constant that represents the macro you want to run. Use `xlAutoOpen` to run the `Auto_Open` procedure; use `xlAutoClose` to run the `Auto_Close` procedure.

For example, the following statements open a workbook named Budget.xls and then run the workbook's `Auto_Open` procedure. (If the workbook doesn't have an `Auto_Open` procedure, Excel just ignores the `RunAutoMacros` statement.)

```
Workbooks.Open "Budget.xls"
ActiveWorkbook.RunAutoMacros xlAutoOpen
```

The following two statements run the Budget.xls workbook's `Auto_Close` macro and then close the workbook:

```
With Workbooks("Budget.xls")
    .RunAutoMacros xlAutoClose
    .Close
End With
```

> **NOTE**
>
> The `RunAutoMacros` method also recognizes two other constants: `xlAutoActivate` and `xlAutoDeactivate`. These constants are used for workbooks that contain the old Excel 4.0 `Auto_Activate` and `Auto_Deactivate` macros. These macros run whenever the user activates or deactivates the workbook. VBA, however, doesn't use these procedures. Instead, it uses the `OnActivate` and `OnDeactivate` properties, described later in this chapter.

Working with Event Handler Procedures

Some VBA objects include properties and methods that enable you to run a procedure when a specific event occurs. You can set up these *event handler* procedures (also called `OnEvent` procedures) to automatically execute, say, when the user activates a worksheet, at a certain time of day, or when a specified key combination is pressed. The next few sections take you through each of VBA's event handlers.

Running a Procedure When You Activate a Sheet

Many of your applications will use multiple workbooks or multiple sheets in a single workbook. For example, you might have a customer database, an invoice entry sheet, and an accounts receivable aging report all in different sheets in a single workbook. As the user activates each sheet, you may need to perform various actions, such as modifying an application menu, displaying a toolbar, or asking the user whether he or she wants to save changes.

You can do this by using the `OnSheetActivate` property to specify an event handler to run when the user activates a sheet. The six objects listed in Table 27.1 use the `OnSheetActivate` property.

Table 27.1. Excel objects that use the `OnSheetActivate` property.

Object	Description
Application	Runs event handler when any sheet in any workbook is activated.
Chart	Runs event handler when a specified chart sheet is activated.
DialogSheet	Runs event handler when a specified dialog sheet is activated.
Module	Runs event handler when a specified VBA module is activated.

continues

Table 27.1. continued

Object	Description
Workbook	Runs event handler when any sheet in a specified workbook is activated.
Worksheet	Runs event handler when a specified worksheet is activated.

For example, Listing 27.1 showed an `ActivateCustomerDatabase` procedure that was set up to run each time the user activates the Customer Database worksheet. This procedure displays the Customer Database toolbar and enables the commands on the **D**ata | Customer **D**atabase submenu.

As another example, Listing 27.3 shows an `Auto_Open` procedure that sets up an event handler for a worksheet named Data Entry. When the user selects the Data Entry tab, the `DataEntryHandler` procedure runs automatically. In this case, the event handler sets up a `While...Wend` loop that displays a dialog box and then runs the `ProcessData` procedure each time the user selects OK. The loop exits only when the user selects the Close button. Notice, as well, that Listing 27.3 includes an `Auto_Close` procedure that cancels the `OnSheetActivate` property by setting it to a null string (`""`).

Listing 27.3. Setting up and processing an event handler for a worksheet.

```
Sub Auto_Open()
    Worksheets("Data Entry").OnSheetActivate = "DataEntryHandler"
End Sub

Sub DataEntryHandler()

    Dim done As Boolean
    done = False

    While Not done
        With DialogSheets("Data Entry Dialog")
            If .Show Then
                ' If the user selects OK, process the data
                ProcessData (.ListBoxes("List Box 5").Value)
            Else
                ' Otherwise, exit the loop
                done = True
            End If
        End With
    Wend

End Sub

Sub ProcessData(item As Integer)

    ' Offset to the appropriate cell and then increment the current value
    With Worksheets("Data Entry").[A1].Offset(item - 1, 1)
        .Value = .Value + 1
```

```
    End With

End Sub

Sub Auto_Close
    Worksheets("Data Entry").OnSheetActivate = ""
End Sub
```

NOTE

Excel doesn't run an OnSheetActivate handler when you open the workbook.

CAUTION

When specifying an OnSheetActivate handler for the Application object, be sure to include the name of the workbook and module where the event handler resides. Otherwise, Excel might not be able to find the procedure, and you'll get an error.

Running a Procedure When You Deactivate a Sheet

The OnSheetDeactivate property enables you to set up an event handler that automatically runs when the user deactivates a sheet. The objects that use OnSheetActivate use OnSheetDeactivate in the same way. (See Table 27.1.)

For example, Listing 27.1 showed a DeactivateCustomerDatabase procedure that runs each time the user deactivates the Customer Database worksheet. This procedure hides the Customer Database toolbar and disables the commands on the **D**ata | Customer **D**atabase submenu.

CAUTION

Avoid using the ActiveWorkbook or ActiveSheet objects with the OnSheetDeactivate property. Excel switches to the new workbook or sheet *before* running the event handler, so the code that references the active workbook or sheet might not run properly.

Running a Procedure When You Activate a Window

The OnWindow property is similar to OnSheetActivate. However, OnWindow specifies an event handler that runs whenever the user activates a window (and not just a sheet). Recall that you can have multiple windows opened for the same worksheet.

You can use the OnWindow property with the Window object (in which case the event handler runs when the user switches to a specified window) or the Application object (the event handler runs when the user switches to any window).

In Listing 27.4, for example, the SetWindowHandler procedure defines an OnWindow handler for the Data.xls:2 window. The event handler, DataWindowHandler, sets several Window object properties.

Listing 27.4. Setting up an OnWindow event handler.

```
Sub SetWindowHandler()
    Windows("Data.xls:2").OnWindow = "DataWindowHandler"
End Sub

Sub DataWindowHandler()
    With Windows("Data.xls:2")
        .SplitVertical = 130
        .DisplayFormulas = True
        .DisplayGridlines = False
        .DisplayZeros = False
        .FreezePanes = True
        .WindowState = xlMaximized
    End With
End Sub
```

To cancel an event handler associated with a window, assign the OnWindow property to the null string (""), like so:

```
Windows("Data.xls:2").OnWindow = ""
```

> **NOTE**
>
> OnSheetActivate or OnSheetDeactivate event handlers execute *after* the OnWindow procedure.

Running a Procedure When You Press a Key

As you learned back in Chapter 21, "Getting Started with VBA," Excel lets you assign a Ctrl-*key* shortcut to a procedure. However, this method has two major drawbacks:

■ Excel uses some Ctrl-*key* combinations internally, so your choices are limited.

■ It doesn't help if you would like your procedures to respond to "meaningful" keys such as Delete and Esc.

To remedy these problems, use the Application object's OnKey method to run a procedure when the user presses a specific key or key combination:

```
Application.OnKey(key,procedure)
```

key

The key or key combination that runs the procedure. For letters, numbers, or punctuation marks, enclose the character in quotes (for example, "a"). For other keys, use the following strings:

Key	What to Use
Backspace	"{BACKSPACE}" or "{BS}"
Break	"{BREAK}"
Caps Lock	"{CAPSLOCK}"
Delete	"{DELETE}" or "{DEL}"
Down arrow	"{DOWN}"
End	"{END}"
Enter (keypad)	"{ENTER}"
Enter	"~" (tilde)
Esc	"{ESCAPE}" or "{ESC}"
Home	"{HOME}"
Insert	"{INSERT}"
Left arrow	"{LEFT}"
Num Lock	"{NUMLOCK}"
Page Down	"{PGDN}"
Page Up	"{PGUP}"
Right arrow	"{RIGHT}"
Scroll Lock	"{SCROLLLOCK}"
Tab	"{TAB}"
Up arrow	"{UP}"
F1 through F12	"{F1}" through "{F12}"

You also can combine these keys with the Shift, Ctrl, and Alt keys. You just precede the preceding codes with one or more of the following:

Key	What to Use
Alt	% (percent)
Ctrl	^ (caret)
Shift	+ (plus)

procedure   The name (entered as text) of the procedure to run when the user presses a key. If you enter the null string (`""`) for *procedure*, a key is disabled. If you omit *procedure*, Excel resets the key to its normal state.

For example, pressing Delete normally wipes out only a cell's contents. If you would like a quick way of deleting everything in a cell (contents, formats, notes, and so on), you could set up (for example) Ctrl-Delete to do the job. Listing 27.5 shows three procedures that accomplish this:

SetKey   Sets up the Ctrl-Delete key combination to run the `DeleteAll` event handler. Notice how the *procedure* argument includes the name of the workbook so this key combination will operate in any workbook.

DeleteAll   Runs the `Clear` method on the current selection.

ResetKey   Resets Ctrl-Delete to its default behavior.

Listing 27.5. Procedures that set and reset a key combination using the OnKey method.

```
Sub SetKey()
    Application.OnKey _
        key:="^{Del}", _
        procedure:="Chap27.xls!DeleteAll"
End Sub

Sub DeleteAll()
    Selection.Clear
End Sub

Sub ResetKey()
    Application.OnKey _
        key:="^{Del}"
End Sub
```

Procedures That Respond to the Mouse

In Excel, double-clicking on an object with the mouse produces different results depending on the object involved. For example, double-clicking on a cell activates in-cell editing, and double-clicking on a graphics object displays the Format Object dialog box for that object. Either of these behaviors could be dangerous because they enable the user to edit cells or objects. To intercept double-clicks, you can set the OnDoubleClick property to run a procedure whenever the user double-clicks.

You can set the OnDoubleClick property for the Application object (to trap double-clicks in any sheet), or for Chart, DialogSheet, Module, and Worksheet objects (to trap double-clicks in specific sheets).

If you just want to disable double-clicks, assign OnDoubleClick to a null string (""). More usefully, you could assign a different behavior to a double-click. For example, Listing 27.6 shows three procedures that take advantage of the OnDoubleClick property:

SetDoubleClick	Sets the Application object's OnDoubleClick property to run the DisplayTime procedure whenever the user double-clicks.
DisplayTime	Uses the MsgBox method to display the time. The Now function returns the current date and time, and the Format function converts the date to text in the specified date format.
ResetDoubleClick	Resets double-clicking to its default behavior.

Listing 27.6. Procedures that display the time when the user double-clicks.

```
Sub SetDoubleClick()
    Application.OnDoubleClick = "Chap27.xls!DisplayTime"
End Sub

Sub DisplayTime()
    MsgBox "The time is " & Format(Now, "h:mm AM/PM")
End Sub

Sub ResetDoubleClick()
    Application.OnDoubleClick = ""
End Sub
```

Running a Procedure at a Specific Time

If you need to run a procedure at a specific time, use the OnTime method:

```
Application.OnTime(earliestTime,procedure,latestTime,schedule)
```

earliestTime	The time (and date, if necessary) you want the procedure to run. Enter a date/time serial number.
procedure	The name (entered as text) of the procedure to run when the *earliestTime* arrives.
latestTime	If Excel isn't ready to run the procedure at *earliestTime* (that is,

if it's not in Ready, Cut, Copy, or Find mode), it will keep trying until *latestTime* arrives. If you omit *latestTime*, VBA waits until Excel is ready. Enter a date/time serial number.

schedule   A logical value that determines whether the procedure runs at ***earliestTime*** or not. If *schedule* is True or omitted, the procedure runs. Use False to cancel a previous OnTime setting.

The easiest way to enter the time serial numbers for ***earliestTime*** and *latestTime* is to use the TimeValue function:

TimeValue(***time***)

time   A string representing the time you want to use (such as "5:00PM" or "17:00").

For example, the following formula runs a procedure called Backup at 5:00 PM:

```
Application.OnTime _
    earliestTime:=TimeValue("5:00PM"), _
    procedure:="Backup"
```

TIP

If you want the OnTime handler to run after a specified time interval (for example, an hour from now), use Now + TimeValue(***time***) for ***earliestTime*** (where ***time*** is the interval you want to use). For example, the following statement schedules a procedure to run in 30 minutes:

```
Application.OnTime _
    earliestTime:=Now + TimeValue("00:30"), _
    procedure:="Backup"
```

Procedures That Respond to Data Entry

To run a procedure when the user enters data in a worksheet, set the OnEntry property of the Application object or a Worksheet object.

Listing 27.7 shows a procedure called SetDataEntry that sets the Statistics worksheet's OnEntry property to run a procedure called VerifyNumbers whenever a user enters data. If the data entered is not a number, the procedure displays a message box to warn the user.

Notice that the VerifyNumbers procedure uses the Application object's Caller property. This property returns a reference to the cell that caused the VerifyNumbers procedure to be called (that is, the cell into which the user entered the data).

Listing 27.7. Procedure to verify data entered in a worksheet.

```
Sub SetDataEntry()
```

```
    Workbooks("Chap27.xls").Worksheets("Statistics").OnEntry = _
        "Chap27.xls!VerifyNumbers"
End Sub

Sub VerifyNumbers()
    Dim dataEntryCell As Range

    dataEntryCellValue = Application.Caller
    If Not IsNumeric(dataEntryCell.Value) Then
        MsgBox "Please enter a number in cell " & _
                dataEntryCell.Address & "!"
    End If
End Sub
```

To cancel a data entry event handler, assign the `OnEntry` property to the null string (`""`):

```
Workbooks("Chap27.xls").Worksheets("Statistics").OnEntry = ""
```

Running a Procedure After Recalculation

On a complex worksheet, changing one variable can affect dozens of formulas. If you can't keep an eye on all these formulas (to check, for example, that a boundary condition is still being met), you can have Excel do it for you. Just set the `OnCalculate` property of the `Application` or a Worksheet object.

For example, the `SetCalculate` procedure in Listing 27.8 sets the Budget worksheet's `OnCalculate` property to run the `CheckMargin` procedure whenever the worksheet recalculates. `CheckMargin` watches a value named `GrossMargin` in Budget. If, after a recalculation, this value dips below 20 percent, the procedure displays a warning message.

Listing 27.8. The `SetCalculate` procedure runs `CheckMargin` whenever the Budget worksheet recalculates.

```
Sub SetCalculate()
    Workbooks("Chap27.xls").Worksheets("Budget").OnCalculate = _
        "Chap27.xls!CheckMargin"
End Sub

Sub CheckMargin()
    With Range("Budget!GrossMargin")
        If .Value < 0.2 Then
            .Select
            MsgBox "Gross Margin is below 20%!"
        End If
    End With
End Sub
```

To cancel an `OnCalculate` event handler, assign the property to the null string (`""`).

A Few More Automatic Procedures

The automatic procedures we've looked at so far are the ones you'll use most often. But Excel also boasts a few more automatic procedures to cover some less common scenarios. Here's a brief review of these other procedures:

OnRepeat and *OnUndo*

OnRepeat sets the name of the **Edit | Repeat** menu item and specifies the procedure that runs when the user selects the **Edit | Repeat** command. Set this property at the end of a procedure so the user can easily repeat the procedure just by selecting **Edit | Repeat**. Here's the syntax:

Application.OnRepeat(*text*,*procedure*)

text	The name of the **Edit	Repeat** menu item. This command normally uses R as its accelerator key, so make sure that the ***text*** argument has an ampersand (&) before the R.
procedure	The procedure to run when the user selects **Edit	Repeat** (this will usually be the name of the procedure that contains the OnRepeat statement).

The OnUndo property is similar to OnRepeat, except that it sets the name of the **Edit | Undo** menu item and specifies the procedure that runs when the user selects **Edit | Undo**:

Application.OnUndo(*text*,*procedure*)

text	The name of the **Edit	Undo** menu item.
procedure	The procedure to run when the user selects **Edit	Undo**.

Listing 27.9 shows an example that uses both OnRepeat and OnUndo. The currCell variable is declared at the top of the module to make it global (in other words, available to all the procedures in the module). The BoldAndItalic procedure makes the font of the active cell bold and italic, and then sets the OnRepeat property (to run BoldAndItalic again) and the OnUndo property (to run the procedure named UndoBoldAndItalic).

Listing 27.9. Procedures that set the OnRepeat and OnUndo properties.

```
Dim currCell As String    ' Global variable
Sub BoldAndItalic()

    With ActiveCell
        .Font.Bold = True
        .Font.Italic = True
        currCell = .Address
    End With

    Application.OnRepeat _
        Text:="&Repeat Bold and Italic", _
```

```
            procedure:="BoldAndItalic"

    Application.OnUndo _
        Text:="&Undo Bold and Italic", _
        procedure:="UndoBoldAndItalic"
End Sub

Sub UndoBoldAndItalic()

    With Range(currCell).Font
        .Bold = False
        .Italic = False
    End With

End Sub
```

OnData and OnSetLinkOnData

The OnData property sets or returns a procedure that runs whenever Excel (the Application.OnData property) or a worksheet (the Worksheet.OnData property) receives DDE or OLE data:

object.OnData(*procedure*)

object	Either the Application object or a Workbook object.
procedure	The name of the procedure.

For example, the following statement tells Excel to run the NewBudgetData procedure whenever external data arrives for any link in the Budget.xls workbook:

```
Workbooks("Budget.xls").OnData procedure:="NewBudgetData"
```

The OnSetLinkData property sets or returns a procedure that runs whenever a particular link in the specified workbook is updated:

object.OnSetLinkData(*name,procedure*)

object	The Workbook object that contains the link.
name	The name of the link (in other words, the name that appears in the formula bar).
procedure	The name of the procedure to run.

For example, the following statement sets up a procedure named UpdateMemo to run whenever the link named WinWord¦'C:\My Documents\Annotation.doc'!DDE_LINK1 is updated:

```
Workbooks("Memo.xls").OnSetLinkData _
    name:="WinWord¦'C:\My Documents\Annotation.doc'!DDE_LINK1", _
    procedure:="UpdateMemo"
```

> **NOTE**
>
> You also can get the name of a link by using the Workbook object's LinkSources method. This method returns an array of strings that contain the names of the links in the specified workbook.

OnSave

OnSave is a Workbook object property that returns or sets a procedure that runs automatically whenever the user selects the File | Save or File | Save As command. There are two things to note about the OnSave property:

- The specified procedure runs *before* the workbook is saved.
- The specified procedure must have a Boolean argument (regardless of whether or not the procedure actually uses the argument).

Listing 27.10 shows several procedures that use the OnSave property. The SetOnSave procedure sets up OnSave to run the AskToSaveAll procedure whenever the user saves the active workbook. AskToSaveAll (note the Boolean argument) asks the user if he wants to save all the open workbooks. If he selects **Yes**, the For Each...Next loop runs the Save method for each workbook. The ResetOnSave procedure disables the OnSave property by setting it equal to the null string.

Listing 27.10. Some procedures that use the OnSave property.

```
Sub SetOnSave()
    ActiveWorkbook.OnSave = "AskToSaveAll"
End Sub

Sub AskToSaveAll(s As Boolean)

    Dim response As Integer, book As Workbook

    response = MsgBox("Save all open workbooks?", vbYesNo + vbQuestion)

    If response = vbYes Then
        For Each book In Workbooks
            book.Save
        Next book
    End If

End Sub

Sub ResetOnSave()
    ActiveWorkbook.OnSave = ""
End Sub
```

Trapping Errors

Properly designed procedures don't leave the user out in the cold if an error occurs. Instead, they designate an *error handling routine* to process errors and (usually) report back to the user.

To trap errors, use the On Error GoTo *line* statement, where *line* is a label that indicates the start of your error handling code. (A *label* is a text string—without spaces or periods—followed by a colon.)

Listing 27.11 shows an example. The BackUpToFloppy procedure is designed to get a drive letter from the user and then save the active workbook to the drive. If a problem occurs (such as having no disk in the drive), the routine displays an error message and gives the user the option of trying again or quitting.

Listing 27.11. A procedure with an error-handling routine.

```
Sub BackUpToFloppy()

    Dim backupDrive As String, backupName As String, msg As String
    Dim done As Boolean, result As Integer

    ' Define the error handling code
    On Error GoTo ErrorHandler

    done = False
    backupDrive = "A:"
    While Not done
        ' Get the drive to use for the backup
        backupDrive = InputBox( _
                    prompt:="Enter the drive letter for the backup:", _
                    Title:="Backup", _
                    default:=backupDrive)

        ' Check to see if OK was selected
        If backupDrive <> "" Then
            ' Make sure that the backup drive contains a colon (:)
            If InStr(backupDrive, ":") = 0 Then
                backupDrive = Left(backupDrive, 1) & ":"
            End If
            ' First save the file
            ActiveWorkbook.Save
            ' Assume the backup will be successful and
            ' so set done to True to exit the loop
            done = True
            ' Concatenate drive letter and workbook name
            backupName = backupDrive & ActiveWorkbook.Name
            ' Make a copy on the specified drive
            ActiveWorkbook.SaveCopyAs filename:=backupName
        Else
            Exit Sub
        End If
    Wend
```

continues

Listing 27.11. continued

```
    Exit Sub    ' Bypass the error handling code

ErrorHandler:    ' Code branches here if an error occurs
    msg = "The following error has occurred:" & Chr(13) & _
        "   Error number:  " & Err & Chr(13) & _
        "   Error message: " & Error(Err) & Chr(13) & Chr(13) & _
        "Select Abort to bail out, Retry to reenter the drive" & Chr(13) & _
        "letter, or Ignore to attempt the backup again."
    result = MsgBox(msg, vbExclamation + vbAbortRetryIgnore)
    Select Case result
        Case vbAbort
            Exit Sub
        Case vbRetry
            done = False
            Resume Next
        Case vbIgnore
            Resume
    End Select

End Sub
```

The error routine is set up with the following statement:

```
On Error GoTo ErrorHandler
```

The ErrorHandler argument refers to the ErrorHandler: label. If an error occurs, the procedure jumps to this label and runs the code between the label and the End Sub statement. In this case, a message is displayed that includes the error number (as given by the Err function) and an error message (as given by the Error(Err) function).

The error handler's MsgBox gives the user three choices, which get processed by the subsequent Select Case statement:

Abort   Selecting this option (Case vbAbort) bails out of the procedure altogether by running the Exit Sub statement.

Retry   Selecting this option (Case vbRetry) means the user wants to reenter the drive letter. The done variable is set to False (done controls the While...Wend loop) and then the Resume Next statement is run. Resume Next tells VBA to continue running the procedure from the statement *after* the statement that caused the error. In this case, the next statement is Wend, so the procedure just loops back (since we set done to False) and runs the InputBox function again.

Ignore Selecting this option (Case vbIgnore) means the user wants to attempt the backup again. For example, if the user forgot to insert a disk in the drive, or if the drive door wasn't closed, he would fix the problem and then select this option. In this case, the error handler runs the Resume statement, which tells VBA to continue the procedure from the statement that caused the error.

NOTE

For more sophisticated error handling, use the Err function in conjunction with Select Case to test for different errors and process the result accordingly. For a list of error codes, load the VBA Help file and use the Index tab to look for the trappable errors topic.

Summary

This chapter showed you how to work with VBA procedures that respond to events. You learned how to create procedures that run when the user opens or closes a workbook, activates or de-activates a worksheet or window, presses a key, double-clicks the mouse, enters data, recalculates a workbook, and more. I also showed you how to trap errors in your procedures. You'll find related material in the following chapters:

- Auto_Open procedures are perfect places to set up the user interface for your application (such as displaying toolbars, adding menus, and initializing dialog boxes). See Chapter 25, "Creating a Custom User Interface," to learn how to create these user interface elements.

- You can prevent many VBA errors by properly debugging your applications before foisting them upon your users. I discuss VBA debugging tips and techniques in Chapter 29, "Debugging VBA Procedures."

Working with Other Applications: OLE, DDE, and More

28

Your VBA code will likely spend most of its time working with Excel objects and their associated properties and methods. However, there will be times when you need your code to interact with other applications. Happily, VBA offers a number of functions and methods for working with other applications inside your procedures. This chapter shows you how to start other programs; how to send them keystrokes; how to work with OLE, OLE automation, and DDE; and how to use DLLs in your procedures.

Starting Another Application

I suppose the most obvious way to work with another application is simply to start it up and work with it directly. As is usually the case with most computer tasks, there is a hard way and an easy way to do this. The "hard" way is to open the Start menu and then either wade through all those submenus to launch the program from its icon or select the **R**un command and enter the program's executable filename in the Run dialog box.

The easy way, especially if you use the other application frequently while working in Excel, is to use the Shell function to start the program from a VBA procedure:

Shell(***pathname***,*windowStyle*)

pathname	The name of the file that starts the application (or the name of a data file associated with the executable file). Unless the file is in the Windows folder, you should include the drive and folder to make sure that VBA can find the file.
windowStyle	A number that specifies how the application window will appear:

windowStyle	*Window Appearance*
1, 5, 9	Normal size with focus
2 (or omitted)	Minimized with focus
3	Maximized with focus
4, 8	Normal without focus
6, 7	Minimized without focus

If successful, Shell returns a number (called the *task ID* number). If unsuccessful, Shell generates an error.

Listing 28.1 shows an example of the Shell function.

Listing 28.1. Using the Shell function to start an application.

```
Sub StartControlPanelIcon(cplFile As String)

    On Error GoTo BadStart

    Shell "CONTROL.EXE " & cplFile, 1
```

```
    Exit Sub

BadStart:
    MsgBox "Could not start Control Panel!", _
        vbOKOnly + vbExclamation
End Sub

' This procedure calls StartControlPanelIcon with
' "ODBCCP32.CPL" to open the Data Sources dialog box
'
Sub ChangeDataSource()
    StartControlPanel ("ODBCCP32.CPL")
End Sub
```

The Windows Control Panel is a frequently used accessory that lets you control many aspects of the Windows environment, including printer settings, fonts, and colors. The `StartControlPanelIcon` procedure takes advantage of the fact that you can start any Control Panel icon directly by using the following command-line syntax:

`CONTROL.EXE cplFile`

Here, `cplFile` is a .CPL (Control Panel Library) file that corresponds to the Control Panel icon you want to start. Table 28.1 lists some of the Control Panel icons and their corresponding .CPL files.

Table 28.1. Control Panel icons and their .CPL files.

Icon	.CPL File
32bit ODBC	ODBCCP32.CPL
Accessibility Options	ACCESS.CPL
Add/Remove Programs	APPWIZ.CPL
Date/Time	TIMEDATE.CPL
Display	DESK.CPL
Find Fast	FINDFAST.CPL
Fonts	MAIN.CPL Fonts
Keyboard	MAIN.CPL Keyboard
Mail and Fax	MLCFG32.CPL
Microsoft Mail Post Office	WGPOCPL.CPL
Modems	MODEM.CPL
Mouse	MAIN.CPL Mouse
Multimedia	MMSYS.CPL

continues

864

Table 28.1. continued

Icon	.CPL File
Network	NETCPL.CPL
Passwords	PASSWORD.CPL
Printers	MAIN.CPL Printers
Regional Settings	INTL.CPL
System	SYSDM.CPL

The StartControlPanelIcon procedure takes a cplFile argument that specifies the Control Panel icon with which you want to work. The procedure sets up an On Error handler just in case Control Panel doesn't start properly. Then it runs the Shell function to load Control Panel and run the module specified by cplFile.

The ChangeDataSource procedure shows an example of how you call StartControlPanelIcon. In this case, the Data Sources dialog box appears so you can set up or modify an ODBC data source (as described in Chapter 15, "Using Microsoft Query").

NOTE

Use the ChDir statement if you need to change to an application's directory before starting the program:

ChDir *Path*

The *Path* argument is a string that specifies the directory to change to.

CAUTION

Don't enter statements after a Shell function if you want the statements to execute only when you've finished with the other application. The Shell statement runs an application *asynchronously,* which means that VBA starts the program and then immediately resumes executing the rest of the procedure.

Activating a Running Application

Once you have some other programs up and running, your VBA application may need to switch between them. For example, you might want the user to switch between Excel and the Control Panel to change various settings. To switch to any running application, use the AppActivate statement:

```
AppActivate(title,wait)
```

title	The name of the application as it appears in the title bar, or its task ID number (as returned by the Shell function).
wait	A logical value that determines when Excel switches to the application. If *wait* is True, AppActivate waits until you activate Excel before switching. If *wait* is False or omitted, AppActivate immediately switches to the application.

Note that, for some applications, the title bar may include both the name of the application and the name of the active document. If ***title*** doesn't match any application's title bar exactly, VBA tries to find a title bar that *begins with* ***title***.

Listing 28.2 shows AppActivate in action.

Listing 28.2. Using the AppActivate statement to switch to a running application.

```
' This procedure loads the Phone Dialer accessory
'
Sub LoadPhoneDialer()

    On Error GoTo BadStart

    ' Start Phone Dialer without the focus
    Shell "DIALER.EXE", 4

    ' Set up the Ctrl+Shift+P shortcut key
    Application.OnKey _
        Key:="^+P", _
        Procedure:="ActivatePhoneDialer"

    MsgBox "Phone Dialer loaded!" & Chr(13) & _
        "Press Ctrl+Shift+P to activate.", _
        vbInformation

    Exit Sub
BadStart:
    MsgBox "Could not start Phone Dialer!", _
        vbOKOnly + vbExclamation

End Sub

' This procedure copies the current cell and activates
' Phone Dialer when the user presses Ctrl+Shift+P
'
Sub ActivatePhoneDialer()

    Dim result As Integer

    On Error GoTo NotRunning

    ' Copy the contents (a phone number?) of the current cell
    ActiveCell.Copy
```

continues

Listing 28.2. continued

```
    ' Activate Phone Dialer
    AppActivate "Phone Dialer"

    Exit Sub

NotRunning:
    result = MsgBox("Phone Dialer is not loaded! " & _
                    "Do you want to load it now?", _
                    vbYesNo + vbExclamation)

    If result = vbYes Then
        LoadPhoneDialer
        Resume
    End If

End Sub
```

In this example, the LoadPhoneDialer procedure loads Windows 95's Phone Dialer accessory and then sets up a shortcut key for activating Phone Dialer.

The Shell function starts Phone Dialer without focus. Then an OnKey method sets up the Ctrl-Shift-P key combination to run the ActivatePhoneDialer procedure. (See Chapter 27, "VBA Procedures That Respond to Events," for the full scoop on the OnKey method.) Finally, a MsgBox function displays a message to tell the user Phone Dialer has been loaded.

If Phone Dialer doesn't load, a different MsgBox function alerts the user to the problem.

The ActivatePhoneDialer procedure copies the contents of the active cell (which contains, ideally, a phone number you want to dial) and then activates Phone Dialer using the AppActivate statement. If an error occurs, the code jumps to the NotRunning label and asks the user if he or she wants to start Phone Dialer.

> **NOTE**
>
> If the application you want to activate is a Microsoft application, you can use the Application object's ActivateMicrosoftApp(*index*) method. Here, *index* is a constant that represents the Microsoft application you want to activate: xlMicrosoftAccess, xlMicrosoftFoxPro, xlMicrosoftMail, xlMicrosoftPowerPoint, xlMicrosoftProject, xlMicrosoftSchedulePlus, or xlMicrosoftWord.
>
> If the application isn't running, ActivateMicrosoftApp starts it. For example, the following statement activates Microsoft Word:
>
> ```
> Application.ActivateMicrosoftApp xlMicrosoftWord
> ```

Sending Keystrokes to an Application

As you'll see later in this chapter, you can use DDE to run a server application's macro commands, and OLE automation makes it easy to program a server application's objects. But the majority of Windows applications don't support OLE automation and don't have a macro language. What's to be done with these less-sophisticated programs?

Well, one solution is to simply load the application using the Shell function and let the user work with the program directly. This is fine if the user is familiar with the application, but your real goal here is to control programs from within a VBA procedure. The solution is to use the SendKeys statement to send keystrokes to the application. You can send any key or key combination (including those that use the Alt, Ctrl, and Shift keys) and the result is exactly the same as if you typed it yourself. Here is the syntax of the SendKeys statement:

SendKeys **string**,wait

string	The key or key combination you want to send to the active application. For letters, numbers, or punctuation marks, enclose the character in quotes (for example, "a"). For other keys, use the strings outlined in Table 28.2.
wait	A logical value that determines whether VBA waits for the keys to be processed before continuing the procedure. If wait is True, VBA waits for the application to finish processing the keys before moving on to the next statement in the procedure. It doesn't wait if the wait argument is False or omitted.

Table 28.2. Strings to use for the SendKeys method's *string* argument.

For...	Use...
Backspace	"{BACKSPACE}" or "{BS}"
Break	"{BREAK}"
Caps Lock	"{CAPSLOCK}"
Delete	"{DELETE}" or "{DEL}"
Down arrow	"{DOWN}"
End	"{END}"
Enter (keypad)	"{ENTER}"
Enter	"~" (tilde)
Esc	"{ESCAPE}" or "{ESC}"
Home	"{HOME}"

continues

Table 28.2. continued

For...	*Use...*
Insert	`"{INSERT}"`
Left arrow	`"{LEFT}"`
Num Lock	`"{NUMLOCK}"`
Page Down	`"{PGDN}"`
Page Up	`"{PGUP}"`
Right arrow	`"{RIGHT}"`
Scroll Lock	`"{SCROLLLOCK}"`
Tab	`"{TAB}"`
Up arrow	`"{UP}"`
F1 through F12	`"{F1}"` through `"{F12}"`

> **NOTE**
>
> For most of the keys listed in Table 28.2, you can send the key multiple times by enclosing a number within the braces. For example, to send the up arrow key three times, use {UP 3}.

By combining these keys with the Alt, Ctrl, and Shift keys, you can create any key combination. Just precede a string from Table 28.2 with one or more of the codes listed in Table 28.3.

Table 28.3. Codes for the Alt, Ctrl, and Shift keys.

For...	*Use...*
Alt	% (percent)
Ctrl	^ (caret)
Shift	+ (plus)

All you have to do is start a program with Shell and then you can send whatever keystrokes you need. (You can sometimes get away with activating a running application with AppActivate and then sending the keys, but I've found this doesn't work consistently. You'll need to experiment with the applications you want to use.) For example, you can close any active Windows application by sending the Alt-F4 key combination, as follows:

```
SendKeys "%{F4}"
```

Listing 28.3 shows a more complex example that dials a phone number using the Phone Dialer accessory.

> **NOTE**
>
> Listing 28.3 is a simplified version of the PhoneCustomer procedure used in the Customer Database application discussed in Chapter 26, "Database and Client/Server Programming" (see the Customer.xls workbook on this book's CD).

Listing 28.3. Controlling an application using the SendKeys statement.

```
Sub LoadAndDialPhoneDialer()

    Dim msg As String, buttons As Integer, response As Integer
    On Error GoTo BadStart

    msg = "About to dial the following number:" & _
        Chr(13) & Chr(13) & _
        "    " & ActiveCell & _
        Chr(13) & Chr(13) & _
        "Please make sure your modem is turned on."
    buttons = vbOKCancel + vbExclamation
    response = MsgBox(msg, buttons)

    If response = vbCancel Then Exit Sub

    ' Copy the contents (a phone number?) of the current cell
    ActiveCell.Copy

    ' Start Phone Dialer without the focus
    Shell "DIALER.EXE", 1

    ' Paste the copied phone number with Ctrl+V and
    ' then press Enter to select the Dial button
    SendKeys "^v~", True

    ' Wait five seconds to give the modem time to dial
    Application.Wait Now + TimeValue("00:00:05")

    ' Close the dialog boxes and exit Phone Dialer
    SendKeys "~{ESC}%{F4}"

    Application.CutCopyMode = False

    Exit Sub

BadStart:
    MsgBox "Could not start Phone Dialer!", _
        vbOKOnly + vbExclamation
End Sub
```

This procedure uses a modem and the Phone Dialer accessory to dial the phone number contained in the active cell. After displaying a `MsgBox` that tells the user the number that will be dialed and to make sure his or her modem is on, the procedure copies the active cell and starts Phone Dialer.

A `SendKeys` statement sends Ctrl-V and then Enter to paste the phone number and select the **D**ial button. After a few seconds, Phone Dialer displays the Call Status dialog box. Go ahead and pick up the receiver, but don't press Enter to clear the dialog box. The procedure waits five seconds to give your phone time to dial and then another `SendKeys` statement sends the following keys: Enter (to remove the dialog box), Esc (to cancel the Dialing dialog box) and Alt-F4 (to exit Phone Dialer). Finally, the `CutCopyMode` property is set to `False` to take Excel out of copy mode.

> **NOTE**
>
> Keep in mind that the `SendKeys` statement is case-sensitive. For example, the strings `"^P"` and `"^+p"` both send the key combination Ctrl-Shift-P. If you just want to send Ctrl-P, `"^p"` is the string to use.

> **TIP**
>
> Include the following characters in braces ({}) to send them in a `SendKeys` string: ~ % ^ ( ) + { } [ ]. For example, you send a percent sign as follows:
>
> ```
> SendKeys "{%}"
> ```

Using Dynamic Data Exchange

Later in this chapter, you'll learn how the advanced technologies of OLE and OLE automation make it easier than ever to work with and exchange data with other Windows applications. However, of the thousands of Windows applications that exist, only a few support the OLE standard and a mere handful (for now) support OLE automation. OLE might one day be the de facto standard for application interoperability, but until that day comes we'll need a few more tricks in our programming bag to work with other applications.

One of those tricks is the predecessor of OLE: *dynamic data exchange* (*DDE*). DDE is an internal communications protocol that enables some Windows applications to exchange data and even execute each other's commands. Because it's implemented unevenly in different applications, DDE is nowhere near as clean (or as straightforward) as OLE, but it's often the only choice we have. The good news is that VBA provides plenty of tools to control the DDE protocol at the procedure level. The next few sections examine each of those tools.

DDE: The Basics

Human conversations can take two forms: static and dynamic. A static conversation—such as the exchange of letters or e-mail—is one where information is passed back and forth intermittently. A dynamic conversation, on the other hand, is one where information is exchanged continuously. Face-to-face meetings or telephone calls are examples of dynamic conversations.

So a *dynamic* data exchange, then, is one where two applications continuously send data and commands to each other. As in OLE, the two applications involved in this process are called client and server. The *client* is the application that initializes the conversation and sends requests for data (the client is also sometimes called the *destination*). The *server* is the application that responds to the client's requests by executing its own commands and sending its data (the server is also called the *source*).

DDE conversations unfold in three stages:

1. **Initiate a link between the client and the server.** This link—it's called a *channel*—is the path along which the two applications will communicate. In our case, VBA will be initiating the conversation, so it will be the client.

2. **Work with the server.** Once the link is established, the client can exchange data with the server and can control the server by invoking its internal macro commands or by sending keystrokes.

3. **Terminate the link.** When the client is finished working with the server, your procedure needs to close the channel.

Initiating a Link Between VBA and a Server Application

Just as you need to call someone before you can have a phone conversation with them, so too must your procedure "call" a server application to initiate a DDE conversation. To establish a channel between VBA and another DDE application, use the DDEInitiate method:

object.DDEInitiate(***app,topic***)

object	The Application object.
app	The DDE name of the server application with which you want to open a link.
topic	This is the "topic of conversation" that the two applications will be using. For most applications, you use either System (the application as a whole) or the name of a document in the application (that is, the name as it appears in the title bar).

DDEInitiate(*App, Topic*)

The DDE name used in the *app* argument depends on the application—it's almost always the name of the executable file that starts the application (without the extension). For example, the DDE name for Excel is Excel, for Word for Windows it's Winword, and for Access it's MSAccess. For other applications, check your documentation or contact the application's technical support department.

Make sure you include the full pathname of a document in the DDEInitiate method's *topic* argument if you're trying to access a document that isn't already open. Here's an example:

```
DDEInitiate("Winword", "C:\WINWORD\MEMO.DOC")
```

If DDEInitiate is successful, it returns an integer identifying the channel. You'll need to refer to this number in all subsequent DDE exchanges between the client and server.

The server application needs to be open before you can initiate a DDE session. So one decision you need to make before running the DDEInitiate method is whether you want to open the server beforehand with the Shell function or whether you want DDEInitiate to handle it for you. In most cases, a Shell function is the way to go because the DDEInitiate startup method has two annoying quirks:

- Excel displays a dialog box similar to the one shown in Figure 28.1. You need to select **Yes** to start the application. If you like, you can prevent this message from appearing by setting the Application.DisplayAlerts property to False.

FIGURE 28.1.

The dialog box Excel displays if you let DDEInitiate *start a server application that isn't already running.*

- If the application isn't in the current directory or the DOS search path, DDEInitiate won't be able to find it. You can solve this problem by first using the ChDir statement to change to the application's directory:

```
ChDir "C:\WINWORD"
```

Listing 28.4 shows a sample Function procedure that uses the DDEInitiate method.

Listing 28.4. Using the DDEInitiate method to open a DDE channel.

```
Function OpenHailingFrequencies() As Integer
    Dim channel As Integer

    On Error GoTo BadConnection

    ' Start WinWord and establish the DDE connection
    Shell "C:\MSOffice\Winword\Winword.exe", 6
    channel = DDEInitiate("Winword", "System")

    MsgBox "A channel to Word is now open.", vbInformation
```

```
    ' Return the channel number
    OpenHailingFrequencies = channel
    Exit Function

BadConnection: _
    MsgBox "Could not open a channel to Word!", vbExclamation
    ' Return 0
    OpenHailingFrequencies = 0

End Function
```

The OpenHailingFrequencies procedure is designed to open a DDE channel between Excel and Word for Windows. A variable named channel is declared to store the channel number returned by the DDEInitiate method. An On Error GoTo handler is established just in case something goes wrong. (This is always a good idea, because DDE connections are notoriously flaky.)

Next, a Shell function starts Word for Windows without focus and then the DDEInitiate method is run. If all goes well, the channel number is stored in the channel variable, a MsgBox function tells the user the connection has been established, and then the channel number is returned. If an error occurs, the code jumps to the BadConnection label, displays an error message, and returns 0.

When your procedure is finished with its DDE conversation, you need to terminate the link between the client and server. You do this by running the DDETerminate method:

DDETerminate *channel*

Here, *channel* is the channel number returned by the DDEInitiate method.

Controlling the Server Application

Once you have an open channel, you can use the DDEExecute method to control the other application. You can send either commands the server application understands (such as commands from its macro language, if it has one) or you can send keystrokes. DDEExecute has the following syntax:

DDEExecute(*channel,string*)

> **channel**   The channel returned by the DDEInitiate method.
>
> **string**   A text string representing the commands to run in the application.

The tricky part of the DDEExecute method is the ***string*** argument; its form entirely depends on the application. Excel and Word for Windows enable you to use their macro commands, provided that you enclose the commands in square brackets ([ ]). Other applications also enable you to use their macro commands, but they don't support the square-brackets standard. Other programs have no macro language, but they do have special DDE commands. Finally, there are applications without special commands to use, but they enable you to control the application by sending keystroke sequences with the DDEExecute method.

NOTE

To send keystrokes with DDEExecute, use the same key formats I showed you earlier for the SendKeys statement. For example, the DDEExecute(Channel,"^v") statement sends the key combination Ctrl-V to the application linked to VBA by Channel. Note, however, that you can't use DDEExecute to send keys to a dialog box. For that you need to use the SendKeys method.

Listing 28.5 uses several examples of the DDEExecute method.

Listing 28.5. Using DDEExecute to control a server application.

```
Sub CreateWordLink()

    Dim channel As Integer
    On Error GoTo BailOut

    ' Start Word
    Application.StatusBar = "Starting Word..."
    Shell "C:\MSOffice\Winword\Winword.exe", 6

    ' Initiate channel with System topic
    Application.StatusBar = "Initiating DDE conversation..."
    channel = DDEInitiate("Winword", "System")

    ' Open the document we want to work with
    Application.StatusBar = "Opening Word document..."
    DDEExecute channel, "[FileOpen ""C:\My Documents\DDE_Test.doc""]"
    DDETerminate channel

    ' Initiate new channel with document
    Application.StatusBar = "Initiating DDE conversation with document..."
    channel = DDEInitiate("Winword", "C:\My Documents\DDE_Test.doc")

    ' Get the text from the first line of the document
    Application.StatusBar = "Getting text..."
    DDEExecute channel, "[StartOfDocument]"
    DDEExecute channel, "[EndOfLine 1]"
    DDEExecute channel, "[EditCopy]"

    ' Paste and link the copied text
    Application.StatusBar = "Pasting and linking text..."
    Worksheets("Sheet1").Activate
    Range("A1").Select
    ActiveSheet.Paste link:=True

    ' Quit Word and terminate channel
    Application.StatusBar = "Quitting Word..."
    DDEExecute channel, "[FileExit 2]"
    DDETerminate channel

    Application.StatusBar = False
    Exit Sub
```

```
BailOut:
    DDETerminate channel
    MsgBox "DDE operation failed!", vbExclamation
    Application.StatusBar = False

End Sub
```

The CreateWordLink procedure loads Word for Windows, executes several Word commands—including copying some text—and then pastes the copied text into Excel with a DDE link.

The procedure begins by setting up an error handler and starting Word. (The Application object's StatusBar property is used throughout the procedure to keep the user abreast of what's happening.) A channel is opened to Word's System topic and the return value is stored in the channel variable. The first DDEExecute method runs WordBasic's FileOpen command to open a file named DDE_Test.doc. You've now finished your conversation with the System topic, so DDETerminate closes the channel.

You can now start up a new conversation, but this time with the DDE_Test.doc file as the topic. The procedure executes three WordBasic commands; these commands move to the start of the document (StartOfDocument), select the entire first line (EndOfLine 1), and copy the selection to the Clipboard (EditCopy).

The next few lines paste and link the copied data. First, the cell where the data will be pasted is selected (this is mandatory when pasting linked data) and then the Paste method uses its link argument to paste the text with a DDE link to Word.

Finally, one last DDEExecute method sends the WordBasic command for quitting Word: FileExit 2. (Note that the 2 means Word doesn't save any documents.) Then, another DDETerminate closes the second channel.

Exchanging Data with the Server Application

As you've seen, each DDE conversation between the client and server is established on a specified topic. Everything else the two applications "discuss" in the current DDE session is limited to subjects related to the topic. For example, in the preceding section you saw how the server's commands are a fit subject to include in the conversation.

We'll now turn to another subject you can use in your DDE dialogues: data items. Each server application that supports DDE defines one or more items that can be shared with the client. For example, a typical spreadsheet item is a cell, and a typical word processor item is a bookmark (that is, a named chunk of text). These items are always composed of simple text and numbers; graphics and other high-level objects can't be transferred in a DDE conversation.

The next two sections show you how to use the DDERequest and DDEPoke methods to exchange data items between the client and server.

Receiving Data from the Server

If the server has data you would like to transfer to a worksheet cell, you can establish a DDE link between the two applications and then use the DDERequest method to retrieve the data:

DDERequest(*channel*, *item*)

> *channel*   The channel returned by the DDEInitiate method.
>
> *item*   A string that specifies the data item you want to retrieve from the server.

Listing 28.6 runs through an example.

Listing 28.6. Using DDERequest to retrieve data from an application.

```
Sub RequestWordData()

    Dim channel As Integer, wordData As Variant
    On Error GoTo BailOut

    ' Start Word
    Application.StatusBar = "Starting Word..."
    Shell "C:\MSOffice\Winword\Winword.exe", 6

    ' Initiate channel with System topic
    channel = DDEInitiate("Winword", "System")

    ' Open the document we want to work with
    Application.StatusBar = "Opening Word document..."
    DDEExecute channel, "[FileOpen ""C:\My Documents\Memo.doc""]"
    DDETerminate channel

    ' Initiate new channel with document
    channel = DDEInitiate("Winword", "C:\My Documents\Memo.doc")

    ' Find keyword and add a bookmark
    DDEExecute channel, "[StartOfDocument]"
    DDEExecute channel, "[EditFind .Find = ""ACME""]"
    DDEExecute channel, "[SelectCurSentence]"
    DDEExecute channel, "[EditBookmark .Name = ""Gotcha""]"

    ' Retrieve the bookmark
    wordData = DDERequest(channel, "Gotcha")
    Worksheets("Sheet1").[A1].Value = wordData

    ' Quit Word and terminate channel
    DDEExecute channel, "[FileExit 1]"
    DDETerminate channel

    Exit Sub

BailOut:
    DDETerminate channel
    MsgBox "DDE operation failed!", vbExclamation

End Sub
```

The idea behind the `RequestWordData` procedure is to find a particular section of text in a word document and then read it into Excel. The procedure begins, as before, by setting up an error handler, starting Word, establishing the channel, and then opening the document.

The first `DDEExecute` method moves to the start of the document; the second `DDEExecute` looks for the text string "ACME" in the document; then the entire sentence containing "ACME" is selected, and a final `DDEExecute` creates a bookmark named "Gotcha" for the selected sentence.

To retrieve the text, the `DDERequest` method asks Word for the "Gotcha" item and stores it in the `wordData` variable. (Note that the `wordData` variable is declared as a `Variant`. This is required because the `DDERequest` method always returns an array.) The retrieved data is stored in cell A1 of Sheet1, and then Word is closed (note the `FileExit 1` saves changes) and the channel is terminated.

> **NOTE**
>
> You can use `DDERequest` to get a list of all the server's open documents. Just initiate a DDE channel on the System topic and then use `DDERequest` to return the Topics item. Here is an example:
>
> ```
> openFiles = DDERequest(channel, "Topics")
> ```
>
> Here, `openFiles` is a `Variant` variable. The server will return the list of open files as an array.

Sending Data to the Server

Like all good conversations, the exchange between the client and server is a two-way street. Therefore, just as your procedures can request data from the server, so too can the client send data to the server. This is handled by the `DDEPoke` method:

`DDEPoke(`*`channel`*`,`*`item`*`,`*`data`*`)`

`channel`	The channel returned by the `DDEInitiate` method.
`item`	A string that specifies the data item to which the data will be sent.
`data`	The data you want to send to the server application (it must be plain text or numbers).

Listing 28.7 shows you an example.

Listing 28.7. Using `DDEPoke` to send data to an application.

```
Sub SendDataToWord()

    Dim channel As Integer, pokeData As Variant
    On Error GoTo BailOut
```

continues

Listing 28.7. continued

```
    ' Start Word
    Application.StatusBar = "Starting Word..."
    Shell "C:\MSOffice\Winword\Winword.exe", 6

    ' Initiate channel with System topic
    channel = DDEInitiate("Winword", "System")

    ' Open the document we want to work with
    Application.StatusBar = "Opening Word document..."
    DDEExecute channel, "[FileOpen ""C:\My Documents\Memo.doc""]"
    DDETerminate channel

    ' Initiate new channel with document
    channel = DDEInitiate("Winword", "C:\My Documents\Memo.doc")

    'Get the data to be sent
    PokeData = Worksheets("Sheet1").[A1].Value

    'Send it to the "Gotcha" bookmark
    DDEPoke Channel, "Gotcha", PokeData

    ' Quit Word and terminate channel
    DDEExecute channel, "[FileExit 1]"
    DDETerminate channel

    Exit Sub

BailOut:
    DDETerminate channel
    MsgBox "DDE operation failed!", vbExclamation

End Sub
```

This procedure performs the opposite function of the procedure we looked at in Listing 28.6. Here, VBA takes text from a cell and sends it to a bookmark in Word. The procedure begins by setting up the error handler, starting Word, and then establishing the link. The cell data to send is stored in the pokeData variable, and then the DDEPoke method sends it to the "Gotcha" bookmark in the Word document. The link is then terminated and the procedure exits.

Adding Linked and Embedded Objects

As you saw in Chapter 7, "Exchanging Data with Other Applications," object linking and embedding (OLE) can add some slick new tricks to your Excel arsenal. However, the price you pay for this advanced technology is added complexity. This is especially true for novice users who might be uncomfortable with the various choices available in a typical OLE operation. For example, if you've copied data from the server application, the client's Paste Special command gives you a number of choices: you can paste the information as an object or, depending on the data, you can paste it as a picture or as text; you can paste the data linked or unlinked, and you can paste the data as an icon or in full view.

VBA can help because it gives you control over each of these decisions at the procedural level. You can give your users a single command or toolbar button that creates an specified OLE object and hides the gory details. The next few sections show you how to create OLE objects with VBA.

Using the *Add* Method for the *OLEObjects* Collection

In Excel, each linked or embedded OLE object is an OLEObject, and the collection of all OLE objects in a worksheet is OLEObjects. To insert a new OLE object in a sheet, use the Add method with the following syntax:

sheet.OLEObjects.Add(*classType,fileName,link,displayAsIcon,iconFileName,*
➡*iconIndex,iconLabel*)

sheet	The worksheet to which you want to add the OLE object.
classType	If you're inserting a new object, use *classType* to specify the type of object you want to insert. For example, to insert a new Word for Windows 6 document, you use "Word.Document.6" for *classType* (see the next section for more information).
fileName	If you're inserting an object from an existing server file, use *fileName* to specify the name of the file. If you use this parameter, don't specify a *classType*.
link	This is a logical value that determines whether or not the object created from *fileName* is linked or embedded. If True, the object is linked to the original file; if False or omitted, the object is embedded.
displayAsIcon	A logical value that determines how the object is displayed. If True, the object is displayed as an icon; if False or omitted, the object is displayed in its normal picture form.
iconFileName	If *displayAsIcon* is True, use *iconFileName* to specify the name of the file that contains the icon you want to display. If you omit *iconFileName*, the default icon for the OLE class is used.
IconIndex	Some files contain multiple icons, so you can use *iconIndex* to select the icon you want to use (where the first icon is 0, the second is 1, and so on). For this to work, *displayIcon* must be True, *iconFileName* must point to a valid icon file, and you must specify the *iconLabel* argument.
iconLabel	If *displayAsIcon* is True, *iconLabel* spells out a text string that appears underneath the icon.

I show you how to use the Add method and its arguments in the next few sections.

Looking Up an Object's Class Type

Before looking at the OLEObject's Add method in action, let's take a quick look at how you find out an object's class type (also known as its *programmatic ID*) for the classType argument.

Windows maintains a *registry* of information about applications installed on your system. This database contains, among other things, data related to applications that support OLE. To find out the class types of the OLE objects available on your system, first open the Registry Editor by displaying the Start menu, selecting the **R**un command, typing regedit in the Run dialog box, and then selecting OK.

The HKEY_CLASSES_ROOT hierarchy contains OLE and DDE information for your installed applications. Open HKEY_CLASSES_ROOT and look for the CLSID key, which contains all the information you need. Here's how to find the class type for an object:

1. Highlight the CLSID key.
2. Select the **E**dit | **F**ind command (or press Ctrl-F) to display the Find dialog box.
3. Enter the name of the object you want to find (for example, Video Clip), activate the Match **w**hole string only check box, and then select **F**ind Next. The Registry searches for the text and then displays the first key that matches the string. (It will be a long string of numbers, such as 00022602-0000-0000-C000-000000000046.)
4. The item appears at the bottom of the window, so you'll need to scroll up to see the subkeys. (Figure 28.2 shows the key for the Video Clip object.) These subkeys contain all the OLE-related information about the object.

FIGURE 28.2.

Look in the CLSID key to find insertable OLE objects.

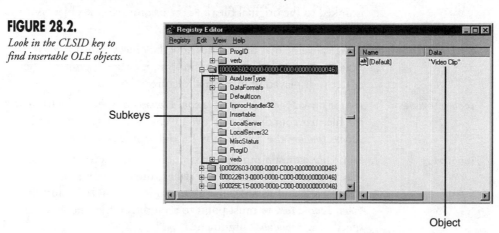

5. To find out the object's class type, highlight the ProgID subkey. As you can see in Figure 28.3, the class type for a Video Clip object is avifile.
6. To search for the class type for another object, press Backspace twice to return to the CLSID key and then repeat steps 2 through 5.

FIGURE 28.3.

The ProgID subkey tells you the class type of the OLE object.

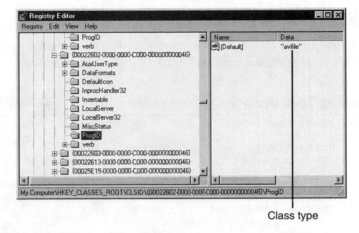

Class type

To save you some legwork, Table 28.4 lists some class types for common objects.

Table 28.4. Class types for common objects.

Object	Class Type
Bitmap Image	Paint.Picture
Calendar Control	MSACAL.MSACALCtrl.7
Media Clip	mplayer
Microsoft ClipArt Gallery	MS_ClipArt_Gallery.2
Microsoft Data Map	MSDataMap.1
Microsoft Equation 2.0	Equation.2
Microsoft Exccl Chart	Exccl.Chart.5
Microsoft Excel Worksheet	Excel.Sheet.5
Microsoft Graph 5.0	MSGraph.Chart.5
Microsoft PowerPoint Presentation	PowerPointShow.7
Microsoft Project 4.0 Project	MSProject.Project.4
Microsoft Word Document	Word.Document.6
Microsoft Word Picture	Word.Picture.6
Microsoft WordArt 2.0	MSWordArt.2
MIDI Sequence	midfile
MS Organization Chart 2.0	OrgPlusWOPX.4
Package	Package
Video Clip	avifile
Wave Sound	SoundRec
WordPad Document	Wordpad.Document.1

Inserting a New Embedded Object

To insert a new embedded object into a worksheet, you need to run the OLEObject's Add method with the *classType* argument. Listing 28.8 provides an example.

Listing 28.8. Using the Add method to embed a new object in a worksheet.

```
Sub InsertNewWordArt()

    Dim msgPrompt As String, msgButtons As Integer
    Dim response As Integer, embeddedArt as Object

    msgPrompt = "Are you sure you want to insert a new WordArt object?"
    msgButtons = vbOKCancel + vbQuestion
    response = MsgBox(msgPrompt, msgButtons)

    If response = vbOK Then
        Application.StatusBar = "Loading WordArt..."
        Set embeddedArt = Worksheets("Sheet1").OLEObjects.Add _
            (classType:="MSWordArt.2")
        Application.StatusBar = False
    End If

End Sub
```

The InsertNewWordArt procedure is designed to insert a new WordArt object into a worksheet. The procedure begins by constructing the prompt and buttons for a MsgBox function, which asks the user if he's sure he wants to insert the object. If OK was selected, the procedure displays a message in the status bar about loading WordArt. Then the Add method inserts the WordArt object into Sheet1 and stores it in the Object variable EmbeddedArt.

Unless you add the object as an icon, the appearance of the object you insert depends largely on the server application. In some cases, the server application loads and presents you with a blank document. Other applications (such as WordArt) display a default object. In most cases, though, you just get a container (that is, a blank picture box) for the object. If you would like to make sure the server application loads so the user can create the new object, add the Activate method to the end of your Add statement, as in this example:

```
Worksheets("Sheet1").OLEObjects.Add (classType:="OrgPlusWOPX.4").Activate
```

(Alternatively, you can assign the new OLEObject to an object variable—as we did in Listing 28.8—and then run the OLEObject's Activate method on the variable: embeddedArt.Activate.)

> **NOTE**
>
> Don't forget to position the active cell appropriately before inserting the new object. Excel uses the active cell to position the top-left corner of the object.

Inserting an Existing File as an Embedded Object

To embed an OLE object from an existing file, you need to run the Add method with the *fileName* argument and you need to either set the *link* argument to False or omit it altogether. Listing 28.9 shows you how it's done.

Listing 28.9. Using the Add method to embed an existing file in a worksheet.

```
Sub EmbedWordDoc()

    Worksheets("Sheet1").OLEObjects.Add _
        fileName:="C:\My Documents\Memo.doc", _
        displayAsIcon:=True, _
        iconFileName:="C:\MSOffice\Winword\Winword.exe", _
        iconIndex:=1, _
        iconLabel:="MEMO.DOC - Double-click to open"

End Sub
```

This procedure embeds a Word for Windows document by specifying the filename in the Add method and by omitting the *link* argument. For good measure, the procedure also displays the object as an icon by setting the *displayAsIcon* argument to True, specifying both an icon file (the Word for Windows executable) and an icon index, and entering a label to appear beneath the icon.

Inserting an Existing File as a Linked Object

If you would rather insert an existing file as linked instead of embedded, you need to set the Add method's *link* argument to True, as shown in Listing 28.10.

Listing 28.10. Using the Add method to insert an existing file as a linked object.

```
Sub InsertPictureAsLinked()

    Application.ScreenUpdating = False
    Worksheets("Sheet1").Activate
    Range("C1").Select
    ActiveWindow.DisplayGridlines = False

    ActiveSheet.OLEObjects.Add _
        fileName:="C:\Windows\Forest.bmp", _
        link:=True

    Application.ScreenUpdating = True

End Sub
```

This procedure inserts a bitmap file into a worksheet as a linked object. The first few statements set up the worksheet: screen updating is turned off, the worksheet is activated, the cell where the upper-left corner of the object will appear is selected, and then the window's gridlines are removed.

Then the Add method is run to insert the file. The *fileName* argument specifies the bitmap file and the *link* argument is set to True to establish the link.

Working with Linked and Embedded Objects

Once you have a linked or embedded object inserted into a worksheet, you can now work with the object using the OLEObject's properties and methods. Among other things, this will enable you to change the object's size and formatting, update the object data, edit the object, and delete it from the worksheet.

Before examining these techniques, though, you need to know how to refer to OLE objects once you've added them to a worksheet. One way is to use the OLEObjects method:

sheet.OLEObjects(*index*)

sheet	The worksheet that contains the OLE object.
index	This argument can be any of the following:

A number representing the OLE object you want to use, where 1 signifies the first object inserted into the worksheet, 2 is the second object inserted, and so on.

The name, as text, of the OLE object you want to use. Excel assigns each object a name of the form "Picture *n*," where *n* means the object was the *n*th item added to the sheet. You can find out the name of any OLE object by clicking on it and looking in the formula bar's Name box.

An array of numbers or names.

> **NOTE**
>
> Try to assign meaningful names to your OLE objects. The problem with the OLEObjects method is that neither form of the *index* argument is particularly enlightening. OLEObjects(3) is just as obscure as OLEObjects("Picture 4"). To remedy this, you can either store the object in a global variable or change the object's Name property (see the next section for details).

CAUTION

Don't confuse regular picture objects (such as those inserted into the worksheet by using the **Insert | Picture** command) with OLE objects. Both have names of the form "Picture *n*," so it's easy to get them mixed up. When in doubt, select the object and look in the formula bar. An OLE object displays information about its class type and, if applicable, its filename.

Some OLE Object Properties

Like most Excel objects, an OLEObject has a number of properties you can take advantage of in your code. Here's a summary of a few of the more commonly used OLEObject properties:

AutoUpdate: This property is True if the object updates automatically when the server data changes. AutoUpdate applies only to linked objects.

Border: Sets the object's border.

Height: Sets or returns the height of the object in points, where there are 72 points in an inch.

Left: Sets or returns the position of the left edge of the object. The distance is measured in points from the left edge of column A.

Name: The name of the object. You can use this property to rename the object and you can then use the new name as the *index* in the OLEObjects method.

Object: Returns the OLE automation object associated with the object. See the section called "Using OLE Automation," later in this chapter.

OLEType: Tells you whether the file is linked (in which case the property returns the constant xlOLELink) or embedded (the property returns the constant xlOLEEmbed).

Shadow: Set this property to True to add a shadow to the object's container. Use False to remove a shadow.

Top: Sets or returns the position of the top edge of the object. The distance is measured in points from the top edge of row 1.

Visible: Set this property to False to hide an object. To unhide the object, set this property to True.

Width: Sets or returns the height of the object in points.

Listing 28.11 shows a procedure that tries out several of these properties.

Listing 28.11. A procedure that uses several OLEObject properties.

```
Sub OLEObjectProperties()

    Dim wordObject As Object

    Worksheets("Sheet1").Activate
    Range("B1").Value = _
        "Double-click to edit text:"
    Range("B2").Select

    Set wordObject = ActiveSheet.OLEObjects.Add _
        (fileName:="C:\My Documents\Memo.doc")

    With wordObject
        .Height = 175
        .Width = 350
        .Border.Weight = xlMedium
        .Name = "Annotation"
        .Shadow = True
    End With

End Sub
```

The OLEObjectProperties procedure inserts a Word document and then sets some properties for the new object. The procedure begins by declaring an Object variable named wordObject to store the new object. The worksheet is set up for the insertion and then the Add method inserts the Memo.doc file (and assigns it to the wordObject variable at the same time).

The With statement uses the wordObject variable to set some properties of the new object, including the Height, Width, Border, Name, and Shadow.

Some OLE Object Methods

OLE objects also come equipped with several methods you can use to manipulate the objects once you've inserted them. Many of these methods (such as Copy, Cut, Delete, and Select) are straightforward. However, two—Update and Verb—have special significance for OLE objects. I'll take a look at both of these methods in the next couple of sections.

The *Update* Method

If you inserted the OLE data as a linked object, the link between the object and the server file is usually automatic. This means that anytime the server file changes, the client object is updated automatically. There are two circumstances in which updating is *not* automatic:

■ If you've changed the link to manual. (You can do this by selecting the **Edit | Links** command, highlighting the source file in the Links dialog box, and then selecting the **Manual** update option.)

■ If you closed and then reopened the client document and selected **No** when Excel asked if you wanted to reestablish the links.

In these situations, you need to update the object using the Update method. Listing 28.12 provides an example.

Listing 28.12. Using the Update method to update an OLE object.

```
Sub UpdateAllObjects()
    Dim sheet As Worksheet, obj As Object

    For Each sheet In ActiveWorkbook.Worksheets
        Application.StatusBar = _
            "Now updating objects in " & sheet.Name
        For Each obj In sheet.OLEObjects
            If obj.OLEType = xlOLELink Then obj.Update
        Next obj
    Next sheet

    Application.StatusBar = False
    MsgBox "Link update complete."

End Sub
```

This procedure trudges through each worksheet in the active workbook and updates all the linked objects. The first For...Next loop uses the sheet variable to cycle through the worksheets in the active workbook. The StatusBar property displays the name of each worksheet in the status bar so you can watch the progress of the operation. Another For...Next statement uses the obj variable to loop through every OLE object in the current worksheet. If the object is linked (that is, its OLEType property equals xlOLELink), then it gets updated with the Update method. When both loops are complete, the procedure resets the status bar and displays a completion message.

The *Verb* Method

Each OLE object has one or more *verbs* that specify what actions you can perform on the object. Unlike methods, which tell you what actions can be performed on the object from the point of view of Excel, verbs tell you what actions can be performed on the object *from the point of view of the server* (that is, the application you used to create the object). For example, a typical verb is "edit." Running this verb opens the server application so you can edit the object.

To run a verb, use the Verb method:

object.OLEObjects(*verb*)

object	The OLE object with which you want to work.
verb	A constant or integer that specifies the verb to run.

Here are some notes to keep in mind when dealing with the *Verb* argument:

■ All OLE objects have a *primary* verb, which is the same as the action taken when you double-click on the object. To specify the primary verb, use the constant xlPrimary or the number 1.

■ For most objects, the primary verb lets you edit the object. If you want to edit an object but you're not sure what its primary verb does, use the constant xlOpen.

■ If the object supports a secondary verb, you can specify this verb by using 2 for the *Verb* argument.

■ For embedded objects that support OLE 2.0, the primary verb (xlPrimary) lets you edit the object in place and the secondary verb (xlOpen) lets you open the object in a separate server window.

NOTE

To find out which verbs are available for an object, look up the object in the Registry Editor, as described earlier. The object's supported verbs are shown in the Verb subkey.

Table 28.5 lists the available verbs for some common OLE objects.

Table 28.5. Verbs for common OLE objects.

Object	Primary Verb	Other Verb
Bitmap Image	Edit	Open
Calendar Control	Edit	Properties
Media Clip	Play	Edit
Microsoft ClipArt Gallery	Replace	None
Microsoft Data Map	Open	Edit
Microsoft Equation 2.0	Edit (in-place)	Open
Microsoft Excel Chart	Edit (in-place)	Open
Microsoft Excel Worksheet	Edit (in-place)	Open
Microsoft Graph 5.0	Edit (in-place)	Open
Microsoft Word Document	Edit (in-place)	Open
Microsoft Word Picture	Edit (in-place)	Open
Microsoft WordArt 2.0	Edit (in-place)	Open
MIDI Sequence	Play	Edit
MS Organization Chart 2.0	Edit	None

Object	Primary Verb	Other Verb
Package	Activate Contents	Edit
Video Clip	Play	Edit
Wave Sound	Play	Edit
WordPad Document	Edit (in-place)	Open

Check out Listing 28.13 to see an example of the Verb method.

Listing 28.13. Using the Verb method to edit an OLE object.

```
Sub InsertAndEditWordDoc()
    Dim msgPrompt As String, msgButtons As Integer
    Dim wordDoc As Object, response As Integer

    Set wordDoc = Worksheets("Sheet1").OLEObjects.Add _
        (classType:="Word.Document.6")

    msgPrompt = "Do you want to insert the document in-place?"
    msgButtons = vbYesNoCancel + vbQuestion
    response = MsgBox(msgPrompt, msgButtons)

    Select Case response
        Case vbYes
            WordDoc.Verb xlPrimary
        Case vbNo
            WordDoc.Verb xlOpen
        Case Else
            Exit Sub
    End Select

End Sub
```

This procedure embeds a new Word for Windows document and then gives the user the choice of editing the document in-place or in a separate window. The embedded document is inserted and stored in the wordDoc variable. Then the MsgBox message asks the user how he or she wants to edit the document. If response is vbYes (that is, the user wants to edit in-place), the Verb method is run with the xlPrimary constant. If response is vbNo, the Verb method uses xlOpen. Otherwise, the procedure exits.

Using OLE Automation

The beauty of OLE (especially OLE 2.0) is not only how easy it is to insert objects in a worksheet, but also the access you have to the object's original tools. With a simple double-click or Verb method, you can edit the object with the full power of the server's menus and commands.

But, until recently, the one thing that's been missing is the ability to control the server through programming. Editing or creating an object, whether it's in-place or in a separate window, has meant that you must at least be familiar with the server application. And while *you* might be willing to spend time and effort learning a new program, the users of your VBA applications might not be.

This has all changed with the advent of OLE automation. Applications that support OLE automation "expose" their objects to VBA (and any other applications and development tools that support the OLE automation standard). So just as VBA can recognize and manipulate, say, an Excel worksheet range (a Range object), it can also recognize and manipulate objects from other OLE automation applications. Visio, for example, exposes a number of objects to VBA, including its documents, pages, shapes, and windows. Access 7.0 exposes dozens of objects, including its forms and reports. Also, the Binder application that ships with Office 95 (discussed in Chapter 7) supports OLE automation and exposes its sections as objects.

Each of these objects has its own collection of methods and properties that can be read or altered, just like Excel's methods and properties. For example, you can use OLE automation to create a new Binder object and then use the Sections object's Add method to add a section to the binder.

Although only a few applications now support OLE automation, it is widely believed that this will be *the* standard for application interoperability in the not-too-distant future. Certainly any other applications that use VBA will be OLE-automated (and Microsoft has stated publicly that VBA will soon be a part of all of its major applications), and many other applications will expose their objects (the way Visio and Binder do).

Accessing OLE Automation Objects

How you access an object from an OLE automation application depends on whether or not the object provides an object library file (an OLB file such as XLEN50.OLB that comes with Excel 5.0). Here's a summary:

- If the application does provide an object library, you can refer to the objects directly, just like you do with Excel's objects. Also, some applications (such as Word for Windows) don't have an object library but do allow some of their objects to be accessed directly.

> **NOTE**
>
> To make sure you can refer to an OLE-automated application's objects, you need to set up a reference to the appropriate *object library*. You do this by selecting the **Tools** | References command from any module and then activating the object library's check box in the References dialog box.

Once you've set up the reference, you can see the library's objects by displaying the Object Browser (select the **V**iew | **O**bject Browser command or press F2). Select the library from the **L**ibraries/Workbooks list and the available objects appear in the **Ob**jects/Modules list.

- If the application doesn't provide an object library and you want to access a new object, use the `CreateObject` method.
- If the application doesn't have a library and you want to access an existing object, use the `GetObject` method.

The next few sections discuss each of these techniques in more detail.

Accessing Objects Directly

Accessing objects directly is the easiest way to work with OLE automation. The syntax for doing so is as follows:

Application.ObjectName

Here, *Application* is the name of the application and *ObjectName* is the name of the object. If you're not sure about what to use for the application name, each `OLEObject` has an `Object` property that can supply you with the application name as follows:

MyOLEObject.Object.Application

In this context, *MyOLEObject* is an existing `OLEObject`. For example, suppose you have an embedded Word for Windows document stored in a variable named `wordObject`. To refer to Word's WordBasic object (the only OLE automation object exposed by Word), you would use a statement such as the following:

```
Set wordBasicObj = wordObject.Object.Application.WordBasic
```

This statement sets an `Object` variable named `wordBasicObj` equal to the WordBasic object that can work directly with the Word document. That is, you can use WordBasic macro commands as methods for the WordBasic object. For example, you can insert text in the document by using WordBasic's `Insert` macro command as a method, like so:

```
wordBasicObj.Insert = "This is the text that will be inserted."
```

Listing 28.14 shows an example.

Listing 28.14. Referring to OLE automation objects directly.

```
Sub AutomateWordObject()

    Dim docObject As Object, wordBasicObj As Object

    'Select the upper-left cell
    Worksheets("Sheet1").Activate
    Range("A2").Select

    'Insert the object
    Set docObject = ActiveSheet.OLEObjects.Add _
        (classType:="Word.Document.6")

    'Work with it
    With docObject
        .Activate
        'Access the WordBasic object directly
        Set wordBasicObj = .Object.Application.WordBasic
        wordBasicObj.Insert "I'm an OLE automated object!"
        wordBasicObj.EditSelectAll
        wordBasicObj.Bold
    End With

    Range("A1").Select

End Sub
```

This procedure embeds a new Word for Windows document and then invokes Word's WordBasic object to edit the document. The procedure begins by declaring two Object variables: docObject will hold the embedded document object and wordBasicObj will hold the WordBasic object. Then the procedure selects a sheet and a location for the embedded document.

An Add method inserts the embedded Word document and initializes the docObject variable. Then a With statement works with docObject. The object is first activated (to start in-place editing), then the WordBasic object is opened. The next three lines run the WordBasic commands Insert, EditSelectAll, and Bold. Finally, a worksheet cell is selected to turn off in-place editing.

Creating a New OLE Automation Object

If an OLE automation application provides an object library, you can use the library functions to create new objects. For example, the Access Application object includes a CreateForm method that enables you to create a new form.

If there is no object library for the application, you can use the CreateObject function to create new OLE automation objects:

```
CreateObject(class)
```

> **class**   The *programmatic identifier* that specifies the server application
> and the type of object to create.

The **class** argument always takes the following form:

```
applicationName.objectType
```

For example, the programmatic identifier for WordBasic is `"Word.Basic"`, and for Binder it's
`"Office.Binder"`.

Listing 28.15 provides an example.

Listing 28.15. Using `CreateObject` to create an OLE automation object.

```
Sub CreateBinderObject()

    Dim objBinder As Object

    Set objBinder = CreateObject("Object.Binder")
    objBinder.SaveAs "C:\My Documents\MyBinder.obd"

End Sub
```

This procedure declares an `Object` variable named `objBinder`, uses `CreateObject` to create a
new Binder object, and then uses the Binder object's `SaveAs` method to save the binder.

Accessing an Existing OLE Automation Object

Instead of creating a new object, you might need to work with an existing object. To do that,
use the `GetObject` method:

```
GetObject(pathName Class)
```

> *pathName*   The full pathname of the file with which you want to work.
>
> *class*   The class type of the object.

Listing 28.16 shows an example of the `GetObject` method in action.

Listing 28.16. Using the `GetObject` method to work with an existing file.

```
Sub CreateBinderSections()

    Dim objBinder As Object

    Set objBinder = GetObject( _
        pathName:="C:\My Documents\MyBinder.obd", _
        class:="Object.Binder")
```

continues

Listing 28.16. continued

```
With objBinder
    ' Add the new sections
    .Sections.Add fileName:="C:\My Documents\Memo.doc"
    .Sections.Add fileName:=ThisWorkbook.FullName

    ' Save the binder
    .Save
End With

End Sub
```

The GetObject method assigns the MyBinder.odb file to the objBinder variable. Then a With section uses the Sections object's Add method to add two new sections to the binder: a Word document and the current workbook. Finally, the Binder object's Save method saves the binder.

Summary

This chapter walked you through a number of techniques for working with other applications. The most straightforward of these techniques is the simple Shell function, which starts another application. You can activate any running application by using the AppActivate statement, and you can send keystrokes to a running application by using the SendKeys method.

You also learned about dynamic data exchange (DDE). This protocol lets DDE-enabled applications "talk" to each other and exchange data items. VBA has several DDE functions that let you initialize a DDE channel, execute the server application's commands, send data back and forth, and terminate the link.

Finally, this chapter showed you how to work with object linking and embedding (OLE) and OLE automation. To insert OLE objects in a worksheet, you learned to use the Add method of the OLEObjects collection. Once you've inserted an object, you can use VBA to work with the object. The OLEObjects method returns individual OLE objects, and several properties (such as AutoUpdate, Border, Name, and OLEType) and methods (such as Update and Verb) are available for OLE objects. The chapter finished with a look at OLE automation. This is a standard that lets applications expose their objects to languages such as VBA. Your procedure can then work with these objects by running their methods and reading or setting their properties. For applications with object libraries, you can refer to their objects directly. Otherwise, use the CreateObject and GetObject functions.

Here's a list of related chapters:

- Chapter 7, "Exchanging Data with Other Applications," shows you how to use DDE and OLE to work with other applications directly.

- To access external databases, you can use Microsoft Query. See Chapter 15, "Using Microsoft Query," and Chapter 16, "Creating Advanced Queries," for details.

■ For VBA database-related chores, use Data Access Objects (DAO) to manipulate external databases. I show you how to use DAO in Chapter 26, "Database and Client/ Server Programming."

■ The OnData and SetLinkOnData properties can set up a procedure to run whenever a DDE or OLE link is updated. See Chapter 27, "VBA Procedures That Respond to Events," for details.

Debugging
VBA Procedures

29

It's usually easy to get short `Sub` and `Function` procedures up and running. However, as your code grows larger and more complex, errors inevitably will creep in. Many will be simple syntax problems you can fix easily, but others will be more subtle and harder to find. For the latter—whether the errors are incorrect values being returned or problems in the overall logic of a procedure—you'll need to be able to look "inside" your code to scope out what's wrong. The good news is that VBA provides you with several reasonably sophisticated debugging tools that can remove some of the burden of program problem solving. This chapter looks at these tools and shows you how to use them to help recover from most programming errors.

> **NOTE**
>
> A *bug* is a logical or syntactical error in a computer program. The term descends from the earliest days of room-size computers, when problems occasionally were traced to insects actually getting stuck between vacuum tubes!

A Basic Strategy for Debugging

Debugging, like most computer skills, involves no great secrets. In fact, all debugging is usually a matter of taking a good, hard, dispassionate look at your code. Although there are no set-in-stone techniques for solving programming problems, you can formulate a basic strategy that will get you started.

When a problem occurs, the first thing you need to determine is what kind of error you're dealing with. There are four basic types:

Syntax errors: These errors arise from misspelled or missing keywords and incorrect punctuation. VBA catches most (but not all) of these errors when you enter your statements.

Compile errors: When you try to run a procedure, VBA takes a quick look at the code to make sure things look right. If it sees a problem (such as an `If...Then` statement without a corresponding `End If`), it highlights the statement where the problem has occurred and displays an error message.

Runtime errors: These errors occur during the execution of a procedure. They generally mean that VBA has stumbled on a statement that it can't figure out. It might be a formula attempting to divide by zero or using a property or method with the wrong object.

Logic errors: If your code zigs instead of zags, the cause is usually a flaw in the logic of your procedure. It might be a loop that never ends or a `Select Case` that doesn't select.

After you've determined what species of error has occurred, you need to decide how to deal with it. Syntax errors are flagged right away by VBA, which means that you just have to read the error message and then clean up the offending statement. Unfortunately, not all of VBA's error messages are helpful. For example, one common syntax error is to forget to include a closing quotation mark in a string. When this happens, VBA reports the following unhelpful message:

```
Expected: To or list separator or )
```

Fixing compile errors is also usually straightforward. Read the error message and see where VBA has highlighted the code. Doing so almost always gives you enough information to fix the problem.

Runtime errors produce a dialog box such as the one shown in Figure 29.1. These error messages usually are a little more vague than the ones you see for syntax and compile errors. It often helps to see the statement where the offense has occurred. You can do this by selecting the **G**oto button. This activates the module and places the insertion point on the line where the error has occurred. If you still can't see the problem, you need to rerun the procedure and pause at or near the point in which the error occurs. This enables you to examine the state of the program when it tries to execute the statement. These techniques are explained later in this chapter.

FIGURE 29.1.

A typical runtime error message.

Logic errors are the toughest to pin down because you don't get any error messages to give you clues about what went wrong and where. To help, VBA enables you to trace through a procedure one statement at a time. This enables you to watch the flow of the procedure and to see if the code does what you want it to do. You also can keep an eye on the values of individual variables and properties to make sure they're behaving as expected.

Pausing a Procedure

Pausing a procedure in midstream enables you to see certain elements, such as the current values of variables and properties. It also enables you to execute program code one statement at a time so that you can monitor the flow of a procedure.

When you pause a procedure, VBA enters *break mode* and displays the Debug window, shown in Figure 29.2. The Debug window is divided into two parts:

The Watch Pane   This area enables you to monitor the values of procedure variables, properties, or expressions. See the section "Monitoring Procedure Values."

The Code Pane   This area shows a section of the currently running procedure. The current statement (that is, the one that VBA will execute next) is surrounded by a box. See the section "Stepping into a Procedure."

FIGURE 29.2.

VBA displays the Debug window when you enter break mode.

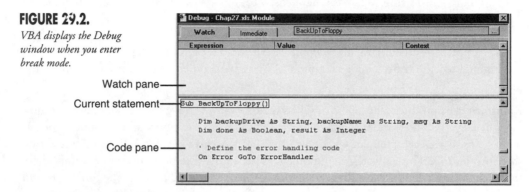

Watch pane

Current statement

Code pane

Entering Break Mode

VBA gives you no less than five ways to enter break mode:

- From a runtime error dialog box
- At the beginning of a procedure
- By pressing Esc or Ctrl-Break while a procedure is running
- By setting *breakpoints*
- By using a Stop statement

Entering Break Mode from an Error Dialog Box

As I mentioned earlier, when a runtime error occurs, you should first try clicking the **G**oto button in the dialog box. This takes you to the statement causing the problem and, in many cases, enables you to fix the error right away.

For more obscure problems, you'll need to enter break mode and take a look around. You can do this by selecting the **D**ebug button from the error message dialog box.

Entering Break Mode at the Beginning of a Procedure

If you're not sure where to look for the cause of an error, you can start the procedure in break mode. Place the insertion point inside the procedure and select the **R**un | Step **I**nto command or click the Step Into button on the Visual Basic toolbar. VBA displays the Debug window and highlights the Sub statement.

The Step Into button.

Entering Break Mode by Pressing the Esc Key

If your procedure isn't producing an error but appears to be behaving strangely, you can enter break mode by pressing Esc (or Ctrl-Break) or by clicking the Step Macro button on the Visual Basic toolbar while the procedure is running. VBA pauses on whatever statement it was about to execute.

 The Step Macro button.

Setting a Breakpoint

If you know approximately where an error or logic flaw is occurring, you can enter break mode at a specific statement in the procedure by setting up a *breakpoint*. The following procedure shows you what to do:

1. Activate the module containing the procedure you want to run.
2. Place the insertion point on the statement where you want to enter break mode. VBA will run every line of code up to, but not including, this statement.
3. Select the **R**un | Toggle **B**reakpoint command or click the Toggle Breakpoint button on the Visual Basic toolbar. VBA highlights the entire line in red, as shown in Figure 29.3.

    The Toggle Breakpoint button.

4. Repeat steps 2 and 3 to set other breakpoints.

FIGURE 29.3.

When you set a breakpoint, VBA highlights the entire line in red.

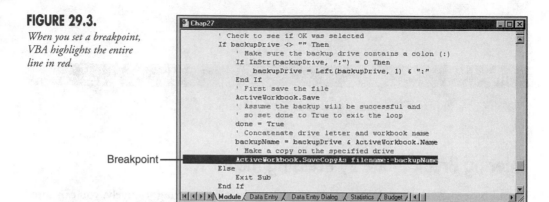

Breakpoint

NOTE

To remove a breakpoint, place the insertion point on the same line and select the **R**un | Toggle **B**reakpoint command, or click the Toggle Breakpoint button, or press F9. To remove all the breakpoints, select the **R**un | **C**lear All Breakpoints command.

Entering Break Mode Using a *Stop* Statement

When developing your applications, you'll often test the robustness of a procedure by sending it various test values or by trying it out under different conditions. In many cases, you'll want to enter break mode to make sure things look okay. You could set breakpoints at specific statements, but you lose them if you close the file. For something a little more permanent, you can include a Stop statement in a procedure. VBA automatically enters break mode whenever it encounters a Stop statement.

Figure 29.4 shows the BackUpToFloppy procedure with a Stop statement inserted just before the statement that runs the SaveCopyAs method.

FIGURE 29.4.

You can insert Stop statements to enter break mode at specific procedure locations.

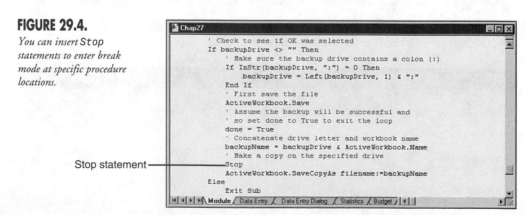

Stop statement

Exiting Break Mode

To exit break mode, you can use either of the following methods:

■ Resume normal program execution by selecting the **R**un | Co**n**tinue command, by clicking the Resume Macro button on the Visual Basic toolbar, or by pressing F5.

 The Resume Macro button.

■ End the procedure by selecting the **R**un | **E**nd command or by clicking the Visual Basic toolbar's Stop Macro button.

The Stop Macro button.

Stepping Through a Procedure

One of the most common (and most useful) debugging techniques is to step through the code one statement at a time. This enables you to get a feel for the program flow to make sure that things such as loops and procedure calls are executing properly. You can either step *into* procedures or step *over* them.

Stepping into a Procedure

Stepping into a procedure means you execute one line at a time. To step into a procedure, first enter break mode as described earlier in this chapter. The Debug window appears, and VBA places a box around the current statement. Now select the **R**un | Step **I**nto command or click the Step Into button on the Visual Basic toolbar. VBA executes the current statement and displays the box around the next statement. Keep stepping through until the procedure ends or until you're ready to resume normal execution.

 The Step Into button.

> **TIP**
>
> You can also step into a procedure by pressing F8.

Stepping over a Procedure

Some statements call other procedures. If you're not interested in stepping through a called procedure, you can step *over* it. This means that VBA executes the procedure normally and then resumes break mode at the next statement *after* the procedure call. Here's how you step over a procedure:

1. Enter break mode as described earlier in this chapter. The Debug window appears, and VBA displays a box around the current statement.

2. Step into the procedure until you come to a procedure call you want to step over.

3. Select the **R**un | Step **O**ver command or click the Visual Basic toolbar's Step Over button. VBA executes the procedure and then places the box around the next statement.

 The Step Over button.

> **TIP**
>
> You also can step over a procedure by pressing Shift-F8.

4. Repeat steps 2 and 3 until the procedure ends or until you're ready to resume normal execution.

> **TIP**
>
> I'm always accidentally stepping into procedures I'd rather step over. If the procedure is short, I just step through it until I'm back in the original procedure. If it's long, however, I don't want to waste time going through every line. Instead, I set a breakpoint at the End Sub (or End Function) statement and then resume normal execution. The procedure reenters break mode at the end of the procedure, and I continue stepping from there.

Monitoring Procedure Values

Many runtime and logic errors are the result of (or, in some cases, can result in) variables or properties assuming unexpected values. If your procedure uses or changes these elements in several places, you'll need to enter break mode and monitor the values of these elements to see where things go awry. VBA enables you to set up *watch expressions* to do just that. These watch expressions appear in the Watch pane of the Debug window.

Adding a Watch Expression

To add a watch expression, you use the Add Watch dialog box, shown in Figure 29.5. This dialog box contains the following elements:

Expression   The watch expression. You can enter a variable name, property, user-defined function name, or any other valid VBA expression.

Context   Specifies the context of the variable (that is, where the variable is used). You enter the **P**rocedure and the **M**odule.

Watch Type   Specifies how VBA watches the expression. The **W**atch Expression option displays the expression in the Watch pane when you enter break mode. Break When Value is **T**rue tells VBA to automatically enter break mode when the expression value becomes True (or nonzero). Break When Value **C**hanges automatically enters break mode whenever the value of the expression changes.

FIGURE 29.5.

Use the Add Watch dialog box to add watch expressions.

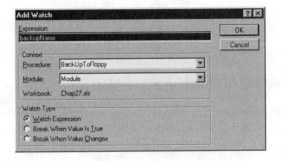

Follow these steps to add a watch expression:

1. If the expression exists inside the procedure (for example, a variable name), select the expression as follows:

   For single-word expressions, place the insert point anywhere inside the word.

   For more complex expressions, highlight the entire expression.

2. Select the **T**ools | **A**dd Watch command to display the Add Watch dialog box.

3. If necessary, enter the expression you want to watch in the **E**xpression text box and select the Context options.

4. Select a Watch Type option.

5. Select OK.

Once you've added a watch expression, you monitor it by entering break mode and selecting the Watch tab in the Debug window. Figure 29.6 shows an example of this.

TIP

The **T**ools | **A**dd Watch command is available when the Debug window is active. Therefore, you can add watch expressions while in break mode.

FIGURE 29.6.

The Debug window with a watch expression.

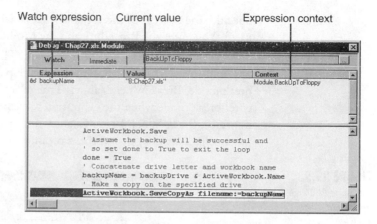

Editing a Watch Expression

You can make changes to a watch expression while in break mode. The following procedure takes you through the necessary steps:

1. Select the Watch pane by clicking it or by pressing Ctrl-F6.
2. Highlight the watch expression you want to edit.
3. Select the **T**ools | **E**dit Watch command. VBA displays the Edit Watch dialog box.

> **TIP**
>
> You also can display the Edit Watch dialog box by double-clicking the watch expression.

4. Make your changes to the watch expression.
5. Select OK to return to the Debug window.

Deleting a Watch Expression

To delete a watch expression you no longer need to monitor, follow these steps:

1. Select the Watch pane by clicking it or by pressing Ctrl-F6.
2. Highlight the watch expression you want to delete.
3. Select the **T**ools | **E**dit Watch command. VBA displays the Edit Watch dialog box.
4. Select the **D**elete button. VBA deletes the expression and returns you to the Debug window.

Displaying an Instant Watch

Many variables and properties are set once, and they don't change for the rest of the procedure. To avoid cluttering the Watch pane with these expressions, you can use an Instant Watch to quickly check the expressions' values. The following procedure shows you how it's done:

1. In the Debug window's Code pane, place the insertion point inside the expression you want to display.

2. Select the **T**ools | Instant **W**atch command or click the Instant Watch button on the Visual Basic toolbar. VBA displays the Instant Watch dialog box, shown in Figure 29.7.

   The Instant Watch button.

FIGURE 29.7.

Use the Instant Watch dialog box to quickly display the value of an expression.

3. If you want to add an expression to the Watch pane, select the **A**dd button. To return to the Debug window without adding the expression, select Cancel.

Using the Immediate Pane

The Watch pane tells you the current value of an expression, but you'll often need more information than this. You also might want to plug in different values for an expression while in break mode. You can perform these tasks with the Debug window's Immediate pane (which you can display by selecting the Immediate tab in the Debug window).

Printing Data in the Immediate Pane

Using the special Debug object, you can use its Print method to print text and expression values in the Immediate pane. There are two ways to do this:

- By running the Print method from the procedure
- By entering the Print method directly into the Immediate pane

The Print method uses the following syntax:

```
Debug.Print outputList
```

> outputList   An expression or list of expressions to print in the Immediate pane. Separate multiple expressions with semicolons. If you omit outputList, a blank line is printed.

Running the *Print* Method from a Procedure

If you know that a variable or expression changes at a certain place in your code, enter a Debug.Print statement at that spot. When you enter break mode, the outputList expressions appear in the Immediate pane. For example, Figure 29.8 shows a procedure in break mode. The information displayed in the Immediate pane was generated by the following statement:

```
Debug.Print "The backup filename is "; backupName
```

FIGURE 29.8.

Use Debug.Print in your code to display information in the Immediate pane.

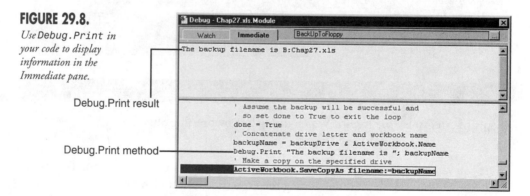

Running the *Print* Method in the Immediate Pane

You can also use the Print method directly in the Immediate pane to display information. Because you're already in the Debug window, you don't need to specify the Debug object.

Figure 29.9 shows a couple of examples. In the first line, I typed Print backupDrive and pressed Enter. VBA responded with B:. In the second example, I typed ? backupName (? is the short form for the Print method), and VBA responded with B:Chap27.xls.

FIGURE 29.9.

You can enter Print *statements directly in the Immediate pane. Note the use of the question mark (?) as a short form for the* Print *method.*

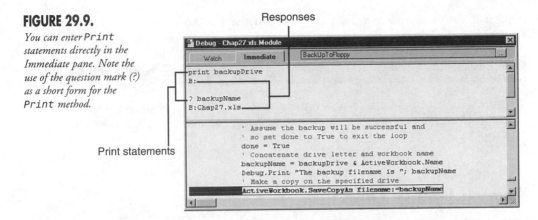

Executing Statements in the Immediate Pane

Perhaps the most effective use of the Immediate pane, however, is to execute statements. There are many uses for this feature:

- To try some experimental statements to see their effect on the procedure.
- To change the value of a variable or property. For example, if you see that a variable with a value of zero is about to be used as a divisor, you could change the variable to a nonzero value to avoid crashing the procedure.
- To run other procedures or user-defined functions to see if they operate properly under the current conditions.

You enter statements in the Immediate pane just as you do in the module itself. For example, entering the following statement in the Immediate pane changes the value of the backupName variable:

```
backupName = "A:Chap27.xls"
```

Debugging Tips

Debugging your procedures can be a frustrating job—even during the best of times. Here are a few tips to keep in mind when tracking down programming problems.

Indent Your Code for Readability

VBA code is immeasurably more readable when you indent your control structures. Readable code is that much easier to trace and decipher, so your debugging efforts have one less hurdle to negotiate. Indenting code is a simple matter of pressing Tab an appropriate number of times at the beginning of a statement.

It helps if VBA's automatic indentation feature is enabled. To check this, select the **Tools |
O**ptions command, select the Module General tab, and activate the **A**uto Indent check box.

> **NOTE**
>
> By default, VBA moves the insertion point four spaces to the right when you press the
> Tab key. You can change the default by entering a new value in the **T**ab Width spinner
> in the Module General tab of the Options dialog box.

Turn on Syntax Checking

VBA's automatic syntax checking is a real time-saver. To make sure this option is turned on,
activate the **D**isplay Syntax Errors check box in the Module General tab of the Options dialog
box.

Require Variable Declarations

To avoid errors caused by using variables improperly, you should always declare your procedure variables. To make VBA display an error if you don't declare a variable, add the following
statement to the top of the module:

```
Option Explicit
```

> **TIP**
>
> To have VBA include the `Option Explicit` statement in every new module, activate
> the **R**equire Variable Declarations check box in the Module General tab of the Options
> dialog box.

Break Down Complex Procedures

Don't try to solve all your problems at once. If you have a large procedure that isn't working
right, test it in small chunks to try and narrow down the problem. To test a piece of a procedure, add an `Exit Sub` statement after the last line of the code you want to test.

Enter VBA Keywords in Lowercase

If you always enter keywords in lowercase letters, you can easily detect a problem when you see
that VBA doesn't change the word to its normal case when you enter the line.

When a Procedure Refuses to Run

If your procedure refuses to run, check the following:

- Make sure the workbook containing the module is open.
- If you're trying to run the procedure by pressing a shortcut key, make sure the shortcut key has been defined.
- Check to see whether another procedure has the same shortcut key. If one does and it appears earlier in the Macro dialog box list, your procedure won't run. You'll need to change the shortcut key for one of the procedures.
- Make sure that another open module doesn't have a procedure with the same name.

Comment Out Problem Statements

If a particular statement is giving you problems, you can temporarily deactivate it by placing an apostrophe at the beginning of the line. This tells VBA to treat the line as a comment.

Break Up Long Statements

One of the most complicated aspects of procedure debugging is making sense out of long statements (especially formulas). The Immediate pane can help (you can use it to print parts of the statement), but it's usually best to keep your statements as short as you can. Once you get things working properly, you often can recombine statements for more efficient code.

Use Range Names Whenever Possible

Procedures are much easier to read and debug if you use range names in place of cell references. Not only is a name such as Expenses!Summary more comprehensible than Expenses!A1:F10, but it's also safer. If you add rows or columns to the Summary range, the name's reference changes as well. With cell addresses, you have to adjust the references yourself.

Take Advantage of User-Defined Constants

If your procedure uses constant values in several different statements, you can give yourself one less debugging chore by creating a user-defined constant for the value. (See Chapter 21, "Getting Started with VBA.") This gives you three important advantages:

- It ensures that you don't enter the wrong value in a statement.
- It's easier to change the value because you have to change only the constant declaration.
- Your procedures will be easier to understand.

Summary

This chapter showed you how to use VBA's debugging facilities to weed out errors in your code. You learned a basic debugging strategy, how to pause and step through a procedure, and how to use breakpoints, watch expressions, and the Immediate pane. Here are some places to go for related information:

■ The best way to stamp out bugs in your VBA code is to become familiar with the basic building blocks of VBA programming. These basics were covered in Chapter 21, "Getting Started with VBA," Chapter 22, "Understanding Objects," and Chapter 23, "Controlling VBA Code and Interacting with the User."

■ To help avoid errors caused by your users, you should set up your application's interface to minimize the possibility of improper data entry and to make it as easy as possible for users to work with the program. Creating a custom user interface is the subject of Chapter 25, "Creating a Custom User Interface."

■ If an error *does* occur in your application, you should trap it and present the user with an explanation of what went wrong. To learn how to do this using the On Error Goto statement, see Chapter 27, "VBA Procedures That Respond to Events."

Check Book:
A Sample Application

30

If you've ever wondered where all your money goes, this chapter's for you. Here we'll look at a checkbook application—called Check Book—that enables you to record all the financial activity from a bank account on a worksheet. You can use Check Book to record checks, deposits, withdrawals, ATM (automated teller machine) transactions, bank charges, and more. You can categorize each transaction so that you can see how much you're spending on clothing, groceries, and entertainment. The application even keeps a running balance for the account so that you know how much money you have before you write a check.

Using Check Book

You'll find the Check Book application in the file Checkbk.xls on this book's CD. When you open this workbook, you'll see the Register worksheet (Figure 30.1 shows the worksheet with a few transactions already filled in). This worksheet is similar to the paper check register you're familiar with, and it's where you enter the information for each transaction. You have the following fields:

Rec: The record number of the transaction. If you use the custom dialog boxes, this field is incremented automatically.

FIGURE 30.1.

The Check Book worksheet.

Rec	Date	Chk Num	Payee/Description	Category	Debit	Credit	✓	Balance
1	8/23/95		Starting balance			5,000.00	✓	5,000.00
2	8/24/95	1	Bell	Phone - L. Dist	(87.25)		✓	4,912.75
3	8/25/95	2	Accountant	L&P Fees	(750.00)		✓	4,162.75
4	8/26/95		Birthday presents	Gifts	(250.00)		✓	3,912.75
5	9/1/95		Paycheck	Salary		1,237.45	✓	5,150.20
6	9/1/95	3	Eaton's	Clothing	(149.37)		✓	5,000.83
7	9/5/95		Food City	Groceries	(187.50)		✓	4,813.33
8	9/12/95		Texaco	Auto - Fuel	(25.00)		✓	4,788.33
9	9/14/95	4	Hockey tickets	Entertainment	(90.00)		✓	4,698.33
10	9/15/95		Paycheck	Salary		1,237.45	✓	5,935.78
11	9/21/95		Win95 Plus Pack	Comp Software	(50.00)		✓	5,885.78
12	9/25/95		Furnace repair	Repairs	(350.00)		✓	5,535.78
13	9/25/95		Last National Bank	Bank Charge	(12.50)		✓	5,523.28
14	9/25/95		Last National Bank	Interest		22.87	✓	5,546.15
15	9/27/95	5	VISA	Clothing	(237.89)			5,308.26
16	9/29/95		Paycheck	Salary		1,237.45		6,545.71

Register / Account Info / Transaction Summary / Tran

Date: The date of the transaction.

Chk Num: The check number (if the transaction is a check).

Payee/Description: If the transaction is a check, use this field to enter the name of the payee. For deposits or withdrawals, enter a short description.

Category: The application comes with more than 50 predefined income and expense categories that cover interest income, salary, clothing, utilities, and more. The dialog boxes list all the categories in drop-down list boxes; therefore, you can easily select the category you want from the list.

Debit: Cash outflows are placed in this column. Although the numbers are formatted to appear in a red font with parentheses around them, they are *not* negative numbers.

Credit: Cash inflows are placed in this column.

✓: The ✓ column is used to indicate transactions that have cleared the bank (that is, transactions that appear on your bank statement). Normally this is done by the Reconciliation feature, but you can enter a check mark by pressing Ctrl-Shift-K or Alt-0252. (You must use the keyboard's numeric keypad to enter the numbers.)

Balance: The running balance in the account. With the exception of cell I2, which contains the formula =G2-F2, the cells in this column contain the following formula:

```
=Balance
```

This is a named formula that computes the balance at the time of the highlighted transaction. This is a relative reference formula, so its definition changes with each cell. For example, here is the formula when cell I3 is selected:

```
=I2 + G3 - F3
```

This translates as follows: take the previous Balance amount, add the current Credit amount, and subtract the current Debit amount.

Entering Account Information

When you first open Check Book, you need to tell the application some basic information about the bank account, such as the name of the bank and the account number. This information, which appears in the transaction dialog boxes, can be handy if you're using the application for more than one account. You also can add or delete categories for the account.

Entering Basic Account Data

The next procedure shows you how to enter basic account data:

1. Select the **Tools | Check Book | Account** Information command or click the Account Information button on the Check Book toolbar. The Account Information dialog box appears, as shown in Figure 30.2.

     The Account Information button on the Check Book toolbar.

2. In the **Bank** text box, enter the name of the bank for this account.

3. In the Account **Number** text box, enter the account number.

4. In the Account **Type** text box, enter the type of account (for example, Checking or Savings).

5. Select OK.

FIGURE 30.2.

Use the Account Informa-tion dialog box to enter basic information about your account.

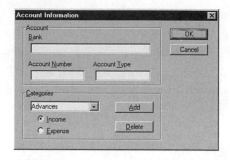

Adding Check Book Categories

As mentioned earlier, the Check Book application comes with dozens of predefined categories for your transactions. However, this list is by no means exhaustive—you might like to add some categories. The following procedure tells you how to do so:

1. Display the Account Information dialog box, as described earlier.

2. Select a type for the new category (**I**ncome or **E**xpense).

3. In the **C**ategories combo box, enter a name for the category. You can enter up to 255 characters, but only about 15 or so will appear in the Register worksheet's Category column.

4. Select the **A**dd button. Check Book adds the new category and displays a message.

5. Select OK to return to the Account Information dialog box.

6. To add other categories, repeat steps 2 through 5.

7. When you're done, select OK.

Deleting Check Book Categories

To keep the category list manageable, you can delete categories you'll never use by following these steps:

1. Display the Account Information dialog box, as described earlier.

2. In the **C**ategories group, activate the type of category you want to delete (**I**ncome or **E**xpense).

3. Select the category in the **C**ategories drop-down list.

4. Select the Delete button. Check Book asks whether you're sure you want to delete the category.

5. Select **Y**es to proceed with the deletion.

6. Repeat steps 2 through 5 to delete other categories.

7. When you've finished deleting, select OK.

Entering a Starting Balance

Before processing any transactions, you should enter a starting balance in the first row of the register. You can enter either the current balance in the account or the balance on your last bank statement. If you choose the latter, you'll also have to enter any subsequent transactions that transpired since the date of the last statement. You need to enter two things:

1. In row 2, enter the appropriate date in the Date field. If you're using the balance from your last statement, enter the statement date.

2. If the account has a positive balance, enter the amount in the Credit field. Otherwise, enter it in the Debit field (remember to enter the debit balance as a positive number). The Balance field automatically lists the new balance.

Recording Checks

If you can write checks on your account, follow the steps in the following procedure to record checks in the Check Book register:

1. Select the **T**ools | Check **B**ook | Record **C**heck command or click the Record Check button on the Check Book toolbar. Check Book displays the Check dialog box, shown in Figure 30.3.

 The Record Check button on the Check Book toolbar.

FIGURE 30.3.

Use the Check dialog box to record a check transaction.

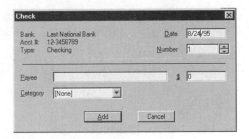

2. Enter the check date in the **D**ate text box. You can use any Excel data format, but the Date field is formatted as *mm/dd/yy.*

3. Enter the check number in the **N**umber spinner.

4. Use the **P**ayee text box to enter the name of the person or company to whom the check is payable.

5. In the **$** text box, enter the check amount.

6. Select a category from the **C**ategory drop-down list. If you don't want to use a category for this transaction, select [None].

7. Select the **A**dd button. Check Book records the check and displays a fresh Check dialog box.

8. Repeat steps 2 through 7 to record other checks.

9. Select Close to return to the register.

Recording Withdrawals

When you withdraw money from the account, follow these steps to record the withdrawal:

1. Select the **T**ools | Check **B**ook | Record **W**ithdrawal command or click the Record Withdrawal button on the Check Book toolbar. The Withdrawal Slip dialog box appears, as shown in Figure 30.4.

 The Record Withdrawal button on the Check Book toolbar.

FIGURE 30.4.

Use the Withdrawal Slip dialog box to record withdrawals from your account.

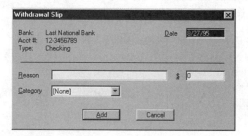

2. Enter the withdrawal date in the **D**ate text box.

3. Enter a reason for the withdrawal in the **R**eason text box.

4. In the **$** text box, enter the amount of the withdrawal.

5. Select a category from the **C**ategory drop-down list (or select [None] to enter no category).

6. Select the **A**dd button. Check Book records the withdrawal and displays a fresh Withdrawal Slip dialog box.

7. Repeat steps 2 through 6 to record other withdrawals.

8. Select Close to return to the register.

Recording Deposits

The following procedure shows you how to record deposits to your account:

1. Select the **T**ools | Check **B**ook | Record **D**eposit command or click the Record Deposit button on the Check Book toolbar. Check Book displays the Deposit Slip dialog box, shown in Figure 30.5.

The Record Deposit button on the Check Book toolbar.

FIGURE 30.5.

Use the Deposit Slip dialog box to record deposits to the account.

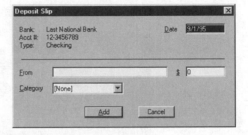

2. Enter the date of the deposit in the **D**ate text box.

3. In the **F**rom text box, enter the source of the deposit.

4. Enter the deposit amount in the **$** text box.

5. Select a category from the **C**ategory drop-down list (or select [None] to enter no category).

6. Select the **A**dd button. Check Book records the deposit and displays a fresh Deposit Slip dialog box.

7. To record other deposits, repeat steps 2 through 6.

8. Select Close to return to the register.

Balancing the Check Book

The Check Book application includes a Reconciliation feature that enables you to balance the account by reconciling the Check Book register with your bank statement. You supply the application with the date and balance of your last statement and the date and balance of your current statement. Check Book then extracts the transactions you entered between those dates (and any older, uncleared transactions) and you check them off (one by one) with your statement.

Figure 30.6 shows the screen you'll be using. The area on the left shows the statement data. The Difference field is the value to watch. The area on the right displays the uncleared transactions that have occurred before or on the current statement date. You use the ✓ field to check off these transactions with the corresponding items on the new statement. If all goes well, the two transaction lists will be identical and the Difference field will show 0.00. You've balanced the account!

If the Difference field is not zero, you need to look for the discrepancy. You might have missed a transaction or you might have entered the wrong amount. If you find the problem, cancel the reconciliation, fix (or add) the transaction, and try again.

FIGURE 30.6.

The Reconciliation screen enables you to compare your transactions with the bank statement.

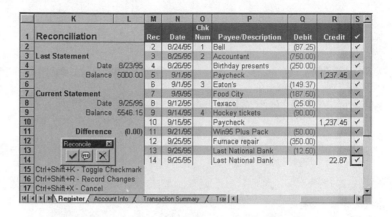

The following procedure takes you through the required steps for completing the reconciliation:

1. With your statement in hand, enter any new bank charges or interest payments that appear in the statement.

2. Select the **T**ools | Check **B**ook | **R**econciliation command or click the Reconciliation button on the Check Book toolbar. The Reconciliation dialog box appears.

    The Reconciliation button on the Check Book toolbar.

3. The Last Bank Statement group displays the information from the last reconciliation. (Or, if this is your first reconciliation, it shows the date and amount of your starting balance.) Edit this data if it's incorrect.

4. In the Current Bank Statement group, use the D**a**te text box to enter the statement date and the Ba**l**ance text box to enter the final balance on the statement.

5. Select OK. The Reconciliation screen appears. (See Figure 30.6.)

6. In the ✓ field, enter check marks for each transaction that appears on the statement. To enter a check mark, press Ctrl-Shift-K or Alt-0252 (make sure you use the keyboard's numeric keypad to enter the numbers) or click the Toggle Check Mark button on the Reconcile toolbar.

    The Toggle Check Mark button on the Reconcile toolbar.

7. If the reconciliation is successful (that is, if the Difference field is 0), press Ctrl-Shift-R or click the Record Reconciliation button on the Reconcile toolbar to record the changes in the register. If you need to cancel the reconciliation and return to the register to make adjustments, press Ctrl-Shift-X or click the Cancel Reconciliation button on the Reconcile toolbar.

The Record Reconciliation button on the Reconcile toolbar.

 The Cancel Reconciliation button on the Reconcile toolbar.

How the Check Book Application Works

Besides the Register worksheet, the Check Book application includes seven other sheets that perform behind-the-scenes duties:

Account Info: This is the sheet where your account information, including the income and expense categories, is stored.

Transaction Reports: This worksheet contains two pivot tables. The Income Report pivot table shows the categories and the sum of the Credit field. The table is sorted in descending order by Sum of Credit so that the income categories appear at the top. The Expense Report pivot table shows the categories and the sum of the Debit field. The table is sorted in descending order by Sum of Debit so that the expense categories appear at the top.

NOTE

To update either pivot table, select a cell inside the table and then select the **Tools |
Refresh Data** command. Both tables were built using the Register range name (which refers to the transactions in the check book register), so a simple refresh will do the job.

Transaction Procedures: This module contains the VBA procedures that support the three Check Book transactions: recording checks, withdrawals, and deposits.

Transaction Dialog: This is a dialog sheet that contains the basic layout of the dialog boxes used for the transactions. Properties such as the dialog box title are modified within the procedures.

Info Procedures: This module contains the VBA procedures behind the Account Information command.

Info Dialog: This dialog sheet defines the layout of the Account Information dialog box.

Reconciliation Procedures: This module contains the VBA procedures used by the Reconciliation feature.

Reconciliation Dialog: This is the dialog sheet for the Reconciliation dialog box.

Understanding the Account Info Worksheet

Figure 30.7 shows the Account Info worksheet. Many of the procedures (which you'll be looking at later) refer to cells or ranges on this sheet, so it's important to understand how the sheet is set up. The worksheet is divided into four areas: Account Data, Reconciliation Data, Income Categories, and Expense Categories.

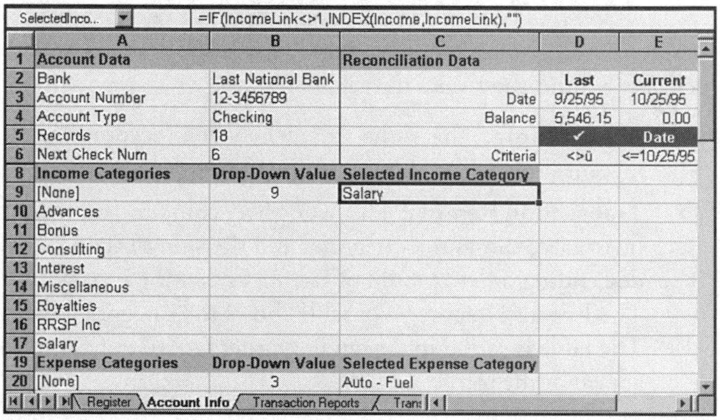

FIGURE 30.7.

The Account Info worksheet.

The Account Data Area

The Account Data area contains the account information and data that applies to the Register worksheet. Here's a summary of the cells, their names, and their descriptions:

Cell	Name	Description
B2	Bank	The name of the bank, as entered into the Account Information dialog box.
B3	AccountNumber	The account number from the Account Information dialog box.
B4	AccountType	The type of account from the Account Information dialog box.
B5	Records	The number of records (transactions) in the Register worksheet. The range of transactions is named Register; therefore, the value in this cell is given by the formula =ROWS(Register-1). (You have to subtract one because the Register range includes the column headings.)
B6	NextCheckNum	The next likely check number you'll be using. This is given by the formula =MAX(Register!C:C)+1. (Column C is the Chk Num column in the Register worksheet.)

The Reconciliation Data Area

This area holds data used by the Reconciliation feature. It contains the following ranges and names:

Range	Name	Description
D3	LastDate	The date of the last bank statement.
D4	LastBalance	The balance on the last statement.
E3	CurrentDate	The date of the current statement.
E4	CurrentBalance	The balance on the current statement.
D5:E6	Criteria	The criteria range used to extract the transactions for the reconciliation. The ✓ field selects the uncleared transactions. (The check mark character is the normal text representation of the ANSI 252 character used to create a check mark.) The Date field selects transactions that were entered on or before the CurrentDate.

The Income Categories Area

This area holds the list of income categories that appear in the Deposit Slip dialog box (or when you select the Income option in the Account Information dialog box). Here's a summary of the defined names in this area:

Range	Name	Description
A9:A17	Income	The range of income categories.
B9	IncomeLink	The linked cell associated with either the Category drop-down list in the Deposit Slip dialog box or the Categories drop-down in the Account Information dialog box when the Income option is selected. The value represents the item number of the list selection (where [None] is 1, Advances is 2, and so on).
C9	SelectedIncome	The category that corresponds to the value in the IncomeLink cell. This value is given by the following formula: `=IF(IncomeLink<>1, INDEX(Income,IncomeLink),"")` If IncomeLink is not 1, use INDEX() to find the category; otherwise, [None] was selected, so display a blank.

The Expense Categories Area

This area holds the list of expense categories that appear in the Check and Withdrawal Slip dialog boxes (or when you select the Expense option in the Account Information dialog box). Here's a summary of the defined names in this area:

Range	Name	Description
A20:A69	Expense	The range of expense categories.
B20	ExpenseLink	The linked cell associated with the Category drop-down list in the Check and Withdrawal Slip dialog boxes or the Categories drop-down in the Account Information dialog box when the Expense option is selected. The value represents the item number of the list selection.
C20	SelectedExpense	The category that corresponds to the value in the ExpenseLink cell. This value is given by the following formula:

```
=IF(ExpenseLink
1,<>1,INDEX
(Expense,
ExpenseLink),"")
```

If `ExpenseLink` is not 1, use `INDEX()` to find the category; otherwise, [None] was selected, so display a blank.

The Transaction Procedures

The Transaction module contains a number of procedures that set up the application, display the transaction dialog boxes, and process the results. The next few sections discuss the procedures related to the transaction dialog boxes.

Recording a Check

When you select the Record Check command, Check Book runs the `RecordCheck` procedure, shown in Listing 30.1. Because the different transactions all use the same basic dialog box layout, most of this procedure (and the similar procedures for recording withdrawals and deposits) is spent modifying the dialog box properties.

Listing 30.1. The `RecordCheck` procedure.

```
Sub RecordCheck()
    Set transDialog = DialogSheets("Transaction Dialog")
    '
    ' Initialize dialog box controls for recording a check
    '
    With transDialog
        .DialogFrame.Caption = "Check"
        .DialogFrame.OnAction = "TransactionDialogShow"
        .Labels("Label 6").Caption = "Payee"
        .Labels("Label 6").Accelerator = "P"
        .Labels("Label 15").Visible = True
        .EditBoxes("Edit Box 16").Visible = True
        .EditBoxes("Edit Box 16").Caption = Range("NextCheckNum")
        .EditBoxes("Edit Box 16").OnAction = "Transaction_EditBox16_Change"
        .Spinners("Spinner 24").Visible = True
        .Spinners("Spinner 24").Value = Range("NextCheckNum")
        .Spinners("Spinner 24").OnAction = "Transaction_Spinner24_Change"
        .DropDowns("Drop Down 14").ListFillRange = "Expenses"
        .DropDowns("Drop Down 14").LinkedCell = "ExpenseLink"
    End With
    '
    ' Display Check dialog box
    '
    transDialog.Show
End Sub
```

The first order of business, however, is to initialize a variable named `transDialog`. This variable is used by most of the procedures in this module, so it was declared with the following statement at the top of the module:

```
Public transDialog As DialogSheet
```

The `Public` keyword makes the variable available to every procedure in the module. In `RecordCheck`, the variable is assigned to the Transaction Dialog dialog sheet.

Then a `With` statement initializes the dialog box properties that apply to the Check dialog box. In particular, note the following:

■ When you set the `OnAction` property of the `DialogFrame`, you're setting up an `OnShow` event handler for the dialog box. This is a procedure that runs automatically whenever you display a dialog box with the `Show` method. In this case, `RecordCheck` defines a procedure named `TransactionDialogShow` as the `OnShow` event handler. (See the section "The `OnShow` Event Handler for the Transaction Dialog Boxes," later in this chapter.)

■ The Withdrawal Slip and Deposit Slip dialog boxes don't use the Number control for entering a check number, so (as you'll see) they hide the label ("Label 15"), text box ("Text box 16"), and spinner ("Spinner 24"). `RecordCheck` sets the `Visible` property for these controls to `True` to make sure they're visible in the Check dialog box.

■ The Number text box ("Text box 16") is initialized to the `NextCheckNum` range from the Account Info worksheet. Also, its `OnAction` property is set to the `Transaction_EditBox16_Change` procedure.

■ The Number spinner ("Spinner 24") is also initialized to the `NextCheckNum` range and its `OnAction` property is set to the `Transaction_Spinner24_Change` procedure. (See the section "The Event Handlers for the Check Dialog Box," later in this chapter.)

■ For the drop-down list ("Drop Down 14"), you change the list of items by changing the `ListFillRange` property (if the list is in a worksheet range). `RecordCheck` sets this property to the `Expenses` range from the Account Info worksheet.

■ The cell linked to the drop-down is governed by the `LinkedCell` property. `RecordCheck` sets this to the Account Info worksheet's `ExpenseLink` cell.

When the dialog box is ready, the `Show` method is run to display it. The next three sections discuss the event handlers associated with this dialog box.

The *OnShow* Event Handler for the Transaction Dialog Boxes

An `OnShow` event handler is useful for statements that initialize common properties in a dialog box. In the Check Book application, each type of transaction has its own specific dialog box properties, but many properties are common to all three. These are set by the `TransactionDialogShow` procedure, shown in Listing 30.2.

Listing 30.2. The `TransactionDialogShow` procedure.

```
Sub TransactionDialogShow()
    '
    ' Initialize dialog box controls
    '
    With transDialog
        .Buttons("Button 2").OnAction = "Transaction_Button2_Click"
        .Buttons("Button 3").Caption = "Cancel"
        .Labels("Label 22").Caption = Range("Bank")
        .Labels("Label 23").Caption = Range("AccountNumber")
        .Labels("Label 26").Caption = Range("AccountType")
        .EditBoxes("Edit Box 7").Caption = ""
        .EditBoxes("Edit Box 9").Caption = Format(Now, "m/d/yy")
        .EditBoxes("Edit Box 12").Caption = 0
        .EditBoxes("Edit Box 12").OnAction = "Transaction_EditBox12_Change"
        .DropDowns("Drop Down 14").Value = 1
        .Focus = .EditBoxes("Edit Box 9").Name
    End With

End Sub
```

As you can see, the entire procedure is spent initializing dialog box properties. Here are some highlights:

- The Add button ("Button 2") has its OnAction property set to the procedure Transaction_Button2_Click. This procedure will then run whenever you select the Add button. (See the section "The Event Handler for Adding a Transaction," later in this chapter.)

- The account information from the Account Info worksheet (Bank, AccountNumber, and AccountType) is assigned to three label captions.

- The Date field ("Text box 9") is initialized to today's date.

- The $ field ("Text box 12") has its OnAction property set to the procedure Transaction_EditBox12_Change. This procedure checks to make sure you enter a number in the $ field.

- The Value property of the drop-down list ("Drop Down 14") is set to 1 (that is, the first item in the list).

- The dialog box Focus property (the *focus* is the currently selected control) is set to the Date field.

The Event Handlers for the Check Dialog Box

The Check dialog box has two event handlers that set up a link between the text box and spinner associated with the Number option. These are shown in Listing 30.3.

Listing 30.3. The event handlers for the Check dialog box.

```
Sub Transaction_Spinner24_Change()
    With transDialog
        .EditBoxes("Edit Box 16").Caption = .Spinners("Spinner 24").Value
    End With
End Sub

' Transaction_EditBox16_Change()
' Event handler for Number edit box in Check dialog box
'
Sub Transaction_EditBox16_Change()
    With transDialog
        .Spinners("Spinner 24").Value = .EditBoxes("Edit Box 16").Caption
    End With
End Sub
```

When you change the value of one control, you want the other to change as well. For example, the Transaction_Spinner24_Change procedure is called whenever you click one of the spinner arrows. The procedure sets the text box caption equal to the new value of the spinner.

Similarly, the Transaction_EditBox16_Change procedure is called whenever you change the value in the text box. The procedure sets the Value property of the spinner equal to the new value in the text box.

The Event Handler for Adding a Transaction

In each transaction dialog box, when you select the Add button, Check Book records the information in the Register and then displays a fresh dialog box for the next transaction. This process is controlled by `Transaction_Button2_Click`—the event handler for the Add button, shown in Listing 30.4.

Listing 30.4. The Add button event handler.

```
Sub Transaction_Button2_Click()
    Dim newTransRow As Integer      ' Row where new transaction will be added
    newTransRow = Range("Register").Row + Range("Register").Rows.Count
    Application.ScreenUpdating = False   ' Turn off screen updating
    '
    ' Change Cancel button caption to "Close"
    '
    transDialog.Buttons("Button 3").Caption = "Close"
    '
    ' Enter transaction in Register
    '
    With transDialog
        Cells(newTransRow, 1).Value = Range("Register").Rows.Count
        Cells(newTransRow, 2).Value = .EditBoxes("Edit Box 9").Caption
        Cells(newTransRow, 4).Value = .EditBoxes("Edit Box 7").Caption
        Cells(newTransRow, 9).Value = "=Balance"
        Select Case .DialogFrame.Caption
            Case "Check"
                Cells(newTransRow, 3).Value = .EditBoxes("Edit Box 16").Caption
                Cells(newTransRow, 5).Value = Range("SelectedExpense")
                Cells(newTransRow, 6).Value = .EditBoxes("Edit Box 12").Caption
            Case "Withdrawal Slip"
                Cells(newTransRow, 5).Value = Range("SelectedExpense")
                Cells(newTransRow, 6).Value = .EditBoxes("Edit Box 12").Caption
            Case "Deposit Slip"
                Cells(newTransRow, 5).Value = Range("SelectedIncome")
                Cells(newTransRow, 7).Value = .EditBoxes("Edit Box 12").Caption
        End Select
    End With
    '
    ' Redefine Register range name
    '
    Names.Add Name:="Register", _
            RefersToR1C1:=Range("Register").Resize(Range("Records") + 2)

    With Range("Register")
        '
        ' Copy transaction formatting
        '
        .Resize(1).Offset(.Rows.Count - 2).Copy
        .Resize(1).Offset(.Rows.Count - 1).PasteSpecial (xlFormats)
        '
        ' Shade odd record numbers
        '
        If Range("Records") Mod 2 = 1 Then
            With .Resize(1).Offset(.Rows.Count - 1)
                .Interior.Pattern = xlSolid
```

```
                    .Interior.ColorIndex = 15
            End With
        Else
            With .Resize(1).Offset(.Rows.Count - 1)
                .Interior.Pattern = xlSolid
                .Interior.ColorIndex = 2
            End With
        End If
    End With
    '
    ' Reset Payee and amount
    '
    With transDialog
        .EditBoxes("Edit Box 7").Caption = ""
        .EditBoxes("Edit Box 12").Caption = 0
        .EditBoxes("Edit Box 16").Caption = Range("NextCheckNum")
        .Spinners("Spinner 24").Value = Range("NextCheckNum")
        .Focus = .EditBoxes("Edit Box 9").Name
    End With

    Cells(newTransRow, 1).Select      ' Select first cell of new transaction
    Application.ScreenUpdating = True ' Turn screen updating back on
End Sub
```

The first two statements declare and initialize a variable named newTransRow. This is the row number in which the new transaction will appear in the Register worksheet. newTransRow is the sum of the Row and Rows.Count properties of the Register range. The next statement changes the caption of the other command button to Close (it appears initially as Cancel). This is standard practice for this kind of dialog box. A Cancel button is supposed to exit a dialog box without doing anything. By clicking Add, you've done something (added a transaction), so you can no longer "cancel" the dialog box; you can only "close" it.

The With statement takes care of adding the dialog box data into the worksheet cells. The various Cells methods return the cells in the new transaction row, and the Value properties of the returned cells are set to the appropriate dialog box properties. Also, the =Balance formula is entered into the Balance field (column 9). To handle the differences between checks, withdrawals, and deposits, a Select Case statement is used:

- For a check, a check number is entered, the Account Info worksheet's SelectedExpense range is used for the Category field, and the amount is entered in the Debit field (column 6).

- For a withdrawal, SelectedExpense is used for the Category, and the amount is entered in the Debit field (column 6).

- For a deposit, SelectedIncome is used for the Category, and the amount is entered into the Credit field (column 7).

When that's done, the Register range name is redefined by using the Name object's Add method. The new range is calculated by using the Resize method to increase the number of rows in the Register range. The number of rows is determined by the following formula:

```
Range("Records") + 2
```

The Records cell, you'll recall, contains the number of transactions in the Check Book register. This number is one less than the number of rows in Register, and because you're adding a row for the new transaction, you have to add 2 to the Records value.

In the next `With` statement, the first two lines copy the transaction above the new transaction and then paste the formatting onto the new transaction cells.

The Register worksheet uses shading on odd-numbered transactions to make them more readable. The next section adds this shading automatically. It first checks to see if the new record number is odd with the following statement:

```
If Range("Records") Mod 2 = 1
```

VBA's `Mod` operator returns the remainder when you divide the number to the left of `Mod` by the number to the right of `Mod`. In this example, the procedure divides the value in the Records range by 2. If the remainder equals 1, the number is odd, so you need to shade the transaction. A combination of the `Resize` and `Offset` methods returns the transaction. Then the `Interior` property is set to a solid pattern (the `xlSolid` constant) and the color is set to gray (15). If the record is not odd, the application colors the transaction cells white (`ColorIndex 2`) instead.

The final `With` statement resets the dialog box controls for the next transaction. The Payee/Reason/From control ("Text box 7") is cleared, the $ text box ("Text box 12") is set to 0, and the Number text box and spinner are set to the new value in the NextCheckNum range. (This value is automatically updated when you add a transaction. See the section "Understanding the Account Info Worksheet," earlier in this chapter.)

Recording a Withdrawal

Recording a withdrawal is handled by the `RecordWithdrawal` procedure. This is almost identical to the `RecordCheck` procedure (discussed earlier). It initializes its specific dialog box properties and then shows the dialog box. Here's a summary of some of the changes it makes:

- The title of the dialog box (the `DialogFrame.Caption` property) is set to "Withdrawal Slip."
- The label that appears as Payee in the Check dialog box is changed to Reason.
- The text box and spinner associated with the Number option are hidden.

Recording a Deposit

As you might expect, the procedure for recording a deposit—`RecordDeposit`—is similar to that for recording a check or a withdrawal. Here are a few of the dialog box properties that get changed in this procedure:

- The title of the dialog box is set to Deposit Slip.
- The label that appears as Payee in the Check dialog box and Reason in the Withdrawal Slip dialog box is set to From.
- The text box and spinner associated with the Number option are hidden.
- The `ListFillRange` property of the drop-down list is set to the `Income` range on the Account Info worksheet. Also the `LinkedCell` property is set to the `IncomeLink` cell.

The Account Information Procedures

The Info Procedures module contains five procedures that display and process the Account Information dialog box. The next few sections look at each of these procedures.

Displaying the Dialog Box

The Account Information command is attached to the `DisplayInfoDialog` procedure, shown in Listing 30.5. The `InfoDialog` variable (which is declared as `Public` at the top of the module) is set to the Info Dialog dialog sheet. Then, a `With` statement initializes the dialog box control properties. Here are some things to note:

- The three text boxes are assigned the account information data from the Account Info worksheet.
- The drop-down list is initialized to contain the items from the `Income` range.
- The Income option ("Option Button 11") is activated (that is, its `Value` property is set to `True`), and its `OnAction` property is set to the `Income_Button_Click` event handler. Also, the Expense option button's `OnAction` property is set to the `Expense_Button_Click` procedure. (Both procedures are discussed in the next section.)
- The `OnAction` properties for the Add and Delete buttons are set to `Add_Button_Click` and `Delete_Button_Click`, respectively. (See the sections "Adding a Category" and "Deleting a Category," later in this chapter.)

Listing 30.5. The `DisplayInfoDialog` procedure.

```
Sub DisplayInfoDialog()
    Set infoDialog = DialogSheets("Info Dialog")
    '
    ' Initialize Account Information dialog box
    '
    With infoDialog
        .EditBoxes("Edit Box 5").Caption = Range("Bank")
        .EditBoxes("Edit Box 7").Caption = Range("AccountNumber")
        .EditBoxes("Edit Box 16").Caption = Range("AccountType")
        .DropDowns("Drop Down 9").ListFillRange = "Income"
        .DropDowns("Drop Down 9").LinkedCell = "IncomeLink"
        .DropDowns("Drop Down 9").Value = 2
```

continues

Listing 30.5. continued

```
        .OptionButtons("Option Button 11").Value = True
        .OptionButtons("Option Button 11").OnAction = "Income_Button_Click"
        .OptionButtons("Option Button 12").OnAction = "Expense_Button_Click"
        .Buttons("Button 13").OnAction = "Add_Button_Click"
        .Buttons("Button 14").OnAction = "Delete_Button_Click"

        If .Show Then
            Range("Bank") = .EditBoxes("Edit Box 5").Caption
            Range("AccountNumber") = .EditBoxes("Edit Box 7").Caption
            Range("AccountType") = .EditBoxes("Edit Box 16").Caption
        End If

    End With
End Sub
```

The Show method displays the dialog box. If you select OK, the three text box captions are entered into the appropriate Account Info worksheet cells.

The Event Handlers for the Option Buttons

The Income_Button_Click and Expense_Button_Click event handlers are shown in Listing 30.6. The Income_Button_Click procedure runs whenever you activate the Income option button. This routine modifies the drop-down list's ListFillRange property to point to the Income range on the Account Info worksheet and the LinkedCell property to point to the IncomeLink cell. The Value is set to 2 to bypass the [None] item.

The Expense_Button_Click procedure is similar to the Income_Button_Click procedure. When you activate the Expenses button, the Expense_Button_Click procedure is executed; this procedure changes the ListFillRange to the Expenses range and the LinkedCell to ExpensesLink.

Listing 30.6. The event handlers for the Income and Expense option buttons.

```
Sub Income_Button_Click()
    With infoDialog.DropDowns("Drop Down 9")
        .ListFillRange = "Income"
        .LinkedCell = "IncomeLink"
        .Value = 2
    End With
End Sub

Sub Expense_Button_Click()
    With infoDialog.DropDowns("Drop Down 9")
        .ListFillRange = "Expenses"
        .LinkedCell = "ExpenseLink"
        .Value = 2
    End With
End Sub
```

Adding a Category

When you select the Add button to add a category, Check Book runs the `Add_Button_Click` procedure, shown in Listing 30.7. The procedure begins by declaring two variables: `newCategory` is the name of the new category, and `rowNum` is the row number in which the new category will be inserted.

The `With` statement adds the new category. The `newCategory` variable is set to the drop-down list's `Caption` property. Then an `If` statement checks to see which type of category you're adding:

■ In an income category (the Income button, "Option Button 11", has the Value 1), `rowNum` is assigned a row within the `Income` range. (The actual location within the `Income` range isn't important, because you'll be sorting the range later.) Then an entire row is inserted at `Cells(rowNum,1)`, `newCategory` is placed in the cell, and the `Income` range is sorted to keep things in alphabetical order.

■ In an expense category, the process is similar. The new row is set within the Expenses range, the new category is inserted, and Expenses is sorted.

The procedure ends by displaying a `MsgBox` function telling the user that the new category has been added.

Listing 30.7. The `Add_Button_Click` event handler.

```
Sub Add_Button_Click()
    Dim newCategory, rowNum As Integer, catType As String
    Application.ScreenUpdating = False

    With infoDialog
        newCategory = .DropDowns("Drop Down 9").Caption
        '
        ' Determine if category is Income or Expense
        '
        If .OptionButtons("Option Button 11").Value = 1 Then
            catType = "Income"
            rowNum = Range("Income").Row + 1
            With Worksheets("Account Info")
                .Cells(rowNum, 1).EntireRow.Insert
                .Cells(rowNum, 1).Value = newCategory
                .Range("Income").Sort Key1:=.Cells(rowNum, 1)
            End With
        Else
            catType = "Expense"
            rowNum = Range("Expenses").Row + 1
            With Worksheets("Account Info")
                .Cells(rowNum, 1).EntireRow.Insert
                .Cells(rowNum, 1).Value = newCategory
                .Range("Expenses").Sort Key1:=.Cells(rowNum, 1)
            End With
        End If
    End With
```

continues

Listing 30.7. continued

```
MsgBox Prompt:="'" & newCategory & "' has been added " & _
       "to the list of " & catType & " categories.", _
       Buttons:=vbOKOnly + vbInformation, _
       Title:="Add Category"
End Sub
```

Deleting a Category

The `Delete_Button_Click` procedure is shown in Listing 30.8. Check Book runs this procedure when you select the Delete button to delete a category.

Listing 30.8. The `Delete_Button_Click` procedure.

```
Sub Delete_Button_Click()
    Dim rowNum As Integer, categoryToDelete, categoryNumber As Integer
    Dim alertMsg As String, alertButtons As Integer, response As Integer
    '
    ' Determine if category is Income or Expense
    '
    With infoDialog
        If .OptionButtons("Option Button 11").Value = 1 Then
            categoryToDelete = Range("SelectedIncome")
            rowNum = Range("Income").Row + .DropDowns("Drop Down 9").Value - 1
        Else
            categoryToDelete = Range("SelectedExpense")
            rowNum = Range("Expenses").Row + .DropDowns("Drop Down 9").Value - 1
        End If
        categoryNumber = .DropDowns("Drop Down 9").Value
    End With
    '
    ' Check for [None] selected
    '
    If categoryToDelete = "" Then
        alertMsg = "Can't delete the [None] category!"
        alertButtons = vbOKOnly + vbExclamation
    Else
        alertMsg = "Are you sure you want to delete the" & _
                   " " & categoryToDelete & " " & "category?"
        alertButtons = vbYesNo + vbQuestion
    End If
    '
    ' Ask for confirmation
    '
    response = MsgBox(Prompt:=alertMsg, _
                    Buttons:=alertButtons, _
                    Title:="Delete Category")
```

```
    If response = vbYes Then
        Worksheets("Account Info").Cells(rowNum, 1).EntireRow.Delete
    ➡        'Delete category
    End If

End Sub
```

The With statement checks to see whether you're deleting an income or expense category:

- In an income category, a variable named categoryToDelete is set to the value in the SelectedIncome range. Then rowNum is set to the row number in the Income range of the category to be deleted.

- In an expense category, categoryToDelete is set to SelectedExpense, and rowNum is set to the appropriate row number within the Expenses range.

The procedure then checks to make sure you don't select the [None] item. The [None] item shouldn't be deleted, because you need it for entering transactions that don't have categories. If [None] is selected, the alertMsg and alertButtons variables are set up to display an appropriate message. Otherwise, these variables are set up to display a confirmation message.

In either case, a MsgBox function displays the constructed message, and the result is stored in the response variable. If you're deleting a legitimate category, the response variable is checked with an If statement. If response equals vbYes, the category's row is deleted.

The Reconciliation Procedures

The Reconciliation Procedures module contains several procedures that support the Check Book's Reconciliation feature. This section takes a look at these procedures.

Displaying the Reconciliation Dialog Box

The DisplayReconciliationDialog procedure, shown in Listing 30.9, displays and processes the Reconciliation dialog box. The reconDialog variable holds the Reconciliation Dialog sheet, and a With statement uses this variable to initialize, show, and process the dialog box. The initialization statements read the appropriate cells from the Account Info worksheet. The If statement runs the Show method and, if you select OK, the procedure records the new data in Account Info. Then the SetUpReconciliation procedure is called to run the reconciliation.

Listing 30.9. The DisplayReconciliationDialog procedure.

```
Sub DisplayReconciliationDialog()
    Set reconDialog = DialogSheets("Reconciliation Dialog")
```

continues

Listing 30.9. continued

```
        'Initialize the dialog box controls and then show it
    With reconDialog
        .EditBoxes("Edit Box 6").Caption = Range("LastDate").Text
        .EditBoxes("Edit Box 8").Caption = Range("LastBalance")
        .EditBoxes("Edit Box 11").Caption = ""
        .EditBoxes("Edit Box 13").Caption = 0

        If .Show Then    'Record new data and set up reconciliation
            Range("LastDate").Value = .EditBoxes("Edit Box 6").Caption
            Range("LastBalance").Value = .EditBoxes("Edit Box 8").Caption
            Range("CurrentDate").Value = .EditBoxes("Edit Box 11").Caption
            Range("CurrentBalance").Value = .EditBoxes("Edit Box 13").Caption
            SetUpReconciliation
        End If
    End With
End Sub
```

Setting Up the Reconciliation Screen

As you'll soon see, Check Book creates the reconciliation transactions by extracting them from the Register (based on the values in the Account Info worksheet's Criteria range). However, Excel doesn't enable you to extract list records to a different worksheet, so the Reconciliation area must reside on the Register worksheet. I've placed the Reconciliation area to the right of the Register range, starting in column K. The problem with this arrangement is that rows might accidentally get deleted if you're performing maintenance within the register.

To guard against this possibility, the SetUpReconciliation procedure reconstructs the entire Reconciliation screen from scratch (see Listing 30.10). The first statement turns off screen updating. Then a With statement adds and formats the labels and data used in the Reconciliation screen. A cell named Reconciliation (cell K1 in the Register worksheet) is the starting point, and the rest of the statements use either Resize or Offset to enter and format the cell values.

Most of the statements are straightforward, but one in particular might create a few furrows in your brow. Toward the end of the With statement, you'll see the following (take a deep breath):

```
With .Offset(10,1).FormulaArray = "=CurrentBalance-LastBalance-
➡SUM(IF(NOT(ISBLANK(Checkmarks)),Credits-Debits,0))"
```

This is the array formula that appears in the Difference cell in the Reconciliation screen (L11). CurrentBalance and LastBalance are the balances from the Account Info sheet. The Checkmarks name refers to the range of cells under the ✓ column in the extracted reconciliation transactions. Similarly, Credits refers to the range of cells under the Credit column, and Debits refers to the cells under the Debit column. The IF() part of the formula translates to the following:

> For each reconciliation transaction, if the ✓ field is not blank (that is, if it contains a check mark), return the difference between the Credit value and the Debit value; otherwise, return 0.

The SUM() function adds up all these values.

Next, SetUpReconciliation sets up the new reconciliation transactions. The With statement—With Range("FirstCheckmark")—uses the cell FirstCheckmark as the starting point (cell T2). The old transactions are cleared by first offsetting the CurrentRegion (the transactions plus the column headings) by one row (to move it off the headings) and by using the Clear method.

The AdvancedFilter method is used to extract the transactions. Notice how the xlFilterCopy constant is used to tell Excel to extract the records to a different location. The new location is governed by the CopyToRange named variable, which in this case is the Extract range (this is the range of column headings in the Reconciliation screen; that is, N1:T1).

The next few statements redefine the Checkmarks, Credits, and Debits names used in the Difference formula, as well as the RecNums name you'll use later on. The size of each range is determined by the number of extracted transactions, and that value is stored in the totalTrans variable (which is declared as Public at the top of the module).

The rest of the procedure hides the Check Book toolbar, displays the Reconcile toolbar, and sets up the shortcut keys for recording or canceling the reconciliation.

Listing 30.10. The SetUpReconciliation procedure.

```
Sub SetUpReconciliation()

    Application.ScreenUpdating = False   'Turn off screen updating

    'Add and format reconciliation labels and data
    With Range("Reconciliation")
        With .Resize(20, 2)
            .Clear
            .Interior.Pattern = xlSolid
            .Interior.ColorIndex = 15
            .BorderAround
        End With
        .Value = "Reconciliation"
        .Font.Bold = True
        .Font.Size = 12
        .Offset(2, 0).Value = "Last Statement"
        .Offset(2, 0).Font.Bold = True
        .Offset(3, 0).Value = "Date"
        .Offset(3, 0).HorizontalAlignment = xlRight
        .Offset(3, 1).Value = Range("LastDate")
        .Offset(3, 1).NumberFormat = "m/d/yy"
        .Offset(4, 0).Value = "Balance"
        .Offset(4, 0).HorizontalAlignment = xlRight
        .Offset(4, 1).Value = Range("LastBalance")
        .Offset(4, 1).NumberFormat = "#,##0.00_);[Red](#,##0.00)"
        .Offset(6, 0).Value = "Current Statement"
        .Offset(6, 0).Font.Bold = True
        .Offset(7, 0).Value = "Date"
        .Offset(7, 0).HorizontalAlignment = xlRight
        .Offset(7, 1).Value = Range("CurrentDate")
        .Offset(7, 1).NumberFormat = "m/d/yy"
```

continues

Listing 30.10. continued

```
        .Offset(8, 0).Value = "Balance"
        .Offset(8, 0).HorizontalAlignment = xlRight
        .Offset(8, 1).Value = Range("CurrentBalance")
        .Offset(8, 1).NumberFormat = "#,##0.00_);[Red](#,##0.00)"
        With .Offset(10, 0)
            .Value = "Difference"
            .HorizontalAlignment = xlRight
            .Font.Bold = True
        End With
        With .Offset(10, 1)
            .FormulaArray = "=CurrentBalance-LastBalance-
            ➥SUM(IF(NOT(ISBLANK(Checkmarks)),Credits-Debits,0))"
            .NumberFormat = "#,##0.00_);[Red](#,##0.00)"
            .Font.Bold = True
        End With
        .Offset(14, 0).Value = "Ctrl+Shift+K - Toggle Checkmark"
        .Offset(15, 0).Value = "Ctrl+Shift+R - Record Changes"
        .Offset(16, 0).Value = "Ctrl+Shift+X - Cancel"
End With

'Display Reconciliation area
Application.Goto Reference:=Range("Reconciliation"), Scroll:=True

'Set up new reconciliation
With Range("FirstCheckmark")
    'Clear the current transactions
    .CurrentRegion.Offset(1, 0).Clear

    'Extract the new ones
    Range("Register").AdvancedFilter _
        Action:=xlFilterCopy, _
        CriteriaRange:=Range("Criteria"), _
        CopyToRange:=Range("Extract")

    'Make sure there are transactions in the reconciliation
    If Range("FirstRec") = "" Then
        MsgBox Prompt:="No transactions to reconcile!", _
                Buttons:=vbOKOnly, _
                Title:="Check Book"
        EndReconciliation
        Exit Sub
    End If

    'Redefine the ranges used by the Difference formula
    totalTrans = .CurrentRegion.Rows.Count - 1
    Names.Add Name:="Checkmarks", RefersToR1C1:=.Resize(totalTrans)
    Names.Add Name:="Credits", RefersToR1C1:=.Offset(0, -1).Resize(totalTrans)
    Names.Add Name:="Debits", RefersToR1C1:=.Offset(0, -2).Resize(totalTrans)
    Names.Add Name:="RecNums", RefersToR1C1:=.Offset(0, -6).Resize(totalTrans)
    .Select
End With

'Set up toolbars
Toolbars("Check Book").Visible = False
With Toolbars("Reconcile")
    .Visible = True
    .Position = xlFloating
```

```
        .Left = 73
        .Top = 223
    End With

    'Set up shortcut keys for recording and canceling
    Application.OnKey Key:="^+r", Procedure:="RecordReconciliation"
    Application.OnKey Key:="^+x", Procedure:="EndReconciliation"
End Sub
```

Recording the Reconciliation

When you record the reconciliation, the RecordReconciliation procedure, shown in Listing 30.11, is executed. The job of the For Each...Next loop is to copy the contents of the Reconciliation screen's ✓ field into the corresponding field in the Register range. The RecNums name refers to the range of cells below the Rec column. Each loop through these cells (each cell is named recCell) does three things:

1. The contents of the ✓ field (offset from recCell by six columns) are stored in checkCell.

2. The MATCH() worksheet function looks for the record number (the Value of recCell) in column A (the Rec column of the Register). The result is the row number of the transaction, which is stored in registerRow.

3. checkCell is stored in the ✓ field of the Register range. (The CheckField name refers to the column heading of the field.)

The next four statements record the statement data in the Account Info worksheet: CurrentDate is moved to LastDate and cleared, and CurrentBalance is moved to LastBalance and set to 0. The final statement calls the EndReconciliation procedure (discussed in the next section).

Listing 30.11. The procedure for recording the reconciliation.

```
Sub RecordReconciliation()
    Dim registerRow As Integer, recCell As Range, checkCell As Variant

    'Record check marks
    For Each recCell In Range("RecNums")
        checkCell = recCell.Offset(0, 6).Value
        registerRow = Application.Match(recCell.Value, [a1].EntireColumn, 0)
        Cells(registerRow, Range("CheckField").Column).Value = checkCell
    Next recCell

    'Record statement data
    Range("LastDate").Value = Range("CurrentDate")
    Range("CurrentDate") = ""
    Range("LastBalance").Value = Range("CurrentBalance")
    Range("CurrentBalance") = 0

    EndReconciliation          'End it all
End Sub
```

Ending the Reconciliation

The EndReconciliation procedure, shown in Listing 30.12, performs several tasks that reset the Register worksheet: the Check Book toolbar is displayed, the Reconcile toolbar is hidden, the first cell of the Register range is selected, and the Ctrl-Shift-R and Ctrl-Shift-K shortcut keys are reset.

Listing 30.12. The procedure for ending the reconciliation.

```
Sub EndReconciliation()
    Toolbars("Reconcile").Visible = False        'Hide Reconcile toolbar
    Toolbars("Check Book").Visible = True         'Display Check Book toolbar
    Cells(Range("Register").Row + 1, 1).Select    'Select first cell
    Application.OnKey Key:="^+r"                   'Reset Ctrl+Shift+R
    Application.OnKey Key:="^+x"                   'Reset Ctrl+Shift+K
End Sub
```

Summary

This chapter finished our look at VBA and spreadsheet applications by taking you through the Check Book application. I showed you how the application works, and then I took you behind the scenes to see the procedures and other plumbing that make up the guts of the application. Here are some other chapters to read for related information:

- To learn how to work with pivot tables, head for Chapter 13, "Creating Pivot Tables," and Chapter 14, "Customizing Pivot Tables."

- I covered Range objects in Chapter 24, "Manipulating Excel with VBA."

- To get the full scoop on custom dialog boxes, menus, and toolbars, see Chapter 25, "Creating a Custom User Interface."

- The Check Book application's menus and toolbars are initialized with an Auto_Open procedure in the Transaction Procedures module. To find out more about Auto_Open and the other automatic procedures used in this application, see Chapter 27, "VBA Procedures That Respond to Events."

Appendixes

VI

PART

An Excel 4.0 Macro Language Primer

A

Excel 5.0 and later versions include Visual Basic for Applications (VBA), Microsoft's common macro language. Microsoft has stated that it will be putting all its macro development efforts behind VBA from now on. So although the Excel macro language will be included in all future versions of Excel, it will receive no further enhancements. You should keep this news in mind when deciding which language to use for your macros.

If you do decide to use the Excel 4 macro language, you can refer to this appendix for a basic introduction to its features and syntax.

What Is a Macro?

A macro is a small program that contains a list of instructions you want Excel to execute. Similar to batch files, macros combine several operations into a single procedure that you can invoke quickly. This list of instructions is composed mostly of *macro functions* that work much like regular worksheet functions. Some of these functions perform specific macro-related tasks, but most just correspond to Excel's menu commands and dialog box options. For example, the FILE.CLOSE macro function works much like the **File | C**lose command.

The Three Types of Macros

Macros come in three flavors: *command macros, function macros,* and *subroutine macros.* The following is a summary of their differences:

- Command macros are the most common type of macro; they usually contain functions that are the equivalent of menu options and other Excel commands. The distinguishing feature of a command macro is that, similar to regular Excel commands, they have an effect on their surroundings (the worksheet, workspace, and so on). Whether you're formatting a range, printing a worksheet, or creating custom menus, command macros *change* things. I'll show you how to create command macros later in this appendix.

- Function macros work similar to Excel's built-in functions. Their distinguishing characteristics are that they accept arguments, manipulate those arguments, and return a result. A properly designed function macro has no effect on the current environment. See "Creating Function Macros," later in this appendix, for more information.

- Subroutine macros are a combination of command and function macros. They can take arguments and return values similar to a function macro, but they also can affect their surroundings similarly to a command macro. Subroutines are invoked from within other macros, and their usual purpose is to streamline macro code. If you need to run a task several times in a macro, you'll typically split off the task into a subroutine instead of cluttering up your macro.

Working with Macro Sheets

You'll be entering your macros on special sheets called *macro sheets.* Your entries will be formulas that contain macro functions. To make macros easier to read, however, a macro sheet doesn't show the results of each formula; it shows the formulas themselves.

As soon as you open a workbook containing a macro sheet, the sheet's macros become available to all other open documents. If, however, you have any macros you think you'll use regularly, consider storing them in a special file called the Personal Macro Workbook (PERSONAL.XLS). Excel keeps this workbook in the XLSTART directory and opens the workbook automatically at startup. This ensures that your regular macros are always available to your worksheets.

Recording a Command Macro

To create a command macro, Excel gives you two choices. Using the Macro Recorder to record the appropriate menu choices and dialog box selections, you can automatically create the macro on a macro sheet. Or you can use a macro sheet to build a macro from scratch. The next few sections show you how to record a command macro.

How to Record a Command Macro

The easiest way to create a command macro is to use the Macro Recorder. With this option, you just run through the task you want to automate (including selecting ranges, menu commands, and dialog box options), and Excel translates everything into the appropriate macro functions. These are copied to a macro sheet in which you can replay the entire procedure any time you like. The following procedure takes you through the steps required to record a command macro.

1. Select the **Tools | R**ecord Macro | **R**ecord New Macro command. Excel displays an abbreviated version of the Record New Macro dialog box.

2. Enter a name and description, if required.

3. Click the **O**ptions button to expand the dialog box.

4. Enter the options you want to use with the macro. In particular, be sure to select the MS **E**xcel 4.0 Macro option.

5. Click OK or press Enter. Excel returns you to the worksheet and displays Recording in the status line.

6. Perform the tasks you want to include in the macro.

7. When you're finished, select the **Tools | R**ecord Macro | **S**top Recording command.

To see your creation, either activate the last sheet in the workbook (if you used the current workbook to store the macro) or open the appropriate workbook. (If you used the Personal Macro Workbook, you need to unhide the workbook by selecting the **W**indow | Un**h**ide command and unhiding PERSONAL.XLS.) As you can see in Figure A.1, Excel translates your actions into macro functions and writes them in a column. A typical macro has the following features:

Macro name	The first cell holds the macro name you entered in the Record New Macro dialog box.
Shortcut key	If you assigned a shortcut key to the macro, that key appears in parentheses beside the macro name. (It's understood that a shortcut key shown as (a) means Ctrl-a.)
Macro functions	The main body of the macro consists of a series of formulas. These are Excel's interpretations of the actions you performed during the recording. Excel replays each task by "calculating" each formula when you run the macro.
RETURN() function	When you stop recording, Excel adds the RETURN() function to designate the end of the macro.

FIGURE A.1.

A typical recorded command macro.

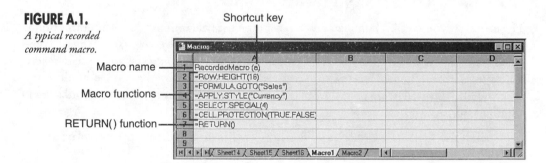

Here are some notes to keep in mind when recording command macros:

■ You can control where a macro appears in a sheet by selecting a cell and then selecting the **T**ools | **R**ecord Macro | **M**ark Position for Recording command. When you're ready to record, select the **T**ools | **R**ecord Macro | **R**ecord at Mark command.

■ The shortcut keys Excel suggests are ones that don't conflict with Excel's built-in shortcuts (such as Ctrl-B for Bold or Ctrl-C for Copy). There are eight letters not assigned to Excel commands that you can use with your macros: *e, j, k, l, m, q, t,* and *y.*

■ You access an extra 26 shortcut keys by using capital letters. For example, Excel differentiates between Ctrl-a and Ctrl-A (or, more explicitly, Ctrl-Shift-a).

- By default, Excel uses absolute references during recording. If you prefer to use relative references, select the **T**ools | **R**ecord Macro | **U**se Relative References command. To change back, select the command again.

- If you perform the wrong action while recording, just continue with the correct sequence. I'll show you later in this appendix how to remove your mistakes. Don't try to fix the problem by selecting the Undo command, because doing so only adds an UNDO() function to the macro.

- You can pause recording by selecting the **T**ools | **R**ecord Macro | **S**top Recording command. To resume, use the **T**ools | **R**ecord Macro | **R**ecord at Mark command.

Procedural Macros Versus Keystroke Macros

If you're familiar with Lotus 1-2-3 or Quattro Pro macros, Excel's macros probably will look a little strange. In Lotus 1-2-3, for example, a macro command to format a number as currency with 0 decimal places appears as follows:

```
/RFC0~
```

This macro command is just a list of the appropriate keystrokes you would use to enter this command (with ~ as the Enter key). Not surprisingly, these kinds of macros are called *keystroke* macros.

Excel, on the other hand, uses *procedural* macros. A procedural macro doesn't care about the individual keystrokes you use to perform an action. Instead, the macro records the final result of each separate procedure. Several examples of this are in the macro shown in Figure A.1. For example, consider the following formula (cell A2):

```
=ROW.HEIGHT(16)
```

I generated this formula by selecting the F**o**rmat | **R**ow | **H**eight command, entering 16 in the **R**ow Height text box, and then selecting OK. Excel ignored the individual keystrokes and mouse clicks I used and, instead, noted what was important: the result of those actions.

Procedural macros operate by compressing an entire procedure (such as selecting a menu command and entering options in a dialog box) into a single macro function. To interpret many of these macro functions properly, you need to know how Excel translates dialog box options into function arguments. Here's a rundown:

- Excel arranges the function arguments in the same order in which they appear in the dialog box. (That is, the order in which you select options when you tab through them.)

- Numbers or text you type in a text box are shown as numeric or text arguments. For example, entering 16 in the Row Height dialog box produces the ROW.HEIGHT(16) macro function. Similarly, selecting **E**dit | **G**o To and entering the name Sales in the **R**eference text box records the function FORMULA.GOTO("Sales").

- A list box selection is shown as a text argument. For example, selecting Format | Style and choosing Currency from the Style Name list produces the function `APPLY.STYLE("Currency")`.

- Option buttons are represented as numeric arguments. The number corresponds to the button's order in its group. For example, if you select the Special button in the Go To dialog box and then choose the Blanks option in the Go To Special dialog box (the fourth button), Excel enters the function `SELECT.SPECIAL(4)`.

- Check box arguments are shown as `TRUE` (if activated) or `FALSE` (if deactivated). For example, if you select Format | Cells and activate the Locked check box (but not the Hidden check box) in the Protection tab, you end up with the function `CELL.PROTECTION(TRUE,FALSE)`.

Keep these guidelines in mind, and you'll find that procedural macros are much easier to understand and debug than their cryptic keystroke cousins.

> **NOTE**
>
> Note that VBA macros are even easier to decipher than Excel 4.0 macros. For example, the macro command `SELECT.SPECIAL(4)` is meaningful only if you know that the 4 stands for the Blanks option. In VBA, the same command looks something like this:
>
> `ActiveCell.SpecialCells(xlBlanks).Select`
>
> As you can see, it's a little more apparent that the command is selecting blank cells.

Editing a Recorded Command Macro

Although procedural macros are almost always cleaner than their keystroke counterparts, you'll have plenty of recorded macros that don't turn out quite right the first time. Whether you give a command you shouldn't have or miss a command altogether, often you must patch things up after the fact.

If your macro contains functions you want to remove, just delete the offending cells from the macro sheet. (To keep things tidy, it's best to delete the cells instead of just clearing them.)

If you left out a step or two, follow the instructions in the next procedure to insert new recorded actions into an existing macro.

> **NOTE**
>
> If you want to just add new actions to the end of your macro, you can skip steps 1 through 3 of the following procedure.

1. Activate the macro sheet that contains the macro you want to change. (If you need to make changes to a macro stored in PERSONAL.XLS, you must first unhide the sheet by selecting the **Window | Unhide** command.)

2. Decide where in the macro you want the new recording to begin, and at that position, insert enough blank cells to hold all of your actions. To be safe, you probably should insert a few more cells than you think you need, as shown in Figure A.2.

FIGURE A.2.

Insert more than enough cells to handle your new recorded actions.

Rows inserted for new recording

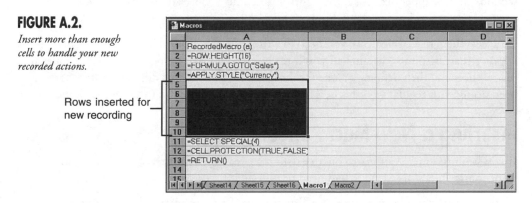

3. Select the topmost blank cell and choose **Tools | Record Macro | Mark** Position for Recording. This command tells Excel where you want the new actions recorded.

4. Activate the worksheet or chart you want to use for the recording.

5. Select the **Tools | Record Macro | Record** at Mark command to resume the recording.

6. Perform the actions you want to add to the macro.

7. When you're done, select **Tools | Record Macro | Stop** Recorder.

8. Activate the macro sheet and clean up things by deleting any remaining blank cells or, if necessary, the extra RETURN() function that Excel added at the end of the insertion (see Figure A.3).

FIGURE A.3.

When you finish inserting your recording, you need to clean up the macro.

New functions

Extra RETURN() function

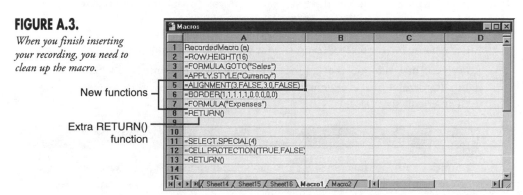

Writing Your Own Command Macro

Although the Macro Recorder makes it easy to create your own homegrown macros, there are plenty of macro features you can't access with mouse or keyboard actions or by selecting menu options. For example, Excel has a couple dozen information macro functions that return data about cells, worksheets, the workspace, and more. (I'll discuss many of these functions in later sections of this appendix.) Also, the control functions enable you to add true programming constructs, such as looping, branching, and decision making.

To access these macro elements, you need to write your own macros from scratch. This process is easier than it sounds, because all you'll really be doing is entering a series of formulas in a macro sheet and then defining a name for the macro. It's not all that different from what you've been doing with regular worksheets. The next few sections take you through the various steps.

Inserting a New Macro Sheet

If you want to enter your macro on an existing macro sheet, just select the sheet's tab. (If you want to use PERSONAL.XLS, you need to unhide it first.)

If you want to start a new macro sheet, first activate the sheet before which you want to insert the macro sheet and then select the **Insert | Macro | MS Excel 4.0 Macro** command. Excel inserts the new sheet.

> **TIP**
>
> You can create a new macro sheet by pressing Ctrl-F11 or Ctrl-Alt-F1.

How to Write a Command Macro

With a macro sheet active, follow these steps to write your own command macro:

1. Select the first cell you want to use for the macro.
2. Enter a name for the macro. (Be sure to use a legal Excel name.)
3. Enter your macro formulas and functions in the column immediately below the macro name. Remember that every macro entry is a formula, so you must begin each cell with an equals sign (=).

> **NOTE**
>
> For complex command functions, it's probably faster to use the Macro Recorder than to try to remember the syntax of something such as FORMAT.FONT(), which has nine arguments.

4. When you're finished, type =RETURN() to mark the end of the macro.

Properly written macros also include documentation that explains each macro step. See "Macro Programming Concepts," later in this appendix, for more information on macro documentation.

Pasting Macro Functions

Some macro functions have very long argument lists. (The WORKSPACE() function, for example, has no fewer than 16 arguments.) Instead of looking up the proper order for these arguments, you can simply paste the function into the cell. The following procedure lists the required steps:

1. In the cell, enter an equals sign (=) and then select the **I**nsert | **F**unction command (or press Shift-F3). The Function Wizard - Step 1 of 2 dialog box appears.

2. Use the Function **C**ategory list to select a category. You'll find that most macro functions are in the Commands, Customizing, and Macro control categories.

3. Select the function you want from the Function **N**ame list.

4. Click the Next > button. If the function has multiple syntaxes, the Function Wizard - Step 1a of 2 dialog box appears. In this case, select the syntax you want and then select the Next > button. Excel displays the Function Wizard - Step 2 of 2 dialog box.

Why would a function have more than one syntax? Some functions can do double (or even triple) duty. For example, you can apply the FORMAT.FONT() function to worksheet cells, graphic objects, or chart items. Each of these applications requires a different argument list.

5. Enter the arguments you want to use with the function.

6. Select **F**inish to paste the function.

If you know the name of the function you want, you can paste its arguments by entering the function name followed by the left parenthesis and then pressing Ctrl-A.

Naming a Command Macro

When you've finished writing your macro, you need to name it (and, optionally, assign a shortcut key). The following procedure shows you how you name a macro:

1. Activate the macro sheet containing the macro you want to name.

2. Select the cell containing the name of the macro.

3. Select the **I**nsert | **N**ame | **D**efine command. The Define Name dialog box appears.

4. If necessary, change the macro name shown in the Names in **W**orkbook edit box.

5. Make sure that the reference in the **R**efers to box is the correct address for the macro name.

6. In the Macro box, select the **C**ommand option.

7. If you want the macro to appear in the Function Wizard's list of functions, select Ca**t**egory and choose the User Defined option. You normally use this option only for function and subroutine macros.

8. If you want to use a shortcut key with the macro, enter a letter in the **K**ey:Ctrl+ text box.

9. Click OK or press Enter.

Running a Command Macro

Excel offers several methods for running your command macros. The next few sections discuss a few of these methods.

Using the Macro Dialog Box

Excel takes all the command macros it finds in the macro sheets of any open workbook and in the PERSONAL.XLS file and stores their names in a list in the Macro dialog box. To run any of these macros, you can select the name from the list, as described in the following steps:

1. Open the workbook with the macro sheet that contains the macro you want to run. (You can skip this step if the macro exists in the Personal Macro Workbook.) Note that the macro sheet just has to be open in memory; it doesn't have to be the active sheet.

2. If the macro will be affecting a worksheet, activate the sheet and position the active cell where you need it.

3. Select the **T**ools | **M**acro command. Excel opens the Macro dialog box, shown in Figure A.4.

4. Select the name of the macro you want to run from the **M**acro Name/Reference list.

FIGURE A.4.

Use the Macro dialog box
to run your macros.

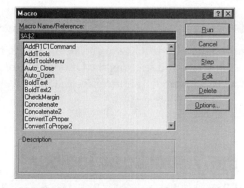

5. Click **R**un or press Enter. Excel runs the macro.

TIP

If the active sheet is a macro sheet, you also can run a macro from a shortcut menu. Right-click on the name of the macro and select the Run command. Excel displays the Macro dialog box and enters the cell address in the **M**acro Name/Reference box. Click **R**un to start the macro.

NOTE

If you want to stop a macro before it's finished, press the Esc key. In the Macro Error dialog box that appears, select **H**alt to shut down the macro or **C**ontinue to resume.

Using Macro Shortcut Keys

Running a macro with a shortcut key is easy. Hold down the Ctrl key and press the letter you assigned to the macro. If the macro doesn't run, check for these possibilities:

- Is the workbook that contains the macro open?
- Did you assign a shortcut key to the macro?
- Is there another macro with the same shortcut key? If two or more macros have the same shortcut key, Excel runs the first macro in the list.
- Did you assign a capital-letter shortcut key? As mentioned earlier, Excel differentiates between Ctrl-a and Ctrl-Shift-A.

TIP

You can assign a shortcut key to an existing macro by highlighting the macro in the Macro dialog box and selecting the **O**ptions button. In the Macro Options dialog box that appears, activate the Shortcut **K**ey check box and enter the letter in the Ctrl+ edit box.

Using the Visual Basic Toolbar

The Visual Basic toolbar includes a Run Macro tool. This procedure explains how to use it:

1. Activate the macro sheet containing the macro you want to run.
2. Select the cell containing the name of the macro.
3. Select the Run Macro tool.

    The Run Macro tool.

TIP

If you don't want the macro to start at the beginning, select whichever cell you want to use as a starting point and then select the Run Macro tool.

Creating Function Macros

Excel comes with hundreds of built-in functions that make up one of the largest function libraries of any spreadsheet. Even with this vast collection, however, you'll still find plenty of applications these functions don't cover. For example, you might need to calculate the area of a circle of a specified radius or the gravitational force between two objects. You could easily make these calculations on a worksheet, of course, but if you need them frequently, it makes sense to create your own functions that you can use any time. This section shows you how to create your own function macros.

As mentioned earlier, the defining characteristic of function macros is that they return a result. They can perform any number of calculations on numbers, text, logical values, and so on, but they're not allowed to affect their surroundings. They can't move the active cell or format a range or change the workspace settings. In fact, anything you can access using the menus is off-limits in a function macro.

What *can* you put in a function macro? All of Excel's built-in worksheet functions are fair game, and you can use any macro function that isn't the equivalent of a menu command or a desktop action. You can, of course, combine these functions and other items to create formulas using Excel's basic operators.

The simplest function macro is one that does nothing but return a value. Figure A.5 shows a function macro called Return57 that consists of a single formula: =RETURN(57). This is the same RETURN() function you used to terminate your command macros earlier. RETURN() performs the same task in a function macro, but it also sends the function result back to the worksheet that called it. And, as you can see in the accompanying worksheet, you use a function macro just like you use a regular function (except, of course, that you must precede the macro name with the name of the macro sheet's workbook so that Excel knows where to find it).

FIGURE A.5.

A simple function macro that only returns a value.

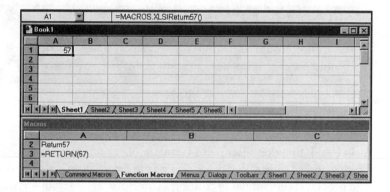

Most function macros (like most of the built-in functions) actually accept *arguments*. This capability enables you to send data to the macro, which then manipulates it and sends back the result. For example, Excel has a SQRT() function for calculating square roots, but it doesn't have a cube root function. Figure A.6 shows a CubeRoot function macro that fits the bill.

FIGURE A.6.

A function macro that calculates cube roots.

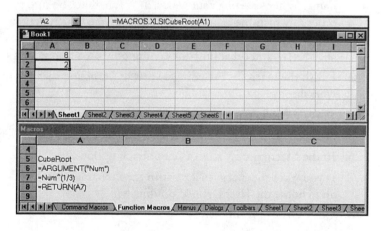

The macro's first line is an ARGUMENT() function that tells Excel to expect an argument with this function. This line also gives the argument a name (Num). As you can see in the accompanying worksheet, the macro is called and a value is sent (the contents of cell A1, in this case). The macro's second line—=Num^(1/3)—takes the Num argument and calculates its cube root. Finally, the RETURN() function sends back the result (from cell A7 in the macro sheet).

All of your function macros will have this basic structure. You therefore need to keep three things in mind when you design these kinds of macros:

- What arguments will the macro take?
- What formulas will you use within the macro?
- What value or values will be returned?

NOTE

You can use arrays to return multiple values from a function macro. See Chapter 2, "Building Better Formulas," to learn about array formulas.

Writing a Function Macro

As I've said, function macros can't contain menu commands or mouse and keyboard actions. This means, of course, that there is no way to record function macros—you have to type them. The process is very similar to creating a command macro from scratch. Follow the steps in this procedure to write a function macro:

1. In the macro sheet you want to use, select the first cell for the macro and enter a name.
2. Enter your macro formulas and functions in the column immediately below the macro name. When entering your ARGUMENT() functions, be sure to place them in the same order in which the arguments will appear when the function is called. (See the section in this appendix titled "Common Function-Macro Functions" to learn more about ARGUMENT() and other functions commonly used in function macros.)
3. Finish the macro by including a RETURN() function that returns a value to the worksheet.
4. Select the cell containing the name of the macro.
5. Select the Insert | Name | Define command to display the Define Name dialog box.
6. In the Macro group, select the Function option.
7. If you want the macro to appear in the FunctionWizard dialog box, select Category and choose the User Defined option.
8. Click OK or press Enter.

Using a Function Macro

You can use function macros only within worksheet or macro sheet formulas. First you need to make sure that the sheet containing the macro is open (unless the macro is stored in PERSONAL.XLS). Then you have two choices:

■ In the formula bar, type the name of the macro's workbook, an exclamation point (!), the macro name, and any arguments enclosed in parentheses.

> **TIP**
>
> If you're entering the formula in a worksheet in the same workbook as the macro, you don't need to include the workbook name and exclamation point.

■ Select the **Insert | Function** command, highlight User Defined in the Function **C**ategory list, and select the macro from the Function **N**ame list. (You can do this only if you saved the macro in the User Defined category when you defined the macro name.)

Common Function-Macro Functions

Despite the function restrictions you face when you're creating function macros, there are still hundreds of functions to choose from. Four functions, however, are used often in function macros: RESULT(), ARGUMENT(), CALLER(), and VOLATILE(). Next we'll take a closer look at each of these important functions.

The *RESULT()* Function

You use the RESULT() function to specify the data type of the value returned by a function macro. Be sure to use RESULT() before any other formulas in the macro (including ARGUMENT() functions), and use the following syntax:

RESULT(*type_num*)

type_num   Indicates the data type of the result according to the values displayed in the following table:

type_num	Data Type
1	Numeric
2	Text
4	Logical
8	Reference
16	Error
64	Array

In most cases, RESULT() is an optional function. You therefore don't have to use it in macros when the data type of the result is obvious, such as in the CubeRoot macro discussed earlier. If you don't include RESULT(), Excel assumes that the data type value is 7. Why 7? That's the sum of the values for the numeric, text, and logical data types. This means that you can return a value that is any of those three types. To specify any other combination of data types, just add the appropriate values together.

> **NOTE**
>
> RESULT() is not optional when a macro returns values that are either references or arrays.

You'll use RESULT() most often in complex macros when there is a chance that you could accidentally return an incorrect value. RESULT() can save you lots of debugging time. For example, it can prevent you from returning text when the calling program is expecting a logical value.

> **CAUTION**
>
> You still might get unexpected results even if you use the RESULT() function. If the returned value is a different type than that specified in the RESULT() function, Excel tries to convert the result to the required data type. This is another example of Excel's *data coercion:* you might end up with numbers converted to text, or something similar. If Excel can't make the conversion, the macro returns the #VALUE! error.

The *ARGUMENT()* Function

You've seen how the ARGUMENT() function adds flexibility to a function macro by enabling the user to input data to the function. The ARGUMENT() function actually serves three important purposes:

- It defines the names of the arguments.
- It determines the order of the arguments between the function's parentheses.
- Optionally, it specifies the data type of each argument.

Unless you're using RESULT(), the ARGUMENT() functions must appear at the beginning of the macro. You have a choice of two syntaxes, depending on how you want to store the arguments.

To store the arguments as names, use the following syntax:

ARGUMENT(***name_text***,*type_num*)

name_text   The name you want to define for the argument.

type_num   The data type value.

After you've defined a name for the argument, any formula in the macro sheet can use the name in its calculations.

If you prefer to store the arguments in cells, use this form:

ARGUMENT(*name_text*,*type_num*,**reference**)

name_text   The name you want to define for the argument.

type_num   The data type value.

reference   A cell address that Excel uses to store the data.

To refer to the argument in other formulas, you can use *name_text* or **reference**. Most macro programmers avoid using **reference** because the arguments take up unnecessary space on the macro sheet. The exception is if your function will be returning an array. In this case, you'll usually want to enter the array values into a range on the macro sheet and then return that range.

When designing your ARGUMENT() functions, keep the following points in mind:

- ■ Function macros can have a maximum of 29 arguments.

- ■ If your function has any optional arguments, put them at the end of the argument list to make things easier for the user.

- ■ Use an IF() function to test for incorrect values entered by the user. For example, if one of your arguments requires a positive number, you should check for negative numbers and report an error if anything is amiss. See "Macros That Make Decisions," later in this appendix, to learn how to use IF() in a macro. See "Displaying Information to the User" to learn how to display error messages.

The *CALLER()* Function

The CALLER() function returns information about which cell, range, menu command, tool, or object called the currently running macro. CALLER() is invaluable for macros that need to behave differently depending on where they were called.

For example, you might have several worksheets that call the same macro. If these sheets have slightly different structures, your macro might have to allow for this situation in some way. The simple macro shown in Figure A.7 passes CALLER() to the GET.CELL() function to determine the name of the calling worksheet. A more advanced macro would test for possible filenames and react accordingly.

FIGURE A.7.

A macro that uses
CALLER( ) *to determine
the name of the worksheet
that called the macro.*

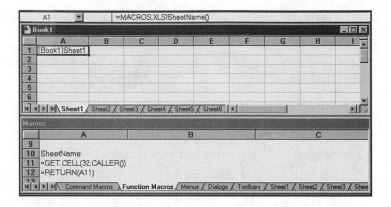

Here are some points you should keep in mind when using CALLER():

- If you want to determine the cell or range from which a macro was called, you can't use CALLER() by itself. Instead, use GET.CELL() or REFTEXT() to convert the reference to text.

- If the macro was chosen from a menu command, CALLER() returns a horizontal array of three elements that includes the command's position number, the menu number, and the menu bar number.

- If the macro was invoked by selecting an object such as a macro button, CALLER() returns a text string that identifies the object.

- If the macro was started from a toolbar, CALLER() returns a horizontal array that includes the tool's position and the toolbar name.

The *VOLATILE()* Function

As you might know, Excel normally recalculates your worksheet formulas only when you change any data that affects the formula either directly or indirectly. Unfortunately, this rule *doesn't* apply to function macros. This means that you might end up with out-of-date results in some of your worksheet formulas that use function macros for their calculations.

To overcome this problem, include the VOLATILE() function in all your function macros. This function tells Excel to always recalculate the macro whenever it recalculates a worksheet. Enter VOLATILE() before all other macro formulas except RESULT() and ARGUMENT().

Macro Programming Concepts

The macros you've seen so far have been simple, linear beasts designed to carry out only a few tasks or calculations. To build truly powerful (and truly useful) macros, you need to learn about Excel's programming features. This is, after all, a programming language (albeit a simple one).

As such, it enables you to make decisions, branch to other parts of a macro, set up loops, and create subroutines. The next few sections show you all these features and more.

Documenting Your Macros

Before diving in to the programming features of Excel's macro language, I want to make a quick point about documentation. As your macros grow more complex, they also grow harder to decipher, either by someone else's looking at the macro for the first time, or by your looking at your code a few months down the road. Excel's often cryptic function arguments (all those numbers and TRUE/FALSE values) can make some macros downright impenetrable.

To avoid this fate, you should enter a short comment into the cell next to each of your macro formulas. This note can be a brief explanation of what the formula is doing or a clarification of the function arguments used. Figure A.8 shows a macro formatted for documentation. Here are some of the features of this format:

- The right column holds the formula documentation.

- The left column lists any cell names used in the macro. (To learn about using names in macros, see the section "Macro Worksheet Skills," later in this appendix.)

- You can include text entries among the macro formulas to add comments that separate each of the macro's tasks. (Excel ignores text cells when processing the macro.) To make the comments easier to spot, use a bold italic font.

- Borders separate the various parts and make the macro easier to read.

FIGURE A.8.

Document your macros to make them easier to understand.

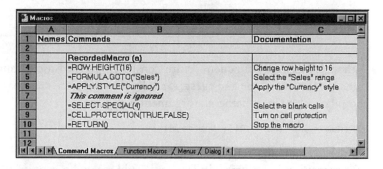

Macros That Make Decisions

A smart macro performs tests on its environment and then, based on the results of each test, decides what to do next. For example, suppose that you've written a function macro that uses one of its arguments as a divisor in a formula. You should test the argument before using it in the formula to ensure that it isn't 0 (to avoid producing a #DIV/0! error). If it is, you could display a message to alert the user to the illegal argument.

Using *IF()* to Make True/False Decisions

Simple true/false decisions are handled by the IF() function. Recall that the IF() function has the following syntax:

IF(***logical_test***,*true_expr*,*false_expr*)

logical_test	A logical expression that evaluates to either TRUE or FALSE.
true_expr	The value returned by the IF() function if ***logical_test*** evaluates to TRUE.
false_expr	The value returned if the ***logical_test*** is FALSE.

Figure A.9 shows a simple function macro that tests an argument and returns a different string based on the results of that test.

FIGURE A.9.

A simple function macro that returns a different value based on a logical test.

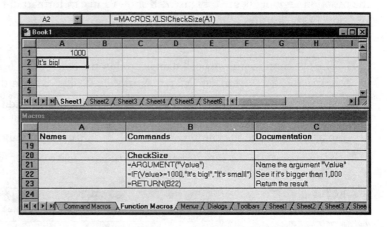

Although most IF() functions return constants, you can use formulas and even other functions for the *true_expr* and *false_expr*. For example, the CubeRoot function you saw earlier should check to see whether the argument is negative:

=IF(Num < 0, "Num < 0!", Num^(1/3))

If the Num argument is negative, the function returns the string Num < 0!; otherwise, the cube root expression is evaluated. In fact, you could make this expression truly efficient by including the RETURN() function right in the IF():

=IF(Num < 0, RETURN("Num < 0!"), RETURN(Num^(1/3)))

Using a Block *IF* to Run Multiple Expressions

Using the IF() function to calculate a formula or run another function adds a powerful new weapon to your macro arsenal. This technique, however, suffers from an important drawback: whatever the result of the logical test, you can execute only a single expression. This limitation is fine in many cases, but at times you'll need to run one group of expressions if the test is `TRUE` and a different group if the test is `FALSE`. To handle such a situation, you need to use a *block* `IF`.

A block `IF` is actually a combination of three functions: `IF()`, `ELSE()`, and `END.IF()`. The block is set up in the following manner:

```
=IF(logical_test)
    (Expressions to run if logical_test is TRUE go here.)
=ELSE()
    (Expressions to run if logical_test is FALSE go here.)
=END.IF()
```

NOTE

In contrast to a block `IF`, the `IF()` function by itself is called an *in-line* `IF`, because everything happens in a single line.

The block begins with the usual `IF()` function, without the *`true_expr`* and *`false_expr`* arguments. If the ***`logical_test`*** returns `TRUE`, all the statements between the `IF()` and `ELSE()` functions are executed (you can insert any number of formulas). If, however, ***`logical_test`*** returns `FALSE`, all the statements between the `ELSE()` and `END.IF()` functions are executed.

For example, suppose that you want to calculate the future value of a series of regular deposits, but you want to differentiate between monthly deposits and quarterly deposits. Figure A.10 shows a function macro called FutureValue that does the job.

FIGURE A.10.

A function macro that uses a block `IF` to differentiate between monthly and quarterly deposits.

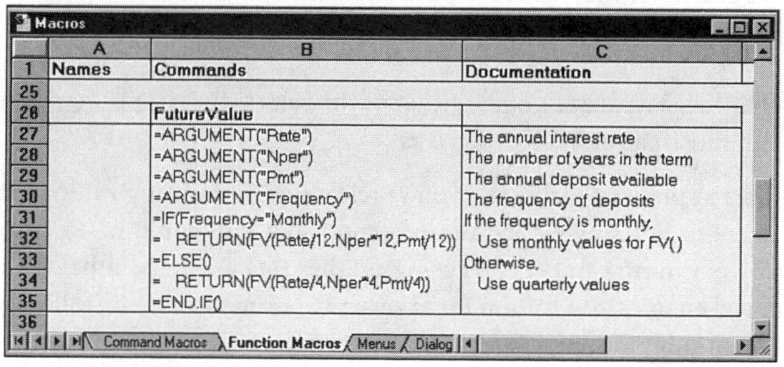

	A	B	C
1	Names	Commands	Documentation
25			
26		FutureValue	
27		=ARGUMENT("Rate")	The annual interest rate
28		=ARGUMENT("Nper")	The number of years in the term
29		=ARGUMENT("Pmt")	The annual deposit available
30		=ARGUMENT("Frequency")	The frequency of deposits
31		=IF(Frequency="Monthly")	If the frequency is monthly,
32		= RETURN(FV(Rate/12,Nper*12,Pmt/12))	Use monthly values for FV()
33		=ELSE()	Otherwise,
34		= RETURN(FV(Rate/4,Nper*4,Pmt/4))	Use quarterly values
35		=END.IF()	
36			

The first three arguments (`Rate`, `Nper`, and `Pmt`) are the annual interest rate, the number of years in the term of the investment, and the total deposit available annually. The fourth argument—`Frequency`—is either `Monthly` or `Quarterly`. The goal is to adjust the first three arguments based on the `Frequency`. For example, if `Frequency` is `Monthly`, you need to divide the interest rate by 12, multiply the term by 12, and divide the annual deposit by 12. The `IF()` function (cell B31) runs a test on the `Frequency` argument:

```
=IF(Frequency = "Monthly")
```

If this argument is true, the function adjusts Rate, Nper, and Pmt accordingly and returns the future value. Otherwise, a quarterly calculation is assumed, and different adjustments are made to the arguments.

Following are some notes on the block IF:

- The ELSE() function is optional. If you can ignore a FALSE result in the IF() function (which is often the case), you can leave out the ELSE() and its associated statements. The structure of the block IF therefore becomes this:

```
=IF(logical_test)
    (Expressions to run if logical_test is TRUE go here.)
=END.IF()
```

- Block IFs are much easier to read if you indent the expressions between IF(), ELSE(), and END.IF(), as shown in Figure A.10. This technique enables you to identify easily which group of statements will be run if the result is TRUE and which group will be run if the result is FALSE. Just add three or four spaces after the equals sign (=).

Using a Block *IF* to Make Multiple Decisions

Another problem with the in-line IF() is that normally you can make only one decision. The function calculates a single logical result and performs one of two actions. Plenty of situations, however, require multiple decisions before you can decide which action to take.

One solution is to use the AND() and OR() functions to evaluate a series of logical tests. For example, the FutureValue macro probably should test the Frequency argument to ensure that it's either Monthly or Quarterly. The following IF() function uses OR() to accomplish this task:

```
IF(OR(Frequency = "Monthly", Frequency = "Quarterly"))
```

If Frequency doesn't equal either of the values, the OR() function returns FALSE, and the macro can return a message to the user.

This approach works, but you're really just performing multiple logical tests; in the end, you make only a single decision. A second solution would be to *nest* IF() functions. Nesting involves running an IF() and using another IF() as part of either the true_expr or the false_expr. Excel enables you to nest up to seven IF() functions. The following is an example that checks the number of days an invoice is past due:

```
IF(PastDue>30, IF(PastDue>90, "Really late!", "Late"), "OK")
```

If the invoice is less than or equal to 30 days past due, the function returns OK. For invoices more than 30 days past due, a second IF() checks to see whether the invoice is more than 90 days past due. If it is, the function returns Really late!. Otherwise, the function returns Late.

At the cost of added complexity, nested IF() functions accomplish the goal of multiple decision making. The further you nest IF() functions, the harder they get to read and understand. The best solution is to return to the block IF and add a new function: ELSE.IF(). This function combines ELSE() and IF() to make it easy to make multiple decisions. The syntax of ELSE.IF() is as follows:

```
ELSE.IF(logical_test)
```

Here is the basic structure of a block IF that includes this function:

```
=IF(logical_test1)
    (Expressions to run if logical_test1 is true)
=ELSE.IF(logical_test2)
    (Expressions to run if logical_test2 is true)
=ELSE()
    (Expressions to run if all tests are false)
=END.IF()
```

As you can see, you keep adding ELSE.IF() functions for each new decision you want to make. For example, suppose that you want to write a function that converts a raw score into a letter grade according to the following table:

Raw Score	Letter Grade
Less than 50	F
Between 50 and 59	D
Between 60 and 69	C
Between 70 and 79	B
80 and over	A

Figure A.11 shows the LetterGrade macro, which uses a block IF with a few ELSE.IF() functions to make the conversion.

FIGURE A.11.

A macro that makes multiple decisions using a block IF with a few ELSE.IF() functions.

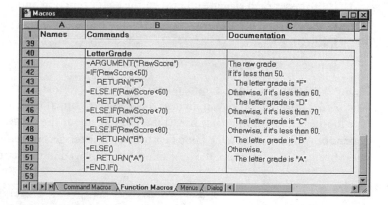

Macros That Loop

If your macro needs to repeat a section of code, you can set up a loop that tells Excel how many times to run through the code. The next few sections look at Excel's three types of loops.

Using *FOR()* Loops

The most common type of loop is the FOR() loop (also called the FOR-NEXT loop). Use this loop when you know how many times you want to repeat a group of formulas. The structure of a FOR() loop is similar to the following syntax:

```
=FOR(counter_text,start_num,end_num,step_num)
    (Statements to be repeated go here.)
=NEXT()
```

counter_text	A text string that defines the name of the loop counter. The loop counter is a number that counts how many times the macro has gone through the loop.
start_num	A value that tells the macro what value the loop counter starts with. (This value usually is 1, but you can enter any number.)
end_num	A value that tells the macro the last number the loop counter can have before exiting the loop.
step_num	A value that defines an increment for the loop counter. (If you leave this out, the default value is 1.)

When Excel encounters the FOR() function, it follows this five-step process:

1. It sets **counter_text** equal to **start_num**.
2. It tests **counter_text** to see whether it's greater than **end_num**. If so, Excel exits the loop (that is, it processes the first statement after the NEXT() function). Otherwise, it continues.
3. It processes each statement between the FOR() function and the NEXT() function.
4. It adds step_num to **counter_text**. (It adds 1 to **counter_text** if step_num is not specified.)
5. It repeats steps 2 through 4 until it's done.

Figure A.12 shows a simple command macro (LoopTest) that uses a FOR() loop. Each time the macro goes through the loop, it invokes the MESSAGE() function to display the value of Counter (the loop counter) in the status bar. (I'll talk more about the MESSAGE() function later in this appendix.) When you run the LoopTest macro, Counter gets incremented by one each time it goes through the loop. Also, the new value gets displayed in the status bar.

FIGURE A.12.

A simple FOR() loop.

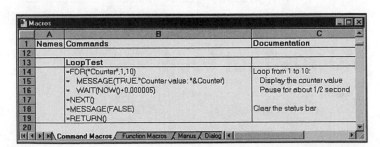

NOTE

The LoopTest macro also uses the WAIT(*serial_text*) function to slow things down a bit. The *serial_text* argument is the time serial number that you want Excel to wait before resuming processing. LoopTest uses the argument NOW() + 0.000005 to pause the macro for about half a second.

Following are some notes on FOR() loops:

- The loop counter doesn't always have to be incremented. By using a negative value for step_num, you can start at a higher number and work down to a lower value.

- As with block IFs, indent the statements inside a FOR() loop for increased readability.

- To keep the number of names defined on a macro sheet to a minimum, always try to use the same name for all your FOR() loop counters. The letters i through n are traditionally used for counters in programming. For greater clarity, names such as Counter are best. The only time you need to be careful is when a FOR() loop statement calls another macro that has its own FOR() loop. If the two loops use the same name for the counter, the results probably won't be what you intended.

- If you need to break out of a FOR() loop before the defined number of repetitions is completed, use the BREAK() function, described in the section titled "Using BREAK() to Exit a Loop."

Using *FOR.CELL()* Loops

A useful variation of the FOR() loop is the FOR.CELL() loop that operates on each cell in a range. You don't need a loop counter, because Excel loops through the individual cells in the range and performs whatever operations are inside the loop on each cell. Following is the syntax of the basic FOR.CELL() loop:

```
=FOR.CELL(cell_name,range_ref,skip_blanks)
    (Statements to be performed on each cell go here.)
=NEXT()
```

cell_name	A defined name that Excel uses to represent the reference for each cell in the range.
range_ref	A reference to the range of cells through which FOR.CELL() will loop. If you leave this out, Excel uses the current selection.
skip_blanks	A logical value that determines whether FOR.CELL() skips blanks. Set *skip_blanks* to TRUE (or omit it) to make FOR.CELL() skip blanks. To include blanks, use FALSE.

For example, you can create a command macro that converts a range of text into proper case (that is, with the first letter of each word capitalized). This is a useful function if you import mainframe data into your worksheets, because mainframe records usually are displayed entirely in uppercase. This macro uses the following three steps:

1. Loop through the selected cells with FOR.CELL().

2. Convert each cell's text to proper case. Use the PROPER() function to handle this:

   PROPER(***text***)

   text   The text to convert to proper case.

3. Enter the converted text into the selected cell. This is the job of the FORMULA() function:

   FORMULA(***formula***,reference)

   formula   The value or formula you want to enter.

   reference   Specifies where you want the formula entered. (If you omit reference, Excel enters ***formula*** in the active cell.)

Figure A.13 shows the resulting macro, ConvertToProper.

FIGURE A.13.

This command macro uses FOR.CELL() to loop through a selection and convert each cell to proper case.

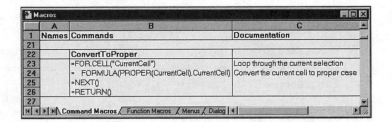

Using *WHILE()* Loops

What do you do if you need to loop, but you don't know in advance how many times to repeat the loop? This could happen, for example, if you want to loop only until a certain condition is met (such as encountering a blank cell). The solution is to use the third type of loop: the WHILE() (or WHILE-NEXT) loop.

Following is the syntax of a WHILE() loop:

```
=WHILE(logical_test)
    (Statements to be repeated go here.)
=NEXT()
```

As long as ***logical_test*** returns TRUE, Excel repeats the loop. As soon as ***logical_test*** changes to FALSE, the loop ends.

Figure A.14 shows a macro called BoldText that runs down a worksheet column and, whenever a cell contains text, adds bold formatting to the cell. The idea is to loop until the macro encounters a blank cell. This action is controlled by the following WHILE() function:

```
=WHILE(NOT(ISBLANK(ACTIVE.CELL())))
```

The ACTIVE.CELL() function returns the reference for the active cell. The ISBLANK() function checks the active cell to see whether it's blank. Entering ISBLANK(ACTIVE.CELL()) inside the NOT() function tells the macro to continue looping while the active cell is not blank. Then, an IF() function uses ISTEXT() to check whether the active cell contains a text value. If the cell does contain text, the FORMAT.FONT(,,TRUE) formula adds bold formatting. The SELECT("R[1]C") function moves down one row, and the whole thing repeats. (For details on the SELECT() function, see "Selecting a Cell or Range," later in this appendix.)

FIGURE A.14.

A macro that uses a WHILE() loop to process cells until it encounters a blank cell.

	A	B	C
1	Names	Commands	Documentation
28			
29		**BoldText**	
30		=WHILE(NOT(ISBLANK(ACTIVE.CELL())))	Loop while the active cell is not blank
31		= IF(ISTEXT(ACTIVE.CELL()))	If the active cell is text,
32		= FORMAT.FONT(,,TRUE)	Set the bold attribute
33		= END.IF()	
34		= SELECT("R[1]C")	Move down one row
35		=NEXT()	
36		=RETURN()	
37			

Using *BREAK()* to Exit a Loop

Most loops run their natural course, and then the macro moves on. At times, however, you might want to exit a loop prematurely—for example, when you find a certain type of cell or an error, or when the user has entered an unexpected value. To exit the loop, include a BREAK() function. (Usually, you also need an IF() function to test for the exit condition.)

Figure A.15 shows a revised version of the preceding macro called BoldText2. This version exits the WHILE() loop when it encounters a cell that doesn't contain text.

FIGURE A.15.

In the BoldText2 macro, the BREAK() function terminates the WHILE() loop if the active cell doesn't contain text.

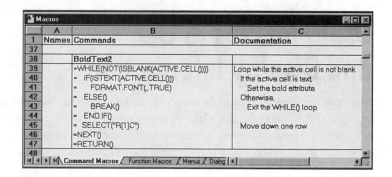

	A	B	C
1	Names	Commands	Documentation
37			
38		**BoldText2**	
39		=WHILE(NOT(ISBLANK(ACTIVE.CELL())))	Loop while the active cell is not blank
40		= IF(ISTEXT(ACTIVE.CELL()))	If the active cell is text,
41		= FORMAT.FONT(,,TRUE)	Set the bold attribute
42		= ELSE()	Otherwise,
43		= BREAK()	Exit the WHILE() loop
44		= END.IF()	
45		= SELECT("R[1]C")	Move down one row
46		=NEXT()	
47		=RETURN()	
48			

Using Subroutine Macros

As you work with macros, you'll find that certain tasks keep cropping up regularly. For example, if you import a lot of mainframe data into your worksheets, you might be constantly using the code from the ConvertToProper macro, discussed earlier. Adding code from frequently used macros to your new macros, however, creates large programs. You should be using *subroutine macros* to streamline your work.

A subroutine is a separate macro that gets invoked from within the main macro. Control is passed over to the subroutine, and the subroutine's macro formulas are then executed. When Excel processes the subroutine's RETURN() function, control is passed back to the main macro, and this macro resumes execution. There are many advantages to using subroutines in this way:

- Your main macro remains uncluttered and easy to read. As long as you give the subroutine a descriptive name, the reader will know what is happening in the macro.

- A well-written subroutine is set up to accomplish only a single, specific task. Keeping subroutines simple and focused makes figuring out what they do and debugging them easier.

- After you have a subroutine working perfectly, you can confidently use it in your other macros. You don't have to reinvent the wheel each time.

You create subroutine macros just like you create any other macro. After you define a macro's name, you can invoke the subroutine from the main program the same way you would a regular Excel function. For example, to run the ConvertToProper macro as a subroutine, you just include the following formula in a macro:

```
=ConvertToProper()
```

If the macro exists in a different workbook, precede the name with the name of the workbook and an exclamation point:

```
=MACROS.XLS!ConvertToProper()
```

Of course, if the subroutine takes arguments, you need to include them as well.

Using Macros to Get and Display Information

Most macros have an essentially antisocial nature. They do their jobs quietly in the background without much fuss or fanfare. Other macros, however, are more gregarious; they tell you things, ask you questions, and even listen to your answers. The next few sections present the macro functions that enable you to display information and get input from the user.

Displaying Information to the User

One of the cardinal rules in successful macro design (indeed, in all of programming) is to keep the user involved. If an operation is going to take a long time, let the user know and keep him informed of its progress. If the user makes an error (for example, by entering the wrong argument in a function macro), he needs to be gently admonished so that he'll be less likely to do it again.

Excel has four functions that display information in one form or another: BEEP(), SOUND.PLAY(), MESSAGE(), and ALERT().

Beeping the Speaker

Excel's most basic form of communication is the simple, attention-getting beep. It's Excel's way of saying "Ahem!" or "Excuse me!" and it's handled, appropriately enough, by the BEEP() function.

BEEP(*tone_num*)

> *tone_num*   A number between 1 and 4 that specifies the sound you want to hear. (To hear different sounds, you need to have a sound driver installed on your system.) Without *tone_num,* BEEP() simply reproduces the usual sound that you hear on your system when, for example, you try to close a file without saving it.

If you have a sound board, you can use BEEP() to produce up to five sounds, depending on what you use for *tone_num.* Table A.1 lists the various values you can use with the BEEP() function and the corresponding system sounds they produce.

Table A.1. System sounds generated by the BEEP() function.

tone_num	*System Sound*
None	Default beep
1	Critical stop
2	Question
3	Exclamation
4	Asterisk

> **CAUTION**
>
> Avoid overusing the BEEP() function. The idea is to get the user's attention, and constant beeping only defeats that purpose. Besides, most users quickly become annoyed at any program that barks at them incessantly. Signaling errors and the ends of long operations are good uses for the BEEP() function.

Using Other Sounds

The BEEP() function is useful, but it's primitive, to say the least. If you have the necessary hardware, you can get your macros to play much more sophisticated sounds and even your own recorded voice.

Adding a Sound to a Cell Note

It all begins with the SOUND.NOTE() function, which has two syntaxes. The first form enables you to import a sound from a sound file into a cell note:

SOUND.NOTE(*cell_ref,file_text*)

cell_ref	A reference to the cell that will receive the sound. If you omit *cell_ref*, Excel enters the note into the active cell.
file_text	The name of the file containing the sound. If you don't include this argument, Excel uses the active worksheet.

For example, the following function imports a sound file called DOGBARK.WAV into the active cell:

=SOUND.NOTE(,"C:\SOUNDS\DOGBARK.WAV")

The second form of the SOUND.NOTE() function enables you to record or erase sounds in a cell note:

SOUND.NOTE(*cell_ref,erase_sound*)

cell_ref	A reference to the cell where the sound will be recorded or erased. Excel uses the active cell if you omit *cell_ref*.
erase_sound	A logical value that determines whether you're recording or erasing a sound note. Set it to TRUE if you want to erase the sound note; set it to FALSE (or omit it) to record a sound note.

NOTE

To record sound notes, you must have the appropriate hardware installed on your system.

If you use the SOUND.NOTE() function to record a sound, you'll see the Record dialog box when you run the macro. Just choose **R**ecord, record your note, choose **S**top when you're done, and click OK.

Playing a Sound

After you have inserted a sound note, you can use the SOUND.PLAY() function to play it (assuming, as usual, that the user's computer has the appropriate hardware):

SOUND.PLAY(*cell_ref,file_text*)

cell_ref	A reference to the cell that contains the sound. Excel uses the active cell if you omit *cell_ref*.
file_text	The name of a file containing the sound you want to play. If you include *cell_ref*, Excel ignores *file_text*.

For example, the following function plays a message recorded in a cell named ErrorMessage in the active worksheet:

=SOUND.PLAY(!ErrorMessage)

> **NOTE**
>
> Prefacing a cell reference or range name with an exclamation mark tells Excel that the reference applies to the active worksheet. See "Working with References," later in this appendix, for more information.

Instead of adding sounds to cell notes, you can play them right from a file. The following function plays the TADA.WAV file:

=SOUND.PLAY(,"C:\WINDOWS\TADA.WAV")

Adding Sound Checks to Your Macros

As you've seen, using sounds in your macros requires special hardware and software. A well-written macro should verify that a computer is capable of playing or recording sounds before trying to use them. You do this by using the GET.WORKSPACE() function, which has the following syntax:

GET.WORKSPACE(*type_num*)

type_num	Tells Excel what type of workspace information you need. Your Excel manual lists the dozens of available values, but Table A.2 shows the two that serve our purpose here.

Table A.2. Values for *type_num* that return system sound information.

type_num	*What It Returns*
42	TRUE if the system is capable of playing sounds, and FALSE otherwise
43	TRUE if the system is capable of recording sounds, and FALSE otherwise

When adding sounds to a cell note, you should always check that no sound note already exists. If one does exist and you try to add another, your macro will crash. Figure A.16 shows a macro that uses the GET.CELL(47) function to first check for the existence of a sound note in the active cell. If one exists, the macro uses SOUND.NOTE() to erase it before proceeding.

FIGURE A.16.

This macro checks for a sound note before adding one.

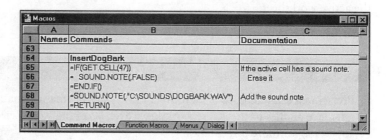

Displaying a Message in the Status Bar

The MESSAGE() function displays text messages on the left side of the status bar at the bottom of the screen. This capability provides you with an easy way to keep the user informed about what the macro is doing or how much is left to process.

Here's the syntax for this function:

```
MESSAGE(logical,message_text)
```

> **logical**   A logical value that controls the message displayed in the status bar. Use TRUE to display the message given by *message_text*. To remove a message and return control of the status bar to Excel, set **logical** to FALSE.
>
> **message_text**   The message you want to display.

As an example of the MESSAGE() function, Figure A.17 shows a revised version of the ConvertToProper macro (called ConvertToProper2). The idea here is to display a message of the form "Converting cell *x* of *y*" in which *x* is the number of cells converted so far, and *y* is the total number of cells to be converted.

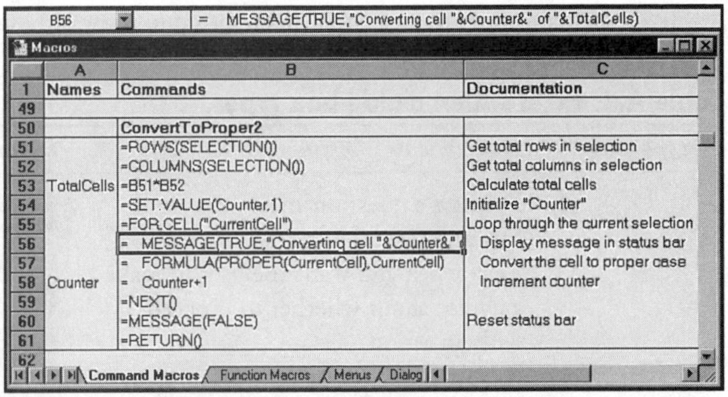

FIGURE A.17.

A macro that uses
MESSAGE( ) to inform the
user of the progress of the
operation.

The first two lines use the ROWS( ) and COLUMNS( ) functions to return the total number of rows and columns in the current selection. The third line (cell B53) multiplies these numbers to get the total number of cells in the selection (cell B53 is named TotalCells). The final bit of preparation requires the SET.VALUE( ) function (which I'll discuss in detail later in this appendix) to initialize a counter variable (named Counter).

In the FOR.CELL( ) loop, the MESSAGE( ) function displays the progress of the operation. (Note the use of the concatenation operator (&) to combine text and values.) Then, before the looping occurs, the Counter variable gets incremented.

NOTE

The ConvertToProper2 macro uses range names in the macro itself (TotalCells and Counter). I'll describe this handy technique in more depth later.

Displaying an Alert Dialog Box

The problem with the MESSAGE( ) display is that it's often a bit too subtle. Unless users know to look down at the status bar, they might miss your messages altogether. For those times when users must see a message, you can use the ALERT( ) function to display an Alert dialog box.

Here is the syntax for the ALERT( ) function:

```
ALERT(message_text,type_num,help_ref)
```

message_text	The message you want to display in the dialog box.
type_num	A specification of which of the three dialog box types you want to use (see Table A.3).
help_ref	A reference to a custom help topic. If you include help_ref, a Help button appears in the dialog box.

Table A.3 explains each type of Alert dialog box and shows an example of each.

Table A.3. Excel's Alert dialog box types.

type_num	Description	Example
1	Displays a question-mark icon and OK and Cancel buttons. Use this Alert when you want the user to make a choice about whether to proceed with an action.	![Microsoft Excel dialog with question-mark icon: A type 1 Alert box, OK and Cancel buttons]
2	Displays an information icon and an OK button. Use this Alert to display important information to the user.	![Microsoft Excel dialog with information icon: A type 2 Alert box, OK button]
3	Displays an exclamation icon and an OK button. Use this Alert to display errors or warnings.	![Microsoft Excel dialog with exclamation icon: A type 3 Alert box, OK button]

TIP

For long alert messages, Excel automatically wraps the text inside the dialog box. If you want to create your own line breaks, use the carriage-return character (ASCII 13) between each line:

```
=ALERT("First line."&CHAR(13)&"Second line.",1)
```

Type 2 and type 3 Alert dialog boxes are straightforward. They simply display information to the user, who must then click OK before the macro will resume.

Type 1 Alert dialog boxes are a little different. In this case, users have a choice between OK and Cancel, which gives them some control over the progress of the macro. If they click OK, the ALERT() function returns TRUE; if they click Cancel, ALERT() returns FALSE. This means that you can use an IF() function to test the user's choice and branch accordingly. The macro fragment shown in Figure A.18 asks users whether they want to see a preview before printing a document.

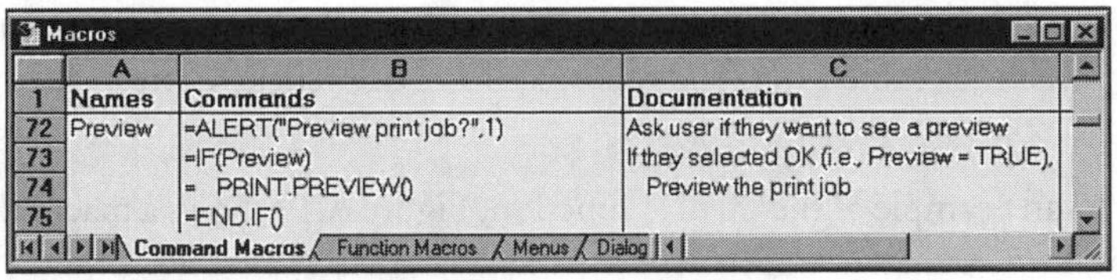

FIGURE A.18.

A macro fragment that uses ALERT() to ask users whether they want to see a preview of a print job.

Getting Input from the User

As you've seen, a type 1 Alert dialog box enables your macros to interact with the user and get some feedback. Unfortunately, this method limits you to simple yes or no answers. For more varied user input, you must use more sophisticated techniques.

Prompting the User for Input

The most common way to get input from the user is through the INPUT() function. This function displays a dialog box with a message that prompts the user to enter data, and it provides an edit box for the data itself. Here is the syntax for this function:

INPUT(**message_text**,*type_num*,*title_text*,*default*,*x_pos*,*y_pos*,*help_ref*)

message_text	The prompt text that appears in the dialog box.
type_num	A number that specifies the type of data to be entered. You can use any of the following values (if the value is omitted, INPUT() assumes a value of 2):

type_num	Data Type
0	Formula
1	Number
2	Text
4	Logical
8	Reference
16	Error
64	Array

title_text	The title of the dialog box. If you omit this argument, Excel uses the title "Input."
default	The default value shown in the edit box.
x_pos,*y_pos*	The horizontal and vertical positions of the upper-left corner of the dialog box. The values are measured in *points;* there are 72 points in an inch. If you omit these values, Excel centers the dialog box.
help_ref	A reference to a custom help topic.

In addition, the dialog box has OK and Cancel buttons. If the user clicks OK, INPUT() returns the value entered into the edit box; if the user clicks Cancel, INPUT() returns the logical value FALSE.

As an example of the INPUT() function, Figure A.19 shows a macro that starts a command macro.

FIGURE A.19.

A macro to start a command macro.

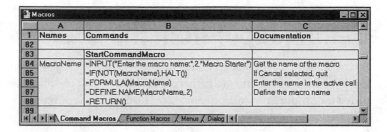

The INPUT() function prompts for the name of the macro, which is stored in MacroName. Figure A.20 shows the dialog box displayed by the INPUT() function. If the user clicks Cancel, INPUT() returns FALSE, the IF() test in cell B85 fails, and the macro runs a HALT() function to stop the macro. Otherwise, the macro enters the name in the appropriate cell (using the FORMULA() function) and then defines the name (using the DEFINE.NAME() function; see the Excel Function Reference for details).

FIGURE A.20.

The dialog box displayed by the INPUT() function in Figure A.19.

NOTE

HALT() stops all running macros. Use of HALT() prevents the current macro from returning to the macro that called it. This precaution probably is not necessary in this case, but it's a good idea to get in the habit of running HALT() whenever the user clicks Cancel.

TIP

You can easily modify this macro to create another that starts a function macro. Just change the 2 in the DEFINE.NAME() function to 1.

Accessing Excel's Standard Dialog Boxes

Many macro functions are known as *dialog box equivalents* because they enable you to select the same options available in Excel's standard dialog boxes. These dialog box equivalents work fine if your macro knows which options to select, but this isn't always the case.

For example, if your macro prints a document (using the PRINT() function), you might need to know how many copies the user wants or how many pages to print. You could use INPUT() functions to get this data, but it's usually easier to display the Print dialog box. All you have to do is add a question mark after the function name. For the Print dialog box, you use the following formula:

```
=PRINT?()
```

If you know *some* of the data beforehand, you can still fill in the appropriate function arguments. This data then appears in the dialog box as the defaults. For example, when you display the Open dialog box, Excel enters *.XL? as the default file specification. If you want to open non-Excel files, you must change the file specification or select a different item from the List Files of Type box. To avoid this situation, you can specify a different file type when you invoke the Open dialog box. For example, to display files with a .TXT extension, you use the following formula:

```
=OPEN?("*.TXT")
```

Macro Worksheet Skills

Most command macros eventually do *something* to a worksheet. It might be selecting a cell or a range, entering a formula, or even copying and moving data. Knowing how a macro interacts with a worksheet is crucial if you ever hope to write useful routines. The rest of this appendix looks closely at that interaction. First I show you how macros use references, and then I show you basic tasks such as selecting ranges, cutting and copying data, and getting cell information.

Working with References

Mastering cell and range references is perhaps the most fundamental of all spreadsheet skills because most worksheet chores involve cells, ranges, and range names. This skill takes on added importance, however, when you work with macros. On a worksheet, for example, you can select cells and ranges easily with the mouse or keyboard, or you can paste range names into formulas. In a macro, though, you are in a sense flying blind. Because most macros operate on some *other* sheet (that is, a sheet other than the one on which the macro resides), you usually end up having to describe—or even calculate—the range you want to work with.

This, unfortunately, tends to add a layer of complexity to macro references, which can sometimes leave even experienced macro jockeys shaking their heads. The good news is that you really have to learn only a few fundamental concepts (and use them often) to get comfortable. The next few sections tell you everything you need to know.

Understanding A1 Versus R1C1 References

Perhaps the biggest source of confusion in macro references is Excel's use of the so-called *R1C1* reference style. The normal A1 style that you're used to numbers a worksheet's rows from 1 to 16384 and assigns the letters A through IV to the worksheet's 256 columns. In R1C1 style, though, Excel numbers both the rows and the columns. In general, the notation $RxCy$ refers to the cell at row x and column y. Here are some examples:

A1 Style	R1C1 Style
$A$1	R1C1
$D$8	R8C4
$B$4:$E$10	R4C2:R10C5
$B:$B	C2 (that is, column B)
$3:$3	R3 (that is, row 3)

As you can see, these are all absolute references. To use relative references in R1C1 notation, enclose the numbers in square brackets. For example, R[2]C[2] refers to the cell two rows down and two columns to the right of the active cell. Similarly, R[–1]C[–3] refers to the cell one row above the active cell and three columns to the left. Here are a few more examples of relative references:

Relative Reference	Description
R[1]C[–1]	One row down and one column left
R[–5]C[3]	Five rows up and three columns right
R[2]C	Two rows down, same column
RC[–1]	Same row, one column left
R	The current row
C	The current column

Should You Use A1 or R1C1 Notation?

The reference style you use in your macros depends on the context. If a formula or function requires a *true* reference (that is, a cell or range address), you can use either A1 or R1C1 notation. Note, though, that using R1C1 for true references requires changing Excel's workspace options. (See the next section.)

Some functions, however, require arguments to be *text* references (that is, a reference in the form of a text string). In this case, you must use R1C1 notation and enclose the reference in quotation marks (for example, `"R[1]C[2]"`).

You're left, then, with two choices:

■ If you want to maintain a consistent notation throughout your macros, use the R1C1 style for true references.

■ If the users of your macros might not be familiar with R1C1 notation, you should stick to A1 style for true references (especially if the user will be selecting ranges).

Switching Excel to R1C1 Notation

If you decide to use R1C1 notation, you need to change your workspace setup to switch true references from the default A1 style to the R1C1 style. Follow these steps:

1. Select the **T**ools | **O**ptions command and select the General tab in the Options dialog box.
2. Activate the R1**C**1 check box.
3. Click OK or press Enter. Excel returns you to the worksheet and converts all the A1 notation in your formulas to the R1C1 style.

Referencing Worksheets

One of the crucial questions to keep asking yourself when building your command macros is, what sheet do I want this formula to affect? When answering this question, you have three choices:

■ The macro sheet. This is called a *local reference*.

■ The active sheet. This is called an *active reference*.

■ A specific sheet. This is called an *external reference*.

The next three sections present each type of reference in more detail.

Using Local References

Local references are straightforward. Because they refer to the sheet on which the macro formula resides, you simply use the appropriate cell or range address in either A1 or R1C1 style. For example, Figure A.21 shows the ConvertToProper2 macro. To calculate the TotalCells variable, cell B53 multiplies the values for the rows (cell B51) and columns (cell B52) in the selection:

```
=B51*B52
```

FIGURE A.21.

For local references, just use the cell or range address.

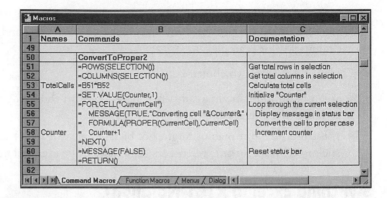

> **CAUTION**
>
> You should always use relative references in macros. This way, if you alter the macro by adding or deleting lines, your existing formulas will adjust accordingly.

Using Active References

Two methods are available for referencing a cell or range on the active worksheet. The method you use depends on whether you need a true reference or a text reference.

For a true reference, enter an exclamation point followed by an absolute address in either A1 or R1C1 style. (Remember, though, that to use R1C1 notation for true references, you need to set up your workspace to handle them, as described earlier, in the section titled "Switching Excel to R1C1 Notation.") For example, the following function enters the label Expenses into cell C3 of the active worksheet:

```
=FORMULA("Expenses",!$C$3)
```

Notice that I said you must use an *absolute* address when entering a true reference. The problem with relative addresses is that, contrary to what you might expect, Excel doesn't assume that the reference is relative to the active cell. Instead, it assumes that the reference is relative *to the cell that contains the formula on the macro sheet.* This assumption can lead to two types of problems. For example, suppose that you're using A1 notation and you enter the following formula in cell B10 of the macro sheet:

```
=FORMULA("Expenses",!C3)
```

This formula works, but if you subsequently delete a line from the macro, the formula changes to this:

```
=FORMULA("Expenses",!C2)
```

The second type of problem occurs when you're using R1C1 notation. Suppose that you enter the following formula in cell R10C2:

```
=FORMULA("Expenses",!R[-1]C)
```

Theoretically, you're trying to enter the label Expenses in the cell above the active cell. Excel, however, interprets the relative address R[–1]C to mean R9C2 (the cell above the one containing the formula), so it enters the label in cell R9C2 of the active worksheet (no matter which cell is active).

If you need to enter a text reference to a cell on the active worksheet, just enter the reference in R1C1 style enclosed in quotation marks. (You don't have to change the workspace options for text references.) The following formula enters the Expenses label in row 3, column 3:

```
=FORMULA("Expenses","R3C3")
```

Unlike true references, relative addresses can be used with text references. For example, the following formula adds the Expenses label to the cell one row above the active cell:

```
=FORMULA("Expenses","R[-1]C")
```

> **NOTE**
>
> Why is there a difference between how Excel sees a true relative reference and how it sees a text relative reference? The reason has to do with *when* Excel calculates the reference. A true relative reference is calculated as soon as you enter the formula (so it's interpreted relative to the formula's cell). A text relative reference, on the other hand, is calculated only when you run the macro (so it's interpreted relative to the active cell).

One of the handiest functions in the Excel 4.0 macro language is the ACTIVE.CELL() function. This function simply returns a reference to the active cell (including the sheet name and workbook filename, if necessary). For example, to find out the row number of the active cell, you use the following formula:

```
=ROW(ACTIVE.CELL())
```

Using External References

To reference a cell or range on a sheet other than the active sheet, enter the name of the sheet, an exclamation point, and the absolute address in either A1 or R1C1 style. If the sheet name uses two or more words, enclose the name in single quotation marks. For example, the following formula enters an Expenses label in cell C3 on a sheet named August Expenses:

```
=FORMULA("Expenses",'August Expenses'!$C$3)
```

If the sheet resides in a different workbook, precede the sheet name with the workbook filename (including the extension and the drive and directory, if necessary) in square brackets:

```
=FORMULA("Expenses",'[BUDGET.XLS]August Expenses'!$C$3)
```

For a text reference, enter the sheet name, an exclamation point, and the absolute cell address in R1C1 style, and then surround everything with quotation marks:

```
=FORMULA("Expenses","'August Expenses'!R3C3")
```

As with referencing the active worksheet, relative references to an external worksheet are dangerous. If you use a true relative reference, the reference is calculated relative to the formula's cell on the macro sheet. For example, if you enter the following formula in cell R10C2 on the macro sheet, it always enters the label in cell R9C2 of August Expenses:

```
=FORMULA("Expenses",'August Expenses'!R[-1]C)
```

If you use a text relative reference, Excel calculates the reference relative to the *active cell* (which could be on any sheet). For example, if the active cell is R5C5, the following formula enters Expenses in cell R6C6 of August Expenses (this assumes that August Expenses is not the active worksheet):

```
=FORMULA("Expenses","'August Expenses'!R[1]C[1]")
```

Calculating References with *OFFSET()*

In the preceding section, you saw that the only way to reference a relative address on the active worksheet was to use a text reference (and you also saw that you can never safely use relative addresses for external references). There are several disadvantages to this approach:

- Excel doesn't check the syntax of references enclosed in quotation marks.

- It's difficult to create relative text references from existing macro variables. (It's not impossible, however: you could just use the concatenation operator (&) to construct the appropriate string. The problem is that these statements are unintuitive and tough to decipher.)

- Only five functions accept text references: ABSREF(), FORMULA(), INDIRECT(), SELECT(), and TEXTREF(). Of these, only ABSREF(), FORMULA(), and SELECT() accept relative text references.

The way to overcome these problems, and add tremendous flexibility to your macros in the process, is to *calculate* references using the OFFSET() function. With this method, you begin with a reference and then specify a certain number of rows and columns to indicate where the new reference should start.

Here is the syntax for this function:

```
OFFSET(reference,rows,cols,height,width)
```

reference	The original reference on which the returned reference is based.
rows	The number of rows (up or down) from the top-left cell of *reference* to where the returned reference will start.
cols	The number of columns (left or right) from the top-left cell of *reference* to where the returned reference will start.
height	The number of rows in the returned reference.
width	The number of columns in the returned reference.

For example, the following OFFSET() function returns a reference to the cell that is one row above and two columns to the right of the active cell:

```
OFFSET(ACTIVE.CELL(),-1,2)
```

Figure A.22 shows a simple macro that concatenates (combines) two text strings. This macro is handy, for instance, if you have a list with separate first-name and last-name fields and you want to combine them. As you can see in Sheet1, the active cell is C2, and the first-name and last-name fields are in columns A and B, respectively.

FIGURE A.22.

A macro that concatenates two text strings.

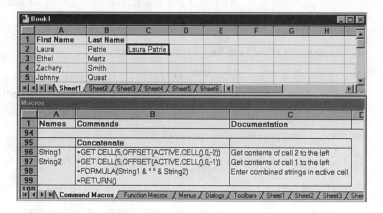

The first GET.CELL() function (its name is String1) returns the contents of the cell two columns to the left of the active cell by using the following OFFSET() function:

```
OFFSET(ACTIVE.CELL(),0,-2)
```

Similarly, the second GET.CELL() function (String2) returns the contents of the cell one column to the left of the active cell. Finally, the FORMULA() function concatenates String1 and String2 (with a space between) and enters the new string in the active cell.

Converting Between Text and True References

Your macros will often have to convert between text and true references. For example, suppose that the active cell contains the string Sales and you want to store the active cell's address in cell C2. You know that the ACTIVE.CELL() function returns a reference to the active cell, so your first guess might be to use the following formula in a macro:

```
=FORMULA(ACTIVE.CELL(),!$C$2)
```

When you run the macro, you get Sales in cell C2 rather than the reference you wanted. This happens because of an assumption Excel makes. For functions that return references, Excel usually assumes that you want to work with the contents of the referenced cell, rather than the reference itself. (The exception to this rule is when you use the function as an argument in another function that accepts a reference argument.) In this case, Excel stores the contents of the active cell (the string Sales) in cell C2.

To get around this, you must convert the reference to text with the REFTEXT() function:

REFTEXT(*reference*,*a1*)

reference	The reference you want to convert.
a1	A logical value that determines whether REFTEXT() returns the text in A1 style (TRUE) or R1C1 style (FALSE or omitted).

To fix the preceding problem, you convert ACTIVE.CELL() to text:

```
=FORMULA(REFTEXT(ACTIVE.CELL(),TRUE),!$C$2)
```

One of the most common uses for REFTEXT() is to capture a reference entered with the INPUT() function. Again, without converting, INPUT() would store the contents of the reference. To capture the reference itself, you must use REFTEXT(), as in the following example:

```
=REFTEXT(INPUT("Enter a reference",8))
```

To convert text references into true references, use the TEXTREF() function:

TEXTREF(*text*,*a1*)

text	The text reference you want to convert.
a1	A logical value that determines whether TEXTREF() returns the text in A1 style (TRUE) or R1C1 style (FALSE or omitted).

For example, the following macro fragment gets a range from the user and then selects the range (assuming that the first formula resides in cell B10):

```
=REFTEXT(INPUT("Enter a range",8))
=SELECT(TEXTREF(B10))
```

> **NOTE**
>
> I'll discuss the SELECT() function later, in the section titled "Using the SELECT() Function."

Working with Names in Macros

Using range names in your macros is generally straightforward. You can refer to names on the active worksheet by preceding the name with an exclamation point (!)—for example, !Database. Or you can refer to names on an external worksheet by preceding the name with the workbook filename, the sheet name, and an exclamation point—for example, '[DATA.XLS]Customer Data'!Database.

You also have access to six functions that are the macro equivalents of Excel's range commands: DEFINE.NAME(), CREATE.NAMES(), LIST.NAMES(), DELETE.NAME(), GET.NAME(), and GET.DEF(). I won't discuss these functions in detail here. There are, however, two other functions you need to look at more closely: SET.NAME() and SET.VALUE().

Defining Macro Sheet Names with *SET.NAME()*

Use the SET.NAME() function to define a name for a value on a macro sheet. Here is its syntax:

SET.NAME(***name_text***,*value*)

> ***name_text***   The name you want to define.
>
> *value*   The value you want to store in ***name_text***. If you omit *value*, Excel deletes ***name_text***.

Figure A.23 shows a revised version of the Concatenate macro (called Concatenate2) that uses SET.NAME(). In this macro, the OFFSET() functions in cells B108 and B109 need to access the active cell. Rather than running the ACTIVE.CELL() function each time, the macro uses the following formula to assign the name Active to the result of the ACTIVE.CELL() function:

=SET.NAME("Active",ACTIVE.CELL())

Thus, any subsequent function that needs to refer to the active cell just uses the name Active. You gain two advantages with this method:

- Substituting shorter names for long-winded functions makes the macro less cluttered and easier to read.
- Because the macro must run the function only once, it executes faster.

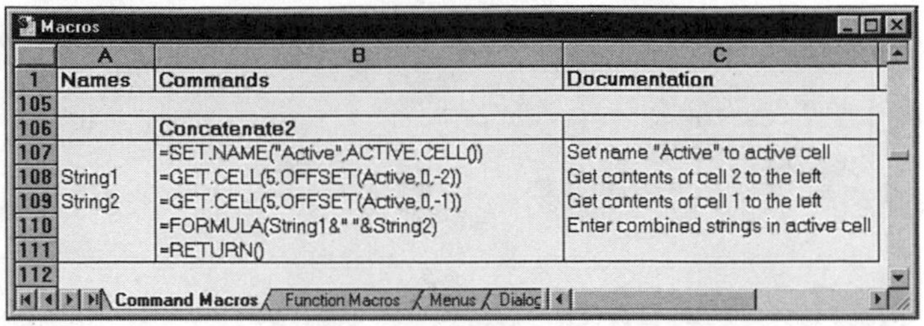

FIGURE A.23.

Use SET.NAME() *to assign a name to a frequently used value.*

TIP

In addition to using the SET.NAME() function, you also can assign names to values using the following syntax:

name_text=*value*

This technique saves you from having to enter the name in a separate cell, and it often makes the macro code easier to read. For example, to assign the value 1 to the name Counter, just type Counter = 1 in a cell. To increment Counter, type the formula Counter = Counter + 1 in another cell.

NOTE

To avoid wasting memory, it's good practice to delete any range names in the macro sheet that are not used by any other macro. Use the DELETE.NAME(**name_text**) function, in which **name_text** is the name you want to delete.

Storing Macro Sheet Values with *SET.VALUE()*

Instead of storing a value in a name, you might need to store it in a cell or range on the macro sheet. You can do this with the SET.VALUE() function:

SET.VALUE(**reference**,*value*)

reference	The cell (or range) on the macro sheet where you want to store the value.
value	The value you want to store.

Note that if **reference** contains a formula, the formula does not change; only the value of the cell changes. To see how this works, take a look at the macro in Figure A.24.

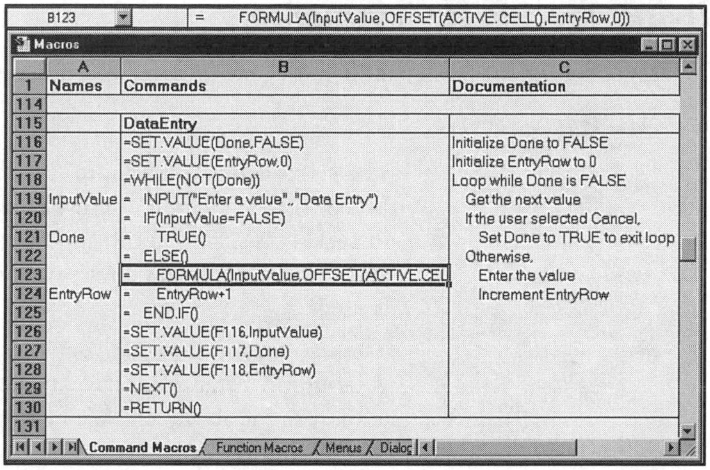

FIGURE A.24.

SET.VALUE( ) initializes Done and EntryRow but doesn't alter their formulas.

	A	B	C
		B123 ▼	= FORMULA(InputValue,OFFSET(ACTIVE.CELL(),EntryRow,0))

Macros

	A Names	B Commands	C Documentation
1	Names	Commands	Documentation
114			
115		DataEntry	
116		=SET.VALUE(Done,FALSE)	Initialize Done to FALSE
117		=SET.VALUE(EntryRow,0)	Initialize EntryRow to 0
118		=WHILE(NOT(Done))	Loop while Done is FALSE
119	InputValue	= INPUT("Enter a value",,"Data Entry")	Get the next value
120		= IF(InputValue=FALSE)	If the user selected Cancel,
121	Done	= TRUE()	Set Done to TRUE to exit loop
122		= ELSE()	Otherwise,
123		= FORMULA(InputValue,OFFSET(ACTIVE.CEL	Enter the value
124	EntryRow	= EntryRow+1	Increment EntryRow
125		= END.IF()	
126		=SET.VALUE(F116,InputValue)	
127		=SET.VALUE(F117,Done)	
128		=SET.VALUE(F118,EntryRow)	
129		=NEXT()	
130		=RETURN()	
131			

Command Macros / Function Macros / Menus / Dialog

The purpose of this macro is to enter numeric data in a column until the user clicks Cancel in the INPUT( ) dialog box. The first SET.VALUE( ) function sets the value of the cell named Done (cell B121) to FALSE:

`=SET.VALUE(Done,FALSE)`

Although this cell contains the formula =TRUE( ), setting Done to FALSE has no effect on the formula. (Remember: Excel doesn't evaluate macro formulas until it comes across them when you run the macro. This means that you're free to assign any value you like to any cell.) The second SET.VALUE( ) function initializes a counter (the cell named EntryRow) that tracks which row the data goes in:

`=SET.VALUE(EntryRow,0)`

Next, a WHILE( ) function loops as long as Done is FALSE (because you don't know in advance how much data the user will enter). As long as the user clicks OK, the macro enters the data (the new cell is offset from the active cell by EntryRow rows) and increments the EntryRow counter. When the user clicks Cancel, however, the INPUT( ) function returns FALSE, and Done is set to TRUE. This exits the loop on the next pass, and you are, literally, done.

Selecting a Cell or Range

Selecting a cell or range is one of the most common worksheet tasks, so you need to be comfortable with the corresponding macro methods. The next two sections take you through the basics.

Using the *SELECT()* Function

The SELECT() function can handle most of your range selection needs. Here is its syntax:

SELECT(*selection,active_cell*)

selection	The cell or range you want to select on the active worksheet. If you use A1 notation, it must be an absolute reference, as in SELECT(!$B$3). You can also use the R1C1 style, as in SELECT("R3C2"). If you omit *selection*, the current selection is used.
active_cell	The cell in *selection* that you want to make the active cell. If you omit this argument, Excel makes the upper-left cell of *selection* the active cell. Again, you can use A1 (absolute) or R1C1 notation.

It's important to remember that SELECT() applies only to the active worksheet. If you try to use it with an external reference, Excel generates an error. If you need to select a range on an external worksheet, use the FORMULA.GOTO() function. (See the section later in this appendix titled "Selecting a Range with FORMULA.GOTO().")

NOTE

If you need to, you can make a worksheet active before using SELECT() by running the WORKBOOK.SELECT(*sheet_name*) function, in which *sheet_name* is the name of a sheet in the active workbook (enclosed in quotation marks). To activate a different workbook, use the ACTIVATE(*window_text*) function, in which *window_text* is the name of the open workbook you want to activate. (Technically, it's the name that appears in the window title bar.) You also can use ACTIVATE.PREV() to activate the previous workbook window and ACTIVATE.NEXT() to activate the next workbook window.

The most basic use of the SELECT() function is to simulate the keys you normally use to navigate through a worksheet. Table A.4 lists some SELECT() functions and their key equivalents.

Table A.4. Some SELECT() functions and their key equivalents.

SELECT() *Function*	*Key Equivalent*
SELECT("RC[1]")	Right arrow or Tab
SELECT("RC[-1]")	Left arrow or Shift-Tab
SELECT("R[1]C")	Down arrow
SELECT("R[-1]C")	Up arrow

If you want to select a range of cells, just enter the range coordinates in SELECT(). For example, the following formula selects the range A1:E10 in the active worksheet:

```
=SELECT(!$A$1:$E$10)
```

TIP

Use the SELECTION() function if you need the reference of the current selection.

CAUTION

SELECT() is fairly slow, so don't use it unless you have to. For many functions that take reference arguments, you often can use an OFFSET() function to specify the reference instead of selecting it in advance. For example, consider the following formula:

```
=FORMULA("Sales",OFFSET(ACTIVE.CELL(),1,1))
```

This formula executes slightly faster than these two formulas:

```
=SELECT("R[1]C[1]")
=FORMULA("Sales")
```

Selecting a Range with *FORMULA.GOTO()*

SELECT() selects ranges only in the active worksheet. If you need to select an external reference, use FORMULA.GOTO() instead:

FORMULA.GOTO(*reference,corner*)

reference	An active or external reference for the cell or range you want to select.
corner	A logical value that determines the position of the upper-left cell of the selection. If *corner* is TRUE, Excel places the upper-left cell of *reference* in the upper-left corner of the window. If *corner* is FALSE (or if you omit it), Excel positions *reference* normally.

FORMULA.GOTO() is the command equivalent of the **Edit | G**o To command, and it works just like the SELECT() function.

TIP

After you select a range with FORMULA.GOTO(), run the function again without the *reference* argument to return to your previous position.

Cutting and Copying Data with Macros

If you need to cut and copy data within your macros, you can do it easily with the CUT() and COPY() functions. These functions have identical syntaxes:

```
CUT(from_reference,to_reference)
COPY(from_reference,to_reference)
```

from_reference	The reference of the source cell or range you want to cut or copy. If you omit *from_reference*, Excel uses the current selection.
to_reference	The reference of the destination cell or range. If you omit *to_reference*, Excel cuts or copies *from_reference* to the Clipboard. You can enter these references in either A1 or R1C1 style for either the active worksheet or an external document.

> **NOTE**
>
> By specifying the *from_reference* argument in CUT() or COPY(), you don't need to use SELECT() to select a cell or range beforehand.

Although Excel has a PASTE() function, you don't need to use it as long as you specify a *to_reference* argument in your CUT() and COPY() functions. However, there is also a PASTE.SPECIAL() function that is the equivalent of selecting the **S**pecial button in the Go To dialog box:

```
PASTE.SPECIAL(paste_num,operation_num,skip_blanks,transpose)
```

paste_num   A number that specifies what you want to paste:

paste_num	Description
1	All
2	Formulas
3	Values
4	Formats
5	Notes

operation_num   A number that specifies what type of operation to perform:

operation_num	Operation
1	None
2	Add
3	Subtract

4	Multiply
5	Divide
skip_blanks	Set this logical value to TRUE if you want to skip blank cells when pasting. Set it to FALSE to paste normally.
transpose	Set this logical value to TRUE if you want Excel to transpose rows and columns when pasting. Set it to FALSE to paste the data without transposing.

NOTE

Before you use PASTE.SPECIAL(), be sure to use SELECT() to select the area where you want the data pasted. Also, be sure not to specify a destination range in your CUT() or COPY() function.

NOTE

In Chapter 2, I showed you a worksheet named Life.xls that implemented a game called Life. The macros that support this application are written in the Excel 4.0 macro language, so you might want to examine them to see how they work. This application also shows you how to work with dialog boxes in the Excel 4.0 macro language.

VBA Statements

B

Throughout our excursion into spreadsheet programming in Part V of this book (Chapters 21 through 30), I introduced you to various VBA statements. These statements appeared on an "as needed" basis whenever I wanted to explain a particular VBA topic (such as the control structures we looked at in Chapter 23, "Controlling VBA Code and Interacting with the User"). Although we covered a few dozen VBA statements in all, there wasn't enough room (or enough of a reason) to cover the full 84 statements that make up the VBA repertoire. (In this context, a *statement* is any VBA keyword or construct that isn't a function, object, property, or method.)

In an effort to put some finishing touches on our VBA coverage, this appendix presents a brief, but complete, look at every VBA statement. I give a short description of each statement and, where appropriate, I refer you to the relevant chapter in Part V where you can get more detailed information. For the other statements, you can get full explanations and examples from the Statements section of the VBA Help file.

Table B.1. VBA statements.

Statement	Chapter	Description
AppActivate *title*,wait	28	Activates the running application with the title or task ID given by *title*.
Beep	23	Beeps the speaker.
Call *name*,*argumentlist*		Calls the *name* procedure. (Because you can call a procedure just by using its name, the Call statement is rarely used in VBA programming.)
ChDir *path*	24	Changes the current directory (folder) to *path*.
ChDrive *drive*	24	Changes the current drive to *drive*.
Close *filenumberlist*		Closes the I/O file opened with the Open statement.
Const *CONSTNAME*	21	Declares a constant variable named *CONSTNAME*.
Date = *date*		Changes the system date to *date*.
Declare *name*		Declares a procedure from a dynamic link library (DLL).
DefBool *letterrange*		A module-level statement that sets the default data type to Boolean for all variables that begin with the letters in *letterrange* (for example, DefBool A-F).
DefCur *letterrange*		Sets the default data type to Currency for all variables that begin with the letters in *letterrange*.

Statement	Chapter	Description
DefDate *letterrange*		Sets the default data type to Date for all variables that begin with the letters in *letterrange*.
DefDbl *letterrange*		Sets the default data type to Double for all variables that begin with the letters in *letterrange*.
DefInt *letterrange*		Sets the default data type to Integer for all variables that begin with the letters in *letterrange*.
DefLng *letterrange*		Sets the default data type to Long for all variables that begin with the letters in *letterrange*.
DefObj *letterrange*		Sets the default data type to Object for all variables that begin with the letters in *letterrange*.
DefSng *letterrange*		Sets the default data type to Single for all variables that begin with the letters in *letterrange*.
DefStr *letterrange*		Sets the default data type to String for all variables that begin with the letters in *letterrange*.
DefVar *letterrange*		Sets the default data type to Variant for all variables that begin with the letters in *letterrange*.
Dim *variablename*	21	Declares a variable named *variablename*.
Do...Loop	23	Loops through one or more statements while a logical condition is True.
DoEvents		Yields execution to the operating system so that it can process pending events from other applications (such as keystrokes and mouse clicks).
End *keyword*	21, 23	Ends a procedure, function, or control structure.
Erase *arraylist*		Frees the memory allocated to a dynamic array or reinitializes a fixed-size array.

continues

Table B.1. continued

Statement	Chapter	Description
Err = *errornumber*		Sets Err (the current error status) to *errornumber*.
Error *errornumber*		Simulates an error by setting Err to *errornumber*.
Exit *keyword*	23	Exits a procedure, function, or control structure.
FileCopy *source,destination*		Copies the *source* file to *destination*.
For Each...Next	23	Loops through each member of a collection.
For...Next	23	Loops through one or more statements until a counter hits a specified value.
Function	21	Declares a user-defined function procedure.
Get #*filenumber,varname*		Reads an I/O file opened by the Open statement into a variable.
GoSub...Return		Branches to and returns from a subroutine within a procedure. (However, creating separate procedures makes your code more readable.)
GoTo *line*		Sends the code to the line label given by *line*.
If...Then...Else	23	Runs one of two sections of code based on the result of a logical test.
Input #*filenumber,varlist*		Reads data from an I/O file into variables.
Kill *pathname*		Deletes the file *pathname* from a disk.
Let *varname=expression*		Sets the variable *varname* equal to *expression*. Let is optional and is almost never used.
Line Input #*filenumber,var*		Reads a line from an I/O file and stores it in *var*.
Load		A restricted keyword.
Lock #*filenumber*		Controls access to an I/O file.
Lset *stringvar = string*		Left-aligns a string within a String variable.

Statement	Chapter	Description
Lset *var1* = *var2*		Copies a variable of one user-defined type into another variable of a different user-defined type.
Mid		Replaces characters in a String variable with characters from a different string.
MkDir *path*		Creates the directory (folder) named *path*.
Name *oldName* As *newname*		Renames a file or directory (folder).
On Error	27	Sets up an error-handling routine.
On...GoSub, On...GoTo		Branches to a line based on the result of an expression.
Open *pathname*		Opens an input/output (I/O) file.
Option Base 0¦1	21	Determines (at the module level) the default lower bound for arrays.
Option Compare Text¦Binary	21	Determines (at the module level) the default mode for string comparisons.
Option Explicit	21	Forces you to declare all variables used in a module. Enter this statement at the module level.
Option Private		Indicates that the module is private and can't be accessed by other procedures outside the module. Enter this statement at the module level.
Print #*filenumber*		Writes data to an I/O file.
Private *varname*	21	Declares the *varname* variable to be a private variable that can be used only in the module in which it's declared. Enter this statement at the module level.
Property Get		Declares a property procedure.
Property Let		Assigns a value to a property in a property procedure.
Property Set		Sets a reference to an object in a property procedure.
Public *varname*		Makes the *varname* variable available to all procedures in a module.

continues

Table B.1. continued

Statement	Chapter	Description
Put #*filenumber,varname*		Writes data from the variable *varname* to an I/O file.
Randomize *number*		Initializes the random-number generator. Omit *number* to get a different random number each time.
ReDim *varname*	21	Reallocates memory in a dynamic array.
Rem *comment*		Tells VBA that the following text is a comment. The apostrophe (') is more widely used.
Reset		Closes all I/O files opened with Open.
Resume	27	After an error, resumes program execution at the line that caused the error.
Return		See GoSub...Return.
RmDir *path*		Deletes a directory (folder).
Rset *stringvar=string*		Right-aligns a string within a String variable.
SavePicture		A restricted keyword.
Seek #*filenumber,position*		Sets the current position in an I/O file.
Select Case	23	Executes one of several groups of statements based on the value of an expression.
SendKeys *string,wait*	28	Sends the keystrokes given by *string* to the active application.
Set *objectvar=object*		Assigns an *object* to an Object variable named *objectvar*.
SetAttr *pathname,attr*		Assigns the attributes given by *attr* (for example, vbReadOnly) to the file given by *pathname*.
Static *varname*		Declares *varname* to be a variable that will retain its value as long as the code is running.
Stop	29	Places VBA in Pause mode.
Sub	21	Declares a procedure.
Time = *time*		Sets the system time to *time*.

Statement	Chapter	Description
Type ***varname***		Declares a user-defined data type. (Used at the module level only.)
Unload		A restricted keyword.
While...Wend	23	Loops through a block of code while a condition is True.
Width #***filenumber,width***		Assigns an output-line width to an I/O file.
With...End With		Executes a block of statements on a specified object.
Write #***filenumber***		Writes data to an I/O file.

VBA Functions

C

Although we discussed quite a few VBA functions in Part V of this book, we were by no means exhaustive in our coverage. In fact, VBA boasts over 150 built-in functions that cover data conversion, dates and times, math, strings, and lots more. This appendix presents a categorical list of each VBA function and the arguments they use. You can get full explanations and examples for all the functions in the Functions section of the VBA Help file.

Table C.1. Conversion functions.

Function	What It Returns
CBool(*expression*)	An *expression* converted to a Boolean value.
CCur(*expression*)	An *expression* converted to a Currency value.
CDate(*expression*)	An *expression* converted to a Date value.
CDbl(*expression*)	An *expression* converted to a Double value.
CInt(*expression*)	An *expression* converted to an Integer value.
CLng(*expression*)	An *expression* converted to a Long value.
CSng(*expression*)	An *expression* converted to a Single value.
CStr(*expression*)	An *expression* converted to a String value.
CVar(*expression*)	An *expression* converted to a Variant value.
CVDate(*expression*)	An *expression* converted to a Date value. (Provided for backward compatibility. Use CDate instead.)
CVErr(*errornumber*)	A Variant of subtype Error that contains *errornumber*.

Table C.2. Database functions (Microsoft Query).

Function	What It Returns
QueryGetData(*connectionStr,etc.*)	A new query in the Microsoft Query add-in.
QueryGetDataDialog(*connectionStr,etc.*)	A new query in the Microsoft Query add-in. This function is equivalent to running the **D**ata	Get External Data command.
QueryRefresh(*ref*)	Refreshed external data in the range given by *ref*.

Table C.3. Date and time functions.

Function	What It Returns
Date	The current system date as a Variant.
Date$()	The current system date as a String.
DateSerial(*year*,*month*,*day*)	A Date value for the specified *year*, *month*, and *day*.
DateValue(*date*)	A Date value for the *date* string.
Day(*date*)	The day of the month given by *date*.
Hour(*time*)	The hour component of *time*.
Minute(*time*)	The minute component of *time*.
Month(*date*)	The month component of *date*.
Now	The current system date and time.
Second(*time*)	The second component of *time*.
Time	The current system time as a Variant.
Time$	The current system time as a String.
Timer	The number of seconds since midnight.
TimeSerial(*hour*,*minute*,*second*)	A Date value for the specified *hour*, *minute*, and *second*.
TimeValue(*time*)	A Date value for the *time* string.
Weekday(*date*)	The day of the week, as a number, given by *date*.
Year(*date*)	The year component of *date*.

Table C.4. Error functions.

Function	What It Returns
Erl	A value that specifies the line number where the most recent error occurred.
Err	A value that specifies the runtime error number of the most recent error.
Error(*errornumber*)	The error message, as a Variant, that corresponds to the *errornumber*.
Error$(*errornumber*)	The error message, as a String, that corresponds to the *errornumber*.

Table C.5. File and directory functions.

Function	What It Returns
CurDir(*drive*)	The current directory as a Variant.
CurDir$(*drive*)	The current directory as a String.
Dir(*pathname*, attributes)	The name, as a Variant, of the file or directory (folder) specified by *pathname* and satisfying the optional *attributes* (for example, vbHidden). Returns Null if the file or directory doesn't exist.
Dir$(*pathname*, attributes)	The name, as a String, of the file or directory (folder) specified by *pathname* and satisfying the optional *attributes* (for example, vbHidden). Returns Null if the file or directory doesn't exist.
EOF(*filenumber*)	True if the end of file specified by *filenumber* has been reached; False otherwise.
FileAttr(*filenumber*, *returnType*)	The file mode (if *returnType* is 1) or the file handle (if *returnType* is 2) of the file given by *filenumber*.
FileDateTime(*pathname*)	The Date that the file given by *pathname* was created or last modified.
FileLen(*pathname*)	The length, in bytes, of the file given by *pathname*.
FreeFile(*rangenumber*)	The next available file number available to the Open statement.
GetAttr(*pathname*)	An integer representing the attributes of the file given by *pathname*.
Loc(*filenumber*)	The current read/write position in an open I/O file.
LOF(*filenumber*)	The size, in bytes, of an open I/O file.
Seek(*filenumber*)	The current read/write position, as a Variant, in an open I/O file.
Seek$(*filenumber*)	The current read/write position, as a String, in an open I/O file.
Shell(*pathname*, *windowstyle*)	The task ID of the executed program given by *pathname*.

Table C.6. Math functions.

Function	What It Returns
Abs(*number*)	The absolute value of *number*.
Atn(*number*)	The arctangent of *number*.
Cos(*number*)	The cosine of *number*.
Exp(*number*)	*e* (the base of the natural logarithm) raised to the power of *number*.
Fix(*number*)	The integer portion of *number*. If *number* is negative, Fix returns the first negative integer greater than or equal to *number*.
Hex(*number*)	The hexadecimal value, as a Variant, of *number*.
Hex$(*number*)	The hexadecimal value, as a String, of *number*.
Int(*number*)	The integer portion of *number*. If *number* is negative, Int returns the first negative integer less than or equal to *number*.
Log(*number*)	The natural logarithm of *number*.
Oct(*number*)	The octal value, as a Variant, of *number*.
Oct$(*number*)	The octal value, as a String, of *number*.
Rnd(*number*)	A random number.
Sgn(*number*)	The sign of *number*.
Sin(*number*)	The sine of *number*.
Sqr(*number*)	The square root of *number*.
Tan(*number*)	The tangent of *number*.

Table C.7. Miscellaneous functions.

Function	What It Returns
Array(*arglist*)	A Variant array containing the values in *arglist*.
Command	Nothing. This is a restricted keyword.
CreateObject(*class*)	An OLE automation object of type *class*.
Format(*expression,*format)	The *expression*, as a Variant, according to the string format.
Format$(*expression,*format)	The *expression*, as a String, according to the string format.

continues

Part VI

Table C.7. continued

Function	*What It Returns*
GetObject(*pathname*,*class*)	The OLE automation object given by *pathname* and *class*.
Input(*number*,#*filenumber*)	*number* characters, as a Variant, from the I/O file given by *filenumber*.
Input$(*number*,#*filenumber*)	*number* characters, as a String, from the I/O file given by *filenumber*.
InputB(*number*,#*filenumber*)	*number* bytes, as a Variant, from the I/O file given by *filenumber*.
InputB$(*number*,#*filenumber*)	*number* bytes, as a String, from the I/O file given by *filenumber*.
InputBox(*prompt*,*etc.*)	Prompts the user for information.
IsArray(*varname*)	True if *varname* is an array.
IsDate(*expression*)	True if *expression* can be converted into a date.
IsEmpty(*expression*)	True if *expression* is empty.
IsError(*expression*)	True if *expression* is an error.
IsMissing(*argname*)	True if the argument specified by *argname* was not passed to the procedure.
IsNull(*expression*)	True if *expression* is the null string ("").
IsNumeric(*expression*)	True if *expression* is a number.
IsObject(*expression*)	True if *expression* is an object.
LBound(*arrayname*,*dimension*)	The lowest possible subscript for the array given by *arrayname*.
LoadPicture()	Nothing. This is a restricted keyword.
MsgBox(*prompt*,*etc.*)	The button a user selects from the MsgBox dialog box.
RGB(*red*,*green*,*blue*)	The color that corresponds to the *red*, *green*, and *blue* components.
Tab(*n*)	Positions output for the Print # statement or the Print method.
TypeName(*varname*)	A string that indicates the data type of the *varname* variable.
UBound(*arrayname*,*dimension*)	The highest possible subscript for the array given by *arrayname*.
VarType(*varname*)	A constant that indicates the data type of the *varname* variable.

Table C.8. Solver functions.

Function	Description
SolverAdd(***cellRef,relation,***formulaText)	Adds a constraint to the current Solver problem.
SolverChange(***cellRef,relation,***formulaText)	Changes an existing Solver constraint.
SolverDelete(***cellRef,relation,***formulaText)	Deletes an existing Solver constraint.
SolverFinish(keepFinal,reportArray)	Tells Excel what to do with the current Solver results.
SolverFinishDialog(keepFinal,reportArray)	Displays the Solver Results dialog box.
SolverGet(***typeNum,***sheetName)	Returns information about the current Solver model.
SolverLoad(***loadArea***)	Loads saved Solver parameters.
SolverOk(setCell,maxMinVal,valueOf,byChange)	Defines a Solver model.
SolverOkDialog(setCell,maxMinVal,valueOf,byChange)	Displays the Solver dialog box.
SolverOptions(***maxTime,***etc.)	Sets the Solver options.
SolverReset()	Resets the current Solver model to the default values.
SolverSave(***saveArea***)	Saves the current Solver model.
SolverSolve(userFinish,showRef)	Starts a Solver solution.

Table C.9. String functions.

Function	What It Returns
Asc(***string***)	The ANSI character code of the first letter in ***string***.
Chr(***charcode***)	The character, as a Variant, that corresponds to the ANSI code given by ***charcode***.
Chr$(***charcode***)	The character, as a String, that corresponds to the ANSI code given by ***charcode***.

continues

Table C.9. continued

Function	What It Returns
InStr(*start*,**string1**,**string2**)	The character position of the first occurrence of **string2** in **string1**, starting at *start*.
InStrB(*start*,**string1**,**string2**)	The byte position of the first occurrence of **string2** in **string1**, starting at *start*.
LCase(**string**)	**string** converted to lowercase as a Variant.
LCase$(**string**)	**string** converted to lowercase as a String.
Left(**string**,**length**)	The leftmost **length** characters from **string** as a Variant.
Left$(**string**,**length**)	The leftmost **length** characters from **string** as a String.
LeftB(**string**)	The leftmost **length** bytes from **string** as a Variant.
LeftB$(**string**)	The leftmost **length** bytes from **string** as a String.
Len(**string**)	The number of characters in **string**.
LenB(**string**)	The number of bytes in **string**.
LTrim(**string**)	A string, as a Variant, without the leading spaces in **string**.
LTrim$(**string**)	A string, as a String, without the leading spaces in **string**.
Mid(**string**,**start**,*length*)	*length* characters, as a Variant, from **string** beginning at **start**.
Mid$(**string**,**start**,*length*)	*length* characters, as a String, from **string** beginning at **start**.
MidB(**string**,**start**,*length*)	*length* bytes, as a Variant, from **string** beginning at **start**.
MidB$(**string**,**start**,*length*)	*length* bytes, as a String, from **string** beginning at **start**.
Right(**string**,**length**)	The rightmost **length** characters from **string** as a Variant.
Right$(**string**,**length**)	The rightmost **length** characters from **string** as a String.
RightB(**string**,**length**)	The rightmost **length** bytes from **string** as a Variant.

Function	What It Returns
RightB$(**string,length**)	The rightmost **length** bytes from **string** as a String.
RTrim(**string**)	A string, as a Variant, without the trailing spaces in **string**.
RTrim$(**string**)	A string, as a String, without the trailing spaces in **string**.
Space(**number**)	A string, as a Variant, with **number** spaces.
Space$(**number**)	A string, as a String, with **number** spaces.
Str(**number**)	The string representation, as a Variant, of **number**.
Str$(**number**)	The string representation, as a String, of **number**.
StrComp(**string2,string2,**compare)	A value indicating the result of comparing **string1** and **string2**.
String(**number,character**)	**character,** as a Variant, repeated **number** times.
String$(**number,character**)	**character,** as a String, repeated **number** times.
Trim(**string**)	A string, as a Variant, without the leading and trailing spaces in **string**.
Trim$(**string**)	A string, as a String, without the leading and trailing spaces in **string**.
UCase(**string**)	**string** converted to uppercase as a Variant.
UCase$(**string**)	**string** converted to uppercase as a String.
Val(**string**)	The number contained in **string**.

The Windows ANSI Character Set

D

This appendix presents the Windows ANSI character set. Table D.1 lists the ANSI numbers from 32 to 255. The first 32 numbers—0 to 31—are reserved for control characters such as ANSI 13, the carriage return. There are three columns for each number:

Text	The ANSI characters that correspond to normal text fonts such as Arial (Excel's default font), Courier New, and Times New Roman.
Symbol	The ANSI characters for the Symbol font.
Wingdings	The ANSI characters for the Wingdings font.

To enter these characters into your worksheets, you can use any of the following four methods:

■ For the ANSI numbers 32 through 127, you can either type the character directly using the keyboard or hold down the Alt key and type the ANSI number using the keyboard's numeric keypad.

■ For the ANSI numbers 128 through 255, hold down the Alt key and use the keyboard's numeric keypad to enter the ANSI number, including the leading 0 shown in the table. For example, to enter the registered trademark symbol (ANSI 174), you would press Alt-0174.

■ Use the CHAR(*number*) worksheet function, where *number* is the ANSI number for the character you want to display.

■ In a Visual Basic procedure, use the Chr(*charcode*) function, where *charcode* is the ANSI number for the character.

Table D.1. The Windows ANSI character set.

ANSI	Text	Symbol	Wingdings
32			
33	!	!	✎
34	"	∀	✂
35	#	#	✀
36	$	∃	✍
37	%	%	⌂
38	&	&	📖
39	'	∋	🕯
40	(	(	☎
41	)	)	✆

ANSI	Text	Symbol	Wingdings
42	*	*	✉
43	+	+	🖃
44	,	,	📪
45	–	–	📫
46	.	.	📬
47	/	/	📭
48	0	**0**	📁
49	1	**1**	📂
50	2	**2**	📄
51	3	**3**	📃
52	4	**4**	📑
53	5	**5**	🖨
54	6	**6**	⌛
55	7	**7**	⌨
56	8	**8**	🖱
57	9	**9**	🖲
58	:	:	💻
59	;	;	🖥
60	<	<	💾
61	=	=	💽
62	>	>	✆
63	?	?	✍
64	@	≅	✎
65	A	**A**	✌
66	B	**B**	👌
67	C	**X**	👍
68	D	**Δ**	👎
69	E	**E**	☜
70	F	**Φ**	☞
71	G	**Γ**	☝
72	H	**H**	☟
73	I	**I**	✋
74	J	**ϑ**	☺

continues

Table D.1. continued

ANSI	Text	Symbol	Wingdings
75	K	Κ	☺
76	L	Λ	☹
77	M	Μ	💣
78	N	Ν	☠
79	O	Ο	🏳
80	P	Π	🏴
81	Q	Θ	✈
82	R	Ρ	☼
83	S	Σ	💧
84	T	Τ	❄
85	U	Υ	✝
86	V	ς	✝
87	W	Ω	✦
88	X	Ξ	✠
89	Y	Ψ	✡
90	Z	Ζ	☾
91	[	[	☯
92	\	∴	ॐ
93	]	]	✺
94	^	⊥	♈
95	_	_	♉
96	`	‾	♊
97	a	α	♋
98	b	β	♌
99	c	χ	♍
100	d	δ	♎
101	e	ε	♏
102	f	φ	♐
103	g	γ	♑
104	h	η	♒
105	i	ι	♓
106	j	φ	🙰
107	k	κ	&

ANSI	Text	Symbol	Wingdings
108	l	λ	●
109	m	μ	○
110	n	ν	■
111	o	ο	□
112	p	π	▫
113	q	θ	□
114	r	ρ	▭
115	s	σ	◆
116	t	τ	◆
117	u	υ	◆
118	v	ϖ	❖
119	w	ω	◆
120	x	ξ	⊠
121	y	ψ	⊠
122	z	ζ	⌘
123	{	{	⊕
124	|	|	✿
125	}	}	"
126	~	~	"
127			▯
0128			⓪
0129			①
0130	'		②
0131	ƒ		③
0132	"		④
0133	...		⑤
0134	†		⑥
0135	‡		⑦
0136	ˆ		⑧
0137	‰		⑨
0138	Š		⑩
0139	‹		❿
0140	Œ		❶

continues

Table D.1. continued

ANSI	Text	Symbol	Wingdings
0141			❷
0142			❸
0143			❹
0144			❺
0145	`		❻
0146	'		❼
0147	"		❽
0148	"		❾
0149	•		❿
0150	–		☞
0151	—		☜
0152	~		☝
0153	™		☞
0154	š		☟
0155	›		☜
0156	œ		☞
0157			☟
0158			·
0159	Ÿ		•
0160			
0161	¡	Υ	○
0162	¢	′	●
0163	£	≤	◉
0164	¤	/	⊙
0165	¥	∞	◎
0166	¦	ƒ	○
0167	§	♣	▪
0168	¨	♦	□
0169	©	♥	▲
0170	ª	♠	✦
0171	«	↔	★
0172	¬	←	✳
0173		↑	✺

ANSI	Text	Symbol	Wingdings
0174	®	→	✻
0175	¯	↓	✳
0176	°	°	⊕
0177	±	±	⊕
0178	²	″	✧
0179	³	≥	⋈
0180	´	×	◈
0181	µ	∝	✪
0182	¶	∂	☆
0183	·	•	◷
0184	¸	÷	◷
0185	¹	≠	◑
0186	º	≡	◔
0187	»	≈	◕
0188	¼	…	◐
0189	½	⎢	◒
0190	¾	⎯	◓
0191	¿	↵	⊕
0192	À	ℵ	◔
0193	Á	ℑ	◕
0194	Â	ℜ	◑
0195	Ã	℘	↩
0196	Ä	⊗	↪
0197	Å	⊕	↰
0198	Æ	∅	↱
0199	Ç	∩	↲
0200	È	∪	↳
0201	É	⊃	↴
0202	Ê	⊇	↵
0203	Ë	⊄	✿
0204	Ì	⊂	▩
0205	Í	⊆	✠
0206	Î	∈	✧

continues

Table D.1. continued

ANSI	Text	Symbol	Wingdings
0207	Ï	∉	⚡
0208	Đ	∠	⚡
0209	Ñ	∇	⚡
0210	Ò	®	⚡
0211	Ó	©	⚡
0212	Ô	™	⚡
0213	Õ	∏	⊠
0214	Ö	√	⊠
0215	×	·	◄
0216	Ø	¬	➤
0217	Ù	∧	▲
0218	Ú	∨	▼
0219	Û	⇔	↻
0220	Ü	⇐	↺
0221	Ý	⇑	∩
0222	Þ	⇒	∪
0223	ß	⇓	←
0224	à	◊	→
0225	á	⟨	↑
0226	â	®	↓
0227	ã	©	↖
0228	ä	™	↗
0229	å	∑	↙
0230	æ	⎛	↘
0231	ç	⎜	←
0232	è	⎝	→
0233	é	⎡	↕
0234	ê	⎢	↓
0235	ë	⎣	↖
0236	ì	⎧	↗
0237	í	⎨	↙
0238	î	⎩	↘
0239	ï	⎪	⇦

ANSI	Text	Symbol	Wingdings
0240	ð		⇨
0241	ñ	⟩	⇧
0242	ò	∫	⇩
0243	ó	⌠	⇔
0244	ô	⎮	⇕
0245	õ	⌡	⬔
0246	ö	⎫	⬈
0247	÷	⎪	⬉
0248	ø	⎬	⬊
0249	ù	⎤	▫
0250	ú	⎥	▪
0251	û	⎦	✘
0252	ü	⎱	✓
0253	ý	⎬	☒
0254	þ	⎭	☑
0255	ÿ		▦

INDEX

PLUG YOURSELF INTO...

THE MACMILLAN INFORMATION SUPERLIBRARY™

Free information and vast computer resources from the world's leading computer book publisher—online!

FIND THE BOOKS THAT ARE RIGHT FOR YOU!

A complete online catalog, plus sample chapters and tables of contents give you an in-depth look at *all* of our books, including hard-to-find titles. It's the best way to find the books you need!

- ● STAY INFORMED with the latest computer industry news through our online newsletter, press releases, and customized Information SuperLibrary Reports.

- ● GET FAST ANSWERS to your questions about MCP books and software.

- ● VISIT our online bookstore for the latest information and editions!

- ● COMMUNICATE with our expert authors through e-mail and conferences.

- ● DOWNLOAD SOFTWARE from the immense MCP library:
    - Source code and files from MCP books
    - The best shareware, freeware, and demos

- ● DISCOVER HOT SPOTS on other parts of the Internet.

- ● WIN BOOKS in ongoing contests and giveaways!

TO PLUG INTO MCP: →   WORLD WIDE WEB: **http://www.mcp.com**

GOPHER: gopher.mcp.com

FTP: ftp.mcp.com

Add to Your Sams Library Today with the Best Books for Programming, Operating Systems, and New Technologies

The easiest way to order is to pick up the phone and call

1-800-428-5331

between 9:00 a.m. and 5:00 p.m. EST.

For faster service please have your credit card available.

ISBN	Quantity	Description of Item	Unit Cost	Total Cost
0-672-30474-0		Windows 95 Unleashed (book/CD)	$35.00	
0-672-30531-3		Teach Yourself Windows 95 Programming in 21 Days, 2E	$39.99	
0-672-30706-5		Programming Microsoft Office (book/CD)	$49.99	
0-672-30647-6		Microsoft Office Developer's Guide (book/disk)	$45.00	
0-672-30596-8		Develop a Professional Visual Basic Application in 14 Days (book/CD)	$35.00	
0-672-30620-4		Teach Yourself Visual Basic 4 in 21 Days, 3E	$29.99	
0-672-30771-5		Essential Visual Basic 4	$25.00	
0-672-30869-X		Essential Access 7	$25.00	
0-672-30792-8		Teach Yourself Access 7 in 14 Days, 3E	$29.99	
0-672-30553-4		Absolute Beginner's Guide to Networking, 2E	$22.00	
0-672-30752-9		Electronic Publishing Unleashed (book/CD)	$49.99	
0-672-30612-3		The Magic of Computer Graphics (book/CD)	$45.00	
0-672-30865-7		Virtual Reality Madness! 1996 (book/3 CDs)	$49.99	
0-672-30456-2		The Magic of Interactive Entertainment (book/CD)	$39.95	
0-672-30513-5		Becoming a Computer Musician (book/CD)	$39.99	
0-672-30524-0		Absolute Beginner's Guide to Multimedia (book/CD)	$29.99	
❑ 3 ½" Disk		Shipping and Handling: See information below.		
❑ 5 ¼" Disk		TOTAL		

Shipping and Handling: $4.00 for the first book, and $1.75 for each additional book. Floppy disk: add $1.75 for shipping and handling. If you need to have it NOW, we can ship product to you in 24 hours for an additional charge of approximately $18.00, and you will receive your item overnight or in two days. Overseas shipping and handling adds $2.00 per book and $8.00 for up to three disks. Prices subject to change. Call for availability and pricing information on latest editions.

201 W. 103rd Street, Indianapolis, Indiana 46290

1-800-428-5331 — Orders   1-800-835-3202 — FAX   1-800-858-7674 — Customer Service

Book ISBN 0-672-30739-1

What's on the CD-ROM

What's on the CD-ROM

The companion CD-ROM contains:

- Sample spreadsheets created by the author
- Version 5.5 of the Baarnes Utilities, the award-winning Excel add-on
- Third-party applications
- Utility demos that work with Excel

Software Installation

If you have Auto Play enabled within Windows 95, a menu program will automatically run when you insert the CD-ROM. This menu allows you to install the example spreadsheets, Baarnes utilities, and demo programs. If you need to create a program group follow these steps:

1. Click the Start button and choose **Run**.

2. Type <*drive*>:SETUP and press Enter. <*drive*> is the drive letter of your CD-ROM drive. For example, if your CD-ROM is drive D, type D:SETUP and press Enter.

3. Follow the on-screen instructions in the setup program. The program will create a new Program group called *Excel Unleashed*. This group contains icons for running the new menu program, installing the example spreadsheets, and installing the Baarnes Utilities.